ELEMENTS OF THE JEWISH AND MUHAMMADAN CALENDARS

ELEMENTS OF THE JEWISH AND MUHAMMADAN CALENDARS

WITH

RULES AND TABLES

AND

EXPLANATORY NOTES ON THE

JULIAN AND GREGORIAN CALENDARS

By the Rev.

SHERRARD BEAUMONT BURNABY

M.A., F.R.A.S.

GYAN

Published by

Gyan Publishing House
5, Ansari Road
Daryaganj, New Delhi-110002
Phone: 011-47034999, 9811692060
E-mail: books@gyanbooks.com

Distribution Network
gyanbooks.com
India, USA, Canada, UK, Australia, France

ISBN : 978-81-212-9828-5 (PB)
First Published, 1901

2nd Impression 2023

Printed at: Gyan Press, Delhi.

ELEMENTS OF THE JEWISH AND MUHAMMADAN CALENDARS
Author: SHERRARD BEAUMONT BURNABY

ELEMENTS OF

THE JEWISH AND MUHAMMADAN CALENDARS

WITH

RULES AND TABLES

AND

EXPLANATORY NOTES ON THE

JULIAN AND GREGORIAN CALENDARS

BY THE REV.

SHERRARD BEAUMONT BURNABY

M.A., F.R.A.S.

MDCCCCI

PREFACE

THE following treatises on the Jewish and Muḥammadan Calendars were not originally intended for separate publication. They were first written as part of a more comprehensive book containing an account of other Calendars and Eras to which reference was frequently made. When, through the kindness of friends among my parishioners at Hampstead, I found it possible to publish this portion of the work, I gladly availed myself of the opportunity, and rearranged the MS. in such a manner that it assumed its present form. This, I thought, rendered it necessary to add some brief explanatory notes on the Julian and Gregorian Calendars, such as might take the place of references made to Articles in the larger work.

A work of this kind must, of necessity, partake more or less of the nature of a compilation. Without claim to originality, I have endeavoured to bring to a focus materials gleaned from many various sources, as indicated by the list of books which I have consulted. There will, consequently, be found herein little, perhaps, which may not be read elsewhere; but many of the books and pamphlets which have been written on these Calendars are not easily accessible to the general reader, and in many, though rules are given and legal enactments respecting them are stated, the reasons for these rules and enactments are not fully and clearly described. This is particularly the case with respect to the Jewish Calendar; while, with regard to the Muḥammadan, the rules for the reduction of Hijra dates to the Christian Era are generally of such a nature that implicit reliance cannot be placed upon them.

I have endeavoured to simplify the rules for both Calendars, and to explain the reasons for them in such a manner that a student who will take the trouble to read this book may not have to encounter the same difficulties which I myself experienced when I commenced the study of the subject. I have perhaps used too much freedom in my criticisms; if that be the case, I can only express the hope that others may be more lenient with respect to errors and imperfections which they may detect in my own work.

I have spared no pains in trying to render the Chronological Tables as accurate as possible by careful revision. The Christian dates corresponding to Tishrî 1, Nîsân 15, and Muḥarram 1 are not usually given beyond A.D. 2000 or thereabouts. I have computed them for an additional thousand years.

I am much indebted to the Rev. Dr. Löwy and to the Very Rev. Dr. Gaster for valuable assistance afforded me with respect to the Jewish Calendar, and particularly to Mr. James Kennedy, of H.M. Bengal Civil Service, in the first place for the suggestion by which the publication of the work has been made possible, and, again, for bringing to my notice many of the books which I have found useful. I have also, through Mr. Kennedy, become indebted to Mr. A. G. Ellis, Curator of Oriental MSS. in the British Museum, who was good enough to correct my transliteration of Arabic words and names. It must not, however, be supposed that any of these gentlemen is answerable for errors or misprints, for none of them has seen either my MS. or the proof sheets.

SHERRARD B. BURNABY,

Late of the Vicarage, Hampstead.

LONGFIELD,
GREAT MISSENDEN.

CONTENTS

PART I

THE JEWISH CALENDAR

CHAPTER I.

CHAPTER II.

CHAPTER III.

CHAPTER IV.

CHAPTER V.

CHAPTER VI.

CHAPTER VII.

CHAPTER VIII.

CHAPTER IX.

GENERAL TABLES.

PART II

THE MUHAMMADAN CALENDAR

CHAPTER I.

CHAPTER II.

CHAPTER VIII.

THE OTTOMAN FINANCIAL CALENDAR.

GENERAL TABLES.

PART III

BRIEF NOTES ON THE JULIAN AND GREGORIAN CALENDARS

INDICES.

PART I

THE JEWISH CALENDAR

ERRATA.

Page 23, line 16, *insert* and *after* months.
„ 29, „ 6, *for* on *read* in the evening of.
„ „ „ 7, *for* 27 *read* 26.
„ 31, „ 5, *for* Koenick *read* Kornick.
„ 45, „ 8, *after September* 26 *insert* that is, *for* 1d. 23h.
„ „ „ 12, *for* which *read* and 6d. 14h. 0ch. — 4d. 8h. 876ch. or 2d. 5h. 204ch. would be, &c.
„ 66, „ 29, *for* ably *read* able.
„ 69, „ 5, *for* Nisân 1 *read* Nisân 15.
„ 72, „ 15, *for* Gregorian *read* Julian.
„ 97, „ 16, *for* requires *read* require.
„ 99, „ 23, *for* superior *read* inferior.
„ 114, „ 18, *read* with a Monday or a Saturday; therefore, in the third line from the bottom and in the last line of the Table, &c.
„ 120, „ 12, *after* required *insert a comma.*
„ 151, „ 11, *for* 995 *read* 905
„ 152, „ 11, *for* 245-231 *read* 241-235.
„ 186, „ 12, *for* Tishri *read* Tishri 1.
„ 197, „ 6, *after* Succoth *insert a semicolon.*
„ 263, „ 18, *for* upon *read* to.
„ 280, *in two last lines of Table V., for* 3775975 *and* 4469944 *read* 2775875 *and* 3469844.
„ 287, *in molad for Cycle* 290, *for feria* 9 *read* 2.
„ 427, *in f.n. for* $\left\{\frac{n}{2}\right\}$ *and* $\left\{\frac{n+1}{2}\right\}$ *read* $\left\{\frac{n}{4}\right\}$ *and* $\left\{\frac{n+1}{4}\right\}$.
„ 439, line 27, *for* 621·509 *read* 621·569.
„ „ *in f.n. second line from bottom, for Muḥammadan* days *read* years.
„ 441, line 9, *for* ·970224 *read* ·970224 Y.
„ 447, *in heading to Ch. VI. for* is *read* said to be.
„ 517, line 17, *after* number *insert* of days.
„ 524, „ 13, *for* 1196 *read* 1196 + 1.
„ 537, „ 12, *for* Megillak *read* Megillath.
„ „ „ 25, *for* Calandar *read* Calęndar.
„ 540, „ 14, *for* 36 *read* 46.
„ 547, „ 21, *for* Ka'ab *read* Ka'ba.

CHAPTER I

1. It is only reasonable to suppose that the Hebrews, when dwelling in the land of Egypt, employed the Egyptian method of reckoning time. They would naturally have acquired the custom from a people with whom they had for a long time been familiar.

It is true that they had actually sojourned in Egypt for only two hundred and ten years,* but their forefathers Abraham, Isaac, and Jacob had been in constant communication with that country.

The Egyptians commenced their year with the month Thoth at the time of the Autumnal Equinox, and whether the Hebrews had or had not adopted this custom, it is quite certain that, so far as their religious ceremonial observances were concerned, a change took place at the time when they obtained their freedom. Just before their departure from Egypt the command of God came to Moses and Aaron that the month then current, which had not long commenced, should be to them "the beginning of months," † that is to say, it was in future to be accounted as the first month of the year. This occurred in the Spring season at or about the time of the Vernal Equinox; and this month has been retained ever since by the Jews as the first of the Legal or Ecclesiastical year for the regulation of all their Fasts and Festivals.

If, however, the Hebrews had been in the habit of commencing their year at the time of the Autumnal Equinox, in common with the Egyptians—of which there can be but little if any doubt—it would be long before the whole nation would become accustomed to the innovation.‡ It was from this cause, in all probability, that for civil

* For the Sojourning of the Hebrews in Egypt, see Note at the end of this Chapter.

† Exodus xii. 1.

‡ Ewald, "Antiquities of Israel," p. 344.

and political purposes the year had another commencement. The first month of this civil year was the seventh of the Legal year, and corresponded to the Thoth of the Egyptians. After the time of the Captivity in Babylon it was called Tishrî.

2. The first month of the Ecclesiastical year, "the beginning of months," is called in the Hebrew Scriptures "the Abib." The article is always used in the Hebrew text, though invariably omitted in the English authorised version. In later times this month was called Nîsân, Nehemiah ii. 1, Esther iii. 7, and so Josephus tells us* that "in the month Xanthicus, so called by the Macedonians, which is by us called Nîsân, on the fourteenth day of the Lunar month when the Sun is in Aries, the Law ordained that we should every year slay that sacrifice which was called the Passover; for in this month it was that we were delivered from bondage under the Egyptians." †

3. In the early Hebrew Scriptures the months are generally described according to their numerical order in the Ecclesiastical year; thus we have—

"The first month," spoken of in Genesis viii. 13, Leviticus xxiii. 5, Numbers xxviii. 16, and in many other passages.

"The second month," Genesis vii. 11, Exodus xvi. 1.

"The third month," Exodus xix. 1.

* "Antiq.," iii. x. 5.

† With respect to the two commencements of the year, compare the Jewish practice with that of both the Anglican and Roman Churches. The civil year now commences on January 1st, the liturgic year on Advent Sunday. "It is the peculiar computation of the Church to begin her year, and to renew the annual course of her service, at the time of Advent, therein differing from all other accounts of time whatsoever. The reason of which is, because she does not number her days, or measure her seasons, so much by the motion of the sun, as by the course of our Saviour: beginning and counting on her year with Him, who, being the true Son of Righteousness, began now to rise upon the world, and as the day-star on high, to enlighten them that sat in spiritual darkness" (Wheatley, "Book of Common Prayer," ch. v. sect. i. p. 203).

"Tempus quod Dominicæ Nativitatis memoriam antecedit, ideo Adventus nuncupatur, quia totus ejus Ecclesiasticus ordo juxta contemplationem Adventus Domini dispositus est" (Rupertus, "De Divin. Offic.," lib. iii. cap. i.).

In the eleventh century the custom of computing the year from Easter was introduced, and became common from about A.D. 1300 to 1500. "Ut autem apud nos duplex anni primordium est, alterum civile a Januario, alterum Ecclesiasticum a mense Paschali, sic illi civilem annum auspicati sunt a Tisri mense Lunari autumnali, Ecclesiasticum a Nisan verno mense" (Petavius, "Rat. Temp.," pt. ii. lib. i. cap. vi.; tom. ii. p. 22).

"The seventh month," Leviticus xxiii. 24, 34, 39, Numbers xxix. 1.

All the twelve months are thus designated by numeration in 1 Chronicles xxvii. 2–5, where the names of David's captains for each month are recorded.

Four times in the Pentateuch "the Abib" is mentioned without the affix "the first month."

Exodus xiii. 4. "This day came ye out in the month Abib."

Exodus xxiii. 15. "In the time appointed of the month Abib."

Exodus xxxiv. 18. "In the time of the month Abib, for in the month Abib thou camest out from Egypt."

Deuteronomy xvi. 1. "Observe the month of Abib."

In the Book of Kings the names of three of the months are given, together with their numerical order—

1 iii. 1. "In the month Zif, which is the second month."

1 viii. 2. "In the month Ethanim, which is the seventh month."

1 vi. 38. "In the month Bul, which is the eighth month."

These four—the Abib, Zif, Ethanim and Bul—are the only months of which the names are specified before the time of the Captivity. The names have reference to the seasons of the year at which they occurred.

The Abib is the month of corn,* or of new fruits; so the Vulgate renders Exodus xiii. 4, "Hodie egredimini mense novarum frugum." And the Septuagint, ἐν μηνὶ τῶν νέων, "the month of new things."

Zif is the month of flowers.

Ethanim may be the month of fruit, but the meaning of the word is doubtful.

Bul is the month of rain.

4. During the Captivity in Babylon, and after that time, mention is made of seven months by name, including Nîsân, as the Abib was now called. The numerical order of the month as it stands in the Ecclesiastical year is also sometimes specified.

Esther iii. 7. "In the first month, that is, in the month Nîsân." In Nehemiah ii. 1 Nîsân is mentioned by name, without the numerical prefix.

* Die Gerstenreife: ripe barley. Laz. Bendavid, "Zur Berechnung des Judischen Kalenders," p. 26, § 15*a*.

Esther vii. 9. "In the third month, that is, in the month Sîván.' In Baruch i. 8, this month is mentioned by name only.

Nehemiah vi. 15, and 1 Maccabees xiv. 27. "The month 'Elûl," without the number.

Zechariah vii. 1. "In the fourth day of the ninth month, even in Chisleu." In Nehemiah i. 1, and 1 Maccabees i. 54, this month is mentioned by name only.

Esther ii. 16. "In the tenth month, which is the month Têbeth."

Zechariah i. 7, and 1 Maccabees xvi. 14. "In the eleventh month, which is the month Schebhât."

Esther viii. 12, and 2 Maccabees xv. 36. "The twelfth month, which is the month Adhâr."

The remaining five months are not mentioned either in the sacred Books or in the Apocrypha. They are found in the Talmud and in other Hebrew writings. One only, Marḥeshwân, the eighth month, is mentioned by Josephus, ("Antiq.," i. iii. 3).

The origin of the names used after the Captivity is said by some writers to be Chaldaic, but is more probably Syrian. Eight of them differ from the Syriac but slightly, as will be seen from the following list. The names are given according to the transliteration of Dr. Sachau in the Athâr-ul-Bâkiya, or "Vestiges of the Past," by al-Bîrûnî.

MONTHS OF THE HEBREW ECCLESIASTICAL YEAR.

	Before the Captivity.	After the Captivity.		Corresponding to
		Hebrew.	Syriac.	
1	The Abib	Nîsân	Nîsân	March—April
2	Zif	Iyâr	Iyâr	April—May
3		Sîwân	Hazîrân	May—June
4		Tammûz	Tammûz	June—July
5		Âbh	Âbh	July—August
6		'Elûl	Ilûl	August—September
7	Ethanim	Tishrî	Teshrîn I.	September—October
8	Bul	Marḥeshwân	Teshrîn II.	October—November
9		Kislêw	Kânûn I.	November—December
10		Têbeth	Kânûn II.	December—January
11		Schebhât	Shebât	January—February
12		Adhâr	Adhâr	February—March

The Syriac names are given by Scaliger,* and by Beveridge; † the latter has them in both Syriac and Roman characters. The variations in spelling are but slight.

Bevan conjectures ‡ that some of the Syriac names were derived from the names of deities, and refers to Ezekiel viii. 14, where Tammûz is mentioned: "Then he brought me to the door of the gate of the Lord's house which was toward the north: and, behold, there sat women weeping for Tammuz."

Jerome interprets the word by Adonis, who, he says, is in Hebrew and Syriac called Tammûz. The Vulgate has "plangentes Adonidem." The Septuagint retains Tammûz, in its Greek form. The worship of Tammûz was general in Asia, particularly in Assyria. It spread to Egypt, Greece, and Italy, and has been identified with that of Adonis, the Sun-god. His death and restoration to life were celebrated by annual festivals.§

Lucian, as quoted by Parkhurst in his Hebrew Lexicon,‖ gives an account of these festivals; he says, "The Syrians affirm that what the boar is reported to have done against Adonis was transacted in their country; and in memory of this accident they every year beat them-

* "De Emen. Temp.," lib. iv. p. 241.

† "Institutiones Chronologicæ," Appendix, p. 259.

‡ In Smith's "Dictionary of the Bible," Art. Month., vol. ii. p. 417.

§ *Cf.* Milton, "Paradise Lost," bk. i. 446:—

"Thammuz came next behind,
Whose annual wound in Lebanon allur'd
The Syrian damsels to lament his fate
In amorous ditties all a summer's day;
While smooth Adonis from his native rock
Ran purple to the sea, suppos'd with blood
Of Thammuz yearly wounded; the love tale
Infected Sion's daughters with like heat;
Whose wanton passions in the sacred porch
Ezekiel saw, when, by the vision led,
His eye surveyed the dark idolatries
Of alienated Judah."

Adonis was said to die and to revive again every year. He was killed by a wild boar in Lebanon, from which the river named after him descends

"Repetitaque mortis imago
Annua plangoris peraget simulamina."
(Ovid, "Met.," x. 726.)

‖ P. 668.

selves and lament, and celebrate frantic rites; and great wailings are appointed throughout the country; and after they have beaten themselves, and lamented, they first perform funeral obsequies to Adonis, as to one dead, and afterwards on the next, or another day, they feign that he is alive, and ascended into the air or heaven, and shave their heads, as the Egyptians do at the death of Apis; and whatever women will not consent to be shaved are obliged, by way of punishment, to prostitute themselves during one day to strangers; and the money thus earned is consecrated to Venus." Parkhurst adds to this translation of the passage, "From this account we may form a tolerably just notion of the manner in which the Jewish idolatresses lamented Thammuz."

It was one of these abominations transacted at Jerusalem that the prophet Ezekiel beheld, in a vision, as he sat in his house with the elders of Judah, in the sixth year of the captivity of Jehoiachin.

Rawlinson, on Herodotus i. 615, says that the Assyrians had a month called Sin, which may correspond to Sîwân.

Marḥeshwân is Hebrew, and indicates a month in which rainy weather prevails.

So far as regards the correspondence between the Hebrew months and our own, the Table just given must be taken with some latitude. Although the Hebrew months now fall usually as therein indicated, partly in one of our months, partly in another, yet it is quite possible that the whole of some Hebrew month may correspond to, or be included by one of our own. Thus in A.D. 1897, Sîwân corresponded with June; Sîwân 1 was June 1, Sîwân 30 was June 30. So, too, the whole of Tammûz was included in July; the first day of that month was July 1, the last day was July 29, Tammûz being a month of twenty-nine days. Such correspondence does not, however, occur frequently.

5. It will be gathered from what has been said that the ancient Hebrew year consisted, usually, of twelve Lunar months;* and, taking the average length of a Lunation at twenty-nine and a half days, there would be 354 days in an ordinary Lunar year. It must, however,

* *Cf.* 1 Kings iv. 7. "Solomon had twelve officers over all Israel, which provided victuals for the King and his household: each man his month in a year made provision." Also, 1 Chron. xxvii. 1-15, where we find described in detail for twelve months, "the courses of those that served the king month by month throughout all the months of the year."

be distinctly understood that the ancient Hebrew calendar was not permanently fixed. The Lunar year falls short of the Solar year by nearly eleven days, and, because the Hebrew festivals were regulated not by the Moon alone, but also by the state of the harvests which depend upon the seasons, that is, upon the influence of the Sun, it became necessary to reconcile the length of the year when measured by Lunations to its length when measured by the motion of the Sun.

For this purpose an extra month was intercalated once in about every three years. In later times seven months were intercalated regularly in the course of every nineteen years. In this way the Lunar year was brought into accord with the Solar, and the calendar was made to correspond to the seasons.

There are indications in the Scripture that this was the case; that the year was accounted by Moses to be governed by the Sun as well as by the Moon. Thus, at the very beginning, in the account of the Creation, we read, Genesis i. 14, 16, "And God said, Let there be lights in the firmament of the heaven to divide the day from the night; and let them be for signs and for seasons; and for days and years. . . . And God made two great lights; the greater light to rule the day, and the lesser light to rule the night." God did not say, "Let the lesser light be for years." Both the greater and the lesser light are included as the signs of the seasons.

There is clear reference to the yearly harvests, and therefore to the seasons which are governed by the sun, in Exodus xxxiv. 22, "Thou shalt observe the feast of ingathering at the year's end." Also in Deuteronomy xiv. 22, "Thou shalt truly tithe all the increase of thy seed that the field bringeth forth year by year."

Scaliger,* and Frank† show that the year was Luni-Solar, from the precise details which are given in Genesis concerning the months and days of the Deluge.

6. It was absolutely necessary for the due observance of the religious ceremonies, the Fasts and Festivals of the Hebrews, that the year should be made Luni-Solar. The great Feast of the Passover, upon which all the other Feasts depend, was, by the Levitical Law, to commence not only "at even" on the fourteenth day of the

* "De Emendatione Temporum," lib. iii. p. 220.

† "Novum Systema Chronologiæ," cap. i. § ix. p. 9.

Abib, but it was to be kept at the same season of the year as that which was current when it was first instituted. All tradition pointed to the Spring season as the time, and accordingly Josephus says, as already stated (Art. 2), that the Festival was kept when the Sun was in Aries. Now the day when the Sun enters the Sign Aries is called the day of the Vernal Equinox, and therefore, in the words of Lindo,* "the proper season for keeping the Passover is the Full Moon of the Vernal Equinox, or after the Sun has entered Aries; it must be kept while the Sun is in that Sign, but it is indifferent at what period of it the Full Moon happens." It has been universally held by the Jewish Rabbis that the fourteenth day of the Abib was intended to mean the day of the Full Moon which came next after the day of the Vernal Equinox, and that it has always been so understood. If that be the case the New Moon itself, of which the fourteenth day was accounted the day of Full Moon, might be before, or upon, or after the day of the Equinox; and although there is a difference of opinion as to whether the Abib began with the New Moon which preceded, or with that which followed the day of the Equinox, it is probable that it was made to begin with whichever of the two Moons were the nearer to the day of the Equinox.

7. However this may be, there is no doubt that the Feast was kept at the time of Full Moon, and the question naturally arises, How did the Hebrews in the old time determine when the Moon was New, so that they might correctly reckon the days to the fourteenth?

The answer must be that in all probability they were sometimes, if not often, wrong by at least one day; perhaps even by two; unless, indeed, some special guidance were given to their Priests in this matter. Of such guidance there is no hint in the Scriptures. No instructions were given in the Books of the Law as to the method by which either the New Moon, or its fourteenth day, were to be found. No doubt it was done from the first, as we know that it was done in later times, by actual observation, that is, the Moon was assumed to be New when its crescent became first visible. Whether this were so or not before and during the time that the first Temple was standing, it is an established fact that it was so after the Captivity in Babylon, and that great care was bestowed upon these observations. Special watchers were appointed, men of good repute, who were sent

* "Jewish Calendar for Sixty-four Years," p. 5.

to the summits of the highest hills in the neighbourhood of Jerusalem to look for the first appearance of the New Moon. So soon as the crescent became visible they lighted fires, the smoke of which could be seen from the city. This method after a time had to be forsaken, for the Samaritans, in their national enmity to the Jews, deceived them by lighting false signal-fires before the crescent of the New Moon had become actually visible. This artifice was soon discovered, and recourse was then had to special messengers.

Professor Graetz states * that while the custom of indicating the first appearance of the crescent by these signals prevailed the fires "could be seen on the Mount of Olives, on Mount Sartaba (Alexandrion), on Mount Tabor, and so on, as far as Beth-Beltis on the Babylonian frontier. On the day when the New Moon was expected the Babylonian community looked out for the signal, and repeated it for the benefit of those who lived afar. The congregations in Egypt, however, Asia Minor, and Greece, could not use bonfires; they were uncertain as to the day on which the New Moon fell, and therefore they kept two days instead of one."

Hence arose the custom, to which further reference will be made hereafter, of observing two Neomeniæ, or days for celebrating the Full Moon † (*v. post*, Article 89).

8. Maimonides in the "Kiddusch hachodesch," caps. ii. and iii., gives an account of the Watchers and of their duties, as well as the results of the reports that they brought to the Council at Jerusalem. Riccioli, quoting from many authorities,‡ but more especially from R. Jehuda, says that when the watchers had made their report to the Synhedrion certain figures delineating the phases of the Moon were exhibited to them. These figures had been drawn by Gamaliel upon the wall of an upper chamber. They were asked by the Priest, pointing to the different figures, which phase, or appearance, they had seen. Is it this? Is it that? If the Rabbis were satisfied that the witnesses had actually seen the crescent they proclaimed the New

* "History of the Jews," vol. ii. p. 366.

† It may be noted here that Latin writers are careful to distinguish between the time of the actual or at least the computed conjunction of Sun and Moon, and the day upon which the festival of the New Moon was observed. For the former the word Novilunium is employed, for the latter Neomenia, from the Greek νουμηνία.

‡ "Chronologia Reformata," lib. xii. p. 13. He says of R. Jehuda, that he was "Author Misnæ Talmudicæ anno fere 100 post Christi ascensionem."

Moon by sound of trumpets, and twice repeated the word *Mekudash*—"Consecrated."* Swift runners were then sent to all places not more than ten days' journey from Jerusalem to give notice that the important day had been determined. Riccioli adds the words, "And yet, as we have shown previously, it is possible that the first appearance of the Moon might not take place till the third or fourth day after the true Conjunction." †

It is quite true that, even if the atmosphere were clear and the sky free from clouds, the New Moon could not possibly be seen before Sunset on at least the second day after the true Conjunction.

If, then, the Hebrews counted the fourteenth day of the Moon from this first visibility, as is generally supposed, it would really be the fifteenth or sixteenth day of the true Moon; and in this way would be actually nearer to the time of the true Full Moon than if they had been able to see the Conjunction itself, and had kept the Feast on the fourteenth day reckoned from that event.

The average interval of time between the actual New and Full Moon is more than fourteen days and eighteen hours, so that the Moon has not only entered upon her fifteenth day at the time she becomes Full, but is within less than six hours of entry upon her sixteenth day.

9. Whatever may have been the method of measuring time adopted by the ancient Hebrews there is a want of any evidence ‡ that, before the time of the Babylonish Captivity, they possessed an acquaintance with even the fundamental laws of astronomy, or of the true motions of the earth and of the heavenly bodies. The names of the four months, which have been given as in use before the Captivity, prove that the year was Solar as well as Lunar, for these names have reference to the seasons at which they respectively occurred.

In 1 Samuel xx. 5 it is recorded that David announced, "To-morrow is the New Moon," and it has been argued from this that he must have had some knowledge of astronomical computation, since the Moon was not visible for one or two days before the Conjunction,

* Maimonides says that the Chief of the Council pronounced the word, and all the people repeated it twice ("Kiddusch hachodesch," cap. i. § vii. p. 348).

† "Posse tamen Lunæ primam phasim non contingere nisi 3 aut 4 die post verum Novilunium ostendimus, lib. iv. Almagesti, cap. 3" ("Chron. Ref.," lib. xii. p. 13).

‡ Except, perhaps, some obscure passages with reference to the tribe of Isachar (*v. post*, Art. 15, p. 21).

and certainly had not yet been proclaimed. Little weight can be attached to this; for, although Lunations vary in length, yet the variation between two successive Lunations never attains to two hours. If David knew, as he would know, when the last New Moon occurred, he must have been ignorant indeed if he could not predict with some certainty the day upon which the next might be expected.

One thing is clear—that the commencements of the Hebrew months were governed by the New Moons, or rather by the first visibility of the Moon—the phase which she was assumed to present when New. We know, also, that the year was rendered Luni-Solar by the intercalation of an extra month as necessity for it arose. In this way the seasons at which the Fasts and Festivals were observed would be, year by year, restored to their proper places.

10. The rules which determined these intercalations were formed as follows:—

One of the Jewish ordinances was that a sheaf of Barley should be offered before the Lord as the first fruits of the harvest. This was to be done in the Abib, or month Nîsân, immediately after the Passover, on the second day of unleavened bread, which is the sixteenth day of the month.* If it were found, before this day had arrived, that the Barley would not be then ripe it was evident that the season, according to the reckoning by Lunar months, had been accounted as arriving too early in the year. It must be made to come later. The first day of the Abib is approaching; the first day of the new year; the beginning of months. But, by the Sun, the Spring season has not arrived; the Barley is not ready for the reapers; the lambs for the Passover are not yet fit to be killed. The first day of

* Josephus, "Antiq.," iii. x. 5. In Leviticus xxiii. 11 it is called "the morrow after the Sabbath." There has always been some difference of opinion as to the meaning of this phrase. It is generally considered, both by Jews and Christians, that the Sabbath here mentioned is the first day of holy convocation of the Passover, to which reference is made in verses 6 and 7 of the same chapter: "In the fifteenth day of the same month is the feast of unleavened bread unto the Lord: seven days ye must eat unleavened bread. In the first day ye shall have an holy convocation: ye shall do no servile work therein."

In the Septuagint version the Hebrew words are rendered by *ἡ ἐπαύριον τῆς πρώτης*, "the morrow of the first day," that is, the day after the first day of the festival.

There is a passage in the Book of Joshua, v. 11, which confirms the view that the day in question was Nîsân 16: "They did eat of the old corn of the land, on the morrow after the Passover, unleavened cakes, and parched corn in the self-same day."

For a full discussion of the question and the opinions of various authorities see the article "Pentecost," by Samuel Clark, in Smith's "Dictionary of the Bible," Note *b*.

the ceremonial year must be postponed till the next Lunation commences. The current year which is coming to a close must be increased in length by another month.

11. Some authorities state that the extra month was intercalated whenever the first day of the Passover happened to occur before the day of the Vernal Equinox.* This may have been the case in later times, but it is probable that the ancient Hebrews were content with noticing that the New Moon which, if no correction were made, would be the first in the Spring season, was coming too soon; that the Spring had not actually arrived; and that, in order to keep the great Festival at the appointed time they must wait for the next Moon.

12. The method of forming the months and years which has been indicated continued in use among the ancient Hebrews only while they dwelt in their own land. After the dispersion † they were compelled to employ astronomical calculations for the purpose of fixing the times of Fasts and Festivals, as they had no means of rapid communication with their co-religionists scattered throughout the civilised world.

For this purpose Cycles were employed. The first that was used appears to have been that of eighty-four years, formed by adding the Octaeteris of Cleostratus to the seventy-six years of the Callippic Cycle.‡ Whether this were so or not must, however, remain

* Prideaux, "Connection of History," vol. i. p. 6.

† The dispersion of the Jews throughout the world is very commonly dated from the siege and fall of Jerusalem, A.D. 70. It had, however, commenced long before this event. Large colonies of Jews were formed in Egypt under the Ptolemies; by Ptolemy Soter in particular. After the death of Alexander the Great, B.C. 323 or 324 (the exact date is disputed) Ptolemy took Jerusalem, and carried many Jews to Alexandria. Strabo says that they occupied a considerable portion of that city, and were so numerous that they had a governor of their own who protected their laws and customs, as though he were a ruler of a free republic. There were also many Jews in Cyrene; we read in Acts of the Apostles vi. 8 that the Cyrenian Jews had a synagogue of their own in Jerusalem. Antiochus the Great, who was very friendly to the Jews, removed two thousand families from Mesopotamia and Babylonia where they were in danger, and settled them in fortified places in Phrygia and Lydia; allotted to them lands and possessions, and discharged them from the liability to taxation for ten years (Josephus, "Antiq.," xii. 3; Prideaux, "Connection of History," vol. iii. p. 155). In the time of Cicero there were many wealthy Jews in Italy ("Orat. pro L. V. Flacco," vol. ii. p. 176). In the Acts of the Apostles, iii. 9-11, there is a long list of countries from which foreign Jews had assembled at Jerusalem.

‡ Ideler, "Handbuch," bd. i. p. 571, gives as the authority for this statement Epiphanius, "Hœres," li. ch. 26, p. 448.

doubtful, because during very many years—more than six centuries after the time when astronomical computations were first made—the method by which the New Moons and Festivals were determined was kept as a profound secret, certain astronomical rules being handed down by tradition from Patriarch to Patriarch,* but not made public.

About the middle of the third century of the Christian Era Rabbi 'Addâ bar Ahabâ of Babylon † was anxious to deliver the foreign communities from their uncertainty as to the precise days on which the Festivals were to be observed. Hitherto they had been entirely dependent upon the messages they received from the Synhedrion in Palestine. With this purpose in view he made astronomical computations, adopting the calculations of Hipparchus (made circâ B.C. 146), for the length of a Lunation, namely, 29d.-12h. 44m. 3·3s., and for the Tropical or true Solar year the mean length of 365d. 5h. 55m. 25·4385s. (*v. post*, Art. 19). About the same time his contemporary, Rabbi Samuel, or Mar-Samuel, called also Arioch and Yarchinai,‡ who had studied astronomy under Persian instructors, drew up a Calendar for determining the New Moons. He refrained, however, from making public the method he employed, fearing to disturb the unity of Judaism, which might suffer if the foreign communities became independent of the chief Council in Palestine with regard to these matters.

He adopted the less scientific Julian year of Sosigenes, 365d. 6h.§

13. In A.D. 358 Rabbi Hillel II. reformed the Jewish Calendar. According to the testimony of Rabbi Hâi Gaon,‖ who lived in the eleventh century, he finally established it as it is now in use among the Jews. Isidore Loeb says that he finds it difficult to believe that this tradition is exact.¶ He does not contest the statement that

* *Cf.* Graetz, vol. ii. p. 579.

† Lazarus Bendavid, p. 32, says that he was President of the Academy of Sora [in Arabia Deserta, on the borders of Mesopotamia] in A.D. 250. Ideler gives the date of his birth as A.D. 183 ("Handbuch," bd. i. p. 574).

‡ Graetz, ii. p. 523. Lazarus Bendavid says that he also was President of the Sora Academy (p. 36). Ideler, bd. i. p. 574, says that he died in A.D. 250.

§ Sosigenes was an Egyptian astronomer who assisted Julius Cæsar in the correction of the Roman Calendar, B.C. 46.

‖ Gaon = Illustrious. It is a title of honour.

¶ "Tables du Calendrier Juif," p. 5. "Nous avons peine à croire cette tradition soit parfaitement exacte. Sans contester que Hillel II. ait contribué, dans une large mesure, à la création du calendrier juif, il nous parait impossible d'admettre que le calendrier actuel ait

Hillel II. contributed in a large measure to the foundation of the Jewish Calendar, but maintains the impossibility of admitting that the actual Calendar, as it now is, could have been formed so early as the time of Hillel. In his opinion it was not finally settled till after the fifth century, when the Talmudic Period, so called, had come to a close.

Whether Hillel II. did really bring the Calendar into its present shape must remain uncertain, in spite of the efforts of many learned scholars to solve the question. It is known that both in Palestine and Babylon the old fashion of observing the Moon remained in use till the middle of the fourth century.* This, in some measure, confirms the opinion of Loeb.

It has been stated † that Hillel II. was a direct descendant from Gamaliel, who was President of the Synhedrion when S. Peter and the Apostles were called before that assembly (Acts of the Apostles, v. 34), and at whose feet S. Paul was brought up and "taught according to the perfect manner of the law of the fathers" (*Ib.*, xxii. 3). L. M. Lewisohn has shown that this tradition is erroneous,‡ though it is true that Hillel became President of the Synhedrion when he was about eighty years of age.

The following account of the circumstances which induced him to make public his Calendar and method of computation is given by Graetz.§ After describing the terrible sufferings of the Jews under Constantius in the middle of the fourth century, this historian continues: "The miserable condition of the Jews was the occasion of an act of self-renunciation on the part of the Patriarch Hillel, which has never yet been thoroughly appreciated. The custom had prevailed up to now of keeping secret the computation of the New-Moon and leap-year, and of making known the times of the Festivals to the communities in the neighbouring lands by announcing them by messengers. During the persecutions under Constantius this method had proved itself both impracticable and useless. Whenever the

existé, tel que nous l'avons, du temps de Hillel. On a de nombreuses preuves que ce calendrier n'était pas encore en usage, au moins dans quelques-unes de ses parties, dans les temps talmudiques. . . . Le calendrier actuel a donc été achevé après l'epoque talmudique, c'est-à-dire après le Ve siecle."

* Hamburger, "Real-Enclycopädie," vol. ii. p. 628.

† Prideaux, vol. iv. p. 616.

‡ "Geschichte des jüdischen Kalenderwesens," p. 23.

§ "History of the Jews," vol. ii. p. 579.

Synhedrion was prevented from fixing the date of the leap-year, the Jewish communities in distant countries were left in utter doubt concerning the most important religious decisions. In order to put a stop to all difficulty and uncertainty, Hillel II. introduced a final and fixed Calendar; that is to say, he placed at every one's disposal the means of establishing the rules which had guided the Synhedrion up till then in the calculation of the Calendar, and the fixing of the festivals. With his own hand the Patriarch destroyed the last bond which united the communities dispersed throughout the Roman and Persian empires with the Patriarchate. He was more concerned for the dignity of the continuance of Judaism than for the dignity of his own house, and therefore abandoned those functions, for which his ancestors, Gamaliel II. and Simon his son, had been so jealous and solicitous. The members of the Synhedrion were favourable to this innovation; they only desired that the second day of the Festivals, which had always been celebrated by the communities not situated in Palestine, should not be disregarded. José addressed to the Alexandrian communities an epistle containing the following words: 'Although we have made you acquainted with the order of the Festivals, nevertheless change not the custom of your ancestors' (*i.e.*, to observe certain of the New Moons and Festivals upon two days). The same recommendation was also made to the Babylonians—'Adhere closely to the customs of your fathers.' This advice was conscientiously followed, and the second day is observed by all the non-Palestinian communities even at the present time."

14. Professor Graetz does not take the same view as Isidore Loeb with respect to any further correction of the form and methods of the Calendar. He says: "The method of calculating introduced by Hillel is so simple and certain that up to the present day it has not required either emendation or amplification, and for this reason is acknowledged to be perfect by all who are competent to express an opinion on the subject, whether Jews or non-Jews. The system is based on a Cycle of nineteen years, in which seven leap-years occur.* Ten months in every year are invariable, and consist alternately of twenty-nine and

* It must not be supposed that these, so called, leap-years are similar to our own. The "leap-years" of the Professor's translator are generally called Embolismic or Intercalary. They have thirteen months, and consist of either 383, 384, or 385 days, according to circumstances which will be explained.

thirty days [this should be thirty and twenty-nine]; the two autumn months which follow Tishri (the most important of all the months), are left variable, as being dependent on certain circumstances in Astronomy and Jewish Law. . . . It has not been ascertained how much of this system was invented by Hillel and how much he owed to tradition; for it is indisputable that certain astronomical rules were regarded as traditional in the patriarchal house; in any case Hillel appears to have laid Samuel's calendar under contribution."

And yet it is certain that Hillel did not adopt the year of R. Samuel, but that of R. 'Addâ. All the authorities are agreed upon this point, and it is the astronomical length of the year which is employed by the Jews to this day. Thus, R. Abraham Zacuth, as quoted by Selden,* says: "The President Hillel, the son of Jehuda the President, composed the annual computus according to the astronomical teaching of R. 'Adda, to be employed by us even till Messiah the Son of David shall come."

Note.—SOJOURN OF THE ISRAELITES IN EGYPT.—There is frequent misapprehension concerning the duration of the sojourn in Egypt. This arises from an imperfect understanding of the references made to it in the Scriptures. We read in Exodus xii. 40, "The sojourning of the children of Israel in Egypt was four hundred and thirty years." In Genesis xv. 13 there is recorded the prediction of God to Abram that "his seed should be afflicted four hundred years." S. Stephen, quoting from Genesis, speaks of the seed of Abram being "evil-entreated in a strange land for four hundred years" (Acts of the Apostles vii. 6).

The four hundred and thirty years of Exodus xii. do not refer to the length of time that the Israelites dwelt in Egypt, reckoned from the date when Jacob and his sons went there out of Canaan; they are the number of years reckoned from the departure of Abram out of Chaldæa. The four hundred years of Genesis xv. are reckoned from the birth of Isaac, when the promise of God was made to Abram thirty years after the patriarch had entered Canaan. This fact is recognised by the Septuagint version of Exodus xii. 40, "The sojourning of the children of Israel, which they sojourned in the land of Egypt, and in

* "Dissertatio," cap. xvii. p. 79. He quotes from the Sepher Iuchasin, fol. 50*a*, and translates the Hebrew thus: "Hillel Princeps filius R. Jehudæ Principis composuit rationem Intercalationis, seu computum annalem juxta doctrinam astronomicam Rab Adda, à nostris adhibendam usque dum venerit Messias filius David."

the land of Canaan, was four hundred and thirty years," where the addition of the words, "and in the land of Canaan," is to be observed.*

This is confirmed by S. Paul, Galatians iii. 17, "This I say, that the law which was four hundred and thirty years after, cannot disannul the covenant that was confirmed before of God in Christ, that it should make the covenant of none effect."

With reference to this, S. Augustin says,† "The prophecy was made to Abram that his seed should sojourn in a strange country, and be afflicted four hundred years—not that they were to be under the Egyptian persecution for four hundred years, but that it would be four hundred years [from the time of the promise] before it came to an end." S. Augustin also says that he computes the four hundred and thirty years from the seventy-fifth year of the age of Abram, when the first promise was made to him by God, till the time when the children of Israel came out of Egypt.

The actual time that elapsed from the entry of Jacob into Egypt to the Exodus was two hundred and ten years,‡ for, according to the Jewish computation,

The interval from the birth of Abram to the birth of Moses, was	420	years.
Moses was eighty years of age when the Exodus took place, Exod. vii. 7	80	,,
	500	,,
And, Abraham was one hundred years old when Isaac was born, Gen. xxi. 5	100	,,
Isaac was sixty when Jacob was born, Gen. xxv. 26	60	,,
Jacob entered Egypt when he was one hundred and thirty years old, Gen. xlvii. 9	130	,,
	290	,,

* ἡ δὲ κατοίκησις τῶν υἱῶν 'Ισραὴλ ἣν κατῴκησαν 'εν γῇ Αἰγύπτῳ καὶ ἐν γῇ χαναάν ἔτη τετρακόσια τριάκοντα.

† "De Civitate Dei," lib. xvi. cap. iv.

‡ Josephus erroneously makes it 215 years, in "Antiq.," ii. xv. 2.

The difference, or 500 − 290 = 210 = the time that the Israelites actually dwelt in Egypt.

It is but fair to add that although this account is very generally received by modern chronologers, yet it is not universally credited as correct. Frankius, for example, maintains strongly that the sojourn in Egypt lasted for four hundred years from the time that Jacob went there, and that the four hundred and thirty is to be reckoned from the time that Joseph was sold into bondage.*

The editors of "L'Art de Vérifier les Dates" are convinced that the belief is well founded which makes the sojourn to have been for four hundred and thirty years from the entry of Jacob to the year of the Exodus, exclusive,† thus adding thirty years to the period assigned by Frankius.

* "Novum Systema Chronologiæ Fundamentalis," p. 155.
† Pt. i. tom. i. p. 364.

CHAPTER II

ELEMENTS OF THE JEWISH CALENDAR

15. THE HOUR is not divided by the Jews into minutes and seconds, but into 1080 equal parts called Chalakim. These are the Ostenta, or Scrupulæ of Scaliger and other writers.

The number 1080 possesses certain advantages; being of the form $2^3 \times 3^3 \times 5$, it has $(3 + 1)(3 + 1)(1 + 1)$, or 32 divisors, including unity and itself.*

Strauchius states † that Aben Ezra (on Exodus xii.), claims these divisions as "the divisions of Israel," and that according to Rabbi Samuel they were brought down from heaven by Isachar, the son of Jacob. Selden quotes ‡ the words of R. Samuel, according to Abraham Zucuth in Iuchasin, fol. 40*a*, which he translates thus: "Isacharem ascendisse in firmamentum, et secum deduxisse partes 1080."

S. Jerome says that "the sons of Isachar were learned and erudite men skilled in the knowledge of time. They were Doctors, Computists, and Masters, both for the celebration of the Festivals, and for other matters; and so in the benediction of Isachar it is said, 'He bowed his shoulder to bear, and became a servant unto tribute'" (Genesis xlix. 15).

The Septuagint Version has ἐγενήθη ἀνὴρ γεωργός, "became an agriculturist." Is it possible that there is a remote reference here to

* Maimonides, "Kiddusch hachodesch," cap. vi. 2; De Veil's trans. p. 368. "Hora autem distribuitur in scrupulos mille et octaginta. Quid ita vero? quia numero in isto licet dimidiam, quartam, et octavam partem reperire; tertiam, sextam, nonans; itemque quintam et decimam, atque alias bene multas, quarum suum quæque nomen habet."

† "Breviarium Chronologicum," lib. i. cap. i. 4.

‡ "Dissertatio," cap. i. p. 2.

the ripening of the Barley, one of the determinants in the old times for the celebration of the Passover?

In Deuteronomy xxxiii. 19, Moses says of Isachar, "They shall call the people unto the mountain: there they shall offer sacrifices of righteousness: for they shall suck of the abundance of the seas, and of treasures hid in the sand." The Jewish commentators understand this to mean "treasures hidden in the Law."

In 1 Chronicles xii. 32 it is said of the children of Isachar that they were men "which had understanding of the times, to know what Israel ought to do." This is explained as meaning that they were skilful in computing the periods of the Sun and Moon, and in ascertaining the proper times for the feasts and solemnities. Josephus paraphrases the passage thus—"who foreknew what was to come hereafter."*

Maimonides refers to those who wrote in the old times, and says that they were learned men of the tribe of Isachar, but that none of their writings have come down to us.

Scaliger † asserts that, although the division of the hour into 1080 parts was claimed by the Jews as their own, it was employed by other Eastern nations, including the Samaritans, Arabians, and Persians. He gives no proof of this, and quotes no authority for the statement.

A still smaller division of time is the Rêga; 76 Rêgaïm are equal to one Chalak.

It is easy to convert Chalaḳim and Rêgaïm into minutes and seconds, or the reverse; for we have—

1 hour = 60 min. = 3600 secs. = 21600 thirds.
= 1080 ch. = 82080 rêg.
So that— 1 min. = 18 ch. = 1,368 rêg.
and— 1 sec. = 22·8 rêg.

Tables I. and II. show, respectively, the equivalents of Chalaḳim in minutes and seconds, and of minutes and seconds in Chalaḳim and Rêgaïm.

16. The Day is divided into twenty-four hours, which are numbered from 0 to 23. The Jews have no special names for the days of the week except for the seventh day, which is Schabbath (Sabbath),

* "Antiquities," vii. 2, § 2 (vol. i. p. 346).
† "De Emend. Temp.," lib. i. p. 5, D.

meaning "a day of rest." For technical purposes the days are numbered 1, 2, 3, 4, 5, 6, 7, Sunday being the first day, Monday the second day, and so on to Saturday, the seventh day, which is the Sabbath.

For Calendar purposes these days may be distinguished as feria 1, feria 2, &c.

The Jewish day commences at Sunset, but for computations of the Calendar it is assumed to commence at 6 p.m., for the Meridian of Jerusalem. This is in the evening of the preceding Christian Civil day, thus anticipating by six hours the commencement, at Midnight, of the Christian Civil day; but six hours later than the commencement of the Astronomical day at Noon. This is in agreement with the ancient record of Genesis i. 5, "The evening and the morning were the first day." Hence the Jewish Sabbath, feria 7, commences in the evening of our Friday and terminates in the evening of Saturday. The commencements of the months of the years, follow the same rule.

It may be well to notice here the difference between "Correspondence" and "Coincidence" as those terms will be employed hereafter. When a Jewish day is said to "correspond" to a Christian day reference is made to the last eighteen hours of the former and to the first eighteen hours of the latter, periods which in both cases include the twelve hours of day-time as distinguished from night-time.

Thus, the Jewish feria 1 is said to "correspond" to our Sunday; but feria 1 does not "coincide" with Sunday. The twenty-four hours of feria 1 "coincide" with the twenty-four hours which elapse between 6 p.m. of our Saturday and 6 p.m. of Sunday.

In the same way, the Jewish year 6179 is said to "correspond" to the Christian year 2419, and that its first day will be Monday, October 1, A.D. 2418. It will be seen at once that the "correspondence" extends only to the last nine months of the Jewish year 6179, and to the first nine of A.D. 2419. The "coincidence" is really from 6 p.m. of Sunday, September 30, 2418, to 6 p.m. of Friday, September 21, 2419.

The following Synopsis for three days may assist in indicating the difference between the Jewish Calendar method of noting the hours and our own ordinary Civil notation:—

Jewish Notation. d.	h.	ch.					Ordinary Civil Notation. h. m
1	0	0	... equivalent to ...		Saturday	...	6 0 p.m.
1	3	0	... ,, ...		,,	...	9 0 p.m.
1	6	0	... ,, ...		Sat.-Sun.	...	Midnight.
1	9	0	... ,, ...		Sunday	...	3 0 a.m.
1	9	540	... ,, ...		,,	...	3 30 a.m.
1	12	0	... ,, ...		,,	...	6 0 a.m.
1	15	0	... ,, ...		,,	...	9 0 a.m.
1	18	0	... ,, ...		,,	...	Noon.
1	18	810	... ,, ...		,,	...	12 45 p.m.
2	0	0	... ,, ...		,,	...	6 0 p.m.
2	6	0	... ,, ...		Sun.-Mon.	...	Midnight.
2	12	0	... ,, ...		Monday	...	6 0 a.m.
2	18	0	... ,, ...		,,	...	Noon.
2	19	270	... ,, ...		,,	...	1 15 p.m.
3	0	0	... ,, ...		,,	...	6 0 p.m.
3	6	0	... ,, ...		Mon.-Tues.	...	Midnight.
3	12	0	... ,, ...		Tuesday	...	6 0 a.m.
&c.					&c.		

It must be very distinctly understood that such an expression as, for example, 7d. 3h. 540ch., when used to indicate the instant of time at which some event takes place on a particular day of the week, means nothing more than that 3 hours 540 chalakim of the seventh day of the week have elapsed. Thus, if any event, such as the time of a Conjunction of the Sun and Moon, be noted as occurring at 7d. 3h. 540ch., this does not mean that seven whole days, together with 3h. 540ch. of the next day have elapsed since some fixed time, but simply that the event takes place upon the seventh day of the week when 3h. 540ch. of that day have elapsed, the instant when the event occurs being equivalent to 9h. 30m. p.m. on a Friday in our own Civil notation, because the seventh Jewish day commences at 6 p.m. on our sixth day.

If, however, it be expressly stated that the interval of time since some fixed standard is 7d. 3h. 540ch., then it does mean that seven whole days, together with 3h. 540 ch. of the eighth day have elapsed.

17. All time, for purposes of the Jewish Calendar, is computed according to local time at Jerusalem; that is, the computations are made for the Meridian of Jerusalem. Maimonides quotes, as the reason for this, Isaiah ii. 3: "Out of Zion shall go forth the law, and the word of the Lord from Jerusalem.*

* "Kiddusch hachodesch," cap. i. viii. (De Veil, trans., p. 344).

At Jerusalem, Solar time is 2h. 21m. in advance of Greenwich time. In other words, when it is 2h. 21m. p.m. at Jerusalem, it is only Noon at Greenwich (*v. post*, Chap. IV. Article 47).

18. The Jewish MONTH is of two forms—Astronomical and Civil.

The Astronomical Month is the mean length of a Lunation, or Synodical Month; its duration is taken as—

29d. 12h. 793ch.,* or 29d. 12h. 44m. 3·3s.,

which only differs from the latest computation of Elger by ·649 of a second.

No variation has ever been made from this computation in the Jewish Calendar. It was adopted, as previously stated, by the Rabbis Samuel and Hillel II. from the computations of Hipparchus.

The Civil months consist of either 30 or 29 days; but, before giving the number of days in each of the months, it will be necessary to speak of the year which, with the Jews, varies in length to a far greater extent than that which exists between the common and Bissextile year of the Christian Calendar.

19. THE YEAR. Although the Jews have adopted as the basis of their Calendar the Metonic Cycle of nineteen years, or 235 mean Lunations, yet their computation is more accurate than that of Meton. He reckoned the mean length of the Tropical year to be 365d. 6h. 19m. 15$\frac{1}{19}$s.; the Rabbis 'Addâ and Hillel II. employed the year of Hipparchus, consisting of 365d. 5h. 55m. 25·4385s., or 365d. 5h. 997ch. 48reg.†

Dr. Sachau, in his Annotations at the end of his translation of al-Bîrûnî, says‡ that there can be no doubt as to the origin of this year, for it can be exactly obtained through dividing by 19 the length of 235 Synodical months of Hipparchus, thus—

235 Lunations = 6939d. 16h. 595ch.
= 19 (365d. 5h. 997ch. 48reg.).

Petavius says § that some assert the year of Rabbi 'Addâ to have been 363d. 5h. 595ch. 48reg. These figures are clearly erroneous.

* Maimonides, "Kid. hach.," viii. i. p. 375. Talmud, Megillath. v. 1.
† Scaliger, lib. iv. p. 279, A. Lazarus Bendavid, Art. 27, p. 32. Ad. Schwarz, p. 65, &c.
‡ P. 387.
§ "De Emen. Temp." lib. ii. cap. xliii. p. 91.

The 3 in the units place for the days must be a misprint for 5, and the 5 in the units place for the chalaḳim should be 7, for, a few lines further on, Petavius says that the difference between the Solar year of R. 'Addâ and twelve Lunations, or 354d. 8h. 876ch., is 10d. 21h. 121ch. If the interval of time which, he says, some have assigned to the year of R. 'Addâ were right, the difference would be only 8d. 21h. 119ch., which is absurd. In other passages he gives the length correctly.*

The nineteen years of the Jewish Cycle, whether they be Civil or Astronomical, are divided into Common and Embolismic years. Of the former there are twelve in every Cycle, each consisting of twelve Lunar months. Of the latter there are seven, each consisting of thirteen Lunar months.

The Embolismic years stand, in the numerical range of the cycle, as,

3, 6, 8, 11, 14, 17, 19.†

This order, according to Dr. Sachau,‡ has only become canonical since the time of Maimonides. It is not mentioned by al-Bîrûnî.

Scaliger,§ and others, give, as a Latin version of the Hebrew memorial for this order of intercalation, the words, "Ter, ter, bis, ter, ter, ter, bis"—"third, third, second, third, third, third, second."

Insomuch as the first year of their Era is accounted by the Jews in their chronology as the first year in the first Cycle of nineteen years, it is only necessary, in order to find the Cycle and position in the Cycle of any given year, to divide the number representing the given year by 19. The quotient will give the Cycle, the remainder will give the position of the year in the Cycle.

If the remainder be one of the numbers given above, then the year is Embolismic. If it be any other number, the year is Common. If there be no remainder the year is the last in the Cycle, and is therefore Embolismic.

This may be reduced to the following general rule: If H denote the year, then it is Embolismic when $\left\{\frac{7\ H + 13}{19}\right\}_r$ ‖ is greater than 11.

* *E.g.*, ii. xlv. p. 93.

† Maimonides, "Kid. hach.," vi. § xi. p. 370.

‡ "Annotations on al-Bîrûnî," p. 390.

§ Lib. vii. p. 626, B.

‖ That is, the remainder after dividing 7 H + 13 by 19.

20. The arrangement, or system, of the Embolismic years in the Cycle is not arbitrary. They are introduced when the accumulated excess in the estimated mean length of the Solar years over the length of twelve mean Lunar months attains to one month, or as near to that point as possible. The exact coincidence of the 19 years of an Astronomical Cycle with 235 Lunations, according to the Jewish estimation of the mean lengths of the true Solar or Tropical year, and of a Lunation, may be shown as follows:—

	d.	h.	ch.	reg.
Estimated length of the Tropical year ...	365	5	997	48
" " of twelve Lunations ...	354	8	876	0
Excess of one Tropical year..................	10	21	121	48
" two " years	21	18	243	20
" three " "	32	15	364	68
Consequently,				
At the end of the 3rd year there would be a deficit	32	15	364	68
But the 3rd year has a thirteenth month	29	12	793	0
So that the deficit is reduced to	3	2	651	68
At the end of the 6th year there would be a further deficit for three years ...	32	15	364	68
	35	17	1016	60
But the 6th year has a thirteenth month	29	12	793	0
So that the deficit is reduced to	6	5	223	60
At the end of the 8th year there would be a further deficit for two years ...	21	18	243	20
	27	23	467	4
But the 8th year has a thirteenth month	29	12	793	0
So that now there is an Excess of	1	13	325	72
During the next three years, the 9th, 10th, 11th, there would accumulate a deficit of	32	15	364	68

	d.	h.	ch.	reg.
So that at the end of the 11th year there would be a deficit	31	2	38	72
But the 11th year has a thirteenth month	29	12	793	0
Which reduces the deficit to	1	13	325	72
At the end of the 14th year there would be a further deficit for three years ...	32	15	364	68
	34	4	690	64
But the 14th year has a thirteenth month	29	12	793	0
So that the deficit is reduced to	4	15	977	64
The deficit for the next three years, 15th, 16th, 17th, is	32	15	364	68
So that at the end of the 17th year it would be..................................	37	7	262	56
But the 17th year has a thirteenth month	29	12	793	0
So that the deficit is reduced to	7	18	549	56
During the next two years, 18th, 19th, there would accumulate a deficit for two years	21	18	243	20
	29	12	793	0
But the 19th has a thirteenth month ...	29	12	793	0
And the Coincidence is exact	0	0	0	0

21. The Jewish computation of the Metonic Cycle differs from that used in the Christian Calendar, for, in the first place, the Jewish Civil year commences in the Autumn, with the first day of the month Tishri. In the second place, the Cycle used by the Jews does not commence simultaneously with the Cycle of our Golden Numbers, but two years and three to four months earlier. Hence every Number in the Jewish Cycle of nineteen years corresponds to two of our Golden Numbers, partly to the one, partly to the other.

For example: The Jewish year 5656 commenced in the evening of

September 18, A.D. 1895, its first day being said to correspond to September 19. It closed in the evening of September 7, A.D. 1896. It was the thirteenth year in a Cycle, for the remainder is 13 when 5656 is divided by 19. But the Golden Number for A.D. 1895 was xv., and for 1896 it was xvi.

So again, the next Jewish year 5657 commenced on September 7, 1896, and ended on September 27, 1897. It was the fourteenth year in a Jewish Cycle; but the Golden Number in the Gregorian Calendar for 1896 is xvi., and for 1897 it is xvii.

In the same way it will be found that every year in the Jewish Cycle has a number which differs by 2 for the first part, and by 3 for the latter and greater portion of the year, from the Golden Numbers of the two corresponding Christian years.

22. There is another and more important difference between the Calendar years of the Jews and Christians. While the latter have only two forms for the Civil year—namely, the common year of 365 days and the Bissextile of 366—the Jews have no less than six. Their Common and Embolismic years are each subject to three different forms. The Common year may contain 353, 354, or 355 days; the Embolismic may have 383, 384, or 385. This variation is rendered necessary by a regulation of the ceremonial law, which will have to be presently explained. It prohibits the first day of the year from falling upon either the first, fourth, or sixth day of the week—Sunday, Wednesday, or Friday. Hence, if the first day of a year fall, by computation, on one of these days, its commencement must be postponed to the following day; in other words, the previous year must be lengthened by one day. Sometimes the commencement of a year has to be postponed for two days, for other reasons which also will be explained.

On these accounts the year has three separate forms, each of which may belong either to a Common or to an Embolismic year, so that there are six forms in all.

COMMON YEARS, of twelve Lunar Months.

(1) The Ordinary, or Regular Common year. The months have thirty and twenty-nine days alternately, six of each. A year of this form has therefore 354 days.

(2) The Imperfect, or Deficient Common year. A year of this form has 353 days. The year is not shortened by taking away its last day, but the third month, Kislêw, is shortened by one day. It has only twenty-nine days, the normal number being thirty.

(3) The Perfect, or Abundant Common year. In a year of this form, which has 355 days, the extra day is obtained by making the second month, Marḥeshwân, to have thirty instead of twenty-nine days.

EMBOLISMIC YEARS, of thirteen Lunar Months.

(4) The Ordinary, or Regular Embolismic year has an intercalated month of thirty days. It therefore contains seven months of thirty, and six of twenty-nine days, or 384 days in all.

(5) The Imperfect, or Deficient Embolismic year. The third month, Kislêw, has only twenty-nine days instead of thirty as in the Deficient Common year. This loss of one day, with the addition of the thirty that are intercalated, gives to a year of this form 383 days.

(6) The Perfect, or Abundant Embolismic year. The second month, Marḥeshwân, is increased in length from twenty-nine to thirty days, as in an Abundant Common year. This increase, with the addition of the thirty intercalated days, gives 385 days to a year of this form.

23. Whenever an additional month is intercalated, that is to say seven times in every nineteen years, it invariably comes next after the fifth month of the Civil year, the last but one of the Ceremonial year. It comes next before Adhâr, whose name and place it takes. Adhâr itself, in these Embolismic years, is called Adhâr scheni, Second Adhâr, or Ve-Adhâr, that is "after Adhâr." The intercalated month has always thirty days, while Adhâr itself, now become Adhâr scheni, retains its usual length of twenty-nine days.*

Al-Bîrûnî † says: "They added these days as a complete month [*i.e.*, thirty days], which they called the first Adhâr, whilst they called the original month of this name the second Adhâr, because of its following immediately behind its namesake."

* Maimonides, "Kid. hach.," viii. § 5. "Anno intercalari, quoniam Adar numerantur duo, primus eorum fit plenus, cavus alter." De Veil, trans., p. 376.

† P. 63.

It is necessary to be particular with respect to this fact, for the very reverse is sometimes stated or implied. But a great mistake is made when it is said that Ve-Adhâr is the intercalated month, and that it has only twenty-nine days, while a thirtieth day is added to Adhâr. With respect to this error, Meier Koenick says that most of the chronologists are mistaken in supposing that Adhâr-II., or Ve-Adhâr, is the intercalary month; the month Adhâr in Common years, and Adhâr II. in Embolismic years are identical. He states distinctly that in Embolismic years Adhâr I. has thirty days and is the intercalary month, and that the second Adhâr, or Ve-Adhâr, has twenty-nine days.*

Al-Bîrûnî says: † "According to another opinion, the first Adhâr is the original month, the name of which, without any addition, was used in the Common year, and the Second Adhâr is to be the Leap-month in order that it should have its place at the end of the year, for this reason, that, according to the command of the Thora,‡ Nîsân was to be the first of their months. This, however, is not the case. That the Second Adhâr is the original month is evident from the fact that its place, and length, the number of its days, the feast and fast-days which occur in it, are not liable to any changes. And of all these days nothing whatsoever occurs in the First Adhâr of a leap-year. Further, they make it a rule that, during the Second Adhâr, the Sun should always stand in the Sign of Pisces, whilst in the First Ahhâr of a leap-year he must be in Sign of Amphora."

The fact that, in an Embolismic year, all the Fasts and Festivals which are proper to Adhâr are observed in Ve-Adhâr is sufficient proof that the additional month is formed by the intercalation of thirty days before Adhâr and not after it. It proves, moreover, that a day is not added to Adhâr in Embolismic years, but that in such

* "System der Zeitrechnung," p. xxviii. "Adar der 1ste hat 30 Tage, ist das Schaltmonat. Der 2te Adar oder Veadar hat 29 Tage. Der meisten Chronologen irren, wenn sie der Meinung sind, dass der Monat Adar der 2te oder Veadar der Schaltmonat sei, wo sei wohl der veränderte Name Veadar dazu verleitete, welcher Name im Hebräischen noch einmal Adar nur bedeutet. Der Monat Adar im gemeinen und der Monat Adar der 2te im Schaltjahr sind identisch, beide haben nur 29 Tage, und in beiden werden auch die Feste, die für diesen Monat angeordnet sind, als z. B. das Hamansfest u. s. w. gefeiert. Der Monat Adar der 1ste ist der Schalt-Monat und hat 30 Tage."

† "Vestiges," p. 63.

‡ The Book of the Law.

years it has still twenty-nine days only; and it is the original Adhâr which, in these years, is called Ve-Adhâr, or Adhâr scheni.

The authors of "L'Art de Vérifier les Dates" * as well as Ideler, † Isidore Loeb, ‡ and Lindo, § appear to be in error in this respect.

24. The table on page 33 gives the number of days in the months for each of the six different forms of the year; the last column contains the names as they are usually written in England.

25. It should be noticed here that the number of days from the beginning of Nîsân to the end of the year never varies. In each of the six forms of the year the last six months contain $3 \times 30 + 3 \times 29$, or 177 days. The variations in the length of the year are caused by the changes made during the first six months. In Common years the months Marḥeshwân and Kislêw vary from their regular length when the year is deficient or abundant. In Embolismic years there is the same variation in the length of these months as well as the greater change caused by the addition of the Intercalary Adhâr.

The following is the arrangement:—

Common Years.

Deficient.	From Tishrî 1, inclusive,	to Nîsân 1,	exclusive,	176 days.
Regular.	,,	,,	,,	,,	177 ,,
Abundant.	,,	,,	,,	,,	178 ,,

In each form: From Nîsân 1, inclusive, to the end of the year, 177 days.

* Pt. ii. tom. ii. p. 115. "Dans leur année extraordinaire il y en avait un treizième qu'on intercalait après *adar*, et qu'on appelait par cette raison *veadar*, le *second adar;* de sorte que l'année extraordinaire avait treize mois."

† Band i. p. 541. "Man sieht also Thischri, Schebat, Adar im Schaltjahr, Nisan Sivan und ab haben immer dreisig, Tebeth, Adar im Gemeinjahr oder Veadar im Schaltjahr, Ijar, Thamus und Elul immer neun und zwanzig Tage."

‡ Tables du Calendrier Juif, Paris, 1866, p. 4. "Dans les années embolismiques le 6° mois a 30 jours au lieu de 29, et le mois supplémentaire a 29 jours; de sorte que les années embolismiques ont 30 jours de plus que les années communes."

§ "Jewish Calendar for Sixty-four Years," p. 5. "In Embolismic years Adar has thirty days, and the Intercalary month, Ve-Adar, twenty-nine."

	Common Years.				Embolismic Years.			
	Regular.	Deficient.	Abundant.		Regular.	Deficient.	Abundant.	
Tishrî	30 days	30 days	30 days	Tishrî	30 days	30 days	30 days	Tisri
Marḥeshwân	29 ,,	29 ,,	30 ,,	Marḥeshwân	29 ,,	29 ,,	30 ,,	Hesvan
Kislêw	30 ,,	29 ,,	30 ,,	Kislêw	30 ,,	29 ,,	30 ,,	Kislef
Ṭêbeth.........	29 ,,	29 ,,	29 ,,	Ṭêbeth.........	29 ,,	29 ,,	29 ,,	Tebet
Shebhâṭ	30 ,,	30 ,,	30 ,,	Shebhâṭ	30 ,,	30 ,,	30 ,,	Sebat
				I Adhâr intercalary	30 ,,	30 ,,	30 ,,	First Adar
Adhâr	29 ,,	29 ,,	29 ,,	Ve-Adhár ...	29 ,,	29 ,,	29 ,,	Second Adar
Nîsân	30 ,,	30 ,,	30 ,,	Nîsân	30 ,,	30 ,,	30 ,,	Nisan
Iyâr	29 ,,	29 ,,	29 ,,	Iyâr	29 ,,	29 ,,	29 ,,	Yiar
Sîwân	30 ,,	30 ,,	30 ,,	Sîwân	30 ,,	30 ,,	30 ,,	Sivan
Tammûz	29 ,,	29 ,,	29 ,,	Tammûz......	29 ,,	29 ,,	29 ,,	Tamuz
Âbh	30 ,,	30 ,,	30 ,,	Âbh	30 ,,	30 ,,	30 ,,	Ab
'Elul	29 ,,	29 ,,	29 ,,	'Elul	29 ,,	29 ,,	29 ,,	Elul
Number of days in year	354	353	355	Number of days in year	384	383	385	

Embolismic Years.

Deficient.	From Tishrî 1, inclusive, to Nîsân 1, exclusive,				206 days.
Regular.	,,	,,	,,	,,	207 ,,
Abundant.	,,	,,	,,	,,	208 ,,

In each form: From Nîsân 1, inclusive, to the end of the year, 177 days.

Also: Because from Nîsân 1, inclusive, of any Civil year, H, to Tishrî 1, exclusive, of the following year, H + 1, there are always 177 days, therefore Tishrî 1 of the year H + 1 is always the 163rd day after Nîsân 15 of the year H. For in every year, whether it be deficient, regular, or abundant, Common, or Embolismic, there are

From Nîsân 16 to 30	15 days.
'Iyâr has always	29 ,,
Sivân ,,	30 ,,
Tammûz ,,	29 ,,
Âbh ,,	30 ,,
'Elûl ,,	29 ,,
	162 ,,

and Tishrî 1 of the next year is the 163rd day. It will be found hereafter that use is made of this fact in computing the date of the Passover.

26. The Astronomical Lunar year is also of two forms—Common and Embolismic. These forms, unlike those of the Civil years, are constant; they are not divided into regular, deficient, and abundant lengths.

The Common Astronomical year is the duration of time occupied by twelve Lunations, namely,

354d. 8h. 876ch.
or, 354d. 8h. 48m. 40s.

The Embolismic Astronomical year is the duration of thirteen Lunations, namely,

383d. 21h. 589ch.
or, 383d. 21h. 32m. 43·3s.

TABLE OF JEWISH YEARS, A.M. 5650 to 5657 = A.D. 1889–90 to 1896–97.

The Hebrew Months.	A.M. 5650 = A.D. 1889-90.		A.M. 5651 = A.D. 1890-91.		A.M. 5652 = A.D. 1891-92.		A.M. 5653 = A.D. 1892-93.	
	Month Commences.	Days.	Month Commences.	Days.	Month Commences.	Days.	Month Commences.	Days.
Tishri	September 26, 1889	30	September 15, 1890	30	October 3, 1891	30	September 22, 1892	30
Marḥeshwan	October 26	29	October 15	29	November 2	29	October 22	29
Kislêw	November 24	30	November 13	29	December 2	30	November 20	30
Têbeth	December 24	29	December 12	29	January 1, 1892	29	December 20	29
Schebhât ...	January 22, 1890	30	January 10, 1891	30	January 30	30	January 18, 1893	30
Adhâr I. ...	February 21	29	February 9	30	February 28	29	February 17	29
Adhâr II ...			March 11	29				
Nîsân	March 22	30	April 9	30	March 29	30	March 18	30
Iyâr	April 21	29	May 9	29	April 27	29	April 17	29
Sîwân	May 20	30	June 7	30	May 26	30	May 16	30
Tammûz ...	June 19	29	July 7	29	June 25	29	June 15	29
Abh	July 18	30	August 5	30	July 24	30	July 14	30
'Elûl	Aug. 17 to Sept. 14	29	Sept. 4 to Oct. 2		Aug. 23 to Sept. 21	29	Aug. 13 to Sept. 10	29
	354 Days.		383 Days.		354 Days.		354 Days.	
	Ordinary Common.		Intercalary Imperfect.		Ordinary Common.		Ordinary Common.	

TABLE OF JEWISH YEARS, A.M. 5650 TO 5657 = A.D. 1889–90 TO 1896–97—*continued.*

The Hebrew Months	A.M. 5654 = A.D. 1893-94.		A.M. 5655 = A.D. 1894-95.		A.M. 5656 = A.D. 1895-96.		A.M. 5657 = A.D. 1896-97.	
	Month Commences.	Days.	Month Commences.	Days.	Month Commences.	Days.	Month Commences.	Days.
Tishri	September 11, 1893	30	October 1, 1894	30	September 19, 1895	30	September 8, 1896	30
Marḥeshwan	October 11	30	October 31	29	October 19	29	October 8	29
Kislêw	November 10	30	November 29	29	November 18	30	November 6	30
Tebêth	December 10	29	December 28	29	December 18	29	December 6	29
Schebhâṭ ...	January 8, 1894	30	January 26, 1895	30	January 16, 1896	30	January 4, 1897	30
Adhâr I. ...	February 7	30	February 25	29	February 15	29	February 3	30
Adhâr II ...	March 9	29					March 5	29
Nisân	April 7	30	March 26	30	March 15	30	April 3	30
Iyâr	May 7	29	April 25	29	April 14	29	May 3	29
Siwân	June 5	30	May 24	30	May 13	30	June 1	30
Tammûz ...	July 5	29	June 23	29	June 12	29	July 1	29
Âbh	August 3	30	July 22	30	July 11	30	July 30	30
'Elûl	Sept. 2 to Sept. 30	29	Aug. 21 to Sept. 18	29	Aug. 10 to Sept. 7	29	Aug. 29 to Sept. 26	29
	385 Days. Intercalary Perfect.		353 Days. Ordinary Imperfect.		354 Days. Ordinary Common.		384 Days. Intercalary Common.	

27. In the preceding Table, which is given as an example of eight consecutive Jewish years, the commencement of each month must be understood as taking place six hours earlier than the corresponding Gregorian day. Thus, Tishrî, A.M. 5650, is entered in the Table as corresponding to September 26, A.D. 1889. It commences at 6 p.m. on September 25,* which is six hours before the commencement of the Civil day, September 26. In fact, Tishrî 1, A.M. 5650, really coincides with six hours of September 25, and eighteen hours of September 26. So it is throughout the Table.

28. It will be useful, for purposes of reference, to collect here in a tabular form the leading elements of the Jewish Calendar.

(1)	The Common Civil year,	Regular	354 days.
		Deficient	353 ,,
		Abundant	355 ,,
	The Embolismic Civil year,	Regular	384 ,,
		Deficient	383 ,,
		Abundant	385 ,,

(2)	The Astronomical month	29d. 12h. 793ch.
		= 29d. 12h. 44m. 3·3s.
(3)	Twelve Astronomical months	354d. 8h. 876ch.
		= 354d. 8h. 48m. 40s.
(4)	Thirteen ,, ,,	383d. 21h. 589ch.
		= 383d. 21h. 32m. 43·3s.
(5)	Cycle of nineteen years	6939d. 16h. 595ch.
		=6939d. 16h. 43m. 3·3s.

From these figures we obtain the remainders after subtracting seven days as often as possible :—

(6)	For the Astronomical month	1d. 12h. 793ch.
(7)	,, Twelve Astronomical months	4d. 8h. 876ch.
(8)	,, Thirteen ,, ,,	5d. 21h. 589ch.
(9)	,, Cycle of nineteen years	2d. 16h. 595ch.
(10)	,, two Cycles	5d. 9h. 110ch.
(11)	,, three Cycles	1d. 1h. 705ch.
(12)	,, four Cycles	3d. 18h. 220ch.

* 6h. 34m. for the Latitude of London.

Compare with these—

a. Mean Julian year	365d. 6h. 0m.
b. Cycle of nineteen mean Julian years	6939d. 18h. 0m.
c. Mean Gregorian year.........................	365d. 5h. 49m. 12s.
d. Cycle of nineteen mean Gregorian years...	6939d. 14h. 34m. 48s.
e. Cycle of 400 Gregorian years...........	146097d.

Hence we have—

(13) The excess of a mean Julian year above a Jewish Common Astronomical year	10d. 21h. 11m. 20s.
	=10d. 21h. 204ch.
(14) The excess of a Jewish Embolismic Astronomical year above a mean Julian year	28d. 15h. 32m. 43·3s.
	=28d. 15h. 589ch.
(15) The excess of nineteen mean Julian years above Cycle of nineteen Jewish years...........................	0d. 1h. 26m. 56·6s.
	= 0d. 1h. 485ch.
(16) The excess of the Jewish Cycle of nineteen years above nineteen mean Gregorian years	0d. 2h. 8m. 15·3s.
	= 0d. 2h. 148·59ch.

29. Inasmuch as the Jewish Cycle of nineteen years is shorter by 1h. 485ch. than nineteen mean Julian years, it follows that ever since the formation of the Jewish Calendar the close of every Cycle has retrogressed from the Julian Calendar. In other words, the commencement of every Jewish Cycle of nineteen years comes a little nearer to the beginning of the Julian year than did the commencement of the previous Cycle. This retrogression will amount to one day in less than 315 years. Hillel formed the Calendar in A.D. 358; since that time 1542 years have elapsed, and therefore (measuring by Jewish Astronomical years) the commencements of the present Jewish years ought to have approached nearer to the commencements of the Julian years by nearly five days.

On the other hand, if the mean length of the true Solar year be taken as 365d. 5h. 48m. 46s., the value of nineteen true Solar years will be 6939d. 14h. 26m. 34s. The length of the Jewish Astronomical Cycle of nineteen years exceeds this interval of time by 2h. 16m. 29·3s. It follows that the commencement of every Jewish Cycle comes a little later, with reference to true Solar time, than the commencement of the preceding Cycle. This advance will amount to a whole day in a little less than 201 years. Assuming, then, that the Calendar of Hillel was correct, both by Sun and Moon, in the year 358, it follows that all the Jewish Fasts and Festivals are now about seven days later in the year —by the Sun—than they were at that time. Unless some correction be made, the time will arrive when the first day of the Jewish year will have left the season of the Autumnal Equinox, and have advanced to the Winter; while the Feast of the Passover instead of being observed in the Spring will be transferred to the Summer. It will not, however, be till A.D. 6372 that the error will amount to a whole month, and may then be easily corrected by dropping an Embolismic month.*

30. Table III. shows the Astronomical duration of time in the Jewish Common and Embolismic years; and Table IV. shows the time elapsed at the close of each year of a Cycle. By Table V. the duration of any given number of Jewish Cycles may be found. These are all according to Astronomical computation, and must not be confused with the lengths of the Civil years and Cycles. Table V. will be used as follows:—

Required the Astronomical duration of 327 Cycles.

300 Cycles	=	2081906d.	21h.	300ch.
20 ,,	=	138793d.	19h.	20ch.
7 ,,	=	48577d.	19h.	925ch.
327 ,,	=	2269278d.	12h.	165ch.

* *Cf.* Isidore Loeb, "Tables de Cal. Juif," p. 6.

CHAPTER III

THE JEWISH MUNDANE ERA

31. MÔLÊD, *pl.* MÔLEDÔTH, is a Hebrew word meaning renewal, rejuvenescence. It would be properly applied to the phase of the Moon at the instant of time when her Conjunction with the Sun takes place. It is, however, commonly used not for the actual time of New Moon, but for the computed time, which governs the commencement of each month, and, thence, the commencement of each year and of each Cycle.

Thus, the Molad* for any month is the computed time of New Moon which determines the Astronomical commencement of the Lunation, as distinguished from the Civil commencement of the month, which is affected by other considerations. The Molad for a year is the Molad for the first month of that year. The Molad for a Cycle is the Molad for the first month of the first year of that Cycle.

The Molads are not expressed in full; that is to say, they do not give the whole interval of time elapsed since the commencement of the Jewish Era, but only the feria, or day of the week, and the time upon that day at which the computed New Moon occurs. Thus:—If it be stated that the Molad for a certain year is 5d. 13h. 259ch. it means that the first New Moon of that year occurs, by computation, on feria 5, at 13h. 259ch. after the commencement of that day, corresponding to Thursday, 7h. 14m. 23⅓s., a.m.

32. It must always be remembered that the computed time of New Moon, for the Jewish Calendar, is not the time of the actual Conjunction of the Sun and Moon. The length of a Lunation, as

* The Anglicised form of the word as it is usually employed.

adopted by the founders of the present permanent Calendar, is a constant quantity, whereas the Lunations of the true Moon of the Heavens are variable in their duration. The Moon of the Jewish Calendar is a mean or average Moon moving uniformly, such as the artificial Moon of Hilarius, which is used in the Julian and Gregorian Calendars of the Christian Church.

The present Calendar is called permanent because no alteration can be made in any Jewish law, including the Calendar, except by the Great Synhedrion, and only when the Assembly is at Jerusalem. The Calendar, therefore, must, of necessity, remain permanent, and can be subjected to no correction until such time as the Synhedrion shall again be able, under the Will of God, to meet in the Holy City—a time to which many look forward with hope and expectation.

33. The Jews do not reckon the commencement of their Mundane Era from the day upon which they believe that the world was created, although the contrary to this is very often erroneously stated.

They hold that the world was created by God at the time of the Autumnal Equinox, September 21, in the year of the Julian Period 954, B.C. 3760, and that the Sun and Moon were formed on the fourth day of the week at 15h. measured from 6h. of the preceding evening, that is, at 9h. in the morning of feria 4, Wednesday.* But the Mundane Era, the Calendar, and the computation for New Moons do not start from this point. They commence from a fictitious or imaginary Moon, the first Moon of an imaginary or anticipative year next preceding the year of the creation of the world.† The first day of this imaginary Moon, if it had existed, would have been in the year of the Julian Period 953, on the second day of the week, feria 2, at 5h. 204ch. after the commencement of that day, that is, at 11h. 204ch. p.m. for the Meridian of Jerusalem.

This day corresponds to Monday, October 7, B.C. 3761, and the time to 11h. 20m. p.m., or 40m. before the close of that Julian day at midnight. This day and hour is the Jewish Epoch, or Commencement of the Era, from which all computations for the Calendar are made.

* Genesis i. 16, 19. "And God made two great lights, and set them in the firmament of heaven . . . and the evening and the morning were the fourth day."

† Compare with this the commencement of the Dionysian Paschal Cycle; it does not commence simultaneously with the first year of the common Christian Era, but is reckoned from the preceding year, its first day being January 1, B.C. 1.

34. It is not clear how the exact day and hour were determined, neither is it known when this Epoch was first introduced. It is possible that Rabbi 'Addâ or Rabbi Samuel may have computed backwards from the Molad of some year or Cycle as actually observed by themselves or by Persian astronomers, and that their reckoning was adopted by Hillel II.; or Hillel himself may have made an independent computation of the New Moons, reckoning backwards from the first New Moon of the Cycle current when he formed the Calendar; that is to say, from the Molad for the Jewish year 4105, the first in the 217th Cycle, which was 2d. 4h. 204ch. The day of the New Moon of Tishrî in that year corresponded to Monday, September 24, A.D. 344.

However this may be, it is from the Molad for Tishrî in the year of the Julian Period 953, 2d. 5h. 204ch., Monday, October 7, B.C. 3761, that the commencements of all the years of the Jewish Calendar, as determined by Hillel, are computed.*

This Molad is said by Scaliger, Petavius, and others to be called the Molad Tohu, answering to the Greek χαός, "confusion," "nothingness."† It is generally called the Molad BeHaRD,‡ or B'HaRaD.§

35. The passage which has just been quoted, in a footnote, from the "Kiddusch hachodesch" may seem opposed to the statement that the Era is reckoned from an imaginary, anticipative year—the year which would have next preceded that of the creation of the world had there been then any measure of time.

The explanation, if indeed the matter can be explained, is somewhat complicated.

* Maimonides, "Kiddusch hachodesch," De Veil's trans., cap. vi. 8, p. 369. "Jam exordium putandi ducendum est ab prima post constitutum mundum luna nova. Ea fuit ad secundam hebdomadæ noctem post horam quintam, et consequentis horæ scrupulum quartum et ducentesimum: character est 2. 5. 204. Ab hac oportet luna nova putandi initium repeti."

† Scaliger, "De Emend. Temp.," lib. vii. p. 631, C. "Tohu enim ipsis est, quod veterebus Græcis χαός."

Petavius, lib. ii. cap. xlvi. tom. i. p. 93. "Novilunium porro conficti illius anni vocant novilunium Tohu, id est confusionis, sive Nihili, quod tunc luna nondum esset a Deo condita. Acciditque novilunium illud feria II., hora 5, 204, ab initio noctis."

So, too, Petav., vii. cap. xvii. p. 387. "Ac novilunium Tohu, hoc est confusionis et inane, sive fictivum, vocant illud istum."

Adolf Schwarz, p. 50.

‡ Isidore Loeb, p. 5. col. 2.

§ L. Bendavid, p. 13, § 12. Adolf Schwarz, p. 50, note 2. According to the Hebrew method of numeration the letter B stands for 2; H for 5; R for 200; D for 4.

De Veil, in a note on the passage quoted, asks the question: "How can it be possible that the first New Moon after the Creation occurred on the second day, when we have it laid down in the Law that the luminaries were created on the fourth day, and man upon the sixth day?" In order to "untie this knot" he consulted the Hebrew Commentaries on Maimonides, and found that it was "very necessary to know that God completed the creation of the first man at the third hour of the sixth day from the foundation of the world." [He evidently means the third hour of the day-time, as distinguished from the night-time; this would be more usually called the fifteenth hour, being measured from six o'clock on the preceding evening]. "For God gathered together the earth out of which He formed the first man during the first [thirteenth] hour of that day; and prepared it during the second [fourteenth]. Since, therefore, from the time of the first foundation of the world to that of the perfected man there had elapsed five whole days and fourteen hours of the sixth day, we must make it our business to know both the month to which those days and hours belong, and also the first New Moon of that year to which the month belongs. From the time therefore of that New Moon, which occurred when the second [fourteenth] hour of the sixth day was ending, there must be subtracted four days, eight hours, and eight hundred and seventy-six chalakim (4d. 8h. 876ch.), which is the excess of a Common Lunar year of twelve months above an exact number of weeks; and we find that the first New Moon of the year which preceded the creation of man occurred on the second day of the week, when five hours and two hundred and four chalakim of its night had elapsed.* Its character [Molad] is therefore 2d. 5h. 204ch. And certainly, by computing those years which have elapsed since the creation of the world, this anticipative year may be determined. In this manner it seems to me that the passage is explained."

The explanation may not be quite so clear to others as it is to De Veil. He does not say why the New Moon, from the Molad of which he subtracts the excess of a Common year, is set down at 6d. 14h. 0ch., that being the time at which the creation of the first man was completed. Scaliger and Petavius profess to throw some light upon this point. The former says† "that the New Moon, whose Molad is 2d. 5h. 204ch., is called Novilunium Tohu. It is a mathe-

* (6d. 14h. 0ch.) − (4d. 8h. 876ch.) = 2d. 5h. 204ch.

† "De Emend. Temp.," viii. p. 631, C.

matical anticipation, προλήπτσις μαθηματική. But by the Jews this New Moon is called Neomenia 'επιπλήξεως; so it is said to be 'επιπληξις σελήνης" [a rebuking, or upbraiding of the Moon]. "For the Jews have a Folk-lore (fingunt) that the Moon, being jealous of the Sun, expostulated with God because the Sun shone together with her. For every ruling power is impatient of a consort. And, being severely rebuked by God, was shut up in darkness, and not permitted to shine until man was created. So for two days she did not appear, which indeed is indicated by their New Moon Tohu."

The way in which Scaliger takes Tohu as indicative of this is clear. If the excess of a Common year, 4d. 8d. 876ch., be subtracted from the time recorded by tradition for the creation of the Moon, namely 4d. 15h. 0ch., then the Molad for the Epoch would be 7d. 6h. 204ch; but it is 4d. 5h. 204ch., which is obtained by subtracting the excess of a Common year from 6d. 14h. 0ch. Therefore the interval of time between 4d. 15h. 0ch. and 6d. 14h. 0ch., or two whole days all but one hour, must have been lost to the Moon. In other words, she was punished by being shut up in darkness for forty-seven hours!

Of course Scaliger places no faith in this Folk-lore. He speaks of it as being utterly ridiculous. And it is hardly necessary to say that no Jewish scholar treats the myth that has been so ingeniously invented with any more respect.

Petavius relates very much the same story.* His method of reasoning is somewhat complicated, but the substance of his account is as follows: He says that such of the Jews as adopt a particular computation (that is, those who take for the Epoch, Monday, October 7, B.C. 3761, which was not always universally adopted), consider that the Sun and Moon were created together in the first year of the world, at the time of the Autumnal Equinox, namely, on feria 4, at the fifteenth hour from the beginning of the night, that is, at 9 in the morning of Wednesday. The Moon was then endowed with a brightness equal to that of the Sun; but, when she spoke contemptuously, and said that one luminary was quite enough for the world, she was punished by God for her presumption, and not suffered to shine for one day and twenty-three hours, nearly two whole days. Consequently the beginning of the first actual Lunar month, and of the first year, was delayed till the fourteenth hour of feria 6, that is to 8 a.m. on Friday morning.

* "De Emend. Temp.," lib. ii. cap. xlv. p. 93.

Assume then, he continues, that the Sun and Moon were created together on September 24, at 9h. a.m., in the year of the Julian Period 954. The Sunday letter was E, and the day was, therefore, Wednesday.

If this had been the commencement of the first actual Lunar month the Molad for Tishri would have been 4d. 15h. 0ch.; but the commencement was delayed to the fourteenth hour of Friday, September 26; and the Molad from which to reckon would become the sum of 4d. 15h. 0ch., and 1d. 23h. 0ch., or 6d. 14h. 0ch.

If there had been a Lunar year preceding this it would have consisted of 354d. 8h. 876ch., the excess of which above an exact number of weeks is 4d. 8h. 876ch., which would be the Molad for Tishri in the fictitious, anticipative year, answering to 953 of the Julian Period. This is the Molad Tohu, from whence the Era is made to commence.

Thus it appears, he continues, that one day and twenty-three hours, being the interval which elapsed between the first shining of the Sun and the first shining of the Moon, is counted as though it were a whole year; and this, Petavius asserts, is the rule of the Jewish Masters—"Dies unus in anno pro anno computatur." The statement is incorrect; the Jewish masters hold no such doctrine. Moreover, the saying does not apply, for the interval to be accounted for is not Dies unus, but two days all but one hour.

The argument from the Molads will be better understood when the method by which they are computed has been developed.

36. The fact is that Jewish chronologists are not in exact agreement as to the year which is to be taken for the commencement of the Era. There are three opinions with respect to it.

First, that which may be taken as the orthodox or generally received view, that Adam was perfected on the sixth day, when five whole days and fourteen hours had elapsed from the first instant of creation. These days belong to the end of a year which terminated at the moment when Adam was perfected by God, and, "Why should they be lost?" Why should they not be reckoned as forming a part of the Era? If they be counted—as they ought to be—we shall have (6d. 14h. 0ch.)−(4d. 8h. 876ch.) as the Molad for the day, which would have been Tishri 1 in this year, and that is the proper Epoch from which the Era should be reckoned.

The second opinion is that the Epoch should be the instant of the perfecting of Adam, namely, the fourteenth hour of the sixth day, and the Era, which then might properly be called Era Adami, must be computed from that Epoch. This would make a difference of one year in dating, so that, for example, Annus Mundi 5657 would be Annus Adami 5656.

The third opinion is that no year ought to be counted at all until it is completed, so that the year of the Creation is the year 0. This makes a difference, from the Calendar, of two years in dating, and those who adopt this view would call A.M. 5657 the year 5655.

This is analogous to the contention of some, who still maintain erroneously that the first year of the Christian Era was the year 0. A fallacy which has been repeatedly exposed.

37. The Jewish Era of the Calendar is, consequently, Mundane, commencing with Monday, October 7, B.C. 3761.

Hence, if 3761 be subtracted from the number representing any Jewish year, then the year of the Lord, which will be found is that which in its Autumn season* begins to coincide with it. Thus: For the Jewish Mundane year, or A.M., 5606, we have 5606 − 3761 = 1845; showing that A.M. 5606 commenced some time in the Autumn of A.D. 1845, and consequently ended some time in the Autumn of 1846.

If the procedure be reversed, the Jewish year coinciding with any given year of the Lord may be found. That is, if 3761 be added to the year of the Lord, then the Jewish year, which commences in the Autumn of the given year, will be known. Thus: For A.D. 1864, we have 1864 + 3761 = 5625, showing that in the Autumn of 1864 the Jewish year 5625 had its commencement.

In establishing the correspondence between Jewish and Christian dates, care must be taken to ascertain precisely the Christian year to which the month in the Jewish date belongs. Suppose, for example, that it were required to find the Christian year in which Nîsân 15, of A.M. 5660, occurs. It would not be correct to say that A.D. 1899 is the year required because 5660−3761=1899. This equation only shows that A.M. 5660 began in the Autumn of 1899.† The last three months of 1899 must have elapsed before Nîsân 15 of A.M. 5660 could have been reached, for this day always occurs in the Spring; accordingly,

* August, September, October. The Jewish Civil years are variable in length, but never of the same length as the Julian or Gregorian Civil years.

† It began six hours before Tuesday, August 24, Julian = September 5, Gregorian.

it is in the Spring of A.D. 1890 that the Nisân 15 in question occurred.*

The first four months of every Jewish Civil year, beginning with Tishrî 1, may have either 117, 118, or 119 days, according to whether the year be Deficient, Regular, or Abundant. This applies both to Common and Embolismic years. Suppose some given year, H, to be abundant, so that its first four months have 119 days, and let Tishrî 1 correspond to September 6 in the Christian year Y. December 31 will be the 118th day of the Jewish year H. These 118 days of the Christian year Y will cover the 30 days of Tishrî, the 30 of Marḥeshwân, the 30 of Kislêw, and 28 of Têbeth. The last, or 29th day of this month Têbeth, and all the remaining months of the Jewish year H, fall within the Christian year Y+1.

It does not appear that the custom of dating from the creation of the world was generally employed by the Jews till towards the end of the fourteenth century. It is possible that this Era may have been originally suggested by Maimonides, who died A.D. 1204. Bartolocci says that it was introduced gradually in his time,† but it is not by any means established that it was used at all in his time.

It is very generally said that previous to the fourteenth century the Jew employed the Era of the Seleucidæ. M. Schwab is strongly opposed to this, and insists that this Era, called by the Jews the Era of Contracts, was only used when it was forced upon them by the Syrian Kings. When they obtained their freedom under the Hasmonæan princes they at once abandoned this method of dating. That is his opinion, the reasons for which are stated hereafter in Chapter IX., Megillath Ta'anith, Day xvi.

The Era of the Seleucidæ is still used by the Jews of Yemen, or Southern Arabia.

38. Schwarz refers‡ to the confusion of ideas that exists with respect to the true meaning of the Molads. In illustration of this he

* Saturday, April 1, Julian = April 14, Gregorian. With regard to the error which may be made see *post*, Article 68.

† "Bibliotheca magna Hebraica," part ii. p. 430. "Æra contractuum maxime fuit in usu apud Hebræos, perduravitque usque ad tempora R. Mosis Bar Maimonis, quo tempore jam paulatim introductus erat mos numerandi ab æra creationis mundi et seorsim dimissa æra contractuum, ita ut hodie omnino cessaverit in Synagoga." The quotation is not taken direct, but from Ideler, "Handbuch," bd. i. p. 568.

‡ "Der Jüdische Kalendar," p. 58, footnote 1.

quotes the definition of the word as given by Ideler. "Molad—that is birth of the new luminary, called New Moon; but not the true Conjunction which we call New Moon, only the time at which the Moon first becomes visible, after the Conjunction, in the evening twilight, which the Greeks call *νουμηνία*. The reckoning gives the Molads so that, as a rule, the crescent of the Moon is visible on the day which the Molad indicates."*

Thus Ideler very distinctly asserts that the Molad gives the day upon which the New Moon first becomes visible—an extraordinary mistake, for, as previously stated, the Molad gives the time of Conjunction with the Sun of an artificial Moon moving uniformly in the heavens, and has nothing to do with the first visibility of the crescent of the true Moon. Ideler is correct in stating that the Molad does not give the time of the true Conjunction; and he is also correct when he says—beyond the passage quoted by Schwarz—"that the interval between any two successive Molads is the mean duration of a Synodical month, 29d. 12h. 793ch." The very fact of this interval being a constant quantity proves that the Moon of the Molads is supposed to move uniformly, which is not the case with the true Moon of the Heavens, whose Lunations are variable in length. But if the Moon of the Molads move uniformly, how can the Molad indicate the first visibility of the true Moon which does not move uniformly? Moreover, even if the true Moon did move uniformly, the interval of time which elapses between her actual Conjunction with the Sun and her first visibility in the evening twilight could not by any possibility be a certain definite, constant quantity.

Schwarz adds that, to his regret, he is unable to refer to Lazarus Bendavid, and therefore he cannot say whether Ideler obtained from Bendavid or from Auerbach this "piece of wisdom"—"Weiseheit."

There is no doubt but that he took it from L. Bendavid, who says: "Moled (birth, *i.e.*, of the Moon), New Moon, that is to say, the instant of the visible Conjunction of the Sun and Moon.† He con-

* "Handbuch," Band 1, p. 543. "Moled, Geburt, nämlich des neuen Lichts, heist der Neumond, aber nicht gerade die Conjunction, die wir unter Neumond verstehen, sondern die Zeit, wo der Mond nach der Conjunction zuerst wieder in der Abenddämmerung sichtbar wird, was die Griechen *νουμηνία* nannten. Die Rechnung gibt nämlich die Moleds so, dass in der Regel die Mondsichel an dem Tage erscheint, auf den der Moled trifft."

† "Zur Berechnung und Geschichte des Jüdischen Kalenders," p. 5, § 6. "Moled (Geburth, sc. des Mondes), Neumond, heist der Augenblick der scheinbaren Conjunction von Sonne und Mond."

tinues, as does Ideler, "The interval from one Molad to another is, according to the Talmudists and Maimonides, fixed at 29d. 12h. 793ch."

39. Computation of the Molads.—The length of a Jewish Astronomical month, 29d. 12h. 793ch., exceeds an exact number of weeks by 1d. 12h. 793ch. Consequently, if the Molad for Tishrî in any given year be known, the Molads for all the months in that year will be found by the successive additions of 1d. 12h. 793ch.* Seven days, and all multiples of 7, are to be rejected whenever the sum of the days, hours, and Chalaḳim amounts to or exceeds 8 days. The 7 is not, however, to be rejected from such a Molad as 7d. 15h. 60ch., for this, as previously explained, indicates a certain time upon the seventh day, and not that the seventh day is completed and the eighth is entered. It is evident that 7 cannot be subtracted until the last hour of the seventh day has elapsed.

It would, perhaps, prevent a confusion of ideas upon this point if the feriæ of Molads were printed in Roman numerals, reserving the Indian numerals for the hours and Chalaḳim, thus:—iv. 7. 819, or vii. 15. 60. This, however, is not the custom.

Take now, for an example, the method of obtaining the Molads for the months of the first year of the Jewish Era, when the Molad for Tishrî was 2d. 5h. 204ch.; in other words, this month commenced, Astronomically, upon the second day of the week, when 5h. 204ch. of that day had elapsed.

	d.	h.	ch.
Molad of Tishrî	2	5	204
Add	1	12	793
" Marḥeshwân	3	17	997
Add	1	12	793
" Kislêw	5	6	710
Add	1	12	793
" Ṭêbeth	6	19	423
Add	1	12	793
" Schebhât	1	8	136
Add	1	12	793

* Maimonides, "Kid. hach.," vi. 7. "Sicque licet consequentium reperire mensium lunam novam vel ad infinitum tempus." De Veil, trans., p. 369.

		d.	h.	ch.
Molad of 'Adhâr		2	20	929
	Add	1	12	793
,, Nîsân		4	9	642
	Add	1	12	793
,, 'Iyâr		5	22	355
	Add	1	12	793
,, Sîwân		7	11	68
	Add	1	12	793
,, Tammuz		1	23	861
	Add	1	12	793
,, Âbh		3	12	574
	Add	1	12	793
,, 'Elûl		5	1	287
	Add	1	12	793
,, Tishrî in the next year		6	14	0

If this process be continued the Molads for all the months from the commencement of the Jewish Era may be found, care being taken to add 1d. 12h. 793ch. for 'Adhâr I., as well as for 'Adhâr II., in the Embolismic years.

The process may be shortened; there is no necessity to make all these successive additions in order to find the Molad for any given month of a year. It is evident that for the sixth month, for example, six times 1d. 12h. 793ch. is to be added to the Molad of the first month of the year; while for the tenth month the addition must be (1d. 12h. 793ch.) × 10; seven, and multiples of seven, being rejected from the days when they exceed seven.

Table VI. shows the additions that are to be made to the Molad of Tishrî in any given year, H, in order to obtain the computed Molad for any month in that year.

For example:—Given that the Molad of Tishrî in the year 5659 is 6d. 4h. 704ch., find the Molad for Tammûz in the same year.

First ascertain whether the year be Common or Embolismic. The division of 5659 by 19 leaves a remainder 16; therefore, the year is common. The addition to be made to the Molad for Tishrî in order to obtain that for Tammûz in a Common year is, by the Table, 6d. 18h. 657ch. The sum is 12d. 23h. 281ch., from which 7d. may be rejected, so that it becomes 5d. 23h. 281ch., the Molad required. The occurrence of New Moon is thus computed, Astronomically, to be on feria 5, at 23h. 281ch. after that day has commenced. Now, feria 5 commences, formally, at 6 p.m. on the Christian fourth day of the week, Wednesday, and when 23h. 281ch. of feria 5 have elapsed, the time arrived at is 5h. 281ch., or 5h. 15m. 36⅔s. p.m. on Thursday, for the meridian of Jerusalem.

40. Molads for Years.—A Jewish Astronomical Common year of twelve months contains 354d. 8h. 876ch.; and an Astronomical Embolismic year of thirteen months contains 383d. 21h. 589ch. These intervals of time exceed an exact number of weeks by 4d. 8h. 876ch. and 5d. 21h. 589ch. respectively. Therefore, if the Molad for any given year be known, the Molads for all succeeding years may be found by the successive additions of 4d. 8h. 876ch. in the case of a Common year, and of 5d. 21h. 589ch. in the case of an Embolismic year.

Take, for an example of the method to be pursued, the first years of the Jewish Era.

	d.	h.	ch.
Molad of first year	2	5	204
This year was Common, therefore add	4	8	876
Molad of second year	6	14	0
This year was Common, add	4	8	876
Molad of third year	3	22	876
This year was Embolismic, add	5	21	589
Molad of fourth year	2	20	385
This year was Common, add	4	8	876
Molad of fifth year	7	5	181
This year was Common, add	4	8	876
Molad of sixth year	4	13	1057
This year was Embolismic, add	5	21	589

	d.	h.	ch.
Molad of seventh year	3	11	566
This year was Common, add	4	8	876
Molad of eighth year	7	20	362

If this process be continued the Molads for all succeeding years may be found.

41. Just as the process for finding the Molad for any month in a given year is shortened by making use of the Table of Additions, Table VI., so the above process may be shortened if it be required to find the Molad for any year of a Cycle, assuming that the Molad for the first year of the Cycle be known. The Common and Embolismic years maintain constant places in every Cycle, so that it is easy to form a Table of Additions to be made to the Molad for the first year of any given Cycle in order to ascertain the Molad for any other year in the same Cycle.

This Table, VII., is obtained as follows:—

Let the Molad for the first year of the given Cycle be M. For the excess of a Common year, which is 4d. 8h. 876ch., write C.

For the excess of an Embolismic year, which is 5d. 21h. 589ch. write E.

Then—

			d.	h.	ch.
Molad for second year.........	=M+ C		=M+4	8	876
Add excess of a Com. year	C		4	8	876
Molad for third year	=M+2C		=M+1	17	672
Add excess of an Emb. year		E	5	21	589
Molad for fourth year	=M+2C	+ E	=M+7	15	181
Add excess of a Com. year	C		4	8	876
Molad for fifth year............	=M+3C	+ E	=M+4	23	1057
Add excess of a Com. year	C		4	8	876
Molad for sixth year	=M+4C	+ E	=M+2	8	853
Add excess of an Emb. year		E	5	21	589
Molad for seventh year	=M+4C	+2E	=M+1	6	362
&c.			&c.		

It will, of course, be noticed that the Molad for the *n*th year of a Cycle is not found by adding ($n-1$) (4d. 8h. 876d.) to the Molad for the first year, because the addition for an Embolismic year differs from that for a Common year.

42. MOLADS OF CYCLES.—A Cycle of nineteen years contains 6939d. 16h. 595ch., according to Jewish Astronomical computation. This interval of time is 2d. 16h. 595ch. in excess of an exact number of weeks. Hence, if the Molad, M, for any Cycle be known, those for all succeeding Cycles will be found by the continued addition of this excess. The Astronomical length of the Cycle being constant, the addition to be made never varies. This, as will be seen hereafter, is not the case with the Civil Cycle, which is of variable length.

A general formula for the addition to be made to the Molad, M, for any Cycle, C, in order to find the Molad for any other Cycle, C+*n*, is easily obtained, for—

Molad for C+1 will be M+2d. 16h. 595ch.
,, C+2 ,, M+2 (2d. 16h. 595ch.)
,, C+3 ,, M+3 (2d. 16h. 595ch.)

And, generally,

,, C+*n* ,, M+*n* (2d. 16h. 595ch.)

Table VIII. shows the required addition for any given number of Cycles from one to six hundred, together with the number of years in such Cycles. It is to be read thus:—For seven more Cycles add to the Molad for the given Cycle 4d. 19h. 925ch. The second column shows that in seven Cycles there are 133 years.

By means of this Table, together with Table VII., the feria and hour of the computed New Moon of Tishri for any year in the Jewish Era is readily found. The additions will, as a rule, be made to the Molad BeHaRD of the first Cycle, namely, 2d. 5h. 204ch.

Example.—Required the Molad for Tishri in the year 5357.

Before the year 5357 commences there have elapsed 5356 years, or 281 Cycles and 17 complete years. Therefore 5357 is the eighteenth year of the 282nd Cycle.

	d.	h.	ch.
Molad BeHaRD	2	5	204
Add, for 200 Cycles	5	22	200
,, 80 ,, ...	5	4	80
,, 1 Cycle	2	16	595
For eighteenth year (Table VII.)	6	10	210
	22	10	209

From the 22 days there are rejected 21, and the Molad required is 1d. 10h. 209ch.; that is to say, the computed New Moon of Tishrî in the year 5357 occurs at 10h. 209ch. after the commencement of feria 1. Feria 1 commences at 6 p.m. on the Christian Saturday, therefore the Christian time of this New Moon will be Sunday at 4h. 209ch. a.m., or 4h. 11m. $36\frac{2}{3}$s.

Example 2.—Required the Molad for Tishrî in the year 5821.

Here 5820 years, or 306 Cycles and 6 years have expired.

	d.	h.	ch.
Molad BeHaRD	2	5	204
300 Cycles	1	21	300
6 ,, ...	2	3	330
For the seventh year	1	6	362
Molad required.....................	7	12	116

43. If the Molad for any year or Cycle be known, that for the preceding year or Cycle will be obtained by subtracting from the known Molad the excess of the preceding year or Cycle; for, if M be the Molad for any year or Cycle, H, then—

$$M = \text{Molad for } (H-1) + \text{excess of } (H-1)$$
$$\therefore \text{Molad for } (H-1) = M - \text{excess of } (H-1).$$

Example.—The Molad for the year 5648 is 1d. 0h. 856ch.; that for the year 5647 is required.

Because $5647 = 19 \times 297 + 4$, it is the fourth in a Cycle, and, therefore, is a Common year. The excess of an Astronomical Common year is 4d. 8h. 876ch. This cannot be subtracted from 1d. 0h. 856ch., which must therefore be increased by 7. This can be done without altering the day of the week. We have, therefore—

	d.	h.	ch.
Molad for 5648	8	0	856
Subtract excess of 5647	4	8	876
Molad for 5647	3	15	1060

44. It should be noticed that the day of the computed, or Astronomical New Moon of Tishrî does not always indicate the day of the week, or feria upon which the Civil year, as distinguished from the Astronomical year, actually commences. There are certain ceremonial regulations, to be hereafter explained, which frequently cause the commencement of the year to be postponed for one day, sometimes for two days. This postponement indeed occurs more often than not. The same thing applies, of course, to the commencement of the Civil Cycle of nineteen years, and has an effect upon the number of days contained in such Cycles.

The method of finding the length of the Civil Cycles will be given when these regulations have been described.

Hence the necessity of attending to the difference between Novilunium, the computed day of New Moon, and Neomenia, the day on which the New Moon is celebrated. (See *post*, Chap. IV., Art. 47.)

45. In Article 36 the additions were indicated which must be made to the Molad BeHaRD in order to find the Molads for subsequent Cycles. These Molads may now be computed. There are certain facts, pointed out by Isidore Loeb,* which greatly facilitate the calculation.

1. For computing the Chalaḳim.

The duration of one Astronomical Cycle is 6939d. 16h. 595ch., and the duration of two Cycles is 13879d. 9h. 110ch. Therefore the duration of two Cycles exceeds an exact number of weeks by 5d. 9h. 110ch.

Hence the Chalaḳim in the Molad for any Cycle, C + 2, will be 110 more in number than in the Molad for the Cycle C.

Now, in the Molad for the First Cycle the number of Chalaḳim is 204; therefore, in the Molad for the Third Cycle there will be 204 + 110, or 314; in the Molad for the Fifth Cycle there will be 204 + 2 (110), or 424; and so on. Hence, for the Molads of the successive Cycles with uneven numbers we have, for the Chalaḳim, an Arithmetical Series of which the first term is 204, and the common difference 110. This series may be easily written down, care being taken to reject 1080 whenever it is possible to do so, this being the number of Chalaḳim in one hour, which will of course be carried to the hours.

The series for the Cycles with uneven numbers will therefore be—

204, 314, 424, 534, 644, 754, 864, 974, (1084 − 1080, or) 4, 114, &c.

* "Tables du Calendrier Juif," p. 6. Problème i.

Again, for the Cycles with even numbers, the first term of the series will be the number of Chalakim in the Molad for the second Cycle; this is found from the sum of—

	d.	h.	ch.
Molad BeHaRD	2	5	204
Addition for one Cycle (Table VIII.)	2	16	595
	4	21	799

The first term of the series for the Cycles with uneven numbers is, therefore, 799; and, just as in the former case, writing now C + 1 for C, and C + 3 for C + 2, the common difference is, as before, 110. Therefore, the series is 799, 909, 1019, (1129 – 1080, or) 49, 159, 269, &c.

A check upon results may be obtained by observing that the nth term of any Arithmetical Series, whose first term is a, and common difference d, is $a + (n - 1)d$. Thus, the nth term of the first series will be $204 + (n - 1)\ 110$, or $110n + 94$. That of the second series, for the even numbers, will be $779 + (n - 1)\ 110$, or $110n + 689$. In both cases 1080 will be rejected as often as possible.

Also, because the 1st, 2nd, 3rd, 4th, &c., terms of the first series belong to the Cycles whose numbers are 1, 3, 5, 7, 9, &c., the nth term of this series will belong to the Cycle whose number is $2n - 1$. Thus, if the number of the Cycle be 99, the term of the series which belongs to it will be the fiftieth, for $99 = 2 \times 50 - 1$. In this case $n = 50$, therefore the number of Chalakim in the Molad of the ninety-ninth Cycle is $110 \times 50 + 94$, or 5594, which becomes 194 when 5×1080 is rejected.

In the same way, because the 1st, 2nd, 3rd, 4th, &c., terms of the second series belong to the Cycles whose numbers are 2, 4, 6, 8, &c., the nth term of this series, for the even numbers, will belong to the Cycle whose number is $2n$. Thus, if the number of the Cycle be 98, the term of the series which belongs to it will be the forty-ninth, for $98 = 2 \times 49$. In this case $n = 49$, and the number of the Chalakim in the ninety-eighth Cycle is $110 \times 49 + 689$, or 6079, which becomes 679 when 1080 has been rejected five times.

The result of this is that the Chalakim in the Molad for any uneven Cycle, as 1, 3, 5, &c., can never be in number other than one of the terms of the Arithmetical Series 4, 14, 24 . . . . 1074, where the common difference is 10; and the Chalaḳim in the Molad for any even Cycle, as 2, 4, 6, &c., can never be in number other than one of the terms of the series 9, 19, 29 .... 1079. For the Chalaḳim in the Molad for any Cycle C + 2 exceed in number those in the Molad for the Cycle C by 110, so that, if we write down the series of which the first term is 204, and common difference is 110, rejecting 1080 from any term when it is possible to do so, we obtain the following system, the terms being written consecutively in the horizontal lines:—

204	314	424	534	644	754	864	974	4	114
224	334	444	554	664	774	884	994	24	134
244	354	464	574	684	794	904	1014	44	154
264	374	484	594	704	814	924	1034	64	174
284	394	504	614	724	834	944	1054	84	194
304	414	524	634	744	854	964	1074	104	214
324	434	544	654	764	874	984	14	124	234
344	454	564	674	784	894	1004	34	144	254
364	474	584	694	804	914	1024	54	164	274
384	494	604	714	824	934	1044	74	184	294
404	514	624	734	844	954	1064	94		

After 94 the next term would be 204, and the series recurs; so that every term here written is included in the series 4, 14, 24 .... 1074. By the substitution of the digit 9 for 4, whenever the latter occurs in the units place, we have a similar system for those Cycles which are evenly numbered, as 2, 4, 6, &c. Every number in this system will be covered by one of terms of the series 9, 19, 29 .... 1079.

2. For Computing the Hours.

The length of three Astronomical Cycles is 3(6939d. 16h. 595ch.), or 20819d. 1h. 705ch. This interval of time is 1d. 1h. 705ch. in excess of an exact number of weeks.

Therefore the number of hours in the Molad for any Cycle, C + 3, is greater by unity than the number in the Molad for the Cycle C, assuming that nothing be carried from the Chalaḳim to the column of hours. If, however, the sum of the Chalaḳim be equal to or be greater than 1080, then 1 hour will be carried from such sum. In this case the number of hours in the Molad for C + 3 will be greater by 2 than the number in the Molad for the Cycle 3.

Now, in order to obtain the Molad for C + 3, the whole amount to be added to that for C, on account of three Cycles, is (by Table VIII.), 1d. 1h. 705ch.; and 705 = 1080 − 375; therefore it is only when the Chalaḳim in Cycle C are in number equal to or greater than 375 that

1 hour will be carried forward. But as no term in either of the series for the Chalaḳim is, or ever can be, 375, it is sufficient to say that the hours in the Molads of the Cycles, C, C + 3, C + 6, C + 9, &c., increase by unity if the Chalaḳim in the respective terms be less than 375, but increase by 2 if the number be equal to or greater than 375, that is if the number be greater than 374.

The computation for the hours may therefore be distributed into three series, namely, those for the Cycles whose numbers are—

1, 4, 7, 10, 13, &c.
2, 5, 8, 11, 14, &c.
3, 6, 9, 12, 15, &c.

And it will be found, when the Computation is made, that for—

Cycle 1		the hours are 5,	and Chalaḳim	less than 375
,, 1 + 3, or 4,	,,	5 + 1, or 6,	,,	more ,,
,, 4 + 3, or 7,	,,	6 + 2, or 8,	,,	,, ,,
,, 7 + 3, or 10,	,,	8 + 2, or 10,	,,	less ,,
,, 10 + 3, or 13,	,,	10 + 1, or 11,	,,	more ,,
,, 13 + 3, or 16,	,,	11 + 2, or 13,	,,	,, ,,
,, 16 + 3, or 19,	,,	13 + 2, or 15,	,,	less ,,
,, 19 + 3, or 22,	,,	15 + 1, or 16,	,,	&c.
&c.		&c.		

So, again, it will be found that for—

Cycle 2		the hours are 21,	and Chalaḳim	more than 375
,, 2 + 3, or 5,	,,	21 + 2, or 23,	,,	,, ,,
,, 5 + 3, or 8,	,,	23 + 2, or 25 = 1d. 1h.	,,	less ,,
,, 8 + 3, or 11,	,,	1 + 1, or 2,	,,	more ,,
,, 11 + 3, or 14,	,,	2 + 2, or 4,	,,	,, ,,
,, 14 + 3, or 17,	,,	4 + 2, or 6,	,,	less ,,
,, 17 + 3, or 20,	,,	6 + 1, or 7,	,,	&c.
&c.		&c.		

Also for—

Cycle 3		the hours are 14,	and Chalaḳim	less than 375
,, 3 + 3, or 6,	,,	14 + 1, or 15,	,,	more ,,
,, 6 + 3, or 9,	,,	15 + 2, or 17,	,,	,, ,,
,, 9 + 3, or 12,	,,	17 + 2, or 19,	,,	less ,,
,, 12 + 3, or 15,	,,	19 + 1, or 20,	,,	more ,,
,, 15 + 3, or 18,	,,	20 + 2, or 22,	,,	,, ,,
,, 18 + 3, or 21,	,,	22 + 2, or 24 = 1d. 0h.	,,	less ,,
,, 21 + 3, or 24,	,,	0 + 1, or 1,	,,	&c.
&c.		&c.		

3. Computation for the Days.

Since the excess of three Cycles over an exact number of weeks is 1d. 1h. 705ch., the number of days in the Molad for any Cycle, C, must be increased by unity in order to find the number of days in the Molad for the Cycle C + 3. But, if the hours and Chalakim in the Molad for Cycle C amount to, or are greater than 22h. 375ch., then the number of days for the Molad of C + 3 will be two more than the number in that for Cycle C; because, if 22h. 375ch., or more, be added to 1d. 1h. 705ch., the sum of the hours and Chalakim will either amount to or be greater than 24h., so that one day would have to be carried to the sum of days.

The computation for the days may, however, be made even more rapidly than by this process, in the following manner:—

Let H and *h* be the hours in the Molads for C and C + 3 respectively. If H be less than *h*, the days in the Molad for C are to be increased by unity to give the days in the Molad for C + 3. If H be greater than *h*, the increase is to be 2.

It is assumed that the columns of hours and Chalakim, as exhibited in Table IX., have been written before the days are computed.

This computation will be distributed into three series, in the same way as the three series for the hours.

Thus we have, for—

Cycle		days are		hours are	this is less than	of Cycle
Cycle 1	days are	2,	hours are	5;	this is less than 6	of Cycle 4
„ 1 + 3, or 4,	„	2 + 1, or 3,	„	6;	„ 8	„ 7
„ 4 + 3, or 7,	„	3 + 1, or 4,	„	8;	„ 10	„ 10
„ 7 + 3, or 10,	„	4 + 1, or 5,	„	10;	„ 11	„ 13
„ 10 + 3, or 13,	„	5 + 1, or 6,	„	11;	„ 13	„ 16
„ 13 + 3, or 16,	„	6 + 1, or 7,	„	13;	„ 15	„ 19
„ 16 + 3, or 19,	„	7 + 1, or 1,	„	15;	„ 16	„ 22
„ 19 + 3, or 22,	„	1 + 1, or 2,	„	16;	„ 18	„ 25
„ 22 + 3, or 25,	„	2 + 1, or 3,		&c.		&c.
&c.		&c.				

Again, it will be found that for—

Cycle		days are		hours are		of Cycle
Cycle 2	the days are	4,	and hours are	21;	less than 23	of Cycle 5
„ 2 + 3, or 5,	„	4 + 1, or 5,	„	23;	more „ 1	„ 8
„ 5 + 3, or 8,	„	5 + 2, or 7,	„	1;	less „ 2	„ 11
„ 8 + 3, or 11,	„	0 + 1, or 1,	„	2;	„ „ 4	„ 14
„ 11 + 3, or 14,	„	1 + 1, or 2,	„	4;	„ „ 6	„ 17
„ 14 + 3, or 17,	„	2 + 1, or 3,	„	6;	„ „ 7	„ 20
„ 17 + 3, or 20,	„	3 + 1, or 4,			&c.	
&c.		&c.				

And, lastly, for—

Cycle 3	the days are 7,	and hours are 14;	less than 15 of Cycle 6
„ 3 + 3, or 6,	„ 7 + 1, or 1,	„ 15;	„ „ 17 „ 9
„ 6 + 3, or 9,	„ 1 + 1, or 2,	„ 17;	„ „ 19 „ 12
„ 9 + 3, or 12,	„ 2 + 1, or 3,	„ 19;	„ „ 20 „ 15
„ 12 + 3, or 15,	„ 3 + 1, or 4,	„ 20;	„ „ 22 „ 18
„ 15 + 3, or 18,	„ 4 + 1, or 5,	„ 22;	more „ 0 „ 21
„ 18 + 3, or 21,	„ 5 + 2, or 7,	„ 0;	less „ 1 „ 24
„ 21 + 3, or 24,	„ 0 + 1, or 1,		&c.
&c.	&c.		

Following the method here described Table IX. is formed. The first column gives the number of the Cycle, from 1 to 528; the second gives the year which, in the Mundane Era, corresponds to the first year of each Cycle; and the third column gives the Molad for the Cycle, commencing with BeHaRD, 2d. 5h. 204ch., the Molad for the first Cycle of the Era.

The Chalakim for all the Cycles with uneven numbers are first written down; next, the Chalakim for all the Cycles with even numbers. The hours are then computed; first, for the series of Cycles with numbers 4, 7, 10, 13, &c.; then, for those with the numbers 2, 5, 8, 11, &c.; and next, for those with the numbers 3, 6, 9, 12, &c. The days in the three series are computed in the same order.

It will be remembered that 1080ch. are always to be carried forward to the column of hours, as 1 hour; that 24 hours are to be carried forward as 1 day; and that 7 is to be rejected from the feria, or number of the day, when the number amounts to or exceeds 8 days.

The results thus obtained may be tested by employing the Table VIII. of Additions to be made to the Molad for any Cycle in order to find the Molad for any subsequent Cycle.

Thus, for Cycle 41,

Molad BeHaRD	2	5	204
Add for 40 Cycles	2	14	40
Molad for Cycle 41	4	19	244

46. It has been demonstrated by René Martin * that the Molads do not recur in the same order until 36288 Cycles, or 689472 years

* "Mémoire sur le calendrier hebraïque." Angers, 1863, p. 106.

have elapsed. The same thing was shown by al-Bîrûnî nine hundred years ago.* The proof is very simple.

An Astronomical Cycle contains 6939d. 16h. 595ch. or $6939 \frac{3575}{5184}$.

The numerator and denominator in the fraction have no common measure, therefore the fraction will not vanish till the whole quantity is multiplied by 5184. In other words, 5184 is the least number of Cycles which contains an interval of time that can be expressed in integral days without any horary appendices. The computed Conjunction of Sun and Moon, for the Molad of Tishrî, will not return to the same day of the week, and same time of the day, until seven times this number of Cycles have elapsed, that is, not till after 36288 Cycles, or 689472 years, have passed.

Observe that $6939 \frac{3575}{5184} \times 5184 = 35975251$, a number which is of the form $7n + 4$; the least multiple which will bring this number to the form $7n$ is 7.

More will be said upon this subject when the question of Perpetual Calendars, so called, is discussed.

The following is the demonstration given by René Martin—

Molad BeHaRD	= 2	5	204 =	57444ch.........*a*.
Cyclical excess	= 2	16	595 =	69715ch..........*b*.
Chalaḳim in 7 days	= 7 ×	24 ×	1,080 =	181440ch..........*c*.

Let x be the required number of the Cycle whose Molad is again to be 2 5 204.

The Molad for Tishrî in year 1 of Cycle 1...... $= a$.
The Molad for Tishrî in year 1 of Cycle 2...... $= a + b$.
The Molad for Tishrî in year 1 of Cycle 3...... $= a + 2b$.

And, generally,
The Molad for Tishrî in year 1 of Cycle x...... $= a + (x - 1)b$.

The value of $a + (x - 1)b$ must be such that, when the greatest possible integral number of weeks is taken away from it, the remainder may be a.

* Dr. Sachau's trans., "Vestiges," p. 153.

Let p be this number of weeks, then cp is the number of Chalaḳim in p weeks, and we have—

$$a + (x - 1)b - cp = a$$

$$\therefore \quad x - 1 = \frac{cp}{b} = \frac{181440}{69715}p = \frac{36288}{13943}p$$

This fraction is in its lowest terms, therefore 13943 is the least possible value of p, since x, and therefore $x - 1$, is an integer. Hence, $x - 1 = 36288$; that is to say, 36288 Cycles, or 689472 years must elapse before the Molad for Tishrî will be again 2 5 204.

CHAPTER IV

RULES OF THE JEWISH CALENDAR AS NOW ESTABLISHED

47. Hitherto the Molads, or the day of the week and the time upon that day, when the computed New Moons will occur for the Cycles, the years of the Cycle, and the months of the year, have been calculated. The instant of time indicated by the Molad is the Astronomical commencement of the month, the year, or the Cycle, according to the estimated mean value of a Lunation in the Jewish computation. This, of necessity, involves in the Molad the fractions of a day; but, as with the Julian and Gregorian Calendars, so with the Jewish—no fractions of a day can be admitted, and the Calendar months commence, as do the days, at a fixed time, namely, at six in the evening for the Meridian of Jerusalem. They do not, however, always, or indeed most frequently, commence upon the day indicated by the Molad. The ancient ordinances which govern the Jewish holy days compel this fluctuation.

When it is said that the Calendar days commence at six in the evening for the Meridian of Jerusalem, it must be understood that this formal time refers to the Calendar and the Calendar only. It does not mean that the Civil days in any given locality, as, for example, in London, or in Canton, commence at that particular local time which coincides with 6 p.m. at Jerusalem. The longitudes of London and Canton differ respectively from that of Jerusalem to the extent that when it is six in the evening at Jerusalem, it is 3h. 39m. in the afternoon at London, and 11h. 12m. in the night at Canton; the former being 2h. 21m. to the west, and the latter 5h. 12m. to the east of Jerusalem.* Roughly speaking, the Civil day commences at sunset, local time, at

* Longitude of Canton, 113° 20′ E. of Greenwich.

any given place; so that, as Lazarus Bendavid says,* "A Calendar composed for the Ganges can be used by the Jews on the Mississippi, as all look to their own Meridian only." He points out that Christopher Wolff is quite wrong with regard to this matter,† and that a similar mistake has been made by many subsequent writers. He says that Waser especially does not seem to have mastered the subject. There are certain laws, to be hereafter explained, which frequently cause the postponement of Tishrî 1 from the feria indicated by the Molad to the next day, and even to the day after the next; Waser, therefore, according to Bendavid, proposes this case: "Assume that the New Moon of Tishrî occurs for the Meridian of Paris on feria 3, at 8h. 40m. 20s.; the local time at Moscow would then be 11h. 4m. 20s. At Paris the New Moon would be celebrated on Tuesday, but the Law which is called GaTRaD—ADU" (see *post*, Article 52 (2)) "would cause the celebration to be postponed at Moscow till the Thursday following." This, of course, could not be permitted, and upon this Wolff founds the hypothesis that everywhere the modern Jews go by the Meridian of Jerusalem. But, says Bendavid, "I should like to know how the Meridian of Paris concerns the Jews in Moscow."

The facts are very simple, and there is no real difficulty involved. The Calendar is formed according to the Meridian of Jerusalem. Its rules are all framed with respect to that Meridian, and that only. If Tishrî 1 be postponed it is because the computed Molad has a particular value at Jerusalem. What may be the corresponding local time at Paris, or Moscow, or on the banks of the Ganges is not considered. The Jews everywhere are to commence their months, and years, and Cycles with the day determined for Jerusalem, but the hour of that day at which they commence their service is determined by the latitude, upon which the time of sunset depends, and the local time at the place where they dwell. We have precisely the same effect in our own Gregorian Calendar. That Calendar is framed for the Meridian of Rome, which is 12° 30′, or, in time, fifty minutes, east of Greenwich; our Easter Sunday does not commence at 50m. past 12h. on Saturday night; it commences at midnight, that is, it commences when it is midnight with us, not when it is midnight at Rome. The Christians

* "Zur Berechnung des Jüdischen Kalenders," p. 51, § *b*. "Ein Kalender am Ganges verfertigt, ist für die Juden am Mississippi-Flutz brauchbar, da alle nur auf ihren Meridian Rücksicht nehmen."

† In the "Elementa Chronologica," § 339, 6.

in Alexandria use the same Calendar and observe Easter on the same day as the Romans and ourselves, but they commence their Sunday 69 minutes earlier than we commence it.

So it is with the Jews; their days and their Festivals begin according to the local time, determined by the position of the place.

In regulating the time when any given day will commence the question of twilight is taken into consideration. It is lawful to lengthen all days, especially those of rejoicing, either at their beginning or their end.* The only exception to this is Kippûr, the great Day of Atonement, which is unalterable. It is observed as a strict Fast, and, as no one is allowed to fast for more than twenty-four hours, this day cannot be lengthened. The service on the eve is sometimes begun a few minutes earlier, but not the Fast. On the other hand, Tishri 1, for example, which is a Festival day, may begin at 5.30 p.m., although sunset does not take place till after six o'clock. So with respect to the Sabbath. It is not announced that "the Sabbath commences" but that "the service commences" at such and such an hour. If any one be engaged, for example, in writing a letter on Friday evening, he is not bound to leave off his occupation at the exact time announced. Although no work is done upon the Sabbath a license of about fifteen minutes is allowed, and the writing, or other occupation, may be continued during the permitted margin.

Inasmuch as the Jewish Civil and religious day is not reckoned from an absolutely fixed time, as with ourselves, but from evening to evening, the commencement of the day varies according to the time of the year and according to the latitude of the place. Thus, if the Sun set for the latitude of London at 8 p.m. in the month of June, it will not set till 10 p.m. in the North of Scotland, and be still later in the Shetland Isles.

Rules for the commencements of the Sabbaths and Festivals for the latitude of London were formed by Rabbi David Nieto,† but there was a difficulty, until recently, as to the time at which these days should close. Dr. Joseph Jacobs, the Editor of the Jewish Year Book, says that the ancient Rabbinical rule is that the day is at an end when three stars of the second magnitude can be seen in the heavens.‡

* With respect to lengthening Feasts and not lengthening Fasts, compare the old maxim of the Canonists—"Favores sunt ampliandi, et odiosa sunt restringenda."

† Haham of the Sephardim, that is, Chief Rabbi of the Spanish Jews. He died in London, January 10, 1728.

‡ Year Book for 5658, A.D. 1897-1898, p. 18.

Within the last twenty years Dr. Friedlander in England, M. Hirsch in France, and Dr. Zuckermann in Germany, have determined astronomically how many degrees below the horizon the Sun must have sunk before three stars of the second magnitude can be seen. This was a point of the Law which had not been previously determined.

The time at which the Sabbaths close in London was settled by the very Rev. Dr. Adler, the late Chief Rabbi, according to the formula of Dr. Friedlander.

48. Under the reformed Calendar the ancient customs are not all observed in their integrity. For instance, in former times watchers were employed to observe the first appearance of the Moon's crescent, and when their report had been received and verified the day of New Moon was publicly proclaimed. But under the reformed Calendar the day, not of the true Moon but of a mean Moon supposed to move uniformly in the heavens, is Astronomically computed; and the New Moon is celebrated, with certain exceptions to be described, upon the day itself when the computed Conjunction occurs. The chief of these exceptions is that if the computed Conjunction take place upon a Sunday, a Wednesday, or a Friday, its celebration is postponed to the following day. For the reason of this rule see *post*, Article 49 (2), and for further exceptions Articles 51, 52.

The reformed Calendar was undoubtedly an innovation, and, as Schwarz observes,* there is nothing in the history of the Jews with which it can be compared. It was a necessity in order to preserve the integrity of their religious observances, and for their very existence as a distinct and separate people. The communities, scattered in different countries, were no longer ably to rely upon the receipt of messages from the chief Council in Palestine, and, without a fixed Calendar, would have been equally unable to determine the time for their solemn Feasts, New Moons, and assemblies, the observance of which upon certain days was enjoined by the Law, to whose dictates they were devotedly attached.

In order to understand how great the innovation was the rules as now established—rules which have been kept undoubtedly since the time of Hillel, and probably for a much longer period—must be considered, and compared so far as possible with the requirements of the Mosaical Law.

* "Der Jüdische Kalender," p. 58.

49. Leading Rules of the Reformed Calendar.

1. The fifteenth day of the month Nîsân, the day observed as that of the Full Moon after the Sun has entered the Sign Aries, generally known as the First Day of the Passover, Azyma, or the First of the Days of Unleavened Bread, is never allowed to fall upon feriæ 2, 4, or 6, Monday, Wednesday, or Friday.

This is a Rabbinical rule. It is a fact, as Stöffler remarks,* that the Levitical Law nowhere expressly prohibits these days for the celebration of the First Day of the Passover. He states that the regulation was not made till after the building of the second Temple. If it were then made it is probable that it was because it was found difficult, without such a rule, to carry into effect the laws which are expressly laid down concerning other Festivals and Fasts. The Passover regulates all other solemnities of the year, just as Easter determines the observance of the Christian holy days; and therefore it is arranged in such a manner that no other Festivals or Fasts should occur upon days when it would be in some cases impossible, in others highly inconvenient to observe them properly.

There are good reasons for the rule. It is necessary to guard against any day upon which work has to be done falling on the Sabbath, feria 7, since work of every description is strictly prohibited on that day.†

Again, it was desirable to prevent a Sabbath, and any other day upon which all work must cease, from following each other consecutively. Two such days coming together would give rise to great practical inconvenience in the social life of the people; no fire could be lighted; no food could be cooked; nothing could be carried from one place to another; no journey could be made exceeding two thousand paces in length. Perhaps the most important consideration was that no dead body could be buried, while in a hot and sultry climate like that of Palestine it was highly essential that burial should take place so soon as possible after death.‡

* In the "Calendarium Romanum Magnum," Prop. xli., F. f. 74. "Deviant enim a Mosaica constitutione quà nunquam Pascha celebrant die Lunæ, die Mercurii, et die Veneris, quos lex nusquam prohibet . . . sed per constitutiones a legis peritis et Judicibus eorum emanatas in secunda templi instauratione, sequentibus intrudunt diebus."

† Exodus xxxv. 2. "Six days shall work be done; but on the seventh day there shall be to you an holy day, a Sabbath of rest to the Lord: whosoever doth work thereon shall be put to death."

Cf. also Exodus xx. 8-11, and xxxi. 14, 15; Leviticus xxiii. 3; Deuteronomy v. 12-15. In Numbers xv. 32-36, there is recorded the stoning of a man who gathered sticks on the Sabbath day.

‡ See *post*, on the Sabbath, Article 75.

The Hebrew letters forming the word BaDU are employed as "memoria technica" to indicate the prohibited feriæ for Nîsân 15, namely 2, 4, and 6, Monday, Wednesday, Friday. In the Hebrew method of numeration B = 2, D = 4, U = 6.

2. It will be remembered that Tishrî 1 in any Jewish Civil year, H + 1, is always the 163rd day after Nîsân 15 in the preceding year, H, (Article 25). Now 163 is of the form $7n + 2$; therefore, rejecting the $7n$ days, or n complete weeks, it is only necessary to add 2 to the feria of Nîsân 15 in any year H, in order to find the feria of Tishrî in the year H + 1.

Hence, if Nîsân 15 were allowed to fall upon either feria 2, 4, or 6, then the following Tishrî 1 would occur either on feria 4, 6, or 1, Wednesday, Friday, or Sunday. These days would be inconvenient. It is the first day of the Civil year, and the first day of the seventh month of the Sacred or Religious year. It is a day upon which all work is strictly prohibited.* Now if it were observed upon a Friday, or a Sunday, there would be two days of rest coming together, for Friday immediately precedes, and Sunday immediately follows the Sabbath.

Moreover, if Tishrî 1 were allowed to fall upon a Sunday, then Tishrî 14 would be a Sabbath, and the next day, Tishrî 15 is Succoth, the Feast of Tabernacles, upon which no work might be done,† so that again there would be two days of rest occurring consecutively.

If Tishrî 1 were observed upon a Wednesday, then the great Day of Atonement, the fast Kippûr, which is observed upon the tenth day of this month, would fall upon a Friday. All work upon this day is forbidden,‡ and because the day following is the Sabbath there would again be two days of rest coming together. It is chiefly with respect to this important day that the arrangements are made.

The social inconvenience arising from the occurrence of two consecutive Sabbaths, or days of rest, would be more especially felt in the

* Leviticus xxiii. 24, 25. "In the seventh month, in the first day of the month, shall ye have a Sabbath . . . ye shall do no servile work therein."

† Leviticus xxiii. 34, 35. "The fifteenth day of this seventh month shall be the Feast of Tabernacles for seven days unto the Lord. On the first day shall be an holy convocation: ye shall do no servile work therein." Also, Numbers xxix. 12.

‡ Leviticus xxiii. 27, 28. "On the tenth day of the seventh month there shall be a day of Atonement: it shall be an holy convocation unto you: and ye shall afflict your souls, and offer an offering made by fire unto the Lord. And ye shall do no work in that same day: for it is a day of Atonement, to make an Atonement for you before the Lord your God."

month Tishrî, which is always in the Autumn. The heat in Palestine is then intense, so that the food cooked on the preceding working day would not keep in good condition for the two non-working days. It must, however, and does, frequently happen at other seasons of the year that there are two consecutive days of rest. Thus, when Nîsân 1 falls upon feria 1, Sunday, which is not prohibited, it follows immediately after the ordinary weekly Sabbath. If it fall upon feria 7, the Sabbath itself, then Schabuoth, the Feast of Weeks, which is fifty days afterwards (Pentecost), must occur upon feria 1, Sunday, which immediately follows the Sabbath.

In fact, the Rabbinical rule with respect to the prohibited days appears to have been made with especial regard to the season of the year at which the month Tishrî occurs; the month of which the tenth day is the great Day of Atonement.

The memorial letters for the days on which it is forbidden to celebrate Tishrî 1 are ADU, feria 1, 4, and 6. A = 1, D = 4, U = 6.

3. Because the First Day of Unleavened Bread, Nisân 15 cannot be upon either feria 2, 4, or 6, therefore Schabuoth, or Ashereth, the Feast of Weeks, which is fifty days after Nîsân 15, cannot be upon either feria 3, 5, or 7, Tuesday, Thursday, or Saturday; for fifty days exceed an exact number of weeks by one day.

This rule is remembered by the letters of the word GaHaZ. G = 3, H = 5, and Z = 7.

4. The Feast of Lots, or Purim, always precedes Nîsân 15 by thirty days, or four weeks and two days; therefore Purim cannot be upon either feria 7, 2, or 4, Saturday, Monday, or Wednesday.

The word for this is ZaBaD.

5. Because Tishrî 1 cannot be upon either feria 1, 4, or 6, therefore Kippûr, the Day of Atonement, observed upon Tishrî 10, cannot be upon either feria 3, 6, or 1, Tuesday, Friday, or Sunday.

The memorial letters are AGU.

Collecting the results of the above rules, it appears that the prohibited days are, for Passover.............. 2, 4, 6. BaDU.

,,	Tishrî 1	1, 4, 6.	ADU.
,,	Kippûr	1, 3, 6.	AGU.
,,	Schabuoth	3, 5, 7.	GaHaZ.
,,	Purim	2, 4, 7.	ZaBaD.

Also, if the feria of Nîsân 15 be	F.
that of Tishrî 1 will be	F + 2.
„ Kippûr „	F + 4.
„ Schabuoth „	F + 1.
„ Purim „	F + 5.

Since F indicates the same week-day as F + 7, therefore F + 4 and F + 5 are respectively equivalent to F − 3 and F − 2. The Purim whose feria is F + 5, or F − 2 is the Purim which precedes Nîsân 15; it is in the same Civil year as Tishrî 1, but in the Sacred or Ecclesiastical year which precedes that commencing with Nîsân 1.

50. These five rules, concerning the feriæ upon which certain of the chief solemnities cannot fall, are Political. There are other rules which may be called Astronomical, inasmuch as they are in a great measure due to the method employed in the construction of the Calendar. They are of importance, for the form or variety of the year, that is the number of days which it contains, depends upon them as well as upon ADU.

This, however, does not apply to the question, Is the year Common or Embolismic? The answer to that question is determined by the position of the year in the Cycle. The places of the Embolismic years are fixed and, as already stated, are those which stand in the numerical order

3, 6, 8, 11, 14, 17, 19,

while the remaining twelve years in the Cycle are Common.

51. Every Jewish year is of the form $7n + x$, where x may be either 3, 4, 5, 6, or 0. No year can have any other value for its number of days, for the six forms of the year are:—

1. Common Deficient, having days 353, or $7n + 3$.
2. „ Regular, „ 354, or $7n + 4$.
3. „ Abundant, „ 355, or $7n + 5$.
4. Embolismic Deficient, „ 383, or $7n + 5$.
5. „ Regular, „ 384, or $7n + 6$.
6. „ Abundant, „ 385, or $7n$

Consideration will first be given to those facts arising from Astronomical computation which, like ADU, frequently cause the first day of the year to differ from the day indicated by the Molad, that is, from the day Astronomically computed for the Conjunction of the Sun and Moon.

The reason why no year is allowed to commence with either feria 1, 4, or 6 has already been assigned. If the feria of the Molad, as found by computation, fall to either of these forbidden days, then Tishrî 1 is postponed to the next day. It will frequently happen that an Astronomical postponement of Tishrî 1 will have to be made from a lawful to an unlawful day; in that case a further postponement takes place, so that there occurs a postponement of two days from the day indicated by the Molad.

The postponement is never made, under any circumstances, for more than two days.

Another fact, to which attention should be given, is that the first day of any year or Cycle is never allowed to retrogress from the feria indicated by the Molad. If it cannot be observed on the day found by computation it is invariably advanced; it is observed a day, or two days later; it is never observed earlier than the day indicated by the Molad.

52. The following are the rules with respect to the Astronomical postponement. They are given in the "Kiddusch hachodesh" of Maimonides, vii. §§ 2–6.

1. If the computed New Moon of Tishrî occur upon any day of the week so late as, or later than, 18h., reckoned from 6 p.m. of the preceding evening (for the Meridian of Jerusalem), that is to say, if it occur upon any day of the week at Noon, or later than Noon, then the following day is to be taken for the celebration of that New Moon, and is to be Tishrî 1, always provided that the following day in question is not one of the days forbidden for Tishrî 1. If it should be one of the forbidden days, namely Sunday, Wednesday, or Friday, then Tishrî 1 must be further postponed to one day later.

The memorial word for this rule is YacH. Y = 10; cH = 8.

The reason for the rule is as follows:—Although the Jewish Civil day commences at 6 p.m., yet, for the purpose of computing the Conjunctions of the Sun and Moon, the days commence at the preceding Noon. The Astronomical time, thus measured, shows an advance of six hours upon Civil time. Hence, if Civil time upon any given day be 18h., it is Astronomically 24h.; or, a whole day from the preceding Noon. On that account the New Moon which occurs at Noon, or later than Noon is not reckoned as falling upon the feria indicated by the Molad, but upon the following feria.

For example:—In the Jewish year 5340 the Molad for Tishrî 1 is by computation 1d. 23h. 1079ch. In other words, 23h. 1079ch. of feria 1, Sunday, have elapsed before the Conjunction takes place. These hours and parts of an hour are reckoned from six in the evening of feria 7, Saturday; and the time at which the computed Conjunction takes place falls just within the limits of the Civil day, feria 1. By Astronomical reckoning feria 1 commenced six hours earlier, and the time elapsed since this Astronomical commencement is 29h. 1079ch.; in other words, feria 2 has not only been entered, but more than five hours of its duration have elapsed.

Tishrî 1 is therefore postponed to the next day; from Sunday, September 20, A.D. 1579, to Monday, September 21; these being the corresponding Gregorian dates.

For another example:—The computed Molad for the New Moon of Tishrî in the year 5797 is 7d. 22h. 35ch., or, the computed Conjunction occurs upon a Saturday at 22h. 35ch., measured from 6 p.m. of Friday. The time measured from Noon of Friday is therefore 28h. 35ch., equivalent to 4h. 35ch. in the afternoon of Saturday. By Astronomical reckoning the next day, Sunday, feria 1, has commenced and more than four hours of its duration have elapsed. The celebration of this New Moon, or Tishrî 1, does not take place upon the day indicated by the Molad, but is postponed to the next day, Sunday, Astronomically. Sunday, however, is forbidden by ADU, and therefore the celebration has to be further postponed, Politically, to feria 2, Monday. This day corresponds to the Gregorian date September 22, A.D. 2036.

2. If in a Common year* the computed Molad for Tishrî fall to a Tuesday, feria 3, so late as, or later than, 9h. 204ch., that is to say, if the Molad be greater than 3d. 9h. 203ch., then Tishrî 1 is to be postponed; and because it cannot be upon feria 4, Wednesday, on account of ADU it must be further postponed to Thursday, feria 5.

If the Molad be less than 3d. 9h. 204ch. by even 1 Chalaḳ there is no need for any postponement.

The memorial word for this rule is GaTRaD. G = 3; T = 9; R = 200; D = 4.

The reason for this rule is as follows:—Let the computed Molad

* Observe that this rule does not apply to Embolismic years. It belongs to Common years only.

for Tishrî in a Common year, H, have a value not less than 3d. 9h. 204ch. The duration of an Astronomical Common year is 354d. 8h. 876ch., which exceeds $7n$ weeks by 4d. 8h. 876ch. The Molad of Tishrî for the following year, H + 1, will have for its minimum value the sum of 3d. 9h. 204ch. and 4d. 8h. 876ch., or 7d. 18h. 0ch.; that is to say, if the computed Molad for H be not less than 3d. 9h. 204ch., then, that for H + 1 will not be less than 7d. 18h. 0ch. The rule YacH, concerning the 18 hours, intervenes. Feria 1 is Astronomically entered, and the celebration of the first New Moon of H + 1 must be postponed to that day, that is, from Saturday to Sunday. But Sunday is a prohibited day, and Tishrî 1 is further postponed Politically to Monday by ADU.

This postponement of the first day of H + 1 lengthens the preceding year, H, by two days. If, therefore, the year H had been allowed to commence with a Tuesday, as indicated by its computed Molad, it would have contained 356 days; for its last day is a Sunday (because H + 1 commences with a Monday), and it is a Common year. But no Common year can have more than 355 days. It must therefore be shortened by at least one day. It cannot be shortened by cutting off its last day, for that would make H + 1 to commence with a Sunday, which is prohibited. It cannot be shortened by cutting off its last two days, for that would make H + 1 to commence with a Saturday; but the feria of H + 1 is not less than 7d. 18h. 0ch., therefore YacH prevents it from commencing with a Saturday. And again H cannot be shortened by cutting off its last three days, for that would not only cause H + 1 to commence with a prohibited day, Friday, but would also cause the first day of H + 1 to retrogress from its Molad, which is never permitted. If H were shortened at its close by more than three days it would have less than 353 days, which is impossible.

It appears, then, that the year H cannot be reduced from 356 days by cutting off any of the days with which it terminates. Nothing therefore remains possible but to shorten it at its commencement. Its first day must be postponed from Tuesday, feria 3, to Wednesday, feria 4; and, because Wednesday is a prohibited day, there must be a further postponement to Thursday, feria 5. This reduces the number of 356 days to 354, the year commencing with a Thursday and terminating with a Sunday. It is, therefore, a Common Regular year, and can be of no other form.

The reason why this rule does not apply to an Embolismic year is that the Astronomical duration of such a year exceeds an exact number of weeks by 5d. 21h. 589ch. Suppose that the Molad of an Embolismic year, H, be, at the least, 3d. 9h. 204ch., and be not greater than 3d. 17h. 1079ch., so that it does not come under the rule YacH. The Molad of the following year, H + 1, will vary from 2d. 6h. 793ch. to 2d. 15h. 588ch,* and however it may vary between these limits the year H + 1 will commence with feria 2, Monday, to which there is no impediment. Consequently the year H will end with a Sunday, and if it commence with a Tuesday, as indicated by the Molad, it will have six more days than an exact number of weeks. Being Embolismic its form will be $7n + 6$, and it will have 384 days, which is quite consistent with the length of an Embolismic Regular year. Such a year may therefore commence with a Tuesday, feria 3, even if the Molad exceed 3d. 9h. 204ch., so long as it do not exceed 3d. 17h. 1079ch.

As an example, take the Embolismic year 5660. It is the seventeenth year of the 298th Cycle. Its computed Molad is 3d. 13h. 300ch. By the addition of 5d. 21h. 589ch. the Molad for the next year, 5661, is found to be 2d. 11h. 9ch. Therefore, 5661 commences with feria 2, Monday, and 5660 must terminate with a Sunday. This being the case, if 5660 commence with a Tuesday, as indicated by the Molad, it has $7n + 6$, or 384 days. It is an Embolismic Regular year, and no rule of the Calendar is transgressed.

But suppose now that the rule GaTRaD were applied to this Embolismic year, and that it were not allowed to commence till Thursday. It must still end with a Sunday, on account of the Molad for the following year falling to a Monday. It could only have 382 days, which is impossible because no Embolismic year ever has less than 383 days.

3. If the computed Molad for Tishri in a Common year which follows next after an Embolismic year exceed 2d. 15h. 588ch., that is to say, if it amount to 2d. 15h. 589ch., or be greater than this, then Tishri 1 is to be postponed from feria 2, Monday, to feria 3, Tuesday.

If the Molad be less than 2d. 15h. 589ch. by even one Chalak then there is no need for any postponement.

* 3	9	204	....	3	17	1079
5	21	589	....	5	21	589
2	6	793		2	15	588

The memorial words for this rule are BaTU ThaKPhaT. B = 2; TU = 15; Th = 400; K = 100; Ph = 80; T = 9.

The reason for the rule is as follows:—Let the Molad for some given year, H, be 2d. 15h. 589ch., or be greater than this, and let the preceding year, H – 1, be Embolismic. The excess of an Astronomical Embolismic year over an exact number of weeks is 5d. 21h. 589ch.; if this excess be subtracted from the Molad of H, which may be increased by 7 without altering the feria, the remainder will be the Molad for H – 1. The minimum value of this remainder will be 3d. 18h. 0ch.* The first day of H – 1 must therefore be postponed to feria 4, Wednesday, because the limit 18h. is reached. It must be further postponed to feria 5, Thursday, on account of ADU.

If, therefore, the Molad of H attain to, or be greater than 2d. 15h. 589ch., the preceding year, H – 1, must have commenced with a Thursday, feria 5, and being Embolismic, that is to say, being of one of the forms $7n + 5$, $7n + 6$, or $7n$ days, it must have had for its last day either a Monday, a Tuesday, or a Wednesday. Consequently the next year, H, could only have for its first day a Tuesday, a Wednesday, or a Thursday. Wednesday is impossible, it is forbidden by ADU. Thursday, feria 5, is impossible, for the Molad of H falls to feria 2, and postponement can never take place for more than two days. The only alternative is Tuesday, feria 3.

Hence the rule is that if the Molad of any year which follows an Embolismic year fall to feria 2, and the hours and Chalakim exceed 15h. 588ch., then, Tishrî 1 must be postponed to feria 3.

4. The five rules, BaDU, ADU, YacH, GaTRaD, and BaTU ThaKPhaT, which have reference to the postponement of Tishrî 1, are called the five Dechiyyôth of the Jewish Calendar. It will be convenient to place their results in a collective form:—

(1) BaDU. . . . Nîsân 15, never on Monday, Wednesday, or Friday.

(2) ADU. . . . Tishrî 1, never on Sunday, Wednesday, or Friday.

(3) YacH. . . . If the Molad for Tishrî fall to any day so late as or later than 18h., Tishrî 1 is postponed to the next day.

	d.	h.	ch.
* Minimum value = 2d. 15h. 589ch., equivalent ...	9	15	589
Subtract	5	21	589
	3	18	0

(4) GaTRaD. . . . If the Molad for Tishrî fall, in a Common year, on a Tuesday so late as or later than 9h. 204ch., Tishrî 1 is postponed to the next day, and thence by ADU to Thursday.

(5) BaTU ThaKPhaT. . . . If in a Common year which follows next after an Embolismic year the Molad for Tishrî fall upon a Monday so late as or later than 15h. 589ch., Tishrî 1 is postponed to Tuesday.

53. The rules which determine the feria with which any given year can possibly commence must now be considered. These rules will, for convenience of reference, be first stated in a tabulated form; the reasons for them will be given afterwards. They are partly Political, partly Astronomical.

The length or form of any given year is found by ascertaining, in the first place, whether it be a Common or an Embolismic year, and in the second place, by finding the feriæ with which it commences and terminates.

An example will illustrate the method to be employed.

Find the form of the Jewish year 5616.

(*a*) The division of 5616 by 19 gives a remainder 11, with a quotient 295. The year is therefore the eleventh in the 296th Cycle. Its place in the Cycle shows that it is Embolismic, and must be of the form 378 + x, where the value of x has to be found.

(*b*) To find the feria with which the year commences.

Molad BeHaRD	2	5	204
Add for 200 Cycles elapsed	5	22	200*
,, 90 ,, ,,	4	1	630
,, 5 ,, ,,	6	10	815
,, the eleventh year	6	6	339†
Molad for Tishrî, 5616	3	22	28

The computed New Moon occurs on feria 3, or Tuesday, and as the hours and Chalakim attain to 18h. and more, the celebration is postponed by YacH to Wednesday, and is further postponed by ADU to Thursday.

The first day of the year 5616 is therefore a Thursday.

(*c*) To find the feria with which the year terminates we must find that with which the next commences.

* Table VIII. † Table VII.

Molad for Tishri, 5616	3	22	28
Add the excess of an Embolismic year	5	21	589
Molad for Tishrî, 5617	2	19	617

The computed New Moon for Tishrî, 5617, falls to feria 2, or Monday, and Tishrî 1 is postponed to Tuesday by BaTU PhaKPhaT as well as by YacH.

(*d*) Insomuch as the first day of 5617 is a Tuesday the last day of 5616 must be a Monday. But it commences with a Thursday, as shown by (*b*). Therefore, its integral number of weeks, or 378 days, terminate with a Wednesday. It has five more days, namely Thursday, Friday, Saturday, Sunday, and Monday. Its length is therefore 378 + 5, or 383 days. Its form is $7n + 5$. It is an Embolismic Deficient year.

Example 2.

Lacoine in his "Tables de Concordance des Dates," p. 36, gives the form of the year 4668 as C.D., that is "Commune déficiente." Isidore Loeb in his "Tables du Calendrier Juif" (Tableau XII.) gives the form as 5a, that is, "Commune abondante," commencing with feria 5, or Thursday. Meier Kornick in his "System der Zeitrechnung," p. 117, makes Nîsân 15 in 4667 to be March 31, and in 4668 to be March 20, from which it may be deduced that he considers Tishrî 1 in 4668 and 4669 to have corresponded respectively to Thursday September 10, A.D. 907 and Tuesday, August 30, A.D. 908. He therefore makes the year 4668 to commence with a Thursday and terminate with a Monday, and therefore to be a Common Abundant year.

Is Lacoine right, or are Isidore Loeb and Kornick right?

The division of 4668 by 19 gives a quotient 245, and a remainder 13. The year in question is therefore the 13th of the 246th Cycle.

BeHaRD	2	5	204
Add for 200 Cycles	5	22	200
,, 40 ,,	2	14	40
,, 5 ,,	6	10	815
,, thirteenth year	2	12	724
Molad for Tishrî, 4668	5	16	903
Add excess of a Common year	4	8	876
Molad, for Tishrî, 4669	3	1	699

From this it is evident that the year 4668 commenced with feria 5, Thursday, and the next year with feria 3, Tuesday; so that 4668 must have terminated with a Monday. It therefore has five days more than an exact number of weeks, and is a Common Abundant Year. Isidore Loeb and Kornick are right; Lacoine is in error.

Example 3.

Lazarus Bendavid, in "Zur Berechnung des Jüdischen Kalenders," p. 97, gives a so-called "Calendarium Perpetuum," from which it appears that the year 4868 is to have its first day and its length determined by the symbol hR, which means that it commences with a Thursday and is "regel mässige," or regular. Is this correct?

This year is found in the usual way to be the fourth in the 257th Cycle.

BeHaRD	2	5	204
Add for 200 Cycles	5	22	200
„ 50 „	1	11	590
„ 6 „	2	3	330
„ fourth year	7	15	181
Molad for Tishri, 4868	5	9	425
Excess of a Common year	4	8	876
Molad for Tishri, 4869	2	18	221

Consequently the year 4868 commences with a Thursday, and it must terminate with a Monday; for the Molad of 4869 falling to feria 2, or Monday, but having more than 18 hours, comes under the rule YacH, causing Tishri 1 in this year to be Tuesday. The year 4868 has therefore 355 days, and ought to be marked h.U, meaning Thursday, "uebershussig," or abundant.*

54. The following Table shows the week-day with which a year of given form, $7n + x$, can commence and terminate, and the consequent week-day with which the year that follows it will commence.

It may be read thus:—A year of 353 days can only commence with

* This is not a misprint in the "Calendarium Perpetuum"; hU, cannot be substituted for hR, without vitiating the result for other years. It is a failure in this form of Perpetual Calendar, which passes under a title to which it has no real claim. The error arises from a source which will be explained when "Perpetual Calendars" are considered in Chapter VI.

a Monday or a Saturday. If it commence with a Monday it will terminate with a Wednesday; if it commence with a Saturday it will terminate with a Monday. The following year must then commence in the one case with a Thursday, in the other with a Tuesday.

The Proof of the Statements contained in the Table will be given directly afterwards.

FIRST AND LAST DAYS POSSIBLE FOR THE JEWISH YEARS, AND FIRST DAYS OF THE FOLLOWING YEAR.

	Length of the year H, in days.	First day of H.	Last day of H.	First day of H + 1.
1	$353 = 7n + 3$	Monday	Wednesday	Thursday
	,, ,,	Saturday	Monday	Tuesday
2	$354 = 7n + 4$	Tuesday	Friday	Saturday
	,, ,,	Thursday	Sunday	Monday
3	$355 = 7n + 5$	Monday	Friday	Saturday
	,, ,,	Thursday	Monday	Tuesday
	,, ,,	Saturday	Wednesday	Thursday
4	$383 = 7n + 5$	Monday	Friday	Saturday
	,, ,,	Thursday	Monday	Tuesday
	,, ,,	Saturday	Wednesday	Thursday
5	$384 = 7n + 6$	Tuesday	Sunday	Monday
6	$385 = 7n$	Monday	Sunday	Monday
	,, ,,	Thursday	Wednesday	Thursday
	,, ,,	Saturday	Friday	Saturday

PROOF OF THE STATEMENTS CONTAINED IN THE TABLE.

1. A Common Deficient year of 353 days can only commence with a Monday or a Saturday.

It cannot commence with a Sunday, a Wednesday, or a Friday, because these days are prohibited by ADU.

It cannot commence with feria 3, Tuesday, because if it did so commence, its $7n$ days, containing n complete weeks, would terminate with a Monday, and the last of its three remaining days would be a

Thursday. In that case the following year would commence with a Friday, which is a forbidden day for Tishri 1.

It cannot commence with feria 5, Thursday, for if it did so commence its completed weeks would end with a Wednesday, and the last of its three remaining days would be a Saturday. The next year would then commence with feria 1, Sunday, which is a forbidden day.

There is, however, nothing to prevent it from commencing with feria 2, Monday, or with feria 7, Saturday, and with one or other of these days it must commence. It will then end with a Wednesday or a Monday, and the next year will commence with a Thursday or a Tuesday, which are both lawful days.

2. A Common Regular year, of 354 days, can only commence with a Tuesday or a Thursday.

Such a year cannot commence with a Monday, feria 2, for if it did so commence its $7n$ days would end with Sunday, feria 1, and the last of its four remaining days would be a Thursday. The next year would begin with a Friday, which is prohibited by ADU.

It cannot commence with a Saturday, feria 7, for its $7n$ days would end with a Friday; the last of the remaining four days would be a Tuesday, and the next year would begin with a Wednesday, which is prohibited.

There is nothing to prevent it from commencing with feria 3, Tuesday, or feria 5, Thursday, in which case it would terminate with a Friday or a Sunday, and the next year would commence with a lawful day, Saturday or Monday.

3. A Common Abundant year, of 355 days, can only commence with a Monday, a Thursday, or a Saturday.

Such a year commencing with one of these three days would terminate either with a Friday, a Monday, or a Wednesday. The next year would commence with one or other of the lawful days Saturday, Tuesday, or Thursday.

But a year of 355 days cannot begin with a Tuesday, for its $7n$ days would end with a Monday, and the last of the remaining five days would be a Saturday. No year can end with a Saturday, because the next year would begin with a prohibited Sunday.

4. An Embolismic Deficient year, of 383 days, contains, like a Common Abundant year, five days more than an exact number of weeks. It is therefore subject to the same restraint as a Common Abundant

year, and cannot begin with a Tuesday. There is nothing to interfere with its first day being a Monday, a Thursday, or a Saturday, and with one or other of these three days it must begin.

5. An Embolismic Regular year, of 384 days, can only commence with a Tuesday.

Such a year cannot commence with a Monday, a Thursday, or a Saturday, for its $7n + 6$ days would terminate with a Saturday, a Tuesday, or a Thursday. The next year would begin with one of the forbidden days, a Sunday, a Wednesday, or a Friday.

The only remaining day with which it can commence is feria 3, Tuesday. In this case its $7n$ days would terminate with a Monday; the last of its remaining six days would be a Sunday. The next year would then commence with a Monday, to which there is no impediment.

6. An Embolismic Abundant year, of 385 days, can only commence with a Monday, a Thursday, or a Saturday.

With respect to the years of the other five forms it has not been necessary to consider any Astronomical reason why they cannot commence with certain days. The Political rule ADU has sufficed. The present case is different. A year of 385 days contains an exact number of weeks, so that with whatever feria it may commence it will terminate with the next preceding feria. Why, then, is it restricted as to its commencement to the three days Monday, Thursday, and Saturday? Why cannot it commence with a Tuesday? It would end with a Monday, and the next year would begin with a Tuesday, which is possible for a year of 354, or of 384 days. The latter is excluded because there are never two consecutive Embolismic years. But why should it not commence with a Tuesday, and be followed by a year of 354 days commencing also with a Tuesday?

The reason is Astronomical. The impossibility arises from the way in which the Calendar is constructed by the computation of Molads.

In order that any year, H, may commence with a Tuesday, feria 3, its Molad must not be less than 2d. 15h. 589ch., and not more than 3d. 17h. 1079ch. For if the Molads were less than 2d. 15h. 589ch. the year would commence with a Monday, feria 2, as indicated by the Molad, since the rule BaTU ThaKPhaT would not intervene to postpone Tishrî 1 to feria 3. Also, if the Molad were greater than 3d. 17h. 1079ch., that is to say, if it were 3d. 18h. 0ch., or more, then

YacH would intervene, and Tishrî 1 would be postponed from Tuesday, feria 3, to Thursday, feria 4.

Now the excess of an Astronomical Embolismic year above an exact number of weeks is 5d. 21h. 589ch. If, therefore, the Molad of the Embolismic year, H, be from 2d. 15h. 589ch. to 3d. 17h. 1079ch., that of H + 1 will be from 1d. 13h. 98ch. to 2d. 15h. 588ch.,* and, whatever may be the variation between these limits, H + 1 will commence with feria 2, Monday. But Monday is the day with which H terminates, and it is impossible that this day can belong to both of the years. Therefore H cannot terminate with a Monday, which is equivalent to saying that it cannot commence with a Tuesday, for it is a year of 385 days, an exact number of weeks.

It can, however, commence with either a Monday, a Thursday, or a Saturday, for the following year will commence with the same day, and there is nothing to prevent its being followed by a year of 353 or of 355 days, either of which may commence with a Monday or a Saturday; while a year of 355 days can also commence with a Tuesday.

55. Collecting the results obtained from these rules it will appear that the years, governed by their Molads and by the rules of the Calendar, will commence with certain fixed days of the week according to the annexed Table, which is to be thus read :—

Tishrî 1 will occur upon a Monday, when the Molad of the year is not less than 7d. 18h. 0ch., and not greater than 2d. 15h. 588ch. This rule applies to those Common years which follow next after an Embolismic year, namely, the years whose numerical positions in a Cycle are 1, 4, 7, 9, 12, 15, or 18.

It must be understood that in this, and in similar Tables, the Rêgäim are neglected. There are 76 Rêgäim in a Chalak, and when the limit is given as, for example, 2d. 17h. 1079ch., the actual limit is 2d. 17h. 1079ch. 75r. It means that 2d. 18h. 0ch. (= 2d. 17h. 1080ch.) must not be attained. This is the method adopted by Maimonides, and, following him, by Petavius and others. Some modern writers, as Dr. Adolf Schwarz or Dr. Sachau, the translator of al-Bîrunî, would

* 2	15	589	....	3	17	1079
5	21	589	....	5	21	589
1	13	98		2	15	588

TABLE OF WEEK-DAYS WITH WHICH THE JEWISH YEARS COMMENCE ACCORDING TO THEIR MOLADS.

Tishri 1.	Molads: the Limits are inclusive.	Years to which the Rule Applies.	Place of the Year in a Cycle.
Monday	7 18 0 to 2 15 588	Common following Embolismic	1, 4, 7, 9, 12, 15, 18
,, ...	7 18 0 to 2 17 1079	Common which follow Common, and all Embolismic	2, 5, 10, 13, 16 and 3, 6, 8, 11, 14, 17, 19
Tuesday	2 15 589 to 3 9 203	Common following Embolismic	1, 4, 7, 9, 12, 15, 18
,, ...	2 18 0 to 3 9 203	Common following Common	2, 5, 10, 13, 16
,, ...	2 18 0 to 3 17 1079	All Embolismic	3, 6, 8, 11, 14, 17, 19
Thursday ...	3 9 204 to 5 17 1079	All Common	1, 2, 4, 5, 7, 9, 10, 12, 13, 15, 16, 18
,, ...	3 18 0 to 5 17 1079	All Embolismic	3, 6, 8, 11, 14, 17, 19
Saturday......	5 18 0 to 7 17 1079	All Years	1 to 19

give the limits thus, from 2d. 18h. 0ch. up to 2d. 15h. 589ch. When given in this way there is some risk of supposing that the 589ch. may be reached; the fact being that if the Molad be greater than 2 15 588, that is, if 2 15 589 be attained, the year will commence with a Tuesday, and not with a Monday.

56. FURTHER REGULATIONS WITH RESPECT TO THE COMMENCEMENT AND FORM OF THE YEARS.

Hitherto, the days have been considered with which the Jewish years can commence; these days have been determined thus far by the Molads, and the rules ADU, YacH, GaTRaD, and BaTuThaKPhaT.

We now come to those which determine the length or form of the successive years. These rules include the former, but they are further developed, and place yet more restriction on the limits of the Molads. They are given in Table X., called the Table of Day-Limits.

I. COMMON YEARS.

1. A Common year will commence with a Monday, and be Deficient, 353 days, if its Molad is found by computation to be so great as 7d. 18h. 0ch., and be not greater than 1d. 9h. 203ch.

(*a*) The year will commence with a Monday if its Molad be so great as or greater than 7d. 18h. 0ch., for Tishrî 1 is postponed from feria 7 to feria 1 by YacH, and from feria 1 to feria 2 by ADU.

(*b*) The length of a Common year, H, is found by the addition to its Molad of the excess of a Common year above an exact number of weeks, by which means the commencement of the next year, H + 1, is found.

Molad of H	7	18	0 to	1	9	203
Excess of H............................	4	8	876	4	8	876
Molad of H + 1	5	2	876 to	5	17	1079

The feria for H + 1 being 5, and the maximum value of the hours and Chalakim in the Molad not amounting to 5d. 18h., the year commences with Thursday, the day indicated by the Molad. Therefore the last day of H must have been a Wednesday. As H commenced with a Monday the last day of its completed weeks is a Sunday; it therefore contains three days more than an exact number of weeks, namely, Monday, Tuesday, and Wednesday. It is therefore of the form 350 + 3, or 353 days. It is Deficient.

It will be seen at once that if the superior limit of the Molad of H had been so great as 1d. 9h. 204ch., that is, if it had been even 1 Chalaḳ greater than it is, then the limit for the Molad of H + 1 would have become 5d. 18h. 0ch. In such a case the commencement of H + 1 would be postponed from feria 5, Thursday, to feria 7, Saturday. This would have lengthened H by two days, making it to consist of 355 days. Therefore the extreme limit for the Molad of a Common year which commences with a Monday, and is Deficient, is 1d. 9h. 203ch.

2. A Common year which follows an Embolismic year will commence with a Monday, and be Abundant, 355 days, if its Molad be not less than 1d. 9h. 204ch., and not greater than 2d. 15h. 588ch.

(*a*) Any year, whether it follows an Embolismic year or not, whose Molad has these limits, will commence with a Monday. If the feria be 1, then Tishrî 1 is postponed from Sunday to Monday, by ADU. If the feria be 2, Tishrî 1 falls naturally to Monday; it is only postponed by BaTU PhaKPhaT to Tuesday, when the Molad attains to 2d. 15h. 589ch.

The year in question therefore commences with a Monday.

(*b*) Molad of H........................	1	9	204	to	2	15	588
Excess of H........................	4	8	876		4	8	876
Molad of H + 1..................	6	18	0	to	7	0	384

Therefore, H + 1 commences with a Saturday, and the last day of the year H must be a Friday. As H commences with a Monday its completed weeks terminate with a Saturday, and it has an excess of five over $7n$ days, namely, Monday, Tuesday, Wednesday, Thursday, and Friday. It has therefore 355 days.

3. A Common year which follows a Common year will commence with a Monday, and will be Abundant, 355 days, if its Molad be not less than 1d. 9h. 204ch., and not greater than 2d. 17h. 1079ch.

(*a*) If the feria be 1, Tishrî 1 is postponed to feria 2, Monday, by ADU. If the feria be 2, Tishrî 1 is not postponed by BaTU PHaKPhaT from Monday to Tuesday, because the year in question does not follow an Embolismic year. Also, Tishrî 1 is not postponed to Tuesday by YacH because the maximum value of its Molad does not attain to 2d. 18h. 0ch.

The year will therefore commence with a Monday.

(b) Molad of H	1	9	204 to	2	17	1079
Excess of H	4	8	876	4	8	876
Molad of H + 1	6	18	0 to	7	2	875

Therefore H + 1 commences with a Saturday, and the last day of H must be Friday. As H commences with a Monday it must have 355 days.

(c) But why is 1 9 204 the minimum Molad with which a Common year following a Common year, and commencing with a Monday, can have 355 days? Simply because all Common years whose Molad is less than this have been proved under Rule 1 to have only 353 days.

(d) And why is 2 17 1079 the maximum Molad for such a year? Because if the Molad attain to 2 18 0 Tishri 1 will be postponed to Tuesday; so that the year could not fulfil the condition of commencing with a Monday, no matter how many or how few days it might have.

4. A Common year which follows an Embolismic year will commence with a Tuesday, and be Regular, or have 354 days, if its Molad be not less than 2d. 15h. 589ch., and be not greater than 3d. 9h. 203ch.

(a) If the feria be 2, and the hours and Chalakim be not less than 15h. 589ch. Tishri 1 is postponed from Monday to Tuesday, in a year which follows an Embolismic year, by BaTU PHaKPhaT. If the feria be 3, Tishri 1 falls naturally to Tuesday so long as the maximum value of the Molad does not attain to 3d. 9h. 204ch.

Therefore the year in question will commence with a Tuesday.

(b) Molad of H	2	15	589 to	3	9	203
Excess of H	4	8	876	4	8	876
Molad of H+1	7	0	385 to	7	17	1079

H+1, therefore, commences with a Saturday, and H ends with a Friday. As it commenced with a Tuesday it has four days more than an exact number of weeks. It has 354 days.

5. A Common year which follows a Common year will commence

with a Tuesday, and be Regular, 354 days, if its Molad be not less than 2d. 18h. 0ch., and be not greater than 3d. 9h. 203ch.

(*a*) Such a year will commence with Tuesday for the reason given in (4, *a*). Its Molad cannot be less than 2d. 18h. 0ch., for if it be less than this it will commence with a Monday.

(*b*) Molad of H	2	18	0	to	3	9	203
Excess of H	4	8	876		4	8	876
Molad of H + 1	7	2	876	to	7	17	1079

H+1, therefore, commences with a Saturday, and the last day of H is a Friday. As H commences with a Tuesday it must have 354 days.

From (4) and (5) it appears that all Common years which commence with a Tuesday are Regular, or have 354 days; and it may be noted here that no year, whether it be Common or Embolismic, can commence with a Tuesday except such years as are Regular—that is, no year commences with a Tuesday unless it have 354 or 384 days.

6. Every Common year whose Molad is not less than 3d. 9h. 204ch., and not greater than 5d. 9h. 203ch., commences with a Thursday, and is Regular, 354 days.

(*a*) If the feria be 3, and the hours and Chalakim are not less than 9d. 204ch. Tishri 1 is postponed from Tuesday to Wednesday by GaTRaD, and further postponed to Thursday by ADU. If the feria be 5, and the Molad be, as in this case, anything less than 5d. 18h. 0ch., Tishri 1 falls naturally to Thursday.

The year in question commences, therefore, with a Thursday.

(*b*) Molad of H	3	9	204	to	5	9	203
Excess of H	4	8	876		4	8	876
Molad of H + 1	1	18	0	to	2	17	1079

Therefore, H + 1 commences with Monday, for if the Molad of H + 1 be not less than 1d. 18h. 0ch. its first day is postponed from Sunday to Monday; also, Tishri 1 falls naturally to Monday if the feria be 2, although the hours and Chalakim exceed 15h. 589ch., for H is, by hypothesis, a Common year, so that H + 1 does not follow an Embolismic year, and BaTU PHaKPhaT does not apply to it.

Because H + 1 commences with a Monday, H must end with a

Sunday. It has therefore 354 days, for it commences with a Thursday.

7. Every Common year whose Molad is not less than 5d. 9h. 204ch., and not greater than 5d. 17h. 1079ch., commences with a Thursday, and is Abundant, 355 days.

(*a*) Such a year commences naturally with a Thursday, feria 5, as indicated by the Molad, for YacH causes no postponement till the Molad 5d. 18h. 0ch. be attained.

(*b*)							
Molad of H	5	9	204	to 5	17	1079
Excess of H	4	8	876	4	8	876
Molad of H + 1	2	18	0	to 3	2	875

Therefore, H + 1 commences with a Tuesday, and H terminates with a Monday. As H commences with a Thursday it has five days more than an exact number of weeks. It has 355 days.

8. Every Common year whose Molad is not less than 5d. 18h. 0ch. and not greater than 6d. 0h. 407ch., will commence with a Saturday, and be Deficient, 353 days.

(*a*) Since the minimum Molad is 5d. 18h. 0ch. Tishrî 1 is postponed by YacH from Thursday to Friday so long as the feria in the Molad is 5. It is further postponed by ADU from Friday to Saturday. If the Molad be 6, Tisrhî 1 is postponed from Friday to Saturday.

Therefore all such years must commence with a Saturday.

(*b*)						
Molad of H	5	18	0	to 6	0	407
Excess of H	4	8	876	4	8	876
Molad of H + 1	3	2	876	to 3	9	203

H + 1 commences with Tuesday, because the Molad is always less than 3d. 9h. 204ch. H ends with Monday. It commences with Saturday; its 7*n* days end with Friday. It has three more days, and therefore contains 353 days.

9. A Common year which is followed by an Embolismic year will commence with a Saturday, and be Deficient, 353 days, if its Molad be not less than 5d. 18h. 0ch., and be not greater than 6d. 9h. 203ch.

(*a*) Such a year must commence with a Saturday for the reason assigned in (8, *a*).

(*b*) Molad of H	5	18	0 to	6	9	203
Excess of H	4	8	876	4	8	876
Molad of H + 1	3	2	876 to	3	17	1079

H + 1 is, by hypothesis, an Embolismic year. Although its maximum Molad is more than 3d. 9h. 204ch. its first day is not postponed by GaTRaD, which applies to Common years only.

The year H + 1 therefore commences with feria 3, Tuesday, as indicated by the Molad, and H ends with a Monday. As H commences with a Saturday it has three days more than an exact number of weeks. It has 353 days.

10. A Common year which is followed by a Common year will commence with a Saturday, and be Abundant, 355 days, if its Molad be not less than 6d. 0h. 408ch., and be not greater than 7d. 17h. 1079ch.

(*a*) If the feria be 6, Tishrī 1 is postponed from Friday to Saturday by ADU. If the feria be 7 there is no postponement from Saturday because the maximum value of the Molad is less than 7d. 18h. 0ch.

The year, therefore, commences with a Saturday.

(*b*) Molad of H........................	6	0	408 to	7	17	1079
Excess of H	4	8	876	4	8	876
Molad of H + 1..................	3	9	204 to	5	2	875

The year H + 1 is, by hypothesis, a Common year. Therefore when the feria is 3, and the Molad not less than 3d. 9h. 204ch., as in this case, Tishrī 1 is postponed by GaTRaD, from Tuesday to Wednesday, and thence to Thursday by ADU. When the feria becomes 4, Tishrī 1 is postponed to Thursday by ADU. If the feria be 5 Tishrī 1 falls naturally to Thursday so long as the Molad be less than 5d. 18h. 0ch., as it is here.

The year H + 1 begins, therefore, with a Thursday, and H ends with a Wednesday. H, therefore, has 355 days, for it begins with a Saturday and has five days more than an exact number of weeks.

(*c*) If the Molad be less than 6d. 0h. 408ch., even by one Chalaḳ, the Molad of H + 1 will not attain to 3d. 9h. 204ch. In such a case H + 1 would begin with a Tuesday instead of with a Thursday. This would shorten H by two days, reducing its number to 353. If, therefore, H be followed by a Common year it cannot be Abundant if its Molad be less than 6d. 0h. 408ch.

11. Every Common year whose Molad is not less than 6d. 9h. 204ch., and not greater than 7d. 17h. 1079ch., will commence with a Saturday, and be Abundant, 355 days.

(*a*) Such years commence with Saturday, because if the feria be 6 Tishrî 1 is postponed by ADU from Friday to Saturday; and if the feria be 7 there is no postponement so long as the maximum value of the Molad is less than 7d. 18h. 0ch.

(*b*) Molad of H	6	9	204	to 7	17	1079
Excess of H	4	8	876	4	8	876
Molad of H + 1	3	18	0	to 5	2	875

Therefore H + 1 commences with a Thursday, and H ends with a Wednesday. It commences with a Saturday, its 7*n* days end with a Friday. Its extra days are five, Saturday, Sunday, Monday, Tuesday, and Wednesday. It has 355 days.

Rules Respecting the Commencement and Form of Embolismic Years.

12. Every Embolismic year commences with a Monday and is Deficient, 383 days, if its Molad be not less than 7d. 18h. 0ch., and be not greater than 1d. 20h. 490ch.

(*a*) The year commences with Monday for the reason assigned in (1, *a*).

(*b*) Molad of H	7	18	0	to 1	20	490
Excess of H, Emb.	5	21	589	5	21	589
Molad of H + 1	6	15	589	to 7	17	1079

Therefore H + 1 commences with a Saturday, and H ends with a Friday. As it begins with a Monday, and is Embolismic, it has 383 days.

13. Every Embolismic year commences with a Monday and is Abundant, 385 days, if its Molad be not less than 1d. 20h. 491ch., and be not greater than 2d. 17h. 1079ch.

(*a*) ADU postpones Tishrî 1 to Monday when the feria is 1. BaTU THaKPhaT does not affect Embolismic years, therefore Tishrî 1 falls naturally to Monday when the feria is 2.

(*b*) Molad of H........................	1	20	491	to 2	17	1079
Excess of H	5	21	589	5	21	589
Molad of H + 1	7	18	0	to 1	15	588

H + 1, therefore, commences with Monday, for Tishrî 1 is postponed to that day whether the feria be 7 or 1. H ends with a Sunday, and as it begins with a Monday it must have 385 days.

14. Every Embolismic year whose Molad is not less than 2d. 18h. 0ch., and not greater than 3d. 17h. 1079ch., commences with a Tuesday, and is Regular, 384 days.

(*a*) Because the minimum value of the Molad is 2d. 18h. 0ch. Tishrî 1 is postponed by YacH from Monday to Tuesday. When the Molad becomes 3d. 0h. 0ch., but does not attain to 3d. 18h. 0ch., Tishrî 1 falls naturally to Tuesday in an Embolismic year.

(*b*) Molad of H	2	18	0	to 3	17	1079
Excess of H	5	21	589	5	21	589
Molad of H + 1	1	15	589	to 2	15	588

H + 1, commences with a Monday, and H must end with a Sunday. It therefore has six days more that an exact number of weeks. It has 384 days.

15. Every Embolismic year whose Molad is not less than 3d. 18h. 0ch., and not greater than 4d. 11h. 694ch., commences with a Thursday, and is Deficient, 383 days.

(*a*) When the Molad is not less than 3d. 18h. 0ch., Tishrî 1 is postponed by YacH, and ADU, from Tuesday to Thursday. When the feria is 4, it is postponed by ADU from Wednesday to Thursday.

Such a year must therefore commence with a Thursday.

(*b*) Molad of H	3	18	0	to 4	11	694
Excess of H	5	21	589	5	21	589
Molad of H + 1	2	15	589	to 3	9	203

H + 1 follows H which is, by hypothesis, an Embolismic year;

therefore H + 1 is a Common year following an Embolismic year, and must commence with a Tuesday, as demonstrated by (4, *a*). Consequently H must end with a Monday, and, as it commences with a Thursday, its $7n$ days end with a Wednesday. It has therefore five extra days, Thursday, Friday, Saturday, Sunday, Monday, and its form is $7n + 5$, or it has $378 + 5 = 383$ days.

This proof is given in some detail because both Dr. Adolf Schwarz in "Der Jüdischer Kalender" p. 64, Table B, and Dr. Sachau in his translation of the Athâr-ul-Bâkiya of al-Bîrûnî, p. 152, who are authorities, state that a year whose Molad has these limits consists, when Embolismic, of 384 days. The former describes it as "5r," the figure indicating the feria, the letter standing for regelmässige, or Regular. The latter says that it commences with feria 5, and is "Intermediate," the term employed by this author for a Regular year. It is beyond dispute that a year whose Molad is from 3 18 0 to 4 11 694, both inclusive, must commence with feria 5, Thursday, whether it be Common or Embolismic; and it is equally beyond dispute that an Embolismic year of 384 days, would, if it commenced with a Thursday, end with a Tuesday; for, $384 = 7n + 6$; the last day of the completed weeks is a Wednesday; the remaining days are Thursday, Friday, Saturday, Sunday, Monday, and Tuesday. If therefore a year which has 384 days commenced with a Thursday, that which next follows would begin with a Wednesday, which is impossible.

Moreover, it has been proved in Article 54, par. 5, that a year of 384 days can only commence with a Tuesday, so that an Embolismic year which commences with a Thursday must have either 383 or 385 days.

That this is an error in the Table B, given by Dr. Schwarz at p. 64, is made clear by an inspection of his Table K, pp. 82, 83, which gives the sixty-one possible arrangements, or sequence of years for the Jewish Cycle. This includes not only every possible form of a Cycle, but also every possible form of a Jewish year; there is not a single Embolismic year which is marked 5R. Every Embolismic year in that Table which commences with feria 5 is marked either as M., mangelhaft, Deficient, or U, überschüssig, Abundant. In fact, nothing else is possible.

Petavius, in "De Doctrina Temporum," lib. vii. cap. xviii., under the heading "Canones neomeniæ Tisri in Embolimæis annis," states correctly that a year whose Molad has these limits commences with a Thursday and is Deficient.

16. Every Embolismic year whose Molad is not less that 4d. 11h. 695ch., and not greater than 5d. 17h. 1079ch., will commence with a Thursday, and be Abundant, 385 days.

(*a*) If the feria be 4 Tishrî 1 is postponed to Thursday; if it be 5 and the Molad be anything less than 5d. 18h. 0ch., Tishrî 1 falls naturally to Thursday.

(*b*)							
Molad of H	4	11	695	to 5	17	1079
Excess of H	5	21	589	5	21	589
Molad of H + 1	3	9	204	to 4	15	588

H + 1 is a Common year, for it follows an Embolismic year, therefore Tishrî 1 is postponed by GaTRaD from feria 3 to feria 4, and thence by ADU to feria 5; also when the Molad attains to 4d. 0h. 0ch. there is a postponement to feria 5. If the feria be 5, and the Molad be not so great as 5d. 18h. 0ch., Tishrî 1 falls naturally to Thursday. H + 1 therefore, commences with a Thursday; H ends with a Wednesday, and as it commenced with a Thursday it has an exact number of weeks, or 385 days.

17. Every Embolismic year whose Molad is not less than 5d. 18h. 0ch., and not greater than 6d. 20h. 490ch., commences with a Saturday, and is Deficient, 383 days.

(*a*) The minimum value of the Molad being 5d. 18h. 0ch., Tishrî 1 is postponed from Thursday to Saturday by YacH and ADU. With the Molad 6d. 0h. 0ch. to 6d. 17h. 1079ch. it is postponed by ADU from Friday to Saturday, and if it be greater than 6d. 17h. 1079ch., both YacH and ADU are effective to postpone it from Friday to Saturday. The year therefore begins with Saturday.

(*b*)						
Molad of H........................	5	18	0	to 6	20	490
Excess of H	5	21	589	5	21	589
Molad of H + 1..................	4	15	589	to 5	17	1079

H + 1 commences with a Thursday; the last day of H is a Wednesday, therefore it has 383, or $7n + 5$ days for it commences with a Saturday.

18. Every Embolismic year whose Molad is not less than 6d. 20h. 491ch., and not greater than 7d. 17h. 1079ch., commences with a Saturday, and is Abundant, 385 days.

(*a*) When the feria is 6, Tishrî 1 is postponed by ADU from Friday to Saturday. When the feria is 7, Tishrî 1 falls naturally to Saturday, so long as the Molad does not exceed 7d. 17h. 1079ch. The year, therefore, commences with a Saturday.

(*b*) Molad of H....................	6	20	491 to	7	17	1079
Excess of H	5	21	589	5	21	589
Molad of H + 1	5	18	0 to	6	15	588

H + 1 commences with a Saturday, and the last day of H is a Friday. It commences with a Saturday, therefore it has $7n + 0$, or 385 days.

These results are called the Day-Limits of the years. They are collected in Table X. The vertical argument in that Table refers to the numbering of the demonstrations above.

It is important to notice that there are further restrictions on the Day-Limits for a Common year following an Embolismic when it is the first year in a Cycle. These restrictions will be explained in Article 58.

57. Besides the commencement of the Civil year with Tishrî, and of the Ecclesiastical year with Nîsân, the Jews have, for a particular purpose, a third commencement, Schebhât 15, called Laylanot, the First Day of the year of Trees, which occurs generally in one of the Christian months January or February. It is unlawful to eat of the fruit of a tree until the third crop is produced; but because the crop is produced annually, this law is so interpreted that it is made lawful to eat of the crop of the third year. These years are reckoned from Schebhât 15. Hence if a tree be planted at any time before that day its first year is reckoned as terminating with that day, although the tree may in fact have been planted for only a few weeks, or even a few days. Its third year would then commence when it had been in position only one year and a portion of another, and the fruit which is produced during this nominal third year may be lawfully eaten.

To find the Length of any Given Cycle.

58. This is done in a similar way to that by which the length of any given year is found, namely, by ascertaining the feriæ with which the Cycle commences and terminates.

An Astronomical Cycle of nineteen years is a constant quantity, consisting of 6939d. 16h. 595ch., but a Civil Cycle of nineteen years is variable in length. It must of necessity consist of an integral number of days, and this number may be either 6939, 6940, 6941, or 6942 days, that is, its length may be of one of the four forms 7N + 2, 7N + 3, 7N + 4, or 7N + 5, according to the feria with which it commences and the number of times that Tishrî 1 is postponed by the Dechiyyôth in the course of the nineteen years.

6939 Days.

A Cycle of 6939, or $7n + 2$ days cannot commence with a Monday, because if it did so commence it would terminate with a Tuesday, and the first year of the next Cycle would commence with a Wednesday, which is a day forbidden for Tishrî 1.

It may commence with either a Tuesday, a Thursday, or a Saturday.

Tuesday. Let C be the Cycle. It will commence with this day if its Molad be not less than 2 15 589, and not greater than 3 1 484.

Molad of C	2	15	589	to 3	1	484
Add excess of C	2	16	595	2	16	595
Molad of C + 1	5	8	104	to 5	17	1079

C + 1, therefore, commences with a Thursday and C ends with a Wednesday; as, by hypothesis, it commences with a Tuesday, it has $7n + 2$, or 6939 days.

With reference to the limits assigned here to the Molad of C, it must be noticed that although a Common year which follows an Embolismic (as the first year of every Cycle), can commence with a Tuesday if its Molad be from 2 15 589 to 3 9 203, (Article 56(4)), yet when such a year is the first of a Cycle which has only 6939 days the superior limit is reduced from 3 9 203 to 3 1 484. This limit is obtained as follows:—The next Cycle, C + 1, must commence with a Thursday if C commence with a Tuesday, and have $7n + 2$ days. The maximum Molad for year or Cycle which commences with a Thursday is 5 17 1079, for if the Molad be greater than this by one Chalaḳ the year will commence with a Saturday. Hence we have—

Maximum Molad for C + 1	5	17	1079
Subtract excess of C	2	16	595
Maximum Molad for C	3	1	484

THURSDAY. A Cycle of 6939 days can commence with this day if its Molad be from 3 9 204 to 5 1 484.

Molad of C	3	9	204 to	5	1	484
Add excess of C	2	16	595	2	16	595
Molad of C + 1	6	1	799 to	7	17	1079

C + 1 commences with a Saturday, therefore C terminates with a Friday, and has $7n + 2$, or 6939 days.

Here, again, the superior limit of the Molad for C is reduced, namely, from 5 9 203 (Article 56(6)), to 5 1 484, obtained by subtracting the excess of C from the maximum Molad which permits a year to commence with a Saturday, that is, 7 17 1079. If this Molad were increased by only one Chalaḳ the first year of C + 1 would commence with a Monday; C would terminate with a Sunday, and instead of having only 6939 days it would have 6941.

SATURDAY. A Cycle of 6939 days can commence with this day if its Molad be from 5 18 0 to 6 22 1073.

Molad of C	5	18	0 to	6	22	1073
Add excess of C	2	16	595	2	16	595
Molad of C + 1	1	10	595 to	2	15	588

C + 1 commences with a Monday, therefore C terminates with a Sunday, and has $7n + 2$ days.

The superior limit for the Molad of C is reduced from 7 17 1079 to 6 22 1073 in order that C + 1 may commence with a Monday. The maximum limit for the Molad of C + 1, which follows an Embolismic year, is therefore 2 15 588, for if it were one Chalak greater than this it would commence with a Tuesday. Subtracting the excess of C from 2 15 588, to which 7 days may be added without altering the feria, the remainder is 6 22 1073.

6940 Days.

A Cycle of 6940, or $7n + 3$ days cannot commence with a Tuesday, because it would terminate with a Thursday, and the next Cycle would commence with a Friday, which is impossible.

It cannot commence with a Thursday, because the next Cycle would commence with a Sunday, which is also impossible.

It may commence with a Monday or a Saturday.

Monday. A Cycle of 6940 days can commence with a Monday if its Molad be from 7 18 0 to 2 15 588.

Molad of C	7	18	0 to	2	15	588
Excess of C	2	16	595	2	16	595
Molad of C + 1	3	10	595 to	5	8	103

C + 1 commences with a Thursday, and therefore C terminates with a Wednesday, and has $7n + 3$ or 6940 days.

In this case the ordinary limits for a Common year commencing with a Monday requires no reduction.

Saturday. It can commence with this day if its Molad be from 6 22 1074 to 7 16 688.

Molad of C	6	22	1074 to	7	16	688
Excess of C	2	16	595	2	16	595
Molad of C + 1	2	15	589 to	3	9	203

C + 1 commences with a Tuesday, therefore C terminates with a Monday, and has $7n + 3$ days.

The ordinary limits for the Molad of a Common year following an Embolismic year, to commence with Saturday, are 5 18 0 to 7 17 1079. Both of these limits have to be restricted for the first year of a Cycle which is to have 6940 days. If the inferior Molad of C + 1 were less than 2 15 589 by even one Chalak the year and the Cycle would commence with a Monday, C would terminate with a Sunday and have only 6939 days. The minimum limit for the Molad of C is therefore 6 22 1074. With regard to the superior limit, if it were one Chalak greater than 7 16 688 the Molad for C + 1 would attain to 3 9 204, and in that case C + 1 would commence with a Thursday, so that C would have $7n + 5$ days.

6941 Days.

A Cycle of 6941, or $7n + 4$ days cannot commence with a Monday or a Saturday because, if it did so commence, it would terminate with a Thursday or a Tuesday, and the next Cycle would commence with a forbidden day, Friday or Wednesday.

It can commence with a Tuesday or a Thursday.

Tuesday. It can commence with Tuesday if the limits for its Molad be 3 1 485 and 3 9 203.

Molad of C	3	1	485	to	3	9	203
Excess of C	2	16	595		2	16	595
	5	18	0	to	6	1	798

C + 1 commences with Saturday; C ends with Friday, and has $7n + 4$, or 6941 days.

The inferior limit for a Common year following an Embolismic year is 2 15 589; but if it is to be the first year of a Cycle which has 6941 days, this limit must not be less than 3 1 485, for if it were even one Chalak less the Molad of C + 1 would not attain to 5 18 0; in that case Tishri 1 would not be postponed from feria 5 to Saturday; C would terminate with a Wednesday, and have only 6939 days.

The superior limit requires no alteration.

Thursday. The ordinary limits are 3 9 204 and 5 17 1079, but if a Cycle is to be one of 6941 days its inferior limit cannot be less than 5 1 485.

Molad of C	5	1	485	to	5	17	1079
Excess of C	2	16	595		2	16	595
Molad of C + 1	7	18	0	to	1	10	594

C + 1 commences with Monday; C terminates with Sunday, and has $7n + 4$, or 6941 days.

If the Molad of C were anything less than 5 1 485, that of C + 1 would be less than 7 18 0 and Tishri 1 would not be postponed from Saturday to Monday.

6942 Days.

A Cycle which has 6942 or $7n+5$ days can commence with a Saturday only.

It cannot commence with a Monday, for the Day-Limits which permit of a year commencing with a Monday are 7 18 0 to 2 15 588, and it has been shown that with these limits a Cycle is one of only 6940 days.

It cannot commence with a Tuesday, because it would terminate with a Saturday, and the next Cycle would commence with a Sunday, which is impossible.

It cannot commence with a Thursday, because the limits for the Molad of a Common year so commencing are 3 9 204 to 5 17 1079.

Molad of C	3	9	204	to	5	17	1079
Excess of C	2	16	595		2	16	595
Molad of C + 1	6	1	799	to	1	10	594

C + 1 would, therefore, commence with a Saturday, or with a Monday. In the former case C would terminate with a Friday, and have only $7n+2$ days; in the latter case, it would end with a Sunday and have only $7n+4$ days.

Saturday. A Cycle of 6942 days can commence with this day.

The ordinary limits for the Molad of any year which commences with a Saturday are 5 18 0 and 7 17 1079. In order that a Cycle so commencing may have 6942 days the superior limit for the Molad of its first year must be increased to 7 16 689, for if it be anything less than this the next Cycle will not commence with a Thursday.

Molad of C	7	16	689	to	7	17	1079
Excess of C	2	16	595		2	16	595
Molad of C + 1	3	9	204	to	3	10	594

C + 1 begins with a Thursday; C ends with a Wednesday, and has $7n+5$, or 6942 days.

The fact that it is possible for a Cycle to contain so many as 6942 days is not always recognised. Dr. Schwarz, in one passage, speaks of Cycles as though they could only contain 6939, 6940, or 6941 days,* but in line 61 of his "Tabel K," p. 83, he gives, as a possible form of a Cycle, one which has its first year marked 7u, meaning that it is a Common Abundant year, and commences with a Saturday; the last year of the same Cycle is marked as 5υ, meaning that this nineteenth year commences with a Thursday, and is an Embolismic Abundant year. It therefore contains 385 days, or an exact number of weeks, and because it commences with a Thursday it must terminate with a Wednesday. In other words, the Cycle itself terminates with a Wednesday, and as it commences with a Saturday it must contain 7N + 5, or 6942 days.

Such a Cycle is, however, of very rare occurrence. The only Cycles which have had 6942 days since the commencement of the Era are the 154th, and the 167th, and that only when the computation is made according to the rules of the reformed Calendar.

The same thing will not occur again till the 547th Cycle is reached; its Molad is 7 17 1074. After that the 560th Cycle, whose Molad is 7 17 169, will also have 6942 days; see Example 3, below.

The results which have been obtained are collected in the following Table:—

LIMITS FOR THE MOLADS OF CYCLES ACCORDING TO THE NUMBER OF DAYS IN THE CYCLE.

Days in Cycle.	First Day of Cycle C.	Molads: The Limits are inclusive.	First Day of Cycle C + 1.
6939	Tuesday	2 15 589 to 3 1 484	Thursday
	Thursday	3 9 204 to 5 1 484	Saturday
	Saturday	5 18 0 to 6 22 1073	Monday
6940	Monday	7 18 0 to 2 15 588	Thursday
	Saturday	6 22 1074 to 7 16 688	Tuesday
6941	Tuesday	3 1 485 to 3 9 203	Saturday
	Thursday	5 1 485 to 5 17 1079	Monday
6942	Saturday	7 16 689 to 7 17 1079	Thursday

* In the German text, "Der Jüdische Kal.," p. 78, the figures are 3639, 3640, and 3641. "Daher rührt auch die veränderliche Länge des Mondcyclus, der bald 3639, bald 3640, zuweilen gar 3641 Tage zählt." These are evidently misprints for 6939, 6940, and 6941.

The method of finding the lengths of any given Cycle is illustrated by the following examples:—

Example 1.—Required the number of days in the 295th Cycle.

BeHaRD	2	5	204
Add for 200 Cycles elapsed	5	22	200
" 90 " "	4	1	630
" 4 " "	3	18	220
Molad for 295th Cycle	1	23	174
Add for 1 Cycle	2	16	595
Molad for 296th Cycle	4	15	769

From this it appears that the 295th Cycle commences with a Monday, because feria 1, to which the Molad falls, is forbidden by ADU. Also it must terminate with a Wednesday, for the next Cycle commences with feria 5, Thursday, because feria 4, Wednesday, is forbidden.

The 295th Cycle has therefore three days more than an exact number of weeks, and is of the form 7n + 3, or has 6940 days.

Example 2.—Find upon what date the 154th Cycle of the Era would have commenced, and the number of days it would have contained, if the rules of the Jewish Calendar, as now established, had been then in force.

BeHaRD	2	5	204
Add for 100 Cycles elapsed	2	23	100
" 50 " "	1	11	590
" 3 " "	1	1	705
Molad of 154th Cycle	7	17	519
Add for 1 Cycle	2	16	595
Molad of 155th Cycle	3	10	34

The 154th Cycle would, therefore, have commenced with a Saturday, and it must have terminated with a Wednesday, because the feria in the Molad for the next Cycle is 3 and the hours and Chalaḳim exceed 9h. 204ch., so that the rules GaTRaD and ADU postpone the commencement of the first year of this Cycle to Thursday.*

The 154th Cycle had, therefore, five days more than an exact number of weeks, and if the rules had been in force would have had 6,942 days.

Example 3.—Find the feria with which the 560th Cycle will commence, and the length of the Cycle.

BeHaRD	2	5	204
Add for 500 Cycles elapsed	7	19	500
,, 50 ,, ,,	1	11	590
,, 9 ,, ,,	3	4	1035
Molad of 560th Cycle	7	17	169
Add for 1 Cycle	2	16	595
Molad of 561st Cycle	3	9	764

The 560th Cycle will commence with a Saturday, and it will terminate with a Wednesday, for the next Cycle begins with a Thursday, Tishrî 1 being postponed by GaTRaD and ADU from feria 3 to feria 5. The Cycle will, therefore, have five days above an exact number of weeks, and be of the form 7n + 5, or will have 6942 days.

* The first year of every Cycle is a Common year following an Embolismic year, and therefore comes within the rule GaTRaD.

CHAPTER V

THE SEQUENCE OF YEARS

59. The following statements, which refer to the possible and impossible sequence of years, may be deduced from the rules which have been previously given. They result, in fact, from the method in which the Calendar is constructed by means of Molads, and from the law which prohibits the celebration of Tishrî 1 upon certain days of the week.

The Numbers and Letters in the margin refer to the proofs. These will be given after the statements have been made.

I. A Deficient year, whether it be either Common or Embolismic, cannot be followed by a Deficient year.

a. b. 353 cannot be followed by 353.
c. d. 353 cannot be followed by 383.
e. f. g. 383 cannot be followed by 353.

II. A Regular year, whether Common or Embolismic, cannot be followed by a Regular year.

a. b. 354 cannot be followed by 354.
c. d. 354 cannot be followed by 384.
e. 384 cannot be followed by 354.

III. An Abundant year, whether Common or Embolismic, can, with certain exceptions, be followed by an Abundant year.

a. 355, commencing with Monday, can be followed by 355.

b. c. Not, if it commence with Thursday or Saturday.
d. e. 355, commencing with Monday or Saturday, can be followed by 385.
f. Not, if it commence with Thursday.
g. h. 385, commencing with Monday or Saturday, can be followed by 355.
i. Not, if it commence with Thursday.

IV. A Deficient year, whether Common or Embolismic, can, with certain exceptions, be followed by a Regular year.
a. b. 353, whether commencing with Monday or Saturday, can be followed by 354.
c. 353, commencing with Saturday, can be followed by 384.
d. Not, if it commence with Monday.
e. f. 383, commencing with Thursday or Saturday, can be followed by 354.
g. Not, if it commence with Monday.

V. A Regular Common year can be followed by a Deficient year, with certain exceptions.
a. 354, if it commence with Thursday, can be followed by 353.
b. Not, if it commence with Tuesday.
c. 354, if it commence with Thursday, can be followed by 383.
d. Not, if it commence with Tuesday.

VI. A Regular Embolismic year cannot be followed by a Deficient year.
a. 384 cannot be followed by 353.

VII. A Deficient year can, with certain exceptions, be followed by an Abundant year.
a. 353, if it commence with Monday, can be followed by 355.
b. Not, if it commence with Saturday.
c. 353, if it commence with Monday, can be followed by 385.
d. Not, if it commence with Saturday.
e. f. 383, commencing with Monday or Saturday, can be followed by 355.
g. Not, if it commence with Thursday.

VIII. An Abundant year can, with certain exceptions, be followed by a Deficient year.

a. 355, if it commence with Monday, can be followed by 353.

b. c. Not, if it commence with Thursday or Saturday.

d. e. 355, if it commence with Monday or Saturday, can be followed by 383.

f. Not, if it commence with Thursday.

g. h. 385, if it commence with Monday or Saturday, can be followed by 353.

i. Not, if it commence with Thursday.

IX. An Abundant year, with certain exceptions, can be followed by a Regular year.

a. b. 355, if it commence with Thursday or Saturday, can be followed by 354.

c. Not, if it commence with Monday.

d. 355, if it commence with Thursday, can be followed by 384.

e. f. Not, if it commence with Monday or Saturday.

g. 385, if it commence with Thursday, can be followed by 354.

h. i. Not, if it commence with Monday or Saturday.

X. A Regular year, whether it commence with Tuesday or Thursday, can be followed by an Abundant year.

a. b. 354, commencing with Tuesday or Thursday, can be followed by 355.

c. d. 354, commencing with Tuesday or Thursday, can be followed by 385.

e. 384, which can only commence with Tuesday, can be followed by 355.

It is hardly necessary to add that, according to the arrangement of the Cycle in the established Calendar, it is impossible for two Embolismic years, or for three Common years, to be consecutive.

Proofs of the Foregoing Statements.

The days of the week upon which the Jewish years, according to their form, can commence, will be found in Article 54, page 79.

The limits of the Molads are taken from the collected Table X. They result from the rules specified in Article 56.

In the following proofs H is the given year, H + 1 the next year, and H + 2 the year after H + 1.

I. 353 cannot be followed by 353.

a. Let 353 commence with a Monday, and, if possible, let it be followed by 353.

Molad of H...............	7	18	0	to	1	9	203	
Excess of H, Com. ...	4	8	876		4	8	876	
Molad of H + 1.........	5	2	876	to	5	17	1079	Begins Thursday.
Excess of H + 1	4	8	876		4	8	876	
Molad of H + 2.........	2	11	672	to	3	2	875	

Therefore H + 2 must begin with a Monday or Tuesday, and H + 1 must end with a Sunday or Monday. It commences with a Thursday, and may therefore have 354 or 355 days, but it cannot have 353.

b. Let 353 commence with a Saturday, and, if possible, let it be followed by 353.

Molad of H...............	5	18	0	to	6	0	407	
Excess of H, Com. ...	4	8	876		4	8	876	
Molad of H + 1.........	3	2	876	to	3	8	203	Begins Tuesday.
Excess of H + 1, Com.	4	8	876		4	8	876	
Molad of H + 2.........	7	11	672	to	7	16	1079	

Therefore H + 2 must begin with a Saturday, and H + 1 must end with a Friday. It commences with a Tuesday, and may therefore have 354 days, but it cannot have 353 or 355.

353 cannot be followed by 383.

c. Let 353 commence with a Monday, and, if possible, let it be followed by 383.

Molad of H + 1.........	5	2	876	to	5	17	1079	See *a*, above. Begins Thursday.
Excess of H + 1, Emb.	5	21	589		5	21	589	
Molad of H + 2.........	4	0	385	to	4	15	588	

Therefore H + 2 commences with a Thursday, and H + 1 must end with a Wednesday. It begins with Thursday, and therefore has 385 days, but it cannot have 383 or 384.

d. Let 353 commence with a Saturday.

Molad of H + 1.........	3	2	876	to 3	8	203		See *b*, above. Begins Thursday.
Excess of H + 1, Emb.	5	21	589	5	21	589		
Molad of H + 2.........	1	0	385	to 2	5	792		

Therefore H + 2 begins with a Monday, and H + 2 must end with a Sunday. It begins with Tuesday, and therefore has 384 days, but it cannot have 383 or 385.

383 cannot be followed by 353.

e. Let 383 commence with a Monday, and, if possible, let it be followed by 353.

Molad of H..............	7	18	0	to 1	20	490	
Excess of H, Emb. ...	5	21	589	5	21	589	
Molad of H + 1.........	6	15	589	to 7	17	1079	Begins Saturday.
Excess of H + 1, Com.	4	18	876	4	18	876	
Molad of H + 2.........	4	0	385	to 5	2	875	

Therefore H + 2 commences with a Thursday, and H + 1 must end with a Wednesday. It commences with a Saturday, and can only have 355 days. It cannot have 353 or 354.

f. Let 383 commence with a Thursday, and, if possible, let it be followed by 353.

Molad of H..............	3	18	0	to 4	11	694	
Excess of H, Emb. ...	5	21	589	5	21	589	
Molad of H + 1.........	2	15	589	to 3	8	203	Begins Tuesday.
Excess of H + 1, Com.	4	8	876	4	8	876	
Molad of H + 2.........	7	0	385	to 7	16	1079	

Therefore H + 2 commences with a Saturday, and H + 1 must end with a Friday. It commences with a Tuesday, and can only have 354 days. It cannot have 353 or 355.

g. Let 383 commence with a Saturday, and, if possible, let it be followed by 353.

Molad of H..............	5	18	0	to	6	20	490	
Excess of H, Emb. ...	5	21	589		5	21	589	
Molad of H + 1.........	4	15	589	to	5	17	1079	Begins Thursday.
Excess of H + 1, Com.	4	8	876		4	8	876	
Molad of H + 2.........	2	0	385	to	3	2	875	

Therefore H + 2 will commence with a Monday, or a Tuesday, and H + 1 must end with a Sunday or a Monday. It commences with Thursday, so that it may have 354 or 355 days, but it cannot have 353.

II. 354 cannot be followed by 354.

a. Let 354 commence with a Tuesday, and, if possible, let it be followed by 354.

Molad of H..............	2	15	589	to	3	9	203	
Excess of H, Com. ...	4	8	876		4	8	876	
Molad of H + 1.........	7	0	385	to	7	17	1079	Begins Saturday.
Excess of H + 1, Com.	4	8	876		4	8	876	
Molad of H + 2.........	4	9	181	to	5	2	875	

Therefore H + 2 must commence with a Thursday, and H + 1 must end with a Wednesday. It commences with a Saturday, and therefore must have 355 days; but it cannot have 354 or 353.

b. Let 354 commence with a Thursday, and, if possible, let it be followed by 354.

Molad of H..............	3	9	204	to	5	9	203	
Excess of H, Com. ...	4	8	876		4	8	876	
Molad of H + 1.........	7	18	0	to	2	17	1079	Begins Monday.
Excess of H + 1, Com.	4	8	876		4	8	876	
Molad of H + 2.........	5	2	876	to	7	2	875	

Therefore H + 2 must commence either with a Thursday or a

Saturday, and H + 1 must end with a Wednesday or a Friday. It commences with a Monday; so that it may have 353 or 355 days, but it cannot have 354.

354 cannot be followed by 384.

c. Let 354 commence with a Tuesday, and, if possible, let it be followed by 384.

Molad of H + 1.........	7	0	385	to	7	17	1079	See *a*, above. Saturday.
Excess of H + 1, Emb.	5	21	589		5	21	589	
Molad of H + 2.........	5	21	974	to	6	15	588	

Therefore H + 2 must commence with a Saturday, and H + 1 must end with a Friday. It commences with Saturday, and therefore has 385 days; but it cannot have 384 or 383.

d. Let 354 commence with a Thursday, and, if possible, let it be followed by 384.

Molad of H + 1.........	7	18	0	to	2	17	1079	See *b*, above. Monday.
Excess of H + 1, Emb.	5	21	589		5	21	589	
Molad of H + 2.........	6	15	589	to	1	15	588	

Therefore H + 2 must commence with a Saturday or with a Monday, and H + 1 must end with a Friday or a Sunday. It commences with a Monday. Therefore it may have either 383 or 385 days, but it cannot have 384.

384 cannot be followed by 354.

e. A year of 384 days can only commence with a Tuesday, and, if possible, let it be followed by 354.

Molad of H..............	2	18	0	to	3	17	1079	
Excess of H, Emb. ...	5	21	589		5	21	589	
Molad of H + 1	1	15	589	to	2	15	588	Begins Monday.
Excess of H + 1, Com.	4	8	876		4	8	876	
Molad of H + 2	6	0	385	to	7	0	384	

Therefore H + 2 must begin with a Saturday, and H + 1 must end with a Friday. It commences with Monday, and can only have 355 days. It cannot have 354 or 353.

III. 355, if it commence with Monday, can be followed by 355.

a. Molad of H	1	9	204 to	2	15	588*	
Excess of H, Com. ...	4	8	876	4	8	876	
Molad of H + 1	5	18	0 to	7	0	384	Begins Saturday.
Excess of H + 1, Com.	4	8	876	4	8	876	
Molad of H + 2	3	2	876 to	4	9	180	

Therefore H + 2 commences with a Tuesday, or with a Thursday, and H + 1 must end with a Monday or a Wednesday. It commences with a Saturday, so that it may have 353 or 355 days, but it cannot have 354.

b. Let 355 commence with a Thursday.

Molad of H...............	5	9	204 to	5	17	1079	
Excess of H, Emb. ...	4	8	876	4	8	876	
Molad of H + 1.........	2	18	0 to	3	2	875	Begins Tuesday.
Excess of H + 1, Com.	4	8	876	4	8	876	
Molad of H + 2.........	7	2	876 to	7	11	671	

Therefore H + 2 commences with a Saturday, and H + 1 must end with a Friday. It commences with a Tuesday, and therefore can only have 354 days; it cannot have 355 or 353.

c. Let 355 commence with a Saturday.

Molad of H...............	6	0	408 to	7	17	1079	
Excess of H, Com. ...	4	8	876	4	8	876	
Molad of H + 1.........	3	9	204 to	5	2	875	Begins Thursday.
Excess of H + 1 Com.	4	8	876	4	8	876	
Molad of H + 2.........	7	18	0 to	2	11	671	

Therefore H + 2 must commence with a Monday, and H + 1 must

* Notice that H must follow an Embolismic year, because it is assumed to be itself followed by a Common year. The superior limit is therefore 2 15 588.

end with a Sunday. It begins with a Thursday, so that it has 354 days, and cannot have 355 or 353.

355, if it commence with Monday or Saturday, can be followed by 385.

d. Let 355 commence with Monday.

Molad of H	1	9	204	to 2	17	1079*		
Excess of H. Com. ...	4	8	876	4	8	876		
Molad of H + 1	5	18	0	to 7	2	875	} Begins Saturday.	
Excess of H + 1 Emb.	5	21	589	5	21	589		
Molad of H + 2	4	15	589	to 6	0	384		

Therefore H + 2 commences with a Thursday, or with a Saturday, and H + 1 must end with a Wednesday or a Friday. It begins with Saturday; so that it may have 383 or 385 days; but it cannot have 384.

e. Let 355 commence with a Saturday.

Molad of H...............	6	9	204	to 7	17	1079	
Excess of H, Com. ...	4	8	876	4	8	876	
Molad of H + 1.........	3	18	0	to 5	2	875	} Begins Thursday.
Excess of H + 1, Emb.	5	21	589	5	21	589	
Molad of H + 2.........	2	15	589	to 4	0	384	

Therefore H + 2 commences with a Tuesday, or with a Thursday, and H + 1 must end with a Monday or a Wednesday. It begins with a Thursday, and may have 385 or 383 days. It cannot have 384.

f. Let 355 commence with a Thursday.

Molad of H...............	5	9	204	to 5	17	1079	
Excess of H, Com......	4	8	876	4	8	876	
Molad of H + 1.........	2	18	0	to 3	2	875	} Begins Tuesday.
Excess of H + 1, Emb.	5	21	589	5	21	589	
Molad of H + 2.........	1	15	589	to 2	0	384	

* H may follow either a Common or an Embolismic year because H + 1 is, by hypothesis, Embolismic.

Therefore H + 2 must begin with a Monday, and H + 1 must end with a Sunday. It begins with Tuesday, and therefore has 384 days. Hence, 355 commencing with a Thursday cannot be followed by 385 or by 383.

385, commencing with Monday or Saturday, can be followed by 355.

g. Let 385 commence with Monday.

Molad of H	1	20	491	to 2	17	1079		
Excess of H, Emb. ...	5	21	589		5	21	589	
Molad of H + 1.........	7	18	0	to 1	15	588	Begins Monday.
Excess of H + 1, Com.	4	8	876	4	8	876	
Molad of H + 2.........	5	2	876	to 6	0	384	

Therefore H + 2 may commence with a Thursday or a Saturday, and H + 1 must end with a Wednesday or a Friday. It commences with a Monday, and therefore can have 355 or 353 days; but it cannot have 354.

h. Let 385 commence with Saturday.

Molad of H	6	20	491	to 7	17	1079	
Excess of H, Emb. ...	5	21	589	5	21	589	
Molad of H + 1.........	5	18	0	to 6	15	588	Begins Saturday.
Excess of H + 1, Com.	4	8	876	4	8	876	
Molad of H + 2.........	3	2	876	to 4	0	384	

Therefore H + 2 begins with a Tuesday or a Thursday, and H + 1 must end with a Monday or a Wednesday. It commences with a Saturday, and can have 355 or 353 days, but it cannot have 354.

i. Let 385 commence with Thursday.

Molad of H	4	11	695	to 5	17	1079	
Excess of H, Emb. ...	5	21	589	5	21	589	
Molad of H + 1.........	3	9	204	to 4	15	588	Begins Thursday.
Excess of H + 1, Com.	4	8	876	4	8	876	
Molad of H + 2.........	7	18	0	to 2	0	384	

Therefore H + 2 must begin with a Monday, and H + 1 must end with a Sunday. It commences with a Thursday; it can therefore only have 354 days, so that if 385 commence with a Thursday it cannot be followed by 355 or by 353.

IV. to X. It will be found that the proofs of these statements are included in those which have been given above.

IV.	*a*.	Proof included in	I.*a*.
	b.	„	I.*b*.
	c.	„	I.*d*.
	d.	„	I.*c*.
	e.	„	I.*f*.
	f.	„	I.*g*.
	g.	„	I.*e*.
V.	*a*.	„	II.*b*.
	b.	„	II.*a*.
	c.	„	II.*d*.
	d.	„	II.*c*.
VI.		„	II.*e*.
VII.	*a*.	„	I.*a*.
	b.	„	I.*b*.
	c.	„	I.*e*.
	d.	„	I.*d*.
	e.	„	I.*e*.
	f.	„	I.*g*.
	g.	„	I.*f*.
VIII.	*a*.	„	III.*a*.
	b.	„	III.*b*.
	c.	„	III.*c*.
	d.	„	III.*d*.
	e.	„	III.*e*.
	f.	„	III.*f*.
	g.	„	III.*g*.
	h.	„	III.*h*.
	i.	„	III.*i*.
IX.	*a*.	„	III.*b*.
	b.	„	III.*c*.
	c.	„	III.*a*.
	d.	„	III.*f*.

e. Proof included in III.*d*.
f. „ III.*e*.
g. „ III.*i*.
h. „ III.*g*.
i. „ III.*h*.
X. *a*. „ II.*a*.
b. „ II. *b*.
c. „ II.*c*.
d. „ II.*d*.
e. „ II.*e*.

In the following Table of collected results all those years are entered which can possibly follow a year of the form given in the first column when the latter commences upon the day of the week given in the second column.

It is to be understood that no sequence of years, other than such as are here expressed, is possible. Thus: It is impossible that a year of 354 days can follow a year of 385 days when the latter commences with a Saturday; therefore, in the third line from the bottom of the Table, 354 does not appear.

A Year of Days.	Having for First Day.	Can be followed by a Year having Days in Number.						Reference to Proof.
353	Monday		354	355			385	I.*a* I.*c*
„	Saturday		354			384		I.*b* I.*d*
354	Tuesday			355			385	II.*a* II.*c*
„	Thursday	353		355	383		385	II.*b* II.*d*
355	Monday....................	353		355	383		385	III.*a* III.*d*
	Thursday		354			384		III.*b* III.*f*
	Saturday		354		383		385	III.*c*. III.*e*
383	Monday			355				I.*e*
	Thursday		354					I.*f*
	Saturday		354	355				I.*g*
384	Tuesday			355				II.*e*
385	Monday....................	353		355				III.*g*
	Thursday		354					III.*i*
	Saturday	353		355				III.*h*

60. It may be well to observe here that, in attempting to prove statements such as the foregoing, there may be a temptation to adopt a method which will seem to be both short and simple. It might be said, for example—If a year of 354 days commence with a Tuesday its last day must be a Friday, and the next year will commence with a Saturday; this is a day which is possible for the commencement of years having 353, 355, 383, or 385 days; therefore 354 can be followed by either of these years.

It has, however, been proved, in V.*a*, that, when the Molads are considered, it is impossible for 354, commencing with a Tuesday, to be followed by 353; and, in V.*c*, that it is impossible for it to be followed by 383.

The method, if attempted, therefore fails in this case. It fails also in three other cases. It would show that 353 commencing with a Monday might be followed by 383; that 383 commencing with a Monday might be followed by 353; and that 384 commencing, as it always does, with a Tuesday, might be followed by 353. Each of these sequences is proved by the Molads to be impossible.

Reliance, therefore, must not be placed upon such a method, although it gives correct results in ten out of fourteen cases. Thus:—It will show that 353 commencing with a Saturday can be followed by 354 or by 384. For if 353 commence with a Saturday it must end with a Monday, and the next year will commence with a Tuesday; this is a day which is possible for the commencement of both 354 and 384, but not possible for the commencement of any other year. This method therefore proves, in this instance correctly, that not only can 353 be followed by 354 or by 384, but also that such must be the sequence; the former, if 353 be followed by a Common year; the latter, if it be followed by an Embolismic year.

Correspondence Between Jewish and Christian Dates.

61. Guided by the foregoing regulations the Christian dates corresponding to Tishrī 1, for any consecutive number of years, may be computed. If the computation be not made from the commencement of the Jewish Era it must begin from some year in which the Christian date of Tishrī 1 is known. Assuming that no such date is known, it may be found by means of the formula of Dr. Gauss, which will be described hereafter, or by the method of "Days Elapsed," of which examples will now be given.

Required the Christian date corresponding to Tishrî 1 of the year 5611.

Let it be assumed as known that the Molad BeHaRD is 2d. 5h. 204ch., that is, the Era commenced at 5h. 204ch. after the commencement of feria 2, and that the day corresponded to Monday, October 7, B.C., 3761.* The Jewish feria commences six hours earlier than our own Civil week-day, that is to say, it commences at 6 p.m.

It is also known that, according to Jewish Astronomical computation the mean length

	d.	h.	ch.
Of a Lunation is..............................	29	12	793
Of a Common year..........................	354	8	876
Of an Embolismic year....................	383	21	589
Of a Cycle	6939	16	595

These, then, are the known facts by means of which the Christian date of Tishrî 1 in the given year is to be found. Attention must, of course, be paid to the established rules of the Jewish Calendar.

1. The Christian year, in the Autumn of which A.M. 5611 commences, is A.D. (5611–3761), or 1850; † the Jewish year terminates in the Autumn of 1851.

2. The division of 5611 by 19 gives a quotient 295, and a remainder 6, showing that the given year is the sixth in the 296th Cycle. Consequently there had elapsed 295 complete Astronomical Cycles and 5 complete Astronomical years before the New Moon occurred by which Tishrî 1, A.M. 5611, is governed.

3. To find the time in days, hours, and Chalakim, contained in these 295 Cycles and five years.

In the first five years of every Cycle there are four Common years, and one Embolismic year.

We have then, by actual multiplication,

		d.	h.	ch.
295 Astronomical Cycles	=	2047208	10	565
4 Astro. Com. years	=	1417	11	264
1 Astro. Emb. year	=	383	21	589
The sum	=	2049009	19	338

* Article 33, p. 41. † Article 37, p. 46.

The same result is obtained if the values be taken from the Tables V. and IV., thus:—

	d.	h.	ch.
200 Cycles	1387937	22	200
90 „	624572	1	630
5 „	34698	10	815
First 5 years of next Cycle	1801	8	583
The sum......	2049009	19	338

This, then, is the actual interval of time elapsed, according to Jewish Astronomical computation, since the commencement of the Era up to the occurrence of the New Moon of Tishrî, A.M. 5611.

If we add 5h. 204ch. to this interval of time the sum will denote the time elapsed from 6 p.m. on Monday, October 7, B.C. 3761, up to the occurrence of the New Moon of Tishrî, A.M. 5611. This sum is 2049010d. 0h. 542ch. The New Moon therefore occurred upon the 2049011th day, at 542ch. after the commencement of that day.

4. This number of days, when divided by 7, is found to contain 6 days more than an exact number of weeks. The days commenced with a Monday, feria 2, and the complete weeks terminated, therefore, with a Sunday, feria 1. The last of the 6 remaining days would be a Saturday, feria 7, and the Molad for Tishrî A.M. 5611 is expressed by 7 0 542, or, Saturday at 0h. 242ch. past six o'clock in the evening.

As the same Molad is found for Tishrî 1, A.M. 5611, by the ordinary method (Article 42), it may be concluded that the work up to this point is correct, thus:—

Molad BeHaRD	2	5	204
Excess of 200 Cycles	5	22	200
„ 90 „	4	1	630
„ 5 „	6	10	815
„ for sixth year	2	8	153
	7	0	542

The feria in this Molad being 7, and the hours and Chalakim not amounting to 18h., no postponement is required by any of the rules of the Calendar. Tishrî 1 is celebrated upon the day indicated, namely, the Saturday which has been found to be the 2049011th day of the Era; Monday, October 7, B.C. 3761 being the first of these days.

5. The corresponding day in the Christian Calendar must now be found. This will be done, as usual, by Julian computation, in order to avoid any difficulty which might be caused through the nominal days dropped in the Gregorian Calendar.

Dividing 2049011 by 1461, the quotient gives 1402 quadriennial periods, and 689 days which = 1 year + 324 days.

The interval of time is therefore 4 × 1461 + 1, or 5609 Julian years + 324 days.

From October 7 to December 31, both inclusive, B.C. 3761 is a period of 86 days; therefore 3760 Julian years and 86 days elapsed before the Christian Era commenced; there remain 1849 complete years and 238 days of the next year, A.D. 1850.

The Julian date corresponding to Tishri 1, A.M. 5611 is, therefore, the 238th day, or August 26, in A.D. 1850. The corresponding Gregorian date is August (26 + 12), or September 7.

This demonstration has been given in considerable detail in the hope that it may be thoroughly understood. In actual practice the work would be much abbreviated, thus:—

(1) A.M. 5611 = A.D. (5611−3761) = 1850.

(2) Jewish years elapsed = 5610 = 295 Cycles + 5 years.
= 2049009d. 19h. 338ch.
Add .... 5h. 304ch. in order to obtain the time elapsed, by Astronomical computation, from 6 p.m. Monday, October 7, B.C. 3761. The sum is—
2049010d. + 0h. + 542ch.

The New Moon occurred, therefore, very shortly after the commencement of the 2049011th day of the Era.

(3) For the corresponding Julian date, which is in the Autumn of A.D. 1850.

From October 7 to Dec. 31, B.C. 3761, both inclusive =	86 d.
From January 1, B.C. 3760, to December 31, A.D. 1849 there are 5609 Julian years .... =	2048687 „
	2048773 „

Subtracting this number of days from the total number required, namely 2049011, the remainder is 238. The day required is therefore the 238th of the Julian year 1850; or August 26, A.D. 1850, Julian = September 7, Gregorian.

As another example, with the calculation made from a different basis, let the date be required at which Tishrî 1 occurred in A.D. 1897, to be computed from the Molad 2d. 4h. 204ch. as adopted by Hillel for Tishrî 1, A.M. 4105, corresponding to the Julian date, Monday, September 24, A.D. 344.

(1) A.D. 1897 = A.M. (1897 + 3761) = 5658.

(2) The number of Astronomical years elapsed between the New Moons of Tishrî, A.M. 4105 and A.M. 5658, is 1553, or 81 Cycles + 14 years.

These 14 years are the first fourteen in a Cycle because the division of 4105 by 19 shows that 4105 was the first year in a Cycle. Five of the fourteen years are therefore Embolismic, and nine are Common.

The interval of time between the computed New Moons is, therefore, the sum of

	d.	h.	ch.
80 Cycles	555175	4	80 *
1 Cycle..	6939	16	595
9 Common years............................	3189	7	324 †
5 Embolismic years	1919	11	785
	567223	15	704

that is, the New Moon of Tishrî, A.M. 5658, occurred on the 567224th day, at 15h. 204ch. after that day had commenced.

This number of days is an exact number of weeks, and because the first of these days was a Monday, the last of them was a Sunday; but if the computed New Moon occur upon a Sunday Tishrî 1 is postponed to Monday, which will be the 567225th day. This feria is confirmed by the Molad of A.M. 5658, which may be found in the usual way.

Dividing 5658 by 19 the quotient is 297, and the remainder is 15. It is therefore the fifteenth year of the 298th Cycle.

BeHaRD..	2	5	204
Add for 200 Cycles............................	5	22	200
,, 90 ,, ...	4	1	630
,, 7 ,, ...	4	19	925
,, fifteenth year	5	19	29
	7	19	908

* Table V. † Table III.

As the hours exceed 18, Tishrî 1 is postponed to Sunday, and thence to Monday.

(3) The time elapsed from Monday, September 24, A.D. 344, inclusive, to the end of that year is 99 days, and from the commencement of 345 to the end of 1896 there are 1552 Julian years, or 566868 days. The total number of days up to the end of 1896 is, therefore, 566967.

Subtracting this total from 567225, the remainder is 258. The required date for Tishrî 1 is, therefore, the 258th day of A.D. 1897, Monday, September 15, Julian; the corresponding Gregorian date is Monday, September 27. The week-day is found to be correct, if a further test be required by the Sunday Letter for 1897, Julian E, Gregorian C.

TO FIND THE CHRISTIAN DATE CORRESPONDING TO NÎSÂN 15 OF ANY GIVEN JEWISH YEAR.

62. It will be remembered that Nîsân 15 in any Jewish year, H, invariably precedes Tishrî 1 of the year H + 1 by 163 days.

Consequently, to find the date of Nîsân 15 in the year H nothing more is required than to subtract 163 from the Christian date of Tishrî 1 in the year H + 1, this date being expressed by its serial number as a day of the year.

The idea may occur to some that it would be just as easy to add to the date of Tishrî 1 the number of days that elapse before Nîsân 15 in the same Jewish year is reached. This indeed may be done; but it must be kept in mind that the number of days from Nîsân 15 to Tishrî 1 is constant, while the number from Tishrî 1 to Nîsân 15 is variable. Thus :—

Tishrî 1 to Nîsân 15 in a year of	353 days	190 days.
,, ,,	354 ,, ...	191 ,,
,, ,,	355 ,, ...	192 ,,
,, ,,	383 ,, ...	220 ,,
,, ,,	384 ,, ...	221 ,,
,, ,,	385 ,, ...	222 ,,

The former method is therefore to be preferred as less liable to error. Much less labour is involved, especially when the work is consecutive.

A Table of consecutive days, for which it is only necessary to calculate (by subtraction of 163) the first line, may very easily be formed; by its means the date of Nîsân 15 may be written down at once when the date of Tishrî 1 is known.

It must always be remembered that the months of Nîsân and Tishrî which occur in any one given Christian year belong, the former to the Jewish year H−1, the latter to the Jewish year H.

Calculation for the first line of the Table.

August 20 = January 232 in a Christian Common year,
Subtract 163
January 69 = March 10.
August 20 = January 233 in a Leap-year.
163
January 70 = March 10.

In fact, no difference in the date assigned to Nîsân 15 can, in any case, arise from Leap-years, because the intercalated day occurs before the interval between March and September.

The Table is to be read thus:—If, in any given Christian year the Tishrî 1 which belongs to the Jewish year H occur upon August 20, then, in the same Christian year the Nîsân 15 which belongs to the preceding Jewish year H − 1 will have occurred upon March 10.

TABLE FOR CORRESPONDENCE OF DATES BETWEEN TISHRÎ 1 AND NISAN 15.

Tishri 1 of year H.	Nisân 15 of H−1.	Tishri 1 of year H.	Nisân 15 of H−1.	Tishri 1 of year H.	Nisân 15 of H−1.
August 20	March 10	September 6	March 27	September 23	April 13
„ 21	„ 11	„ 7	„ 28	„ 24	„ 14
„ 22	„ 12	„ 8	„ 29	„ 25	„ 15
„ 23	„ 13	„ 9	„ 30	„ 26	„ 16
„ 24	„ 14	„ 10	„ 31	„ 27	„ 17
„ 25	„ 15	„ 11	April 1	„ 28	„ 18
„ 26	„ 16	„ 12	„ 2	„ 29	„ 19
„ 27	„ 17	„ 13	„ 3	„ 30	„ 20
„ 28	„ 18	„ 14	„ 4	October 1	„ 21
„ 29	„ 19	„ 15	„ 5	„ 2	„ 22
„ 30	„ 20	„ 16	„ 6	„ 3	„ 23
„ 31	„ 21	„ 17	„ 7	„ 4	„ 24
September 1	„ 22	„ 18	„ 8	„ 5	„ 25
„ 2	„ 23	„ 19	„ 9	„ 6	„ 26
„ 3	„ 24	„ 20	„ 10	„ 7	„ 27
„ 4	„ 25	„ 21	„ 11	„ 8	„ 28
„ 5	„ 26	„ 22	„ 12	„ 9	„ 29

From these figures it appears that if D be the day of September in any Christian year which corresponds to Tishrî 1, then D + 21 is the day of March which corresponds to the Nîsân 15 which occurs in the same Christian year. Thus:—

Let Tishrî 1 = October 3 = September 33 = D
Then Nîsân 1 = March (D − 21) = March 54 = April 23.

On the other hand, if d be the day of March which corresponds to Nîsân 15, then d−21 is the day of September which corresponds to Tishrî 1. Thus:—

Let Nîsân 15 = April 4 = March 35 = d
Then Tishrî 1 = September (d−21) = September (35−21) = 14.

As a check upon the feria, or week-day found for Nîsân 15, it may be noticed that, because 163 is of the form $7n + 2$, the feria of Nîsân 15 in any given Christian year is always less by 2 than the feria of the Tishrî 1 which occurs in the same Christian year. In other words the feria of Nîsân 15 in the Jewish year H is less by 2 than the feria of Tishrî 1 in the year H + 1. Thus:—

If Tishrî 1 be on	Monday, feria	2, (or 9),	Nîsân 15 is on	Saturday, feria 7.
"	Tuesday, "	3,	"	Sunday, " 1.
"	Thursday, "	5,	"	Tuesday, " 3.
"	Saturday, "	7,	"	Thursday, " 5.

63. The computation for a series of years may now be made. This will be done, by way of example, for three Cycles, the 296th, 297th, and 298th, commencing with A.M. 5606 (see pp. 123–125).

The first object is to find the Molads for the successive years, by means of which the feria for Tishrî 1 is determined. This will be effected by, first, finding the Molad for A.M. 5606, and then, as usual, by the successive additions of 4d. 8h. 876ch. as the excess for Common years, and of 5d. 21h. 589ch. as the excess for Embolismic years.

As the work now proposed is consecutive it will not be necessary to employ the shortened method of finding the Molads, which was described in Article 41. If, however, there be any doubt as to the correctness of the results obtained they may be tested from time to

CYCLE 296.

Years of Cycle.	A.M.	Molad.	Week-day.	Tishri 1.	Cause of Postponement, if any take place.
1	5606	4 15 769 4 8 876	Wednesday	Thursday	ADU.
2	5607	2 0 565 4 8 876	Monday	Monday	
3 Emb.	5608	6 9 361 5 21 589	Friday	Saturday	ADU.
4	5609	5 6 950 4 8 876	Thursday	Thursday	
5	5610	2 15 746 4 8 876	Monday	Monday	
6 Emb.	5611	7 0 542 5 21 589	Saturday	Saturday	
7	5612	5 22 51 4 8 876	Thursday	Saturday	YacH and ADU.
8 Emb.	5613	3 6 927 5 21 589	Tuesday	Tuesday	
9	5614	2 4 436 4 8 876	Monday	Monday	
10	5615	6 13 232 4 8 876	Friday	Saturday	ADU.
11 Emb.	5616	3 22 28 5 21 589	Tuesday	Thursday	YacH and ADU.
12	5617	2 19 617 4 8 876	Monday	Tuesday	YacH.
13	5618	7 4 413 4 8 876	Saturday	Saturday	
14 Emb.	5619	4 13 209 5 21 589	Wednesday	Thursday	ADU.
15	5620	3 10 798 4 8 876	Tuesday	Thursday	GaTRaD and ADU.
16	5621	7 19 594 4 8 876	Saturday	Monday	YacH and ADU.
17 Emb.	5622	5 4 390 5 21 589	Thursday	Thursday	
18	5623	4 1 979 4 3 876	Wednesday	Thursday	ADU.
19 Emb.	5624	1 10 775	Sunday	Monday	ADU.

Test for the last Molad				
	Molad of 5606	4	15	769
	Add for 19th year	3	19	6
	Molad of 5624	1	10	775

CYCLE 297.

Years of Cycle.	A.M.	Molad.	Week-day.	Tishri 1.	Cause of Postponement, if any take place.
19	5624	1 10 775 5 21 589			
1	5625	7 8 284 4 8 876	Saturday	Saturday	
2	5626	4 17 80 4 8 876	Wednesday	Thursday	ADU.
3 Emb.	5627	2 1 956 5 21 589	Monday	Monday	
4	5628	7 23 465 4 8 876	Saturday	Monday	YacH and ADU.
5	5629	5 8 261 4 8 876	Thursday	Thursday	
6 Emb.	5630	2 17 57 5 21 589	Monday	Monday	
7	5631	1 14 646 4 8 876	Sunday	Monday	ADU.
8 Emb.	5632	5 23 442 5 21 589	Thursday	Saturday	YacH and ADU.
9	5633	4 20 1031 4 8 876	Wednesday	Thursday	ADU.
10	5634	2 5 827 4 8 876	Monday	Monday	
11 Emb.	5635	6 14 623 5 21 589	Friday	Saturday	ADU.
12	5636	5 12 132 4 8 876	Thursday	Thursday	
13	5637	2 20 1008 4 8 876	Monday	Tuesday	YacH.
14 Emb.	5638	7 5 804 5 21 589	Saturday	Saturday	
15	5639	6 3 313 4 8 876	Friday	Saturday	ADU.
16	5640	3 12 109 4 8 876	Tuesday	Thursday	GaTRaD and ADU.
17 Emb.	5641	7 20 985 5 21 589	Saturday	Monday	YacH and ADU.
18	5642	6 18 494 4 8 876	Friday	Saturday	ADU.
19 Emb.	5643	4 3 290	Wednesday	Thursday	ADU.

Test for the last Molad				
	Molad of 5624	1	10	775
	Add for 1 Cycle	2	16	595
	Molad of 5643	4	3	290

CYCLE 298

Years of Cycle.	A.M.	Molad.	Week-day.	Tishri 1.	Cause of Postponement if any take place.
19	5643	4 3 290 5 21 589			
1	5644	3 0 879 4 8 876	Tuesday	Tuesday	
2	5645	7 9 675 4 8 876	Saturday	Saturday	
3 Emb.	5646	4 18 471 5 21 589	Wednesday	Thursday	ADU.
4	5647	3 15 1060 4 8 876	Tuesday	Thursday	GaTRaD and ADU.
5	5648	1 0 856 4 8 876	Sunday	Monday	ADU.
6 Emb.	5649	5 9 652 5 21 589	Thursday	Thursday	
7	5650	4 7 161 4 8 876	Wednesday	Thursday	ADU.
8 Emb.	5651	1 15 1037 5 21 589	Monday	Monday	
9	5652	7 13 546 4 8 876	Saturday	Saturday	
10	5653	4 22 342 4 8 876	Wednesday	Thursday	ADU.
11 Emb.	5654	2 7 138 5 21 589	Monday	Monday	
12	5655	1 4 727 4 8 876	Sunday	Monday	ADU.
13	5656	5 13 523 4 8 876	Thursday	Thursday	
14 Emb.	5657	2 22 319 5 21 589	Monday	Tuesday	YacH.
15	5658	1 19 908 4 8 876	Sunday	Monday	ADU.
16	5659	6 4 704 4 8 876	Friday	Saturday	ADU.
17 Emb.	5660	3 13 500 5 21 589	Tuesday	Tuesday	
18	5661	2 11 9 4 8 876	Monday	Monday	
19 Emb.	5662	6 19 885 5 21 589	Friday	Saturday	ADU.
1 of next Cycle		5 17 394	Thursday	Thursday	

Test for Molad of 5626				
	Molad of 5643	4	3	290
	Add for 1 Cycle	2	16	595
	Molad of 5662	6	19	885

time by means of Table VIII. of "Additions to be Made." It will certainly be wise to test the Molad of every last year of a Cycle, for if a mistake be made anywhere in this consecutive work it will of necessity run on unless it be corrected.

To find the Molad for Tishrî, A.M. 5606.

The division of 5606 by 19 gives a quotient 295, and a remainder 1. The year is therefore the first in the 296th Cycle, and 295 complete Cycles had elapsed before its commencement.

	d.	h.	ch.
Molad BeHaRD..	2	5	204
Excess for 200 Cycles	5	22	200
,, 90 ,, ...	4	1	630
,, 5 ,, ...	6	10	815
Molad for Tishrî, A.M. 5606 =	4	15	769

This affords a point of departure, and the computation for the feriæ of Tishrî 1 can now be made for the whole Cycle.

64. The corresponding Christian dates for Tishrî 1 must now be found. Reference should be made to the method of finding the length of the Jewish year described in Article 53. The question whether the Christian year in which Tishrî 1 occurs be Bissextile or not must be taken into account.

The year with which the computation commences is A.M. 5606. It is necessary to find, by the process illustrated in Article 61, the Christian date of Tishrî 1 for this year.

1. A.M. 5606 = A.D. (5606 − 3761) = 1845.
2. Years elapsed = 5605 = 295 Cycles.

	d.	h.	ch.
200 Cycles =	1387937	22	200
90 ,, =	624572	1	630
5 ,, =	34698	10	815
295 Cycles =	2047208	10	565

This is the actual time elapsed from the commencement of the Era to the computed New Moon of Tishri, 5606.

The day of New Moon by computation is therefore the 2047209th day of the Era = $(7n + 3)$rd day; it must be a Wednesday, because the first day of the Era was a Monday, so that the completed weeks end with a Sunday. The celebration of this Moon, on Tishri 1, is postponed by ADU to Thursday, day 2047210 of the Era.

3. The Christian date required is in the Autumn of A.D. 1845. From October 7, B.C. 3761, to the end of that year = 86 days, and from the commencement of B.C. 3760 to the close of A.D. 1844 there are 5604 Julian years, or 2046861 days; the sum of the two intervals is 2046947 days. The difference between this number and 2047210 is 263. The day required is, therefore, the 263rd of A.D. 1845 = Thursday, September 20, Julian = October 2, Gregorian. The Julian Sunday Letter is G; the Gregorian is E.

Having thus obtained a basis from which the computation can commence, the work may proceed. Gregorian dates will be now employed, the years being subsequent to A.D. 1582. The Sunday Letter of the Christian year is added, in order that the day of the week, as given, may be verified if it be thought necessary.

A.M. 5606. The first day is Thursday; the last must be Sunday, for the next year has been found (Table, above) to commence with a Monday. The form of the year is, therefore, $7n + 4$, so that it has 354 days, being a Common year, for it is the first in a Cycle.

The Gregorian date for Tishri 1 in this year has been found to be October 2, 1845.

The date for Nisân 15 will be found when that for Tishri 1 in the next year has been determined.

A.M. 5607. First day Monday. This day must be October (2 + 354), A.D. 1845, because the last year, A.M. 5606, was found to contain 354 days.

October (2 + 354) = October 356 = September 386 *
Subtract for the year 1846 †...... 365

Tishri 1, 5607 = September 21, 1846. Monday. D.

* The 356th of October is the 386th of September; the latter is used because 365 cannot be subtracted from 356.

† This subtraction is really for the number of days from September 1, 1845, to September 1, 1846, including the month of February, 1846, which has no day intercalated.

For the length of the year:—It begins with a Monday, and ends with a Friday because Tishrî 1, in the next year, has been found to be a Saturday. It, therefore has 5 days more than an exact number of weeks, and being a Common year its form is 350 + 5. It has 355 days.

Nîsân 15 of 5606 occurs 163 days earlier than Tishrî 1 of 5607, and may now be found.

September 21, 1846 = January 264
Subtract...... 163

January 101 = April 11, Saturday.

This date might be taken direct from the Table in Article 62, and, because by the use of that Table, the dates for Nîsân 15 can be written down at once when the results of the computation are collected, it will not be necessary to continue calculating them.

5608 Emb. First day, Saturday. This day must be September 21, 1846 + 355 days, for the last year was found to contain 355 days.

September 21 + 355 = September 376
Subtract for 1847 365

Tishrî 1, 5608 = September 11, 1847. Saturday. C.

Length of the year:—It commences with a Saturday, and ends with a Wednesday, for the next year has been found to begin with a Thursday. It is Embolismic, and is of the form $7n + 5$. It has 383 days.

The method of computing ought now to be understood, and the work may be continued in an abbreviated manner. It should be remarked that the Last day, and the Length of each year is not to be written until the first day of the following year has been noted.

Years of Cycle.	A.M.	First Day.	Sunday Letter.	Last Day.	Length.
4	5609	Thursday, Sep. 11+383=Sep. 394			
		Days in 1848... 366			
		September 28, 1848	A	Sunday	350+4=354
5	5610	Monday, Sep. 28+354=Sep. 382			
		365			
		September 17, 1849	G	Friday	350+5=355
6	5611 Emb.	Saturday, Sep. 17+355=Sep. 372			
		365			
		September 7, 1850	F	Friday	378+7=385
7	5612	Saturday, Sep. 7+385=Sep. 392			
		365			
		September 27, 1851	E	Monday	350+3=353
8	5613 Emb.	Tuesday, Sep. 27+353=Sep. 380			
		Days in 1852... 366			
		September 14, 1852	C	Sunday	378+6=384
9	5614	Monday, Sep. 14+384=Sep. 398			
		365			
		Sep. 33			
		=October 3, 1853	B	Friday	350+5=355
10	5615	Saturday, Sep. 33+355=Sep. 388			
		365			
		September 23, 1854	A	Wednesday	350+5=355
11	5616 Emb.	Thursday, Sep. 23+355=Sep. 378			
		365			
		September 13, 1855	G	Monday	378+5=383
12	5617	Tuesday, Sep. 13+383=Sep. 396			
		Days in 1856... 366			
		September 30, 1856	E	Friday	350+4=354

Years of Cycle.	A.M.	First Day.	Sunday Letter.	Last Day.	Length.
13	5618	Saturday, Sep. 30+354=Sep. 384 365			
		September 19, 1857	D	Wednesday	350+5=355
14	5619 Emb.	Thursday, Sep. 19+355=Sep. 374 365			
		September 9, 1858	C	Wednesday	378+7=385
15	5620	Thursday, Sep. 9+385=Sep. 394 365			
		September 29, 1859	B	Sunday	350+4=354
16	5621	Monday, Sep. 29+354=Sep. 383 Days in 1860... 366			
		September 17, 1860	G	Wednesday	350+3=353
17	5622 Emb.	Thursday, Sep. 17+353=Sep. 370 365			
		September 5, 1861	F	Wednesday	378+7=385
18	5623	Thursday, Sep. 5+385=Sep. 390 365			
		September 25, 1862	E	Sunday	350+4=354
19	5624 Emb.	Monday, Sep. 25+354=Sep. 379 365			
		September 14, 1863	D	Friday	378+5=383
		CYCLE 297.			
1	5625	Saturday, Sep. 14+383=Sep. 397 Days in 1864... 366			
		Sep. 31 =October 1, 1864	B	Wednesday	350+5=355
2	5626	Thursday, Sep. 31+355=Sep. 386 365			
		September 21, 1865	A	Sunday	350+4=354

Years of Cycle.	A.M.	First Day.	Sun-day Letter.	Last Day.	Length.
3	5627 Emb.	Monday, Sep. 21+354=Sep. 375 365 September 10, 1866	G	Sunday	378+7=385
4	5628	Monday, Sep. 10+385=Sep. 395 365 September 30, 1867	F	Wednesday	350+3=353
5	5629	Thursday, Sep. 30+353=Sep. 383 Days in 1868... 366 September 17, 1868	D	Sunday	350+4=354
6	5630 Emb.	Monday, Sep. 17+354=Sep. 371 365 September 6, 1869	C	Sunday	378+7=385
7	5631	Monday, Sep. 6+385=Sep. 391 365 September 26, 1870	B	Friday	350+5=355
8	5632 Emb.	Saturday, Sep. 26+355=Sep. 381 365 September 16, 1871	A	Wednesday	378+5=383
9	5633	Thursday, Sep. 16+383=Sep. 399 Days in 1872... 366 Sep. 33 =October 3, 1872	F	Sunday	350+4=354
10	5634	Monday, Sep. 33+354=Sep. 387 365 September 22, 1873	E	Friday	350+5=355
11	5635 Emb.	Saturday, Sep. 22+355=Sep. 377 365 September 12, 1874	D	Wednesday	378+5=383

Years of Cycle.	A.M.	First Day.	Sunday Letter.	Last Day.	Length.
12	5636	Thursday, Sep. 12+383=Sep. 395 365 September 30, 1875	C	Monday	350+5=355
13	5637	Tuesday, Sep. 30+355=Sep. 385 Days in 1876... 366 September 19, 1876	A	Friday	350+4=354
14	5638 Emb.	Saturday, Sep. 19+354=Sep. 373 365 September 8, 1877	G	Friday	378+7=385
15	5639	Saturday, Sep. 8+385=Sep. 393 365 September 28, 1878	F	Wednesday	350+5=355
16	5640	Thursday, Sep. 28+355=Sep. 383 365 September 18, 1879	E	Sunday	350+4=354
17	5641 Emb.	Monday, Sep. 18+354=Sep. 372 Days in 1880... 366 September 6, 1880	C	Friday	378+5=383
18	5642	Saturday, Sep. 6+383=Sep. 389 365 September 24, 1881	B	Wednesday	350+5=355
19	5643 Emb.	Thursday, Sep. 24+355=Sep. 379 365 September 14, 1882	A	Monday	378+5=383

CYCLE 298.

Years of Cycle.	A.M.	First Day.	Sunday Letter.	Last Day.	Length.
1	5644	Tuesday, Sep. 14+383=Sep. 397 365 Sep. 32 =October 2, 1883	G	Friday	350+4=354
2	5645	Saturday, Sep. 32+354=Sep. 386 Days in 1884... 366 September 20, 1884	E	Wednesday	350+5=355
3	5646 Emb.	Thursday, Sep. 20+355=Sep. 375 365 September 10, 1885	D	Wednesday	378+7=385
4	5647	Thursday, Sep. 10+385=Sep. 395 365 September 30, 1886	C	Sunday	350+4=354
5	5648	Monday, Sep. 30+354=Sep. 384 365 September 19, 1887	B	Wednesday	350+3=353
6	5649 Emb.	Thursday, Sep. 19+353=Sep. 372 Days in 1888... 366 September 6, 1888	G	Wednesday	378+7=385
7	5650	Thursday, Sep. 6+385=Sep. 391 365 September 26, 1889	F	Sunday	350+4=354
8	5651 Emb.	Monday, Sep. 26+354=Sep. 380 365 September 15, 1890	E	Friday	378+5=383

Years of Cycle.	A.M.	First Day.	Sunday Letter.	Last Day.	Length.
9	5652	Saturday, Sep. 15+385=Sep. 398 365 Sep. 33 =October 3, 1891	D	Wednesday	350+5=355
10	5653	Thursday, Sep. 33+355=Sep. 388 Days in 1892... 366 September 22, 1892	B	Sunday	350+4=354
11	5654 Emb.	Monday, Sep. 22+354=Sep. 376 365 September 11, 1893	A	Sunday	378+7=385
12	5655	Monday, Sep. 11+385=Sep. 396 365 Sep. 31 =October 1, 1894	G	Wednesday	350+3=353
13	5656	Thursday, Sep. 31+353=Sep. 384 365 September 19, 1895	F	Monday	350+5=355
14	5657 Emb.	Tuesday, Sep. 19+355=Sep. 374 Days in 1896... 366 September 8, 1896	D	Sunday	378+6=384
15	5658	Monday, Sep. 8+384=Sep. 392 365 September 27, 1897	C	Friday	350+5=355
16	5659	Saturday, Sep. 27+355=Sep. 382 365 September 17, 1898	B	Monday	350+3=353

Years of Cycle.	A.M.	First Day.	Sunday Letter.	Last Day.	Length.
17	5660 Emb.	Tuesday, Sep. 17+353=Sep. 370 365			
		September 5, 1899	A	Sunday	378+6=384
18	5661	Monday, Sep. 5+384=Sep. 389 Days in 1900, Greg.... 365			
		September 24, 1900	G	Friday	350+5=355
19	5662 Emb.	Saturday, Sep. 24+355=Sep. 379 365			
		September 14, 1901	F	Wednesday	378+5=383
1	5663	Thursday			

Collecting the results thus found, we obtain the following Calendar, with respect to Tishrî 1 and Nîsân 15, for the three Cycles 296, 297, 298, A.M. 5606 to 5662; A.D. 1845 to 1901. Julian and Gregorian dates are now both inserted.

TISHRÎ 1 AND NÎSÂN 15.

CYCLE 296. A.M. 5606–5624. A.D. 1845–1864.

A.M.		Molad for Tishri.				Tishri 1.		Nisân 15.		Length of Year.
1	5606	4	15	769	Wednesday	Thursday, Sept. 20–Oct. 2,	1845	Saturday, March 30–April 11,	1846	354
2	5607	2	0	565	Monday	Monday, Sept. 9–21,	1846	Thursday, March 20–April 2,	1847	355
3 Emb.	5608	6	9	361	Friday	Saturday, Aug. 30–Sept. 11,	1847	Tuesday, April 6–18,	1848	383
4	5609	5	6	950	Thursday	Thursday, Sept. 16–28,	1848	Saturday, March 26–April 7,	1849	354
5	5610	2	15	746	Monday	Monday, Sept. 5–17,	1849	Thursday, March 16–28,	1850	355
6 Emb.	5611	7	0	542	Saturday	Saturday, Aug. 26–Sept. 7,	1850	Thursday, April 5–17,	1851	385
7	5612	5	22	51	Thursday	Saturday, Sept. 15–27,	1851	Sunday, March 23–April 4,	1852	353
8 Emb.	5613	3	6	927	Tuesday	Tuesday, Sept. 2–14,	1852	Saturday, April 11–23,	1853	384
9	5614	2	4	436	Monday	Monday, Sept. 21–Oct. 3,	1853	Thursday, April 1–13,	1854	355
10	5615	6	13	232	Friday	Saturday, Sept. 11–23,	1854	Tuesday, March 22–April 3,	1855	355
11 Emb.	5616	3	22	28	Tuesday	Thursday, Sept. 1–13,	1855	Sunday, April 8–20,	1856	383
12	5617	2	19	617	Monday	Tuesday, Sept. 18–30,	1856	Thursday, March 28–April 9,	1857	354
13	5618	7	4	413	Saturday	Saturday, Sept. 7–19,	1857	Tuesday, March 18–30,	1858	355
14 Emb.	5619	4	13	209	Wednesday	Thursday, Aug. 28–Sept. 9,	1858	Tuesday, April 7–19,	1859	385
15	5620	3	10	798	Tuesday	Thursday, Sept. 17–29,	1859	Saturday, March 26–April 7,	1860	354
16	5621	7	19	594	Saturday	Monday, Sept. 5–17,	1860	Tuesday, March 14–26,	1861	353
17 Emb.	5622	5	4	390	Thursday	Thursday, Aug. 24–Sept. 5,	1861	Tuesday, April 3–15,	1862	385
18	5623	4	1	979	Wednesday	Thursday, Sept. 13–25,	1862	Saturday, March 23–April 4,	1863	354
19 Emb.	5624	1	10	775	Sunday	Monday, Sept. 2–14,	1863	Thursday, April 9–21,	1864	383

TISHRÎ 1 AND NÎSÂN 15.

CYCLE 297. A.M. 5625–5643. A.D. 1864–1882.

	A.M.	Molad for Tishri.				Tishri 1.			Nisân 15.			Length of Year.
1	5625	7	8	284	Saturday	Saturday,	Sept. 19–Oct. 1,	1864	Tuesday,	March 30–April 11,	1865	355
2	5626	4	17	80	Wednesday	Thursday,	Sept. 9–21,	1865	Saturday,	March 19–31,	1866	354
3 Emb.	5627	2	1	956	Monday	Monday,	Aug. 29–Sept. 10,	1866	Saturday,	April 8–20,	1867	385
4	5628	7	23	465	Saturday	Monday,	Sept. 18–30,	1867	Tuesday,	March 26–April 7,	1868	353
5	5629	5	8	261	Thursday	Thursday,	Sept. 5–17,	1868	Saturday,	March 15–27,	1869	354
6 Emb.	5630	2	17	57	Monday	Monday,	Aug. 25–Sept. 6,	1869	Saturday,	April 4–16,	1870	385
7	5631	1	14	646	Sunday	Monday,	Sept. 14–26,	1870	Thursday,	March 25–April 6,	1871	355
8 Emb.	5632	5	23	442	Thursday	Saturday,	Sept. 4–16,	1871	Tuesday,	April 11–23,	1872	383
9	5633	4	20	1031	Wednesday	Thursday,	Sept. 21–Oct. 3,	1872	Saturday,	March 31–April 12,	1873	354
10	5634	2	5	827	Monday	Monday,	Sept. 10–22,	1873	Thursday,	March 21–April 2,	1874	355
11 Emb.	5635	6	14	623	Friday	Saturday,	Aug. 31–Sept. 12,	1874	Tuesday,	April 8–20,	1875	383
12	5636	5	12	132	Thursday	Thursday,	Sept. 18–30,	1875	Sunday,	March 28–April 9,	1876	355
13	5637	2	20	1008	Monday	Tuesday,	Sept. 7–19,	1876	Thursday,	March 17–29,	1877	354
14 Emb.	5638	7	5	804	Saturday	Saturday,	Aug. 27–Sept. 8,	1877	Thursday,	April 6–18,	1878	385
15	5639	6	3	313	Friday	Saturday,	Sept. 16–28,	1878	Tuesday,	March 27–April 8,	1879	355
16	5640	3	12	109	Tuesday	Thursday,	Sept. 6–18,	1879	Saturday,	March 15–27,	1880	354
17 Emb.	5641	7	20	985	Saturday	Monday,	Aug. 25–Sept. 6,	1880	Thursday,	April 2–14,	1881	383
18	5642	6	18	494	Friday	Saturday,	Sept. 12–24,	1881	Tuesday,	March 23–April 4,	1882	355
19 Emb.	5643	4	3	290	Wednesday	Thursday,	Sept. 2–14,	1882	Sunday,	April 10–22,	1883	383

TISHRÎ 1 AND NÎSÂN 15.

CYCLE 298. A.M. 5644–5662. A.D. 1883–1901.

A.M.		Molad for Tishri.				Tishri 1.			Nisân 15.			Length of Year.
1	5644	3	0	879	Tuesday	Tuesday,	Sept. 20–Oct. 2,	1883	Thursday,	March 29–April 10,	1884	354
2	5645	7	9	675	Saturday	Saturday,	Sept. 8–20,	1884	Tuesday,	March 19–31,	1885	355
3 Emb.	5646	4	18	471	Wednesday	Thursday,	Aug. 29–Sept. 10,	1885	Tuesday,	April 8–20,	1886	385
4	5647	3	15	1060	Tuesday	Thursday,	Sept. 18–30,	1886	Saturday,	March 28–April 9,	1887	354
5	5648	1	0	856	Sunday	Monday,	Sept. 7–19,	1887	Tuesday,	March 15–27,	1888	353
6 Emb.	5649	5	9	652	Thursday	Thursday,	Aug. 25–Sept. 6,	1888	Tuesday,	April 4–16,	1889	385
7	5650	4	7	161	Wednesday	Thursday,	Sept. 14–26,	1889	Saturday,	March 24–April 5,	1890	354
8 Emb.	5651	1	15	1037	Sunday	Monday,	Sept. 3–15,	1890	Thursday,	April 11–23,	1891	383
9	5652	7	13	546	Saturday	Saturday,	Sept. 21–Oct. 3,	1891	Tuesday,	March 31–April 12,	1892	355
10	5653	4	22	342	Wednesday	Thursday,	Sept. 10–22,	1892	Saturday,	March 20–April 1,	1893	354
11 Emb.	5654	2	7	138	Monday	Monday,	Aug. 30–Sept. 11,	1893	Saturday,	April 9–21,	1894	385
12	5655	1	4	727	Sunday	Monday,	Sept. 19–Oct. 1,	1894	Tuesday,	March 28–April 9,	1895	353
13	5656	5	13	523	Thursday	Thursday,	Sept. 7–19,	1895	Sunday,	March 17–29,	1896	355
14 Emb.	5657	2	22	319	Monday	Tuesday,	Aug. 27–Sept. 8,	1896	Saturday,	April 5–17,	1897	384
15	5658	1	19	908	Sunday	Monday,	Sept. 15–27,	1897	Thursday,	March 26–April 7,	1898	355
16	5659	6	4	704	Friday	Saturday,	Sept. 5–17,	1898	Sunday,	March 14–26,	1899	353
17 Emb.	5660	3	13	500	Tuesday	Tuesday,	Aug. 24–Sept. 5,	1899	Saturday,	April 1–14,	1900	384
18	5661	2	11	9	Monday	Monday,	Sept. 11–24,	1900	Thursday,	March 22–April 4,	1901	355
19 Emb.	5662	6	19	885	Friday	Saturday,	Sept. 1–14,	1901	Tuesday,	April 9–22,	1902	383

Checks upon Results.

65. In addition to the tests suggested in Article 62 for the feria of Nîsân 15, and for the Molads in Article 63, a useful check upon the form or length of the successive years is obtained in the following manner:—

Let the seven feriæ be treated as in repeated order, thus:—

1, 2, 3, 4, 5, 6, 7, 1, 2, 3, 4, 5, 6, 7, 1, &c.

Take the feria of any year H, and count from it, exclusive, in the positive direction, that is to say, from left to right, to the place of the feria, inclusive, of the next year, H + 1. Call the number of places so counted "the difference" of the year H.

For example: Let H commence with a Thursday, feria 5, and H + 1 with a Monday, feria 2. The number of places counted in the positive direction from 5 exclusive, to 2, inclusive, is four. Again, if H commence with a Saturday, feria 7, and H + 1 with a Tuesday, feria 3, the difference in the number of places from 7 to 3 is three.

Then, for a Common year, H:—

If difference be 3,	H is	Deficient	353 days.
,, 4,	,,	Regular	354 ,,
,, 5,	,,	Abundant	355 ,,

For an Embolismic year, H:—

If difference be 5,	H is	Deficient	383 days.
,, 6,	,,	Regular	384 ,,
,, 7,	,,	Abundant	385 ,,

Thus, for Cycle 297,

A M. 5625	begins with feria 7,	next year with 5,	d = 5	... 355
5626	5,	2,	4	... 354
5627 Emb.	2,	2,	7	... 385
5628	2,	5,	3	... 353
5629	5,	2,	4	... 354
5630 Emb.	2,	2,	7	... 385
5631	2,	7,	5	... 355
5632 Emb.	7,	5,	5	... 383
5633	5,	2,	4	... 354
5634	2,	7,	5	... 355
5635 Emb.	7,	5,	5	... 383
5636	5,	3,	5	... 355

5637 begins with feria	3, next year with	7, d =	4 ... 354
5638 Emb.	7,	7,	7 ... 385
5639	7,	·5,	5 ... 355
5640	5,	2,	4 ... 354
5641 Emb.	2,	7,	5 ... 383
5642	7,	5,	5 ... 355
5643 Emb.	5,	3,	5 ... 383

66. A check upon the Christian dates found, in successive years, for Tishrî 1 is obtained from a consideration of the respective lengths of the Jewish and Christian years. There are only two forms of the latter, 365 and 366 days, while there are six different forms of the Jewish year—353, 354, 355, 383, 384, and 385 days. Hence, there are twelve possible combinations that can be made between a Jewish and a Christian year; for the months which are covered by the Jewish year, commencing and terminating always in the Autumn, invariably include the whole of the month of February, and this February may, or may not, have an intercalated day.

Let the Jewish year H have 353 days, and let Tishrî 1 of the year H occur on a day whose serial number is D in the Christian Y. Then—

1. If Y + 1 be a common Christian year of 365 days, February 29 will not occur in the course of the 353 days of H, and H + 1 must commence in Y + 1 earlier than H commences in Y, that is, earlier than D, by 365−353, or 12 days.

2. But if Y + 1 be a Bissextile year, February 29 will be included in the course of the 353 days of H, and H + 1 must commence in the year Y + 1 earlier than D by 366−353, or 13 days.

3, 4. If the year H have 354 days, H + 1 will commence in Y + 1 earlier than H commences in Y by 365−354, or 11 days, if Y + 1 be a Common year, but 366−354, or 12 days, if Y + 1 be Bissextile.

5, 6. If the year H have 355 days, H + 1 will commence in Y + 1 earlier than H commences in Y by 365−355, or by 366−355, that is, by 10, or by 11 days according to whether Y + 1 be a Common or a Bissextile year.

7, 8. On the other hand, if the Jewish year H be Embolismic, and have 383 days, then Tishrî 1 of H + 1 will occur later than Tishrî 1 of H by either 383−365, or 383−366 days, that is, by 18 or by 17 days, according to whether Y + 1 be a Common or a Bissextile year.

9, 10, 11, 12. So too with respect to the Jewish years of 384 and 385 days. In the one case Tishrî 1 of H + 1 will be either 19 or 18 days later than Tishrî 1 of H; in the other case it will be either 20 or 19 days later.

These twelve possible combinations may be reduced to a very simple rule.

Let $7n + x$ be the value in days of a Jewish Common year, H, so that x may be either 3, 4, or 5. Also, let $7N + x$ be the value in days of a Jewish Embolismic year, so that x may be either 5, 6, or zero. Then—

For Common years,

(*a*) If H commence in the Christian year Y, and Y + 1 has 365 days, H + 1 will commence in Y + 1 earlier than H commenced in Y by $365-(7n+x)$ days.

(*b*) If Y + 1 has 366 days, H + 1 commences in it earlier than H commenced in Y by $366-(7n+x)$ days.

For Embolismic years,

(*c*) If Y + 1 has 365 days, then H + 1 commences in it later than H commenced in Y by $(7N+x)-365$ days.

(*d*) If Y + 1 has 366 days, then H + 1 commences in it later than H commenced in Y by $(7N+x)-366$ days.

67. It appears from the Tables given in Articles 54, 55, pp. 79, 83, that there are fourteen possible combinations of the forms of the year with the week-days upon which those years can commence. A Table can be formed which will show the week-day for every day in every month of these fourteen combinations.

The first two columns in Part I. of this Table XI. are a repetition of the first two in the Tables above. The remaining columns, headed with the names of the months, show which column of week-days in Part II. is to be employed.

Although thirty days are given in each of these seven columns, only twenty-nine, of course, are required for those months which have only that number of days. It must also be remembered that in Deficient years, whether Common or Embolismic, Kislêw has only twenty-nine days instead of the thirty which it contains in Regular and Abundant years; while in Abundant years, both Common and Embolismic, Marḥeshwân has thirty days instead of the twenty-nine which it has in Deficient and Regular years.

The following example, of which the full work is given, will illustrate the way in which the Table is to be used.

Find the week-day for Kislêw 13 in the Jewish year 5611.

a. The division of 5611 by 19 gives a quotient 295, and a remainder 6. It is therefore an Embolismic year.

b. The Molad of 5611 is the sum of

	d.	h.	ch.
BeHaRD	2	5	204
Excess of 200 Cycles	5	22	200
" 90 "	4	1	630
" 5 "	6	10	815
For a sixth year	2	8	853
	7	0	542

There is no reason for postponing Tishrî 1 from feria 7; the first day of the given year is, therefore, Saturday.

c. An Embolismic year which commences with a Saturday may be one of either 383 or 385 days. To ascertain which of these forms appertains to A.M. 5611 it will be necessary to find the day of the week with which the next year commenced.

Molad for 5611	7	0	542
Excess of an Emb. year	5	21	589
Molad for 5612	5	22	51

Tishrî 1 is postponed by YacH and ADU from feria 5 to feria 7, Saturday. The previous year, 5611, therefore, ended with a Friday, and as it commenced with a Saturday, it is of the form $7n + 0$, or has 385 days.

All the required facts are now established, and we may proceed to use the Table.

Refer to Line 14 of Part I., which is for an Embolismic year of 385 days commencing with a Saturday. Under the heading Kislêw the figure 4 appears in this line. Therefore, Column 4 in Part II. is to be employed. It shows that Kislêw 13 is a Monday.

If the question had been proposed with the required facts given, the day would have been found thus:—

Tishrî 1, 5611 is a Saturday	= feria	7
Add for Tishrî 2 to Tishrî 30		29
„ „ Marḥeshwân		30
„ „ Kislêw 1 to Kislêw 13		13
		79

and because $79 = 7n + 2$, the week-day required is Monday.

68. If the feria, or week-day, be required for any date in a Jewish month occurring in some given Christian year, care must be taken to ascertain precisely the year to which the Jewish month belongs (see Article 37, p. 46); if this be not done there is liability to error.

Example.

Upon which day of the week does Nîsân 15 occur in A.D. 1900?

By the addition of 3761 to 1900, we find that the Jewish year corresponding in part to A.D. 1900 is 5661; that is, the year 5661 commences at some time in the Autumn of A.D. 1900.

It is very clear that the Nîsân 15 which occurred during the course of A.D. 1900 must have belonged to the Jewish year 5660.

The division of 5660 by 19 gives a quotient 297, and a remainder 17. The year is therefore the seventeenth in a Cycle, and is Embolismic. Its Molad is the sum of:—

	d.	h.	ch.
BeHaRD	2	5	204
Excess of 200 Cycles	5	22	200
„ 90 „	4	1	630
„ 7 „	4	19	925
And, for a seventeenth year	7	12	701
	3	13	500

There is nothing to cause the postponement of Tishrî 1 from feria 3, Tuesday.

For the Molad of the next year, the addition of 5 21 589 gives 2 11 9, and Tishrî 1 is a Monday. Consequently 5660 must have ended with a Sunday; and, as it begins with a Tuesday and is Embolismic, it is of the form $7n + 6$, or has 384 days.

Line 11 of the Table, Part I., refers us to Column 7 of Part II. for the month Nîsân, from which it is seen that Nîsân 15 occurs upon a Saturday.

It may perhaps be well to show how the error may arise, to the possibility of which reference was made at the commencement of this Article, and in Article 37.

Suppose that the Nîsân 15 occurring in A.D. 1900 has been erroneously taken as belonging to the Jewish year 1900 + 3761, or 5661; the week-day would have been found to be Thursday, which is, of course, wrong. Thus:—

$$\left\{\frac{5661}{19}\right\} = 297\text{; and } r = 18.$$

BeHaRD	2	5	204
Excess for 297 Cycles	7	19	675
,, 17 years elapsed	6	10	210
Molad of 5661	2	11	9 Monday.
Add for a Com. year	4	8	876
Molad of 5662	6	19	985

Tishrî 1 of 5662 is postponed by ADU from feria 6, Friday, to feria 7, Saturday. Therefore 5661 terminates with a Friday; and, as it began with a Monday and is a Common year, it is of the form 350 + 5, or has 355 days.

Refer to Line 5 of Part I. of the Table; it tells us that Column 5 of Part II. is to be used for Nîsân; the 15th day of the month appears to be Thursday, which is wrong.

69. There is, however, a simpler method even than this; for, by the employment of the seven first letters of the Alphabet as Day-Letters, a Calendar may be formed—Table XVI.—which will show the day of the week for any day of any month when the feria for Tishrî 1 and the form of the year are known.

Numerical values must be given to the seven Letters according to the feria for Tishrî 1:—Thus, if Tishrî 1 be feria 5, A will be 5 and be the Thursday Letter, B will be 6 and be the Friday Letter, C will be 7 and be the Saturday Letter, &c., according to the following system:—

TISHRI 1.

= Feria 2.	= Feria 3.	= Feria 5.	= Feria 7.
A .. 2	A .. 3	A .. 5	A .. 7
B .. 3	B .. 4	B .. 6	B .. 1
C .. 4	C .. 5	C .. 7	C .. 2
D .. 5	D .. 6	D .. 1	D .. 3
E .. 6	E .. 7	E .. 2	E .. 4
F .. 7	F .. 1	F .. 3	F .. 5
G .. 1	G .. 2	G .. 4	G .. 6

The Calendar, Table XVI., is to be used as in the following examples:—

1. Required the week-day for Kislêw 13 in the year 5611, which has 385 days; Tishrî 1 is a Saturday.

Part VI. of the Calendar, which belongs to a year of this form, must be used.

Because Tishrî 1 = feria 7, and Kislêw 13 is in a line with C, it is a Monday, for C = 2 when A = 7.

2. Required the week-day for Tammûz 29 in the year 5659, which commenced with a Saturday, and had 353 days.

Part I. of the Calendar must be used.

Here again Tishrî 1 is on feria 7, ∴ A = 7, and Tammûz 29, which is on the line with G, is feria 6, or Friday.

3. Nisân 15, in the year 5660, which commenced with a Tuesday and had 384 days.

Part V. of the Table. A = 3; Nisân 15 = E = 7 = Saturday.

CHAPTER VI

KEBÎÔTH. PERPETUAL CALENDARS. SIXTY-ONE FORMS OF THE CYCLE

70. It is usual in Jewish Calendars and Year-Books to describe the year by means of three characters. The first on the right (the Hebrew language is written from right to left), gives the feria with which the year commences; that in the middle is the initial letter of the word which defines the form or length of the year; and that on the left gives the feria for Nisân 15, the First Day of Unleavened Bread.

The combination of these three characters is called the Kebîa of the year, a word derived from the Aramaic root Keba, meaning "Settlement," or "Determination (*sc.*, of the Feasts)."*

Tables have been formed of the Kebîôth for a series of years. One of these is given by al-Bîrûnî† for A.M. 4754 to 5285 inclusive, A.D. 993 to 1524. This Table, however, so far as the Jewish years are concerned, contains only the feria for Tishri 1, and the form of the year.

The old chronologists seem to have believed that such Tables, formed for a period of 247 (= 13 × 19) years, would serve in perpetuity, because they thought that after that time had elapsed all the Kebîôth would return in the same cyclical order as before. This, however, is erroneous, as will be proved.

The fourteen possible combinations of the year, in its different forms, with the four week-days which are lawful for Tishrî 1, would be expressed as Kebîôth in the following manner, the feriæ for Tishrî 1 and Nîsân 15 being here transposed, in order that the Table

* Ideler, i. p. 561. † Sachau, trans. p. 154.

may be read according to the customary way, that is, from left to right:—

The small letters indicate Common, and the capital letters indicate Embolismic years: a, A = Abundant; r, R = Regular; d, D = Deficient.

1	....	1 a 5
2	....	1 d 7
3	....	1 D 5
4	....	3 d 2
5	....	3 a 7
6	....	3 D 7
7	....	3 A 5
8	....	5 a 2
9	....	5 r 3
10	....	5 D 2
11	....	5 A 7
12	....	7 r 5
13	....	7 A 2
14	....	7 R 3

If, therefore, a year were described as having the Kebîa, or Sign, 1, a, 5, it would indicate that Tishrî 1 occurs on feria 1, Monday, that the year is Common Abundant, or has 355 days, and that Nîsân 15 is on feria 5, Thursday.

Perpetual Calendars.

71. It is almost self-evident, perhaps quite self-evident, that the old chronologists must have been perfectly aware of the fact that the duration of the Civil Cycle of nineteen Civil years is a variable, while that of the Astronomical Cycle is a constant quantity. Schwarz says* that they consoled themselves under the idea that after every thirteen Cycles, that is, after every 247 years, there takes place almost an exact equalisation. In other words, they believed not only that every such Cycle of 247 years contained the same number of days, but also that after every such 247 years the Kebîôth would all return in the same

* "Der Jüdische Kalender," p. 78. "Schon die alten Chronologen fühlten diese Unebenheit, und sie beruhigten sich über dieses Schwanken bei dem Gedanken, dass nach 13 Mondcykeln, d. h. nach 247 Jahren, ein möglichst genauer Ausgleich eintritt. Ja, man ging in dieser Behauptung so weit, anzunehmen, dass in dem unter dem Namen Iggul des R. Nachshon Gaon bekannten grossen Cyklus alle Conjunctionen sich in derselben Ordnung wiederholen."

order. He says that this Cycle is known as the Iggul of Rabbi Nachson Gaon (A.D. 881–889), and that they even went so far as to believe that all the Conjunctions of the Sun and Moon were repeated in the same order, after every 247 years.

Scaliger fell into this error. Though he is explicit in stating that the Conjunctions do not return in the same order with respect to the hours and the Chalakim, till after the lapse of many centuries,* yet he positively asserts that after every 247 years the celebrations of the New Moons will come back to the same days of the week.† As he particularly addresses his communications to the young students it is possible that he intends it for them only. If his statement were allowed to pass without notice it might probably mislead some who would not be at the trouble of ascertaining whether it can be verified.

The fact is that the commencement of the first year of these, so-called, Great Cycles of 247 years has already changed its week-day five times since the commencement of the Era, and a change will take three times more before the year 7678 commences in A.D. 3917.

The changes which have already taken place are as follows:—

Cycle 35	commenced with	Tuesday;	Cycle 48	with	Monday.
,, 83	,,	Saturday;	,, 96	,,	Thursday.
,, 141	,,	Monday;	,, 154	,,	Saturday.
,, 168	,,	Thursday;	,, 181	,,	Tuesday.
,, 238	,,	Tuesday;	,, 251	,,	Monday.

Those which will take place are—

Cycle 286	commenced with	Saturday;	Cycle 299	with	Thursday.
,, 344	will commence with	Monday;	,, 357	,,	Saturday.
,, 358	,, ,,	Thursday;	,, 371	,,	Tuesday.

The feriæ are computed according to the mean length of a Lunation as estimated by Hipparchus, and adopted by Hillel II. for the Jewish Calendar. They are also assumed as subject to the Dechiyyôth, or

* "De Emend. Temp.," lib. ii. p. 134, B. "Cum dico neomeniarum ferias in orbem redire periodo 247 annorum, intelligo feriam, non autem horas. Nam in decem millibus, aut amplius annorum, nunquam reperies duas neomenias, feria, horis, et scrupulis inter se convenientes."

† *Ib.*, p. 132, C et D. "Sciant igitur, adolescentes, in 247 annis, hoc est, Cyclis xiii, omnes neomenias in easdem ferias recurrere. Nam periodus Judaica est annorum 6916, qui 28 divisi dant 247 annos, in quibus fit orbis neomeniarum et feriarum, sicut feriarum tantum in 28 annis Solaribus."

rules which govern the postponement of Tishrî 1; for it is upon these data that the statement of Scaliger is based.

72. Lazarus Bendavid, to whom reference is frequently made by Dr. Sachau in his Annotations on al-Bîrûnî, though he is not considered a great authority by the majority of Hebrew scholars, is equally misleading. He gives a "Kalendarium Perpetuum," so called, by means of which, he says, may be found the feria for the first day of any year in the Jewish Era, as well as the form of any such year. He furnishes full directions as to the way in which it is to be used, together with several examples.*

This Calendar consists of thirteen lines for thirteen ordinary Cycles, divided into nineteen columns for the years of the Cycle, thus forming 247 cells in which are placed the feria of Tishrî 1, and the letter indicating the form of the year for 247 consecutive years.

Bendavid goes beyond this. At p. 58, § 45, he states plainly that the Kebîôth return after every 247 years, that is, after every thirteen Cycles; in other words, that the year P is in every respect identical with the year P + 247. To show that this is so (which it is not), he says that in 13 × 19 years there are 13 × 19 × 235 Lunations, or New Moons, and, because the excess of a Lunation is 1d. 12h. 793ch. above an exact number of weeks, the retrograde movement of the feria in the Molad after 247 years will be (1d. 12h. 793ch.) × 3055, or 4695d. 23h. 175ch., which is 6d. 23h. 175ch., or very nearly one whole week, above an exact number of weeks. And so, the first day of P + 247 must fall to the same feria as the first day of P; also, that which is true for P and P + 247 is true for P + 1 and P + 248; for P + 2 and P + 249; and so on throughout.

To this argument he adds a footnote,† "The Perpetual Calendar attached to this work is based upon the above [argument]. It is taken out of the book 'Lebusch Haschacor' (The Black Robe), No. 428, p. 151, by the Rabbi Mardochai Japhi. The inventor of this Calendar,

* "Zur Berechnung und Geschichte des Jüdischen Kalenders," p. 97, "Calendarium Perpetuum;" and pp. 98, 99, "Schlüssel und Gebrauch des ewigen Kalenders."

† P. 61. "Darauf gründet sich das Calendarium Perpetuum, das diesem Werke angehängt ist. Es ist aus dem Buche Lebushch Haschachor (Schwarzes Gewand), No. 428, p. 151, des R. Mardochai Japhi entnommen. Der Erfinder desselben ist nach Bartoloccius ein mir unbekannter R. Gabriel de Sorano. Nirgends findet man aber einen Beweis dafür. Ich weist nicht, was Waser, a. a. o. meint, wenn er sagt: 'Es komme erst alles in 689472 Jahren wieder in Ordnung.'"

according to Bartolocci, was Rabbi Gabriel de Sorano,* but I have never found a proof of that. I know not what Waser, in another passage, means when he says: 'It comes all over again in order in 689472 years.'"

All this is most remarkable. No account whatever is taken of the 905 Chalakim required to bring 6d. 23h. 175ch. up to seven complete days; and yet these 905ch., occurring as they do once in every 247 years, must in process of time accumulate till they amount to an interval of time sufficient to shift the week-day, and so entirely destroy the perpetuity of the Calendar.

Our author's difficulty about the 689742 years, to which Waser makes reference, would have been removed if he had made the simple calculation which was given in Article 46, page 61.

73. It is quite easy to show that the belief of the old chronologers, and the statements of Scaliger and Lazarus Bendavid are erroneous.

The duration of an Astronomical Cycle of 235 Lunations, or 19 years, is 6939d. 16h. 595ch. Its excess above a complete number of weeks is 2d. 16h. 595ch. Consequently, the excess of thirteen Astronomical Cycles will be (2 16 595) × 13, or 34 23 175; this is 6d. 23h. 175ch. more than an exact number of weeks, as Bendavid says, and will be the excess after 13 × 19, or 247, years have elapsed. The addition of 905ch. would bring the excess to exactly one week.

This being the case, it is evident that the Molad for Tishrî at the commencement of every Cycle of 247 years will have retrogressed, or been diminished, by 905ch., and the question becomes, simply, How long can this retrogression continue before it has amounted to a length of time sufficient to change the week-day for Tishrî 1? In some cases the retrogression may continue for many hundreds, even thousands, of years, without producing a change. In other cases the change will occur after a comparatively short period.

Assume, for the sake of the argument, that the Molad of some year H is 7 18 904; then, the Molad of the year H + 247 will be 905ch. less, that is, it will be 7 17 1079. Clearly, H will commence with a Monday, and H + 247 with a Saturday. Here a period of one Great Cycle of 247 years has been sufficient to shift the week-day for Tishrî 1.

Assume, again, that the Molad of H is 7 20 554; the year will

* Rabbi Gabriel de Sorano is utterly unknown.

commence with a Monday. Before the week-day for Tishrî 1 can be shifted to Saturday this Molad must be reduced, at least, to 7 17 1079. The necessary reduction amounts to 2h. 555ch., or 2715 Chalaḳim. This is exactly 3 × 905. Therefore the retrogression must take place three times, which will occupy 3 × 247, or 741 years.

Once more, assume that the Molad of H is 7 17 1079; this year will commence with a Saturday; in order that the week-day for Tishrî 1 may be shifted to the next possible day in retrogression, namely, Thursday, the Molad must retrogress to, at least, 5 17 1079; that is, it must retrogress to the extent of 48 hours, or 51840 Chalaḳim. Now, 57 × 995 is not sufficient to cover this amount, and therefore it will require no less than 58 × 13 × 19, or 14326 years to effect the change.

This is a long period; but, however long it may be, the change must come—if time endure. And no Calendar can be properly called "Perpetual" whether it fail after 247, or after a thousand times 247 years.

From the examples thus given it will be seen that, in order to find when a change of week-day for the commencement of a Great Cycle of 13 × 19 years will take place, it is only necessary to consider the limits of the Molad which, together with the Dechiyyôth, or five laws, determine the feria for Tishrî 1. Take the difference between these limits; reduce the days and hours to Chalaḳim; divide the whole number of Chalaḳim by 905. If there be no remainder the quotient will give the number of times that 247 years must be repeated before a change of the week-day, which will always be retrogressive, can take place. If there be any remainder, even of only one Chalaḳ, the quotient must be increased by unity, for in that case it will take another Cycle of 247 years to effect the change.

74. In Table XII., which is a scheme for showing when the changes have taken place, and when they will again take place, the horizontal argument gives the number of the ordinary Cycles of nineteen years, from 1 up to 391, in an Arithmetical Series whose common difference is 13. The vertical argument gives the intermediate years.

It may be used for finding the feria with which any Cycle of the Jewish Era commences, up to the 403rd, that is, up to the year 7639 inclusive.

If the number of the given Cycle, for which the feria of Tishrî 1 is required, be amongst the numbers in the horizontal argument, then the feria is found immediately beneath it in the first line of the Table, which is marked by the zero in the vertical argument. If, however, the number of the given Cycle be not found in the horizontal argument, search for the next less number which does appear; and, in the vertical argument, find the number representing the difference between the given Cycle and the next less. In the same line with this number, and in the column under the next less number to that of the given Cycle, will be found the feria with which the given Cycle commences.

Thus:—For the 241st Cycle—The next less number in the horizontal argument is 235, and 245 – 231 = 6. In the line which is marked 6, and in the column under 235, is the figure 5. The 241st Cycle commences with feria 5, Thursday.

The feriæ are in Roman characters when a change takes place, namely, for Cycles 48, 96, 154, 181, and 251, which have already elapsed, and for Cycles 299, 357, and 371, which are in the future.

The feriæ are calculated according to the reformed Calendar, that is, on the assumption that the Molad of the first Cycle of the Jewish Era was 2 5 204, that the excess of a Cycle above an exact number of weeks is 2 16 595, and that, for purposes of computation, the Dechiyôth have always been in force. This method of computation is analogous to that for the Julian Period, which assumes that Leap-years have been observed regularly once in every four years, from B.C. 4713, and will so continue to be observed for a total period of 7980 years.

The following is the computation for the Molads of Cycles where changes of the feria occur.

Cycle 35.			
BeHaRD	2	5	204
30 Cycles	3	16	570
4 "	3	18	220
35th Cycle	2	15	994

Tishri 1 is postponed by BaTU ThaKPhaT to feria 3.

Cycle 48.			
BeHaRD	2	5	204
40 Cycles	2	14	40
7 "	4	19	925
48th Cycle	2	15	89

Tishri 1 is not postponed from feria 2.

Cycle 83.			
BeHaRD	2	5	204
80 Cycles	5	4	80
2 "	5	9	110
83rd Cycle	5	18	394

Tishri 1 is postponed by YacH to feria 6, and by ADU to feria 7.

Cycle 96.			
BeHaRD	2	5	204
90 Cycles	4	1	630
5 "	6	10	815
96th Cycle	5	17	569

Tishri 1 is not postponed from feria 5.

Cycle 141.				
	BeHaRD	2	5	204
	100 Cycles	2	23	100
	40 „	2	14	40
	141st Cycle	7	18	344

Tishri 1 is postponed by YacH and ADU to feria 2.

Cycle 154.				
	BeHaRD	2	5	204
	100 Cycles	2	23	100
	50 „	1	11	590
	3 „	1	1	705
	154th Cycle	7	17	519

Tishri 1 is not postponed from feria 7.

Cycle 168.				
	BeHaRD	2	5	204
	100 Cycles	2	23	100
	60 „	7	9	60
	7 „	4	19	925
	168th Cycle	3	9	209

Tishri 1 is postponed to feria 5, by GaTRaD.

Cycle 181.				
	BeHaRD	2	5	204
	100 Cycles	2	23	100
	80 „	5	4	80
	181st Cycle	3	8	384

Tishri 1 is not postponed from feria 3.

Cycle 238.				
	BeHaRD	2	5	204
	200 Cycles	5	22	200
	30 „	3	16	570
	7 „	4	19	925
	238th Cycle	2	15	819

Tishri 1 is postponed to feria 3 by BaTU PhaKPhaT.

Cycle 251.				
	BeHaRD	2	5	204
	200 Cycles	5	22	200
	50 „	1	11	590
	251st Cycle	2	14	994

Tishri 1 is not postponed from feria 2.

Cycle 286.				
	BeHaRD	2	5	204
	200 Cycles	5	22	200
	80 „	5	4	80
	5 „	6	10	815
	286th Cycle	5	18	219

Tishri 1 is postponed by YacH and ADU to feria 7.

Cycle 299.				
	BeHaRD	2	5	204
	200 Cycles	5	22	200
	90 „	4	1	630
	8 „	7	12	440
	299th Cycle	5	17	394

Tishri 1 is not postponed from feria 5.

Cycle 344.				
	BeHaRD	2	5	204
	300 Cycles	1	21	300
	40 „	2	14	40
	3 „	1	1	705
	344th Cycle	7	18	169

Tishri 1 is postponed to feria 2, by YacH and ADU.

Cycle 370.				
	BeHaRD	2	5	204
	300 Cycles	1	21	300
	60 „	7	9	60
	9 „	3	4	1035
	370th Cycle	7	16	519

Tishri 1 is not postponed from feria 7.

Cycle 358.					Cycle 371.				
	BeHaRD	2	5	204		370th Cycle as above	7	16	519
	300 Cycles	1	21	300		1 Cycle	2	16	595
	50 "	1	11	590					
	7 "	4	19	925					
	358th Cycle	3	9	939		371st Cycle	3	9	34

Tishrî 1 is postponed from feria 3 to feria 5 by GaTRaD.

Tishrî 1 is not postponed from feria 3.

The change of style in the Christian Calendar, made in October, A.D. 1582, took place during the course of the 282nd Jewish Cycle just after the year 5343, the fourth of that Cycle, had commenced. This change does not affect the present question, for it made no alteration in the feriæ or current names of the week-days, but affects their monthly date only.

75. It should now be evident that the only way in which any approach to a Perpetual Calendar can be made is by considering the Molads of the successive Cycles, and the limits to which they are confined in order that the first year of a Cycle may commence with one of the four days which are not forbidden by ADU, and also that the remaining eighteen years of the Cycle may follow each other according to some particular sequence.

Such a Calendar, instead of containing only thirteen lines, will be found to contain sixty-one.

The limiting values for the Molads which allow Tishrî 1 to fall upon a given week-day, and also the form or length of the year when Tishrî 1 does so fall, are given in Table X. This, however, is not sufficient for the present purpose. It is necessary that the limits be further developed; for it is quite possible that the Molad for Tishrî may be such as would cause the first day of a Cycle to be, say, Monday, the number of days in the first year to be 355, the total number of days in the Cycle to be 6940,* and yet the forms of the remaining years vary in their sequence.

It remains, then, to investigate the Molads, and to ascertain the

* There are no less than 4624 variations in the Molad for Tishrî which permit of these three conditions being fulfilled. The Molad, as will be seen hereafter, may be from 1 9 204 to 2 15 589, both inclusive; that is to say, it may be 1 9 204, 1 9 209, 1 9 214, 1 9 219, &c., up to 2 15 589. The figure in the units place of the Chalaḳim must always be either a 4 or a 9, for the first year in a Cycle.

sequence of years which they, in connection with the Dechiyyôth, will permit. In other words, it is required to find the limits within which the Molads must be confined in order that a Cycle may be of a particular type.

The work may appear somewhat tedious, and will involve some repetition of what has been said before; but the subject requires careful attention if it is to be understood.

In the first place, consider the limiting values of the Molads which, combined with the Dechiyyôth, cause a year to commence with a given week-day. These are explained in Article 55, and stated in the Table on page 83, as well as in Table X.; it will save trouble if those Tables be repeated in an abbreviated form here.

The twentieth year, which is the first of the next Cycle, is included because the length of the nineteenth depends, when its first day is fixed, upon the day with which the next year commences.

TABLE A.

Years of the Cycle.	Monday.	Tuesday.	Thursday.	Saturday.
3 6 8 11 14 17 19	7 18 0	2 18 0	3 18 0	5 18 0
1 4 7 9 12 15 18 20	7 18 0	2 15 589	3 9 204	5 18 0
2 5 10 13 16	7 18 0	2 18 0	3 9 204	5 18 0

The Table is to be read thus:—The years 3, 6, 8, &c., . . . 19, will commence with a Monday if the Molad be so great as or greater than 7 18 0, but so soon as the Molad attains to 2 18 0, that is, when it exceeds 2 17 1079, the year will commence with a Tuesday. The column for Monday is supposed to recur after that for Saturday.

76. Take now the very earliest limit which will permit a year to commence with a Monday, that is, 7 18 0, and commencing with this limit compute the Molads for the successive years of the Cycle, adding also that for the twentieth year, which is the first of the next Cycle.

Note the week-day with which each year commences, and thence deduce the length of the year, thus determining the Sign for the year, as 2 d, 5 r, &c.

The following is the result of the computation, the Molads being obtained in the usual way by the addition of 4 8 876 for a Common and of 5 21 589 for an Embolismic year.

The sixth and last columns of this computation, though inserted here with the object of saving space, cannot be added at present.

TABLE B. TYPE 1.

Year of the Cycle.	Molads.	First Day of the Year.	Days in Year.	Sign of Year.	Molad might be.	Possible Addition.
1	7 18 0	Monday	353	2 d	2 15 588	1 21 588
2	5 2 876	Thursday	354	5 r	5 17 1079	0 15 203
3 E	2 11 672	Monday	385	2 A	2 17 1079	0 6 407
4	1 9 181	Monday	353	2 d	2 15 588	1 6 407
5	5 17 1057	Thursday	355	5 a	5 17 1079	0 0 22
6 E	3 2 853	Tuesday	384	3 R	3 17 1079	0 15 226
7	2 0 362	Monday	355	2 a	2 15 588	0 15 226
8 E	6 9 158	Saturday	383	7 D	7 17 1079	1 8 921
9	5 6 747	Thursday	354	5 r	5 17 1079	0 11 332
10	2 15 543	Monday	355	2 a	2 17 1079	0 2 536
11 E	7 0 339	Saturday	385	7 A	7 17 1079	0 17 740
12	5 21 928	Saturday	353	7 d	7 17 1079	1 14 151
13	3 6 724	Tuesday	354	3 r	3 9 203	0 2 559
14 E	7 15 520	Saturday	385	7 A	7 17 1079	0 2 559
15	6 13 29	Saturday	355	7 a	7 17 1079	1 4 1050
16	3 21 905	Thursday	354	5 r	5 17 1079	1 14 174
17 E	1 6 701	Monday	383	2 D	2 17 1079	1 11 378
18	7 4 210	Saturday	355	7 a	7 17 1079	0 13 860
19 E	4 13 6	Thursday	385	5 A	5 17 1079	1 4 1073
20	3 10 595	Thursday			5 17 1079	2 7 484

Every Cycle, the Molad of whose first year is 7 18 0, assuming for the moment the possibility of such a Molad, will be of this Type, which may be called the first Type.

TYPE 1.

Year of Cycle...	1	2	3	4	5	6	7	8	9	10	11	12	13	14	15	16	17	18	19
Sign of year ...	2d	5r	2A	2d	5a	3R	2a	7D	5r	2a	7A	7d	3r	7A	7a	5r	2D	7a	5A

No Cycle, however, can possibly have 7 18 0 for its Molad. The Molad may be 7 18 4, 7 18 9, 7 18 14, &c., and the question arises whether any, and, if so, what addition may be made to the Molad of the first year without altering the Type, that is, without altering the feria with which any year in the Cycle commences, and without altering the length of any year: in fact, without altering the Sign of any one of the years: remembering always that any addition made to the Molad of the first year will be the source of a similar increment to the Molads of all the remaining years, including the twentieth, or first of the next Cycle.

Such alteration will take place if the increment be sufficient to raise the Molad of any one of the years to that limit which would cause its first day to pass from its present to another feria.

We must therefore now ascertain what increment each of the Molads can receive without causing any such passage to occur. This must be done for each year throughout the Cycle. The least of all the increments that can be made to the respective years will evidently be the maximum increment that the original limit, 7 18 0, with which we start, can receive. The sixth and last columns of Table B can now be added as the computation goes on.

1. The first year will still commence with a Monday if its Molad be increased from 7 18 0 to 2 15 588, which is the same as 9 15 588, since feria 2 and feria 9 represent the same week-day. The first Molad may therefore be increased by 1 21 588.

2. The Molad of the second year is 5 2 876; this might be increased to 5 17 1079 without altering the day, Thursday, with which this year commences, and therefore without altering the length of the first year. The possible increment is therefore 0 15 203.

The computation for the first two years in Table B would then become—

7 18 0 + 0 15 203 = 1 9 203.........Monday.
Add for a Common year... 4 8 876

Molad of second year...... 5 17 1079.........Thursday.

3. The Molad of the third year is 2 11 672; this might be increased to 2 17 1079, without altering the day, Monday, with which the third year commences, and therefore without altering the length of the second year. Consequently the possible increment to the Molad of this third year is 0 6 407, and the original Molad,

7 18 0, may be increased by this amount without causing, as yet, any alteration: notice that it has already been ascertained that the Molad of the second year, and therefore of the first so far as the second is concerned, may be increased by 0 15 203; much more then may it be increased by 0 6 407.

The computation for the first three years in Table B will now become—

7 18 0 + 0 6 407 =	1	0	407	.........Monday.
	4	8	876	
Molad of second year......	5	9	203	.........Thursday.
	4	8	876	
Molad of third year	2	17	1079	.........Monday.

There is no alteration, as yet, in the days with which these three years respectively commence, and therefore no alteration in the lengths of the first two years.

4. The Molad of the fourth year is 1 9 181; this may be increased to 2 15 588 without altering the day, Monday, with which this year commences, and therefore without altering the length of the preceding year. The possible increment is 1 6 407. This increment is greater than can be allowed. It can only accrue through the addition of 1 6 407 to the original Molad, 7 18 0; and we have seen that any addition greater than 0 6 407 to that Molad would alter the Type of the Cycle.

This will be seen at once if we compute the first four years under the idea that this larger addition can be made:—

7 18 0 + 1 6 407 =	2	0	407	.........Monday.
	4	8	876	
Molad of second year ...	6	9	203	.........Saturday.
	4	8	876	
Molad of third year, E....	3	17	1079	.........Tuesday.
	5	21	589	
Molad of fourth year......	2	15	588	.........Monday.

The Type is altered; instead of being 2 d, 5 r, 2 A, 2 d, it becomes 2 a, 7 d, 3 R, 2 a.

Clearly this addition is too great, and it need not be further considered.

5. The Molad of the fifth year is 5 17 1057; this might be increased to 5 17 1079 without altering the day, Thursday, with which the year commences, and therefore without altering the length of the fourth year. The possible increment is 0 0 22. This increment, being less than that which has been already found possible for the preceding years, will not make any alteration in the Type, as yet. The computation will become—

7 18 0 + 0 0 22 =	7	18	22	.........Monday.
	4	8	876	
Molad of second year ...	5	2	898	.........Thursday.
	4	8	876	
Molad of third year, E...	2	11	694	.........Monday.
	5	21	589	
Molad of fourth year ...	1	9	203	.........Monday.
	4	8	876	
Molad of fifth year......	5	17	1079	.........Thursday.

The sequence of the Signs of the years remains precisely the same. The Type is not altered.

If the increase to the original Molad, 7 18 0, were only one Chalak more than 0 0 22, then the Type would be altered; the Molad of the fifth year would become 5 18 0, and this year would commence with a Saturday. The length of the fourth year would be increased by two days; its Sign would become 2 a instead of 2 d; the Type would be vitiated.

It is evident, then, that, so far as we have yet ascertained, the maximum increment to the Molad of the first year can only be 22 Chalakim, if the Type is to be preserved. As this is but a small increment it is not unlikely that nothing smaller will be required. The remaining years must, however, be tested.

It is not necessary to give the full details for the remaining years. The possible increments for each of them are set down in the last column of Table B. They are all greater than 0 0. 22, and therefore they are all too great.

It appears, then, that this addition of 22 Chalakim still retains the function of being the maximum that can be made to the original Molad, 7 18 0, without altering the Sign of any one of the years of the Cycle. In other words, all Cycles which have for the Molad of their first year any value which is not less than 7 18· 0, and not greater than 7 18 22, will be of the same Type. This is given as Type I. in the first line of the collected Types, Table XIII.

By adding together the number of days specified by the Signs of the years, or the number pertaining to each year as actually stated in Table B, above, the total number of days in the Cycle is ascertained. In the present case—Type 1—the sum of the days is 6940; and every Cycle whose Molad is within the limits 7 18 0 and 7 18 22, both inclusive, will consist of this number of days according to the Civil computation.

The possible Molads within these limits are 7 18 4, 7 18 9, 7 18 14, and 7 18 19. It so happens that during the first 7650 years of the Jewish Era there is no Cycle which commences with a Monday whose Molad comes within this range. There is consequently no Cycle, amongst all those years, which is of Type 1, so far as the arrangement or sequence of the years is concerned, though there are many which, with a different sequence, have 6940 days.

77. Type 2.

The inferior limit for the Molad of the first year of a Cycle of the second Type will be 7 18 23. The superior limit will be found in a similar way to that for Type 1.

The computation is given below, by which it will be seen that the increment, 0 2 513, which may be made to the Molad of the tenth year is the least, and therefore this is the greatest that can be made to the original Molad, 7 18 23, which then becomes 7 20 536.

The limits for a Cycle of Type 2 are therefore 7 18 23 and 7 20 536, both inclusive.

Type 2.

Year of the Cycle.	Molads.			First Day of the Year.	Days in Year.	Sign of Year,	Molad might be.			Possible Addition.		
1	7	18	23	Monday	353	2 d	2	15	588	1	21	565
2	5	2	890	Thursday	354	5 r	5	17	1079	0	15	180
3 E	2	11	695	Monday	385	2 A	2	17	1079	0	6	384
4	1	9	204	Monday	355	2 a	2	15	588	0	6	384
5	5	18	0	Saturday	353	7 d	7	17	1079	1	23	1079
6 E	3	2	876	Tuesday	384	3 R	3	17	1079	0	15	203
7	2	0	385	Monday	355	2 a	2	15	588	0	15	203
8 E	6	9	181	Saturday	383	7 D	7	17	1079	1	8	898
9	5	6	770	Thursday	354	5 r	5	17	1079	0	11	309
10	2	15	566	Monday	355	2 a	2	17	1079	0	2	513
11 E	7	0	362	Saturday	385	7 A	7	17	1079	0	17	717
12	5	21	951	Saturday	353	7 d	7	17	1079	1	14	128
13	3	6	747	Tuesday	354	3 r	3	9	203	0	2	536
14 E	7	15	543	Saturday	385	7 A	7	17	1079	0	2	536
15	6	13	52	Saturday	355	7 a	7	17	1079	1	4	1027
16	3	21	928	Thursday	354	5 r	5	17	1079	1	14	151
17 E	1	6	724	Monday	383	2 D	2	17	1079	1	11	355
18	7	4	233	Saturday	355	7 a	7	17	1079	0	13	846
19 E	4	13	29	Thursday	385	5 A	5	17	1079	1	4	1050
20	3	10	618	Thursday			5	17	1079	2	7	461

If the course of the years be traced through any Cycle whose Molad is not less than 7 18 23 and not greater than 7 20 536, it will be found that such Cycle is of this Type, and, like Type 1, has 6940 days.

This forms the second line in Table XIII.

78. Type 3.

This Type will commence with 7 20 537 as the inferior limit for the Molad of the first year of the Cycle.

The computation, made as before, gives the following result:—

Year of the Cycle.	Molads.			First Day of the Year.	Days in Year.	Sign of Year.	Molad might be.			Possible Addition.		
1	7	20	537	Monday	353	2 d	2	15	588	1	19	51
2	5	5	333	Thursday	354	5 r	5	17	1079	0	12	746
3 E	2	14	129	Monday	385	2 A	2	17	1079	0	3	950
4	1	11	718	Monday	355	2 a	2	15	588	0	3	950
5	5	20	514	Saturday	353	7 d	7	17	1079	1	21	565
6 E	3	5	310	Tuesday	384	3 R	3	17	1079	0	12	769
7	2	2	899	Monday	355	2 a	2	15	588	0	12	769
8 E	6	11	695	Saturday	383	7 D	7	17	1079	0	6	384
9	5	9	204	Thursday	355	5 a	5	17	1079	0	8	875
10	2	18	0	Tuesday	354	3 r	3	9	203	0	15	203
11	7	2	876	Saturday	385	7 A	7	17	1079	0	15	203
12	6.	0	385	Saturday	353	7 d	7	17	1079	0	17	694
13	3	9	181	Tuesday	354	3 r	3	9	203	0	0	22
14 E	7	17	1057	Saturday	385	7 A	7	17	1079	0	0	22
15	6	15	566	Saturday	355	7 a	7	17	1079	1	2	513
16	4	0	362	Thursday	354	5 r	5	17	1079	1	17	717
17 E	1	9	158	Monday	383	2 D	2	17	1079	1	8	921
18	7	6	747	Saturday	355	7 a	7	17	1079	0	11	332
19 E	4	15	543	Thursday	385	5 A	5	17	1079	0	2	537
20	3	13	52	Thursday			5	17	1079	2	4	1027

From this computation it appears that the least of all the increments that can be made is 0 0 22, which can be added to the Molads of both the years 10 and 11. The original Molad with which this Type commences may therefore be increased by this amount, and the limits for Type 3 are 7 20 537, and 7 20 559, both inclusive.

There are only six possible Molads which can come within these limits; the feria and hours being in each 7 20, and the Chalaḳim, respectively, 534, 539, 544, 549, 554, 559.

In the first 403 Cycles, covering 7647 years of the Era, there occurs no Cycle of this Type.

The fourth Type will commence with 7 20 560 as the inferior limit for the Molad of its first year.

79. If this process be continued it will be found that there are, in all, 61 possible Types for the Cycles, and 61 only. It is perhaps unnecessary to give the computations for the remaining Types, as the method has been sufficiently indicated. The computation for Type 61 will, however, be stated. It starts with 7 16 689 for the Molad of its first year, and it will be seen that the maximum increment which this Molad can receive, without changing the Type, is 0 1 390, being the increment that can be made to the Molad of the first year.

This raises the superior limit to 7 17 1079, and the next Type would start with 7 18 0, which is the inferior limit for Type 1, so that the whole series of Types will now recur in the same order as before.

Type 61.

Year of the Cycle.	Molads.	First Day of the Year.	Days in Year.	Sign of Year.	Molad might be.	Possible Addition.
1	7 16 689	Saturday	355	7 a	7 17 1079	0 1 390
2	5 1 485	Thursday	354	5 r	5 17 1079	0 16 594
3 E	2 10 281	Monday	385	2 A	2 17 1079	0 7 798
4	1 7 870	Monday	353	2 d	2 15 588	0 7 798
5	5 16 666	Thursday	355	5 a	5 17 1079	0 1 413
6 E	3 1 462	Tuesday	384	3 R	3 17 1079	0 16 617
7	1 22 1051	Monday	353	2 d	2 15 588	0 16 617
8 E	6 7 847	Saturday	383	7 D	7 17 1079	0 10 232
9	5 5 356	Thursday	354	5 r	5 17 1079	0 12 723
10	2 14 152	Monday	355	2 a	2 17 1079	0 3 927
11 E	6 22 1028	Saturday	385	7 A	7 17 1079	0 19 51
12	5 20 537	Saturday	383	7 d	7 17 1079	1 21 542
13	3 5 333	Tuesday	354	3 r	3 9 203	0 9 950
14 E	7 14 129	Saturday	385	7 A	7 17 1079	0 3 950
15	6 11 718	Saturday	355	7 a	7 17 1079	0 6 361
16	3 20 514	Thursday	354	5 r	5 17 1079	1 21 565
17 E	1 5 310	Monday	383	2 D	2 17 1079	1 12 769
18	7 2 899	Saturday	355	7 a	7 17 1079	0 15 180
19 E	4 11 695	Thursday	385	5 A	5 17 1079	0 6 384
20	3 9 204	Thursday			5 17 1079	2 8 875

The final results for all the Types are set out in Table XIII.

80. The following Table C will, so far as the limits are concerned, supply the want of the computations for Types 4 to 60. It shows, in the last column, the year of the Cycle which is capable of receiving that increment which is the least. It will be observed that in nineteen of the Types there are two years, each of which may receive the same increment. This is an important fact of which further notice will be taken.

Table C.

Type.	First Limit.			Possible Increment.			Second Limit.			Year, of which Molad may be increased.
1	7	18	0	0	0	22	7	18	22	5
2	7	18	23	0	2	513	7	20	536	10
3	7	20	537	0	0	22	7	20	559	13 or 14
4	7	20	560	0	3	927	1	0	407	3
5	1	0	408	0	4	1004	1	5	332	9
6	1	5	333	0	2	536	1	7	869	18
7	1	7	870	0	1	413	1	9	203	2
8	1	9	204	0	0	22	1	9	226	6 or 7
9	1	9	227	0	2	513	1	11	740	10 or 11
10	1	11	741	0	11	309	1	22	1050	15
11	1	22	1051	0	0	22	1	22	1073	19
12	1	22	1074	0	1	413	2	0	407	3 or 4
13	2	0	408	0	2	513	2	2	921	7 or 8
14	2	2	922	0	2	536	2	5	378	17
15	2	5	379	0	8	852	2	14	151	12
16	2	14	152	0	0	22	2	14	174	16
17	2	14	175	0	1	413	2	15	588	1
18	2	15	589	0	2	513	2	18	22	4 or 5
19	2	18	23	0	2	536	2	20	559	14
20	2	20	560	0	4	1004	3	1	484	20
21	3	1	485	0	3	927	3	5	332	9
22	3	5	333	0	0	22	3	5	355	13
23	3	5	356	0	0	22	3	5	378	17 or 18
24	3	5	379	0	3	904	3	9	203	1 or 2
25	3	9	204	0	0	22	3	9	226	6
26	3	9	227	0	2	513	3	11	740	11
27	3	11	741	0	8	875	3	20	536	10
28	3	20	537	0	0	22	3	20	559	14 or 15
29	3	20	560	0	2	513	3	22	1073	18 or 19
30	3	22	1074	0	1	413	4	0	407	3
31	4	0	408	0	2	513	4	2	921	8
32	4	2	922	0	8	875	4	11	717	7
33	4	11	718	0	0	22	4	11	740	11 or 12
34	4	11	741	0	2	513	4	14	174	15 or 16
35	4	14	175	0	3	927	4	18	22	5
36	4	18	23	0	7	461	5	1	484	20
37	5	1	485	0	1	413	5	2	898	4
38	5	2	899	0	0	22	5	2	921	8 or 9
39	5	2	922	0	2	513	5	5	355	12 or 13
40	5	5	356	0	0	22	5	5	378	17
41	5	5	379	0	3	904	5	9	203	2
42	5	9	204	0	0	22	5	9	226	5 or 6
43	5	9	227	0	8	852	5	17	1079	1
44	5	18	0	0	2	536	5	20	536	9 or 10
45	5	20	537	0	0	22	5	20	559	14

TABLE C. (*continued*).

Type.	First Limit.			Possible Increment.			Second Limit.			Year, of which Molad may be increased.
46	5	20	560	0	2	513	5	22	1073	19
47	5	22	1074	0	1	413	6	0	407	2 or 3
48	6	0	408	0	7	461	6	7	869	18
49	6	7	870	0	3	927	6	11	717	7
50	6	11	718	0	0	22	6	11	740	11
51	6	11	741	0	2	513	6	14	174	16
52	6	14	175	0	8	875	6	22	1050	15
53	6	22	1051	0	0	22	6	22	1073	19 or 20
54	6	22	1074	0	3	904	7	2	898	4
55	7	2	899	0	0	22	7	2	921	8
56	7	2	922	0	2	513	7	5	355	13
57	7	5	356	0	0	22	7	5	378	16 or 17
58	7	5	379	0	3	927	7	9	226	6
59	7	9	227	0	4	1004	7	14	151	12
60	7	14	152	0	2	536	7	16	688	20
61	7	16	689	0	1	390	7	17	1079	1
1	7	18	0	The Types now recur in order.						

81. Professor Nesselmann, in his "Beiträge zur Chronologie,"* gives a method of finding the sixty-one limits for the Molads of first years which determine the sixty-one types of the Cycles. This method is adopted by Adolf Schwarz, † who refers also to the "Jesod Olam," ‡ p. 21*b*, and to Berl Goldberg's Chronological Tables, but relies chiefly upon Nesselmann. The reckoning is not given by either of these writers, but both supply the Table of results, which is similar to Table XIII., though not precisely in the same form. It is not very easy to follow their explanations of the process pursued.

Starting with the earliest Molad which permits a year to commence with a Monday, 7 18 0, the successive years of a Cycle are computed precisely as for Type 1, Table B, above.

Although an Astronomical, as distinguished from a Civil Cycle, may commence with any one of the seven days of the week, as indicated by its Molad (see Table IX.), yet a Civil Cycle can only commence with some one of the four days which are lawful for Tishrî 1. Also, before

* "Crelle Journal für die Mathematik," Band 26, p. 59. Berlin, 1843.

† "Der Jüdische Kalender," p. 79.

‡ By Rabbi Isaac Israeli; an edition in Hebrew and German was published in Berlin in 1848.

any change can take place from one day to another, whether it be for the first or for any subsequent year of the Cycle, the Molad for the year must pass the limit which confines Tishrî 1 to the former of the two days.

Thus: If the Molad for the year be 5 17 1079, the first day of the year will be a Thursday, but so soon as the Molad passes this limit, and attains to 5 18 0, the first day of the year is changed to Saturday.

Now, there is nothing to prevent a Molad from indicating any one of the seven week-days as the commencement of some Astronomical year, and there is nothing to prevent a Civil year from commencing with some one or other of the four possible week-days.

Thus, the first year of a Cycle may commence with a Monday, as in Type 1; or it may commence with a Tuesday, as in Type 18; or with a Thursday, as in Type 25; or with a Saturday, as in Type 44.

The same thing applies to every other year of the nineteen of the Cycle, and also to the twentieth year, which must be taken into consideration, because the day with which it commences is one of the factors that determine the length of the nineteenth year.

Again: The value of the Molad for the first year of a Cycle, and the week-day with which that year commences, determine the whole Type, that is to say, determine the Molad, and thence the week-day, for each of the remaining years of the Cycle, as well as for the twentieth year, because the Molads of the successive years are found by making certain additions, which are constant, to the Molad of the first year. These additions are 4 8 876 for every Common year, and 5 21 589 for every Embolismic year. The result of these additions for any particular year of the Cycle has been given in Table VII.

It is evident, therefore, that there are 20 × 4, or 80 variations which can take place in the Types, because a change in the Sign for any one year will cause a change in the Type, and each one of the twenty years is capable of commencing with any one of four different days.

It is, however, found, when the computation is made, that nineteen of these 80 variations occur twice, thus reducing the total number of different Types to 61.

The limits, within which the Molads of the Cycles must fall, for these sixty-one Types are found by Nesselmann in the following manner:—

The Molad of each year in Type 1, Table B (Article 76), is to be subtracted from the particular day-limit (Table A, Article 75), the attainment to which would cause the postponement of Tishri 1. The remainder is to be added to 7 18 0, the Molad taken for the origin of the computation, and the sum gives the inferior limit for the first year of one of the Types. The superior limit will, of course, be less by one Chalak than the inferior limit of the next succeeding Type; not of the next Type that is found, but of the next Type after all the inferior limits have been found and arranged in the numerical order of their magnitude.

For example: A year will commence with a Saturday, whatever may be its position in the Cycle, if the Molad be so great as or greater than 5 18 0. Therefore all the Molads in Type 1, Table B, are to be subtracted from 5 18 0, and the remainder is to be added to 7 18 0. Thus, the Molad of year 11 in Type 1 is 7 0 339; if this be subtracted from 5 18 0, the minimum day-limit for Saturday, the remainder is 5 17 741.* This, being added to 7 18 0, gives the sum 6 11 741 as the inferior limit for one of the sixty-one Types. When the Types are numbered in order of the magnitudes of the Molads, it will be found that this is number 51.

With respect to Tuesday and Thursday, care must be taken to make the subtractions from those day-limits which are proper to the different years of the Cycle. Thus, Table B shows that those Common years which follow next after an Embolismic year will commence with a Tuesday if the Molad attain to 2 15 589: this is under the rule BaTU ThaKPhaT; all other years, whether Common or Embolismic, commence with a Tuesday, when the Molad attains to 2 18 0.

82. The process thus described will, perhaps, be better understood when the following computations, which I have thought it well to give, are examined. The numbers on the left are the years of the

* Observe that 5 18 0, treated as a Molad, is identical with 12 18 0, because feria 5 and feria 12 are identical; so we have—

12	18	0
− 7	0	339
5	17	741
+ 7	18	0
6	11	741

Cycle, and the twentieth year, the first of the next Cycle, is added. The numbers on the right are the numbers which are attached to the Types when they are arranged in order of magnitude, as in Tables C (Article 80), and XIII.

I. Monday.

The day-limit for Monday in all years is 7 18 0.

All the Molads in Table B are to be subtracted from 7 18 0, and the remainder is to be increased by 7 18 0.

This is equivalent to subtracting each of the Molads from 15 12 0, or, for it is the same thing, from 15 11 1080.

No.	d	h	p	Type
1.	15	12	0	
	7	18	0	
	7	18	0	 1
2.	15	11	1080	
	5	2	876	
	3	9	204	25
3.	15	11	1080	
	2	11	672	
	6	0	408	48
4.	15	11	1080	
	1	9	181	
	7	2	899	55
5.	15	11	1080	
	5	17	1057	
	2	18	23	19
6.	15	11	1080	
	3	2	853	
	5	9	227	43
7.	15	11	1080	
	2	0	362	
	6	11	718	50
8.	15	11	1080	
	6	9	158	
	2	2	922	14
9.	15	11	1080	
	5	6	747	
	3	5	333	22
10.	15	11	1080	
	2	15	543	
	5	20	537	45
11.	15	11	1080	
	7	0	339	
	1	11	741	10
12.	15	11	1080	
	5	21	928	
	2	14	152	16
13.	15	11	1080	
	3	6	724	
	5	5	356	40
14.	15	11	1080	
	7	15	520	
	7	20	560	 4
15.	15	11	1080	
	6	13	29	
	1	22	1051	11
16.	15	11	1080	
	3	21	905	
	4	14	175	35
17.	15	11	1080	
	1	6	701	
	7	5	379	58
18.	15	11	1080	
	7	4	210	
	1	7	870	 7
19.	15	11	1080	
	4	13	6	
	3	22	1074	30
20.	15	11	1080	
	3	10	595	
	5	1	485	

II. Tuesday.

The day-limit for years 1, 4, 7, 9, 12, 15, 18, and 20 is 2 15 589.
For years 2, 3, 5, 6, 8, 10, 11, 13, 14, 16, 17, and 19 it is 2 18 0.

All the Molads in Table B which belong to the former years are to be subtracted from 2 15 589, and the remainder is to be added to 7 18 0. This is equivalent to subtracting these Molads from 10 9 589, or, for it is the same thing, from 10 8 1669.

All the Molads in Table B which belong to the remaining years are to be subtracted from 2 18 0, and this, through the addition of 7 18 0 to the remainders, is equivalent to the subtraction of the Molads from 10 12 0, or from the same value, 10 11 1080.

1.	10	9	589	
	7	18	0	
	2	15	589	18
4.	10	9	589	
	1	9	181	
	2	0	408	13
7.	10	9	589	
	2	0	362	
	1	9	227	9
9.	10	8	1669	
	5	6	747	
	5	2	922	39
12.	10	8	1669	
	5	21	928	
	4	11	741	34
15.	10	9	589	
	6	13	29	
	3	20	560	29
18.	10	9	589	
	7	4	210	
	3	5	379	24
20.	10	8	1669	
	3	10	595	
	6	22	1074	54
2.	10	11	1080	
	5	2	876	
	5	9	204	42
3.	10	11	1080	
	2	11	672	
	1	0	408	5
5.	10	11	1080	
	5	17	1057	
	4	18	23	36
6.	10	11	1080	
	3	2	853	
	7	9	227	59
8.	10	11	1080	
	6	9	158	
	4	2	922	32
10.	10	11	1080	
	2	15	543	
	7	20	537	3
11.	10	11	1080	
	7	0	339	
	3	11	741	27
13.	10	11	1080	
	3	6	724	
	7	5	356	57
14.	10	11	1080	
	7	15	520	
	2	20	560	20
16.	10	11	1080	
	3	21	905	
	6	14	175	52
17.	10	11	1080	
	1	6	701	
	2	5	379	15
19.	10	11	1080	
	4	13	6	
	5	22	1074	47

III. Thursday.

The day-limit for the years 1, 2, 4, 5, 7, 9, 10, 12, 13, 15, 16, 18, and 20 is 3 9 204.

For the years 3, 6, 8, 11, 14, 17, and 19, the day-limit is 3 18 0.

The Molads in Table B which belong to the former years are to be subtracted from 3 9 204, and when 7 18 0 is added to the remainder, the equivalent will be subtracting the Molads from 11 3 204, which is the same as 11 2 1284.

The Molads which belong to the latter years are to be subtracted from 3 18 0, and when 7 18 0 is added to the remainder an equivalent is obtained by subtracting the Molads from 11 12 0.

1.	11	3	204		12.	11	2	1284		3.	11	11	1080	
	7	18	0			5	21	928			2	11	672	
	3	9	204	25		5	5	356	40		2	0	408	13
2.	11	2	1284		13.	11	2	1284		6.	11	11	1080	
	5	2	876			3	6	724			3	2	853	
	6	0	408	48		7	20	560	 4		1	9	227	 9
4.	11	3	204		15.	11	3	204		8.	11	11	1080	
	1	9	181			6	13	29			6	9	158	
	2	18	23	 9		4	14	175	35		5	2	922	39
5.	11	2	1284		16.	11	2	1284		11.	11	11	1080	
	5	17	1057			3	21	905			7	0	339	
	5	9	227	43		7	5	379	58		4	11	741	34
7.	11	2	1284		18.	11	2	1284		14.	11	11	1080	
	2	0	362			7	4	210			7	15	520	
	2	2	922	14		3	22	1074	30		3	20	560	29
9.	11	2	1284		20.	11	2	1284		17.	11	11	1080	
	5	6	747			3	10	595			1	6	701	
	5	20	537	45		7	16	689	61		3	5	379	24
10.	11	2	1284							19.	11	11	1080	
	2	15	543								4	13	6	
	1	11	741	10							6	22	1074	54

IV. SATURDAY.

The day-limit for Saturday in all years is 5 18 0.

All the Molads in Table B are to be subtracted from 5 18 0, and the remainder is to be added to 7 18 0.

This is equivalent to subtracting the Molads from 13 12 0, and insomuch as the subtractions for the Monday day-limit were all made from 15 12 0, all that need be done is to throw back the feria in each of the limits so found by two days. This gives the following result:—

1.	5	18	0	44
2.	1	9	204	8
3.	4	0	408	31
4.	5	2	899	38
5.	7	18	23	2
6.	3	9	227	26
7.	4	11	718	33
8.	7	2	922	56
9.	1	5	333	6
10.	3	20	537	28
11.	6	11	741	51
12.	7	14	152	60
13.	3	5	356	23
14.	5	20	560	46
15.	6	22	1051	53
16.	2	14	175	17
17.	5	5	379	41
18.	6	7	870	49
19.	1	22	1074	12
20.	3	1	485	21

Eighty limits, or variations, have thus been found; but when they come to be arranged, and numbered in the order of their magnitude, so as to form a Table identical with the first and second columns of Table C, it is found that only 61 numbers are required, for 19 of these variations occur twice.

Those which occur twice, and the computations under which they occur, are the following:—

Types.	Computations.	Types.	Computations.
4	Monday, 14, and Thursday, 13	34	Tuesday, 12, and Thursday, 11
9	Tuesday, 7, „ „ 6	35	Monday, 16, „ „ 15
10	Monday, 11, „ „ 10	39	Tuesday, 9, „ „ 8
13	Tuesday, 4, „ „ 3	40	Monday, 13, „ „ 12
14	Monday, 8, „ „ 7	43	Monday, 6, „ „ 5
19	Monday, 5, „ „ 4	45	Monday, 10, „ „ 9
24	Tuesday, 18, „ „ 17	48	Monday, 3, „ „ 2
25	Monday, 2, „ „ 1	54	Tuesday, 20, „ „ 19
29	Tuesday, 15, „ „ 14	58	Monday, 17, „ „ 16
30	Monday, 19, „ „ 18		

The numbers attached to the feriæ in this Table are those of the years of the Cycle, under the headings Monday, Tuesday, Thursday, and Saturday, in the Computations I. II., III., and IV., which have just been made. If this Table be compared with Table C, it will be noticed that the Types which are here found to be duplicated are always in advance by unity of those Types in Table C against which are written, in the last column of that Table, the years of which the Molads are capable of receiving the same increment.

The process of Nesselmann, which I have thus endeavoured to explain, may appear to be shorter and simpler than that previously suggested. It is shorter, so far as obtaining the limits for the Types is concerned; but, insomuch as each Type has afterwards to be computed in full to obtain the Signs of the years, the work is not in reality abbreviated.

It would be interesting to obtain a mathematical proof that there must be sixty-one Types for the Cycles, and that there are not more than sixty-one. This, however, cannot be done by any direct method. The number can only be ascertained by actually counting how many out of the 4 × 20 occur twice; this number being found to be nineteen, the fact that there are sixty-one Types, and not more, must be accepted as an arithmetical coincidence.

A check upon results which have been obtained may be made by the use of Table XIII. combined with Tables XIV. and XV.

The first column, A, of Table XIV. is an Arithmetical Series having zero for its first term, and 13 × 19, or 247, for its common difference.

The second column, B, commencing with the Molad BeHaRD, is an Arithmetical Series whose terms decrease regularly by 905 Chalakim, the amount by which the Molads of Tishri retrogress after every 247 years (Article 73, page 150).

The first column, C, of Table XV. is an Arithmetical Series whose first term is zero, and common difference 19.

The second column, D, of this Table is a repetition of part of Table VIII., and shows the addition which has to be made to the Molads for the multiples of 19.

These Tables are especially intended for finding the feria with which any given Jewish year commences, and the form or length of the year; but, in the course of the process, there will also be found the Molad for the first year of the Cycle to which the given year belongs, the Type of the Cycle, and the position of the given year in the Cycle.

The following is the method of using the Tables:—

Let H be the given year.

1. In the first column, A, of Table XIV. search for the next less number, N, to H, and note the Molad attached to it in column B, which may be called b.

2. Subtract the number, N, from H, and note the remainder, R.

3. Find the number, n, next less to R in column C of Table XV., and note, in column D, the addition to be made, which may be called d.

4. Add d to b; the Sum, $b + d$, is the Molad of the Cycle to which the given year H belongs.

5. Subtract n from R; the remainder, r, is the place of the given year in the Cycle.

6. In the column headed "Limits of the Molads," Table XIII., find among the inferior limits that which is next less to $b + d$. The Type of the Cycle is that in a line with this limit, and the form of the year is that in the column headed by the number r, being the place of the given year in the Cycle.

Examples.

(1) The year 1279.

H = ... 1279 = 19 × 67 + 6.

N = next less in Table XIV. = 1235 ... 2 0 1079 = b

R = 44

n = next less in Table XV. = 38 ... 5 9 110 = d

r = 6 ... 7 10 109 = $b + d$.

= Molad of first year of the 68th Cycle.

The next limit less than $b + d$ in Table XV. is 7 9 227, which belongs to Type 59. This then is the Type to which the 68th Cycle belongs.

The form of a sixth year in a Cycle of this Type is 3R; therefore, the given year 1279 commences with feria 3, Tuesday, and is a Regular Embolismic year of 384 days. It therefore ends with a Sunday, and the next year commences with a Monday, feria 2. Therefore Nîsân 15 in the given year occurs on feria 2 – 2, or 9 – 2, = 7 = Saturday.

(2) The year 4372.

$$\begin{array}{lrl} H = 4372 = 19 \times 230 + 2 & & \\ N = 4199 \ldots\ldots\ldots\ldots\ldots & 1 \quad 14 \quad 1019 & = b. \\ R = 173 & & \\ n = 171 \ldots\ldots\ldots\ldots\ldots & 3 \quad 4 \quad 1035 & = d. \\ \hline r = 2 & 4 \quad 19 \quad 974 & = \text{Molad of Cycle 231.} \end{array}$$

The given year is the second in a Cycle.

The next less limit is 4 18 23, Type 36. The form of a second year in a Cycle of this Type is 2a; the given year commences with a Monday and has 355 days. It therefore ends with a Friday, and the next year commences with feria 7. Nîsân 15 in 4372 occurs on feria 7 – 2, or Thursday.

(3) The year 5665 = 19 × 298 + 3.

$$\begin{array}{lrl} H = 5665 & & \\ N = 5434 \ldots\ldots\ldots\ldots\ldots & 1 \quad 10 \quad 814 & = b. \\ R = 231 & & \\ n = 228 \ldots\ldots\ldots\ldots\ldots & 4 \quad 6 \quad 660 & = d. \\ \hline r = 3 & 5 \quad 17 \quad 394 & = \text{Molad of Cycle 299.} \end{array}$$

The given year is the third in a Cycle.

The next less limit is 5 9 227, Type 43. The form of a third year in a Cycle of this Type is 7A. The year begins with a Saturday, has 385 days, and ends with a Friday. The next year begins with a Saturday, and Nîsân 15 in 5665 is on feria 7 – 2, or Thursday.

CHAPTER VII

JEWISH FASTS AND FESTIVALS

83. One of the leading features of the Jewish Law is the strict observance demanded for the seventh day. It is to be a Sabbath, or Day of Rest from work of every kind. Brief reference was made to this in Article 49, page 67.

It is impossible to determine with any positive accuracy whether one day in seven was or was not observed by the Patriarchs. Some consider that the "sanctification" of the day mentioned in Genesis ii.* is only proleptic, or in anticipation, and is therefore to be understood of the Sabbath which was afterwards enjoyed. This is supposed to be the case because it is never mentioned during the time covered by the patriarchal narrative. This, however, is but negative evidence, and is no proof of the non-existence of the Sabbath as an institution from the earliest times, any more than against its existence during the four hundred and forty years from the time of Moses to that of David during which, also, it is not mentioned.

The first actual record of the institution of the day as one to be kept holy by the Israelites is in Exodus xvi. 22–30, in connection with the gathering of manna. But, in that passage, Moses seems to speak as though the institution had been previously made, and as though it were already clearly known and recognised: "This is that which the Lord hath said, To-morrow is the rest of the holy sabbath unto the LORD." Others think there is reason for believing that "the statute and ordinance" which God made, when He proved the people by the

* Genesis ii. 3. "And God blessed the seventh day and sanctified it: because that in it He had rested from all His work which God created and made."

waters of Marah, were with respect to the observance of this day, Exodus xv. 25.

In the Fourth Commandment, which was given shortly after the event at Marah, the ordinance is set forth distinctly, Exodus xxi. 8–11; the reason there assigned for it being that "in six days the LORD made heaven and earth, the sea, and all that in them is, and rested the seventh day: wherefore the LORD blessed the seventh day and hallowed it." When Moses, not long before his death, called all Israel together, and rehearsed to them the statutes and judgments of the LORD, he did not repeat this reason for the commandment, but substituted the words, "Remember that thou wast a servant in the land of Egypt, and that the LORD thy God brought thee out thence through a mighty hand and by a stretched out arm, therefore the LORD thy God commanded thee to keep the sabbath day," Deuteronomy v. 15.

84. We may gather from other passages in the Old Testament of what kind were the provisions and penalties made respecting the abstinence from labour. There are many such passages, but it is not necessary to refer to more than a few of the most striking.

1. It was forbidden to do any work therein, and the penalty for transgression was death.

Exodus xxxv. 2. "Whosoever doeth work therein shall be put to death." We have an instance of the way in which this law was carried into effect, Numbers xv. 32: "And while the children of Israel were in the wilderness, they found a man that gathered sticks upon the sabbath day. And all the congregation brought him without the camp, and stoned him with stones, and he died: as the LORD commanded Moses."

2. No fire might be lighted.

Exodus xxxv. 3. "Ye shall kindle no fire throughout your habitations upon the sabbath day."

3. No burden might be carried.

Jeremiah xvii. 21. "Thus saith the LORD: Take heed to yourselves and bear no burden on the sabbath day, nor bring it in by the gates of Jerusalem. Neither carry forth a burden out of your houses on the sabbath day, neither do ye any work, but hallow ye the sabbath day, as I commanded your fathers."

4. It was forbidden to buy or sell goods.

Nehemiah x. 31. "If the people of the land bring ware or any victuals on the sabbath day to sell, that we would not buy it of them on the sabbath, or on the holy day."

Ib. xiii. 15. "In those days saw I in Judah some treading winepresses on the sabbath, and bringing in sheaves, and lading asses; as also wine, grapes, and figs, and all manner of burdens, which they brought into Jerusalem on the sabbath day: and I testified against them in the day wherein they sold victuals."

5. Travelling was forbidden.

Exodus xvi. 29. "Abide ye every man in his place, let no man go out of his place on the seventh day. So the people rested on the seventh day."

The Jews were not permitted to make a journey on the Sabbath, or on any of the great festivals which were kept as Sabbaths. The distance that it was lawful to travel is not mentioned by Moses, but it was considered by the Rabbins that it must never exceed two thousand cubits, about seven hundred and fifty paces, or two-thirds of a mile. Josephus, "Antiquities," xviii. cap. viii. 4, "Nor is it lawful for us to journey, either on the sabbath day, or on a festival day."

Reference to this rule is made by Christ in His address to His Apostles, S. Matthew xxiv. 20, "Pray that your flight be not in the winter, neither on the sabbath day." It was usual to close the gates of the cities and towns on this day, so that Christ might have had in view the actual impediments that would have to be encountered if the flight were on the Sabbath; *cf.* Nehemiah xiii. 19: "And it came to pass, that when the gates of Jerusalem began to be dark before the sabbath, I commanded that the gates should be shut, and charged that they should not be opened till after the sabbath."

On the other hand, a blessing was promised to those who duly observed the Sabbath.

Isaiah lviii. 13, 14. "If thou turn away thy foot from the sabbath, from doing thy pleasure upon My holy day; and call the sabbath a delight, the holy of the Lord, honourable; and shalt honour Him, not doing thine own ways, nor finding thine own pleasure, nor speaking thine own words; Then shall thou delight thyself in the Lord; and I will cause thee to ride upon the high places of the earth, and feed thee with the heritage of Jacob thy father: for the mouth of the Lord hath spoken it."

In Ezekiel xx. 12-24, the pollution of the Sabbath is described as one of the great national sins which brought the wrath of God upon the people. In verse 15 it is set down as one of the reasons why those who rebelled in the wilderness were not allowed to enter the promised land.

85. From the time when Nehemiah, after the return from the Captivity in Babylon, "made a sure covenant, and wrote it, and the princes, Levites, and priests set their seal unto it" (Nehemiah ix. 38), from that time forward the Sabbath was most strictly observed. The national sin, in this respect was eliminated. There was indeed one sad exception in the apostacy, when "Wicked men went out of Israel, who persuaded many, saying, Let us go and make a covenant with the heathen that are round about us" [the Greeks under Antiochus Epiphanes], 1 Maccabees i. 11; and when, six years later, Antiochus in the hundred forty and third year of the kingdom of the Greeks,* went up against Jerusalem, and defiled the sanctuary, and two years afterwards burnt the city, so that "her feasts were turned into mourning, her sabbaths into reproach, her honour into contempt," 1 Maccabees i. 39. Yet even in this time of woe and desolation there were many in Israel who remained faithful, "who were fully resolved and confirmed in themselves, not to eat any unclean thing. Wherefore they chose rather to die, that they might not be defiled with meats, and that they might not profane the holy covenant: so then they died," 1 Maccabees i. 62, 63.

The Sabbath was then, indeed, so scrupulously observed by the faithful, that they would not even defend themselves from their enemies on that day; and we are told in 1 Maccabees ii. 34–38, as well as by Josephus, "Antiquities," xii. cap. vi. 2, that "there were about a thousand with their wives and children, who were smothered and burnt in certain caves to which they had fled, without resistance, and without so much as stopping up the entrances into the caves. They avoided to defend themselves on that day, because they were not willing to break in upon the honour they owed the sabbath, even in such distresses, for our law requires that we rest upon that day."

Mattathias the Hasmonæan, the father of the great Judas who was called Maccabæus, decreed, in consequence of this event, that it was lawful to fight even on the Sabbath. He told his followers "that unless they would do so they would become their own enemies, by so

* Era of the Seleucidæ, B.C. 170.

rigorously observing the law, while their adversaries would still assault them on this day, and they would not then defend themselves, and that nothing could then hinder but they all must perish without fighting," "Antiq.," xii. cap. vi. 2. "At that time therefore they decreed saying, Whosoever shall come to make battle with us on the sabbath day, we will fight against him: neither will we die all, as our brethren that were murdered in the secret places," 1 Maccabees ii. 41.

86. Josephus tells us that in later times it was usual to spend the Sabbath day in the study of the Law. When Herod and Agrippa were in Ionia, Nicolaus pleaded before them for the privileges of the Jews, and said in the course of his speech, "The seventh day is set apart from labour; it is dedicated to the learning of our customs and our laws, we thinking it proper to reflect on them as well as on any [good] thing else, in order to our avoiding of sin," "Antiquities," xvi. cap. ii. 3. In fact, from the time when the New Testament history opens the strict observance of the Sabbath had become one of the Jewish characteristics, so that in whatever country a Jew might be found his nationality could be recognised by this alone.

Hospitality was encouraged on the Sabbath day. Indeed it was not unusual for rich men to give a dinner upon the day; but everything had to be eaten cold, since nothing might be cooked upon a Sabbath. It was such a feast that was attended by our Lord, "when He went into the house of one of the chief Pharisees to eat bread on the sabbath day," S. Luke xiv. 1. Nehemiah expressly desired the people not to mourn and weep, but "Go your way, eat the fat, and drink the sweet, and send portions unto them for whom nothing is prepared: for this day is holy unto the Lord: neither be ye sorry; for the joy of the LORD is your strength," viii. 10.

Josephus, in the "Wars of the Jews," iv. cap ix. 12, speaks of the announcement of the beginning and ending of the Sabbath by the sounding of a trumpet. This ceremony is not mentioned elsewhere. He had been narrating the methods adopted by the Zealots against Simon, during the sedition and civil war when Vespasian was preparing to besiege the city. He says, "The Zealots threw their darts easily from a superior place, and seldom failed of hitting their enemies; but having the advantage of situation, and having withal erected four very large towers aforehand, that their darts might come from higher places, one at the north-east corner of the court, one above the Xystus, the third at another corner, over against the lower city, and the last was erected above the top of the Pastophoria, where one of the priests stood, and gave a signal beforehand, with a trumpet at the beginning of every seventh day, in the evening twilight, as also at the evening when that day was finished, as giving notice to the people when they were to leave off work, and when they were to go to work again."

Whiston, in his note upon this passage, vol. iv. p. 112, says that Reland's conjecture here is not improbable that this was the very place that has puzzled our commentators so long, called "Musach Sabbati," the "Covert of the Sabbath," if that be the true reading of 2 Kings xvi. 18, "And the covert for the sabbath that they had built in the house, and the king's entry without, turned he from the house of the LORD for the king of Assyria"; because here the appointed priest stood under a "covering" to proclaim the beginning and ending of every Jewish Sabbath.

87. In addition to specifying especially the seventh day as a Day of Rest, the word Sabbath is also used for all the Jewish Feasts and Fasts upon which work was forbidden. Thus:—

Leviticus xix. 3. "Ye shall fear every man his father and his mother, and keep my sabbaths," and verse 30, "Ye shall keep my sabbaths, and reverence my sanctuary."

Leviticus xvi. 30, 31. "That day (the Day of Atonement), shall be a sabbath of rest unto you, and ye shall afflict your souls by a statute for ever." Also xxiii. 32.

Leviticus xxiii. 24. "In the seventh month, in the first day of the month (Tishrî 1), shall ye have a sabbath, a memorial of blowing of trumpets, an holy convocation."

From the fifteenth day of the same month to the twenty-second, inclusive, was the Feast of Tabernacles; "On the first day shall be a sabbath, and on the eighth day shall be a sabbath," Leviticus xxiii. 39.

88. THE FEASTS OF THE NEW MOONS.

Rôsh-chôdesh, or Renewal of the Month. On the first day of every month the New Moon is celebrated with great ceremony, in accordance with the Mosaical law, though these Festivals are not enumerated among the days of solemn Feasts in Leviticus xxiii. In fact, the days of New Moon are not mentioned at all in that Book, or in Exodus, or in Deuteronomy. Reference is, however, made to them in Numbers, and frequently in other parts of the Scriptures. From the fact of their being generally mentioned specifically it would seem that they were distinguished from the other Feasts, and from the Sabbaths. Thus, in 1 Chronicles xxiii. 31, "And to offer all burnt sacrifices unto the LORD in the sabbaths, in the new moons, and on the set feasts by number." So also 2 Chronicles ii. 4, ". . . for the burnt offerings morning and evening, on the sabbaths, and on the new moons, and on the solemn feasts of the LORD our God." They are separately mentioned in the same way in 2 Chronicles viii. 13 and xxxi. 3; Ezra iii. 5; Nehemiah x. 33; Isaiah i. 13, 14; Ezekiel xiv. 17; Hosea ii. 11, and elsewhere.

S. Paul recognises that there is a distinction, "Let no man judge you in respect of an holy day, or of the new moon, or of the sabbath days," Colossians ii. 16.

With respect to the ceremonies upon these days, they were—

1. The sounding of trumpets. Numbers x. 10. "In the beginnings of your months ye shall blow with the trumpets over your burnt offerings, and over your peace offerings that they may be to you a memorial before your God."

Psalms lxxxi. 3. "Blow up the trumpet in the new moon, in the time appointed, and on our solemn feast day."

Isaiah x. 10. "In the beginnings of your months ye shall blow with the trumpets over your burnt offerings."

Cf. also 1 Samuel xx. 5; 2 Chronicles ii. 4; Ezra iii. 5; Nehemiah x. 33.

2. Additions to the daily sacrifice were made, namely, two young bullocks, a ram, and seven lambs, as a burnt offering, a kid as a sin offering, with wine, and flour mingled with oil. Numbers xxviii. 11-15.

3. The purchase and sale of merchandise was stopped, as upon the Sabbath.

Amos viii. 5. "When will the new moon be gone, that we may sell corn?"

It would appear that it was customary for the people to attend the service in the Temple, and to receive instruction in their religion and laws from their prophets and teachers, for we read, in 2 Kings iv. 23, that when the Shunammite was about to visit Elisha her husband asked her, "Wherefore wilt thou go to him to-day? It is neither new moon nor sabbath."

Isaiah lxvi. 23. "And it shall come to pass that from one new moon to another, and from one sabbath to another, shall all flesh come to worship before Me, saith the LORD."

Ezekiel xlvi. 3. "Likewise the people of the land shall worship at the door of this gate before the LORD, in the sabbaths and in the new moons."

89. The manner in which the day of New Moon, so called, was determined by actual observation, and then consecrated, has been described in Article 7, page 10. Although Hillel II. in A.D. 358 had made known the method of Astronomical computation, yet the custom of watching the heavens for the first appearance of the crescent was retained for many years, and the New Moons were announced as heretofore, messengers being dispatched to carry the information. Special permission was given to these messengers to break the law concerning the limit of a Sabbath-day's journey with respect to the months Tishrî and Nîsân, the most important as regards the Festivals. It is reported that on a certain occasion Rabbi Akiba kept back no less than eighty messengers at Lydda, on account of the Sabbath day, to the great indignation of Gamaliel II.

Those who lived in the neighbourhood of the Holy City kept the celebration during one day; but those who lived farther off, in places which could not be reached by messengers, observed two days on certain occasions, namely, the last day of every month which had thirty days, as well as the first day of the next month.*

Maimonides says † that there were six months of which the New Moons were indicated by messengers:—

Nîsân	on account of the		Passover.
Abh	,,	,,	Fast for the destruction of the Temple.
Elûl	,,	,,	New Moon of Tishrî.
Tishrî	,,	,,	Feast of Tabernacles.
Kislêw	,,	,,	Feast of Purification.
Adhâr	,,	,,	Purim.

* Horace refers to this custom in Sat. i. 9:—

"Memini bene; sed meliore
Tempore dicam: hodie tricesima Sabbata: vin' tu
Curtis Judæis oppedere?"

† "Kiddusch hachodesch," cap. 3.

While the Temple was standing Iyâr was added on account of the Second Passover, which those who were unable to keep the Feast on Nîsân 15 were allowed to celebrate on Iyâr 15.

The following are the months which have two Rôsh-chôdesh, namely, their own first day, and the last day of the preceding month:—

Marḥeshwân, in all years.

Kislêw, in Abundant years, both Common and Embolismic.

Têbeth, in Regular and Abundant years, both Common and Embolismic.

Adhâr I., in Embolismic years.

Adhâr II., in all years.

Iyâr, in all years.

Tammûz, in all years.

'Elûl, in all years.

The five months Tishrî, Schebhât, Nîsân, Sîwân, and Abh have only one Rôsh-chôdesh.

90. The reason why two Rôsh-chôdesh were observed for certain months, as explained by al-Bîrûnî,* Lazarus Bendavid,† and Lindo,‡ was this:—A mean Lunar month, by Jewish Astronomical computation, consists of 29d. 12h. 793ch., so that a Civil month of twenty-nine days is 12h. 793ch. shorter, while one of thirty days is 11h. 287ch. longer than a Lunation. If, then, a Civil month has thirty days, these 11h. 287ch. really belong to the Lunar month which follows it, and this part of a day ought to be observed as part of the first actual twenty-four hours of the Lunation; but it is contrary to principle to keep a holy day during part only of a day, therefore the whole of the thirtieth day must be kept. Again, the remaining 12h. 793ch. of the first actual twenty-four hours of the Lunation fall within the first day of the next Civil month; these hours must be kept sacred; and, for the same reason that the whole of the thirtieth day is kept, the whole of the first day is kept also.

Another cause for assuming the two Rôsh-chôdesh, especially after the method of Astronomical computation had come into use, would be the scrupulous anxiety of the Jews to fulfil the Law. The observance of the New Moons was required, and if any error had crept into the computation by which the day was determined, the observance of two days would tend to its elimination.

* P. 156. † P. 11, § 2. ‡ P. 6.

In this connection an extra day is allotted to certain of the Festivals.

Tishrî 1 and 2 are both observed as Rôsh Ha-schanah, the Commencement of the year.

Tishrî 15 and 16, as Succoth, or the Feast of Tabernacles.

Tishrî 22 and 23. Feast of the Eighth day; but the second day is called the Feast of the Law.

The Passover has eight days in all, instead of seven, Nîsân 15 to 22 inclusive.

Sîwân 6 and 7 are both kept as Schabuoth, the Feast of Weeks.

This custom has existed since the time of the Babylonish Captivity, and is still practised by the strict Jews. In the reformed Synagogue the Festivals are observed upon one day only.

91. A detailed list of the days observed in each month of the Jewish year will now be given.

All the Hebrew Sabbaths, Festivals, and Fasts commence in the evening which precedes the midnight from which the corresponding Christian Civil day begins.

TISHRÎ.

The first month of the Civil Year. The seventh month of the Sacred or Religious year. The Sabbatical year, and the year of Jubilee, both commence with this month.

Tishrî has 30 days in all years.

Day of the month.

1 and 2. Rôsh Ha-schanah, "Caput Anni," or New Year. The first and second days of this month are treated as though they were but one day. In their combination they are termed "Yoma Arichta," that is, "A day lengthened out," or "A long day." Both days are kept with equal solemnity.

The Feast of Trumpets. Leviticus xxiii. 24, 25. "In the seventh month, in the first day of the month, shall ye have a sabbath, a memorial of blowing of trumpets, an holy convocation. Ye shall do no servile work therein, but ye shall offer an offering made by fire unto the LORD." *Cf.* also Numbers xxix. 1-6; Ezra iii. 1; Nehemiah vii. 2, 9.

Day of the month.

This Feast differed in several respects from the ordinary Festivals of the New Moon. In addition to the usual daily sacrifices, and to those which were offered at the celebration of every New Moon, namely, two young bullocks, one ram, seven lambs of the first year, and a kid,* it appears from Numbers xxix. 1-6, that the latter offerings were doubled with the exception of one bullock.

This was one of the seven days of Holy Convocation, Leviticus xxiii. 24; the other six being Tishrî 10, Tishrî 15, Tishrî 22, Nîsân 15, Nîsân 21, and Sîwân 6.

On ordinary occasions trumpets were blown in the Temple at the time when the sacrifices were offered, but this was to be "a day of blowing of trumpets," Numbers xxix. 1. There were trumpets of two kinds, the straight and the ram's horn. The former were used in the Temple only, but it was lawful for any one, even for a child, to blow the ram's horn during this festival unless it happened to fall upon the Sabbath day; in that case, the trumpets were blown in the Temple only.†

It was upon this day, according to tradition, that Abraham prepared to offer his son Isaac for a burnt offering, Genesis xxii. 2.

Theodoret, Comment. in Leviticus, Quœstio xxxii., says that the feast was kept in commemoration of the thunder and lightning on Mount Sinai at the giving of the Law.

The Rabbins have taught that upon these two days God judges all men with respect to their actions during the past year, and disposes the events of the year which is commencing. Hence, these days have been called Days of Judgment, Days of Remembrance, Days of Tribulation, Days of Penitence, and Terrible days.

3. Fast of Guedaliah. In memory of his slaughter, and that of the Jews who were with him at Mizpah, by Ishmael, "of the seed royal." After King Zedekiah had been blinded and carried away to Babylon, Guedaliah was appointed by Nebuchadnezzar to rule over the people that were left in the land. Josephus describes him as being of a kind and gentle disposition. He was

* Numbers xxviii. 11-15.

† Maimonides, "Rôsh Ha-schanah," bk. iv. 1.

Day of the month.

warned by Johanan and others that Ishmael had been sent by Baalis, King of the Ammonites, to kill him in order that Ishmael himself, who was of the royal family, might rule in Israel. He did not believe what they said, and was slain by Ishmael and ten men who were his accomplices, after a great feast at which he had entertained them; 2 Kings xxv. 22–26; Jeremiah xli. 1–3; Josephus, "Antiquities," x. cap. ix. 2, 3.

Al-Bîrûnî says that Guedaliah was killed, together with eighty-two people who were with him, in a cistern in which the water collected until it rose above their heads.*

If this Fast fall upon the Sabbath, which will be the case when Tishrî falls upon a Thursday, it is observed on the following day.

It appears from Megillath Ta'anith (see *post*, Article 115, Day xvii.), that in the time of the Hasmonæans, Tishrî 3 was appointed to be a semi-festival on account of the suppression of the Divine name from official documents.

7. Fast for the Golden Calf which the people compelled Aaron to make in Horeb, when Moses was in the Mount. Exodus xxxii. 1–35; Deuteronomy ix. 12–21; Nehemiah ix. 18; Psalms cvi. 19.

10. Fast of Kippûr, called also Ashûrâ. The great day of Atonement, or Expiation. One of the days of Holy Convocation. The Fast commences half an hour before sunset on the evening of the ninth day, and lasts till half an hour after sunset on the tenth. It is sometimes called the White Fast. It is observed in commemoration of the day upon which Moses came down from Mount Sinai with the renewed Tables of the Law, after he had obtained pardon for the sin of the Israelites in making and worshipping the Golden Calf. The Fast was instituted that atonement might be made for all the sins committed during the past year, from the High Priest down to the humblest of the people.† The account is given in Leviticus xvi. 29, xxiii. 27; and Numbers xxix. 7.

* "Vestiges," p. 269.

† Al-Bîrûnî, p. 270, says sins "committed by mistake," as opposed to wilful sin.

Day of the month.

Fasting upon this day is observed with the utmost strictness. It is obligatory, while all other Fasts are voluntary. It is kept as a Sabbath, or day of rest; it is not lawful to wash, to anoint oneself with oil, even to put on leather shoes. Women who have been recently confined, invalids who are dangerously ill, and children under three years of age, are exempted from the rule.

In the Talmud, Tishrî 10 is called simply "the day." In Acts xxvii. 9, it is ἡ νηστεία, "the fast"—"when sailing was now dangerous because the fast was now already past." The Rhems New Testament * has a marginal note on this passage: "It may signify the Jews' fast of the seventh month, September, after which navigation was perilous, winter approaching." So Elsley, "Annotations," *in loco*, "This was the great fast of Expiation." Dean Alford, *in loco*, says the same, and in his "Chronology of the Book of the Acts," Prolegomena, ch. i. § vi. he gives the date as A.D. 58, A.U.C. 811. The corresponding Jewish year, commencing with Tishrî, was therefore A.M. 3819, which was Embolismic. Consequently A.M. 3818 was a Common year, and had only one Adhâr. Therefore Tishrî 10 in 3819 must have fallen about the time of the Autumnal Equinox, when the weather is often stormy, and "sailing was now dangerous." Dean Alford quotes Vegetius, "De Re Militari," iv. 39, to show that the usual season for sailing did not as a rule close so early, "Ex die igitur tertio iduum Novembris (November 11), usque in diem sextum iduum Martiarum, maria clauduntur."

It was upon the Day of Atonement that the Scape-goat was sent out into the wilderness, Leviticus xxi. 15, 20, 21. Two goats were presented to the High Priest, at the door of the Tabernacle, for a sin offering. He cast lots as to which should be sacrificed, and which should be set at liberty. The latter, after certain prayers had been said, and ceremonies performed, was charged with all the transgressions of the children of Israel, was taken to the wilderness by a man appointed for the purpose, and was then suffered to escape.

* Fol. Ed. "printed in the year 1737," p. 319.

Day of the month.

This is the only fast which was actually ordained by Moses. All the other Fasts were instituted at later times.

15 and 16. Succoth. First and second days of the Feast of Tabernacles, or ingathering of harvest. Gk. σκηνοπηγία. This was one of the three great Feasts upon which every male of the children of Israel was commanded to appear before the Lord, and to make their offerings, Exodus xxiii. 14–17; Deuteronomy xvi. 16, "Three times in a year shall all thy males appear before the Lord thy God in the place that he shall chose: in the feast of unleavened bread, and in the feast of weeks, and in the feast of tabernacles: and they shall not appear before the Lord empty: every man shall give as he is able."

The Feast was kept in memory of the dwelling in tents in the wilderness. Leviticus xxiii. 34–43; Deuteronomy xvi. 13; Ezra iii. 4; Nehemiah ix. 15, 18. Josephus, "Antiq.," iii. cap. x. 4.

The Feast lasted for seven days, but the first and last days were the most solemn. The first day, Tishrî 15, is a day of Holy Convocation.

21. Hosana Raba, the Great Hosana. The seventh day of the Feast of Tabernacles, which now lasts for nine days, the next two being reckoned as a part of the Feast.

22. Schemeni Azereth. The Feast of Benediction. The day of Solemn Assembly of the Congregation after the Feast of Tabernacles had been kept for seven days. Leviticus xxiii. 36, "Seven days ye shall offer an offering made by fire unto the Lord: on the eighth day shall be an holy convocation unto you: it is a solemn assembly: and ye shall do no servile work therein." *Cf.* also Nehemiah viii. 18. This is sometimes called the Feast of the Eighth Day, *i.e.*, of Tabernacles.

23. Simchath Thorah, the Feast of Rejoicing for the Law; the ninth day of the Feast of Tabernacles.

30. First Rôsh-chôdesh of Marḥeshwân.

Day of the month.

92. MARḤESHWÂN.

Second month of the Civil, Eighth of the Sacred year. It has thirty days in Abundant years: in Regular and Deficient years it has only twenty-nine.

1. Second day of Rôsh-chôdesh.

6. Fast of Zedekia. His children were slain in his presence by Nebuchadnezzar, and his own eyes were then put out; 2 Kings xxv. 7; Jeremiah xxxix. 6, and lii. 10, 11.

30. In Abundant years only, this intercalated day is the first Rôsh-chôdesh of Kislêw.

93. KISLÊW.

Third month of the Civil year; ninth month of the Sacred year.

It has thirty days in a Regular and in an Abundant year. It has only twenty-nine in a Deficient year.

1. Rôsh-chôdesh. In Abundant years this is the second Rôsh-chôdesh of Kislêw.

8. Fast on account of the burning of the book written by Baruch at the dictation of Jeremiah the prophet. Jeremiah xxxvi. 20–25.

20. Day of Prayer for rain.

25. Chanukkâ. First day of the Feast of the Dedication, or Purification of the Temple. Lat. *Encoenia*. This Feast was instituted by Judas Maccabæus, and is celebrated for eight days in honour of the restoration of the Temple after it had been profaned by Antiochus Epiphanes, A.M. 3632, B.C. 128; 1 Maccabees i. 59, Josephus, "Antiq.," xii. cap. v. 4. Antiochus had taken away all the treasures of the Temple. See *post*, Article 115, Megillath Ta'anîth, Day vi.

30. Eliminated in Deficient years. In Abundant and Regular years it is the first Rôsh-chôdesh of Têbeth.

Day of the month.

94. TÊBETH.

Fourth month of the Civil, tenth of the Sacred year. It has twenty-nine days in all years.

1. In Deficient years this month has only one Rôsh-chôdesh. In Regular and Abundant years this day is the second Rôsh-chôdesh.

8. Fast on account of the translation of the Holy Scriptures into the Greek language: the Septuagint version.

Al-Bîrûnî gives an interesting account of the transaction.* "After Nebukadnezar had conquered Jerusalem part of the Israelites emigrated from their country, took refuge with the King of Egypt, and lived there under his protection till the time when Ptolimæus Philadelphus ascended the throne. This King heard of the Thora,† and its divine origin. Therefore he gave orders to search for this community and found them at last in a place numbering 30,000 men. He afforded them protection, and took them into his favour, he treated them with kindness, and allowed them to return to Jerusalem, which meantime had been rebuilt by Cyrus, who had also revived the culture of Syria. They left Egypt, accompanied by a body of his (Ptolimæus Philadelphus') servants for their protection. The King said to them: 'I want to ask you for something. If you grant me the favour, you acquit yourselves of all obligations towards me. Let me have a copy of your book, the Thora.' This the Jews promised, and confirmed their promise by an oath. Having arrived at Jerusalem, they fulfilled their promise by sending him a copy of it, but in Hebrew. He however did not know Hebrew. Therefore he addressed himself again to them, asking for people who knew both Hebrew and Greek, who might translate the book for him, promising them gifts and presents in reward. Now the Jews selected seventy-two men out of their twelve tribes, six men of each tribe, from among the Rabbis and priests. These men translated the Thora into Greek, after they had been housed separately, and each couple had got a servant to take care of them. This went on till they

* "Vestiges," p. 24. † The Books of the Law.

Day of the month.

had finished the translation of the whole book. Now the King had in his hands thirty-six translations. These he compared with each other, and did not find any difference in them, except those which always occur in the rendering of the same ideas. Then the King gave them what he had promised, and provided them with everything of the best. The Jews asked him to make them a present of one of these copies, of which they wished to make a boast before their own people. And the King complied with their wish. Now this is the copy of the Christians, and people think that in it no alteration or transposition has taken place. The Jews however give quite a different account, viz., that they made the translation under compulsion, and that they yielded to the King's demand only from fear of violence and maltreatment, and not before having agreed upon inverting and confounding the text of the book."

Josephus gives very much the same account, though some of the details are varied.* He quotes a letter from Ptolemæus to Eleazar, the High Priest, in which the King expresses a wish to do what he can for the benefit of the Jews settled in Egypt, and to obtain for them a copy of the Hebrew Scriptures translated into Greek. He asks that seventy-two elders may be chosen out and sent to him for this purpose. Eleazer complied with the request, and sent the elders with a copy of the Law written in golden letters, of which "they made an accurate interpretation, with great zeal, and great pains."

In consequence of this translation being made darkness was spread over the world during three days and nights. The eighth day of Têbeth was the last of the three dark days, and is observed as a Fast.

There is some confusion of ideas with respect to this Fast, for by some authors it is spoken of as a Feast; thus Philo, who lived in the first century, in the reign of Caligula, says that down to his day there was a great annual festival held on the Island of Pharos, in which not only Jews but others also took part, and that it was celebrated in honour of the translation.†

Graetz, i., ch. xxiv. p. 530, makes the matter quite clear, and explains the origin of the different views. "The Greek trans-

* "Antiquities," xii. cap. ii. 5.

† "De Vita Mosis," lib.ii.

Day of the month.

lation of the Torah might be looked upon as a temple erected to the glory of God in a foreign land. The accomplishment of this task filled the Alexandrian and Egyptian Judæans with intense delight: and they thought, with no little pride, that now the vainglorious Greeks would at last be obliged to concede that the wisdom taught by Judaism was at once more elevating and of more ancient date than the philosophy of Greece. Their satisfaction was doubtless enhanced by the fact that the noble work owed in part its successful termination to the warm sympathy of the friendly King, who then, as it were, opened a new path for Judaism into Greece. It was natural, therefore, that great rejoicings should take place among the Egyptian Judæans on the day of presentation of the version to the King, and that its anniversaries should be observed as holidays. On that day it was customary for the Judæans to repair to the Island of Pharos, where they offered up prayers of joyful thanksgiving. . . . Later on this anniversary became a national holiday, in which even the heathen Alexandrians took part.

"But far different was the effect produced by the translation of the Torah into Greek upon the pious inhabitants of Judæa. Greece was the object of their hatred on account of the sufferings they had endured at her hands, and the indignities she had inflicted upon their sanctuaries; and they now feared, not unnaturally, that the Law would be disfigured and perverted by its translation into Greek. The Hebrew language in which God had revealed Himself upon Mount Sinai, alone appeared to them worthy of being the means by which to transmit the Divine teaching of the Torah. When the Law was presented in a foreign tongue, the pious Judæans deemed Judaism itself altered and profaned. Consequently the commemoration of the translation, which was celebrated as a festival by the Judæans in Egypt, was kept by their brethren in Judæa as a day of national mourning, similar to that upon which the golden calf had been worshipped in the desert, and the day became numbered amongst their fasts."

For further information concerning the Septuagint version, and the traditions connected with it, reference may be made to Ewald, "The History of Israel," vol. v. p. 249. He shows that the translation effected under Ptolemy Philadelphus was

Day of the month.

confined to the Pentateuch, and perhaps the Book of Joshua. The remaining Books of the Old Testament were translated at a later, unknown time, and by unknown authors.

9. The Fast of Têbeth. The origin is unknown.

10. Fast. Nebuchadnezzar arrived at Jerusalem and commenced the siege. Asarah Beteketh. 2 Kings xxv. 1, 2, "It came to pass in the tenth month, in the tenth day of the month, that Nebuchadnezzar, king of Babylon, came, he, and all his host, against Jerusalem and pitched against it; and they built forts against it round about. And the city was besieged unto the eleventh year of king Zedekiah."

95. SCHEBHÂT.

Fifth month of the Civil, eleventh month of the Sacred year. It has thirty days.

1. Rôsh-chôdesh.

5. Fast for the death of the Elders who were coeval with Joshua, the son of Nûn. Judges ii. 10, "All that generation were gathered unto their fathers: and there arose another generation after them, which knew not the LORD, nor yet the works which he had done for Israel."

15. Laylanot, First day of the new year of trees. See Article 57, p. 94.

23. Fast for the rebellion of the tribe of Benjamin. Judges xix. 16 to xxi. 24.

30. First Rôsh-chôdesh of Adhâr in Common years.

96. ADHÂR I.

The intercalary month in Embolismic years. It has no number as a month; that is, it is not called the sixth month of the Civil year, or the eleventh of the Sacred year. It has thirty days.

Day of the month.

There are no Festivals or Fasts observed in this month.

30. First Rôsh-chôdesh of Adhar II. in Embolismic Years.

97. Adhâr II., or Adhâr Sheni.

The sixth month of the Civil year, the twelfth and last of the Sacred year. This month is the original Adhâr, and in Common years is simply so called. It has twenty-nine days.

1. Rôsh-chôdesh, second day.

7. Fast for the death of Moses. Deuteronomy xxxiv. 5, 6, "So Moses, the servant of the Lord, died there in the land of Moab, according to the word of the Lord. And He buried him in a valley in the land of Moab, over against Beth-peor; but no man knoweth of his sepulchre unto this day."

9. Fast in memory of the schism between the followers of Shammâi and Hillel. Al-Bîrûnî says that 28,000 men were killed, but this number is a great exaggeration.

Hillel, a Babylonian, was appointed by Herod in the year B.C. 31 to be one of the presidents of the Synhedrion. He was born about B.C. 75, and traced his descent on the mother's side from the house of David. He was distinguished for extraordinary gentleness, and for a profound trust in God, that never wavered in the midst of trouble. The presidency of the Synhedrion became hereditary in his family during four generations. The second place of honour, that of deputy to Hillel, was given, at Herod's request, to Menahem, an Essene. He soon withdrew in favour of Shammâi, who was strict even to excess in his religious observances.

The two Synhedrists, Hillel and Shammâi, founded separate schools, opposed to one another in many religious, social, and judicial questions.* Graetz says nothing of the warfare which, according to al-Bîrûnî occurred between their respective followers. The latter may perhaps refer to the subsequent strife of the Zealots—Kannaim—a religious faction of whom Zadok, of the school of Shammâi, was the head.

* Graetz, vol. ii. pp. 96, 100, 131.

Day of the month.

13. Thanith Esther. Fast of Esther. Esther iv. 16 and ix. 31. Josephus, "Antiq.," xi. cap. vi. 8, 9, "Esther sent to Mordecai [to desire him] to go to Shushan, and to gather the Jews that were there together to a congregation, and to fast and abstain from all sorts of food, on her account, and [to let him know that] she with her maidens would do the same. . . . Accordingly, Mordecai did as Esther had enjoined him, and made the people fast."

If the thirteenth be a Sabbath this Fast is kept on the eleventh day.

14. Purim. The Feast of Lots. In memory of the deliverance of the Jews from the plot of Haman. Esther iii. 7, and ix. 24. Haman, the Agagite, the enemy of the Jews, had devised a plan for their destruction, and had cast lots, that is, Pur (a Persian word), "to consume them and to destroy them." These lots were cast by Haman in the first month of the year, and the lot fell upon the twelfth month as favourable for his design. The Jews therefore had time to prepare, and by help of Esther to remove the bad impressions against them which had been raised in the mind of Ahasuerus. It was upon Adhâr 14 that the Jews, led by Mordecai, smote their enemies and the ten sons of Haman. Esther ix. 5-17.

15. Schuschan Purim. The second Purim; the feast was kept at Susa on the day after Adhâr 14. Esther ix. 18.

On this day the half-shekel, payable by every Israelite, was collected in the cities; but on the twenty-fifth day in the Temple. Exodus xxx. 13, "This they shall give, every one that passeth among them that are numbered, half a shekel, after the shekel of the sanctuary: an half shekel shall be the offering of the LORD."

98. NÎSÂN.

The seventh month of the Civil year, the first of the Sacred year. It has thirty days.

1. Rôsh-chôdesh.

Day of the month.

2. Fast for the sons of Aaron, Nadab and Abihu, who "died before the LORD, when they offered strange fire before the LORD in the wilderness of Sinai," Numbers iii. 4, and xxvi. 61. The story of the offering of strange fire is told in Leviticus x. 1–7.

10. Fast for the death of Miriam, the sister of Moses and Aaron, Numbers iii. 4.

The lamb of the Passover selected, and "kept up until the fourteenth day," Exodus xii. 3, 6.

In the year when the Israelites were delivered from the Egyptian bondage, this tenth day of Nîsân fell upon the Sabbath. The Sabbath next before the Passover is, upon that account, called the Great Sabbath, and it is lawful to select the lamb for the Paschal service even on the Sabbath day, should the 10th of the month fall upon such a day, because the day of the month when this was to be done is precisely specified,* without reference to the fact that the tenth may be a Sabbath.

14. The Eve of the Passover. The lamb is slain and eaten in the evening. Exodus xii. 2–10, Leviticus xxiii. 5, Josephus, "Antiq." iii. cap. x. 5.

15. Pesach. The first day of the Feast of the Passover. First Day of Unleavened Bread. In the New Testament it is called *ἡ ἑορτὴ τῶν ἀζύμων*, and the days from the fourteenth to the twenty-first inclusive, *ἡμέραι τῶν αζύμων*.

The feast was instituted to commemorate the deliverance of the Israelites from their bondage in Egypt, with special reference to the fact that when the angel of the Lord smote all the first-born in Egypt, he passed over the dwellings of the Israelites, the two sides being sprinkled with the blood of the lamb. Exodus xii. 3–20, xiii. 6; Leviticus xxiii. 6. Josephus, "Antiq." iii. cap. x. 5.

The modern Jews do not continue the actual sacrifice of the Paschal lamb, which is represented in their service by the roasted shankbone of a lamb.

* Maimonides, "Tractatus de Sacrificio Paschali," De Veil, trans. i. 19. p. 9. "Jam victima paschalis ut sabbato consecraretur, concessum erat, quòd huic sacrificio dies status esset: similiter nihil erat, cur suum quisquam solemne sacrum ipso die festo consecrare religioni haberet."

Day of the month.

The Samaritans alone observe the rite according to the ancient ceremonial. The High Priest, now resident at Nablus, on the site of the ancient Samaria, performs the sacrifice.*

The Passover was one of the three great Feasts at which every male was to appear before the Lord. Deuteronomy xvi. 16. See Tishrî 15 and 16, Succoth and Sîwan 6, Schabuoth.

The Jews who do not dwell in Palestine add an additional day to the seven between Nîsân 15 and 22, in order to ensure that all, throughout the world, should keep the festival at the same time. The first two and the last two days are kept as Holy Days of Solemn Assembly.

16. The second day of the Passover. The first sheaf of barley harvest, gathered after sunset on the previous evening, to be offered before the LORD. This rite was instituted before the Israelites had reached the promised land, but it was not to be actually celebrated until they had come thither. Leviticus xxiii. 10, 11. Josephus, "Antiq.," iii. cap. x. 5. See Article 10, p. 13.

From this day commences the Sephira, or counting the days of the Omer, the seven weeks which elapse between the Passover and the Feast of Weeks, or Pentecost. No marriages are performed during these days, except on the thirty-third day. See Iyâr 18, Lag b'Omer. A special prayer is said in the evening of Nîsân 16, and is continued throughout the fifty days, with a declaration of the number of the day as it stands in the numerical order of the fifty.

17–20. Third, Fourth, Fifth, and Sixth days of Unleavened Bread.

21. The last day of Unleavened Bread. A day of Holy Convocation. Exodus xii. 16, "In the first day there shall be an holy convocation, and in the seventh day there shall be an holy convocation to you; no manner of work shall be done in them, save that which every man must eat, that only may be done by you."

* Jewish Year Book, 5659, A.D. 1898, pp. 285, 292.

Day of the month.

22. Eighth day of the Passover. This is the additional day observed by the Jews "of the exile," or those who dwell outside of Palestine.

26. Fast for the death of Joshua, the son of Nûn. Joshua xxiv. 29.

30. First Rôsh-chôdesh of Iyâr.

99. IYÂR.

Eighth month of the Civil, second month of the Sacred year. It has twenty-nine days.

1. Second Rôsh-chôdesh.

7. If the 7th be a Monday it is observed as the First Fast of Iyâr: a Fast of three days for any wrong done during the Feast of Passover. The three days are the Monday, the following Thursday, and the next Monday. If Iyâr 7 be not a Monday, then the Fast is kept in a similar way, but its first day is the Monday next after the 7th. Thus, in the year 5659, A.D. 1899, the Fast was kept on Monday, Iyâr 7 = April 17. In the preceding year it was Monday, Iyâr 10 = May 2.

10. Fast for the death of the High Priest Eli, and for the loss of the Ark which was taken by the Philistines. 1 Samuel iv. 11–18.

14. Pesach Scheni. Second Passover, ordained for those who, through uncleanness or from other causes, are prevented from keeping the Feast at the proper time in the month Nîsân. See Article 115.

18. Lag b'Omer. Feast of the thirty-third of the Omer, reckoned from Nîsân 16, the second day of the Passover inclusive.

Ideler states * that an old tradition belongs to this day concerning the pupils of the Rabbi Akîbâ, but he does not narrate it.

* "Handbuch," i. 566.

Day of the month.

The tradition is that a great mortality broke out among the pupils of the Rabbi, on the first day of the Omer, and that it ceased on this thirty-third day. Many of the stricter Jews retain the custom of not cutting the hair during these days to mark the mourning for the disciples of Akîbâ. He lived in the second century of the Christian Era. He was put to death with the most cruel torture by Turnus Rufus, the Governor under the Emperor Hadrian, in or about A.D. 139. Graetz says * that "the number of his hearers is exaggerated by tradition, which recounts them as twelve thousand, and even double that number; but a more modest record represents them as amounting to three hundred." He was one of the first compilers of the Mishna, was considered the head of the spiritual regeneration of Judaism, and was honoured as a legendary second Moses.†

28. Fast for the death of the prophet Samuel. 1 Samuel xxv. 1.

100. SÎWÂN.

Ninth month of the Civil, third of the Sacred year. It has thirty-one days.

1. Rôsh-chôdesh.

4, 5. Sanctification of the people before the Giving of the Law. Exodus xix. 10, 11, "And the LORD said unto Moses, Go unto the people and sanctify them to-day and to-morrow, and let them wash their clothes, And be ready against the third day."

6. Schabuoth. The Feast of the Congregation, or the Feast of Weeks, called also Asartha = Pentecost, because it was appointed to be held seven weeks, a week of weeks, after the Passover, Exodus xxxiv. 22. It is the fiftieth day after Nîsân 15, therefore called in Greek ἡμέρα τῆς πεντηκοστῆς, the reckoning being from "the morrow after the Sabbath," Leviticus xxiii. 15, 16, that is, from the first day of Holy Convocation of the Passover,

* Vol. ii. p. 357.

† "The Emperor Hadrian," by Ferdinand Gregorovicus; trans. by Mary E. Robinson. p. 145.

Day of the month.

Nîsân 15, inclusive; the word Sabbath being here used not for feria 7, but for "a day of rest."

This was one of the three great Festivals at which every male was to appear before the Lord.

The wheat harvest being now complete, one of the ceremonies of the day was the offering of two loaves of leavened bread "made from fine wheat flour, as first fruits unto the LORD," Leviticus xxiii. 17. This bread was eaten in the Temple in the evening, and nothing of it allowed to remain to the next day.

7. Second day of the Feast. According to the Law the Feast of the Congregation lasted for one day only, but since the time of the Babylonish Captivity the Jews in countries foreign to Palestine have observed it during two days, to meet the possibility of an error.

22. Fast in memory of the idolatry and rebellion under Jeroboam son of Nebat, who made Israel to sin. 1 Kings xii. 26–33, xiv. 16.

27. Fast for the death of Chananyâ who was burned with the scroll of the Law wrapped round him. He was the fourth of the seven martyrs executed by Turnus Rufus, the Governor, in the time of Hadrian; Akîbâ, previously mentioned, being the third. This was in or about A.D. 139.*

30. First Rôsh-chôdesh of Tammûz.

101. TAMMÛZ.

Tenth month of the Civil, fourth of the Sacred year. It has twenty-nine days.

1. Second Rôsh-chôdesh.

17. Scheba asar bethamuz. The Fast of Tammûz, kept in memory of five great misfortunes, though they did not all occur upon this day.

(1) Moses broke in pieces the first Tables of the Law. Exodus xxxii. 19.

* Graetz, vol. ii. p. 431.

Day of the month.

(2) Antiochus Epiphanes set up an image, "the abomination of desolation," upon the altar. 1 Maccabees i. 54. This was on the fifteenth day of the month Kislêw.

(3) The Greeks under Antiochus destroyed the Books of the Law. 1 Maccabees i. 56.

(4) The lamp which burned day and night in the Temple was extinguished by King Ahaz. Al-Bîrûnî ascribes this to Abh 28, "in the days of the prophet Ahaz," * which, Sachau says, "seems to be a mistake for Ahaz the King." *Cf.* 2 Chronicles xxix. 7, "They have shut up the doors of the porch, and have put out the lamps, and have not burned incense nor offered burnt offerings in the holy place unto the Lord God of Israel." Scaliger, also, gives the day as Abh 28.†

(5) The destruction of the fortifications of Jerusalem when Nebuchadnezzar besieged the city. This was on the ninth day of the month at midnight.

If this Fast fall upon the Sabbath it is kept upon the next day.

102. Abh.

Eleventh month of the Civil, fifth of the Sacred year. It has thirty days.

1. Rôsh-chôdesh. Fast for the death of Aaron the High Priest. Numbers xx. 28.

9. Fast of Abh on account of the decree against the Fathers in the wilderness that they should not enter into the promised land, Numbers xiv. 23. *Cf.* Zechariah vii. 5, "When ye fasted and mourned in the fifth and seventh month, even those seventy years, did ye at all fast unto Me, even to Me?"

This Fast is still observed. If the ninth day of the month fall upon the Sabbath, it is kept upon the next day.

On the same day took place the destruction of the first Temple by Nebuchadnezzar, A.M. 3338, B.C. 422; and of the second Temple by Titus, A.D. 70. It is called the Black Fast.

15. Tubeab. A minor Festival to commemorate the feast at

* "Vestiges," p. 276.

† "De Emend. Temp.," lib. vii. p. 651,C.

Day of the month.

Shiloh, and the reconciliation of the tribe of Benjamin. Judges xxi. 13–23.

22. Commemoration of the wood-offering "to burn upon the altar of the Lord," Nehemiah x. 34; xiii. 31. Called Xylophoria by the Greeks. Josephus, "Wars," ii. cap. xvii. 6, "Now the next day was the festival of Xylophoria, upon which the custom was for every one to bring wood for the altar, that there might never be a want of fuel for that fire which was unquenchable, and always burning." (See *post*, Article 115. Day IV.)

30. First Rôsh-chôdesh of 'Elûl.

103. 'Elûl.

Twelfth month of the Civil, sixth of the Sacred year. It has twenty-nine days.

1. Rôsh-chôdesh, second day.

7. Fast for the death of the Spies, who, with the exception of Joshua and Caleb, brought an evil report of the promised land to Moses, Numbers xiv. 36–38. Selden * places this Fast on the seventeenth day of the month. Al-Bîrûnî says that some Jews place this fast on the Monday or Thursday which falls within the last seven days before the beginning of the next year." †

According to Jacob ben Ascher this fast should be on 'Elûl 17. In the Megillath Ta'anith, 'Elûl 7 is given as a semi-festival in commemoration of the rebuilding of the Walls of Jerusalem by Nehemiah. (See *post*, Article 115. Day II.)

104. In the following Calendar for the months the serial numbers are given for the days of the years of all six forms. By means of these numbers the feria for any day of any month may be found, if the form of the year and the feria for Tishrî 1 be known.

For example:—Let the year be Common and Deficient, commencing with a Monday. In such a year Tammûz 17 has 282 for its serial number, which $= 7n + 2$. The n complete weeks beginning with a Monday must terminate with a Sunday, feria 1, and feria $(1 + 2)$ = feria 3 = Tuesday.

* "De Anno Civili," 1644, p. 36. † "Vestiges," p. 277.

Again:—Let the year be Embolismic and Abundant, commencing with a Thursday. In such a year the serial number for II. Adhar 14 is $193 = 7n + 4$. The complete weeks beginning with a Thursday terminate with a Wednesday, feria 4; and feria $(4 + 4) =$ feria 1 = Sunday.

105. The two Tables which follow the monthly Calendar show the feriæ for the Rôsh-chôdesh of each month, and for the principal Feasts and Fasts. Under the headings "Deficient," "Regular," &c., the leading numbers give the feriæ with which each form of year is able to commence. The remaining numbers in each column show the feriæ for the different days against which they are written.

Thus:—If the year be Common and Deficient, and commence with feria 7, the Fast of Guedaliah will be on feria 2; the Rôsh-chôdesh of Têbeth on feria 4, &c.

Table XVII. gives the Christian dates for the chief Feasts and Fasts, governed by that of Nîsân 15.

	TISHRÍ.	Common Year.			Embolismic.		
		Def.	Reg.	Ab.	Def.	Reg.	Ab.
1	Rôsh-Ha-schana. Feast of Trumpets	1	1	1	1	1	1
2	Second day of the Feast ,, ...	2	2	2	2	2	2
3	Fast of Guedaliah..............................	3	3	3	3	3	3
4		4	4	4	4	4	4
5		5	5	5	5	5	5
6		6	6	6	6	6	6
7	Fast for the decree against those who made the golden calf	7	7	7	7	7	7
8		8	8	8	8	8	8
9		9	9	9	9	9	9
10	Âshûrâ = Fast of Kippûr. Day of Atonement	10	10	10	10	10	10
11		11	11	11	11	11	11
12		12	12	12	12	12	12
13		13	13	13	13	13	13
14		14	14	14	14	14	14
15	Succoth = Feast of Tabernacles = Scenopegia	15	15	15	15	15	15
16	Second day of the Feast	16	16	16	16	16	16
17	Third ,, ,, ...	17	17	17	17	17	17
18	Fourth ,, ,, ...	18	18	18	18	18	18
19	Fifth ,, ,, ...	19	19	19	19	19	19
20	Sixth ,, ,, ...	20	20	20	20	20	20
21	Seventh ,, Hoshana Rabba..............	21	21	21	21	21	21
22	Schemeni Azereth = Feast of Benediction	22	22	22	22	22	22
23	Simchath Thorah = Rejoicing for the Law	23	23	23	23	23	23
24	(These eight days are all now reckoned as forming the Feast of Tabernacles.)	24	24	24	24	24	24
25		25	25	25	25	25	25
26		26	26	26	26	26	26
27		27	27	27	27	27	27
28		28	28	28	28	28	28
29		29	29	29	29	29	29
30	First Rôsh-chôdesh of Marheshwân	30	30	30	30	30	30

	MARḤESHWÂN.	Common Year. Def.	Common Year. Reg.	Common Year. Ab.	Embolismic. Def.	Embolismic. Reg.	Embolismic. Ab.
1	Second Rôsh-chôdesh	31	31	31	31	31	31
2		32	32	32	32	32	32
3		33	33	33	33	33	33
4		34	34	34	34	34	34
5		35	35	35	35	35	35
6	Fast of Zedekia	36	36	36	36	36	36
7		37	37	37	37	37	37
8		38	38	38	38	38	38
9		39	39	39	39	39	39
10		40	40	40	40	40	40
11		41	41	41	41	41	41
12		42	42	42	42	42	42
13		43	43	43	43	43	43
14		44	44	44	44	44	44
15		45	45	45	45	45	45
16		46	46	46	46	46	46
17		47	47	47	47	47	47
18		48	48	48	48	48	48
19		49	49	49	49	49	49
20		50	50	50	50	50	50
21		51	51	51	51	51	51
22		52	52	52	52	52	52
23		53	53	53	53	53	53
24		54	54	54	54	54	54
25		55	55	55	55	55	55
26		56	56	56	56	56	56
27		57	57	57	57	57	57
28		58	58	58	58	58	58
29		59	59	59	59	59	59
30	Intercalated day, and First Rôsh-chôdesh of Kislêw, in Abundant years	—	—	60	—	—	60

	KISLÊW.	Common Year.			Embolismic.		
		Def.	Reg.	Ab.	Def.	Reg.	Ab.
1	Rôsh-chôdesh. Second day in Abundant years	60	60	61	60	60	61
2		61	61	62	61	61	62
3		62	62	63	62	62	63
4		63	63	64	63	63	64
5		64	64	65	64	64	65
6		65	65	66	65	65	66
7		66	66	67	66	66	67
8	Fast. Yehoyakim burned the book written by the prophet Jeremiah	67	67	68	67	67	68
9		68	68	69	68	68	69
10		69	69	70	69	69	70
11		70	70	71	70	70	71
12		71	71	72	71	71	72
13		72	72	73	72	72	73
14		73	73	74	73	73	74
15		74	74	75	74	74	75
16		75	75	76	75	75	76
17		76	76	77	76	76	77
18		77	77	78	77	77	78
19		78	78	79	78	78	79
20	Prayer for rain	79	79	80	79	79	80
21		80	80	81	80	80	81
22		81	81	82	81	81	82
23		82	82	83	82	82	83
24		83	83	84	83	83	84
25	Chanukkâ = Feast of Purification of the Temple = Encoenia	84	84	85	84	84	85
26		85	85	86	85	85	86
27		86	86	87	86	86	87
28		87	87	88	87	87	88
29	Eliminated in a deficient year. First Rôsh-chôdesh of Têbeth in Regular and Abundant years	88	88	89	88	88	89
30		—	89	90	—	89	90

	TÊBETH.	Common Year. Def.	Reg.	Ab.	Embolismic. Def.	Reg.	Ab.
1	Rôsh-chôdesh. Second day in Regular and Abundant years	89	90	91	89	90	91
2		90	91	92	90	91	92
3		91	92	93	91	92	93
4		92	93	94	92	93	94
5	First appearance of the darkness of three days	93	94	95	93	94	95
6		94	95	96	94	95	96
7		95	96	97	95	96	97
8	Fast, for Greek translation of the Scriptures	96	97	98	96	97	98
9		97	98	99	97	98	99
10	Asarah Beteketh. Fast of Têbeth. Nebuchadnezzar commenced the siege of Jerusalem	98	99	100	98	99	100
11		99	100	101	99	100	101
12		100	101	102	100	101	102
13		101	102	103	101	102	103
14		102	103	104	102	103	104
15		103	104	105	103	104	105
16		104	105	106	104	105	106
17		105	106	107	105	106	107
18		106	107	108	106	107	108
19		107	108	109	107	108	109
20		108	109	110	108	109	110
21		109	110	111	109	110	111
22		110	111	112	110	111	112
23		111	112	113	111	112	113
24		112	113	114	112	113	114
25		113	114	115	113	114	115
26		114	115	116	114	115	116
27		115	116	117	115	116	117
28		116	117	118	116	117	118
29		117	118	119	117	118	119

	SHEBHÂT.	Common Year.			Embolismic.		
		Def.	Reg.	Ab.	Def.	Reg.	Ab.
1	Rôsh-chôdesh	118	119	120	118	119	120
2		119	120	121	119	120	121
3		120	121	122	120	121	122
4		121	122	123	121	122	123
5	Death of the Fathers in the time of Joshua	122	123	124	122	123	124
6		123	124	125	123	124	125
7		124	125	126	124	125	126
8		125	126	127	125	126	127
9		126	127	128	126	127	128
10		127	128	129	127	128	129
11		128	129	130	128	129	130
12		129	130	131	129	130	131
13		130	131	132	130	131	132
14		131	132	133	131	132	133
15	Rôsh-Ha-shana = Laylanot, New year of Trees	132	133	134	132	133	134
16		133	134	135	133	134	135
17		134	135	136	134	135	136
18		135	136	137	135	136	137
19		136	137	138	136	137	138
20		137	138	139	137	138	139
21		138	139	140	138	139	140
22		139	140	141	139	140	141
23	Fast for rebellion of tribe of Benjamin	140	141	142	140	141	142
24		141	142	143	141	142	143
25		142	143	144	142	143	144
26		143	144	145	143	144	145
27		144	145	146	144	145	146
28		145	146	147	145	146	147
29		146	147	148	146	147	148
30	First Rôsh-chôdesh of Adhâr	147	148	149	147	148	149

ADHAR I.		Common Year.		Embolismic.		
				Def.	Reg.	Ab.
1	Rôsh-chôdesh			148	149	150
2	Intercalated month in Embolismic years. It has no Fast or Feast Day, except the Rôsh-chôdesh.			149	150	151
3				150	151	152
4				151	152	153
5				152	153	154
6				153	154	155
7				154	155	156
8				155	156	157
9				156	157	158
10				157	158	159
11				158	159	160
12				159	160	161
13				160	161	162
14				161	162	163
15				162	163	164
16				163	164	165
17				164	165	166
18				165	166	167
19				166	167	168
20				167	168	169
21				168	169	170
22				169	170	171
23				170	171	172
24				171	172	173
25				172	173	174
26				173	174	175
27				174	175	176
28				175	176	177
29				176	177	178
30	First Rôsh-chôdesh of Adhâr II.			177	178	179

	ADHÂR II.	Common Year.			Embolismic.		
		Def.	Reg.	Ab.	Def.	Reg.	Ab.
1	Rôsh-chôdesh, second day	148	149	150	178	179	180
2		149	150	151	179	180	181
3		150	151	152	180	181	182
4		151	152	153	181	182	183
5		152	153	154	182	183	184
6		153	154	155	183	184	185
7	Fast for death of Moses	154	155	156	184	185	186
8		155	156	157	185	186	187
9	Fast for the strife between followers of Hillel and Shammâi........................	156	157	158	186	187	188
10		157	158	159	187	188	189
11		158	159	160	188	189	190
12		159	160	161	189	190	191
13	Thanith Esther. Fast of Esther	160	161	162	190	191	192
14	Purim. Fast of Lots	161	162	163	191	192	193
15	Schuschan Purim. Second Purim	162	163	164	192	193	194
16		163	164	165	193	194	195
17		164	165	166	194	195	196
18		165	166	167	195	196	197
19		166	167	168	196	197	198
20		167	168	169	197	198	199
21		168	169	170	198	199	200
22		169	170	171	199	200	201
23		170	171	172	200	201	202
24		171	172	173	201	202	203
25		172	173	174	202	203	204
26		173	174	175	203	204	205
27		174	175	176	204	205	206
28		175	176	147	205	206	207
29		176	177	178	206	207	208

ISAN.		Common Year.			Embolismic.		
		Def.	Reg.	Ab.	Def.	Reg.	Ab.
1	Rôsh-chôdesh. Fast for death of Nadab and Abihu	177	178	179	207	208	209
2		178	179	180	208	209	210
3		179	180	181	209	210	211
4		180	181	182	210	211	212
5		181	182	183	211	212	213
6		182	183	184	212	213	214
7		183	184	185	213	214	215
8		184	185	186	214	215	216
9		185	186	187	215	216	217
10	Fast for death of Miriam, sister of Moses...	186	187	188	216	217	218
11		187	188	189	217	218	219
12		188	189	190	218	219	220
13		189	190	191	219	220	221
14	Eve of Passover. Paschal Lamb slain......	190	191	192	220	221	222
15	Pesach. First day of Passover. First day of Unleavened Bread	191	192	193	221	222	223
16	Second day..	192	193	194	222	223	224
17	Third ,, ...	193	194	195	223	224	225
18	Fourth ,, ...	194	195	196	224	225	226
19	Fifth ,, ...	195	196	197	225	226	227
20	Sixth ,, ...	196	197	198	226	227	228
21	Seventh ,, Last day of Unleavened Bread	197	198	199	227	228	229
22	Eighth ,, observed by the Jews "of the Exile"..	198	199	200	228	229	230
23		199	200	201	229	230	231
24		200	201	202	230	231	232
25		201	202	203	231	232	233
26	Fast for death of Joshua, son of Nûn	202	203	204	232	233	234
27		203	204	205	233	234	235
28		204	205	206	234	235	236
29		205	206	207	235	236	237
30	First Rôsh-chôdesh of Iyâr....................	206	207	208	236	237	238

	IYÂR.	Common Year. Def.	Reg.	Ab.	Embolismic. Def.	Reg.	Ab.
1	Rôsh-chôdesh, second day	207	208	209	237	238	239
2		208	209	210	238	239	240
3	NOTE.—First, Second, and Third Fast of Iyâr on first Monday, and on the following Thursday and Monday.	209	210	211	239	240	241
4		210	211	212	240	241	242
5		211	212	213	241	242	243
6		212	213	214	242	243	244
7		213	214	215	243	244	245
8		214	215	216	244	245	246
9		215	216	217	245	246	247
10	Fast for death of Eli the High Priest, and the taking of the Ark	216	217	218	246	247	248
11		217	218	219	247	248	249
12		218	219	220	248	249	250
13		219	220	221	249	250	251
14		220	221	222	250	251	252
15		221	222	223	251	252	253
16		222	223	224	252	253	254
17		223	224	225	253	254	255
18	Lag b'omer. Feast of the thirty-third day of the Omer........................	224	225	226	254	255	256
19		225	226	227	255	256	257
20		226	227	228	256	257	258
21		227	228	229	257	258	259
22		228	229	230	258	259	260
23		229	230	231	259	260	261
24		230	231	232	260	261	262
25		231	232	233	261	262	263
26		232	233	234	262	263	264
27		233	234	235	263	264	265
28	Fast for death of Samuel the Prophet ...	234	235	236	264	265	266
29		235	236	237	265	266	267

	SIWÂN.	Common Year. Def.	Common Year. Reg.	Common Year. Ab.	Embolismic. Def.	Embolismic. Reg.	Embolismic. Ab.
1	Rôsh-chôdesh	236	237	238	266	267	268
2		237	238	239	267	268	269
3		238	239	240	268	269	270
4	Scheloschah jeme hagbalah. Sanctification of the People	239	240	241	269	270	271
5	Second day of Sanctification	240	241	242	270	271	272
6	Schabuoth. Feast of the Congregation. Pentecost	241	242	243	271	272	273
7	Second day of the Feast	242	243	244	272	273	274
8		243	244	245	273	274	275
9		244	245	246	274	275	276
10		245	246	247	275	276	277
11		246	247	248	276	277	278
12		247	248	249	277	278	279
13		248	249	250	278	279	280
14		249	250	251	279	280	281
15		250	251	252	280	281	282
16		251	252	253	281	282	283
17		252	253	254	282	283	284
18		253	254	255	283	284	285
19		254	255	256	284	285	286
20		255	256	257	285	286	287
21		256	257	258	286	287	288
22	Fast for Golden Calves of Jeroboam	257	258	259	287	288	289
23		258	259	260	288	289	290
24		259	260	261	289	290	291
25		260	261	262	290	291	292
26		261	262	263	291	292	293
27	Fast for death of R. Chananyâ	262	263	264	292	293	294
28		263	264	265	293	294	295
29		264	265	266	294	295	296
30	First Rôsh-chôdesh of Tammûz	265	266	267	295	296	297

TAMMÚZ.		Common Year.			Embolismic.		
		Def.	Reg.	Ab.	Def.	Reg.	Ab.
1	Rôsh-chôdesh, second day	266	267	268	296	297	298
2		267	268	269	297	298	299
3		268	269	270	298	299	300
4		269	270	271	299	300	301
5		270	271	272	300	301	302
6		271	272	273	301	302	303
7		272	273	274	302	303	304
8		273	274	275	303	304	305
9		274	275	276	304	305	306
10		275	276	277	305	306	307
11		276	277	278	306	307	308
12		277	278	279	307	308	309
13		278	279	280	308	309	310
14		279	280	281	309	310	311
15		280	281	282	310	311	312
16		281	282	283	311	312	313
17	Fast of Tammûz	282	283	284	312	313	314
18		283	284	285	313	314	315
19		284	285	286	314	315	316
20		285	286	287	315	316	317
21		286	287	288	316	317	318
22		287	288	289	317	318	319
23		288	289	290	318	319	320
24		289	290	291	319	320	321
25		290	291	292	320	321	322
26		291	292	293	321	322	323
27		292	293	294	322	323	324
28		293	294	295	323	324	325
29		294	295	296	324	325	326

	ABH.	Common Year. Def.	Reg.	Ab.	Embolismic. Def.	Reg.	Ab.
1	Rôsh-chôdesh. Fast for death of Aaron	295	296	297	325	326	327
2		296	297	298	326	327	328
3		297	298	299	327	328	329
4		298	299	300	328	329	330
5		299	300	301	329	330	331
6		300	301	302	330	331	332
7		301	302	303	331	332	333
8	Fast for Decree against the Israelites in the wilderness, and destruction of First and Second Temples: called Fast of Âbh	302	303	304	332	333	334
9		303	304	305	333	334	335
10		304	305	306	334	335	336
11		305	306	307	335	336	337
12		306	307	308	336	337	338
13		307	308	309	337	338	339
14		308	309	310	338	339	340
15	Tubeab. Reconciliation of tribe of Benjamin	309	310	311	339	340	341
16		310	311	312	340	341	342
17		311	312	313	341	342	343
18		312	313	314	342	343	344
19		313	314	315	343	344	345
20		314	315	316	344	345	346
21		315	316	317	345	346	347
22	Xylophoria. Wood offering for the Altar	316	317	318	346	347	348
23		317	318	319	347	348	349
24		318	319	320	348	349	350
25		319	320	321	349	350	351
26		320	321	322	350	351	352
27		321	322	323	351	352	353
28		322	323	324	352	353	354
29		323	324	325	353	354	355
30	First Rôsh-chôdesh of Elûl	324	325	326	354	355	356

	ELÛL.	Common Year.			Embolismic.		
		Def.	Reg.	Ab.	Def.	Reg.	Ab.
1	Rôsh-chôdesh, Second day	325	326	327	355	356	357
2		326	327	328	356	357	358
3		327	328	329	357	358	359
4		328	329	330	358	359	360
5		329	330	331	359	360	361
6		330	331	332	360	361	362
7	Fast, Death of the Spies who brought an evil report to Moses	331	332	333	361	362	363
8		332	333	334	362	363	364
9		333	334	335	363	364	365
10		334	335	336	364	365	366
11		335	336	337	365	366	367
12		336	337	338	366	367	368
13		337	338	339	367	368	369
14		338	339	340	368	369	370
15		339	340	341	369	370	371
16		340	341	342	370	371	372
17		341	342	343	371	372	373
18		342	343	344	372	373	374
19		343	344	345	373	374	375
20		344	345	346	374	375	376
21		345	346	347	375	376	377
22		346	347	348	376	377	378
23		347	348	349	377	378	379
24		348	349	350	378	379	380
25		349	350	351	379	380	381
26		350	351	352	380	381	382
27		351	352	353	381	382	383
28		352	353	354	382	383	384
29		353	354	355	383	384	385

FERIÆ FOR NEW MOONS AND DAYS TO BE OBSERVED.
(ARTICLE 105.)

Month, and Day of Month.		Days to be observed. R.C.=Rôsh-Chôdesh.	Common Years. Deficient.		Regular.		Abundant.		
Tishri	1	R.C. of Tishri	2	7	3	5	2	5	7
"	3	Fast of Guedaliah	4	2	5	1*	4	1*	2
"	10	Day of Atonement	4	2	5	7	4	7	2
"	15	Feast of Tabernacles	2	7	3	5	2	5	7
"	21	Hoshana Raba.....................	1	6	2	4	1	4	6
"	23	Feast of the Law	3	1	4	6	3	6	1
"	30	First R.C. of Marheshwan......	3	1	4	6	3	6	1
Marheshwan	1	Second " "	4	2	5	7	4	7	2
"	30	First R.C. of Kislêw	—	—	—	—	5	1	3
Kislêw	1	Second " "	—	—	—	—	6	2	4
Kislêw	1	R.C. of Kislêw.....................	5	3	6	1	—	—	—
"	25	Purification of Temple	1	6	2	4	2	5	7
"	30	First R.C. of Têbeth	—	—	7	2	7	3	5
Têbeth	1	Second " "	—	—	1	3	1	4	6
Têbeth	1	R.C. of Têbeth.....................	6	4	—	—	—	—	—
"	10	Fast of Têbeth.....................	1	6	3	5	3	6	1
Schebhât	1	R.C. of Schêbhat	7	5	2	4	2	5	7
"	30	First R.C. of Adhâr	1	6	3	5	3	6	1
Adhâr	1	Second " "	2	7	4	6	4	7	2
"	13	Fast of Esther.....................	5†	5	2	4	2	5	5†
"	14	Purim	1	6	3	5	3	6	1
"	15	Schushan Purim..................	2	7	4	6	4	7	2
Nisân	1	R.C. of Nisân	3	1	5	7	5	1	3
"	15	Passover	3	1	5	7	5	1	3
"	21	Seventh day of Passover	2	7	4	6	4	7	2
"	30	First R.C. of Iyâr	4	2	6	1	6	2	4
Iyâr	1	Second " "	5	3	7	2	7	3	5
"	18	Lag b'Omer	1	6	3	5	3	6	1
Siwân	1	R.C. of Siwân	6	4	1	3	1	4	6
"	6	Feast of Weeks	4	2	6	1	6	2	4
"	30	First R.C. of Tammûz	7	5	2	4	2	5	7
Tammûz	1	Second " "	1	6	3	5	3	6	1
"	17	Fast of Tammûz..................	3	1	5	1	5	1	3
Abh	1	R.C. of Abh	2	7	4	6	4	7	2
"	9	Destruction of Temple	3	1	5	7	5	1	3
"	30	First R.C. of 'Elûl	3	1	5	7	5	1	3
'Elûl	1	Second " "	4	2	6	1	6	2	4

* The Fast of Guedaliah falls to feria 7, and is observed on the next day.

† The Fast of Esther falls to feria 7, and is therefore kept on the previous Thursday.

FERIÆ FOR NEW MOONS AND DAYS TO BE OBSERVED.

Month, and Day of Month.		Days to be observed. R.C. = Rôsh-Chôdesh.	Embolismic Years.						
			Deficient.			Regular.	Abundant.		
Tishrî	1	R.C. of Tishrî	2	5	7	3	2	5	7
,,	3	Fast of Guedaliah	4	1*	2	5	4	1	2
,,	10	Day of Atonement	4	7	2	5	4	7	2
,,	15	Feast of Tabernacles	2	5	7	3	2	5	7
,,	21	Hoshana Raba	1	4	6	2	1	4	6
,,	23	Feast of the Law	3	6	1	4	3	6	1
,,	30	First R.C. of Marḥeshwan ...	3	6	1	4	3	6	1
Marḥeshwan	1	Second ,, ,, ...	4	7	2	5	4	7	2
,,	30	First R.C. of Kislêw	—	—	—	—	5	1	3
Kislêw	1	Second ,, ,, ...	—	—	—	—	6	2	4
Kislêw	1	R.C. of Kislêw....................	5	1	3	6	—	—	—
,,	25	Purification of the Temple ...	1	4	6	2	2	5	7
,,	30	First R.C. of Têbeth	—	—	—	7	7	3	5
Têbeth	1	Second ,, ,, ...	—	—	—	1	1	4	6
Têbeth	1	R.C. of Têbeth....................	6	2	4	—	—	—	—
,,	10	Fast of Têbeth....................	1	4	6	3	3	6	1
Schebhât	1	R.C. of Schebhât	7	3	5	2	2	5	7
,,	30	First R.C. of Adhâr I.	1	4	6	3	3	6	1
Adhâr I.	1	Second ,, ,, ...	2	5	7	4	4	7	2
,,	30	First R.C. of Adhar II.	3	6	1	5	5	1	3
Adhâr II.	1	Second ,, ,, ...	4	7	2	6	6	2	4
,,	13	Fast of Esther....................	2	5	5‡	4	4	5‡	2
,,	14	Purim	3	6	1	5	5	1	3
,,	15	Schushan Purim.................	4	7	2	6	6	2	4
Nîsân	1	R.C. of Nîsân	5	1	3	7	7	3	5
,,	15	Passover	5	1	3	7	7	3	5
,,	21	Seventh day of Passover	4	7	2	6	6	2	4
,,	30	First R.C. of Iyâr	6	2	4	1	1	4	6
Iyâr	1	Second ,, ,, ...	7	3	5	2	2	5	7
,,	18	Lag b'Omer	3	6	1	5	5	1	3
Sîwân	1	R.C. of Sîwân	1	4	6	3	3	6	1
,,	6	Feast of Weeks	6	2	4	1	1	4	6
,,	30	First R.C. of Tammûz	2	5	7	4	4	7	2
Tammûz	1	Second ,, ,, ...	3	6	1	5	5	1	3
,,	17	Fast of Tammûz.................	5	1	3	1†	1†	3	5
Abh	1	R.C. of Abh........................	4	7	2	6	6	2	4
,,	9	Destruction of Temple	5	1	3	1†	1†	3	5
,,	30	First R.C. of 'Elûl	5	1	3	7	7	3	5
'Elûl	1	Second ,, ,, ...	6	2	4	1	1	4	6

* Fast of Guedaliah falls to feria 7; therefore observed on the next day.
† Fast of Tammûz, and fast of Abh fall to feria 7; therefore observed on the next day.
‡ Fast of Esther falls to feria 7; therefore kept on previous Thursday.

CHAPTER VIII

THE FORMULA OF DR. GAUSS FOR FINDING THE CHRISTIAN DATE OF THE JEWISH PASSOVER

106. The "Berechnung des Jüdischen Osterfestes," by Dr. Gauss, the celebrated German mathematician, was published in the "Monatliche Correspondenz vom Freyherrn von Zach," b. 5, p. 435. Gotha, 1802.

The formula is there given without any demonstration of the method by which it was obtained. This demonstration was, however, supplied by M. le Chevalier Casa Gresy in the "Correspondance Astronomique, etc., du Baron de Zach," tom. i. p. 556. Gênes, 1818.

The formula is given also by Dr. Adolf Schwarz in "Der Jüdische Kalender," p. 72 (Breslau, 1872), but without demonstration.

The following is by no means a literal translation or transcript of the contribution by Casa Gresy, neither does it pursue precisely the same lines, but it must be understood that, with certain modifications, it is derived from his paper upon the subject.

He commences with an account of the elements of the Jewish Calendar, which need not be here repeated; they have already been fully described. It is only necessary to state again that the Jewish Era commences with the Molad 2d. 5h. 204ch., or the fictitious New Moon which is supposed to have occurred on Monday, October 7, in the year of the Julian Period 953, B.C. 3761, at 5h. 204ch. after 6 in the evening, that is, at 11h. 204ch. p.m.; and that the Christian Era commenced at the midnight which was the commencement of the year 4714 of the Julian Period, or Saturday, January 1, A.D. 1.

Every subsequent Julian year has commenced with the same day of the month, but the commencement of the Jewish years is variable. Tishrî 1 may occur in either August, September, or October; that is to say, the year commences in the Autumnal season, but the actual day with which it commences has to be determined for each year.

It follows that, because $4714 - 953 = 3761$, any given Jewish year, H, must commence in the Autumn of the Julian year $H - 3761$. Also, if B be the Julian year in which the Jewish year H terminates and $H + 1$ commences in the Autumn, then $B = H + 1 - 3761 = H - 3760$.

There is a reason for introducing the Jewish year $H + 1$. There are invariably 163 days from the Passover in any year H to Tishrî 1 of the next year $H + 1$; so that if the Julian date of Tishrî 1 in the year $H + 1$ be found, the date of the Passover in the year H is obtained at once by the subtraction of 163 days.

107. The day upon which Tishrî 1 is to be observed is governed by the day of the computed New Moon of Tishrî, and in order to find the Julian date for this New Moon in any given year $H + 1$, it is necessary, in the first place, to ascertain the interval of time which has elapsed since the commencement of the Jewish Era up to the close of the year H. This interval must be measured in Julian Civil years and parts of a year. The addition of one day to this interval will give the date for the first day in the year $H + 1$.

Measured in Jewish years, the interval will, of course, be exactly H years. Some of these H years will be Common, and some will be Embolismic.

Let e = the number of Common years in these H years,
and E = ,, Embolismic ,, ,,
so that $e + E = H$, or $E = H - e$.

Each of the Common years is shorter by 10d. 21h. 204ch., and each of the Embolismic years is longer by 18d. 15h. 589ch. than a mean Julian year of 365d. 6h., the Jewish years being Astronomically computed.

If, therefore, there be an interval of time which contains exactly H Jewish years, the same interval when measured by Julian mean years will contain—

(*a*).........H − e (10d. 21h. 204ch.) + E (18d. 15h. 589ch.).

Also, because in every number of Julian Civil years, such number not being a multiple of 4, there may be 18, or 12, or 6 hours less than in the same number of Julian mean years, it follows that H Julian mean years have, for their equivalent in Civil years, H + 6h. × (the remainder after dividing H by 4). In other words—

$$\text{H mean Julian years} = \left(\text{H} + 6\text{h.} \times \left\{\frac{\text{H}}{4}\right\}_r\right) \text{ Civil Julian years.}$$

The interval of time under consideration must be measured by Julian Civil years, and therefore this value must be substituted for H in expression (*a*), which then becomes—

$$(b) \ldots\ldots \text{H} + 6\text{h.}\left\{\frac{\text{H}}{4}\right\}_r - e\,(10\text{d. } 21\text{h. } 204\text{ch.})^{*} + \text{E}\,(18\text{d. } 15\text{h. } 589\text{ch.}).$$

This, then, is the interval of time, measured in Julian Civil years and parts of a year, from 11h. 204ch. p.m. on Monday, October 7, B.C. 3761, up to the termination of the Jewish year H, by the Astronomical computation, that is, up to the termination of the last Lunation of the year. By the addition of one day to this interval, the integral part of the sum of the terms in the expression will give the computed first day for the Moon of Tishrî in the next Jewish year, H + 1, which is therefore indicated by—

$$(c) \ldots 1\text{d.} + \text{H} + 6\text{h.}\left\{\frac{\text{H}}{4}\right\}_r - e\,(10\text{d. } 21\text{h. } 204\text{ch.}) + \text{E}\,(18\text{d. } 15\text{h. } 589\text{ch.}).$$

It will be more convenient to reckon from Noon of October 1, B.C. 3761, than from 11h. 204ch. p.m. of October 7. The interval of time between these two bases is 6 whole days and 11h. 204ch. of another day. Consequently, if the reckoning be made from Noon, October 1, the Julian date for the first day of the computed Moon of Tishrî in the Jewish year H + 1 will be indicated by the integral part of the sum of the terms in the expression—

$$(d) \ldots\ldots\ldots\ldots 7\text{d. } 11\text{h. } 204\text{ch.} + \text{H} + 6\text{h.}\left\{\frac{\text{H}}{4}\right\}_r - e\,(10\text{d. } 21\text{h. } 204\text{ch.}) + \text{E}\,(18\text{d. } 15\text{h. } 589\text{ch.}),$$

* There is a self-evident misprint here in the demonstration of Casa Gresy as given in the "Correspondance du Zach." The third term of the expression is made +^{e} instead of —^{e}.

in which the first term, 1d., of expression (*c*) is increased by 6d. 11h. 204ch.

There is, however, no necessity for reckoning from so distant a base as the Noon of October 1, B.C. 3761. The reckoning may be made from the Noon of October 1 in the Julian year B, in which the Jewish year H terminates, which is H years nearer to the required date. If the reckoning be thus made, these H years must be dropped from the expression (*d*), which then becomes—

$$(e)\ldots\ldots\ldots\ldots 7\text{d. }11\text{h. }204\text{ch.} + 6\text{h.}\left\{\frac{H}{4}\right\}_r - e\,(10\text{d. }21\text{h. }204\text{ch.}) + E\,(18\text{d. }15\text{h. }589\text{ch.}),$$

indicating the first day of the Moon of Tishrî in the Jewish year H + 1, measured from Noon, October 1, of the Julian year B.

If, in this expression, there be substituted for E its equivalent $H - e$, we have—

$$7\text{d. }11\text{h. }204\text{ch.} + 6\text{h.}\left\{\frac{H}{4}\right\}_r - e\,(10\text{d. }21\text{h. }204\text{ch.}) - e\,(18\text{d. }15\text{h. }589\text{ch.}) + H\,(18\text{d. }15\text{h. }589\text{ch.}),$$

or—

$$(f)\ldots\ldots\ldots 7\text{d. }11\text{h. }204\text{ch.} + 6\text{h.}\left\{\frac{H}{4}\right\}_r - e\,(29\text{d. }12\text{h. }793\text{ch.}) + H\,(18\text{d. }15\text{h. }589\text{ch.}).$$

The number of Common years in H Jewish years, which number is expressed by *e*, is the integral part of the quotient when $12H + 17$ is divided by 19; or—

$$e = \left\{\frac{12H + 17}{19}\right\}.^*$$

By substituting this value of *e* in the last expression, it becomes—

$$(g)\ldots 7\text{d. }11\text{h. }204\text{ch.} + 6\text{h.}\left\{\frac{H}{4}\right\}_r - \left\{\frac{12H + 17}{19}\right\}(29\text{d. }12\text{h. }793\text{ch.}) + H\,(18\text{d. }15\text{h. }589\text{ch.}).$$

* See Note at the end of this Chapter.

In order to reduce this expression to the formula of Gauss, it must be noticed that—

$$\left\{\frac{12\,\mathrm{H}+17}{19}\right\} = \frac{1}{19}\left(12\,\mathrm{H}+17-\left\{\frac{12\,\mathrm{H}+17}{19}\right\}_r\right)^*$$
$$= \frac{12}{19}\mathrm{H}+\frac{17}{19}-\frac{1}{19}\left\{\frac{12\,\mathrm{H}+17}{19}\right\}_r.$$

Substitute this value of $\left\{\frac{12\,\mathrm{H}+17}{19}\right\}$ in expression (g), and it becomes—

$$7\text{d. }11\text{h. }204\text{ch.} + 6\text{h.}\left\{\frac{\mathrm{H}}{4}\right\}_r - \frac{12}{19}\mathrm{H}\,(29\text{d. }12\text{h. }793\text{ch.})$$
$$-\frac{17}{19}(29\text{d. }12\text{h. }793\text{ch.}) + \frac{1}{19}\left\{\frac{12\,\mathrm{H}+17}{19}\right\}_r \times (29\text{d. }12\text{h. }793\text{ch.})$$
$$+\,\mathrm{H}\,(18\text{d. }15\text{h. }589\text{ch.}),$$

where the integral part of the sum of the terms expresses the number of days reckoned from October 1 of the Julian year B to the first day of the Moon of Tishrî in the Jewish year H + 1, both days inclusive.

But the Moon of Tishrî and the first day of the Jewish year most frequently occur before October 1, and sometimes before September 1; it will therefore be convenient to reckon the days from the first day of some month before the Autumnal season commences. It is a matter of indifference, thus far, which of the earlier months be taken, but as the Passover always occurs after March 1, it will be well to take that day for the point of departure. If this basis be adopted, 214 days must be added to the expression above, on account of the number of days, contained in the Christian months, from March 1 to September 30, both inclusive.

Let this addition be made; the first term of the expression then becomes 221d. 11h. 204ch.

* The equivalent of $\left\{\frac{12\,\mathrm{H}+17}{19}\right\}$ is thus obtained:—

Let the integral part of the quotient of $12\,\mathrm{H}+17$ when divided by 19 be n, and the remainder, or $\left\{\frac{12\,\mathrm{H}+17}{19}\right\}_r$ be r.

Then— $12\,\mathrm{H}+17 = 19n + r$, or $12\,\mathrm{H}+17-r = 19n$.

The value of $\left\{\frac{12\,\mathrm{H}+17}{19}\right\}$ is therefore found by dividing $12\,\mathrm{H}+17-r$ by 19.

Also, for greater simplicity, write a for $\left\{\frac{12\,H + 17}{19}\right\}_r$, and b for $\left\{\frac{H}{4}\right\}_r$.

Collect the similar terms; reduce the hours and Chalaḳim to fractions of a day; and the expression becomes—

$$195\frac{4343}{98496} + \frac{b}{4} + 1\frac{272953}{492480}a - \frac{313}{98496}H,\text{*}$$

or—

(I.)......$195{\cdot}0440932 + {\cdot}25\,b + 1{\cdot}5542418\,a - {\cdot}003177794\,H.$

This is the First Formula of Dr. Gauss, for computing the New Moon of Tishrî of the year H + 1.

If, instead of the Jewish year H, the corresponding Julian year B be employed, we have $H = B + 3760$; consequently—

a, or $\left\{\frac{12\,H + 17}{19}\right\}_r$, becomes $= \left\{\frac{12\,B + 45137}{19}\right\}_r = \left\{\frac{12B + 12}{19}\right\}_r$,

and b, or $\left\{\frac{H}{4}\right\}_r$, becomes $= \left\{\frac{B + 3760}{4}\right\}_r = \left\{\frac{B}{4}\right\}_r$.

In this way both a and b are expressed in terms of B, and it only

* (1) $221\text{d. }11\text{h. }204\text{ch.} - \frac{17}{19}(29\text{d. }12\text{h. }793\text{ch.}) = 221\frac{12084}{1080 \times 24} - 26\frac{207881}{19 \times 1080 \times 24}$

$= 195\frac{229596 - 207881}{19 \times 1080 \times 24} = 195\frac{21715}{19 \times 1080 \times 24} = 195\frac{4343}{98496}.$

(2) $\frac{1}{19}(29\text{d. }12\text{h. }793\text{ch.}) = 1\text{d.} + \frac{10\text{d. }12\text{h. }793\text{ch.}}{19} = 1\frac{272953}{19 \times 1080 \times 24}.$

(3) $-\frac{12}{19}(29\text{d. }12\text{h. }793\text{ch.}) + 18\text{d. }15\text{h. }589\text{ch.}$

$= \frac{1}{19}(354\text{d. }7\text{h. }391\text{ch.} - 354\text{d. }8\text{h. }876\text{ch.})$

$= -\frac{1}{19}(0\text{d. }1\text{h. }485\text{ch.}) = -\frac{1565}{19 \times 1080 \times 24} = -\frac{313}{98496}$

remains to substitute B + 3760 for H in the First Formula, which then becomes—

$$195{\cdot}0440932 + {\cdot}25\,b + 1{\cdot}554218\,a - {\cdot}003177794\,(B + 3760),$$

or—

$$\text{(II.)}\ldots\ldots\ldots 183{\cdot}0955877 + {\cdot}25\,b + 1{\cdot}554218\,a - {\cdot}003177794\,B.$$

This is the Second Formula of Dr. Gauss for the New Moon of Tishrî.

These two formulæ are equivalent. They each give the computed date for the New Moon of Tishrî in the Jewish year H + 1, measured in days reckoned from March 1, inclusive, of the corresponding Julian year B, or H − 3760.

108. As the Feast of the Passover, Nîsân 15, in the year H is 163 days earlier than Tishrî 1 of the year H + 1, it is only necessary to subtract this number of days from each of the two formulæ, and we have the computed date for Nîsân 15 in the year H—

$$\text{(III.)}\ldots\ldots\ldots 32{\cdot}0440932 + {\cdot}25\,b + 1{\cdot}5542418\,a - {\cdot}003177794\,H.$$

$$\text{(IV.)}\ldots\ldots\ldots 20{\cdot}0955877 + {\cdot}25\,b + 1{\cdot}5542418\,a - {\cdot}003177794\,B.$$

It will be noticed that in each of the two formulæ the first term does not involve either H, B, *a*, or *b*, or any other variable. It is a constant in each of the formulæ.

With respect to the decimals: After substituting for H, B, *a*, and *b* their values as determined by the given year in which the Julian date of Nîsân 15 is required, let M be the integral, and *m* the decimal part of the sum of the terms.

M + *m* is obtained from whichever formula be employed; and, neglecting for the present the decimal part, *m*, the Julian date of Tishrî 1 will be the Mth day of March * as obtained from (I.) or (II.), while that of Nîsân 15 will be the Mth day of March as obtained from (III.) or (IV.), assuming that there be nothing in the rules of the Jewish Calendar to cause a postponement from the computed day.

The important question of a possible postponement must now be considered. The feriæ 2, 4, and 6, Monday, Wednesday, and Friday, are forbidden for the Passover, and the feriæ 1, 4, and 6, Sunday, Wednesday, and Friday, are forbidden for Tishrî 1.

The week-day for the Mth day of March can always be ascertained

* April 1, 2, 3, &c., are counted as March 32, 33, 34, &c.

by means of the Sunday Letter for the Christian year corresponding to the given Jewish year, by the ordinary rules of the Julian Calendar. This must first be done, and if a postponement from the Mth to the next day be required, such postponement must be made.

There are, however, other rules besides ADU which may render necessary a postponement of Tishrî 1 from the computed day of New Moon.

(1) Let n be the numerical value of the computed feria for Nîsân 15 in the Jewish year H, counting Sunday as 1, Monday as 2, Tuesday as 3, &c. In other words, let n be the numerical value of the week-day for the Mth day of March as found by the formula.

Let t be the numerical value of the computed feria for Tishrî 1 in the following Jewish year H + 1.

Then—

$$t = \left\{\frac{n+163}{7}\right\}_r = \left\{\frac{n+2}{7}\right\}_r,$$

because Tishrî 1 in the year H + 1 is always 163 days later than Nîsân 15 in the year H.

The rule GaTRaD requires that if the computed time for the New Moon of Tishrî fall upon feria 3, Tuesday, so late as or later than 9h. 204ch. after 6 in the evening, that is, if it fall so late as or later than 15h. 204ch. after Noon, and if also the year be Common, then Tishrî 1 has to be postponed to the next day, feria 4, Wednesday, and thence, by ADU, to feria 5, Thursday.

Now, if it be found by the formula that $t = 3$, it is evident that n must be 1, for—

$$t = 3 = \left\{\frac{n+2}{7}\right\}_r,$$

$$\therefore n = 1, \text{ or } 8, \text{ or } 15, \&c.,$$

each of which numbers indicate feria 1.

If, therefore, $n = 1$, and the decimal part of the sum of the terms in the formula, namely m, be equal to or greater than 15h. 204ch., that is to say, if m be equal to or greater than $\cdot 632870\dot{3}$,* and if also

* Let it be remembered that the formula measures the time elapsed from Noon.

$$\begin{array}{r|l} 1080 & 204 \\ \hline 24 & 15\cdot 188 \\ & \overline{\cdot 632870\dot{3}} \end{array}$$

the year H + 1 be Common, then Nîsân 15 of the year H, which is found by the formula, must be postponed from the day found by the formula to the next day, feria 2, Monday. This day is forbidden by BaDU, and there must be a further postponement to feria 3, Tuesday.

(2) If Tishrî 1 be found by the computation to fall upon feria 2, Monday, so late as or later than 15h. 589ch. after 6 in the evening, that is to say, so late as or later than 21h. 589ch. after Noon, and if also the preceding year be Embolismic, then Tishrî 1 is to be postponed to feria 3, Tuesday.

Now, if it be found by the formula that $t = 2$, it is evident that n must be 7, for—

$$t = 2 = \left\{ \frac{n+2}{7} \right\}_r,$$

$$\therefore n = 0, \text{ or } 7, \text{ or } 14, \&c.,$$

each of which values indicates feria 7.

If, therefore, $n = 7$, and the decimal part of the sum of the terms in the formula be equal to or greater than 21h. 589ch., that is to say, if m be equal to or greater than ·897723765, and if also H be an Embolismic year, then Nîsân 15 must be postponed to the (M + 1)th day, which will be feria 1, or Sunday.

(3) There is one other rule of the Calendar, but it does not affect the date given by the formula.

If the New Moon of Tishrî, as computed, fall upon any day of the week so late as or later than 18h. after 6 in the evening, that is to say, so late as, or later than, Noon, then Tishrî 1 is postponed to the following day.

In this case n, or the feria of Nîsân 15 in the preceding year H, will also be a day later.

In the formula the reckoning of time is from Noon. It is made from a point of departure six hours earlier than that of the Jewish reckoning. But the rule regarding the eighteen hours has reference to the Jewish reckoning. The value of $M + m$ has in fact been augmented by six hours, or ·25 of a day.

No matter how great may be the sum of the decimals in the formula, they can never by any possibility be greater than ·9, and when this sum is diminished by ·25 in order to bring it back to the Jewish Epoch, and so to bring it within the rule, it can never possibly amount to ·75 of a day, that is, to 18h. Therefore the effect of this particular rule is entirely excluded when the formula is employed; and it remains, so far as this rule is concerned, that the Mth day of March will be the date of Nîsân 15, the decimal being neglected whether it be great or small.

In finding the dates of Nîsân 15 in the year H, or of Tishrî 1 in the year H + 1, by means of the formula, it will be seen that a, or $\left\{\frac{12\,H + 17}{19}\right\}_r$, which may be of any value from 0 to 18, has to be multiplied by 1·5542418; also, the multiplier both for H and for B is ·003177794. The following Tables of Products will facilitate the computation:—

a	$a \times$ 1·5542418.	H or B.	·003177794 × H or B.
1	1·5542418	1	·003177794
2	3·1084836	2	·006355588
3	4·6627254	3	·009533382
4	6·2169672	4	·012711176
5	7·7712090	5	·015888970
6	9·3254508	6	·019066764
7	10·8796926	7	·022244558
8	12·4339344	8	·025422352
9	13·9881762	9	·028600146
10	15·5424180	11	·034955734
11	17·0966598	12	·038133528
12	18·6509016	13	·041311322
13	20·2051434	14	·044489116
14	21·7593852	15	·047666910
15	23·3136270	16	·050844704
16	24·8678688	17	·054022498
17	26·4221106	18	·057200292
18	27·9763524	19	·060378086

109. Examples.

1. Find the Christian date corresponding to Nîsân 15, A.M. 5578.

Here, H = 5578.

B = H − 3760 = 1818, for which the Julian Sunday Letter is F, and the Gregorian is D.

The year is Embolismic, for 5578 = 298 × 19 + 16.

By Formula I.—

$$a = \left\{\frac{12\,H + 17}{19}\right\}_r = \left\{\frac{66936 + 17}{19}\right\}_r = 16.$$

$$b = \left\{\frac{H}{4}\right\}_r = \left\{\frac{5578}{4}\right\}_r = 2.$$

The values of the terms in the formula are—

The Constant	=	32·0440932
$a \times 1·5542418$	=	24·8678688
$b \times ·25$	=	0·5
		57·4119620
$H \times ·003177794$	=	17·7257349
		39·6862271

The Julian date is therefore March 39, that is, April 8, a Monday, for the Julian Sunday Letter is F. Feria 2 is forbidden for the Passover, and the Festival is kept on feria 3, Tuesday, April 9.

The corresponding Gregorian date is April (9 + 12) = April 21, A.D. 1818.

By Formula II.—

$$a = \left\{\frac{12\,B + 12}{19}\right\}_r = \left\{\frac{21828}{19}\right\}_r = 16.$$

$$b = \left\{\frac{B}{4}\right\}_r = 2.$$

The Constant	=	20·0955877
$a \times 1·5542418$	=	24·8678688
$b \times ·25$	=	0·5
		45·4634565
$B \times ·003177794$	=	5·7772294
		39·6862271

The same result as that given by Formula I. is obtained.

2. Find the Christian date of Nîsân 15 in A.M. 5616.

H = 5616. B = H − 3760 = 1856.

$$a = \left\{\frac{12\,\mathrm{H} + 17}{19}\right\}_r = \left\{\frac{67409}{19}\right\}_r = 16.$$

$$b = \left\{\frac{\mathrm{H}}{4}\right\}_r = 0.$$

The Constant	....	= 32·0440932
$a \times$ 1·5542418	....	= 24·8678688
$b \times$ ·25	....	= 0
		56·9119620
H × ·003177794	....	= 17·8464911
		39·0654709

March 39 = April 8; the Julian Sunday Letter for A.D. 1856 is G. The day is therefore Sunday, and there is no postponement.

The corresponding Gregorian date is Sunday, April (8 + 12) = April 20.

By Formula II.—

$$a = \left\{\frac{12\,\mathrm{B} + 12}{19}\right\}_r = \left\{\frac{22284}{19}\right\}_r = 16.$$

$$b = \left\{\frac{\mathrm{B}}{4}\right\}_r = \left\{\frac{1856}{4}\right\}_r = 0.$$

The Constant	....	= 20·0955877
$a \times$ 1·5542418	....	= 24·8678688
$b \times$ ·25	....	= 0
		44·9634565
B × ·003177794	....	= 5·8979856
		39·0654709

The same result is obtained as that given by Formula I.

Many of the figures in Example 2 are identical with those in Example 1, for, in both examples, $a = 16$, and $b = 0$. It has been intentionally taken because it affords an opportunity of considering the effect produced by the augmentation of the Constant, which is increased by ·25 of a day above the Jewish reckoning.

Suppose that the Constant had not been thus increased; then, in Example 1 the computed date would have been determined by 39·6862271 – ·25, or 39·4362271. This, being less than 39·75, would not have been affected by the rule with respect to 18h. But March 39, that is, April 8 Julian, April 20 Gregorian, being a Monday, the Festival would still be postponed by BaDU to Tuesday, April 9 Julian, April 21 Gregorian.

In Example 2 the computed date would have been determined by 39·0654709 – ·25, or 38·8154709. This is greater than 38·75, and therefore the day would be postponed to March 39, that is, April 8 Julian, April 20 Gregorian. This is the very day which is found by the formula. It is a Sunday in A.D. 1856, which is not a forbidden day for the Passover.

Thus the Example is an illustration of the fact that the result given by the formula is not affected by the rule respecting the 18h.

3. If the rules of the reformed Jewish Calendar were observed in A.D. 622 upon which days in that year would the Passover and Tishrî 1 have occurred?

Let H be the Jewish year in which Nîsân 15 of the Christian year 622 occurred.

H + 1 will be the Jewish year of which the Tishrî 1 occurring in A.D. 622 was the first day.

$$H = 622 + 3760 = 4382$$

$$a = \left\{\frac{12\,H + 17}{19}\right\}_r = \left\{\frac{52601}{19}\right\}_r = 9$$

$$b = \left\{\frac{4382}{4}\right\}_r = 2$$

The Constant	.... =	32·0440932
a × 1·5542418	.... =	13·9881762
b × ·25	.... =	·50
		46·5322694
H × ·003177794	.... =	13·9250933
		32·6071761

March 32 = April 1.

The Sunday Letter for A.D. 622 is C. April 1 is, therefore, Thursday, and there is no postponement.

Tishrî 1, being the first day of A.M. 4383, or of H + 1, corresponds to March (32 + 163) = March 195. There are 184 days from March 1 to August 31, both inclusive. The day required is Saturday, September (195 − 184) = September 11.

4. The same result is obtained by the method described in Article 61, p. 115. The Jewish year which commenced in the Autumn of A.D. 622 was A.M. (622 + 3761) = 4383.

The years elapsed before its commencement are 4382, or 230 complete Cycles + 12 years.

		d.	h.	ch.
200 Cycles	=	1387937	22	200
30 ,,	=	208120	16	570
First 12 years of next Cycle	=	4370	12	724
		1600499	3	414

This is the actual time elapsed, by Jewish Astronomical computation, from the commencement of the Era to the instant of the New Moon of Tishrî, A.M. 4383. The serial number of the day is, therefore, 1600500; and because this number = $7n + 6$ the day was a Saturday, for the Era commenced with a Monday.

To find the corresponding Christian date.

Days elapsed before the Christian Era commenced, from October 7 to December 31, B.C. 3761	=	86
3760 Julian years	=	1373340
		1373426

But the total number of days to Tishrî 1, A.M. 4383, inclusive, is 1600500. Consequently there remain of the Christian Era—

1600500
1373426

227024 days, or 621 Julian years + 254 days.

The Christian date required is, therefore, the 254th day of A.D. 622, that is to say, September 11, which was a Saturday, for the Sunday Letter is C.

Nîsân 15 is 163 days earlier, or the (254 − 163) = 91st day = Thursday, April 1.

The feria for Tishrî 1 may, if it be considered necessary, be verified by the addition of the Molad BeHaRD to the interval of time elapsed before the occurrence of the New Moon of Tishrî, 4383, and rejecting $7n$ days from the sum.

	1600499	3	414
BeHaRD ...	2	5	204
	1600501	8	618, or 7 8 618.

The day is Saturday.

110. Before leaving the subject it may be well to give the full working for some year.

Find the Christian dates corresponding to Tishrî 1 and Nîsân 15 in the Jewish year 5799.

1. 5799 = 19 × 305 + 4; it is therefore the fourth year of the 306th Cycle, or 305 complete Cycles + 3 years have elapsed.

BeHaRD	= 2	5	204
For 300 Cycles add	1	21	300
For 5 „ „	6	10	815
For the fourth year	7	15	181
Molad for A.M. 5799	= 4	4	420

Feria 4 = Wednesday. Tishrî 1 is postponed by ADU to Thursday.

2. In order to know how many days after the commencement of the year Nîsân 15 will occur, the length of the year must be ascertained.

It is a Common year, for it is the fourth in a Cycle.

To the Molad of 5799, which is	4	4	420
add, for a Common year	4	8	876
Molad for 5880	1	13	216

Feria 1 is Sunday. Tishrî 1 of 5880 is postponed, by ADU, to Monday. Hence 5799, which commences with a Thursday, terminates with a Sunday, and, being a Common year, is of the form 350 + 4, or 354 days. It is a Regular Common year.

Nîsân 15 is therefore the 192nd day of the year, that is to say, 191 days must be added to the date of Tishrî 1 when that day is found; for in a Regular Common year the number of days in the months are—

Tishrî	30
Marḥeshwân	29
Kislêw	30
Têbeth	29
Schebhât	30
Adhâr	29
Nîsân 15	15
	192

3. To find the corresponding Christian dates; first, by the method of "time elapsed"; second, by the formula of Gauss.

Time elapsed since the commencement of the Jewish Era to the New Moon of Tishrî, 5799.

	d.	h.	ch.
300 Cycles =	2081906	21	300
5 ,, =	34698	10	815
Add for fourth year	1092	15	181
	2117697	23	716

That is to say, 2117697 complete days, and 23h. 716ch. of the next day have elapsed up to the time of New Moon of Tishrî 5799. This New Moon therefore occurs upon the day whose serial number is 2117698, which is of the form $7n + 2$, and the day is Tuesday, for the Era commenced with a Monday and the $7n$ days terminate with a Sunday; the remaining two days are Monday and Tuesday.

On account of the 23h. 716ch. belonging to this Tuesday the celebration of this New Moon, or Tishrî 1, is postponed, by YacH, to Wednesday, and thence, by ADU, to Thursday, the serial number of which day will be 2117700.

The total number of Jewish days elapsed before the commencement of the Christian Era is 1373426, so that there remain 744274 days of that Era to be reckoned.

This number of days = 2037 Julian years + 260 days of A.D. 2038.
= September 17, A.D. 2038 ......Julian.
= September 30, ,, ...Gregorian.

The Sunday Letter for 2038, Gregorian, is C; September 30 is, therefore, Thursday.

For Nîsân 15 there are to be added to this date 191 days.

September 17 = day, number 260
191

451
Days in A.D. 2038 365

Day of the year 2039 ... 86
= March 27, Julian.
= April 9, Gregorian.

The Sunday Letter, Gregorian, for 2039 is B; therefore April 9 is Saturday.

The required dates are: for Tishrî 1, September 30, 2038, Thursday; for Nîsân 15, April 9, 2039, Saturday.

By Formula I. of Gauss—

$$H = 5799. \qquad B = 5799 - 3760 = 2039 \text{ A.D.}$$

$$a = \left\{\frac{12a + 17}{19}\right\}r = \left\{\frac{69588 + 17}{19}\right\}r = 8$$

$$b = \left\{\frac{5799}{4}\right\}r = 3$$

The Constant...............	= 32·0440932
a × 1·5542418	= 12·4339344
b × ·25	= ·75
	45·2280276
H × ·003177794	= 18·4280274
	26·8000001
	= March 26

The Christian year is A.D. 2039. The Julian Sunday Letter is C. March 26 is therefore Friday, and Nîsân 15 will be on Saturday, March 27, Julian, = April 9, Gregorian.

By Formula II.—

$$B = 2039.$$

$$a = \left\{\frac{12\,B + 12}{19}\right\}_r = 8$$

$$b = \left\{\frac{B}{4}\right\}_r = 3$$

The Constant	.... =	20·0955877
a × 1·5542418	.... =	12·4339344
b × ·25	.... =	·75
		33·2795221
B × ·003177794	.... =	6·4795220
		26·8000001

The result is the same as by Formula I. Nîsân 15 is postponed from Friday, March 26, to Saturday, March 27, Julian = April 9, Gregorian.

For the date of Tishrî 1.

It has already been shown that Nîsân 15 is the 192nd day of the year; therefore 191 days must be subtracted from the date of Nîsân 15 to give the date of Tishrî 1.

April 9 = January 99, A.D. 2039,
365

= January 464, A.D. 2038,
191

= January 273 = September 30, 2038

NOTE ON THE FORMULA $e = \left\{\frac{12 H + 17}{19}\right\}$.

Neither Dr. Gauss, nor any of his commentators, so far as I am aware, afford any explanation of the method by which this formula may be obtained.*

The problem is—To find an expression, a function of one variable n, which has the property of giving for the successive values $n =$ 1, 2, 3, 4, &c., certain integral values fixed in advance, fractions being neglected, corresponding to the successive values of n.

In seeking such an expression it is, in the first place, clear that, because the first two years in the Cycle are Common, and the third is not Common,

$$e \text{ must} = 1, \text{ when } n = 1,$$
$$\text{and } e \text{ must} = 2, \text{ when } n = \text{either } 2, \text{ or } 3.$$

Again; before the sixth year is reached, only one Embolismic year, namely the third, occurs, therefore,

$$e \text{ must} = 4 - 1, \text{ or } 3, \text{ when } n = 4,$$
$$\text{and } e \text{ must} = 5 - 1, \text{ or } 4, \text{ when } n = \text{either } 5, \text{ or } 6.$$

In the same way, there are two Embolismic years and five Common years before the eighth year is reached, therefore,

$$e \text{ must} = 7 - 2, \text{ or } 5, \text{ when } n = \text{either } 7, \text{ or } 8.$$

Proceeding thus, and tabulating the results, we obtain the first and second columns in the Table which follows.

Now, to find an expression, of which the integral part will give these required fixed values to e, it is natural to assume for the first term $\left\{\frac{12n}{19}\right\}$ because in every Cycle of nineteen years there are twelve which are Common. The question then becomes, What

* René Martin, p. 119, gives a Table for the successive values of $\frac{12 R + 17}{19}$; (he uses R for the H in the formula); but he begins by assuming that $\left\{\frac{12 R + 17}{19}\right\}$ is the correct value for e, and only shows, by his Table, that this expression does satisfy the required conditions.

must be the second term? In other words, What increment, x, may be made to the numerator, $12n$, in order that $\left\{\frac{12n+x}{19}\right\}$ may give the required known integral values to e, corresponding to the successive values of n? We must ascertain what is the minimum, and what the maximum possible value that can be assigned to x in each case.

Thus:—For the first year in a Cycle, when $n=1$, and e must also $=1$, it is necessary to make an increment to $12n$ of 7, at the very least, in order that $\left\{\frac{12n+x}{19}\right\}$ may $=1$; for here $n=1$, and $12+7$ is the minimum possible value of the numerator. If the increment were only 6 we should have $\left\{\frac{12n+6}{19}\right\}=0$, whereas it ought to $=1$.

On the other hand, the increment may be increased by any number greater than 6 up to 25, but the increment must not be more than 25. If it were 26, or 27, or 28, &c., $\left\{\frac{12n+x}{19}\right\}$ would have for its numerator 38, or 39, or 40, &c., and this would give 2 for the value of e, whereas it ought to be not more than 1.

So again, for year 10, that is, when $n=10$, and $12n=120$, the increment must be at least 13, in order that $\left\{\frac{12n+x}{19}\right\}$ may $=7$, which is the required value of e, because there are 7 Common years among the first 10 of the Cycle.

On the other hand, the increment may be any number greater than 13, so long as the maximum does not exceed 31; for if the increment were 32 we should have $\left\{\frac{12\times 10+32}{19}\right\}=8$, for the value of e, whereas e must not be more than 7.

In this way the third and fourth columns of the Table are obtained.

Now from the fifth column it appears that the lowest of all the maxima increments that can be made is that for the eighth year. This increment is 17. Also, from the fourth column it appears that the highest of all the minima increments that can be made is that for the sixteenth year, and this also is 17. In other words, the increment cannot be less than 17, and cannot be greater than 17; therefore it must be 17; and we have $\left\{\frac{12n + x}{19}\right\} = \left\{\frac{12n + 17}{19}\right\}$.

This gives the number of Common years which have occurred in a Cycle when n years of that Cycle have elapsed; by writing H for n we have $\left\{\frac{12\,\text{H} + 17}{19}\right\}$ for the number of Common years which have occurred when H years of the Era have elapsed.

A similar formula, $\text{E} = \left\{\frac{7\,\text{H} + 1}{19}\right\}$, may be obtained in like manner for the number of Embolismic years which have occurred when H years of the Era have elapsed.

Years of the Cycle. $n =$	No. of Common years in n. $e =$	$12n$.	Increments that may be made to $12n$.	
			Least.	Greatest.
1	1	12	7	25
2	2	24	10	32
3 Emb.	2	36	2	20
4	3	48	9	27
5	4	60	16	34
6 Emb.	4	72	4	22
7	5	84	11	29
8 Emb.	5	96	0	17
9	6	108	6	24
10	7	120	13	31
11 Emb.	7	132	1	19
12	8	144	8	26
13	9	156	15	33
14 Emb.	9	168	3	21
15	10	180	10	28
16	11	192	17	25
17 Emb.	11	204	5	23
18	12	216	12	30
19 Emb.	12	228	0	18

CHAPTER IX

Megillath Ta'anîth

111. The following account of the Megillath Ta'anîth, or Scroll of Fasting, is derived from a paper read by M. Moïse Schwab at the eleventh International Congress of Orientalists, held in Paris, 1897. It was published in the following year among the Transactions of that Society.*

Under the title Megillath Ta'anîth there is given a list of commemorative days, or anniversaries to be observed, extending from the commencement of the fourth century before the Christian Era to the time of the Emperor Antoninus Pius, A.D. 138. The text itself has a literary interest, for though not so old as the Bible itself, it is anterior to the Talmudic compositions.

M. Joseph Derenbourg † points out a curious fact connected with the title, for this short Chronicle, instead of giving a list of Fasts, does actually enumerate the days which are celebrated as Festivals, or semi-festivals, upon which it is forbidden to Fast. In this connection Ewald says:‡ "The title of the work should be 'List of the Festivals'; but a late anonymous elucidator designated it 'Book of Fasts,' because he appended to it of his own accord a list of the numerous Fast days to which the Rabbis in the Middle Ages had given the force of law; besides, in the Mishna, Ta'anîth iv. 4 *sqq.*, an enumeration of the Festival days was really begun. The author of the little Festival book is described by the interpreter at the close of his work as the

* Actes du onzième congrès International des Orientalistes; Quatrième Section, 1897, pp. 199-259.

† "Essai sur l'histoire de la Palestine," p. 439.

‡ "History of Israel," vol. v., f.n. 3. p. 381.

'School of Eleazar, son of Haninah, son of Hezekiah, son of Garon.'"

M. Schwab says: "Or rather, as is well expressed elsewhere, the ancient Doctors, disciples of Schammaï and of Hillel, wrote it in the chamber of Eleazar when they went to visit him."

Ewald continues: "This very uncertain expression is to some extent appropriate, for the work could not have been completed in its ultimate form till the time of the Roman wars, for some of its festivals are actually derived from them. But even this late and unhistorical interpreter, who probably did not write till the time of Islâm, had still an obscure feeling that the book first arose in the Asmonean-Greek age, and looks there for an explanation of everything which he could not explain from the Old Testament."

It was at the house of the Eleazar here mentioned that meetings were held, a short time before the destruction of the Temple, for the purpose of discussing what measures could be taken to prevent any intercourse with the heathen. The essential plan of this treatise may, therefore, be referred to that period. Additions have certainly been made to it in later times, for there are two days commemorative of events which occurred after the destruction of Jerusalem and the end of the Jewish state of independence—Adhâr 12, the Day of Trajan, and Adhâr 28, the revocation by Antoninus Pius of the decrees of Hadrian against the Jews, A.D. 139 or 140.

There are but few MSS. of this Chronicle; these are chiefly to be found in the Bodleian Library.* Only a few editions of the text have been printed.†

The Chronicle is composed of three distinct parts:—

1. The original text.
2. The Scholia, or additions.
3. The Explanations.

The two last parts are sometimes blended together. They form that which is hereafter called the Commentary. They are the parts that are

* M. Schwab gives the numbers of the MSS. in the Bodleian—641, 3°; 867, 2°; 882; 902; and 2421, 10*b*.

Of these, 867, 2°, and 902 are entire; the rest are only fragments.

† The best edition is that of Hambourg, with notes by Jacob Israël Emden, 1757.

An edition was published by Ambroise Froben at Bâle in 1580. The text, with a Latin version, is given by I. Meyer, at the end of his "De Temporibus," Amsterdam, 1724. More recently it has been printed in "Anecdota Oxoniensia," Semitic Series vol. i. part vi., pp. 3 to 26.

of more recent date than the original text; the language in which they are written is a mixture of Hebrew and Aramaic, like that of the Talmud. The original text is in the Aramaic dialect.

At the end of the work a certain number of days are enumerated upon which it is recommended to fast. This series appears to be a still later addition; it has no commentary attached. The language is pure Hebrew.

The memorable days recorded in the Chronicle are thirty-five in number. They are not given in chronological order, but follow the order of the months, that is to say, they are given according to the order of days as they stand in the Calendar.

With respect to the "Commentary and Historical Notices" herewith—the former is that given in the treatise itself as rendered by M. Schwab; the Historical Notices are derived partly from Schwab, but chiefly from "The History of the Jews," by Graetz,* from Josephus, and from the books of the Maccabees. The quotations from Graetz are not literal transcripts from that author, but are, as a rule, much abbreviated.

112. Commemorative Days.

1. Nîsân 1 to 8. The expenses of the daily sacrifices ought to be defrayed by the Temple.
   Mourning is forbidden.
2. Nîsân 8 to 22. Restoration of the Feast of Weeks to the fiftieth day.
   Mourning is forbidden.
3. Iyâr 7. Inauguration of the wall of Jerusalem.
   Mourning is forbidden.
4. Iyâr 14. Day for the sacrifice of the Paschal Lamb. [This is the Second Passover, Numbers xi. 1.]
   Mourning is forbidden.
5. Iyâr 23. The defenders of Acra have to leave Jerusalem.
6. Iyâr 27. The crown taxes revoked for Judæa and Jerusalem.
7. Sîwân 15, 16. The dwellers in Bethshean and the Plain are exiled.

* The references are to the English translation by Miss Bella Löwy, Nutt., London, 1891.

8. Sîwân 17. The fortress of Bethsura is taken.
9. Sîwân 25. The [Roman] tax-gatherers are withdrawn from Judah and Jerusalem.
10. Tammûz 14. The Book of Decisions is abrogated. Mourning is forbidden.
11. Âbh 15. Day for the offering of wood to the priests. Mourning is forbidden.
12. Âbh 24. Return to the Law.
13. 'Elûl 7. Inauguration of the wall of Jerusalem. Mourning is forbidden.
14. 'Elûl 17. The Romans retreat from Judæa and Jerusalem.
15. 'Elûl 22. We proceed to kill the Apostates.
16. Tishrî 3. The Divine Name removed from Deeds and Documents.
17. Marḥeshwân 23. The stones of the altar [which had been defiled], are buried in the court of the Temple.
18. Marḥeshwân 25. Samaria was taken.
19. Marḥeshwân 27. Renewal of the offering of loaves of wheat-flour on the altar.
20. Kislêw 3. The stones of the heathen images removed from the court of the Temple.
21. Kislêw 7. A Festival day.
22. Kislêw 21. Day of Mount Gerizim. Mourning is forbidden.
23. Kislêw 25. Commencement of the eight days of the Purification of the Temple [Chanukka]. Mourning is forbidden.
24. Têbeth 28. The Synhedrion re-established according to the Law.
25. Schebhât 2. A Festival day. Mourning is forbidden.
26. Schebhât 22. Counteraction of the work which the enemy had ordered to be done in the Temple. Mourning is forbidden.

27. Schebhât 28. King Antiochus was taken away from Jerusalem.
28. Adhâr 8, 9. Days of rejoicing for rain.
29. Adhâr 12. The Day of Trajan.
30. Adhâr 13. The Day of Nicanor.
31. Adhâr 14, 15. Days of Purim.
Mourning is forbidden.
32. Adhâr 16. Rebuilding of the walls of Jerusalem is commenced.
Mourning is forbidden.
33. Adhâr 17. Israel delivered, when the heathen rose against the Doctors of the Law, in the Province of Seleucia and in Beth-Zebedee.
34. Adhâr 20. The people fasted to obtain rain, and the rain fell.
35. Adhâr 28. The Jews receive the good news that they are no longer to be prevented from following the ordinances of their Law.
Mourning is forbidden.

Nevertheless, every one who had previously made a vow to fast is bound by his prayer.

These, then, are the thirty-five commemorative days for rejoicing, to be observed as minor, or semi-festivals. They may be arranged chonologically in six divisions, as follows:—

Division A. In this division there is but one day, Iyâr 14. This alone of the minor Festivals recalls any of the Mosaical ordinances.

Division B, contains three days: anniversaries instituted previous to the time of the Hasmonæans.
'Elûl 7. Rebuilding the walls of Jerusalem by Nehemiah.
Adhâr 14, 15. The Feast of Purim.
Âbh 3. The Festival of the Wood-offering.

Division C, contains fifteen days, instituted as anniversaries in the time of the Hasmonæans. Some of these recall the victories over the Syrians and Greeks; others are in remembrance of happy events which followed in consequence of those victories. All these days are within the time of the Hasmonæan princes, Judas Maccabæus, Jonathan, Simon, and Johanan Hyrcanus.

Division D, contains ten days; eight of these commemorate events in the reign of Queen Salome Alexandra, B.C. 79–70; two refer to the reigns of Aristobulus and Hyrcanus II.

Division E. Time of the Roman domination, four days; previous to the destruction of the Temple and to the end of the Jewish state of independence.

Division F. Two days, instituted as anniversaries at a later period, Adhâr 12, and Adhâr 28.

The following Index will facilitate reference from the list of Commemorative Days arranged in monthly order to the Historical Notices, which are in chronological order.

The first column contains the numbers attached to the days in the former list; the second has the day of the month; the third, the division under which the day is placed; and the fourth gives the numbers of the days as arranged in the Historical Notices.

1	Nisân	1–8	D	XXIV.	20	Kislêw	3	C	V.
2	,,	8–22	D	XXV.	21	,,	7	D	XXI.
3	Iyâr	7	C	XIX.	22	,,	21	C	XIV.
4	,,	14	A	I.	23	,,	25	C	VI.
5	,,	23	C	X.	24	Têbeth	28	D	XX.
6	,,	27	C	XIII.	25	Schebhât	2	E	XXX.
7	Siwân	15, 16	C	XVI.	26	,,	22	E	XXXI.
8	,,	17	C	XI.	27	,,	28	C	VII.
9	,,	25	E	XXXII.	28	Adhâr	8, 9	D	XXIX.
10	Tammûz	14	D	XXII.	29	,,	12	F	XXXIV.
11	Âbh	15	B	IV.	30	,,	13	C	VIII.
12	,,	24	D	XXIII.	31	,,	14, 15	B	III.
13	'Elûl	7	B	II.	32	,,	16	C	XVIII.
14	,,	17	E	XXXIII.	33	,,	17	D	XXVII.
15	,,	22	C	XII.	34	,,	20	D	XXVIII.
16	Tishri	3	C	XVII.	35	,,	28	F	XXXV.
17	Marheshwân	23	C	IX.					
18	,,	25	C	XV.					
19	,,	27	D	XXVI.					

113. COMMENTARY AND HISTORICAL NOTICES.

Division A.

Mosaical Ordinance.

Day I.

Iyâr 14. This refers to the secondary observance of the Passover on the "fourteenth day of the second month," permitted to those who had been prevented by any material cause from celebrating the Feast on the fourteenth day of the first month. Numbers ix. 9–11, "And the Lord spake unto Moses, saying, Speak unto the children of Israel, saying, If any man of you, or of your posterity shall be unclean by reason of a dead body, or be in a journey afar off, yet he shall keep the Passover unto the Lord. The fourteenth day of the second month at even they shall keep it, and eat it with unleavened bread and bitter herbs."

Division B.

Anterior to the time of the Hasmonæans.

Day II.

'Elûl 7. Restoration of the walls of Jerusalem by Nehemiah. The commentator adds, "The walls of Jerusalem had been thrown down by the Syrians. When Israel again obtained supremacy they were rebuilt, as it is said, 'the wall is finished.'"

Nehemiah vi. 15. "So the wall was finished in the twenty and fifth day of the month 'Elûl, in fifty and two days."

M. Schwab says with respect to this, that 'Elûl 25 is definitely fixed for the date, but without doubt the reconstruction of the wall was well advanced by 'Elûl 7.

Day III.

Adhâr 14 and 15. The Feast of Purim.

"After the death of Moses there was no prophet who had prescribed to the Israelites a new commandment, with this exception —to observe the feast of Purim. There is only one distinction between the feasts prescribed by Moses and this feast. The deliverance from Egypt was celebrated—for example—during seven days, while the feast of Mordecai and Esther had only one day. If we celebrate as a feast the escape from Egypt, where the lives of our children alone were in peril, how much more reason is there for us to be joyful on the anniversary of the day when the miracle was wrought under Mordecai and Esther which delivered from danger men and women, children and aged persons."

Day IV.

Âbh 15. The wood-offering. [Xylophoria.]

According to the Commentary, "this anniversary had for its origin the return from the Babylonish Captivity. By order of the Doctors of the Law the Israelites, when freed, brought wood for the burnt sacrifices. The day was instituted as a commemorative festival because the enemies of Palestine had in vain endeavoured to prevent this from being done."

Nehemiah x. 34. "We cast lots among the priests, the Levites, and the people for the wood-offering, to bring it into the house of our God, after the houses of our fathers, at times appointed year by year, to burn upon the altar of the LORD our God, as it is written in the law."

Josephus, "Wars of the Jews," bk. ii. ch. xvii. §. 6, speaks of this day as a Festival in the time when Florus was governor. See *post*, under 'Elûl 17, Day xxxiii.

It appears that after the return from the Captivity the number of Levites, part of whose duty it was to provide wood for the altar, was so reduced that a regular supply could not be maintained. René Martin * states that the accounts of these Festivals as given by Selden, De Zach, and Le Boyer are not in accord, but he obtained from the chief Rabbi the following information: "The Xylophoria were nine in number, Nîsân 1, Tammûz 20, Âbh 5, 7, 10, 15, 20, 'Elûl 20, and Têbeth 1. The privilege of providing wood for the Temple on the appointed days was accorded to certain families, and the festival celebrated on these occasions was for the family whose turn had arrived."

* "Memoire sur le Calendrier Hébraïque," p. 371.

Division C.

In the time of the Hasmonæans.

Day V.

Kislêw 3. The Simôt, or large stones of the heathen images, are cast out of the Temple. B.C. 165.

The Greeks had erected statues and idols in the outer court, or public precinct of the Temple. Twenty-two days before the reconsecration of the Temple (which Josephus, "Antiq.," xii. vii. 6, says took place on Kislêw 25) the Hasmonæans threw down these idols. The account is given in 1 Maccabees iv. 42, 43, where we are told that Judas Maccabæus "chose priests of blameless conversation, such as had pleasure in the law: who cleansed the sanctuary and bare out the defiled stones into an unclean place."

These were the large stones, Simôt, either of the idols themselves or upon which the images had been placed. The author of the Book of Maccabees makes a distinction between these and the smaller stones, Sôrega, with which the altar was built. The latter were not removed to an unclean place, but were buried in the court of the Temple. See *post*, Marḥeshwân 23, Day ix.

With respect to the defilement of the Temple, Graetz, vol. i. ch. xxii. p. 470, gives the following history:—"Antiochus Epiphanes had issued a decree, which was sent forth to all the towns of Judæa, commanding the people to renounce the laws of their God, and to offer sacrifice only to the Greek gods. In order to strike an effectual blow at Judaism he ordained that unclean animals, particularly swine, should be used at the sacrifices. He forbade, under severe penalty, the three religious rites which outwardly distinguished the Judæans from the heathen, namely, circumcision, the keeping of the Sabbath, and the abstinence from unclean food. . . . The Temple was first desecrated, and Antiochus sent a noble there to dedicate the Sanctuary to Jupiter. A swine was sacrificed on the altar in the fore-court, and its blood was sprinkled in the Holy of Holies on the stone which Antiochus had imagined to be Moses' statue; the flesh was cooked, and the melted grease spilt over the leaves of the Holy Scriptures. . . . The roll of the Law, which was found in the Temple, was not only bespattered, but burnt, because, though it taught purity and morality, Antiochus maintained that it inculcated hatred of mankind.

. . . The statue of Jupiter was placed on the altar, 'the abomination of destruction,' to which sacrifices are now to be offered." This occurred in B.C. 168, on Kislêw 15, according to 1 Maccabees i. 54.

According to M. Derenbourg,* as quoted by M. Schwab, the words Simôt and Sirouga, or Sôrega, are of uncertain signification. It can, however, be gathered that they indicate two different objects in stone, of which one commanded respect, while the other was cast aside without hesitation.

Josephus gives the account of the actions of Antiochus in "Antiquities," xii. v. 4, and of the cleansing of the Temple in xii. vii. 6.

Day VI.

Kislêw 25. Reconsecration of the Temple. B.C. 165.

2 Maccabees x. 5–8. "Upon the same day that the strangers profaned the Temple, on the very same day it was cleansed again, even the five-and twentieth day of the same month, which is Casleu. And they kept eight days with gladness, as in the feast of the tabernacles, remembering that not long afore they had held the feast of the tabernacles, when as they wandered in the mountains and dens like beasts. . . . They ordained also by a common statute and decree, That every year those days should be kept of the whole nation of the Jews."

Josephus, "Antiq.," xii. vii. 7, says that this Festival, Channûkka, was called the Feast of Lights.

Graetz, vol. i. ch. xxiii. p. 488. "All the people from every town of Judæa took part in the festival, and the inhabitants of Jerusalem lit bright lamps in front of their houses as a symbol of the Law, called 'Light' by the poets. The Hasmonæan brothers and the other members of the Great Council decided that in future the week beginning on Kislêw 25 should be held as a joyous festival, to commemorate the consecration of the Temple. Year after year the members of the House of Israel were to be reminded of the victory of a small body of men over a large army, and of the re-establishment of the Sanctuary. This decree was conscientiously carried out. For two thousand years these days have been celebrated as 'the days of Consecration' (Channûkka), and lamps have been lighted in every household in Israel. The days derived their name of 'Feast of Lights' from this custom."

* "Essai sur l'histoire de la Palestine," p. 60.

M. Schwab says that this is the historical basis for the tradition concerning a miraculous supply of pure oil. He says nothing more about this tradition, but it is given by Dr. Bannister in his book, "The Temples of the Hebrews," p. 391: "When they were employed in cleansing the Temple, after it had been profaned by the Greeks, they found there only one small phial of oil, sealed up by the High Priest, which would hardly suffice to keep in the lamps so much as one night; but God permitted that it should last several days, till they had time to make more: in memory of which the Jews lighted up several lamps in their synagogues and at the doors of their houses."

Day VII.

Schebhât 28. Anniversary of the death of Antiochus Epiphanes. B.C. 164.

Graetz, vol. i. ch. xxiii. p. 493. "Suddenly important news came to Palestine concerning Antiochus Epiphanes. The progress of that monarch through Parthia had not been signalised by any military success; nor had he been able to refill his treasury. Driven by want of money he undertook an expedition to the city of Susa in Elymais, to plunder the temple of the goddess Anaitis; but the inhabitants resisted the invader and forced him to retreat. He fell sick in the Persian city of Tabæ, and expired in frenzy."

This account is derived from 1 Maccabees vi. 1–16; another history of his dishonour in Persia, his terrible disease, and his death, with fuller details is recorded in 2 Maccabees ix.

Josephus, "Antiq.," xii. ix. 1, is somewhat brief in his account. Driven away from the siege of Susa in Elymais, "he fled as far as Babylon, and lost a great many of his army. And when he was grieving for this disappointment, some persons told him of the defeat of his commanders whom he had left behind him to fight against Judæa; . . . he was confounded, and by the anxiety he was in, fell into a distemper, which, as it lasted a great while, and as his pains increased upon him, so he at length perceived he should die in a little time; so he called his friends to him, and told them that his distemper was severe upon him for the miseries he had brought on the Jewish nation, while he plundered their Temple and condemned their God; and when he had said this, he gave up the ghost."

Day VIII.

Adhâr 13. Commemorative of the defeat and death of the Syrian general Nicanor at the battle of Adarsa. B.C. 160.

This day is mentioned as one to be observed in both the Books of the Maccabees; I. vii. 49, "Moreover, they ordained to keep yearly this day, being the thirteenth of Adhâr;" and, II. xv. 36, "And they ordered all with a common decree in no case to let that day pass without solemnity, but to celebrate the thirteenth day of the twelfth month, which in the Syrian tongue is called Adhâr."

Demetrius, surnamed Soter, son of Seleucus Philopator, had been sent when a child to Rome, as a hostage, by his father. He remained there during the reign of Antiochus Epiphanes; but after the death of that king he demanded his liberty. This was refused by the Senate, and he fled secretly from Rome, accompanied by his friend Nicanor. He went to Syria, where he was well received. The young king Antiochus Eupator, son of Epiphanes, was put to death by his own guards; and Demetrius obtained from the Romans the recognition of himself as king. Shortly afterwards he sent Nicanor against Judas Maccabæus, and "on the thirteenth day of the month Adhâr the hosts joined battle, but Nicanor's host was discomfited, and he himself was first slain in the battle" (1 Maccabees vii. 43).

Graetz, vol. i. ch. xxiii. p. 501. Nicanor marched out from Jerusalem at the head of an immense army, pitching his camp at Bethoron, whilst Judas, surrounded by 3,000 of his bravest followers, took up his post at Adarsa. Judæan valour was once more triumphant over the superior numbers of the Syrians. Nicanor fell on the battle-field, and his army fled in utter confusion. . . . The battle of Adarsa was of so decisive a character that its anniversary was celebrated in years to come under the name of the Day of Nicanor.

The head and one of the arms of Nicanor were cut off, and hung as trophies upon the walls of Jerusalem. 2 Maccabees xv. 32, 35.

Day IX.

Marḥeshwân 23. Restoration of a partition wall in the Temple which had been cast down by the High Priest Alcimus.

With respect to this day the text says, "They buried the Sôrega in the court of the Temple in order to hide them": it is so rendered by M. Derenbourg, p. 61.

M. Schwab states that the Commentator has not understood the subject upon which he was engaged, and has confused this date with that of Nîsân 1 (? Kislêw 3). The heathen, says the Commentator, had erected in the court a construction for which they had used some of the stones of the sacred edifice (*à laquelle ils avaient aussi employé de bonnes pierres*). It was decided that these stones should be allowed to remain until the arrival of the prophet Elias, in order that he might decide which of them were pure, and which were impure.

Accordingly M. Derenbourg renders the original text as above. In support of this he adds the following argument:—"It is sufficient to compare the passages in the Chronicle with those in the First Book of Maccabees, in order to recognise the fact that the Sôrega must have been a part of the altar of burnt offerings which had been defiled, or a collection of stones erected above the altar upon which the heathen had offered sacrifice. There was an uncertainty about these stones: some of them might have been holy originally, some might have formed a part of the material brought from outside, and erected upon the altar. The decision which was reached is described alike in the First Book of Maccabees, and in the Megillath Ta'anîth. Moreover, there is an indication in the Mishna (Tr. Middoth, i. 6), that the Hasmonæans buried the stones of the altar which the Greek kings had defiled."

M. Schwab says that this explanation is too plausible to be refused admission. Nevertheless, he describes this day as commemorative of the restoration of the wall which Alcimus pulled down, or proposed to pull down. This wall consisted of a wooden partition between the courts of the Gentiles and of the women. It was called Sôreg because made of laths superimposed in the way of grill-work. In 1 Maccabees ix. 54 it is called "the wall of the inner hall of the Sanctuary," τὸ τεῖχος τῆς αὐλῆς τῶν ἁγίων τῆς ἐσωτέρας, and is said to have been the work of the prophets, ἔργα τῶν προφητῶν.

Josephus, "Antiq.," xii. x. 6. "As the High Priest Alcimus was resolving to pull down the wall of the Sanctuary, which had been there of old time, and had been built by the holy prophets, he was smitten suddenly by God and fell down . . . and undergoing torments for many days he at length died."

Alcimus was the Greek name of Jakim, a priest who was nephew to Josê one of the teachers of the Law. He was made High Priest by Demetrius, and was devoted to the interests of the Syrian court. It was through his accusations against the Hasmonæans that Nicanor was sent against them. When Judas Maccabæus fell at the battle of Eleasa, B.C. 160, Alcimus obtained full possession of the Temple and the Holy City.

With respect to the particular act in question Graetz says, i. xxiii. p. 509, "The offence with which he was reproached appears, on closer examination, hardly to have been a sin aimed against the religion of the Judæans. It appears that between the inner and outer courts of the Temple was a kind of screen, named, on account of its fragility, 'Soreg.' This screen, the work of the prophets, as it was called, was used as a boundary, which no heathen might pass to penetrate into the Temple. But Alcimus gave orders for the destruction of this partition, probably with the intention of admitting the heathen within the sacred precincts. The pious Judæans were justly incensed, and when Alcimus was seized, directly after this command, with paralysis of speech and of body, from which he never recovered, they attributed his fatal illness to Heaven's wrath."

Day X.

Iyâr 23. Capture of the Fortress Acra, and expulsion of the Syrians. B.C. 142.

In the text we read, "The sons of Acra retire from Jerusalem." The expression "Sons" for Defenders occurs also in 1 Maccabees iv. 2, where the English version has, "And the men of the fortress were his guides"; the Greek is "*καὶ οἱ υἱοὶ τῆς ἄκρας ἦσαν αὐτῷ ὁδηγοί.*"

The Acra, or Acropolis, was a fortress on the north-west of the Temple which had been erected by the Syrians, and was held by a strong garrison: but Simon, the High Priest, "took the citadel of Jerusalem by siege, and cast it down to the ground, that it might not be any more a place of refuge to their enemies when they took it, to do them a mischief, as it had been till now." Josephus, "Antiq.," xiii. vi. 7.

The casting of the citadel to the ground is not mentioned in 1 Maccabees xiii. 49-52, and is apparently an erroneous statement, founded however on circumstances which are narrated by Graetz, i. ch. xxiv. p. 543, "The newly recovered Acra underwent various changes at the hands of the Hasmonæans. The wrath of the people had been too much excited against this fortress to allow of its standing intact . . . it overtopped the Temple-capped Mount itself, and this was not to be. According to the prophecies of Isaiah, in the last days the Mount on which the Temple stood should rise above all other mountains, and be higher than all other heights. This was literally explained to mean that no mount or building should soar above the Temple, and Simon, if even unconvinced himself, was obliged to bow to that belief. . . . In dealing with it a middle course was hit upon. The towers and bastions were taken down; the walls, courts, and halls were left standing, but the hated name of Acra was no longer used, but changed for that of Birah. In this transformed edifice the Jewish soldiers were quartered, and there they kept their weapons. Simon himself dwelt in the Birah in the midst of his soldiers."

M. Schwab says that the expression "Sons of Acra" has given rise to an etymological error. The Commentator has substituted "Karaites" for the original word Acra. This is a serious anachronism. The Karaites were the followers of Anan, who was recognised as the legitimate "prince of the captivity" by many Jews about the year 765 of the Christian Era.*

Dr. Bannister has followed the Commentator, and fallen into this error; "Temples of the Hebrews," p. 394. In speaking of Iyâr 23, he says, "A feast for the expulsion of the Karaites out of Jerusalem, by the Maccabees; according to the Calendar of Sigonius." In describing the Jewish sects, he says of the Karaites, p. 377, "This sect was an offshoot from the Zadikim" [*i.e.*, "the righteous," who adhered to the written Law of Moses strictly, and who came into existence after the return from Babylon], "but the precise time of its origin is unknown."

Day XI.

Sîwân 17. Fortress of Bethsur taken. B.C. 142.

This was one of the fortresses taken by Simon from the Syrians and Hellenistic apostates. Its capture is mentioned only incidentally in 1 Maccabees xiv. 33, where it is said that Simon "fortified the cities of Judæa, together with Bethsura that lieth upon the borders of Judæa, where the armour of the enemies had been before." At the same time he took Gazara and Joppa.

* Schaff-Herzog, "Religious Encyclopædia," vol. ii. p. 1225. Graetz, vol. iii. ch. v. p. 136 of the English edition. Vol. v. p. 174 of the 2nd German edition. Al-Bîrûnî, p. 68, who, however, gives the date more than one hundred years too late, making it 110 years (about) before he wrote his book in A.D. 1000.

DAY XII.

'Elûl 22. Extermination of the renegades, or Hellenistic apostates.

The Commentator says that so long as they remained under the rule of the heathen [the Syrians], the Jews took no action against these impious persons; but when they attained their freedom they warned the unbelievers, and allowed them three days for reflection and repentance. As no account was taken of this warning, the people rose up and exterminated them.

An indication in 1 Maccabees xiii. 50 seems to contradict this, for it is there narrated that "they of the tower in Jerusalem being in great distress for want of victuals, cried to Simon beseeching him to be at one with them: which thing he granted them." M. Schwab assumes that Simon granted to these people a free passage; but points out that from 1 Maccabees xiv. 14, we may conclude that at least a part of them were annihilated, "Every contemner of the law, and wicked person he took away."

Graetz, i. xxiv. p. 543, says, "It is related that 'Elûl 22 was set apart among the days of victory, because it saw the death of those idolaters who had allowed the respite of three days to elapse without returning to their faith."

DAY XIII.

Iyâr 27. Cessation of the crown taxes collected for the Syrians. B.C. 142.

1 Maccabees xiii. 36, 39–41. "King Demetrius unto Simon the High Priest and friend of kings, as also unto the elders and nation of the Jews, sendeth greeting: . . . As for any oversight or fault committed unto this day, we forgive it, and the crown tax also, which ye owe us: and if there were any other tribute paid in Jerusalem, it shall no more be paid. . . . Thus the yoke of the heathen was taken away from Israel in the hundred and seventieth year."

Graetz, i. ch. xxiv. p. 541. "The people looked upon these concessions of Demetrius as the inauguration of their independence, and from that epoch the customary manner of counting time according to the years of the reigning King of Syria was discontinued. Thus, in all public documents in the year 142 B.C. we read, 'In the first year of the High Priest Commander of the army, and Prince of the nation, Simon.'"

So, also, 1 Maccabees xiv. 42. "Then the people of Israel began to write in their instruments and contracts, 'In the first year of Simon the High Priest, the governor and leader of the Jews.'"

DAY XIV.

Kislêw 21. Destruction of the Samaritan Temple on Mount Gerizim. B.C. (*circa*) 120.

The Samaritan Temple was built in the time of Alexander the Great (Josephus, "Antiq.," xiii. iii. 4). This would be after the march of Alexander into Palestine in B.C. 332. Graetz, i. ch. xx. p. 402, assigns an earlier date, "Thus on the summit of the fruitful Mount Gerizim, at the foot of Shechem, in the very heart of the land of Palestine, Sanballat built his temple, probably after the death of Artaxerxes (420).

About the year 120 B.C. John Hyrcanus, the fourth of the Hasmonæan princes, conquered the Samaritans and utterly demolished their Temple. Graetz, ii. ch. i. 8, says, "The anniversary of the destruction of this temple was to be kept with great rejoicing, as the commemoration of a peculiarly happy event, and no fasting or mourning was ever to mar the brightness of the festival. From this time forth, the glory of the Samaritans waned."

DAY XV.

Marḥeshwân 25. Destruction of Samaria, B.C. 109. Samaria capitulated to Hyrcanus and was given up to him after he had besieged it for a whole year. He caused it to be entirely destroyed, and the ground on which it stood to be intersected by ditches and canals so that not a trace of it should remain. Josephus, "Antiq.," xiii. x. 3. Graetz, ii. ch. i. p. 11.

The day of its surrender was added to the days of thanksgiving.

DAY XVI.

Siwân 15, 16. Recovery of the city of Bethshean (Scythopolis), and of the valley of Jezreel. B.C. 109.

The Syrian king, Antiochus Cyzicenus, manifested a fierce hatred against Hyrcanus. His generals invaded Judæa, took several fortresses near the sea-coast, and placed a garrison in Joppa. Hyrcanus sent five ambassadors to Rome to complain to the Senate, and a decree was promulgated forbidding Antiochus to molest the Judæans, and commanding him to restore the fortresses and territories he had seized. He called to his help the co-regent of Egypt, Ptolemy VIII., called Lathurus, who sent auxiliary troops. These were placed under the command of two generals, Callimandrus and Epicrates; the first lost his life in battle: the second yielded to bribery, and delivered into the hands of the two sons of Hyrcanus the town of Bethshean, with all its environs, and other places in the plain of Jezreel, extending as far as Mount Carmel—that is, the whole valley of Jezreel. Schwab, p. 227. Graetz, ii. i. p. 10.

The anniversaries of the recovery of Bethshean and of the Plain, and their incorporation in the territory of Judæa, were added to the days of Victory.

Day XVII.

Tishrî 3. The mention of the Divine Name is suppressed on official documents.

The Commentator says,—"After their victories the Hasmonæans adopted the custom of placing the Divine Name* on their documents and contracts; as—for an example of their method of writing—'in such a year of the High Priest Jochanan, who served the Supreme Being.' The Doctors of the Law disapproved of this practice, for they said that many a memorandum of indebtedness might be torn up after payment had been made, and the pieces be cast upon the ground. To avoid the risk of this profanation the usage was suppressed, and the day upon which this was done was observed as a Festival."

M. Schwab considers that this gloss is badly founded. He says: "It is inadmissible to suppose that they would think it necessary to glorify a rule of so little importance, made to provide against an exceptional mischance." But surely the strict Jews would not consider this a matter of little importance. A piece of parchment, or other material, with the sacred name written upon it might, if cast upon the ground, be trodden upon. This would be profanation, and would be a thing to be avoided. Schwab, however, gives the following as a more probable reason for the observance of this anniversary:—Under the rule of Simon the enforced use of the Era of the Seleucidæ was suppressed. This Era, called by the Jews the Era of Contracts, because used for all deeds and articles of agreement, was imposed on

* The Tetragrammaton, or Tetragram JHWH.

them by the Syrians. It was odious to them; and their rejoicing at its suppression is explained. He says that Ewald wrongly supposes that in spite of the introduction of a method of computing according to the regnal years of the Hasmonæan princes,* the Era of the Seleucidæ was maintained by the Jews in their ordinary life up to the Middle Ages. This, he says, is incorrect, for neither during the existence of the Temple at Jerusalem, nor under the Roman rule, did the Jews of Palestine employ this Era. On the contrary, its employment annulled any act of divorce which bore such a date; and the use of the Era can only be attributed to the Babylonian Jews, the Middle Ages offering a few scattered examples. He refers to Tr. Guittin, f. 80a, and the Seder 'olam rabba, towards its end.

Days XVIII. and XIX.

Adhâr 16 and Iyâr 7. Restoration of the walls of Jerusalem.

The repair of the walls in the time of the Maccabees was commenced on Adhâr 16, and completed on Iyâr 7. It is not known under which of the Hasmonæan princes these days were appointed as commemorative, for the restoration occupied the whole period of Judas, Jonathan, Simon, and Hyrcanus.

The Commentator has referred this restoration erroneously to that which was done in the time of Nehemiah.

Division D.

After the independence of Judæa had been assured there commenced a long series of disputes between the two sects of the Pharisees and the Sadducees. This was kept up until after the death of Alexander Jannæus, in B.C. 79. Graetz says that the bitter rivalry of the two kingdoms of Judah and Israel, in the days of Rehoboam and Jeroboam, was repeated in the history of the strife between the Pharisees and Sadducees.

Under the reign of Queen Salome Alexandra, B.C. 79-70, who was devoted to the Pharisees, the chief of that sect obtained the ascendancy, and the Pharisees celebrated all the days upon which they had been especially successful against their adversaries.

* See above, Day XIII., Iyâr 27. Ewald's observation is in vol. v. p. 335, f.n. 1.

Day XX.

Têbeth 28. Reorganisation of the Synhedrion in conformity with the Law.

In order that the question herein involved may be understood it will be necessary to give some historical details.

The unfriendly relations between the Pharisees and the Sadducees did not exist, to any extent, in the time of Hyrcanus. He made use of both parties according to their capabilities; the Sadducees as soldiers and diplomatists; the Pharisees as teachers of the Law, judges, and functionaries in civil affairs. The former honoured Hyrcanus as the head of the state, the latter as the pious High Priest. In point of fact Hyrcanus was personally in favour of the Pharisees, but as Prince he could not quarrel with the Sadducees, whose leader, Jonathan, was his devoted friend. Until he was overtaken by old age Hyrcanus managed to solve the difficult problem of keeping in a state of amity two parties who were always on the verge of quarrelling; but in the last years of his life he went quite over to the Sadducees. He had been bitterly offended by a certain Eleazar ben Poira, who had stated that his mother had been taken prisoner by the Syrians, and that it was not fitting for the son of a prisoner to be a priest—much less a High Priest. Hyrcanus then deposed the Pharisees from the various important posts that they had filled; and the offices belonging to the Temple, to the courts of law, and to the High Council were given to the followers of the Sadducees.

Hyrcanus died in B.C. 106, a short time only after these events. He had proclaimed his wife to be Queen, and his eldest son Judah, better known by his Greek name Aristobulus, to be High Priest. Aristobulus supplanted his mother on the throne, and put her in prison, together with three of his four brothers. He died after a reign of one year, in B.C. 105.

He was succeeded by his brother Alexander Jannæus, the third son of Hyrcanus. He reigned for twenty-seven years. During his reign the Pharisees were again allowed to appear at Court. Simon ben Shetach was constantly in the king's presence. He was the brother of Salome Alexandra, the wife of Jannæus, who was a warm partisan of the Pharisees, among whom her brother was a chief leader.

Ever since the secession of Hyrcanus from Pharisaism the Great Council had been composed entirely of Sadducees, but Jannæus was disposed to bring about some kind of equality between the two parties by dividing between them the offices of state. The Pharisees positively refused to act with their opponents. Simon ben Shetach alone allowed himself to be elected as a member of the Council.

After a time, from causes for which various reasons have been suggested, Jannæus became an inveterate opponent of Pharisaic teaching, and made his views public in a most insulting manner. The wrath of the congregation assembled in the outer court of the Temple was stirred up. Jannæus called in the help of his foreign mercenaries, and six thousand of the Judæans were slaughtered within the precincts of the Temple. On another occasion he caused eight hundred Pharisees to be crucified in one day. Eight thousand of those who were left in Jerusalem fled from Judæa to Syria and to Egypt.

Alexander Jannæus died from fever, B.C. 79, during his siege of one of the trans-Jordanic fortresses. On his deathbed he repented of his cruel persecution of the Pharisees, and gave various directions respecting them to his wife, Salome Alexandra, who succeeded him as Queen. She was a woman of gentle nature, and of sincere piety; she was still devoted to the Pharisees, and entrusted them with the management of affairs without persecuting the opposing party. The chief post in the Great Council was given up to them. It was offered in the first place to her brother, Simon ben Shetach, who, however, waived his own claim in favour of Judah ben Tabbaï, then in Egypt. The latter, on his return home, undertook, with the help of Simon, the reorganisation of the Council, and the re-establishment of religious observances. These two celebrated reformers have been called "Rebuilders of the Law," "Restorers of the glory of the crown (of the Law)." Many details which had been partly forgotten, partly neglected, were once more introduced into daily life. Graetz, ii. ii. p. 35–49. Josephus, "Antiq.," xiii. ch. x. p. 5, &c.

The Commentator says that the Sadducæan members of the Council were gradually all deprived of their seats, and Pharisees were substituted in their place.

The day upon which this substitution was rendered complete, Têbeth 28, was instituted by the Pharisees as an anniversary Festival.

Day XXI.

Kislêw 7. A Festival day.

The reason for this day being observed as an anniversary is not assigned in the text.

The Commentator says that it is the anniversary of the death of Herod; but Herod died early in the spring, and it is more probable, in the opinion of M. Schwab, that it commemorates the death of Alexander Jannæus, who had so cruelly persecuted the Pharisees.

Graetz, ii. ch. ii. p. 47, only says that the Pharisees celebrated the anniversary of his death with rejoicing, but gives neither the month nor the day of the month. It was in the year B.C. 79.*

Cassel thinks that Kislêw 7 may be the commemoration of the death of Antiochus Eupator, in B.C. 162. He was son and successor of Epiphanes, and quite as much hated as his father.

Dr. Bannister, p. 391, adopts the error of the Commentator, although at p. 259 he gives correctly the month Kislêw as corresponding to November-December, when most certainly Herod did not die.

Day XXII.

Tammûz 14. Suppression of the penal code of the Sadducees.

Graetz, ii. ch. i. p. 22, 23. In the many points of dispute between the Pharisees and the Sadducees the latter invariably followed the exact letter of the Law, which resulted in their occasionally enforcing stricter rules than the Pharisees. For example, the Sadducees maintained that the punishment ordered by the Pentateuch for the infliction of any bodily injury—"an eye for an eye, a tooth for a tooth"—should be literally interpreted and followed out. They obtained in consequence the reputation of being cruel administrators of justice, whilst the Pharisees, appealing to traditional interpretations of the Scriptures, allowed mercy to preponderate, and only required a pecuniary compensation from the offender.

The Commentator says that the Sadducees had their own code for the punishment of crime, outside of or beyond the penal prescriptions of the Mosaical Law. The Pharisees, when they obtained supremacy [in the Council] rejected this particular code, for the simple reason that it said, "Traditional law ought not be put in the place of Scripture."

M. Schwab thinks that, in addition to this reason, the Pharisees might have wished to repress the great severity shown by the Sadducees. It is known from Josephus, "Antiq.," xiii. x. § 6, that they

* Ewald, v. p. 393, gives this year for the accession of his widow, Queen Salome.

acted with extreme rigour in criminal process, while the Pharisees allowed much room for indulgence.

It amounts to this:—The Sadducees rejected all traditional laws, and traditional interpretations of the written Law. They held that a strict adhesion to the literal words of the Law, as given in Holy Scripture, was to be maintained. The Pharisees, on the contrary, adhered to the traditions of the ancients, which they permitted in some cases to override the written Law, thus making the latter to be of none effect. They compared the written word to water; the traditional explanation of it to the wine which is mingled with water. *Cf.* S. Matthew xv. 6, "Ye make void the Law (τὴν ἐντολὴν) of God through your tradition"; and S. Mark vii. 10, "Full well do ye reject the commandment of God that ye may keep your tradition."

Day XXIII.

Âbh 24. Return to the Law.

In other words, submission of the Sadducees, and introduction of the right of heritage according to the rules of the Pharisees.

A law had been introduced by the Sadducees that daughters as well as sons should inherit the estates of their parents. This law was abolished by the Pharisees.

From Numbers xxvii. 1–11 it would appear that no law had been previously given concerning the right of females to inherit in default of male issue. At verse 8 we read how the Lord spake unto Moses saying, "Thou shalt speak unto the children of Israel saying, If a man die, and have no son, then ye shall cause his inheritance to pass unto his daughter." This seems to imply that if a man died and left sons and daughters the inheritance would pass to the former only. If that were the case, this was one of the Levitical injunctions to which the Sadducees paid little attention. It did not stand alone in this respect: Graetz, ii. i. 23, says they neglected "the injunction to carefully avoid the touch of any person or thing considered unclean, and ridiculed their rivals when the latter purified the vessels of the Temple after they had been subject to any contact of the sort."

Day XXIV.

Nisân 1–8. Commemorative of the Decision of the Pharisees that the expense of the daily sacrifice ought to be provided out of the treasury of the Temple.

Graetz, ii. ii. p. 52. When the Pharisees under Queen Salome Alexandra had obtained supremacy the Synhedrion introduced a measure which was diametrically opposed to the views of their opponents. The Sadducees had declared that the daily offerings, and in fact the requirements of the Temple, should not be drawn from a national revenue, but from individual voluntary contributions; but the Council decreed that every Israelite from the age of twenty—proselytes and freed slaves included—should contribute half a shekel yearly to the maintenance, or treasure-house of the Temple. In this way the daily sacrifices acquired a truly national character, as the whole nation contributed towards them. Three collections were instituted during the year: in Judæa at the beginning of spring; in Egypt and Syria at the Feast of Weeks; and in Babylonia, Media, and Asia Minor at the Feast of Tabernacles.

Day XXV.

Nîsân 8–22. Recalls the ordinance of the Pharisees that the Feast of Weeks—Pentecost—should be celebrated on any day of the week, and not be restricted upon the first day of the week, "the morrow of the Sabbath."

The importance of this victory gained by the Pharisees over their opponents consisted in the principle that tradition is superior to the actual written words of Scripture.

The direction in Leviticus xxiii. 16 is that the Feast should be on the fiftieth day counted from "the morrow after the Sabbath" of the Passover. M. Schwab says, "It must be believed that for a certain time, under the Sadducees, the Feast of Pentecost had been celebrated in conformity with their teaching, that is to say, on "the morrow after the Sabbath."

The Commentator says that when the Pharisees came into power they changed this day to the fiftieth, counted from the second day of the Passover. In remembrance of their triumph they celebrated all the fifteen days, from Nîsân 8 to 23, during which the debates lasted.

It is further stated by the Commentator that the discussion on the meaning of the Biblical expressions took place between R. Jochanan ben Zaccäi, R. Eliezer, R. Ismäil, and R. Juda.

R. Jochanan ben Zaccäi lived in the time of King Agrippa, some fifty or sixty years after the commencement of the Christian Era. It was he who, when in the stormy times of anarchy murders by the

Sicarii became so frequent, found it necessary to abrogate the sin-offering for the shedding of innocent blood, because too many animals would have had to be slaughtered (Graetz, ii. ix. p. 240). Hence, M. Schwab observes, "What an anachronism! The Commentator seems to have referred to the epoch when the Pharisees and Sadducees were in dispute, the various interpretations put forth by Doctors and Rabbis who lived, as is well known, two centuries later."

Day XXVI.

Marḥeshwân 27. An anniversary commemorative of the decision of the Pharisees that the loaves of fine flour, offered as first fruits, were not to be consumed by the priests, but ought to be burnt upon the altar.

The Commentary indicates that the contrary had been the practice of the Sadducees—the priests eat the bread.

This was another triumph of tradition over the Law, for the offering is enjoined in Leviticus xxiii. 15–21, where, at verse 20, it is said of the loaves, "they shall be holy to the Lord, for the priests."

Day XXVII.

Adhâr 17. The Doctors of the Law—Pharisees—being persecuted were delivered.

M. Schwab says that it is impossible to ascertain from the expressions employed with respect to this date whether the persecution to which reference is made occurred under Alexander Jannæus or under some other king.

The Commentary thus explains the reason for this day being made commemorative:—"When Jannæus persecuted the Doctors of the Law they fled to Syria, and sojourned in the province of Seleucia."

Josephus, "Antiq.," xiii. ch. xiv. § 2, attests the flight of eight thousand supporters of the Pharisees, on the night after Jannæus had crucified eight hundred of them (see *ante*, Day xix. Têbeth 28).

M. Schwab says that this day ought not to be taken as commemorating only the escape of the Pharisees from the fury of Jannæus but also their deliverance from the heathen. The Commentator states that the Doctors, in their first place of refuge, had been attacked, and part of them fled for safety to Beth-Zebedee. He gives a further detail:—The fugitives, to avoid the danger, placed before their doors horses fully harnessed as for a journey; this was on the Sabbath day, so that it would be made to appear that they had discarded all religious ordinances; then, favoured by the darkness of night, they started and escaped; or again, it may well have been the case that at the time of the persecution a great inundation devastated the country.

Day XXVIII.

Adhâr 20. Miraculous rain after a long drought.

This was in the time of Aristobulus who succeeded his mother Salome Alexandra.

Josephus, "Antiq.," xiv. ii. § 1. "There was a man whose name was Onias; a righteous man he was, and beloved of God, who, in a certain drought, had prayed to God to put an end to the intense heat, and whose prayers God had heard, and sent them rain."

Day XXIX.

Adhâr 8 and 9. Days of rejoicing for rain.

There is a difficulty about this commemoration. The text does not make any reference to some special occasion when the want of rain had been felt; it does not say, as might have been expected, that prayers had been made, and the Divine succour afforded in response to those prayers: it does not say why there were two days, but only that they were days of rejoicing on account of rain.

M. Schwab, under Adhâr 20, with which he thinks these days must have had some close connection, refers to three years of extreme drought and famine, which occurred after the death of Salome Alexandra, when Onias prayed for rain. He thinks it probable that in those years public prayers and fasting for rain were instituted, and that Adhâr 8 may have been the day so observed in the first of those years, with Adhâr 9 as the day observed in the second year. When, at a later time, the rain fell, the fact that the prayers had been answered may have been commemorated, and the two days of penitence have been transformed into semi-festivals, not now to be observed as days of fasting but as days of joy. In a footnote, p. 242, he says, "It is *à propos* to this that the Commentator recalls the circumstance of the Meghilla being in the order of the months, and not in that of the years."

Josephus, in the passage from which a quotation was given in the notice of the preceding day, xxviii., only mentions "a certain drought," without saying for how long a time it lasted.

Division E.

In the time of the Roman Domination.

Day XXX.

Schebhât 2. A Festival day.

As with Kislêw 7, so with this day, the reason for its being observed as an anniversary is not given in the text. M. Schwab thinks that the Commentator is wrong in taking upon himself to assign —as he does—the commemoration of the death of Herod to Kislêw 7; he considers it to be more probable that the rejoicing for that event was upon this day—Schebhât 2. He says that Herod, according to the received Chronology, did not die in Kislêw, but in Schebhât.

It is now almost universally acknowledged that the death of Herod took place in the year B.C. 4, but the exact day of his death has never been established. It can only be ascertained approximately from the statement by Josephus, "Antiq.," xvii. vi. 4, that it was a few days after the occurrence of an Eclipse of the Moon. An Eclipse actually did occur on March 13, B.C. 4,* year 4710 of the Julian Period, and M. Schwab says that Scaliger places this in the month Schebhât ("De Emendatione Temp.," v. p. 463). That is the case; but M. Schwab omits to add that Scaliger states the Eclipse to have occurred on the fourteenth day of that month, in the year of Nabonassar 747 (coinciding with August 24, B.C. 2 to August 22, B.C. 1), in the Jewish year 3760 (which commenced in the Autumn of B.C. 2, and terminated in the Autumn of B.C. 1), in the Julian year 45, and in the year 4713 of the Julian Period (both of which coincided with B.C. 1). Thus Scaliger is very decisive about the year of Herod's death, namely, that it was B.C. 1. But, Petavius, tom. ii. lib. xi. cap. iv. p. 164, very clearly demonstrates that Scaliger is wrong about the year, and therefore it is quite possible that he may be wrong also about the month.

In fact, it appears that both Schebhât 2 and Schebhât 14 are too early for the date of Herod's death. According to the Table given by

* "L'Art de Vérifier les Dates," pt. i. tom. i. p. 246. Petavius, "De Doctrina Temporum," tom. ii. lib. xi. cap. iv. p. 164.

Gumpach,* Nisân 1 was on March 25, in B.C. 1, and on March 29 in B.C. 4, and as there are 59 days from Schebhât 1 to Nîsân 1, Schebhât 14 would be February 7 in B.C. 1, and February 11 in B.C. 4, for we have the following calculation:—

B.C. 1, Nîsân 1 = March 25 = January 84
Adhâr 1 = January 84 − 29 = January 55
Schebhât 1 = January 55 − 30 = January 25
Schebhât 14 = January 25 + 13 = January 38 = February 7.

In B.C. 4, Schebhât 14 is four days later = February 11.

Now the Eclipse happened on March 13th, which is more than "a few days" after either February 7 or February 11.

Schebhât 2 is yet further removed, by twelve days, from March 13.

I am not aware whether it has ever been suggested that Schebhât 2, if it really has anything to do with the death of Herod, may commemorate, not the day of his death, but the time when he was struck with mortal illness, of which an account is given by Josephus, "Antiq.," xvii. vi. 5. From Schebhât 2 to the Passover, Nîsân 15, there is an interval of 72 days which may possibly have been occupied as follows:—

Illness of Herod before he ordered the execution of his son Antipater; during this time he went to Jericho, and thence to the baths of Callirhoe. Josephus, "Antiq.," xvii. vi. 5	21 days
He died five days after the execution of Antipater. *Ib.* viii. 1, at Jericho. *Ib.* "Wars," i. xxxiii. 6	5 ,,
Reading of his letter to the army, and of his will; and acclamation of Archelaus as king. *Ib.* viii. 2	7 ,,
Preparation for the funeral march from Jericho to Herodium, which was accompanied by the "whole army in the same manner as they used to go out to war." *Ib.* viii. 3 and "Wars," i. xxxiii. 9	7 ,,
March from Jericho to Herodium, 200 stadia, at a daily rate of 8 stadia. *Ib.* viii. 3	25 ,,
Mourning by Archelaus continued for seven days. *Ib.* viii. 4	7 ,,
	72 days

* "Über den Alt Jüdischen Kalender," p. 361. Brüssel, 1848.

And the next day, the Passover.

Graetz, ii. iv. p. 117, without suggesting the day, only says that the nation joyfully celebrated the death of Herod as a semi-festival.

DAY XXXI.

Schebhât 22. Non-execution of the decree to place the statue of the Emperor Cauis Caligula in the Temple, due to his death. A.D. 41.

The Chronicle says, "On Schebhât 22 the work ordered by the Emperor to be carried on in the Temple was interrupted." This refers to the madness of Caligula who desired to be adored as a divinity throughout the Empire.

A full account is given by Graetz, ii. viii. p. 189:—Orders had been sent from Rome that the imperial statues were to be erected not only in the synagogues but in the Temple at Jerusalem. Petronius, who was then Governor of Syria, was directed to enter Judæa with his legions, and to turn the Sanctuary into a pagan temple. On the eve of the Feast of Tabernacles a messenger brought the news to Jerusalem. Petronius was at Acco, on the outskirts of Jerusalem, but as the rainy season was at hand, and an obstinate resistance was expected, he resolved to wait for the Spring before commencing operations. Thousands of Judæans hastened to appear before him, declaring that they would rather suffer death than allow their Temple to be desecrated. Petronius sent a true statement of the case to the Emperor, pacifying the people by telling them that nothing could be effected before fresh edicts arrived from Rome. Before his letter had been received by the Emperor, King Agrippa, who was then at Rome, succeeded in obtaining a reversal of the edict, and letters were sent to Petronius annulling the former decree. Meanwhile the letter from Petronius was received by the Emperor. It detailed the difficulties which would have to be encountered if any attempt were made to execute the orders. More than this was not required to lash Caligula's passionate nature into fury. A new order was given to proceed with the introduction of the statues into the Temple; but before it reached Jerusalem the insane Caligula was killed by the prætor Chereas, January 24, B.C. 41.

Tidings of this came to Jerusalem on Schebhât 22, and the day was celebrated as one of great rejoicing.

Day XXXII.

Sîwân 25. Cessation of payment of taxes to the Romans. A.D. 66.

Josephus, "Wars," ii. xvi. §§ 4, 5, recounts that the first act of open rebellion against Rome consisted in the refusal to pay the tax. King Agrippa reproached the people, and described this action as treason towards Rome.

Graetz, ii. ch. ix. It was in A.D. 66. Gessius Florus had been appointed procurator by Poppæa, the wife of Nero. By his shameless partiality, avarice, and inhumanity he hastened the execution of a plan, to shake off the tyrannical yoke of Rome, which had long been cherished by the Judæans. Terrible acts of cruelty and massacre were perpetrated. On one day, Iyâr 16, more than three thousand six hundred men perished, and at length things arrived at such a pitch that a complete revolt broke out. The war of insurrection actually commenced when the Roman troops, by direction of Florus, were about to attack Fort Antonia and the Temple, with the design of carrying off the treasures. The people broke down the colonnade which connected the fortress with the Temple, and so frustrated the governor's hope. Florus then quitted the city; his courage forsook him before the determined attitude of the people. But there were many among the Judæans who were in favour of peace: the followers of Hillel, who abhorred war on principle; the noble and wealthy, whose possessions would be exposed to jeopardy, and who, though smarting under the insolence of Florus, desired the continuance of the present state of things under the imperial power of Rome.

Meanwhile the leaders of the revolutionary party has so far carried their point that the payment of taxes to Rome was withheld. King Agrippa,* who was in favour of peace, called the people together, and in a long speech (preserved by Josephus, "Wars," ii. xvi. 4) urged every possible argument against war. This made some impression at first. A number of people cried out that they had no ill-will against Rome, and only desired to be delivered from the yoke of Florus. Agrippa then exhorted them to replace the broken columns of the colonnade which they had thrown down, and to pay the taxes due to the Emperor. Then he tried to persuade the people to obey Florus; but this spoilt all.

* The same who said to S. Paul, "Almost thou persuadest me to be a Christian." Acts of Apostles xxvi. 28.

The revolutionary party again obtained the upper hand, and Agrippa was obliged to fly from Jerusalem.

After his departure there was no further question of taxes. The satisfaction at their abolition was universal, and the day upon which it was finally resolved that they should not be paid was henceforth to be kept as an anniversary of victory.

M. Schwab says it is possible to determine the date approximately. It must have been between the departure of Florus, Iyâr 16 or 18, and the time when Agrippa invited the people to submit, and had to fly from Jerusalem. This was before the strife of parties, which was before the month Âbh. Consequently the payment of taxes must have been interrupted between the months Iyâr and Âbh, and nearer to the former than to the latter. It was after Agrippa left that there commenced the cessation of the sacrifice offered for the Emperor, the sending of deputies to Florus and Agrippa, and at last the entry of the troops.

These deputies were sent by the advocates of peace, entreating that a sufficient number of troops might be instantly dispatched to Jerusalem to keep order. Florus refused to comply, hoping that the opposing parties among the Judæans would destroy each other; but Agrippa sent three thousand horsemen. Graetz, ii. ix. p. 260.

Hence Sîwân 25 is well adapted to be the correct date for the expulsion of the tax-gatherers.

Day XXXIII.

'Elûl 7. Expulsion of the Romans from Jerusalem and from Judæa.

Graetz, ii. ix.; Josephus, "Wars," ii. xvii. In continuation of the preceding narrative:—When the troops sent by Agrippa arrived at Jerusalem they found the Mount on which the Temple stood, as well as the lower town, in possession of the revolutionary party, the Zealots. A fierce combat took place, and fighting continued for seven days with no decided result. At the time of the Festival of Wood-carrying, Âbh 15, the Zealots barred the entrance to the Temple against any one belonging to the peace party, and gained over to their side the masses of people who had brought wood for the altar. Strengthened in numbers they drove away their opponents, and became masters of the upper town. They set fire to the houses of King

Agrippa and the Princess Berenice, and of the High Priest Ananias, and burned the public archives. They then attacked the Roman guards in Fort Antonia, overcame them, and put them to the sword, Âbh 17. They next proceeded to storm the palace of Herod, which was defended by the combined troops of Rome and Agrippa, under the command of Metilius. After eighteen days' fighting the garrison capitulated. The remaining Romans then retired to the three towers in the wall, where they were besieged, and were at last obliged to sue for mercy. They were all destroyed with the exception of Melitius himself, who, in fear of death, promised to adopt the Judæan faith.

The day on which Jerusalem was thus delivered from the Romans was appointed to be from henceforth one of the festive anniversaries.

Division E.

After the destruction of the Temple of Jerusalem, and the end of the independence of the Jewish people.

Day XXXIV.

Adhâr 12. The Day of Trajan.

Graetz, ii. ch. xv. In the Spring of A.D. 116 the Jews of Babylon, Egypt, Cyrenaica, Lybia, and Cyprus were seized with the idea of shaking off the Roman yoke. The leaders of the rebellion were two brothers, Julianus Alexander and Pappus.

Amongst other operations with a view to quell the rebellion, the chief command in the district of the Euphrates was given by Trajan to his favourite general, Quintus Lucius Quietus, a Moorish prince. His orders were to annihilate the Jews entirely, but it was not till after a contest of long duration that the Romans became masters of the situation. Quietus destroyed many thousands, and laid waste the towns inhabited by the Jews. As a reward for his services Trajan named him Governor of Palestine, with absolute power.

When Hadrian succeeded Trajan, A.D. 117, he granted to the Jews many of their requests. Among these was one for the removal of Quietus. He was deposed, and although the jealousy of the new Emperor with regard to this powerful ruler was the chief reason for his removal, it was made to appear that it had been done as a favour to the Jews. Before he fell into disgrace Quietus was about to pass sentence of death on the two Jewish leaders, Julianus and Pappus, who had fallen into his hands, and were to be executed at Loadicea.

The Commentary relates that Quietus addressed them thus: "If you are of the nation of Hananias, Michael, and Azaria, your God can come and deliver you out of my hands, as He delivered those three men from the hands of Nebuchadnezzar." The brothers answered: "Hananias, Michael, and Azaria were of a truth righteous men, and Nebuchadnezzar was in fact a king, who deserved to be the occasion of so great a miracle. If we have deserved death in the sight of Heaven, and you do not slay us, God has at His disposal abundant means for striking us down—bears, lions, serpents, and scorpions in numbers. If you do slay us God will some day require from you an account of our blood which you will have shed."

At the very moment when the two brothers were being led to a martyr's death the order came from Rome which deposed their executioner from the governorship of Judæa.

The day of their release, Adhâr 12, was celebrated as memorable, and appointed to be a semi-festival under the name of the Day of Trajan.

Day XXXV.

Adhâr 28. End of the persecution which was commenced by Hadrian. A.D. 139 or 140.

"On this day the good news reached the Jews that they were no longer to be persecuted for following the ordinances of their law."

The Commentator refers these words to the retractation of the edicts of Hadrian, which put an end to the persecution. The foreign governors, he says, had forbidden the Jews to observe their Law, to circumcise their children, or to keep the Sabbaths, and had ordained the practice of idolatry.

Jehuda ben Shamua and his companions were advised by a certain noble Roman lady to petition the governor. This they did, and their lamentations induced him to beseech the Emperor that a milder course of conduct might be pursued towards the Jews. Graetz, ii. xvi. p. 435.

This Emperor was Titus Aurelius Antoninus, surnamed Pius, the adopted son of Hadrian, whom he succeeded in A.D. 138. He conceded to the Jews the right of circumcision, but they were not allowed to make proselytes. It was in March, A.D. 139 or 140, on Adhâr 28, that the joyful news arrived of the revocation of the decrees of Hadrian, and this day was made commemorative.

Hadrian commenced his war against the Jews in A.D. 131. It was carried on with the utmost fury on both sides, and was not brought to an end till A.D. 136. Hadrian died in July, A.D. 138.

M. Schwab, p. 251, observes that there are passages in the Talmud to prove that all these days were piously observed in the third century of the Christian Era.* Notice of them is also found in the first half of the fourth century, for it is said of Rabbi Zeïra that he fasted three hundred days in the year, and did not abstain from fasting even on the days of the semi-festivals.

This must have been the Zeïra II. who, according to Graetz, vol. ii. ch. xxi. p. 590, was chosen as one of the four from among whom was to be elected the head of the Academy of Pumbeditha in Persia, after the death of Joseph ben Chiya, about A.D. 333. Graetz does not speak of the fasting mentioned by Schwab, and the latter does not give his authority for the statement.

In the fourth century a distinction was made between the days of Purim and Chanukka on the one part, and the other Festivals in the list on the other part. The former were maintained; the latter fell out of use.

114. Days of Fasting.

The Chronicle ends with a list of twenty-five days of mourning, for which fasting is recommended. The language is Hebrew, and too correct to belong to the same period as the preceding list. There is no Commentary to explain these days, and few traces of them are to be found in the Talmud. The following is the list:—

On the following days, says the Chronicle, fasting is prescribed by the Law, and on these days it is not right either to eat or to drink before the night. The Chronicle does not give the Scriptural references attached.

1. Nisân 1. Death of the sons of Aaron.

    Leviticus x. 1, 2. Nadab and Abihu: "There went out fire from the Lord and devoured them, and they died before the Lord."

* Tr. Taanith, ii. 15, f. 15b. B tr. Rosch haschâna, f. 10b, and 19a. B. tr. Taanith, f. 18a.

2. Nîsân 20. Death of Miriam, the sister of Moses; and the wells are closed.

Numbers xx. 1, 2. "The people abode in Kadesh; and Miriam died there; and was buried there. And there was no water for the congregation."

M. Schwab has a footnote, "This is the only historical source, besides the Bible, which mentions this fact (that is, the want of water), without date."

3. Nîsân 26. Death of Joshua, the son of Nûn. Joshua xxiv. 29.

4. Iyâr 20. Death of the High Priest Eli, and of his two sons. The ark of the Covenant taken by the Philistines. 1 Samuel v. 11–18.

5. Iyâr 29. Death of Samuel.

1 Samuel xxv. 1 and xxviii. 3.

Instead of Iyâr 29, the chronology of al-Bîrûni ("Vestiges," p. 275) gives Iyâr 28—a date which Schwab says is also found in Jacob ben Ascher, Tour Oraḥ Hayim, No. 580.

6. Sîwân 23. First fruits cease to be brought to Jerusalem, in consequence of the obstacles placed in the way by Jeroboam, son of Nebat.

1 Kings xii. 16–19. The fact of the children of Israel ceasing to bring the first fruits to Jerusalem is not actually mentioned, but it may be gathered from the expressions used: "To your tents, O Israel: now see to thine own house, David. So Israel departed unto their tents." "So Israel rebelled against the house of David unto this day."

7. Sîwân 25. They put to death (by Roman tortures) R. Simon ben Gamaliel, R. Ishmaël ben Elischa, and R. Chananyâ.

Simon ben Gamaliel was president of the Synhedrion when Jochanan ben Zaccaï was vice-president. Graetz, vol. ii. ch. ix. p. 241; about A.D. 60. See Notices, Day xxv.

8. Sîwân 27. Rabbi Chananyâ ben Teradion is burned, by order of the same tyrants, and with him the roll of the Law.

This was done by Rufus, in the time of Hadrian. The account is given by Graetz, ii. xvi. p. 432.

9. Tammûz 17. The first Tables of the Law were broken; Exodus xxxii. 19. The offering of the daily sacrifice was interrupted; 1 Maccabees 1, 45. Apostomos (Antiochus Epiphanes), burns the Law, and sets up an idol in the Sanctuary.

   In 1 Maccabees i. 54–56 this is said to have been done on the fifteenth day of the month Kislêw.

10. Âbh 1. Death of the High Priest Aaron. Numbers xxxiii. 38.

11. Âbh 9. It was forbidden that the Israelites in the wilderness should enter Palestine. Numbers xiv. 23.

   The first Temple was destroyed [by Nebuchadnezzar]. The city of Bethar was taken, and then Jerusalem was ravaged and destroyed [by Titus].

12. Âbh 18. The light placed in the west of the Temple is extinguished in the time of Ahaz.

   Compare 2 Chronicles xxviii. 24 with xxix. 7. Al-Bîrûnî makes this event to have happened on Âbh 28.

13. 'Elûl 7. The explorers (spies) in the time of Moses having made an evil report of Palestine, die of pestilence in the desert. Numbers xiv. 37.

   According to Jacob ben Ascher this should be 'Elûl 17.

14. Tishrî 3. Assassination of Guedaliah, and of the Jews who were with him at Mizpah.

   2 Kings xxv. 25. Jeremiah xli. 2.

15. Tishrî 5. Death of twenty notable persons in Israel. R. Akîbâ ben Joseph was cast into prison, where he died.

   Some account of this has been previously given in Article 99, under Iyâr 18.

16. Tishrî 7–10. The famine and the sword afflict Israel on account of the golden calf.

   Exodus xxxii. 27 and 35.

17. Marḥeshwân 6. The eyes of Zedekia were put out after his sons had been slain before him.

   2 Kings xxv. 7.

18. Kislêw 7. Jehoiachim burns the roll written by Baruch ben Neria at the dictation of Jeremiah.

Jeremiah xxxvi. 20–25. Al-Bîrûnî places this Fast at Kislêw 8. Others, on Kislêw 28.

19. Têbeth 8. The Thora was translated into Greek under King Ptolemy. During three days darkness was spread over the world.

Al-Bîrûnî makes Têbeth 5 the first and Têbeth 8 the last of the three days of darkness. See the account in Article 94.

20. Têbeth 9. A Fast for which the Rabbis give no reason.

No further explanation is given. Al-Bîrûnî says, "A fast, of whose origin they are ignorant."

At a later time the death of Ezra was attributed to this day.

21. Têbeth 10. The King of Babylon makes his hand heavy against Jerusalem to destroy it.

See Article 94.

22. Schebhât 8. The just men who survived Joshua the son of Nûn die in their turn.

Al-Bîrûnî places this Fast at Schebhât 5, and says that others fix it on the Monday between the tenth and fifteenth of this month.

23. Schebhât 23. The indignant Israelites attack the tribe of Benjamin on the affair of the concubine.

Judges xix. 16 to xxi. 24. They oppose the idol of Micah. Judges xviii. 14.

24. Adhâr 7. Death of Moses, our Divine Master. Deuteronomy xxxiv. 5.

Al-Bîrûnî adds that the manna and the quails ceased to appear.

25. Adhâr 9. A Fast instituted in memory of the strife between Schammaï and Hillel.

See Article 96.

"Such are the days of fasting legally accepted by Israel. In addition to these our Doctors have prescribed minor fasts:—The Monday and Thursday which follow the days of the great fasts in memory of the destruction of the Temple, of the burning of the Law and of the blasphemies against God. But, 'The days of mourning shall be changed to days of joy,' saith the Eternal. Amen."

The Chronicle is closed with these words. The reference here is to Jeremiah xxxi. 13. "For I will turn their mourning into joy, and will comfort them, and make them rejoice from their sorrow."

M. Schwab adds: "It may be noticed that it is with the fasts as with the semi-festivals. Just as they only maintain [from these lists] the feasts of Chanukka and Purim, so the strict Israelites fast not except on the four following days: Tammûz 17, Âbh 9, Tishrî 3, and Tebêth 10 (besides the vigil of Purim) [that is, the fast of Esther]."

GENERAL TABLES

Table I.

EQUIVALENTS OF CHALAKIM IN MINUTES AND SECONDS.

Chalakim.	Minutes.	Seconds.	Or Min.	Or Sec.	Or Thirds.
1		3⅓		3	20
2		6⅔		6	40
3		10		10	0
4		13⅓		13	20
5		16⅔		16	40
6		20		20	0
7		23⅓		23	20
8		26⅔		26	40
9		30		30	0
10		33⅓		33	20
20	1	6⅔	1	6	40
30	1	40	1	40	0
40	2	13⅓	2	13	20
50	2	46⅔	2	46	40
60	3	20	3	20	0
70	3	53⅓	3	53	20
80	4	26⅔	4	26	40
90	5	0	5	0	0
100	5	33⅓	5	33	20
200	11	6⅔	11	6	40
300	16	40	16	40	0
400	22	13⅓	22	13	20
500	27	46⅔	27	46	40
600	33	20	33	20	0
700	38	53⅓	38	53	20
800	44	26⅔	44	26	40
900	50	0	50	0	0
1000	55	33⅓	55	33	20
1080	60	0	60	0	0

Table II.

EQUIVALENTS OF MINUTES AND SECONDS IN CHALAKIM AND RÊGÄIM.

Minutes.	Seconds.	Chalakim.	Or Chal.	Or Reg.
	1	·3		22·8
	2	·6		45·6
	3	·9		68·4
	4	1·2	1	15·2
	5	1·5	1	38
	6	1·8	1	60·8
	7	2·1	2	7·6
	8	2·4	2	30·4
	9	2·7	2	53·2
	10	3		
	20	6		
	30	9		
	40	12		
	50	15		
1		18		
2		36		
3		54		
4		72		
5		90		
6		108		
7		126		
8		144		
9		162		
10		180		
20		360		
30		540		
40		720		
50		900		
60		1080		

Table III.

DURATION OF JEWISH ASTRONOMICAL LUNAR YEARS.

COMMON YEARS OF 12 LUNATIONS.				EMBOLISMIC YEARS OF 13 LUNATIONS.			
Years.	Days.	H.	Chal.	Years.	Days.	H.	Chal.
1	354	8	876	1	383	21	589
2	708	17	672	2	767	19	98
3	1063	2	468	3	1151	16	687
4	1417	11	264	4	1535	14	196
5	1771	20	60	5	1919	11	785
6	2126	4	936	6	2303	9	294
7	2480	13	732	7	2687	6	883
8	2834	22	528				
9	3189	7	324				
10	3543	16	120				
11	3898	0	996				
12	4252	9	792				

The sum of 12 Common years.................	4252	9	792
and of 7 Embolismic years	2687	6	883
amounts to 1 Cycle .... =	6939	16	595

Care must be taken that this Table be not used in a wrong manner, by assuming, for example, that the interval of time contained in the first twelve years of a Cycle is 4252d. 9h. 792ch. The first twelve years contain

8 Common years .... =	2834d.	22h.	528ch.
and 4 Embolismic years .... =	1535	14	196
The first twelve years therefore contain...	4370d.	12h.	724ch.

as will be seen by the next Table.

Table IV.

TIME ELAPSED AT THE CLOSE OF EACH YEAR OF AN ASTRONOMICAL CYCLE.

Year.	Days.	Hours.	Chal.
1	354	8	876
2	708	17	672
3 Emb.	1092	15	181
4	1446	23	1057
5	1801	8	853
6 Emb.	2185	6	362
7	2539	15	158
8 Emb.	2923	12	747
9	3277	21	543
10	3632	6	339
11 Emb.	4016	3	928
12	4370	12	724
13	4724	21	520
14 Emb.	5108	19	29
15	5463	3	905
16	5817	12	701
17 Emb.	6201	10	210
18	6555	19	6
19 Emb.	6939	16	595

Table V.

ASTRONOMICAL DURATION OF JEWISH CYCLES OF NINETEEN YEARS.

Cycles.	Days.	H.	Ch.	Cycles.	Days.	H.	Ch.
1	6939	16	595	17	117974	17	395
2	13879	9	110	18	124914	9	990
3	20819	1	705	19	131854	2	505
4	27758	18	220	20	138793	19	20
5	34698	10	815	30	208190	16	570
6	41638	3	330	40	277587	14	40
7	48577	19	925	50	346984	11	590
8	55517	12	440	60	416381	9	60
9	62457	4	1035	70	485778	6	610
10	69396	21	550	80	555175	4	80
11	76336	14	65	90	624572	1	630
12	83276	6	660	100	693968	23	100
13	90215	23	175	200	1387937	22	200
14	97155	15	770	300	2081906	21	300
15	104095	8	285	400	3775975	20	400
16	111035	0	880	500	4469944	19	500

Table VI.

ADDITIONS TO BE MADE TO THE MOLAD, M. FOR TISHRÎ IN ANY GIVEN YEAR, IN ORDER TO OBTAIN THE MOLADS FOR OTHER MONTHS IN THE SAME YEAR.

For the Month	In a Common year add			For the Month.	In an Embolismic year add		
	D.	H.	Ch.		D.	H.	Ch.
Marḥeshwân............	1	12	793	Marḥeshwân............	1	12	793
Kislêw	3	1	506	Kislêw	3	1	506
Têbeth	4	14	219	Têbeth	4	14	219
Schebhât	6	2	1012	Schebhât	6	2	1012
				Adhâr I.	0	15	725
Adhâr......................	0	15	725	Adhâr II.	2	4	438
Nîsân.....................	2	4	438	Nîsân.....................	3	17	151
Iyâr	3	17	151	Iyâr	5	5	994
Sîwân.....................	5	5	944	Sîwân.....................	6	18	657
Tammûz	6	18	657	Tammûz	1	7	370
Abh	1	7	370	Abh.............	2	20	83
'Elul	2	20	83	'Elûl	4	8	876
Tishrî in the next year	4	8	876	Tishrî in the next year	5	21	589

Table VII.

ADDITIONS TO BE MADE TO THE MOLAD FOR THE FIRST YEAR IN ANY CYCLE TO OBTAIN THAT FOR ANY OTHER YEAR IN THE SAME CYCLE.

For the Year.	Add		
	D.	H.	Ch.
Second	4	8	876
Third	1	17	672
Fourth	0	15	181
Fifth	4	23	1057
Sixth	2	8	853
Seventh	1	6	362
Eighth	5	15	158
Ninth	4	12	747
Tenth	1	21	543
Eleventh	6	6	339
Twelth	5	3	928
Thirteenth	2	12	724
Fourteenth	6	21	520
Fifteenth	5	19	29
Sixteenth	3	3	905
Seventeenth	0	12	701
Eighteenth	6	10	210
Nineteenth	3	19	6
First year of next Cycle	2	16	595

TABLE VIII.

ADDITIONS TO BE MADE TO THE MOLAD FOR ANY GIVEN CYCLE IN ORDER TO OBTAIN THAT FOR ANY SUBSEQUENT CYCLE.

Cycles.*	Collected Years.	D.	H.	Ch.
1	19	2	16	595
2	38	5	9	110
3	57	1	1	705
4	76	3	18	220
5	95	6	10	815
6	114	2	3	330
7	133	4	19	925
8	152	0	12	440
9	171	3	4	1035
10	190	5	21	550
11	209	1	14	65
12	228	4	6	660
13	247	6	23	175
14	266	2	15	770
15	285	5	8	285
16	304	1	0	880
17	323	3	17	395
18	342	6	9	990
19	361	2	2	505
20	380	4	19	20
30	570	3	16	570
40	760	2	14	40
50	950	1	11	590
60	1140	0	9	60
70	1330	6	6	610
80	1520	5	4	80
90	1710	4	1	630
100	1900	2	23	100
200	3800	5	22	200
300	5700	1	21	300
400	7600	4	20	400
500	9500	0	19	500
600	11400	3	18	600

* That is, Number of Cycles on account of which the Addition is to be made. Thus, for the second Cycle, add the excess of one Cycle to that of the first. For the eighth Cycle add that of 7 Cycles to the first.

Table IX.

MOLADS FOR THE CYCLES 1 TO 528. A.M. 1 TO 10014.

Cycle.	A.M.	D.	H.	Ch.	Cycle.	A.M.	D.	H.	Ch.
1	1	2	5	204	43	799	3	4	354
2	20	4	21	799	44	818	5	20	949
3	39	7	14	314	45	837	1	13	464
4	58	3	6	909	46	856	4	5	1059
5	77	5	23	424	47	875	6	22	574
6	96	1	15	1019	48	894	2	15	89
7	115	4	8	534	49	913	5	7	684
8	134	7	1	49	50	932	1	0	199
9	153	2	17	644	51	951	3	16	794
10	172	5	10	159	52	970	6	9	309
11	191	1	2	754	53	989	2	1	904
12	210	3	19	269	54	1008	4	18	419
13	229	6	11	864	55	1027	7	10	1014
14	248	2	4	379	56	1046	3	3	529
15	267	4	20	974	57	1065	5	20	44
16	286	7	13	489	58	1084	1	12	639
17	305	3	6	4	59	1103	4	5	154
18	324	5	22	599	60	1122	6	21	749
19	343	1	15	114	61	1141	2	14	264
20	362	4	7	709	62	1160	5	6	859
21	381	7	0	224	63	1179	7	23	374
22	400	2	16	819	64	1198	3	15	969
23	419	5	9	334	65	1217	6	8	484
24	438	1	1	929	66	1236	2	0	1079
25	457	3	18	444	67	1255	4	17	594
26	476	6	10	1039	68	1274	7	10	109
27	495	2	3	554	69	1293	3	2	704
28	514	4	20	69	70	1312	5	19	219
29	533	7	12	664	71	1331	1	11	814
30	552	3	5	179	72	1350	4	4	329
31	571	5	21	774	73	1369	6	20	924
32	590	1	14	289	74	1388	2	13	439
33	609	4	6	884	75	1407	5	5	1034
34	628	6	23	399	76	1426	7	22	549
35	647	2	15	994	77	1445	3	15	64
36	666	5	8	509	78	1464	6	7	659
37	685	1	1	24	79	1483	2	0	174
38	704	3	17	619	80	1502	4	16	769
39	723	6	10	134	81	1521	7	9	284
40	742	2	2	729	82	1540	3	1	879
41	761	4	19	244	83	1559	5	18	394
42	780	7	11	839	84	1578	1	10	989

TABLE IX. (*continued*).

Cycle.	A.M.	D.	H.	Ch.	Cycle.	A.M.	D.	H.	Ch.
85	1597	4	3	504	129	2433	3	11	764
86	1616	6	20	19	130	2452	6	4	279
87	1635	2	12	614	131	2471	1	20	874
88	1654	5	5	129	132	2490	4	13	389
89	1673	7	21	724	133	2509	7	5	984
90	1692	3	14	239	134	2528	2	22	499
91	1711	6	6	834	135	2547	5	15	14
92	1730	1	23	349	136	2566	1	7	609
93	1749	4	15	944	137	2585	4	0	124
94	1768	7	8	459	138	2604	6	16	719
95	1787	3	0	1054	139	2623	2	9	234
96	1806	5	17	569	140	2642	5	1	829
97	1825	1	10	84	141	2661	7	18	344
98	1844	4	2	679	142	2680	3	10	939
99	1863	6	19	194	143	2699	6	3	454
100	1882	2	11	789	144	2718	1	19	1049
101	1901	5	4	304	145	2737	4	12	564
102	1920	7	20	899	146	2756	7	5	79
103	1939	3	13	414	147	2775	2	21	674
104	1958	6	5	1009	148	2794	5	14	189
105	1977	1	22	524	149	2813	1	6	784
106	1996	4	15	39	150	2832	3	23	299
107	2015	7	7	634	151	2851	6	15	894
108	2034	3	0	149	152	2870	2	8	409
109	2053	5	16	744	153	2889	5	0	1004
110	2072	1	9	259	154	2908	7	17	519
111	2091	4	1	854	155	2927	3	10	34
112	2110	6	18	369	156	2946	6	2	629
113	2129	2	10	964	157	2965	1	19	144
114	2148	5	3	479	158	2984	4	11	739
115	2167	7	19	1074	159	3003	7	4	254
116	2186	3	12	589	160	3022	2	20	849
117	2205	6	5	104	161	3041	5	13	364
118	2224	1	21	699	162	3060	1	5	959
119	2243	4	14	214	163	3079	3	22	474
120	2262	7	6	809	164	3098	6	14	1069
121	2281	2	23	324	165	3117	2	7	584
122	2300	5	15	919	166	3136	5	0	99
123	2319	1	8	434	167	3155	7	16	694
124	2338	4	0	1029	168	3174	3	9	209
125	2357	6	17	544	169	3193	6	1	804
126	2376	2	10	59	170	3212	1	18	319
127	2395	5	2	654	171	3231	4	10	914
128	2414	7	19	169	172	3250	7	3	429

TABLE IX. (*continued*).

Cycle.	A.M.	D.	H.	Ch.	Cycle.	A.M.	D.	H.	Ch.
173	3269	2	19	1024	217	4105	2	4	204
174	3288	5	12	539	218	4124	4	20	799
175	3307	1	5	54	219	4143	7	13	314
176	3326	3	21	649	220	4162	3	5	909
177	3345	6	14	164	221	4181	5	22	424
178	3364	2	6	759	222	4200	1	14	1019
179	3383	4	23	274	223	4219	4	7	534
180	3402	7	15	869	224	4238	7	0	49
181	3421	3	8	384	225	4257	2	16	644
182	3440	6	0	979	226	4276	5	9	159
183	3459	1	17	494	227	4295	1	1	754
184	3478	4	10	9	228	4314	3	18	269
185	3497	7	2	604	229	4333	6	10	864
186	3516	2	19	119	230	4352	2	3	379
187	3535	5	11	714	231	4371	4	19	974
188	3554	1	4	229	232	4390	7	12	489
189	3573	3	20	824	233	4409	3	5	4
190	3592	6	13	339	234	4428	5	21	599
191	3611	2	5	934	235	4447	1	14	114
192	3630	4	22	449	236	4466	4	6	709
193	3649	7	14	1044	237	4485	6	23	224
194	3668	3	7	559	238	4504	2	15	819
195	3687	6	0	74	239	4523	5	8	334
196	3706	1	16	669	240	4542	1	0	929
197	3725	4	9	184	241	4561	3	17	444
198	3744	7	1	779	242	4580	6	9	1039
199	3763	2	18	294	243	4599	2	2	554
200	3782	5	10	889	244	4618	4	19	69
201	3801	1	3	404	245	4637	7	11	664
202	3820	3	19	999	246	4656	3	4	179
203	3839	6	12	514	247	4675	5	20	774
204	3858	2	5	29	248	4694	1	13	289
205	3877	4	21	624	249	4713	4	5	884
206	3896	7	14	139	250	4732	6	22	399
207	3915	3	6	734	251	4751	2	14	994
208	3934	5	23	249	252	4770	5	7	509
209	3953	1	15	844	253	4789	1	0	24
210	3972	4	8	359	254	4808	3	16	619
211	3991	7	0	954	255	4827	6	9	134
212	4010	2	17	469	256	4846	2	1	729
213	4029	5	9	1064	257	4865	4	18	244
214	4048	1	2	579	258	4884	7	10	839
215	4067	3	19	94	259	4903	3	3	354
216	4086	6	11	689	260	4922	5	19	949

TABLE IX. (*continued*).

Cycle.	A.M.	D.	H.	Ch.	Cycle.	A.M.	D.	H.	Ch.
261	4941	1	12	464	305	5777	7	20	724
262	4960	4	4	1059	306	5796	3	13	239
263	4979	6	21	574	307	5815	6	5	834
264	4998	2	14	89	308	5834	1	22	349
265	5017	5	6	684	309	5853	4	14	944
266	5036	7	23	199	310	5872	7	7	459
267	5055	3	15	794	311	5891	2	23	1054
268	5074	6	8	309	312	5910	5	16	569
269	5093	2	0	904	313	5929	1	9	84
270	5112	4	17	419	314	5948	4	1	679
271	5131	7	9	1014	315	5967	6	18	194
272	5150	3	2	529	316	5986	2	10	789
273	5169	5	19	44	317	6005	5	3	304
274	5188	1	11	639	318	6024	7	19	899
275	5207	4	4	154	319	6043	3	12	414
276	5226	6	20	749	320	6062	6	4	1009
277	5245	2	13	264	321	6081	1	21	524
278	5264	5	5	859	322	6100	4	14	39
279	5283	7	22	374	323	6119	7	6	634
280	5302	3	14	969	324	6138	2	23	149
281	5321	6	7	484	325	6157	5	15	744
282	5340	1	23	1079	326	6176	1	8	259
283	5359	4	16	594	327	6195	4	0	854
284	5378	7	9	109	328	6214	6	17	369
285	5397	3	1	704	329	6233	2	9	964
286	5416	5	18	219	330	6252	5	2	479
287	5435	1	10	814	331	6271	7	18	1074
288	5454	4	3	329	332	6290	3	11	589
289	5473	6	19	924	333	6309	6	4	104
290	5492	9	12	439	334	6328	1	20	699
291	5511	5	4	1034	335	6347	4	13	214
292	5530	7	21	549	336	6366	7	5	809
293	5549	3	14	64	337	6385	2	22	324
294	5568	6	6	659	338	6404	5	14	919
295	5587	1	23	174	339	6423	1	7	434
296	5606	4	15	769	340	6442	3	23	1029
297	5625	7	8	284	341	6461	6	16	544
298	5644	3	0	879	342	6480	2	9	59
299	5663	5	17	394	343	6499	5	1	654
300	5682	1	9	989	344	6518	7	18	169
301	5701	4	2	504	345	6537	3	10	764
302	5720	6	19	19	346	6556	6	3	279
303	5739	2	11	614	347	6575	1	19	874
304	5758	5	4	129	348	6594	4	12	389

TABLE IX. (*continued*).

Cycle.	A.M.	D.	H.	Ch.	Cycle.	A.M.	D.	H.	Ch.
349	6613	7	4	984	393	7449	6	13	164
350	6632	2	21	499	394	7468	2	5	759
351	6651	5	14	14	395	7487	4	22	274
352	6670	1	6	609	396	7506	7	14	869
353	6689	3	23	124	397	7525	3	7	384
354	6708	6	15	719	398	7544	5	23	979
355	6727	2	8	234	399	7563	1	16	494
356	6746	5	0	829	400	7582	4	9	9
357	6765	7	17	344	401	7601	7	1	604
358	6784	3	9	939	402	7620	2	18	119
359	6803	6	2	454	403	7639	5	10	714
360	6822	1	18	1049	404	7658	1	3	229
361	6841	4	11	564	405	7677	3	19	824
362	6860	7	4	79	406	7696	6	12	339
363	6879	2	20	674	407	7715	2	4	934
364	6898	5	13	189	408	7734	4	21	449
365	6917	1	5	784	409	7753	7	13	1044
366	6936	3	22	299	410	7772	3	6	559
367	6955	6	14	894	411	7791	5	23	74
368	6974	2	7	409	412	7810	1	15	669
369	6993	4	23	1004	413	7829	4	8	184
370	7012	7	16	519	414	7848	7	0	779
371	7031	3	9	34	415	7867	2	17	294
372	7050	6	1	629	416	7886	5	9	889
373	7069	1	18	144	417	7905	1	2	404
374	7088	4	10	739	418	7924	3	18	999
375	7107	7	3	254	419	7943	6	11	514
376	7126	2	19	849	420	7962	2	4	29
377	7145	5	12	364	421	7981	4	20	624
378	7164	1	4	959	422	8000	7	13	139
379	7183	3	21	474	423	8019	3	5	734
380	7202	6	13	1069	424	8038	5	22	249
381	7221	2	6	584	425	8057	1	14	844
382	7240	4	23	99	426	8076	4	7	359
383	7259	7	15	694	427	8095	6	23	954
384	7278	3	8	209	428	8114	2	16	469
385	7297	6	0	804	429	8133	5	8	1064
386	7316	1	17	319	430	8152	1	1	579
387	7335	4	9	914	431	8171	3	18	94
388	7354	7	2	429	432	8190	6	10	689
389	7373	2	18	1024	433	8209	2	3	204
390	7392	5	11	539	434	8228	4	19	709
391	7411	1	4	54	435	8247	7	12	314
392	7430	3	20	649	436	8266	3	4	909

TABLE IX. (*continued*).

Cycle.	A.M.	D.	H.	Ch.	Cycle.	A.M.	D.	H.	Ch.
437	8285	5	21	424	483	9159	3	14	794
438	8304	1	13	1019	484	9178	6	7	309
439	8323	4	6	534	485	9197	1	23	904
440	8342	6	23	49	486	9216	4	16	419
441	8361	2	15	644	487	9235	7	8	1014
442	8380	5	8	159	488	9254	3	1	529
443	8399	1	0	754	489	9273	5	18	44
444	8418	3	17	269	490	9292	1	10	639
445	8437	6	9	864	491	9311	4	3	154
446	8456	2	2	379	492	9330	6	19	749
447	8475	4	18	974	493	9349	2	12	264
448	8494	7	11	489	494	9368	5	4	859
449	8513	3	4	4	495	9387	7	21	374
450	8532	5	20	599	496	9406	3	13	969
451	8551	1	13	114	497	9425	6	6	484
452	8570	4	5	709	498	9444	1	22	1079
453	8589	6	22	224	499	9463	4	15	594
454	8608	2	14	819	500	9482	7	8	109
455	8627	5	7	334	501	9501	3	0	704
456	8646	7	23	929	502	9520	5	17	219
457	8665	3	16	444	503	9539	1	9	814
458	8684	6	8	1039	504	9558	4	2	329
459	8703	2	1	554	505	9577	6	18	924
460	8722	4	18	69	506	9596	2	11	439
461	8741	7	10	664	507	9615	6	3	1034
462	8760	3	3	179	508	9634	7	20	549
463	8779	5	19	774	509	9653	3	13	64
464	8798	1	12	289	510	9672	6	5	659
465	8817	4	4	884	511	9691	1	22	174
466	8836	6	21	399	512	9710	4	14	769
467	8855	2	13	994	513	9729	7	7	284
468	8874	5	6	509	514	9748	2	23	879
469	8893	7	23	24	515	9767	5	16	394
470	8912	3	15	619	516	9786	1	8	989
471	8931	6	8	134	517	9805	4	1	504
472	8950	2	0	729	518	9824	6	18	19
473	8969	4	17	244	519	9843	2	10	614
474	8988	7	9	839	520	9862	5	3	129
475	9007	3	2	354	521	9881	7	19	724
476	9026	5	18	949	522	9900	3	12	239
477	9045	1	11	464	523	9919	6	4	834
478	9064	4	3	1059	524	9938	1	21	349
479	9083	6	20	574	525	9957	4	13	944
480	9102	2	13	89	526	9976	7	6	459
481	9121	5	5	684	527	9995	2	22	1054
482	9140	7	22	199	528	10014	5	15	569

Table X.

TABLE OF DAY-LIMITS SHOWING THE WEEK-DAY FOR TISHRÎ I., AND THE FORM OF THE YEAR ACCORDING TO THE MOLADS.

Article 56. For Exceptions see Article 58.

Common Years.

	Tishri.	Molads: the Limits are inclusive.						Form of the Year.	Years to which the Rule applies.	Place of the Year in a Cycle.
1	Monday	7	18	0 to 1	9	203		353	All Common years	1, 2, 4, 5, 7, 9, 10, 12, 13, 15, 16, 18
2	,,	1	9	204 ,, 2	15	588		355	Common following Embolismic	1, 4, 7, 9, 12, 15, 18
3	,,	1	9	204 ,, 2	17	1079		355	Common following Common	2, 5, 10, 13, 16
4	Tuesday	2	15	589 ,, 3	9	203		354	Common following Embolismic	1, 4, 7, 9, 12, 15, 18
5	,,	2	18	0 ,, 3	9	203		354	Common following Common	2, 5, 10, 13, 16
6	Thursday	3	9	204 ,, 5	9	203		354	All Common years	As line 1
7	,,	5	9	204 ,, 5	17	1079		355	All Common years	As line 1
8	Saturday	5	18	0 ,, 6	0	407		353	All Common years	As line 1
9	,,	5	18	0 ,, 6	9	203		353	Common followed by Embolismic	2, 5, 7, 10, 13, 16, 18
10	,,	6	0	408 ,, 7	17	1079		355	Common followed by Common	1, 4, 9, 12, 15
11	,,	6	9	204 ,, 7	17	1079		355	All Common years	As line 1

Embolismic Years.

	Tishri.	Molads: the Limits are inclusive.					Form of the Year.	Years to which the Rule applies.	Place of the Year in a Cycle.
12	Monday	7	18	0 to 1	20	490	383	All Embolismic years	3, 6, 8, 11, 14, 17, 19
13	,,	1	20	491 ,, 2	17	1079	385	,, ,, ,,	,, ,,
14	Tuesday	2	18	0 ,, 3	17	1079	384	,, ,, ,,	,, ,,
15	Thursday	3	18	0 ,, 4	11	694	383	,, ,, ,,	,, ,,
16	,,	4	11	695 ,, 5	17	1079	385	,, ,, ,,	,, ,,
17	Saturday	5	18	0 ,, 6	20	490	383	,, ,, ,,	,, ,,
18	,,	6	20	491 ,, 7	17	1079	385	,, ,, ,,	,, ,,

TABLE XI.

TABLE FOR FINDING THE WEEK-DAY FOR ANY DAY IN A JEWISH YEAR.

PART I. ARTICLE 67.

	Days in the Year.	Tishri 1	Tishri.	Marheshwân.	Kislêw.	Têbeth.	Schebhât.	Adhâr I.	Adhâr II.	Nisân.	Iyâr.	Siwân.	Tammûz.	Âbh.	'Elul.
1	353	Monday	2	4	5	6	7		2	3	5	6	1	2	4
2		Saturday	7	2	3	4	5		7	1	3	4	6	7	2
3	354	Tuesday	3	5	6	1	2		4	5	7	1	3	4	6
4		Thursday	5	7	1	3	4		6	7	2	3	5	6	1
5	355	Monday	2	4	6	1	2		4	5	7	1	3	4	6
6		Thursday	5	7	2	4	5		7	1	3	4	6	7	2
7		Saturday	7	2	4	6	7		2	3	5	6	1	2	4
8	383	Monday	2	4	5	6	7	2	4	5	7	1	3	4	6
9		Thursday	5	7	1	2	3	5	7	1	3	4	6	7	2
10		Saturday	7	2	3	4	5	7	2	3	5	6	1	2	4
11	384	Tuesday	3	5	6	1	2	4	6	7	2	3	5	6	1
12	385	Monday	2	4	6	1	2	4	6	7	2	3	5	6	1
13		Thursday	5	7	2	4	5	7	2	3	5	6	1	2	4
14		Saturday	7	2	4	6	7	2	4	5	7	1	3	4	6

TABLE XI.

PART II. ARTICLE 67.

1	2	3	4	5	6	7
1 Sunday	1 Monday	1 Tuesday	1 Wednesday	1 Thursday	1 Friday	1 Saturday
2 Monday	2 Tuesday	2 Wednesday	2 Thursday	2 Friday	2 Saturday	2 Sunday
3 Tuesday	3 Wednesday	3 Thursday	3 Friday	3 Saturday	3 Sunday	3 Monday
4 Wednesday	4 Thursday	4 Friday	4 Saturday	4 Sunday	4 Monday	4 Tuesday
5 Thursday	5 Friday	5 Saturday	5 Sunday	5 Monday	5 Tuesday	5 Wednesday
6 Friday	6 Saturday	6 Sunday	6 Monday	6 Tuesday	6 Wednesday	6 Thursday
7 Saturday	7 Sunday	7 Monday	7 Tuesday	7 Wednesday	7 Thursday	7 Friday
8 Sunday	8 Monday	8 Tuesday	8 Wednesday	8 Thursday	8 Friday	8 Saturday
9 Monday	9 Tuesday	9 Wednesday	9 Thursday	9 Friday	9 Saturday	9 Sunday
10 Tuesday	10 Wednesday	10 Thursday	10 Friday	10 Saturday	10 Sunday	10 Monday
11 Wednesday	11 Thursday	11 Friday	11 Saturday	11 Sunday	11 Monday	11 Tuesday
12 Thursday	12 Friday	12 Saturday	12 Sunday	12 Monday	12 Tuesday	12 Wednesday
13 Friday	13 Saturday	13 Sunday	13 Monday	13 Tuesday	13 Wednesday	13 Thursday
14 Saturday	14 Sunday	14 Monday	14 Tuesday	14 Wednesday	14 Thursday	14 Friday
15 Sunday	15 Monday	15 Tuesday	15 Wednesday	15 Thursday	15 Friday	15 Saturday
16 Monday	16 Tuesday	16 Wednesday	16 Thursday	16 Friday	16 Saturday	16 Sunday
17 Tuesday	17 Wednesday	17 Thursday	17 Friday	17 Saturday	17 Sunday	17 Monday
18 Wednesday	18 Thursday	18 Friday	18 Saturday	18 Sunday	18 Monday	18 Tuesday
19 Thursday	19 Friday	19 Saturday	19 Sunday	19 Monday	19 Tuesday	19 Wednesday
20 Friday	20 Saturday	20 Sunday	20 Monday	20 Tuesday	20 Wednesday	20 Thursday
21 Saturday	21 Sunday	21 Monday	21 Tuesday	21 Wednesday	21 Thursday	21 Friday
22 Sunday	22 Monday	22 Tuesday	22 Wednesday	22 Thursday	22 Friday	22 Saturday
23 Monday	23 Tuesday	23 Wednesday	23 Thursday	23 Friday	23 Saturday	23 Sunday
24 Tuesday	24 Wednesday	24 Thursday	24 Friday	24 Saturday	24 Sunday	24 Monday
25 Wednesday	25 Thursday	25 Friday	25 Saturday	25 Sunday	25 Monday	25 Tuesday
26 Thursday	26 Friday	26 Saturday	26 Sunday	26 Monday	26 Tuesday	26 Wednesday
27 Friday	27 Saturday	27 Sunday	27 Monday	27 Tuesday	27 Wednesday	27 Thursday
28 Saturday	28 Sunday	28 Monday	28 Tuesday	28 Wednesday	28 Thursday	28 Friday
29 Sunday	29 Monday	29 Tuesday	29 Wednesday	29 Thursday	29 Friday	29 Saturday
30 Monday	30 Tuesday	30 Wednesday	30 Thursday	30 Friday	30 Saturday	30 Sunday

TABLE XII.

TABLE FOR FINDING THE FERIA WITH WHICH THE FIRST YEAR OF ANY CYCLE COMMENCES. A.M. 1 TO 7639.

ARTICLE 74.

Intermediate Cycles.	1	14	27	40	53	66	79	92	105	118	131	144	157	170	183	196	209	222	235	248	261	274	287	300	313	326	339	352	365	378	391
	Number of the Cycle.																														
0	2	2	2	2	2	2	2	2	2	2	2	2	2	2	2	2	2	2	2	2	2	2	2	2	2	2	2	2	2	2	2
1	5	5	5	5	5	5	5	5	5	5	5	5	5	5	5	5	5	5	5	5	5	5	5	5	5	5	5	5	5	5	5
2	7	7	7	7	7	7	7	7	7	7	7	7	7	7	7	7	7	7	7	7	7	7	7	7	7	7	7	7	7	7	7
3	3	3	3	3	3	3	3	3	3	3	3	3	3	3	3	3	3	3	3	II.	2	2	2	2	2	2	2	2	2	2	2
4	7	7	7	7	7	7	7	V.	5	5	5	5	5	5	5	5	5	5	5	5	5	5	5	5	5	5	5	5	5	5	5
5	2	2	2	2	2	2	2	2	2	2	2	2	2	2	2	2	2	2	2	2	2	2	2	2	2	2	2	VII.	7	7	7
6	5	5	5	5	5	5	5	5	5	5	5	5	5	5	5	5	5	5	5	5	5	5	5	5	5	5	5	5	III	3	3
7	7	7	7	7	7	7	7	7	7	7	7	7	7	7	7	7	7	7	7	7	7	7	7	7	7	7	7	7	7	7	7
8	3	3	3	II.	2	2	2	2	2	2	2	2	2	2	2	2	2	2	2	2	2	2	2	2	2	2	2	2	2	2	2
9	5	5	5	5	5	5	5	5	5	5	5	5	5	5	5	5	5	5	5	5	5	5	5	5	5	5	5	5	5	5	5
10	2	2	2	2	2	2	2	2	2	2	2	VII.	7	7	7	7	7	7	7	7	7	7	7	7	7	7	7	7	7	7	7
11	5	5	5	5	5	5	5	5	5	5	5	5	5	III.	3	3	3	3	3	3	3	3	3	3	3	3	3	3	3	3	3
12	7	7	7	7	7	7	7	7	7	7	7	7	7	7	7	7	7	7	7	7	7	7	V.	5	5	5	5	5	5	5	5

TABLE XIII.

TYPES OF THE CYCLE, ACCORDING TO THE MOLAD OF THE FIRST YEAR.

ARTICLES 76–79, pp. 155–163.

No. of the Type.	Limits of the Molads. Both inclusive.							Years of the Cycle.																			Days in Cycle.
								1	2	3	4	5	6	7	8	9	10	11	12	13	14	15	16	17	18	19	
1	7	18	0	to	7	18	22	2 d	5 r	2 A	2 d	5 a	3 R	2 a	7 D	5 r	2 a	7 A	7 d	3 r	7 A	7 a	5 r	2 D	7 a	5 A	6940
2	7	18	23	,,	7	20	536	2 d	5 r	2 A	2 a	7 d	3 R	2 a	7 D	5 r	2 a	7 A	7 d	3 r	7 A	7 a	5 r	2 D	7 a	5 A	,,
3	7	20	537	,,	7	20	559	2 d	5 r	2 A	2 a	7 d	3 R	2 a	7 D	5 r	2 a	7 A	7 d	3 r	7 A	7 a	5 r	2 D	7 a	5 A	,,
4	7	20	560	,,	1	0	407	2 d	5 r	2 A	2 a	7 d	3 R	2 a	7 D	5 a	3 r	7 A	7 d	3 r	7 A	7 a	5 r	2 D	7 a	5 A	,,
5	1	0	408	,,	1	5	332	2 d	5 a	3 R	2 a	7 d	3 R	2 a	7 D	5 a	3 r	7 A	7 a	5 r	2 D	7 a	5 r	2 D	7 a	5 A	,,
6	1	5	333	,,	1	7	869	2 d	5 a	3 R	2 a	7 d	3 R	2 a	7 D	5 a	3 r	7 A	7 a	5 r	2 D	7 a	5 r	2 D	7 a	5 A	,,
7	1	7	870	,,	1	9	203	2 d	5 a	3 R	2 a	7 d	3 R	2 a	7 A	7 d	3 r	7 A	7 a	5 r	2 D	7 a	5 r	2 D	7 a	5 A	,,
8	1	9	204	,,	1	9	226	2 a	7 d	3 R	2 a	7 d	3 R	2 a	7 A	7 d	3 r	7 A	7 a	5 r	2 D	7 a	5 r	2 A	2 d	5 A	,,
9	1	9	227	,,	1	11	740	2 a	7 d	3 R	2 a	7 d	3 R	2 a	7 A	7 d	3 r	7 A	7 a	5 r	2 D	7 a	5 r	2 A	2 d	5 A	,,
10	1	11	741	,,	1	22	1050	2 a	7 d	3 R	2 a	7 a	5 D	3 r	7 A	7 d	3 r	7 A	7 a	5 r	2 D	7 a	5 r	2 A	2 d	5 A	,,
11	1	22	1051	,,	1	22	1073	2 a	7 d	3 R	2 a	7 a	5 D	3 r	7 A	7 a	5 r	2 D	7 a	5 r	2 D	7 a	5 r	2 A	2 d	5 A	,,
12	1	22	1074	,,	2	0	407	2 a	7 d	3 R	2 a	7 a	5 D	3 r	7 A	7 a	5 r	2 D	7 a	5 r	2 A	2 d	5 r	2 A	2 d	5 A	,,
13	2	0	408	,,	2	2	921	2 a	7 a	5 D	3 r	7 a	5 D	3 r	7 A	7 a	5 r	2 D	7 a	5 r	2 A	2 d	5 r	2 A	2 a	7 D	,,
14	2	2	922	,,	2	5	378	2 a	7 a	5 D	3 r	7 a	5 D	3 r	7 A	7 a	5 r	2 D	7 a	5 r	2 A	2 d	5 r	2 A	2 a	7 D	,,
15	2	5	379	,,	2	14	151	2 a	7 a	5 D	3 r	7 a	5 A	5 r	2 D	7 a	5 r	2 D	7 a	5 r	2 A	2 d	5 r	2 A	2 a	7 D	,,
16	2	14	152	,,	2	14	174	2 a	7 a	5 D	3 r	7 a	5 A	5 r	2 D	7 a	5 r	2 D	7 a	5 r	2 A	2 d	5 a	3 R	2 a	7 D	,,
17	2	14	175	,,	2	15	588	2 a	7 a	5 D	3 r	7 a	5 A	5 r	2 D	7 a	5 r	2 A	2 d	5 r	2 A	2 d	5 a	3 R	2 a	7 D	,,
18	2	15	589	,,	2	18	22	2 a	7 a	5 D	3 r	7 a	5 A	5 r	2 D	7 a	5 r	2 A	2 d	5 r	2 A	2 a	7 d	3 R	2 a	7 D	,,
19	2	18	23	,,	2	20	559	3 r	7 a	5 D	3 r	7 a	5 A	5 r	2 D	7 a	5 r	2 A	2 d	5 r	2 A	2 a	7 d	3 R	2 a	7 D	6939
20	2	20	560	,,	3	1	484	3 r	7 a	5 A	5 r	2 d	5 A	5 r	2 D	7 a	5 r	2 A	2 d	5 r	2 A	2 a	7 d	3 R	2 a	7 D	,,
21	3	1	485	,,	3	5	332	3 r	7 a	5 A	5 r	2 d	5 A	5 r	2 D	7 a	5 r	2 A	2 d	5 a	3 R	2 a	7 d	3 R	2 a	7 D	,,
22	3	5	333	,,	3	5	355	3 r	7 a	5 A	5 r	2 d	5 A	5 r	2 D	7 a	5 r	2 A	2 d	5 a	3 R	2 a	7 d	3 R	2 a	7 A	6941
23	3	5	356	,,	3	5	378	3 r	7 a	5 A	5 r	2 d	5 A	5 r	2 A	2 d	5 r	2 A	2 d	5 a	3 R	2 a	7 d	3 R	2 a	7 A	,,
24	3	5	379	,,	3	9	203	3 r	7 a	5 A	5 r	2 d	5 A	5 r	2 A	2 d	5 r	2 A	2 a	7 d	3 R	2 a	7 d	3 R	2 a	7 A	,,
25	3	9	204	,,	3	9	226	3 r	7 a	5 A	5 r	2 d	5 A	5 r	2 A	2 d	5 r	2 A	2 a	7 d	3 R	2 a	7 a	5 D	3 r	7 A	,,
26	3	9	227	,,	3	11	740	5 r	2 d	5 A	5 r	2 d	5 A	5 r	2 A	2 d	5 r	2 A	2 a	7 d	3 R	2 a	7 a	5 D	3 r	7 A	6939
27	3	11	741	,,	3	20	536	5 r	2 d	5 A	5 r	2 a	7 D	5 r	2 A	2 d	5 r	2 A	2 a	7 d	3 R	2 a	7 a	5 D	3 r	7 A	,,
28	3	20	537	,,	3	20	559	5 r	2 d	5 A	5 r	2 a	7 D	5 r	2 A	2 d	5 a	3 R	2 a	7 d	3 R	2 a	7 a	5 D	3 r	7 A	,,
29	3	20	560	,,	3	20	1073	5 r	2 d	5 A	5 r	2 a	7 D	5 r	2 A	2 a	7 d	3 R	2 a	7 a	5 D	3 r	7 a	5 D	3 r	7 A	,,

TYPES OF THE CYCLE, ACCORDING TO THE MOLAD OF THE FIRST YEAR (*continued*)—

No. of the Type.	Limits of the Molads. Both inclusive.		Years of the Cycle.																			Days in Cycle.
	From	To	1	2	3	4	5	6	7	8	9	10	11	12	13	14	15	16	17	18	19	
30	3 22 1074	4 0 407	5 r	2 d	5 A	5 r	2 a	7 D	5 r	2 A	2 a	7 d	3 R	2 a	7 a	5 D	3 r	7 a	5 A	5 r	2 D	6939
31	4 0 408	4 2 921	5 r	2 a	7 D	5 r	2 a	7 D	5 r	2 A	2 a	7 d	3 R	2 a	7 a	5 D	3 r	7 a	5 A	5 r	2 D	„
32	4 2 922	4 11 717	5 r	2 a	7 D	5 r	2 a	7 D	5 a	3 R	2 a	7 d	3 R	2 a	7 a	5 D	3 r	7 a	5 A	5 r	2 D	„
33	4 11 718	4 11 740	5 r	2 a	7 D	5 r	2 a	7 A	7 d	3 R	2 a	7 d	3 R	2 a	7 a	5 D	3 r	7 a	5 A	5 r	2 D	„
34	4 11 741	4 14 174	5 r	2 a	7 D	5 r	2 a	7 A	7 d	3 R	2 a	7 d	5 D	3 r	7 a	5 D	3 r	7 a	5 A	5 r	2 D	„
35	4 14 175	4 18 22	5 r	2 a	7 D	5 r	2 a	7 A	7 d	3 R	2 a	7 a	5 D	3 r	7 a	5 A	3 r	2 d	5 A	5 r	2 D	„
36	4 18 23	5 1 484	5 r	2 a	7 D	5 a	3 r	7 A	7 d	3 R	2 a	7 a	5 D	3 r	7 a	5 A	5 r	2 d	5 A	5 r	2 D	„
37	5 1 485	5 2 898	5 r	2 a	7 D	5 a	3 r	7 A	7 d	3 R	2 a	7 a	5 D	3 r	7 a	5 A	5 r	2 d	5 A	5 r	2 A	6941
38	5 2 899	5 2 921	5 r	2 a	7 A	7 d	3 r	7 A	7 d	3 R	2 a	7 a	5 D	3 r	7 a	5 A	5 r	2 d	5 A	5 r	2 A	„
39	5 2 922	5 5 355	5 r	2 a	7 A	7 d	3 r	7 A	7 a	5 D	3 r	7 a	5 D	3 r	7 a	5 A	5 r	2 d	5 A	5 r	2 A	„
40	5 5 356	5 5 378	5 r	2 a	7 A	7 d	3 r	7 A	7 a	5 D	3 r	7 a	5 A	5 r	2 d	5 A	5 r	2 d	5 A	5 r	2 A	„
41	5 5 379	5 9 203	5 r	2 a	7 A	7 d	3 r	7 A	7 a	5 D	3 r	7 a	5 A	5 r	2 d	5 A	5 r	2 a	7 D	5 r	2 A	„
42	5 9 204	5 9 226	5 a	3 r	7 A	7 d	3 r	7 A	7 a	5 D	3 r	7 a	5 A	5 r	2 d	5 A	5 r	2 a	7 D	5 r	2 A	„
43	5 9 227	5 17 1079	5 a	3 r	7 A	7 a	5 r	2 D	7 a	5 D	3 r	7 a	5 A	5 r	2 d	5 A	5 r	2 a	7 D	5 r	2 A	„
44	5 18 0	5 20 536	7 d	3 r	7 A	7 a	5 r	2 D	7 a	5 D	3 r	7 a	5 A	5 r	2 d	5 A	5 r	2 a	7 D	5 r	2 A	6939
45	5 20 537	5 20 559	7 d	3 r	7 A	7 a	5 r	2 D	7 a	5 A	5 r	7 a	5 A	5 r	2 d	5 A	5 r	2 a	7 D	5 r	2 A	„
46	5 20 560	5 22 1073	7 d	3 r	7 A	7 a	5 r	2 D	7 a	5 A	5 r	7 a	5 A	5 r	2 a	7 D	5 r	2 a	7 D	5 r	2 A	„
47	5 22 1074	6 0 407	7 d	3 r	7 A	7 a	5 r	2 D	7 a	5 A	5 r	7 a	5 A	5 r	2 a	7 D	5 r	2 a	7 D	5 a	3 R	„
48	6 0 408	6 7 869	7 a	5 r	2 D	7 a	5 r	2 D	7 a	5 A	5 r	7 a	5 A	5 r	2 a	7 D	5 r	2 a	7 D	5 a	3 R	„
49	6 7 870	6 11 717	7 a	5 r	2 D	7 a	5 r	2 D	7 a	5 A	5 r	7 a	5 A	5 r	2 a	7 D	5 r	2 a	7 A	7 d	3 R	„
50	6 11 718	6 11 740	7 a	5 r	2 D	7 a	5 r	2 A	7 a	5 A	5 r	7 a	5 A	5 r	2 a	7 D	5 r	2 a	7 A	7 d	3 R	„
51	6 11 741	6 14 174	7 a	5 r	2 D	7 a	5 r	2 A	7 a	5 A	5 r	2 a	7 D	5 r	2 a	7 D	5 r	2 a	7 A	7 d	3 R	„
52	6 14 175	6 22 1050	7 a	5 r	2 D	7 a	5 r	2 A	7 a	5 A	5 r	2 a	7 D	5 r	2 a	7 D	5 a	3 r	7 A	7 d	3 R	„
53	6 22 1051	6 22 1073	7 a	5 r	2 D	7 a	5 r	2 A	7 a	5 A	5 r	2 a	7 D	5 r	2 a	7 A	7 d	3 r	7 A	7 d	3 R	„
54	6 22 1074	7 2 898	7 a	5 r	2 D	7 a	5 r	2 A	7 a	5 A	5 r	2 a	7 D	5 r	2 a	7 A	7 d	3 r	7 A	7 a	5 D	6940
55	7 2 899	7 2 921	7 a	5 r	2 A	2 d	5 r	2 A	2 d	5 A	5 r	2 a	7 D	5 r	2 a	7 A	7 d	3 r	7 A	7 a	5 D	„
56	7 2 922	7 5 355	7 a	5 r	2 A	2 d	5 r	2 A	2 d	7 D	5 r	2 a	7 D	5 r	2 a	7 A	7 d	3 r	7 A	7 a	5 D	„
57	7 5 356	7 5 378	7 a	5 r	2 A	2 d	5 r	2 A	2 d	7 D	5 r	2 a	7 D	5 a	3 r	7 A	7 d	3 r	7 A	7 a	5 D	„
58	7 5 379	7 9 226	7 a	5 r	2 A	2 d	5 r	2 A	2 d	7 D	5 r	2 a	7 D	5 a	3 r	7 A	7 a	5 r	2 D	7 a	5 D	„
59	7 9 227	7 14 151	7 a	5 r	2 A	2 d	5 a	3 R	2 d	7 D	5 r	2 a	7 D	5 a	3 r	7 A	7 a	5 r	2 D	7 a	5 D	„
60	7 14 152	7 16 688	7 a	5 r	2 A	2 d	5 a	3 R	2 d	7 D	5 r	2 a	7 A	7 d	3 r	7 A	7 a	5 r	2 D	7 a	5 D	„
61	7 16 689	7 17 1079	7 a	5 r	2 A	2 d	5 a	3 R	2 d	7 D	5 r	2 a	7 A	7 d	3 r	7 A	7 a	5 r	2 D	7 a	5 A	6942

Table XIV.

Article 82.

A.	B.		
0	2	5	204
247	2	4	379
494	2	3	554
741	2	2	729
988	2	1	904
1235	2	0	1079
1482	2	0	174
1729	1	23	349
1976	1	22	524
2213	1	21	699
2470	1	20	874
2717	1	19	1049
2964	1	19	144
3211	1	18	319
3458	1	17	494
3705	1	16	669
3952	1	15	844
4199	1	14	1019
4446	1	14	114
4693	1	13	289
4940	1	12	464
5187	1	11	639
5434	1	10	814
5681	1	9	989
5928	1	9	84
6175	1	8	259
6422	1	7	434
6669	1	6	609
6916	1	5	784
7163	1	4	959
7410	1	4	54

Table XV.

Article 82.

C.	D.		
0	0	0	0
19	2	16	595
38	5	9	110
57	1	1	705
76	3	18	220
95	6	10	815
114	2	3	330
133	4	18	925
152	7	12	440
171	3	4	1035
190	5	21	550
209	1	14	65
228	4	6	660

Table XVI. (Article 69, p. 144.)

COMMON DEFICIENT YEAR. 353 DAYS.

Part I.

	Tishri.	Marḥeshwân.	Kislêw.	Têbeth.	Schebhât.	Adhâr.	
A	1 8 15 22 29	6 13 20 27	5 12 19 26	4 11 18 25	3 10 17 24	1 8 15 22 29	A
B	2 9 16 23 30	7 14 21 28	6 13 20 27	5 12 19 26	4 11 18 25	2 9 16 23	B
C	3 10 17 24	1 8 15 22 29	7 14 21 28	6 13 20 27	5 12 19 26	3 10 17 24	C
D	4 11 18 25	2 9 16 23	1 8 15 22 29	7 14 21 28	6 13 20 27	4 11 18 25	D
E	5 12 19 26	3 10 17 24	2 9 16 23	1 8 15 22 29	7 14 21 28	5 12 19 26	E
F	6 13 20 27	4 11 18 25	3 10 17 24	2 9 16 23	1 8 15 22 29	6 13 20 27	F
G	7 14 21 28	5 12 19 26	4 11 18 25	3 10 17 24	2 9 16 23 30	7 14 21 28	G

	Nisân.	Iyâr.	Siwân.	Tammûz.	Âbh.	'Elûl.	
A	7 14 21 28	5 12 19 26	4 11 18 25	2 9 16 23	1 8 15 22 29	6 13 20 27	A
B	1 8 15 22 29	6 13 20 27	5 12 19 26	3 10 17 24	2 9 16 23 30	7 14 21 28	B
C	2 9 16 23 30	7 14 21 28	6 13 20 27	4 11 18 25	3 10 17 24	1 8 15 22 29	C
D	3 10 17 24	1 8 15 22 29	7 14 21 28	5 12 19 26	4 11 18 25	2 9 16 23	D
E	4 11 18 25	2 9 16 23	1 8 15 22 29	6 13 20 27	5 12 19 26	3 10 17 24	E
F	5 12 19 26	3 10 17 24	2 9 16 23 30	7 14 21 28	6 13 20 27	4 11 18 25	F
G	6 13 20 27	4 11 18 25	3 10 17 24	1 8 15 22 29	7 14 21 28	5 12 19 26	G

COMMON REGULAR YEAR. 354 DAYS.

Part II.

	Tishri.	Marḥeshwân.	Kislêw.	Têbeth.	Schebhât.	Adhâr.	
A	1 8 15 22 29	6 13 20 27	5 12 19 26	3 10 17 24	2 9 16 23 30	7 14 21 28	A
B	2 9 16 23 30	7 14 21 28	6 13 20 27	4 11 18 25	3 10 17 24	1 8 15 22 29	B
C	3 10 17 24	1 8 15 22 29	7 14 21 28	5 12 19 26	4 11 18 25	2 9 16 23	C
D	4 11 18 25	2 9 16 23	1 8 15 22 29	6 13 20 27	5 12 19 26	3 10 17 24	D
E	5 12 19 26	3 10 17 24	2 9 16 23 30	7 14 21 28	6 13 20 27	4 11 18 25	E
F	6 13 20 27	4 11 18 25	3 10 17 24	1 8 15 22 29	7 14 21 28	5 12 19 26	F
G	7 14 21 28	5 12 19 26	4 11 18 25	2 9 16 23	1 8 15 22 29	6 13 20 27	G

	Nisan.	Iyâr.	Siwân.	Tammûz.	Âbh.	'Elûl.	
A	6 13 20 27	4 11 18 25	3 10 17 24	1 8 15 22 29	7 14 21 28	5 12 19 26	A
B	7 14 21 28	5 12 19 26	4 11 18 25	2 9 16 23	1 8 15 22 29	6 13 20 27	B
C	1 8 15 22 29	6 13 20 27	5 12 19 26	3 10 17 24	2 9 16 23 30	7 14 21 28	C
D	2 9 16 23 30	7 14 21 28	6 13 20 27	4 11 18 25	3 10 17 24	1 8 15 22 29	D
E	3 10 17 24	1 8 15 22 29	7 14 21 28	5 12 19 26	4 11 18 25	2 9 16 23	E
F	4 11 18 25	2 9 16 23	1 8 15 22 29	6 13 20 27	5 12 19 26	3 10 17 24	F
G	5 12 19 26	3 10 17 24	2 9 16 23 30	7 14 21 28	6 13 20 27	4 11 18 25	G

COMMON ABUNDANT YEAR. 355 DAYS. PART III.

	Tishri.	Marḥoswân.	Kislêw.	Têbeth.	Schebhât.	Adhâr.	
A	1 8 15 22 29	6 13 20 27	4 11 18 25	2 9 16 23	1 8 15 22 29	6 13 20 27	A
B	2 9 16 23 30	7 14 21 28	5 12 19 26	3 10 17 24	2 9 16 23 30	7 14 21 28	B
C	3 10 17 24	1 8 15 22 29	6 13 20 27	4 11 18 25	3 10 17 24	1 8 15 22 29	C
D	4 11 18 25	2 9 16 23 30	7 14 21 28	5 12 19 26	4 11 18 25	2 9 16 23	D
E	5 12 19 26	3 10 17 24	1 8 15 22 29	6 13 20 27	5 12 19 26	3 10 17 24	E
F	6 13 20 27	4 11 18 25	2 9 16 23 30	7 14 21 28	6 13 20 27	4 11 18 25	F
G	7 14 21 28	5 12 19 26	3 10 17 24	1 8 15 22 29	7 14 21 28	5 12 19 26	G

	Nisân.	Iyâr.	Siwân.	Tammûz.	Âbh.	'Elûl.	
A	5 12 19 26	3 10 17 24	2 9 16 23 30	7 14 21 28	6 13 20 27	4 11 18 25	A
B	6 13 20 27	4 11 18 25	3 10 17 24	1 8 15 22 29	7 14 21 28	5 12 19 26	B
C	7 14 21 28	5 12 19 26	4 11 18 25	2 9 16 23	1 8 15 22 29	6 13 20 27	C
D	1 8 15 22 29	6 13 20 27	5 12 19 26	3 10 17 24	2 9 16 23 30	7 14 21 28	D
E	2 9 16 23 30	7 14 21 28	6 13 20 27	4 11 18 25	3 10 17 24	1 8 15 22 29	E
F	3 10 17 24	1 8 15 22 29	7 14 21 28	5 12 19 26	4 11 18 25	2 9 16 23	F
G	4 11 18 25	2 9 16 23	1 8 15 22 29	6 13 20 27	5 12 19 26	3 10 17 24	G

EMBOLISMIC DEFICIENT YEAR. 383 DAYS. PART IV.

	Tishri.	Marḥoshwân.	Kislêw.	Têbeth.	Schebhât.	Adhâr I.	Adhâr II.	
A	1 8 15 22 29	6 13 20 27	5 12 19 26	4 11 18 25	3 10 17 24	1 8 15 22 29	6 13 20 27	A
B	2 9 16 23 30	7 14 21 28	6 13 20 27	5 12 19 26	4 11 18 25	2 9 16 23 30	7 14 21 28	B
C	3 10 17 24	1 8 15 22 29	7 14 21 28	6 13 20 27	5 12 19 26	3 10 17 24	1 8 15 22 29	C
D	4 11 18 25	2 9 16 23	1 8 15 22 29	7 14 21 28	6 13 20 27	4 11 18 25	2 9 16 23	D
E	5 12 19 26	3 10 17 24	2 9 16 23	1 8 15 22 29	7 14 21 28	5 12 19 26	3 10 17 24	E
F	6 13 20 27	4 11 18 25	3 10 17 24	2 9 16 23	1 8 15 22 29	6 13 20 27	4 11 18 25	F
G	7 14 21 28	5 12 19 26	4 11 18 25	3 10 17 24	2 9 16 23 30	7 14 21 28	5 12 19 26	G

	Nisân.	Iyâr.	Siwân.	Tammûz.	Âbh.	'Elûl.	
A	5 12 19 26	3 10 17 24	2 9 16 23 30	7 14 21 28	6 13 20 27	4 11 18 25	A
B	6 13 20 27	4 11 18 25	3 10 17 24	1 8 15 22 29	7 14 21 28	5 12 19 26	B
C	7 14 21 28	5 12 19 26	4 11 18 25	2 9 16 23	1 8 15 22 29	6 13 20 27	C
D	1 8 15 22 29	6 13 20 27	5 12 19 26	3 10 17 24	2 9 16 23 30	7 14 21 28	D
E	2 9 16 23 30	7 14 21 28	6 13 20 27	4 11 18 25	3 10 17 24	1 8 15 22 29	E
F	3 10 17 24	1 8 15 22 29	7 14 21 28	5 12 19 26	4 11 18 25	2 9 16 23	F
G	4 11 18 25	2 9 16 23	1 8 15 22 29	6 13 20 27	5 12 19 26	3 10 17 24	G

EMBOLISMIC REGULAR YEAR. 384 DAYS. PART V.

	Tishri.	Marheshwân.	Kislêw.	Têbeth.	Schebhât.	Adhâr I.	Adhâr II.	
A	1 8 15 22 29	6 13 20 27	5 12 19 26	3 10 17 24	2 9 16 23 30	7 14 21 28	5 12 19 26	A
B	2 9 16 23 30	7 14 21 28	6 13 20 27	4 11 18 25	3 10 17 24	1 8 15 22 29	6 13 20 27	B
C	3 10 17 24	1 8 15 22 29	7 14 21 28	5 12 19 26	4 11 18 25	2 9 16 23 30	7 14 21 28	C
D	4 11 18 25	2 9 16 23	1 8 15 22 29	6 13 20 27	5 12 19 26	3 10 17 24	1 8 15 22 29	D
E	5 12 19 26	3 10 17 24	2 9 16 23 30	7 14 21 28	6 13 20 27	4 11 18 25	2 9 16 23	E
F	6 13 20 27	4 11 18 25	3 10 17 24	1 8 15 22 29	7 14 21 28	5 12 19 26	3 10 17 24	F
G	7 14 21 28	5 12 19 26	4 11 18 25	2 9 16 23	1 8 15 22 29	6 13 20 27	4 11 18 25	G

	Nisân.	Iyâr.	Siwân.	Tammûz.	Âbh.	'Elûl.	
A	4 11 18 25	2 9 16 23	1 8 15 22 29	6 13 20 27	5 12 19 26	3 10 17 24	A
B	5 12 19 26	3 10 17 24	2 9 16 23 30	7 14 21 28	6 13 20 27	4 11 18 25	B
C	6 13 20 27	4 11 18 25	3 10 17 24	1 8 15 22 29	7 14 21 28	5 12 19 26	C
D	7 14 21 28	5 12 19 26	4 11 18 25	2 9 16 23	1 8 15 22 29	6 13 20 27	D
E	1 8 15 22 29	6 13 20 27	5 12 19 26	3 10 17 24	2 9 16 23 30	7 14 21 28	E
F	2 9 16 23 30	7 14 21 28	6 13 20 27	4 11 18 25	3 10 17 24	1 8 15 22 29	F
G	3 10 17 24	1 8 15 22 29	7 14 21 28	5 12 19 26	4 11 18 25	2 9 16 23	G

EMBOLISMIC ABUNDANT YEAR. 385 DAYS. PART VI.

	Tishri.	Marheshwân.	Kislêw.	Têbeth.	Schebhât.	Adhâr I.	Adhâr II.	
A	1 8 15 22 29	6 13 20 27	4 11 18 25	2 9 16 23	1 8 15 22 29	6 13 20 27	4 11 18 25	A
B	2 9 16 23 30	7 14 21 28	5 12 19 26	3 10 17 24	2 9 16 23 30	7 14 21 28	5 12 19 26	B
C	3 10 17 24	1 8 15 22 29	6 13 20 27	4 11 18 25	3 10 17 24	1 8 15 22 29	6 13 20 27	C
D	4 11 18 25	2 9 16 23 30	7 14 21 28	5 12 19 26	4 11 18 25	2 9 16 23 30	7 14 21 28	D
E	5 12 19 26	3 10 17 24	1 8 15 22 29	6 13 20 27	5 12 19 26	3 10 17 24	1 8 15 22 29	E
F	6 13 20 27	4 11 18 25	2 9 16 23 30	7 14 21 28	6 13 20 27	4 11 18 25	2 9 16 23	F
G	7 14 21 28	5 12 19 26	3 10 17 24	1 8 15 22 29	7 14 21 28	5 12 19 26	3 10 17 24	G

	Nisân.	Iyâr.	Siwân.	Tammûz.	Âbh.	'Elûl.	
A	3 10 17 24	1 8 15 22 29	7 14 21 28	5 12 19 26	4 11 18 25	2 9 16 23	A
B	4 11 18 25	2 9 16 23	1 8 15 22 29	6 13 20 27	5 12 19 26	3 10 17 24	B
C	5 12 19 26	3 10 17 24	2 9 16 23 30	7 14 21 28	6 13 20 27	4 11 18 25	C
D	6 13 20 27	4 11 18 25	3 10 17 24	1 8 15 22 29	7 14 21 28	5 12 19 26	D
E	7 14 21 28	5 12 19 26	4 11 18 25	2 9 16 23	1 8 15 22 29	6 13 20 27	E
F	1 8 15 22 29	6 13 20 27	5 12 19 26	3 10 17 24	2 9 16 23 30	7 14 21 28	F
G	2 9 16 23 30	7 14 21 28	6 13 20 27	4 11 18 25	3 10 17 24	1 8 15 22 29	G

TABLE XVII.

CHRISTIAN DATES OF JEWISH HOLY DAYS, DETERMINED BY THE DATE OF NÎSÂN 15.

PURIM. One day later in Leap-years.	NÎSÂN 15.	Feast of Weeks.	Fast of ABH.	TISHRÎ I.	Day of Atonement.	Feast of Tabernacles.	Eighth day of the Feast.	Feast of The Law.
Feb. 13	March 15	May 4	July 5	Aug. 25	Sept. 3	Sept. 8	Sept. 15	Sept. 16
,, 14	,, 16	,, 5	,, 6	,, 26	,, 4	,, 9	,, 16	,, 17
,, 15	,, 17	,, 6	,, 7	,, 27	,, 5	,, 10	,, 17	,, 18
,, 16	,, 18	,, 7	,, 8	,, 28	,, 6	,, 11	,, 18	,, 19
,, 17	,, 19	,, 8	,, 9	,, 29	,, 7	,, 12	,, 19	,, 20
,, 18	,, 20	,, 9	,, 10	,, 30	,, 8	,, 13	,, 20	,, 21
,, 19	,, 21	,, 10	,, 11	,, 31	,, 9	,, 14	,, 21	,, 22
,, 20	,, 22	,, 11	,, 12	Sept. 1	,, 10	,, 15	,, 22	,, 23
,, 21	,, 23	,, 12	,, 13	,, 2	,, 11	,, 16	,, 23	,, 24
,, 22	,, 24	,, 13	,, 14	,, 3	,, 12	,, 17	,, 24	,, 25
,, 23	,, 25	,, 14	,, 15	,, 4	,, 13	,, 18	,, 25	,, 26
,, 24	,, 26	,, 15	,, 16	,, 5	,, 14	,, 19	,, 26	,, 27
,, 25	,, 27	,, 16	,, 17	,, 6	,, 15	,, 20	,, 27	,, 28
,, 26	,, 28	,, 17	,, 18	,, 7	,, 16	,, 21	,, 28	,, 29
,, 27	,, 29	,, 18	,, 19	,, 8	,, 17	,, 22	,, 29	,, 30
,, 28	,, 30	,, 19	,, 20	,, 9	,, 18	,, 23	,, 30	Oct. 1
Mar. 1	,, 31	,, 20	,, 21	,, 10	,, 19	,, 24	Oct. 1	,, 2
,, 2	April 1	,, 21	,, 22	,, 11	,, 20	,, 25	,, 2	,, 3
,, 3	,, 2	,, 22	,, 23	,, 12	,, 21	,, 26	,, 3	,, 4
,, 4	,, 3	,, 23	,, 24	,, 13	,, 22	,, 27	,, 4	,, 5
,, 5	,, 4	,, 24	,, 25	,, 14	,, 23	,, 28	,, 5	,, 6
,, 6	,, 5	,, 25	,, 26	,, 15	,, 24	,, 29	,, 6	,, 7
,, 7	,, 6	,, 26	,, 27	,, 16	,, 25	,, 30	,, 7	,, 8
,, 8	,, 7	,, 27	,, 28	,, 17	,, 26	Oct. 1	,, 8	,, 9
,, 9	,, 8	,, 28	,, 29	,, 18	,, 27	,, 2	,, 9	,, 10
,, 10	,, 9	,, 29	,, 30	,, 19	,, 28	,, 3	,, 10	,, 11
,, 11	,, 10	,, 30	,, 31	,, 20	,, 29	,, 4	,, 11	,, 12
,, 12	,, 11	,, 31	Aug. 1	,, 21	,, 30	,, 5	,, 12	,, 13
,, 13	,, 12	June 1	,, 2	,, 22	Oct. 1	,, 6	,, 13	,, 14
,, 14	,, 13	,, 2	,, 3	,, 23	,, 2	,, 7	,, 14	,, 15
,, 15	,, 14	,, 3	,, 4	,, 24	,, 3	,, 8	,, 15	,, 16
,, 16	,, 15	,, 4	,, 5	,, 25	,, 4	,, 9	,, 16	,, 17
,, 17	,, 16	,, 5	,, 6	,, 26	,, 5	,, 10	,, 17	,, 18
,, 18	,, 17	,, 6	,, 7	,, 27	,, 6	,, 11	,, 18	,, 19
,, 19	,, 18	,, 7	,, 8	,, 28	,, 7	,, 12	,, 19	,, 20
,, 20	,, 19	,, 8	,, 9	,, 29	,, 8	,, 13	,, 20	,, 21
,, 21	,, 20	,, 9	,, 10	,, 30	,, 9	,, 14	,, 21	,, 22
,, 22	,, 21	,, 10	,, 11	Oct. 1	,, 10	,, 15	,, 22	,, 23
,, 23	,, 22	,, 11	,, 12	,, 2	,, 11	,, 16	,, 23	,, 24
,, 24	,, 23	,, 12	,, 13	,, 3	,, 12	,, 17	,, 24	,, 25
,, 25	,, 24	,, 13	,, 14	,, 4	,, 13	,, 18	,, 25	,, 26
,, 26	,, 25	,, 14	,, 15	,, 5	,, 14	,, 19	,, 26	,, 27
,, 27	,, 26	,, 15	,, 16	,, 6	,, 15	,, 20	,, 27	,, 28
,, 28	,, 27	,, 16	,, 17	,, 7	,, 16	,, 21	,, 28	,, 29
,, 29	,, 28	,, 17	,, 18	,, 8	,, 17	,, 22	,, 29	,, 30

NOTE.—Purim is always the thirtieth day before Nîsân 15; therefore, in Bissextile years the date for Purim, when it occurs in the month of February, must be increased by unity. Thus:—In A.D. 2192, Nîsân 15 will be upon March 29, and Purim on February 27 + 1, or 28.

TABLE OF
CORRESPONDING JEWISH AND CHRISTIAN DATES,
TISHRÎ 1 AND NÎSÂN 15.

A.D. 610 to 3003.

THE Table is divided into Cycles. The heading of each Cycle contains—

The number of the Cycle.
The Molad for the first year of the Cycle—on the left.
The number of days in the Cycle—on the right.

The first column gives the numerical order of the years of the Cycle. Embolismic years are marked E.

The second column gives the years of the Jewish Mundane Era from 4371 to 6764.

The third column contains the Week-day and Christian date corresponding to Tishrî 1.

After A.D. 1582, the Julian and Gregorian dates are both given.

The Sunday Letter of the Christian year is added in order that the Week-day may be verified. In Bissextile years that Letter alone is given which applies to the last ten months of the year.

The Sunday Letter up to A.D. 1582, inclusive, is that of the Julian Calendar; after 1582 the Gregorian Letter is given.

The fourth column contains the Week-day and Christian date of Nîsân 15, occurring in the Jewish Civil year which is in the same line.

The last column contains the number of days in the Jewish Civil year.

Note that the "corresponding" Christian days to Tishrî 1 and to Nîsân 15 are the corresponding times of daylight. The Jewish day commences at 6 p.m., or 6 o'clock in the evening of the preceding Christian day for the Meridian of Jerusalem. Thus: when Tishrî 1 is said to "correspond" with Thursday, September 24, it must be understood that Tishrî 1 commences at 6 in the evening of Wednesday, September 23, and terminates at 6 in the evening of Thursday, September 24. It is with these twenty-four hours that the day coincides. This difference between coincidence and correspondence must be observed.

MOLAD 4 19 974. CYCLE 231. DAYS, 6939.

1	4371	Thurs.	Sept. 24	610	D	Sat.	April 3	611	354
2	4372	Mon.	„ 13	611	C	Thurs.	March 23	612 b	355
3 E	4373	Sat.	„ 2	612	A	Tues.	April 10	613	383
4	4374	Thurs.	„ 20	613	G	Sun.	March 31	614	355
5	4375	Tues.	„ 10	614	F	Thurs.	„ 20	615	354
6 E	4376	Sat.	Aug. 30	615	E	Thurs.	April 8	616 b	385
7	4377	Sat.	Sept. 18	616	C	Sun.	March 27	617	353
8 E	4378	Tues.	„ 6	617	B	Sat.	April 15	618	384
9	4379	Mon.	„ 25	618	A	Thurs.	„ 5	619	355
10	4380	Sat.	„ 15	619	G	Tues.	March 25	620 b	355
11 E	4381	Thurs.	„ 4	620	E	Sun.	April 12	621	383
12	4382	Tues.	„ 22	621	D	Thurs.	„ 1	622	354
13	4383	Sat.	„ 11	622	C	Tues.	March 22	623	355
14 E	4384	Thurs.	„ 1	623	B	Tues.	April 10	624 b	385
15	4385	Thurs.	„ 20	624	G	Sat.	March 30	625	354
16	4386	Mon.	„ 9	625	F	Tues.	„ 18	626	353
17 E	4387	Thurs.	Aug. 28	626	E	Tues.	April 7	627	385
18	4388	Thurs.	Sept. 17	627	D	Sat.	March 26	628 b	354
19 E	4389	Mon.	„ 5	628	B	Thurs.	April 13	629	383

MOLAD 7 12 489. CYCLE 232. DAYS, 6940.

1	4390	Sat.	Sept. 23	629	A	Tues.	April 3	630	355
2	4391	Thurs.	„ 13	630	G	Sat.	March 23	631	354
3 E	4392	Mon.	„ 2	631	F	Sat.	April 11	632 b	385
4	4393	Mon.	„ 21	632	D	Tues.	March 30	633	353
5	4394	Thurs.	„ 9	633	C	Sun.	„ 20	634	355
6 E	4395	Tues.	Aug. 30	634	B	Sat.	April 8	635	384
7	4396	Mon.	Sept. 18	635	A	Thurs.	March 28	636 b	355
8 E	4397	Sat.	„ 7	636	F	Tues.	April 15	637	383
9	4398	Thurs.	„ 25	637	E	Sat.	„ 4	638	354
10	4399	Mon.	„ 14	638	D	Thurs.	March 25	639	355
11 E	4400	Sat.	„ 4	639	C	Tues.	April 11	640 b	383
12	4401	Thurs.	„ 21	640	A	Sun.	„ 1	641	355
13	4402	Tues.	„ 11	641	G	Thurs.	March 21	642	354
14 E	4403	Sat.	Aug. 31	642	F	Thurs.	April 10	643	385
15	4404	Sat.	Sept. 20	643	E	Tues.	March 30	644 b	355
16	4405	Thurs.	„ 9	644	C	Sat.	„ 19	645	354
17 E	4406	Mon.	Aug. 29	645	B	Thurs.	April 6	646	383
18	4407	Sat.	Sept. 16	646	A	Tues.	March 27	647	355
19 E	4408	Thurs.	„ 6	647	G	Sun.	April 13	648 b	383

MOLAD 3 5 4. CYCLE 233. DAYS, 6941.

1	4409	Tues.	Sept. 23	648	E	Thurs.	April 2	649	354
2	4410	Sat.	„ 12	649	D	Tues.	March 23	650	355
3 E	4411	Thurs.	„ 2	650	C	Tues.	April 12	651	385
4	4412	Thurs.	„ 22	651	B	Sat.	March 31	652 b	354
5	4413	Mon.	„ 10	652	G	Tues.	„ 19	653	353
6 E	4414	Thurs.	Aug. 29	653	F	Tues.	April 8	654	385
7	4415	Thurs.	Sept. 18	654	E	Sat.	March 28	655	354
8 E	4416	Mon.	„ 7	655	D	Thurs.	April 14	656 b	383
9	4417	Sat.	„ 24	656	B	Tues.	„ 4	657	355
10	4418	Thurs.	„ 14	657	A	Sat.	March 24	658	354
11 E	4419	Mon.	„ 3	658	G	Sat.	April 13	659	385
12	4420	Mon.	„ 23	659	F	Tues.	March 31	660 b	353
13	4421	Thurs.	„ 10	660	D	Sun.	„ 21	661	355
14 E	4422	Tues.	Aug. 31	661	C	Sat.	April 9	662	384
15	4423	Mon.	Sept. 19	662	B	Thurs.	March 30	663	355
16	4424	Sat.	„ 9	663	A	Sun.	„ 17	664 b	353
17 E	4425	Tues.	Aug. 27	664	F	Sat.	April 5	665	384
18	4426	Mon.	Sept. 15	665	E	Thurs.	March 26	666	355
19 E	4427	Sat.	„ 5	666	D	Thurs.	April 15	667	385

MOLAD 5 21 599. CYCLE 234. DAYS, 6939.

1	4428	Sat.	Sept. 25	667	C	Sun.	April 2	668 b	353
2	4429	Tues.	„ 12	668	A	Thurs.	March 22	669	354
3 E	4430	Sat.	„ 1	669	G	Thurs.	April 11	670	385
4	4431	Sat.	„ 21	670	F	Tues.	„ 1	671	355
5	4432	Thurs.	„ 11	671	E	Sat.	March 20	672 b	354
6 E	4433	Mon.	Aug. 30	672	C	Thurs.	April 7	673	383
7	4434	Sat.	Sept. 17	673	B	Tues.	March 28	674	355
8 E	4435	Thurs.	„ 7	674	A	Tues.	April 17	675	385
19	4436	Thurs.	„ 27	675	G	Sat.	„ 5	676 b	354
10	4437	Mon.	„ 15	676	E	Tues.	March 24	677	353
11 E	4438	Thurs.	„ 3	677	D	Tues.	April 13	678	385
12	4439	Thurs.	„ 23	678	C	Sat.	„ 2	679	354
13	4440	Mon.	„ 12	679	B	Thurs.	March 22	680 b	355
14 E	4441	Sat.	„ 1	680	G	Tues.	April 9	681	383
15	4442	Thurs.	„ 19	681	F	Sat.	March 29	682	354
16	4443	Mon.	„ 8	682	E	Thurs.	„ 19	683	355
17 E	4444	Sat.	Aug. 29	683	D	Tues.	April 5	684 b	383
18	4445	Thurs.	Sept. 15	684	B	Sat.	March 25	685	354
49 E	4446	Mon.	„ 4	685	A	Sat.	April 14	686	385

MOLAD 1 14 111. CYCLE 235. DAYS, 6940.

1	4447	Mon.	Sept. 24	686	G	Thurs.	April 4	687	355
2	4448	Sat.	" 14	687	F	Sun.	March 22	688 b	353
3 E	4449	Tues.	" 1	688	D	Sat.	April 10	689	384
4	4450	Mon.	" 20	689	C	Thurs.	March 31	690	355
5	4451	Sat.	" 10	690	B	Tues.	" 21	691	355
6 E	4452	Thurs.	Aug. 31	691	A	Sun.	April 7	692 b	383
7	4453	Tues.	Sept. 17	692	F	Thurs.	March 27	693	354
8 E	4454	Sat.	" 6	693	E	Thurs.	April 16	694	385
9	4455	Sat.	" 26	694	D	Tues.	" 6	695	355
10	4456	Thurs.	" 16	695	C	Sat.	March 25	696 b	354
11 E	4457	Mon.	" 4	696	A	Thurs.	April 12	697	383
12	4458	Sat.	" 22	697	G	Tues.	" 2	698	355
13	4459	Thurs.	" 12	698	F	Sat.	March 22	699	354
14 E	4460	Mon.	" 1	699	E	Thurs.	April 8	700 b	383
15	4461	Sat.	" 18	700	C	Tues.	March 29	701	355
16	4462	Thurs.	" 8	701	B	Sat.	" 18	702	354
17 E	4463	Mon.	" 28	702	A	Sat.	April 7	703	385
18	4464	Mon.	Sept. 17	703	G	Tues.	March 25	704 b	353
19 E	4465	Thurs.	" 4	704	E	Tues.	April 14	705	385

MOLAD 4 6 709. CYCLE 236. DAYS, 6939.

1	4466	Thurs.	Sept. 24	705	D	Sat.	April 3	706	354
2	4467	Mon.	" 13	706	C	Thurs.	March 24	707	355
3 E	4468	Sat.	" 3	707	B	Tues.	April 10	708 b	388
4	4469	Thurs.	" 20	708	G	Sat.	March 30	709	354
5	4470	Mon.	" 9	709	F	Thurs.	" 20	710	355
6 E	4471	Sat.	Aug. 30	710	E	Tues.	April 7	711	383
7	4472	Thurs.	Sept. 17	711	D	Sun.	March 27	712 b	355
8 E	4473	Tues.	" 6	712	B	Sat.	April 15	713	384
9	4474	Mon.	" 25	713	A	Thurs.	" 5	714	355
10	4475	Sat.	" 15	714	G	Sun.	March 24	715	353
11 E	4476	Tues.	" 3	715	F	Sat.	April 11	716 b	384
12	4477	Mon.	" 21	716	D	Thurs.	" 1	717	355
13	4478	Sat.	" 11	717	C	Tues.	March 22	718	355
14 E	4479	Thurs.	" 1	718	B	Sun.	April 9	719	383
15	4480	Tues.	" 19	719	A	Thurs.	March 28	720 b	354
16	4481	Sat.	" 7	720	F	Tues.	" 18	721	355
17 E	4482	Thurs.	Aug. 28	721	E	Tues.	April 7	722	385
18	4483	Thurs.	Sept. 17	722	D	Sat.	March 27	723	354
19 E	4484	Mon.	" 6	723	C	Thurs.	April 13	724 b	383

MOLAD 6 23 224. CYCLE 237. DAYS, 6940.

1	4485	Sat.	Sept. 23	724	A	Tues.	April 3	725	355
2	4486	Thurs.	„ 13	725	G	Sat.	March 23	726	354
3 E	4487	Mon.	„ 2	726	F	Thurs.	April 10	727	383
4	4488	Sat.	„ 20	727	E	Tues.	March 30	728 b	355
5	4489	Thurs.	„ 9	728	C	Sat.	„ 19	729	354
6 E	4490	Mon.	Aug. 29	729	B	Sat.	April 8	730	385
7	4491	Mon.	Sept. 18	730	A	Tues.	March 27	731	353
8 E	4492	Thurs.	„ 6	731	G	Tues.	April 15	732 b	385
9	4493	Thurs.	„ 25	732	E	Sat.	„ 4	733	354
10	4494	Mon.	„ 14	733	D	Thurs.	March 25	734	355
11 E	4495	Sat.	„ 4	734	C	Tues.	April 12	735	383
12	4496	Thurs.	„ 22	735	B	Sat.	March 31	736 b	354
13	4497	Mon.	„ 10	736	G	Thurs.	„ 21	737	355
14 E	4498	Sat.	Aug. 31	737	F	Thurs.	April 10	738	385
15	4499	Sat.	Sept. 20	738	E	Sun.	March 29	739	353
16	4500	Tues.	„ 8	739	D	Thurs.	„ 17	740 b	354
17 E	4501	Sat.	Aug. 27	740	B	Thurs.	April 6	741	385
18	4502	Sat.	Sept. 16	741	A	Tues.	March 27	742	355
19 E	4503	Thurs.	„ 6	742	G	Sun.	April 14	743	383

MOLAD 2 15 819. CYCLE 238. DAYS, 6939.

1	4504	Tues.	Sept. 24	743	F	Thurs.	April 2	744 b	354
2	4505	Sat.	„ 12	744	D	Tues.	March 23	745	355
3 E	4506	Thurs.	„ 2	745	C	Sun.	April 10	746	383
4	4507	Tues.	„ 20	746	B	Thurs.	March 30	747	354
5	4508	Sat.	„ 9	747	A	Tues.	„ 19	748 b	355
6 E	4509	Thurs.	Aug. 29	748	F	Tues.	April 8	749	385
7	4510	Thurs.	Sept. 18	749	E	Sat.	March 28	750	354
8 E	4511	Mon.	„ 7	750	D	Thurs.	April 15	751	383
9	4512	Sat.	„ 25	751	C	Tues.	„ 4	752 b	355
10	4513	Thurs.	„ 14	752	A	Sat.	March 24	753	354
11 E	4514	Mon.	„ 3	753	G	Sat.	April 13	754	385
12	4515	Mon.	„ 23	754	F	Tues.	„ 1	755	353
13	4516	Thurs.	„ 11	755	E	Sat.	March 20	756 b	354
14 E	4517	Mon.	Aug. 30	756	C	Sat.	April 9	757	385
15	4518	Mon.	Sept. 19	757	B	Thurs.	March 30	758	355
16	4519	Sat.	„ 9	758	A	Sun.	„ 18	759	353
17 E	4520	Tues.	Aug. 28	759	G	Sat.	April 5	760 b	384
18	4521	Mon.	Sept. 15	760	E	Thurs.	March 26	761	355
19 E	4522	Sat.	„ 5	761	D	Tues.	April 13	762	383

Molad 5 8 334. CYCLE 239. Days, 6941.

1	4523	Thurs.	Sept. 23	762	C	Sat.	April 2	763	354
2	4524	Mon.	„ 12	763	B	Thurs.	March 22	764 b	355
3 E	4525	Sat.	„ 1	764	G	Thurs.	April 11	765	385
4	4526	Sat.	„ 21	765	F	Sun.	March 30	766	353
5	4527	Tues.	„ 9	766	E	Thurs.	„ 19	767	354
6 E	4528	Sat.	Aug. 29	767	D	Thurs.	April 7	768 b	385
7	4529	Sat.	Sept. 17	768	B	Tues.	March 28	769	355
8 E	4530	Thurs	„ 7	769	A	Sun.	April 15	770	383
9	4531	Tues.	„ 25	770	G	Thurs.	„ 4	771	354
10	4532	Sat.	„ 14	771	F	Tues.	March 24	772 b	355
11 E	4533	Thurs.	„ 3	772	D	Tues.	April 13	773	385
12	4534	Thurs.	„ 23	773	C	Sun.	„ 2	774	354
13	4535	Mon.	„ 12	774	B	Tues.	March 21	775	353
14 E	4536	Thurs.	Aug. 31	775	A	Tues.	April 9	776 b	385
15	4537	Thurs.	Sept. 19	776	F	Sat.	March 29	777	354
16	4538	Mon.	„ 8	777	E	Thurs.	„ 19	778	355
17 E	4539	Sat.	Aug. 29	778	D	Tues.	April 6	779	383
18	4540	Thurs.	Sept. 16	779	C	Sat.	March 25	780 b	354
19 E	4541	Mon.	„ 4	780	A	Sat.	April 14	781	385

Molad 1 0 929. CYCLE 240. Days, 6940.

1	4542	Mon.	Sept. 24	781	G	Tues.	April 2	782	353
2	4543	Thurs.	„ 12	782	F	Sun.	March 23	783	355
3 E	4544	Tues.	„ 2	783	E	Sat.	April 10	784 b	384
4	4545	Mon.	„ 20	784	C	Thurs.	March 31	785	355
5	4546	Sat.	„ 10	785	B	Sun.	„ 19	786	353
6 E	4547	Tues.	Aug. 29	786	A	Sat.	April 7	787	384
7	4548	Mon.	Sept. 17	787	G	Thurs.	March 27	788 b	355
8 E	4549	Sat.	„ 6	788	E	Tues.	April 14	789	383
9	4550	Thurs.	„ 24	789	D	Sun.	„ 4	790	355
10	4551	Tues.	„ 14	790	C	Thurs.	March 24	791	354
11 E	4552	Sat.	„ 3	791	B	Thurs.	April 12	792 b	385
12	4553	Sat.	„ 22	792	G	Tues.	„ 2	793	355
13	4554	Thurs.	„ 12	793	F	Sat.	March 22	794	354
14 E	4555	Mon.	„ 1	794	E	Thurs.	April 9	795	383
15	4556	Sat.	„ 19	795	D	Tues.	March 29	796 b	355
16	4557	Thurs.	„ 8	796	B	Sat.	„ 18	797	354
17 E	4558	Mon.	Aug. 28	797	A	Thurs.	April 5	798	383
18	4559	Sat.	Sept. 15	798	G	Tues.	March 26	799	355
19 E	4560	Thurs.	„ 5	799	F	Tues.	April 14	800 b	385

MOLAD 3 17 444 CYCLE 241. DAYS, 6939.

1	4561	Thurs.	Sept. 24	800	D	Sat.	April 3	801	354
2	4562	Mon.	„ 13	801	C	Tues.	March 22	802	353
3 E	4563	Thurs.	„ 1	802	B	Tues.	April 11	803	385
4	4564	Thurs.	„ 21	803	A	Sat.	March 30	804 b	354
5	4565	Mon.	„ 9	804	F	Thurs.	„ 20	805	355
6 E	4566	Sat.	Aug. 30	805	E	Tues.	April 7	806	383
7	4567	Thurs.	Sept. 17	806	D	Sat.	March 27	807	354
8 E	4568	Mon.	„ 6	807	C	Sat.	April 15	808 b	385
9	4569	Mon.	„ 25	808	A	Tues.	„ 3	809	353
10	4570	Thurs.	„ 13	809	G	Sun.	March 24	810	355
11 E	4571	Tues.	„ 3	810	F	Sat.	April 12	811	384
12	4572	Mon.	„ 22	811	E	Thurs.	„ 1	812 b	355
13	4573	Sat.	„ 11	812	C	Sun.	March 20	813	353
14 E	4574	Tues.	Aug. 30	813	B	Sat.	April 8	814	384
15	4575	Mon.	Sept. 18	814	A	Thurs.	March 29	815	355
16	4576	Sat.	„ 8	815	G	Tues.	„ 18	816 b	355
17 E	4577	Thurs.	Aug. 28	816	E	Sun.	April 5	817	383
18	4578	Tues.	Sept. 15	817	D	Thurs.	March 25	818	354
19 E	4579	Sat.	„ 4	818	C	Thurs.	April 14	819	385

MOLAD 6 9 1039. CYCLE 242. DAYS, 6939.

1	4580	Sat.	Sept. 24	819	B	Tues.	April 3	820 b	355
2	4581	Thurs.	„ 13	820	G	Sat.	March 23	821	354
3 E	4582	Mon.	„ 2	821	F	Thurs.	April 10	822	383
4	4583	Sat.	„ 20	822	E	Tues.	March 31	823	355
5	4584	Thurs.	„ 10	823	D	Sat.	„ 19	824 b	354
6 E	4585	Mon.	Aug. 29	824	B	Thurs.	April 6	825	383
7	4586	Sat.	Sept. 16	825	A	Tues.	March 27	826	355
8 E	4587	Thurs.	„ 6	826	G	Tues.	April 16	827	385
9	4588	Thurs.	„ 26	827	F	Sat.	„ 4	828 b	354
10	4589	Mon.	„ 14	828	D	Tues.	March 23	829	353
11 E	4590	Thurs.	„ 2	829	C	Tues.	April 12	830	385
12	4591	Thurs.	„ 22	830	B	Sat.	„ 1	831	354
13	4592	Mon.	„ 11	831	A	Thurs.	March 21	832 b	355
14 E	4593	Sat.	Aug. 31	832	F	Tues.	April 8	833	383
15	4594	Thurs.	Sept. 18	833	E	Sat.	March 28	834	354
16	4595	Mon.	„ 7	834	D	Thurs.	„ 18	835	355
17 E	4596	Sat.	Aug. 28	835	C	Thurs.	April 6	836 b	385
18	4597	Sat.	Sept. 16	836	A	Sun.	March 25	837	353
19 E	4598	Tues.	„ 4	837	G	Sat.	April 13	838	384

MOLAD 2 2 554. CYCLE 243. DAYS, 6940.

1	4599	Mon.	Sept. 23	838	F	Thurs.	April 3	839	355
2	4600	Sat.	„ 13	839	E	Tues.	March 23	840 b	355
3 E	4601	Thurs.	„ 2	840	C	Sun.	April 10	841	383
4	4602	Tues.	„ 20	841	B	Thurs.	March 30	842	354
5	4603	Sat.	„ 9	842	A	Tues.	„ 20	843	355
6 E	4604	Thurs.	Aug. 30	843	G	Sun.	April 6	844 b	383
7	4605	Tues.	Sept. 16	844	E	Thurs.	March 26	845	354
8 E	4606	Sat.	„ 5	845	D	Thurs.	April 15	846	385
9	4607	Sat.	„ 25	846	C	Tues.	„ 5	847	355
10	4608	Thurs.	„ 15	847	B	Sat.	March 24	848 b	354
11 E	4609	Mon.	„ 3	848	G	Thurs.	April 11	849	383
12	4610	Sat.	„ 21	849	F	Tues.	„ 1	850	355
13	4611	Thurs.	„ 11	850	E	Sat.	March 21	851	354
14 E	4612	Mon.	Aug. 31	851	D	Sat.	April 9	852 b	385
15	4613	Mon.	Sept. 19	852	B	Tues.	March 28	853	353
16	4614	Thurs.	„ 7	853	A	Sat.	„ 17	854	354
17 E	4615	Mon.	Aug. 27	854	G	Sat.	April 6	855	385
18	4616	Mon.	Sept. 16	855	F	Thurs.	March 26	856 b	355
19 E	4617	Sat.	„ 5	856	D	Tues.	April 13	857	383

MOLAD 4 19 69. CYCLE 244. DAYS, 6939.

1	4618	Thurs.	Sept. 23	857	C	Sat.	April 2	858	354
2	4619	Mon.	„ 12	858	B	Thurs.	March 23	859	355
3 E	4620	Sat.	„ 2	859	A	Tues.	April 9	860 b	383
4	4621	Thurs.	„ 19	860	F	Sun.	March 30	861	355
5	4622	Tues.	„ 9	861	E	Thurs.	„ 19	862	354
6 E	4623	Sat.	Aug. 29	862	D	Thurs.	April 8	863	385
7	4624	Sat.	Sept. 18	863	C	Sun.	March 26	864 b	353
8 E	4625	Tues.	„ 5	864	A	Sat.	April 14	865	384
9	4626	Mon.	„ 24	865	G	Thurs.	„ 4	866	355
10	4627	Sat.	„ 14	866	F	Tues.	March 25	867	355
11 E	4628	Thurs.	„ 4	867	E	Sun.	April 11	868 b	383
12	4629	Tues.	„ 21	868	C	Thurs.	March 31	869	354
13	4630	Sat.	„ 10	869	B	Tues.	„ 21	870	355
14 E	4631	Thurs.	Aug. 31	870	A	Tues.	April 10	871	385
15	4632	Thurs.	Sept. 20	871	G	Sat.	March 29	872 b	354
16	4633	Mon.	„ 8	872	E	Tues.	„ 17	873	353
17 E	4634	Thurs.	Aug. 27	873	D	Tues.	April 6	874	385
18	4635	Thurs.	Sept. 16	874	C	Sat.	March 26	875	354
19 E	4636	Mon.	„ 5	875	B	Thurs.	April 12	876 b	383

MOLAD 7 11 664. CYCLE 245. DAYS, 6940.

1	4637	Sat.	Sept. 22	876	G	Tues.	April 2	877	355
2	4638	Thurs.	„ 12	877	F	Sat.	March 22	878	354
3 E	4639	Mon.	„ 1	878	E	Sat.	April 11	879	385
4	4640	Mon.	„ 21	879	D	Tues.	March 29	880 b	353
5	4641	Thurs.	„ 8	880	B	Sun.	„ 19	881	355
6 E	4642	Tues.	Aug. 29	881	A	Sat.	April 7	882	384
7	4643	Mon.	Sept. 17	882	G	Thurs.	March 28	883	355
8 E	4644	Sat.	„ 7	883	F	Tues.	April 14	884 b	383
9	4645	Thurs.	„ 24	884	D	Sat.	„ 3	885	354
10	4646	Mon.	„ 13	885	C	Thurs.	March 24	886	355
11 E	4647	Sat.	„ 3	886	B	Tues.	April 11	887	383
12	4648	Thurs.	„ 21	887	A	Sun.	March 31	888 b	355
13	4649	Tues.	„ 10	888	F	Thurs.	„ 20	889	354
14 E	4650	Sat.	Aug. 30	889	E	Thurs.	April 9	890	385
15	4651	Sat.	Sept. 19	890	D	Tues.	March 30	891	355
16	4652	Thurs.	„ 9	891	C	Sat.	„ 18	892 b	354
17 E	4653	Mon.	Aug. 28	892	A	Thurs.	April 5	893	383
18	4654	Sat.	Sept. 15	893	G	Tues.	March 26	894	355
19 E	4655	Thurs.	„ 5	894	F	Sun.	April 13	895	383

MOLAD 3 4 179. CYCLE 246. DAYS, 6941.

1	4656	Tues.	Sept. 23	895	E	Thurs.	April 1	896 b	354
2	4657	Sat.	„ 11	896	C	Tues.	March 22	897	355
3 E	4658	Thurs.	„ 1	897	B	Tues.	April 11	898	385
4	4659	Thurs.	„ 21	898	A	Sat.	March 31	899	354
5	4660	Mon.	„ 10	899	G	Tues.	„ 18	900 b	353
6 E	4661	Thurs.	Aug. 28	900	E	Tues.	April 7	901	385
7	4662	Thurs.	Sept. 17	901	D	Sat.	March 27	902	354
8 E	4663	Mon.	„ 6	902	C	Thurs.	April 14	903	383
9	4664	Sat.	„ 24	903	B	Tues.	„ 3	904 b	355
10	4665	Thurs.	„ 13	904	G	Sat.	March 23	905	354
11 E	4666	Mon.	„ 2	905	F	Sat.	April 12	906	385
12	4667	Mon.	„ 22	906	E	Tues.	March 31	907	353
13	4668	Thurs.	„ 10	907	D	Sun.	„ 20	908 b	355
14 E	4669	Tues.	Aug. 30	908	B	Sat.	April 8	909	384
15	4670	Mon.	Sept. 18	909	A	Thurs.	March 29	910	355
16	4671	Sat.	„ 8	910	G	Sun.	„ 17	911	353
17 E	4672	Tues.	Aug. 27	911	F	Sat.	April 4	912 b	384
18	4673	Mon.	Sept. 14	912	D	Thurs.	March 25	913	355
19 E	4674	Sat.	„ 4	913	C	Thurs.	April 14	914	385

Molad 5 20 774. CYCLE 247. Days, 6939.

1	4675	Sat.	Sept. 24	914	B	Sun.	April 2	915	353
2	4676	Tues.	„ 12	915	A	Thurs.	March 21	916 b	354
3 E	4677	Sat.	Aug. 31	916	F	Thurs.	April 10	917	385
4	4678	Sat.	Sept. 20	917	E	Tues.	March 31	918	355
5	4679	Thurs	„ 10	918	D	Sat.	„ 20	919	354
6 E	4680	Mon.	Aug. 30	919	C	Thurs.	April 6	920 b	383
7	4681	Sat.	Sept. 16	920	A	Tues.	March 27	921	355
8 E	4682	Thurs.	„ 6	921	G	Tues.	April 16	922	385
9	4683	Thurs.	„ 26	922	F	Sat.	„ 5	923	354
10	4684	Mon.	„ 15	923	E	Tues.	March 23	924 b	353
11 E	4685	Thurs.	„ 2	924	C	Tues.	April 12	925	385
12	4686	Thurs.	„ 22	925	B	Sat.	„ 1	926	354
13	4687	Mon.	„ 11	926	A	Thurs.	March 22	927	355
14 E	4688	Sat.	„ 1	927	G	Tues.	April 8	928 b	383
15	4689	Thurs.	„ 18	928	E	Sat.	March 28	929	354
16	4690	Mon.	„ 7	929	D	Thurs.	„ 18	930	355
17 E	4691	Sat.	Aug. 28	930	C	Tues.	April 5	931	383
18	4692	Thurs.	Sept. 15	931	B	Sat.	March 24	932 b	354
19 E	4693	Mon.	„ 3	932	G	Sat.	April 13	933	385

Molad 1 13 289. CYCLE 248. Days, 6940.

1	4694	Mon.	Sept. 23	933	F	Thurs.	April 3	934	355
2	4695	Sat.	„ 13	934	E	Sun.	March 22	935	353
3 E	4696	Tues.	„ 1	935	D	Sat.	April 9	936 b	384
4	4697	Mon.	„ 19	936	B	Thurs.	March 30	937	355
5	4698	Sat.	„ 9	937	A	Tues.	„ 20	938	355
6 E	4699	Thurs.	Aug. 30	938	G	Sun.	April 7	939	383
7	4700	Tues.	Sept. 17	939	F	Thurs.	March 26	940 b	354
8 E	4701	Sat.	„ 5	940	D	Thurs.	April 15	941	385
9	4702	Sat.	„ 25	941	C	Tues.	„ 5	942	355
10	4703	Thurs.	„ 15	942	B	Sat.	March 25	943	354
11 E	4704	Mon.	„ 4	943	A	Thurs.	April 11	944 b	383
12	4705	Sat.	„ 21	944	F	Tues.	„ 1	945	355
13	4706	Thurs.	„ 11	945	E	Sat.	March 21	946	354
14 E	4707	Mon.	Aug. 31	946	D	Thurs.	April 8	947	383
15	4708	Sat.	Sept. 18	947	C	Tues.	March 28	948 b	355
16	4709	Thurs.	„ 7	948	A	Sat.	„ 17	949	354
17 E	4710	Mon.	Aug. 27	949	G	Sat.	April 6	950	385
18	4711	Mon.	Sept. 16	950	F	Tues.	March 25	951	353
19 E	4712	Thurs.	„ 4	951	E	Tues.	April 13	952 b	385

MOLAD 4 5 884. CYCLE 249. DAYS, 6939.

1	4713	Thurs.	Sept. 23	952	C	Sat.	April 2	953	354
2	4714	Mon.	„ 12	953	B	Thurs.	March 23	954	355
3 E	4715	Sat.	„ 2	954	A	Tues.	April 10	955	383
4	4716	Thurs.	„ 20	955	G	Sat.	March 29	956 b	354
5	4717	Mon.	„ 8	956	E	Thurs.	„ 19	957	355
6 E	4718	Sat.	Aug. 29	957	D	Tues.	April 6	958	383
7	4719	Thurs.	Sept. 16	958	C	Sun.	March 27	959	355
8 E	4720	Tues.	„ 6	959	B	Sat.	April 14	960 b	384
9	4721	Mon.	„ 24	960	G	Thurs.	„ 4	961	355
10	4722	Sat.	„ 14	961	F	Sun.	March 23	962	353
11 E	4723	Tues.	„ 2	962	E	Sat.	April 11	963	384
12	4724	Mon.	„ 21	963	D	Thurs.	March 31	964 b	355
13	4725	Sat.	„ 10	964	B	Tues.	„ 21	965	355
14 E	4726	Thurs.	Aug. 31	965	A	Sun.	April 8	966	383
15	4727	Tues.	Sept. 18	966	G	Thurs.	March 28	967	354
16	4728	Sat.	„ 7	967	F	Tues.	„ 17	968 b	355
17 E	4729	Thurs.	Aug. 27	968	D	Tues.	April 6	969	385
18	4730	Thurs.	Sept. 16	969	C	Sat.	March 26	970	354
19 E	4731	Mon.	„ 5	970	B	Thurs.	April 13	971	383

MOLAD 6 22 399. CYCLE 250. DAYS, 6939.

1	4732	Sat.	Sept. 23	971	A	Tues.	April 2	972 b	355
2	4733	Thurs.	„ 12	972	F	Sat.	March 22	973	354
3 E	4734	Mon.	„ 1	973	E	Thurs.	April 9	974	383
4	4735	Sat.	„ 19	974	D	Tues.	March 30	975	355
5	4736	Thurs.	„ 9	975	C	Sat.	„ 18	976 b	354
6 E	4737	Mon.	Aug. 28	976	A	Sat.	April 7	977	385
7	4738	Mon.	Sept. 17	977	G	Tues.	March 26	978	353
8 E	4739	Thurs.	„ 5	978	F	Tues.	April 15	979	385
9	4740	Thurs.	„ 25	979	E	Sat.	„ 3	980 b	354
10	4741	Mon.	„ 13	980	C	Thurs.	March 24	981	355
11 E	4742	Sat.	„ 3	981	B	Tues.	April 11	982	383
12	4743	Thurs.	„ 21	982	A	Sat.	March 31	983	354
13	4744	Mon.	„ 10	983	G	Thurs.	„ 20	984 b	355
14 E	4745	Sat.	Aug. 30	984	E	Tues.	April 7	985	383
15	4746	Thurs.	Sept. 17	985	D	Sun.	March 28	986	355
16	4747	Tues.	„ 7	986	C	Thurs.	„ 17	987	354
17 E	4748	Sat.	Aug. 27	987	B	Thurs.	April 5	988 b	385
18	4749	Sat.	Sept. 15	988	G	Sun.	March 24	989	353
19 E	4750	Tues.	„ 3	989	F	Sat.	April 12	990	384

MOLAD 2 14 994. CYCLE 251. DAYS, 6940.

1	4751	Mon.	Sept. 22	990	E	Thurs.	April 2	991	355
2	4752	Sat.	„ 12	991	D	Tues.	March 22	992 b	355
3 E	4753	Thurs.	„ 1	992	B	Sun.	April 9	993	383
4	4754	Tues.	„ 19	993	A	Thurs.	March 29	994	354
5	4755	Sat.	„ 8	994	G	Tues.	„ 19	995	355
6 E	4756	Thurs.	Aug. 29	995	F	Tues.	April 7	996 b	385
7	4757	Thurs.	Sept. 17	996	D	Sat.	March 27	997	354
8 E	4758	Mon.	„ 6	997	C	Thurs.	April 14	998	383
9	4759	Sat.	„ 24	998	B	Tues.	„ 4	999	355
10	4760	Thurs.	„ 14	999	A	Sat.	March 23	1000 b	354
11 E	4761	Mon.	„ 2	1000	F	Sat.	April 12	1001	385
12	4762	Mon.	„ 22	1001	E	Tues.	March 31	1002	353
13	4763	Thurs.	„ 10	1002	D	Sat.	„ 20	1003	354
14 E	4764	Mon.	Aug. 30	1003	C	Sat.	April 8	1004 b	385
15	4765	Mon.	Sept. 18	1004	A	Thurs.	March 29	1005	355
16	4766	Sat.	„ 8	1005	G	Sun.	„ 17	1006	353
17 E	4767	Tues.	Aug. 27	1006	F	Sat.	April 5	1007	384
18	4768	Mon.	Sept. 15	1007	E	Thurs.	March 25	1008 b	355
19 E	4769	Sat.	„ 4	1008	C	Tues.	April 12	1009	383

MOLAD 5 7 509. CYCLE 252. DAYS, 6941.

1	4770	Thurs.	Sept. 22	1009	B	Sat.	April 1	1010	354
2	4771	Mon.	„ 11	1010	A	Thurs.	March 22	1011	355
3 E	4772	Sat.	„ 1	1011	G	Thurs.	April 10	1012 b	385
4	4773	Sat.	„ 20	1012	E	Sun.	March 29	1013	353
5	4774	Tues.	„ 8	1013	D	Thurs.	„ 18	1014	354
6 E	4775	Sat.	Aug. 28	1014	C	Thurs.	April 7	1015	385
7	4776	Sat.	Sept. 17	1015	B	Tues.	March 27	1016 b	355
8 E	4777	Thurs.	„ 6	1016	G	Sun.	April 14	1017	383
9	4778	Tues.	„ 24	1017	F	Thurs.	„ 3	1018	354
10	4779	Sat.	„ 13	1018	E	Tues.	March 24	1019	355
11 E	4780	Thurs.	„ 3	1019	D	Tues.	April 12	1020 b	385
12	4781	Thurs.	„ 22	1020	B	Sat.	„ 1	1021	354
13	4782	Mon.	„ 11	1021	A	Tues.	March 20	1022	353
14 E	4783	Thurs.	Aug. 30	1022	G	Tues.	April 9	1023	385
15	4784	Thurs.	Sept. 19	1023	F	Sat.	March 28	1024 b	354
16	4785	Mon.	„ 7	1024	D	Thurs.	„ 18	1025	355
17 E	4786	Sat.	Aug. 28	1025	C	Tues.	April 5	1026	383
18	4787	Thurs.	Sept. 15	1026	B	Sat.	March 25	1027	354
19 E	4788	Mon.	„ 4	1027	A	Sat.	April 13	1028 b	385

MOLAD 1 0 24. CYCLE 253. DAYS, 6940.

1	4789	Mon.	Sept. 23	1028	F	Tues.	April 1	1029	353
2	4790	Thurs.	„ 11	1029	E	Sat.	March 21	1030	354
3 E	4791	Mon.	Aug. 31	1030	D	Sat.	April 10	1031	385
4	4792	Mon.	Sept. 20	1031	C	Thurs.	March 30	1032 b	355
5	4793	Sat.	„ 9	1032	A	Sun.	„ 18	1033	353
6 E	4794	Tues.	Aug. 28	1033	G	Sat.	April 6	1034	384
7	4795	Mon.	Sept. 16	1034	F	Thurs.	March 27	1035	355
8 E	4796	Sat.	„ 6	1035	E	Tues.	April 13	1036 b	383
9	4797	Thurs.	„ 23	1036	C	Sun.	„ 3	1037	355
10	4798	Tues.	„ 13	1037	B	Thurs.	March 23	1038	354
11 E	4799	Sat.	„ 2	1038	A	Thurs.	April 12	1039	385
12	4800	Sat.	„ 22	1039	G	Tues.	„ 1	1040 b	355
13	4801	Thurs.	„ 11	1040	E	Sat.	March 21	1041	354
14 E	4802	Mon.	Aug. 31	1041	D	Thurs.	April 8	1042	383
15	4803	Sat.	Sept. 18	1042	C	Tues.	March 29	1043	355
16	4804	Thurs.	„ 8	1043	B	Sat.	„ 17	1044 b	354
17 E	4805	Mon.	Aug. 27	1044	G	Thurs.	April 4	1045	383
18	4806	Sat.	Sept. 14	1045	F	Tues.	March 25	1046	355
19 E	4807	Thurs.	„ 4	1046	E	Tues.	April 14	1047	385

MOLAD 3 16 619. CYCLE 254. DAYS, 6939.

1	4808	Thurs.	Sept. 24	1047	D	Sat.	April 2	1048 b	354
2	4809	Mon.	„ 12	1048	B	Tues.	March 21	1049	353
3 E	4810	Thurs.	Aug. 31	1049	A	Tues.	April 10	1050	385
4	4811	Thurs.	Sept. 20	1050	G	Sat.	March 30	1051	354
5	4812	Mon.	„ 9	1051	F	Thurs.	„ 19	1052 b	355
6 E	4813	Sat.	Aug. 29	1052	D	Tues.	April 6	1053	383
7	4814	Thurs.	Sept. 16	1053	C	Sat.	March 26	1054	354
8 E	4815	Mon.	„ 5	1054	B	Sat.	April 15	1055	385
9	4816	Mon.	„ 25	1055	A	Tues.	„ 2	1056 b	353
10	4817	Thurs.	„ 12	1056	F	Sun.	March 23	1057	355
11 E	4818	Tues.	„ 2	1057	E	Sat.	April 11	1058	384
12	4819	Mon.	„ 21	1058	D	Thurs.	„ 1	1059	355
13	4820	Sat.	„ 11	1059	C	Sun.	March 19	1060 b	353
14 E	4821	Tues.	Aug. 29	1060	A	Sat.	April 7	1061	384
15	4822	Mon.	Sept. 17	1061	G	Thurs.	March 28	1062	355
16	4823	Sat.	„ 7	1062	F	Tues.	„ 18	1063	355
17 E	4824	Thurs.	Aug. 28	1063	E	Sun.	April 4	1064 b	383
18	4825	Tues.	Sept. 14	1064	C	Thurs.	March 24	1065	354
19 E	4826	Sat.	„ 3	1065	B	Thurs.	April 13	1066	385

MOLAD 6 9 134. CYCLE 255. DAYS, 6939.

1	4827	Sat.	Sept. 23	1066	A	Tues.	April 3	1067	355
2	4828	Thurs	„ 13	1067	G	Sat.	March 22	1068 b	354
3 E	4829	Mon.	„ 1	1068	E	Thurs.	April 9	1069	383
4	4830	Sat.	„ 19	1069	D	Tues.	March 30	1070	355
5	4831	Thurs.	„ 9	1070	C	Sat.	„ 19	1071	354
6 E	4832	Mon.	Aug. 29	1071	B	Thurs.	April 5	1072 b	383
7	4833	Sat.	Sept. 15	1072	G	Tues.	March 26	1073	355
8 E	4834	Thurs.	„ 5	1073	F	Tues.	April 15	1074	385
9	4835	Thurs.	„ 25	1074	E	Sat.	„ 4	1075	354
10	4836	Mon.	„ 14	1075	D	Tues.	March 22	1076 b	353
11 E	4837	Thurs.	„ 1	1076	B	Tues.	April 11	1077	385
12	4838	Thurs.	„ 21	1077	A	Sat.	March 31	1078	354
13	4839	Mon.	„ 10	1078	G	Thurs.	„ 21	1079	355
14 E	4840	Sat.	Aug. 31	1079	F	Tues.	April 7	1080 b	383
15	4841	Thurs.	Sept. 17	1080	D	Sat.	March 27	1081	354
16	4842	Mon.	„ 6	1081	C	Thurs.	„ 17	1082	355
17 E	4843	Sat.	Aug. 27	1082	B	Thurs.	April 6	1083	385
18	4844	Sat.	Sept. 16	1083	A	Sun.	March 24	1084 b	353
19 E	4845	Tues.	„ 3	1084	F	Sat.	April 12	1085	384

MOLAD 2 1 729. CYCLE 256. DAYS, 6940.

1	4846	Mon.	Sept. 22	1085	E	Thurs.	April 2	1086	355
2	4847	Sat.	„ 12	1086	D	Tues.	March 23	1087	355
3 E	4848	Thurs.	„ 2	1087	C	Sun.	April 9	1088 b	383
4	4849	Tues.	„ 19	1088	A	Thurs.	March 29	1089	354
5	4850	Sat.	„ 8	1089	G	Tues.	„ 19	1090	355
6 E	4851	Thurs.	Aug. 29	1090	F	Sun.	April 6	1091	383
7	4852	Tues.	Sept. 16	1091	E	Thurs.	March 25	1092 b	354
8 E	4853	Sat.	„ 4	1092	C	Thurs.	April 14	1093	385
9	4854	Sat.	„ 24	1093	B	Tues.	„ 4	1094	355
10	4855	Thurs.	„ 14	1094	A	Sat.	March 24	1095	354
11 E	4856	Mon.	„ 3	1095	G	Thurs.	April 10	1096 b	353
12	4857	Sat.	„ 20	1096	E	Tues.	March 31	1097	355
13	4858	Thurs.	„ 10	1097	D	Sat.	„ 20	1098	354
14 E	4859	Mon.	Aug. 30	1098	C	Sat.	April 9	1099	385
15	4860	Mon.	Sept. 19	1099	B	Tues.	March 27	1100 b	353
16	4861	Thurs.	„ 6	1100	G	Sat.	„ 16	1101	354
17 E	4862	Mon.	Aug. 26	1101	F	Sat.	April 5	1102	385
18	4863	Mon.	Sept. 15	1102	E	Thurs.	March 26	1103	355
19 E	4864	Sat.	„ 5	1103	D	Tues.	April 12	1104 b	383

MOLAD 4 18 244. CYCLE 257. DAYS, 6939.

1	4865	Thurs.	Sept. 22	1104	B	Sat.	April 1	1105	354
2	4866	Mon.	„ 11	1105	A	Thurs.	March 22	1106	355
3E	4867	Sat.	„ 1	1106	G	Tues.	April 9	1107	383
4	4868	Thurs.	„ 19	1107	F	Sun.	March 29	1108 b	355
5	4869	Tues.	„ 8	1108	D	Thurs.	„ 18	1109	354
6E	4870	Sat.	Aug. 28	1109	C	Thurs.	April 7	1110	385
7	4871	Sat.	Sept. 17	1110	B	Sun.	March 26	1111	353
8E	4872	Tues.	„ 5	1111	A	Sat.	April 13	1112 b	384
9	4873	Mon.	„ 23	1112	F	Thurs.	„ 3	1113	355
10	4874	Sat.	„ 13	1113	E	Tues.	March 24	1114	355
11E	4875	Thurs.	„ 3	1114	D	Sun.	April 11	1115	383
12	4876	Tues.	„ 21	1115	C	Thurs.	March 30	1116 b	354
13	4877	Sat.	„ 9	1116	A	Tues.	„ 20	1117	355
14E	4878	Thurs.	Aug. 30	1117	G	Tues.	April 9	1118	385
15	4879	Thurs.	Sept. 19	1118	F	Sat.	March 29	1119	354
16	4880	Mon.	„ 8	1119	E	Tues.	„ 16	1120 b	353
17E	4881	Thurs.	Aug. 26	1120	C	Tues.	April 5	1121	385
18	4882	Thurs.	Sept. 15	1121	B	Sat.	March 25	1122	354
19E	4883	Mon.	„ 4	1122	A	Thurs.	April 12	1123	383

MOLAD 7 10 839. CYCLE 258. DAYS, 6940.

1	4884	Sat.	Sept. 22	1123	G	Tues.	April 1	1124 b	355
2	4885	Thurs.	„ 11	1124	E	Sat.	March 21	1125	354
3E	4886	Mon.	Aug. 31	1125	D	Sat.	April 10	1126	385
4	4887	Mon.	Sept. 20	1126	C	Tues.	March 29	1127	353
5	4888	Thurs.	„ 8	1127	B	Sun.	„ 18	1128 b	355
6E	4889	Tues.	Aug. 28	1128	G	Sat.	April 6	1129	384
7	4890	Mon.	Sept. 16	1129	F	Thurs.	March 27	1130	355
8E	4891	Sat.	„ 6	1130	E	Tues.	April 14	1131	383
9	4892	Thurs.	„ 24	1131	D	Sat.	„ 2	1132 b	354
10	4893	Mon.	„ 12	1132	B	Thurs.	March 23	1133	355
11E	4894	Sat.	„ 2	1133	A	Tues.	April 10	1134	383
12	4895	Thurs.	„ 20	1134	G	Sun.	March 31	1135	355
13	4896	Tues.	„ 10	1135	F	Thurs.	„ 19	1136 b	354
14E	4897	Sat.	Aug. 29	1136	D	Thurs.	April 8	1137	385
15	4898	Sat.	Sept. 18	1137	C	Tues.	March 29	1138	355
16	4899	Thurs.	„ 8	1138	B	Sat.	„ 18	1139	354
17E	4900	Mon.	Aug. 28	1139	A	Thurs.	April 4	1140 b	383
18	4901	Sat.	Sept. 14	1140	F	Tues.	March 25	1141	355
19E	4902	Thurs.	„ 4	1141	E	Sun.	April 12	1142	383

MOLAD 3 3 354. CYCLE 259. DAYS, 6941.

1	4903	Tues.	Sept. 22	1142	D	Thurs.	April 1	1143	354
2	4904	Sat.	„ 11	1143	C	Tues.	March 21	1144 b	355
3 E	4905	Thurs.	Aug. 31	1144	A	Tues.	April 10	1145	385
4	4906	Thurs.	Sept. 20	1145	G	Sat.	March 30	1146	354
5	4907	Mon.	„ 9	1146	F	Tues.	„ 18	1147	353
6 E	4908	Thurs.	Aug. 28	1147	E	Tues.	April 6	1148 b	385
7	4909	Thurs.	Sept. 16	1148	C	Sat.	March 26	1149	354
8 E	4910	Mon.	„ 5	1149	B	Thurs.	April 13	1150	383
9	4911	Sat.	„ 23	1150	A	Tues.	„ 3	1151	355
10	4912	Thurs.	„ 13	1151	G	Sat.	March 22	1152 b	354
11 E	4913	Mon.	„ 1	1152	E	Sat.	April 11	1153	385
12	4914	Mon.	„ 21	1153	D	Tues.	March 30	1154	353
13	4915	Thurs.	„ 9	1154	C	Sun.	„ 20	1155	355
14 E	4916	Tues.	Aug. 30	1155	B	Sat.	April 7	1156 b	384
15	4917	Mon.	Sept. 17	1156	G	Thurs.	March 28	1157	355
16	4918	Sat.	„ 7	1157	F	Sun.	„ 16	1158	353
17 E	4919	Tues.	Aug. 26	1158	E	Sat.	April 4	1159	384
18	4920	Mon.	Sept. 14	1159	D	Thurs.	March 24	1160 b	355
19 E	4921	Sat.	„ 3	1160	B	Thurs.	April 13	1161	385

MOLAD 5 19 949. CYCLE 260. DAYS, 6939.

1	4922	Sat.	Sept. 23	1161	A	Sun.	April 1	1162	353
2	4923	Tues.	„ 11	1162	G	Thurs.	March 21	1163	354
3 E	4924	Sat.	Aug. 31	1163	F	Thurs.	April 9	1164 b	385
4	4925	Sat.	Sept. 19	1164	D	Tues.	March 30	1165	355
5	4926	Thurs.	„ 9	1165	C	Sat.	„ 19	1166	354
6 E	4927	Mon.	Aug. 29	1166	B	Thurs.	April 6	1167	383
7	4928	Sat.	Sept. 16	1167	A	Tues.	March 26	1168 b	355
8 E	4929	Thurs.	„ 5	1168	F	Sun.	April 13	1169	383
9	4930	Tues.	„ 23	1169	E	Thurs.	„ 2	1170	354
10	4931	Sat.	„ 12	1170	D	Tues.	March 23	1171	355
11 E	4932	Thurs.	„ 2	1171	C	Tues.	April 11	1172 b	385
12	4933	Thurs.	„ 21	1172	A	Sat.	March 31	1173	354
13	4934	Mon.	„ 10	1173	G	Tues.	„ 19	1174	353
14 E	4935	Thurs.	Aug. 29	1174	F	Tues.	April 8	1175	385
15	4936	Thurs.	Sept. 18	1175	E	Sat.	March 27	1176 b	354
16	4937	Mon.	„ 6	1176	C	Thurs.	„ 17	1177	355
17 E	4938	Sat.	Aug. 27	1177	B	Tues.	April 4	1178	383
18	4939	Thurs.	Sept. 14	1178	A	Sat.	March 24	1179	354
19 E	4940	Mon.	„ 3	1179	G	Sat.	April 12	1180 b	385

MOLAD 1 12 464. CYCLE 261. DAYS, 6940.

1	4941	Mon.	Sept. 22	1180	E	Thurs.	April 2	1181	355
2	4942	Sat.	„ 12	1181	D	Sun.	March 21	1182	353
3 E	4943	Tues.	Aug. 31	1182	C	Sat.	April 9	1183	384
4	4944	Mon.	Sept. 19	1183	B	Thurs.	March 29	1184 b	355
5	4945	Sat.	„ 8	1184	G	Tues.	„ 19	1185	355
6 E	4946	Thurs.	Aug. 29	1185	F	Sun.	April 6	1186	383
7	4947	Tues.	Sept. 16	1186	E	Thurs.	March 26	1187	354
8 E	4948	Sat.	„ 5	1187	D	Thurs.	April 14	1188 b	385
9	4949	Sat.	„ 24	1188	B	Tues.	„ 4	1189	355
10	4950	Thurs.	„ 14	1189	A	Sat.	March 24	1190	354
11 E	4951	Mon.	„ 3	1190	G	Thurs.	April 11	1191	383
12	4952	Sat.	„ 21	1191	F	Tues.	March 31	1192 b	355
13	4953	Thurs.	„ 10	1192	D	Sat.	„ 20	1193	354
14 E	4954	Mon.	Aug. 30	1193	C	Thurs.	April 7	1194	383
15	4955	Sat.	Sept. 17	1194	B	Tues.	March 28	1195	355
16	4956	Thurs.	„ 7	1195	A	Sat.	„ 16	1196 b	354
17 E	4957	Mon.	Aug. 26	1196	F	Sat.	April 5	1197	385
18	4958	Mon.	Sept. 15	1197	E	Tues.	March 24	1198	353
19 E	4959	Thurs.	„ 3	1198	D	Tues.	April 13	1199	385

MOLAD 4 4 1059. CYCLE 262. DAYS, 6939.

1	4960	Thurs.	Sept. 23	1199	C	Sat.	April 1	1200 b	354
2	4961	Mon.	„ 11	1200	A	Thurs.	March 22	1201	355
3 E	4962	Sat.	„ 1	1201	G	Tues.	April 9	1202	383
4	4963	Thurs.	„ 19	1202	F	Sat.	March 29	1203	354
5	4964	Mon.	„ 8	1203	E	Thurs.	„ 18	1204 b	355
6 E	4965	Sat.	Aug. 28	1204	C	Tues.	April 5	1205	383
7	4966	Thurs.	Sept. 15	1205	B	Sun.	March 26	1206	355
8 E	4967	Tues.	„ 5	1206	A	Sat.	April 14	1207	384
9	4968	Mon.	„ 24	1207	G	Thurs.	„ 3	1208 b	355
10	4969	Sat.	„ 13	1208	E	Sun.	March 22	1209	353
11 E	4970	Tues.	„ 1	1209	D	Sat.	April 10	1210	384
12	4971	Mon.	„ 20	1210	C	Thurs.	March 31	1211	355
13	4972	Sat.	„ 10	1211	B	Tues.	„ 20	1212 b	355
14 E	4973	Thurs.	Aug. 30	1212	G	Sun.	April 7	1213	383
15	4974	Tues.	Sept. 17	1213	F	Thurs.	March 27	1214	354
16	4975	Sat.	„ 6	1214	E	Tues.	„ 17	1215	355
17 E	4976	Thurs.	Aug. 27	1215	D	Tues.	April 5	1216 b	385
18	4977	Thurs.	Sept. 15	1216	B	Sat.	March 25	1217	354
19 E	4978	Mon.	„ 4	1217	A	Thurs.	April 12	1218	383

MOLAD 6 21 574. CYCLE 263. DAYS, 6939.

1	4979	Sat.	Sept. 22	1218	G	Tues.	April 2	1219	355
2	4980	Thurs.	„ 12	1219	F	Sat.	March 21	1220 b	354
3 E	4981	Mon.	Aug. 31	1220	D	Thurs.	April 8	1221	383
4	4982	Sat.	Sept. 18	1221	C	Tues.	March 29	1222	355
5	4983	Thurs.	„ 8	1222	B	Sat.	„ 18	1223	354
6 E	4984	Mon.	Aug. 28	1223	A	Sat.	April 6	1224 b	385
7	4985	Mon.	Sept. 16	1224	F	Tues.	March 25	1225	353
8 E	4986	Thurs.	„ 4	1225	E	Tues.	April 14	1226	385
9	4987	Thurs.	„ 24	1226	D	Sat.	„ 3	1227	354
10	4988	Mon.	„ 13	1227	C	Thurs.	March 23	1228 b	355
11 E	4989	Sat.	„ 2	1228	A	Tues.	April 10	1229	383
12	4990	Thurs.	„ 20	1229	G	Sat.	March 30	1230	354
13	4991	Mon.	„ 9	1230	F	Thurs.	„ 20	1231	355
14 E	4992	Sat.	Aug. 30	1231	E	Tues.	April 6	1232 b	383
15	4993	Thurs.	Sept. 16	1232	C	Sun.	March 27	1233	355
16	4994	Tues.	„ 6	1233	B	Thurs.	„ 16	1234	354
17 E	4995	Sat.	Aug. 26	1234	A	Thurs.	April 5	1235	385
18	4996	Sat.	Sept. 15	1235	G	Sun.	March 23	1236 b	353
19 E	4997	Tues.	„ 2	1236	E	Sat.	April 11	1237	384

MOLAD 2 14 89. CYCLE 264. DAYS, 6940.

1	4998	Mon.	Sept. 21	1237	D	Thurs.	April 1	1238	355
2	4999	Sat.	„ 11	1238	C	Tues.	March 22	1239	355
3 E	5000	Thurs.	„ 1	1239	B	Sun.	April 8	1240 b	383
4	5001	Tues.	„ 18	1240	G	Thurs.	March 28	1241	354
5	5002	Sat.	„ 7	1241	F	Tues.	„ 18	1242	355
6 E	5003	Thurs.	Aug. 28	1242	E	Tues.	April 7	1243	385
7	5004	Thurs.	Sept. 17	1243	D	Sat.	March 26	1244 b	354
8 E	5005	Mon.	„ 5	1244	B	Thurs.	April 13	1245	383
9	5006	Sat.	„ 23	1245	A	Tues.	„ 3	1246	355
10	5007	Thurs.	„ 13	1246	G	Sat.	March 23	1247	354
11 E	5008	Mon.	„ 2	1247	F	Thurs.	April 9	1248 b	383
12	5009	Sat.	„ 19	1248	D	Tues.	March 30	1249	355
13	5010	Thurs.	„ 9	1249	C	Sat.	„ 19	1250	354
14 E	5011	Mon.	Aug. 29	1250	B	Sat.	April 8	1251	385
15	5012	Mon.	Sept. 18	1251	A	Tues.	March 26	1252 b	353
16	5013	Thurs.	„ 5	1252	F	Sun.	„ 16	1253	355
17 E	5014	Tues.	Aug. 26	1253	E	Sat.	April 4	1254	384
18	5015	Mon.	Sept. 14	1254	D	Thurs.	March 25	1255	355
19 E	5016	Sat.	„ 4	1255	C	Tues.	April 11	1256 b	383

MOLAD 5 6 684. CYCLE 265. DAYS, 6941.

1	5017	Thurs.	Sept. 21	1256	A	Sat.	March 31	1257	354
2	5018	Mon.	„ 10	1257	G	Thurs.	„ 21	1258	355
3 E	5019	Sat.	Aug. 31	1258	F	Thurs.	April 10	1259	385
4	5020	Sat.	Sept. 20	1259	E	Sun.	March 28	1260 b	353
5	5021	Tues.	„ 7	1260	C	Thurs.	„ 17	1261	354
6 E	5022	Sat.	Aug. 27	1261	B	Thurs.	April 6	1262	385
7	5023	Sat.	Sept. 16	1262	A	Tues.	March 27	1263	355
8 E	5024	Thurs.	„ 6	1263	G	Sun.	April 13	1264 b	383
9	5025	Tues.	„ 23	1264	E	Thurs.	„ 2	1265	354
10	5026	Sat.	„ 12	1265	D	Tues.	March 23	1266	355
11 E	5027	Thurs.	„ 2	1266	C	Tues.	April 12	1267	385
12	5028	Thurs.	„ 22	1267	B	Sat.	March 31	1268 b	354
13	5029	Mon.	„ 10	1268	G	Tues.	„ 19	1269	353
14 E	5030	Thurs.	Aug. 29	1269	F	Tues.	April 8	1270	385
15	5031	Thurs.	Sept. 18	1270	E	Sat.	March 28	1271	354
16	5032	Mon.	„ 7	1271	D	Thurs.	„ 17	1272 b	355
17 E	5033	Sat.	Aug. 27	1272	B	Tues.	April 4	1273	383
18	5034	Thurs.	Sept. 14	1273	A	Sat.	March 24	1274	354
19 E	5035	Mon.	„ 3	1274	G	Sat.	April 13	1275	385

MOLAD 7 23 199. CYCLE 266. DAYS, 6940.

1	5036	Mon.	Sept. 23	1275	F	Tues.	March 31	1276 b	353
2	5037	Thurs.	„ 10	1276	D	Sat.	„ 20	1277	354
3 E	5038	Mon.	Aug. 30	1277	C	Sat.	April 9	1278	385
4	5039	Mon.	Sept. 19	1278	B	Thurs.	March 30	1279	355
5	5040	Sat.	„ 9	1279	A	Sun.	„ 17	1280 b	353
6 E	5041	Tues.	Aug. 27	1280	F	Sat.	April 5	1281	384
7	5042	Mon.	Sept. 15	1281	E	Thurs.	March 26	1282	355
8 E	5043	Sat.	„ 5	1282	D	Tues.	April 13	1283	383
9	5044	Thurs.	„ 23	1283	C	Sun.	„ 2	1284 b	355
10	5045	Tues.	„ 12	1284	A	Thurs.	March 22	1285	354
11 E	5046	Sat.	„ 1	1285	G	Thurs.	April 11	1286	385
12	5047	Sat.	„ 21	1286	F	Tues.	„ 1	1287	355
13	5048	Thurs.	„ 11	1287	E	Sat.	March 20	1288 b	354
14 E	5049	Mon.	Aug. 30	1288	C	Thurs.	April 7	1289	383
15	5050	Sat.	Sept. 17	1289	B	Tues.	March 28	1290	355
16	5051	Thurs.	„ 7	1290	A	Sat.	„ 17	1291	354
17 E	5052	Mon.	Aug. 27	1291	G	Thurs.	April 3	1292 b	383
18	5053	Sat.	Sept. 13	1292	E	Tues.	March 24	1293	355
19 E	5054	Thurs.	„ 3	1293	D	Tues.	April 13	1294	385

Molad 3 15 794. CYCLE 267. Days, 6939.

1	5055	Thurs.	Sept. 23	1294	C	Sat.	April 2	1295	354
2	5056	Mon.	„ 12	1295	B	Tues.	March 20	1296 b	353
3 E	5057	Thurs.	Aug. 30	1296	G	Tues.	April 9	1297	385
4	5058	Thurs.	Sept. 19	1297	F	Sat.	March 29	1298	354
5	5059	Mon.	„ 8	1298	E	Thurs.	„ 19	1299	355
6 E	5060	Sat.	Aug. 29	1299	D	Tues.	April 5	1300 b	383
7	5061	Thurs.	Sept. 15	1300	B	Sat.	March 25	1301	354
8 E	5062	Mon.	„ 4	1301	A	Sat.	April 14	1302	385
9	5063	Mon.	„ 24	1302	G	Tues.	„ 2	1303	353
10	5064	Thurs.	„ 12	1303	F	Sun.	March 22	1304 b	355
11 E	5065	Tues.	„ 1	1304	D	Sat.	April 10	1305	384
12	5066	Mon.	„ 20	1305	C	Thurs.	March 31	1306	355
13	5067	Sat.	„ 10	1306	B	Sun.	„ 19	1307	353
14 E	5068	Tues.	Aug. 29	1307	A	Sat.	April 6	1308 b	384
15	5069	Mon.	Sept. 16	1308	F	Thurs.	March 27	1309	355
16	5070	Sat.	„ 6	1309	E	Tues.	„ 17	1310	355
17 E	5071	Thurs.	Aug. 27	1310	D	Sun.	April 4	1311	383
18	5072	Tues.	Sept. 14	1311	C	Thurs.	March 23	1312 b	354
19 E	5073	Sat.	„ 2	1312	A	Thurs.	April 12	1313	385

Molad 6 8 309. CYCLE 268. Days, 6939.

1	5074	Sat.	Sept. 22	1313	G	Tues.	April 2	1314	355
2	5075	Thurs.	„ 12	1314	F	Sat.	March 22	1315	354
3 E	5076	Mon.	„ 1	1315	E	Thurs.	April 8	1316 b	383
4	5077	Sat.	„ 18	1316	C	Tues.	March 29	1317	355
5	5078	Thurs.	„ 8	1317	B	Sat.	„ 18	1318	354
6 E	5079	Mon.	Aug. 28	1318	A	Thurs.	April 5	1319	383
7	5080	Sat.	Sept. 15	1319	G	Tues.	March 25	1320 b	355
8 E	5081	Thurs.	„ 4	1320	E	Tues.	April 14	1321	385
9	5082	Thurs.	„ 24	1321	D	Sat.	„ 3	1322	354
10	5083	Mon.	„ 13	1322	C	Tues.	March 22	1323	353
11 E	5084	Thurs.	„ 1	1323	B	Tues.	April 10	1324 b	385
12	5085	Thurs.	„ 20	1324	G	Sat.	March 30	1325	354
13	5086	Mon.	„ 9	1325	F	Thurs.	„ 20	1326	355
14 E	5087	Sat.	Aug. 30	1326	E	Tues.	April 7	1327	383
15	5088	Thurs.	Sept. 17	1327	D	Sat.	March 26	1328 b	354
16	5089	Mon.	„ 5	1328	B	Thurs.	„ 16	1329	355
17 E	5090	Sat.	Aug. 26	1329	A	Thurs.	April 5	1330	385
18	5091	Sat.	Sept. 15	1330	G	Sun.	March 24	1331	353
19 E	5092	Tues.	„ 3	1331	F	Sat.	April 11	1332 b	384

MOLAD 2 0 904. CYCLE 269. DAYS, 6940.

1	5093	Mon.	Sept. 21	1332	D	Thurs.	April 1	1333	355
2	5094	Sat.	„ 11	1333	C	Tues.	March 22	1334	355
3 E	5095	Thurs.	„ 1	1334	B	Sun.	April 9	1335	383
4	5096	Tues.	„ 19	1335	A	Thurs.	March 28	1336 b	354
5	5097	Sat.	„ 7	1336	F	Tues.	„ 18	1337	355
6 E	5098	Thurs.	Aug. 28	1337	E	Sun.	April 5	1338	383
7	5099	Tues.	Sept. 15	1338	D	Thurs.	March 25	1339	354
8 E	5100	Sat.	„ 4	1339	C	Thurs.	April 13	1340 b	385
9	5101	Sat.	„ 23	1340	A	Tues.	„ 3	1341	355
10	5102	Thurs.	„ 13	1341	G	Sat.	March 23	1342	354
11 E	5103	Mon.	„ 2	1342	F	Thurs.	April 10	1343	383
12	5104	Sat.	„ 20	1343	E	Tues.	March 30	1344 b	355
13	5105	Thurs.	„ 9	1344	C	Sat.	„ 19	1345	354
14 E	5106	Mon.	Aug. 29	1345	B	Sat.	April 8	1346	385
15	5107	Mon.	Sept. 18	1346	A	Tues.	March 27	1347	353
16	5108	Thurs.	„ 6	1347	G	Sat.	„ 15	1348 b	354
17 E	5109	Mon.	Aug. 25	1348	E	Sat.	April 4	1349	385
18	5110	Mon.	Sept. 14	1349	D	Thurs.	March 25	1350	355
19 E	5111	Sat.	„ 4	1350	C	Tues.	April 12	1351	383

MOLAD 4 17 419. CYCLE 270. DAYS, 6939.

1	5112	Thurs.	Sept. 22	1351	B	Sat.	March 31	1352 b	355
2	5113	Mon.	„ 10	1352	G	Thurs.	„ 21	1353	355
3 E	5114	Sat.	Aug. 31	1353	F	Tues.	April 8	1354	383
4	5115	Thurs.	Sept. 18	1354	E	Sat.	March 28	1355	354
5	5116	Mon.	„ 7	1355	D	Thurs.	„ 17	1356 b	355
6 E	5117	Sat.	Aug. 27	1356	B	Thurs.	April 6	1357	383
7	5118	Sat.	Sept. 16	1357	A	Sun.	March 25	1358	354
8 E	5119	Tues.	„ 4	1358	G	Sat.	April 13	1359	385
9	5120	Mon.	„ 23	1359	F	Thurs.	„ 2	1360 b	355
10	5121	Sat.	„ 12	1360	D	Tues.	March 23	1361	354
11 E	5122	Thurs.	„ 2	1361	C	Sun.	April 10	1362	383
12	5123	Tues.	„ 20	1362	B	Thurs.	March 30	1363	355
13	5124	Sat.	„ 9	1363	A	Tues.	„ 19	1364 b	354
14 E	5125	Thurs.	Aug. 29	1364	F	Tues.	April 8	1365	385
15	5126	Thurs.	Sept. 18	1365	E	Sat.	March 28	1366	353
16	5127	Mon.	„ 7	1366	D	Tues.	„ 16	1367	354
17 E	5128	Thurs.	Aug. 26	1367	C	Tues.	April 4	1368 b	385
18	5129	Thurs.	Sept. 14	1368	A	Sat.	March 24	1369	355
19 E	5130	Mon.	„ 3	1369	G	Thurs.	April 11	1370	383

MOLAD 7 9 1014. CYCLE 271. DAYS, 6940.

1	5131	Sat.	Sept. 21	1370	F	Tues.	April 1	1371	355
2	5132	Thurs.	„ 11	1371	E	Sat.	March 20	1372 b	354
3 E	5133	Mon.	Aug. 30	1372	C	Sat.	April 9	1373	385
4	5134	Mon.	Sept. 19	1373	B	Tues.	March 28	1374	353
5	5135	Thurs.	„ 7	1374	A	Sun.	„ 18	1375	355
6 E	5136	Tues.	Aug. 28	1375	G	Sat.	April 5	1376 b	384
7	5137	Mon.	Sept. 15	1376	E	Thurs.	March 26	1377	355
8 E	5138	Sat.	„ 5	1377	D	Tues.	April 13	1378	383
9	5139	Thurs.	„ 23	1378	C	Sat.	„ 2	1379	354
10	5140	Mon.	„ 12	1379	B	Thurs.	March 22	1380 b	355
11 E	5141	Sat.	„ 1	1380	G	Tues.	April 9	1381	383
12	5142	Thurs.	„ 19	1381	F	Sun.	March 30	1382	355
13	5143	Tues.	„ 9	1382	E	Thurs.	„ 19	1383	354
14 E	5144	Sat.	Aug. 29	1383	D	Thurs.	April 7	1384 b	385
15	5145	Sat.	Sept. 17	1384	B	Tues.	March 28	1385	355
16	5146	Thurs.	„ 7	1385	A	Sat.	„ 17	1386	354
17 E	5147	Mon.	Aug. 27	1386	G	Thurs.	April 4	1387	383
18	5148	Sat.	Sept. 14	1387	F	Tues.	March 24	1388 b	355
19 E	5149	Thurs.	„ 3	1388	D	Sun.	April 11	1389	383

MOLAD 3 2 529. CYCLE 272. DAYS, 6941.

1	5150	Tues.	Sept. 21	1389	C	Thurs.	March 31	1390	354
2	5151	Sat.	„ 10	1390	B	Tues.	„ 21	1391	355
3 E	5152	Thurs.	Aug. 31	1391	A	Tues.	April 9	1392 b	385
4	5153	Thurs.	Sept. 19	1392	F	Sat.	March 29	1393	354
5	5154	Mon.	„ 8	1393	E	Tues.	„ 17	1394	353
6 E	5155	Thurs.	Aug. 27	1394	D	Tues.	April 6	1395	385
7	5156	Thurs.	Sept. 16	1395	C	Sat.	March 25	1396 b	354
8 E	5157	Mon.	„ 4	1396	A	Thurs.	April 12	1397	383
9	5158	Sat.	„ 22	1397	G	Tues.	„ 2	1398	355
10	5159	Thurs.	„ 12	1398	F	Sat.	March 22	1399	354
11 E	5160	Mon.	„ 1	1399	E	Sat.	April 10	1400 b	385
12	5161	Mon.	„ 20	1400	C	Tues.	March 29	1401	353
13	5162	Thurs.	„ 8	1401	B	Sun.	„ 19	1402	355
14 E	5163	Tues.	Aug. 29	1402	A	Sat.	April 7	1403	384
15	5164	Mon.	Sept. 17	1403	G	Thurs.	March 27	1404 b	355
16	5165	Sat.	„ 6	1404	E	Sun.	„ 15	1405	353
17 E	5166	Tues.	Aug. 25	1405	D	Sat.	April 3	1406	384
18	5167	Mon.	Sept. 13	1406	C	Thurs.	March 24	1407	355
19 E	5168	Sat.	„ 3	1407	B	Thurs.	April 12	1408 b	385

MOLAD 5 19 44. CYCLE 273. DAYS, 6939.

1	5169	Sat.	Sept. 22	1408	G	Sun.	March 31	1409	353
2	5170	Tues.	„ 10	1409	F	Thurs.	„ 20	1410	354
3 E	5171	Sat.	Aug. 30	1410	E	Thurs.	April 9	1411	385
4	5172	Sat.	Sept. 19	1411	D	Tues.	March 29	1412 b	355
5	5173	Thurs.	„ 8	1412	B	Sat.	„ 18	1413	354
6 E	5174	Mon.	Aug. 28	1413	A	Thurs.	April 5	1414	383
7	5175	Sat.	Sept. 15	1414	G	Tues.	March 26	1415	355
8 E	5176	Thurs.	„ 5	1415	F	Sun.	April 12	1416 b	383
9	5177	Tues.	„ 22	1416	D	Thurs.	„ 1	1417	354
10	5178	Sat.	„ 11	1417	C	Tues.	March 22	1418	355
11 E	5179	Thurs.	„ 1	1418	B	Tues.	April 11	1419	385
12	5180	Thurs.	„ 21	1419	A	Sat.	March 30	1420 b	354
13	5181	Mon.	„ 9	1420	F	Tues.	„ 18	1421	353
14 E	5182	Thurs.	Aug. 28	1421	E	Tues.	April 7	1422	385
15	5183	Thurs.	Sept. 17	1422	D	Sat.	March 27	1423	354
16	5184	Mon.	„ 6	1423	C	Thurs.	„ 16	1424 b	355
17 E	5185	Sat.	Aug. 26	1424	A	Tues.	April 3	1425	383
18	5186	Thurs.	Sept. 13	1425	G	Sat.	March 23	1426	354
19 E	5187	Mon.	„ 2	1426	F	Sat.	April 12	1427	385

MOLAD 1 11 639. CYCLE 274. DAYS, 6940.

1	5188	Mon.	Sept. 22	1427	E	Thurs.	April 1	1428 b	355
2	5189	Sat.	„ 11	1428	C	Sun.	March 20	1429	353
3 E	5190	Tues.	Aug. 30	1429	B	Sat.	April 8	1430	384
4	5191	Mon.	Sept. 18	1430	A	Thurs.	March 29	1431	355
5	5192	Sat.	„ 8	1431	G	Tues.	„ 18	1432 b	355
6 E	5193	Thurs.	Aug. 28	1432	E	Sun.	April 5	1433	383
7	5194	Tues.	Sept. 15	1433	D	Thurs.	March 25	1434	354
8 E	5195	Sat.	„ 4	1434	C	Thurs.	April 14	1435	385
9	5196	Sat.	„ 24	1435	B	Sun.	„ 1	1436 b	353
10	5197	Tues.	„ 11	1436	G	Thurs.	March 21	1437	354
11 E	5198	Sat.	Aug. 31	1437	F	Thurs.	April 10	1438	385
12	5199	Sat.	Sept. 20	1438	E	Tues.	March 31	1439	355
13	5200	Thurs.	„ 10	1439	D	Sat.	„ 19	1440 b	354
14 E	5201	Mon.	Aug. 29	1440	B	Thurs.	April 6	1441	383
15	5202	Sat.	Sept. 16	1441	A	Tues.	March 27	1442	355
16	5203	Thurs.	„ 6	1442	G	Sat.	„ 16	1443	354
17 E	5204	Mon.	Aug. 26	1443	F	Sat.	April 4	1444 b	385
18	5205	Mon.	Sept. 14	1444	D	Tues.	March 23	1445	353
19 E	5206	Thurs.	„ 2	1445	C	Tues.	April 12	1446	385

MOLAD 4 4 154. CYCLE 275. DAYS, 6939.

1	5207	Thurs.	Sept. 22	1446	B	Sat.	April 1	1447	354
2	5208	Mon.	„ 11	1447	A	Thurs.	March 21	1448 b	355
3 E	5209	Sat.	Aug. 31	1448	F	Tues.	April 8	1449	383
4	5210	Thurs.	Sept. 18	1449	E	Sat.	March 28	1450	354
5	5211	Mon.	„ 7	1450	D	Thurs.	„ 18	1451	355
6 E	5212	Sat.	Aug. 28	1451	C	Tues.	April 4	1452 b	383
7	5213	Thurs.	Sept. 14	1452	A	Sun.	March 25	1453	355
8 E	5214	Tues.	„ 4	1453	G	Sat.	April 13	1454	384
9	5215	Mon.	„ 23	1454	F	Thurs.	„ 3	1455	355
10	5216	Sat.	„ 13	1455	E	Sun.	March 21	1456 b	353
11 E	5217	Tues.	Aug. 31	1456	C	Sat.	April 9	1457	384
12	5218	Mon.	Sept. 19	1457	B	Thurs.	March 30	1458	355
13	5219	Sat.	„ 9	1458	A	Tues.	„ 20	1459	355
14 E	5220	Thurs.	Aug. 30	1459	G	Sun.	April 6	1460 b	383
15	5221	Tues.	Sept. 16	1460	E	Thurs.	March 26	1461	354
16	5222	Sat.	„ 5	1461	D	Tues.	„ 16	1462	355
17 E	5223	Thurs.	Aug. 26	1462	C	Tues.	April 5	1463	385
18	5224	Thurs.	Sept. 15	1463	B	Sat.	March 24	1464 b	354
19 E	5225	Mon.	„ 3	1464	G	Thurs.	April 11	1465	383

MOLAD 6 20 749. CYCLE 276. DAYS, 6939.

1	5226	Sat.	Sept. 21	1465	F	Tues.	April 1	1466	355
2	5227	Thurs.	„ 11	1466	E	Sat.	March 21	1467	354
3 E	5228	Mon.	Aug. 31	1467	D	Thurs.	April 7	1468 b	383
4	5229	Sat.	Sept. 17	1468	B	Tues.	March 28	1469	355
5	5230	Thurs.	„ 7	1469	A	Sat.	„ 17	1470	354
6 E	5231	Mon.	Aug. 27	1470	G	Sat.	April 6	1471	385
7	5232	Mon.	Sept. 16	1471	F	Tues.	March 24	1472 b	353
8 E	5233	Thurs.	„ 3	1472	D	Tues.	April 13	1473	385
9	5234	Thurs.	„ 23	1473	C	Sat.	„ 2	1474	354
10	5235	Mon.	„ 12	1474	B	Thurs.	March 23	1475	355
11 E	5236	Sat.	„ 2	1475	A	Tues.	April 9	1476 b	383
12	5237	Thurs.	„ 19	1476	F	Sat.	March 29	1477	354
13	5238	Mon.	„ 8	1477	E	Thurs.	„ 19	1478	355
14 E	5239	Sat.	Aug. 29	1478	D	Tues.	April 6	1479	383
15	5240	Thurs.	Sept. 16	1479	C	Sun.	March 26	1480 b	355
16	5241	Tues.	„ 5	1480	A	Thurs.	„ 15	1481	354
17 E	5242	Sat.	Aug. 25	1481	G	Thurs.	April 4	1482	385
18	5243	Sat.	Sept. 14	1482	F	Sun.	March 23	1483	353
19 E	5244	Tues.	„ 2	1483	E	Sat.	April 10	1484 b	384

MOLAD 2 13 264. CYCLE 277. DAYS, 6940.

1	5245	Mon.	Sept.	20	1484	C	Thurs.	March 31	1485	355
2	5246	Sat.	„	10	1485	B	Tues.	„ 21	1486	355
3 E	5247	Thurs.	Aug.	31	1486	A	Sun.	April 8	1487	383
4	5248	Tues.	Sept.	18	1487	G	Thurs.	March 27	1488 b	354
5	5249	Sat.	„	6	1488	E	Tues.	„ 17	1489	355
6 E	5250	Thurs.	Aug.	27	1489	D	Tues.	April 6	1490	385
7	5251	Thurs.	Sept.	16	1490	C	Sat.	March 26	1491	354
8 E	5252	Mon.	„	5	1491	B	Thurs.	April 12	1492 b	383
9	5253	Sat.	„	22	1492	G	Tues.	„ 2	1493	355
10	5254	Thurs.	„	12	1493	F	Sat.	March 22	1494	354
11 E	5255	Mon.	„	1	1494	E	Thurs.	April 9	1495	383
12	5256	Sat.	„	19	1495	D	Tues.	March 29	1496 b	355
13	5257	Thurs.	„	8	1496	B	Sat.	„ 18	1497	354
14 E	5258	Mon.	Aug.	28	1497	A	Sat.	April 7	1498	385
15	5259	Mon.	Sept.	17	1498	G	Tues.	March 26	1499	353
16	5260	Thurs.	„	5	1499	F	Sun.	„ 15	1500 b	355
17 E	5261	Tues.	Aug.	25	1500	D	Sat.	April 3	1501	384
18	5262	Mon.	Sept.	13	1501	C	Thurs.	March 24	1502	355
19 E	5263	Sat.	„	3	1502	B	Tues.	April 11	1503	383

MOLAD 5 5 859. CYCLE 278. DAYS, 6941.

1	5264	Thurs.	Sept.	21	1503	A	Sat.	March 30	1504 b	354
2	5265	Mon.	„	9	1504	F	Thurs.	„ 20	1505	355
3 E	5266	Sat.	Aug.	30	1505	E	Thurs.	April 9	1506	385
4	5267	Sat.	Sept.	19	1506	D	Sun.	March 28	1507	353
5	5268	Tues.	„	7	1507	C	Thurs.	„ 16	1508 b	354
6 E	5269	Sat.	Aug.	26	1508	A	Thurs.	April 5	1509	385
7	5270	Sat.	Sept.	15	1509	G	Tues.	March 26	1510	355
8 E	5271	Thurs.	„	5	1510	F	Sun.	April 13	1511	383
9	5272	Tues.	„	23	1511	E	Thurs.	„ 1	1512 b	354
10	5273	Sat.	„	11	1512	C	Tues.	March 22	1513	355
11 E	5274	Thurs.	„	1	1513	B	Tues.	April 11	1514	385
12	5275	Thurs.	„	21	1514	A	Sat.	March 31	1515	354
13	5276	Mon.	„	10	1515	G	Tues.	„ 18	1516 b	353
14 E	5277	Thurs.	Aug.	28	1516	E	Tues.	April 7	1517	385
15	5278	Thurs.	Sept.	17	1517	D	Sat.	March 27	1518	354
16	5279	Mon.	„	6	1518	C	Thurs.	„ 17	1519	355
17 E	5280	Sat.	Aug.	27	1519	B	Tues.	April 3	1520 b	383
18	5281	Thurs.	Sept.	13	1520	G	Sat.	March 23	1521	354
19 E	5282	Mon.	„	2	1521	F	Sat.	April 12	1522	385

MOLAD 7 22 374. CYCLE 279. DAYS, 6940.

1	5283	Mon.	Sept. 22	1522	E	Tues.	March 31	1523	353
2	5284	Thurs.	,, 10	1523	D	Sat.	,, 19	1524 b	354
3 E	5285	Mon.	Aug. 29	1524	B	Sat.	April 8	1525	385
4	5286	Mon.	Sept. 18	1525	A	Thurs.	March 29	1526	355
5	5287	Sat.	,, 8	1526	G	Sun.	,, 17	1527	353
6 E	5288	Tues.	Aug. 27	1527	F	Sat.	April 4	1528 b	384
7	5289	Mon.	Sept. 14	1528	D	Thurs.	March 25	1529	355
8 E	5290	Sat.	,, 4	1529	C	Tues.	April 12	1530	383
9	5291	Thurs.	,, 22	1530	B	Sun.	,, 2	1531	355
10	5292	Tues.	,, 12	1531	A	Thurs.	March 21	1532 b	354
11 E	5293	Sat.	Aug. 31	1532	F	Thurs.	April 10	1533	385
12	5294	Sat.	Sept. 20	1533	E	Tues.	March 31	1534	355
13	5295	Thurs.	,, 10	1534	D	Sat.	,, 20	1535	354
14 E	5296	Mon.	Aug. 30	1535	C	Thurs.	April 6	1536 b	383
15	5297	Sat.	Sept. 16	1536	A	Tues.	March 27	1537	355
16	5298	Thurs.	,, 6	1537	G	Sat.	,, 16	1538	354
17 E	5299	Mon.	Aug. 26	1538	F	Thurs.	April 3	1539	383
18	5300	Sat.	Sept. 13	1539	E	Tues.	March 23	1540 b	355
19 E	5301	Thurs.	,, 2	1540	C	Tues.	April 12	1541	385

MOLAD 3 14 969. CYCLE 280. DAYS, 6939.

1	5302	Thurs.	Sept. 22	1541	B	Sat.	April 1	1542	354
2	5303	Mon.	,, 11	1542	A	Tues.	March 20	1543	353
3 E	5304	Thurs.	Aug. 30	1543	G	Tues.	April 8	1544 b	385
4	5305	Thurs.	Sept. 18	1544	E	Sat.	March 28	1545	354
5	5306	Mon.	,, 7	1545	D	Thurs.	,, 18	1546	355
6 E	5307	Sat.	Aug. 28	1546	C	Tues.	April 5	1547	383
7	5308	Thurs.	Sept. 15	1547	B	Sat.	March 24	1548 b	354
8 E	5309	Mon.	,, 3	1548	G	Sat.	April 13	1549	385
9	5310	Mon.	,, 23	1549	F	Tues.	,, 1	1550	353
10	5311	Thurs.	,, 11	1550	E	Sun.	March 22	1551	355
11 E	5312	Tues.	,, 1	1551	D	Sat.	April 9	1552 b	384
12	5313	Mon.	,, 19	1552	B	Thurs.	March 30	1553	355
13	5314	Sat.	,, 9	1553	A	Sun.	,, 18	1554	353
14 E	5315	Tues.	Aug. 28	1554	G	Sat.	April 6	1555	384
15	5316	Mon.	Sept. 16	1555	F	Thurs.	March 26	1556 b	355
16	5317	Sat.	,, 5	1556	D	Tues.	,, 16	1557	355
17 E	5318	Thurs.	Aug. 26	1557	C	Sun.	April 3	1558	383
18	5319	Tues.	Sept. 13	1558	B	Thurs.	March 23	1559	354
19 E	5320	Sat.	,, 2	1559	A	Thurs.	April 11	1560 b	385

MOLAD 6 7 484. CYCLE 281. DAYS, 6939.

1	5321	Sat.	Sept. 21	1560	F	Tues.	April 1	1561	355
2	5322	Thurs.	„ 11	1561	E	Sat.	March 21	1562	354
3 E	5323	Mon.	Aug. 31	1562	D	Thurs.	April 8	1563	383
4	5324	Sat.	Sept. 18	1563	C	Tues.	March 28	1564 b	355
5	5325	Thurs.	„ 7	1564	A	Sat.	„ 17	1565	354
6 E	5326	Mon.	Aug. 27	1565	G	Thurs.	April 4	1566	383
7	5327	Sat.	Sept. 14	1566	F	Tues.	March 25	1567	355
8 E	5328	Thurs.	„ 4	1567	E	Tues.	April 13	1568 b	385
9	5329	Thurs.	„ 23	1568	C	Sat.	„ 2	1569	354
10	5330	Mon.	„ 12	1569	B	Tues.	March 21	1570	353
11 E	5331	Thurs.	Aug. 31	1570	A	Tues.	April 10	1571	385
12	5332	Thurs.	Sept. 20	1571	G	Sat.	March 29	1572 b	354
13	5333	Mon.	„ 8	1572	E	Thurs.	„ 19	1573	355
14 E	5334	Sat.	Aug. 29	1573	D	Tues.	April 6	1574	383
15	5335	Thurs.	Sept. 16	1574	C	Sat.	March 26	1575	354
16	5336	Mon.	„ 5	1575	B	Thurs.	„ 15	1576 b	355
17 E	5337	Sat.	Aug. 25	1576	G	Tues.	April 2	1577	383
18	5338	Thurs.	Sept. 12	1577	F	Sun.	March 23	1578	355
19 E	5339	Tues.	„ 2	1578	E	Sat.	April 11	1579	384

MOLAD 1 23 1079. CYCLE 282. DAYS, 6940.

After A.D. 1582 the Sunday Letters in the Table are Gregorian.

1	5340	Mon.	Sept. 21	1579	D	Thurs.	March 31	1580 b	355
2	5341	Sat.	„ 10	1580	B	Sun.	„ 19	1581	353
3 E	5342	Tues.	Aug. 29	1581	A	Sat.	April 7	1582	384
4	5343	Mon.	Sept. 17	1582	G	Thurs.	March 28 .. April 7	1583	355
5	5344	Sat.	Sept. 7 .. 17	1583	B	Tues.	„ 17 .. 27	1584 b	355
6 E	5345	Thurs.	Aug. 27 .. Sept. 6	1584	G	Sun.	April 4 .. 14	1585	383
7	5346	Tues.	Sept. 14 .. 24	1585	F	Thurs.	March 24 .. April 3	1586	354
8 E	5347	Sat.	„ 3 .. 13	1586	E	Thurs.	April 13 .. 23	1587	385
9	5348	Sat.	„ 23 .. Oct. 3	1587	D	Tues.	„ 2 .. 12	1588 b	355
10	5349	Thurs.	Sept. 12 .. 22	1588	B	Sat.	March 22 .. April 1	1589	354
11 E	5350	Mon.	„ 1 .. 11	1589	A	Thurs.	April 9 .. 19	1590	383
12	5351	Sat.	„ 19 .. 29	1590	G	Tues.	March 30 .. April 9	1591	355
13	5352	Thurs.	„ 9 .. 19	1591	F	Sat.	„ 18 .. 28	1592 b	354
14 E	5353	Mon.	Aug. 28 .. Sept. 7	1592	D	Sat.	April 7 .. 17	1593	385
15	5354	Mon.	Sept. 17 .. 27	1593	C	Tues.	March 26 .. April 5	1594	353
16	5355	Thurs.	„ 5 .. 15	1594	B	Sat.	„ 15 .. 25	1595	354
17 E	5356	Mon.	Aug. 25 .. Sept. 4	1595	A	Sat.	April 3 .. 13	1596 b	385
18	5357	Mon.	Sept. 13 .. 23	1596	F	Thurs.	March 24 .. April 3	1597	355
19 E	5358	Sat.	„ 3 .. 13	1597	E	Tues.	April 11 .. 21	1598	383

MOLAD 4 16 594 CYCLE 283. DAYS, 6939.

1	5359	Thurs.	Sept. 21 .. Oct. 1	1598	D	Sat.	March 31 .. April 10	1599	354
2	5360	Mon.	„ 10 .. 20	1599	C	Thurs.	„ 20 .. 30	1600 b	355
3 E	5361	Sat.	Aug. 30 .. Sept. 9	1600	A	Tues.	April 7 .. 17	1601	383
4	5362	Thurs.	Sept. 17 .. 27	1601	G	Sat.	March 27 .. April 6	1602	354
5	5363	Mon.	„ 6 .. 16	1602	F	Thurs.	„ 17 .. 27	1603	355
6 E	5364	Sat.	Aug. 27 .. Sept. 6	1603	E	Thurs.	April 5 .. 15	1604 b	385
7	5365	Sat.	Sept. 15 .. 25	1604	C	Sun.	March 24 .. April 3	1605	353
8 E	5366	Tues.	„ 3 .. 13	1605	B	Sat.	April 12 .. 22	1606	384
9	5367	Mon.	„ 22 .. Oct. 2	1606	A	Thurs.	„ 2 .. 12	1607	355
10	5368	Sat.	„ 12 .. 22	1607	G	Tues.	March 22 .. April 1	1608 b	355
11 E	5369	Thurs.	„ 1 .. 11	1608	E	Sun.	April 9 .. 19	1609	383
12	5370	Tues.	„ 19 .. 29	1609	D	Thurs.	March 29 .. April 8	1610	354
13	5371	Sat.	„ 8 .. 18	1610	C	Tues.	„ 19 .. 29	1611	355
14 E	5372	Thurs.	Aug. 29 .. Sept. 8	1611	B	Tues.	April 7 .. 17	1612 b	385
15	5373	Thurs.	Sept. 17 .. 27	1612	G	Sat.	March 27 .. April 6	1613	354
16	5374	Mon.	„ 6 .. 16	1613	F	Tues.	„ 15 .. 25	1614	353
17 E	5375	Thurs.	Aug. 25 .. Sept. 4	1614	E	Tues.	April 4 .. 14	1615	385
18	5376	Thurs.	Sept. 14 .. 24	1615	D	Sat.	March 23 .. April 2	1616 b	354
19 E	5377	Mon.	„ 2 .. 12	1616	B	Thurs.	April 10 .. 20	1617	383

MOLAD 7 9 109 CYCLE 284. DAYS, 6940.

1	5378	Sat.	Sept. 20 .. 30	1617	A	Tues.	March 31 .. April 10	1618	355
2	5379	Thurs.	„ 10 .. 20	1618	G	Sat.	„ 20 .. 30	1619	354
3 E	5380	Mon.	Aug. 30 .. Sept. 9	1619	F	Sat.	April 8 .. 18	1620 b	385
4	5381	Mon.	Sept. 18 .. 28	1620	D	Tues.	March 27 .. April 6	1621	353
5	5382	Thurs.	„ 6 .. 16	1621	C	Sat.	„ 16 .. 26	1622	354
6 E	5383	Mon.	Aug. 26 .. Sept. 5	1622	B	Sat.	April 5 .. 15	1623	385
7	5384	Mon.	Sept. 15 .. 25	1623	A	Thurs.	March 25 .. April 4	1624 b	355
8 E	5385	Sat.	„ 4 .. 14	1624	F	Tues.	April 12 .. 22	1625	383
9	5386	Thurs.	„ 22 .. Oct. 2	1625	E	Sat.	„ 1 .. 11	1626	354
10	5387	Mon.	„ 11 .. 21	1626	D	Thurs.	March 22 .. April 1	1627	355
11 E	5388	Sat.	„ 1 .. 11	1627	C	Tues.	April 8 .. 18	1628 b	383
12	5389	Thurs.	„ 18 .. 28	1628	A	Sun.	March 29 .. April 8	1629	355
13	5390	Tues.	„ 8 .. 18	1629	G	Thurs.	„ 18 .. 28	1630	354
14 E	5391	Sat.	Aug. 28 .. Sept. 7	1630	F	Thurs.	April 7 .. 17	1631	385
15	5392	Sat.	Sept. 17 .. 27	1631	E	Tues.	March 27 .. April 6	1632 b	355
16	5393	Thurs.	„ 6 .. 16	1632	C	Sat.	„ 16 .. 26	1633	354
17 E	5394	Mon.	Aug. 26 .. Sept. 5	1633	B	Thurs.	April 3 .. 13	1634	383
18	5395	Sat.	Sept. 13 .. 23	1634	A	Tues.	March 24 .. April 3	1635	355
19 E	5396	Thurs.	„ 3 .. 13	1635	G	Sun.	April 10 .. 20	1636 b	383

MOLAD 3 1 704 — CYCLE 285. — DAYS, 6941.

1	5397	Tues.	Sept. 20 .. 30	1636	E	Thurs.	March 30 .. April 9	1637	354
2	5398	Sat.	„ 9 .. 19	1637	D	Tues.	„ 20 .. 30	1638	355
3 E	5399	Thurs.	Aug. 30 .. Sept. 9	1638	C	Tues.	April 9 .. 19	1639	385
4	5400	Thurs.	Sept. 19 .. 29	1639	B	Sat.	March 28 .. April 7	1640 b	354
5	5401	Mon.	„ 7 .. 17	1640	G	Tues.	„ 16 .. 26	1641	353
6 E	5402	Thurs.	Aug. 26 .. Sept. 5	1641	F	Tues.	April 5 .. 15	1642	385
7	5403	Thurs.	Sept. 15 .. 25	1642	E	Sat.	March 25 .. April 4	1643	354
8 E	5404	Mon.	„ 4 .. 14	1643	D	Thurs.	April 11 .. 21	1644 b	383
9	5405	Sat.	„ 21 .. Oct. 1	1644	B	Tues.	„ 1 .. 11	1645	355
10	5406	Thurs.	„ 11 .. 21	1645	A	Sat.	March 21 .. 31	1646	354
11 E	5407	Mon.	Aug. 31 .. Sept. 10	1646	G	Sat.	April 10 .. 20	1647	385
12	5408	Mon.	Sept. 20 .. 30	1647	F	Tues.	March 28 .. April 7	1648 b	353
13	5409	Thurs.	„ 7 .. 17	1648	D	Sun.	„ 18 .. 28	1649	355
14 E	5410	Tues.	Aug. 28 .. Sept. 7	1649	C	Sat.	April 6 .. 16	1650	384
15	5411	Mon.	Sept. 16 .. 26	1650	B	Thurs.	March 27 .. April 6	1651	355
16	5412	Sat.	„ 6 .. 16	1651	A	Sun.	„ 14 .. 24	1652 b	353
17 E	5413	Tues.	Aug. 24 .. Sept. 3	1652	F	Sat.	April 2 .. 12	1653	384
18	5414	Mon.	Sept. 12 .. 22	1653	E	Thurs.	March 23 .. April 2	1654	355
19 E	5415	Sat.	„ 2 .. 12	1654	D	Thurs.	April 12 .. 22	1655	385

MOLAD 5 18 219 — CYCLE 286. — DAYS, 6939.

1	5416	Sat.	Sept. 22 .. Oct. 2	1655	C	Sun.	March 30 .. April 9	1656 b	353
2	5417	Tues.	„ 9 .. 19	1656	A	Thurs.	„ 19 .. 29	1657	354
3 E	5418	Sat.	Aug. 29 .. Sept. 8	1657	G	Thurs.	April 8 .. 18	1658	385
4	5419	Sat.	Sept. 18 .. 28	1658	F	Tues.	March 29 .. April 8	1659	355
5	5420	Thurs.	„ 8 .. 18	1659	E	Sat.	„ 17 .. 27	1660 b	354
6 E	5421	Mon.	Aug. 27 .. Sept. 6	1660	C	Thurs.	April 4 .. 14	1661	383
7	5422	Sat.	Sept. 14 .. 24	1661	B	Tues.	March 25 .. April 4	1662	355
8 E	5423	Thurs.	„ 4 .. 14	1662	A	Sun.	April 12 .. 22	1663	383
9	5424	Tues.	„ 22 .. Oct. 2	1663	G	Thurs.	March 31 .. April 10	1664 b	354
10	5425	Sat.	„ 10 .. 20	1664	E	Tues.	„ 21 .. 31	1665	355
11 E	5426	Thurs.	Aug. 31 .. Sept. 10	1665	D	Tues.	April 10 .. 20	1666	385
12	5427	Thurs.	Sept. 20 .. 30	1666	C	Sat.	March 30 .. April 9	1667	354
13	5428	Mon.	„ 9 .. 19	1667	B	Tues.	„ 17 .. 27	1668 b	353
14 E	5429	Thurs.	Aug. 27 .. Sept. 6	1668	G	Tues.	April 6 .. 16	1669	385
15	5430	Thurs.	Sept. 16 .. 26	1669	F	Sat.	March 26 .. April 5	1670	354
16	5431	Mon.	„ 5 .. 15	1670	E	Thurs.	„ 16 .. 26	1671	355
17 E	5132	Sat.	Aug. 26 .. Sept. 5	1671	D	Tues.	April 2 .. 12	1672 b	383
18	5433	Thurs.	Sept. 12 .. 22	1672	B	Sat.	March 22 .. April 1	1673	354
19 E	5434	Mon.	„ 1 .. 11	1673	A	Sat.	April 11 .. 21	1674	385

MOLAD 1 10 814. CYCLE 287. DAYS, 6940.

1	5435	Mon.	Sept. 21	.. Oct. 1	1674	G	Thurs.	April 1	.. 11	1675	355
2	5436	Sat.	„ 11	.. 21	1675	F	Sun.	March 19	.. 29	1676 b	353
3E	5437	Tues.	Aug. 29	.. Sept. 8	1676	D	Sat.	April 7	.. 17	1677	384
4	5438	Mon.	Sept. 17	.. 27	1677	C	Thurs.	March 28	.. April 7	1678	355
5	5439	Sat.	„ 7	.. 17	1678	B	Tues.	March 18	.. 28	1679	355
6 E	5440	Thurs.	Aug. 28	.. Sept. 7	1679	A	Sun.	April 4	.. 14	1680 b	383
7	5441	Tues.	Sept. 14	.. 24	1680	F	Thurs.	March 24	.. April 3	1681	354
8 E	5442	Sat.	„ 3	.. 13	1681	E	Thurs.	April 13	.. 23	1682	385
9	5443	Sat.	„ 23	.. Oct. 3	1682	D	Sun.	„ 1	.. 11	1683	353
10	5444	Tues.	„ 11	.. 21	1683	C	Thurs.	March 20	.. 30	1684 b	354
11 E	5445	Sat.	Aug. 30	.. Sept. 9	1684	A	Thurs.	April 9	.. 19	1685	385
12	5446	Sat.	Sept. 19	.. 29	1685	G	Tues.	March 30	.. April 9	1686	355
13	5447	Thurs.	„ 9	.. 19	1686	F	Sat.	„ 19	.. 29	1687	354
14 E	5448	Mon.	Aug. 29	.. Sept. 8	1687	E	Thurs.	April 5	.. 15	1688 b	383
15	5449	Sat.	Sept. 15	.. 25	1688	C	Tues.	March 26	.. April 5	1689	355
16	5450	Thurs.	„ 5	.. 15	1689	B	Sat.	„ 15	.. 25	1690	354
17 E	5451	Mon.	Aug. 25	.. Sept. 4	1690	A	Sat.	April 4	.. 14	1691	385
18	5452	Mon.	Sept. 14	.. 24	1691	G	Tues.	March 22	.. April 1	1692 b	353
19 E	5453	Thurs.	„ 1	.. 11	1692	E	Tues.	April 11	.. 21	1693	385

MOLAD 4 3 329. CYCLE 288. DAYS, 6939.

1	5454	Thurs.	Sept. 21	.. Oct. 1	1693	D	Sat.	March 31	.. April 10	1694	354
2	5455	Mon.	„ 10	.. 20	1694	C	Thurs.	„ 21	.. 31	1695	355
3 E	5456	Sat.	Aug. 31	.. Sept. 10	1695	B	Tues.	April 7	.. 17	1696 b	383
4	5457	Thurs.	Sept. 17	.. 27	1696	G	Sat.	March 27	.. April 6	1697	354
5	5458	Mon.	„ 6	.. 16	1697	F	Thurs.	„ 17	.. 27	1698	355
6 E	5459	Sat.	Aug. 27	.. Sept. 6	1698	E	Tues.	April 4	.. 14	1699	383
7	5460	Thurs.	Sept. 14	.. 24	1699	D	Sun.	March 24	.. April 4	1700	355
8 E	5461	Tues.	„ 3	.. 14	1700	C	Sat.	April 12	.. 23	1701	384
9	5462	Mon.	„ 22	.. Oct. 3	1701	B	Thurs.	„ 2	.. 13	1702	355
10	5463	Sat.	„ 12	.. 23	1702	A	Sun.	March 21	.. April 1	1703	353
11 E	5464	Tues.	Aug. 31	.. Oct. 11	1703	G	Sat.	April 8	.. 19	1704 b	384
12	5465	Mon.	Sept. 18	.. 29	1704	E	Thurs.	March 29	.. April 9	1705	355
13	5466	Sat.	„ 8	.. 19	1705	D	Tues.	„ 19	.. 30	1706	355
14 E	5467	Thurs.	Aug. 29	.. Sept. 9	1706	C	Sun.	April 6	.. 17	1707	383
15	5468	Tues.	Sept. 16	.. 27	1707	B	Thurs.	March 25	.. April 5	1708 b	354
16	5469	Sat.	„ 4	.. 15	1708	G	Tues.	„ 15	.. 26	1709	355
17 E	5470	Thurs.	Aug. 25	.. Sept. 5	1709	F	Tues.	April 4	.. 15	1710	385
18	5471	Thurs.	Sept. 14	.. 25	1710	E	Sat.	March 24	.. April 4	1711	354
19 E	5472	Mon.	„ 3	.. 14	1711	D	Thurs.	April 10	.. 21	1712 b	383

MOLAD 6 19 924. CYCLE 289. DAYS, 6939.

1	5473	Sat.	Sept. 20 .. Oct. 1	1712	B	Tues.	March 31 .. April 11	1713	355
2	5474	Thurs.	„ 10 .. 21	1713	A	Sat.	„ 20 .. 31	1714	354
3 E	5475	Mon.	Aug. 30 .. Sept. 10	1714	G	Thurs.	April 7 .. 18	1715	383
4	5476	Sat.	Sept. 17 .. 28	1715	F	Tues.	March 27 .. April 7	1716	355
5	5477	Thurs.	„ 6 .. 17	1716	D	Sat.	„ 16 .. 27	1717	354
6 E	5478	Mon.	Aug. 26 .. Sept. 6	1717	C	Sat.	April 5 .. 16	1718	385
7	5479	Mon.	Sept. 15 .. 26	1718	B	Tues.	March 24 .. April 4	1719	353
8 E	5480	Thurs.	„ 3 .. 14	1719	A	Tues.	April 12 .. 23	1720	385
9	5481	Thurs.	„ 22 .. Oct. 3	1720	F	Sat.	„ 1 .. 12	1721	354
10	5482	Mon.	„ 11 .. 22	1721	E	Thurs.	March 22 .. April 2	1722	355
11 E	5483	Sat.	„ 1 .. 12	1722	D	Tues.	April 9 .. 20	1723	383
12	5484	Thurs.	„ 19 .. 30	1723	C	Sat.	March 28 .. April 8	1724	354
13	5485	Mon.	„ 7 .. 18	1724	A	Thurs.	„ 18 .. 29	1725	355
14 E	5486	Sat.	Aug. 28 .. Sept. 8	1725	G	Tues.	April 5 .. 16	1726	383
15	5487	Thurs.	Sept. 15 .. 26	1726	F	Sun.	March 26 .. April 6	1727	355
16	5488	Tues.	„ 5 .. 16	1727	E	Thurs.	„ 14 .. 25	1728	354
17 E	5489	Sat.	Aug. 24 .. Sept. 4	1728	C	Thurs.	April 3 .. 14	1729	385
18	5490	Sat.	Sept. 13 .. 24	1729	B	Sun.	March 22 .. April 2	1730	353
19 E	5491	Tues.	„ 1 .. 12	1730	A	Sat.	April 10 .. 21	1731	384

MOLAD 2 12 439. CYCLE 290. DAYS, 6940.

1	5492	Mon.	Sept. 20 .. Oct. 1	1731	G	Thurs.	March 30 .. April 10	1732	355
2	5493	Sat.	„ 9 .. 20	1732	E	Tues.	„ 20 .. 31	1733	355
3 E	5494	Thurs.	Aug. 30 .. Sept. 10	1733	D	Sun.	April 7 .. 18	1734	383
4	5495	Tues.	Sept. 17 .. 28	1734	C	Thurs.	March 27 .. April 7	1735	354
5	5496	Sat.	„ 6 .. 17	1735	B	Tues.	„ 16 .. 27	1736	355
6 E	5497	Thurs.	Aug. 26 .. Sept. 6	1736	G	Tues.	April 5 .. 16	1737	385
7	5498	Thurs.	Sept. 15 .. 26	1737	F	Sat.	March 25 .. April 5	1738	354
8 E	5499	Mon.	„ 4 .. 15	1738	E	Thurs.	April 12 .. 23	1739	383
9	5500	Sat.	„ 22 .. Oct. 3	1739	D	Tues.	„ 1 .. 12	1740	355
10	5501	Thurs.	„ 11 .. 22	1740	B	Sat.	March 21 .. April 1	1741	354
11 E	5502	Mon.	Aug. 31 .. Sept. 11	1741	A	Thurs.	April 8 .. 19	1742	383
12	5503	Sat.	„ 18 .. 29	1742	G	Tues.	March 29 .. April 9	1743	355
13	5504	Thurs.	„ 8 .. 19	1743	F	Sat.	„ 17 .. 28	1744	354
14 E	5505	Mon.	„ 27 .. Sept. 7	1744	D	Sat.	April 6 .. 17	1745	385
15	5506	Mon.	Sept. 16 .. 27	1745	C	Tues.	March 25 .. April 5	1746	353
16	5507	Thurs.	„ 4 .. 15	1746	B	Sun.	„ 15 .. 26	1747	355
17 E	5508	Tues.	Aug. 25 .. Sept. 5	1747	A	Sat.	April 2 .. 13	1748	384
18	5509	Mon.	Sept. 12 .. 23	1748	F	Thurs.	March 23 .. April 3	1749	355
19 E	5510	Sat.	„ 2 .. 13	1749	E	Tues.	April 10 .. 21	1750	383

MOLAD 5 4 1034. CYCLE 291. DAYS, 6941.

1	5511	Thurs.	Sept. 20 ..	Oct. 1	1750	D	Sat.	March 30 ..	April 10	1751	354
2	5512	Mon.	„ 9 ..	20	1751	C	Thurs.	„ 19 ..	30	1752b	355
3 E	5513	Sat.	Aug. 29 ..	Sept. 9	1752	A	Thurs.	April 8 ..	19	1753	385
4	5514	Sat.	Sept. 18 ..	29	1753	G	Sun.	March 27 ..	April 7	1754	353
5	5515	Tues.	„ 6 ..	17	1754	F	Thurs.	„ 16 ..	27	1755	354
6 E	5516	Sat.	Aug. 26 ..	Sept. 6	1755	E	Thurs.	April 4 ..	15	1756b	385
7	5517	Sat.	Sept. 14 ..	25	1756	C	Tues.	March 25 ..	April 5	1757	355
8 E	5518	Thurs.	„ 4 ..	15	1757	B	Sun.	April 12 ..	23	1758	383
9	5519	Tues.	Sept. 22 ..	Oct. 3	1758	A	Thurs.	„ 1 ..	12	1759	354
10	5520	Sat.	„ 11 ..	22	1759	G	Tues.	March 21 ..	April 1	1760b	355
11 E	5521	Thurs.	Aug. 31 ..	Sept. 11	1760	E	Sun.	April 8 ..	19	1761	383
12	5522	Tues.	Sept. 18 ..	29	1761	D	Thurs.	March 28 ..	April 8	1762	354
13	5523	Sat.	„ 7 ..	18	1762	C	Tues.	„ 18 ..	29	1763	355
14 E	5524	Thurs.	Aug. 28 ..	Sept. 8	1763	B	Tues.	April 6 ..	17	1764b	385
15	5525	Thurs.	Sept. 16 ..	27	1764	G	Sat.	March 26 ..	April 6	1765	354
16	5526	Mon.	„ 5 ..	16	1765	F	Tues.	„ 14 ..	25	1766	353
17 E	5527	Thurs.	Aug. 24 ..	Sept. 4	1766	E	Tues.	April 3 ..	14	1767	385
18	5528	Thurs.	Sept. 13 ..	24	1767	D	Sat.	March 22 ..	April 2	1768b	354
19 E	5529	Mon.	„ 1 ..	12	1768	B	Sat.	April 11 ..	22	1769	385

MOLAD 7 21 549. CYCLE 292. DAYS, 6940.

1	5530	Mon.	Sept. 21 ..	Oct. 2	1769	A	Tues.	March 30 ..	April 10	1770	353
2	5531	Thurs.	„ 9 ..	20	1770	G	Sat.	„ 19 ..	30	1771	354
3 E	5532	Mon.	Aug. 29 ..	Sept. 9	1771	F	Sat.	April 7 ..	18	1772b	385
4	5533	Mon.	Sept. 17 ..	28	1772	D	Thurs.	March 28 ..	April 8	1773	355
5	5534	Sat.	„ 7 ..	18	1773	C	Sun.	„ 16 ..	27	1774	353
6 E	5535	Tues.	Aug. 26 ..	Sept. 6	1774	B	Sat.	April 4 ..	15	1775	384
7	5536	Mon.	Sept. 14 ..	25	1775	A	Thurs.	March 24 ..	April 4	1776b	355
8 E	5537	Sat.	„ 3 ..	14	1776	F	Tues.	April 11 ..	22	1777	383
9	5538	Thurs.	„ 21 ..	Oct. 2	1777	E	Sun.	„ 1 ..	12	1778	355
10	5539	Tues.	Sept. 11 ..	22	1778	D	Thurs.	March 21 ..	April 1	1779	354
11 E	5540	Sat.	Aug. 31 ..	Sept. 11	1779	C	Thurs.	April 9 ..	20	1780b	385
12	5541	Sat.	Sept. 19 ..	30	1780	A	Tues.	March 30 ..	April 10	1781	355
13	5542	Thurs.	„ 9 ..	20	1781	G	Sat.	„ 19 ..	30	1782	354
14 E	5543	Mon.	Aug. 29 ..	Sept. 9	1782	F	Thurs.	April 6 ..	17	1783	383
15	5544	Sat.	Sept. 16 ..	27	1783	E	Tues.	March 26 ..	April 6	1784b	355
16	5545	Thurs.	„ 5 ..	16	1784	C	Sat.	„ 15 ..	26	1785	354
17 E	5546	Mon.	Aug. 25 ..	Sept. 5	1785	B	Thurs.	April 2 ..	13	1786	383
18	5547	Sat.	Sept. 12 ..	23	1786	A	Tues.	March 23 ..	April 3	1787	355
19 E	5548	Thurs.	„ 2 ..	13	1787	G	Tues.	April 11 ..	22	1788b	385

Molad 3 14 64. CYCLE 293. Days, 6939.

1	5549	Thurs.	Sept. 21 .. Oct. 2	1788	E	Sat.	March 31 .. April 11	1789	354
2	5550	Mon.	„ 10 .. 21	1789	D	Tues.	„ 19 .. 30	1790	353
3 E	5551	Thurs.	Aug. 29 .. Sept. 9	1790	C	Tues.	April 8 .. 19	1791	385
4	5552	Thurs.	Sept. 18 .. 29	1791	B	Sat.	March 27 .. April 7	1792 b	354
5	5553	Mon.	„ 6 .. 17	1792	G	Thurs.	„ 17 .. 28	1793	355
6 E	5554	Sat.	Aug. 27 .. Sept. 7	1793	F	Tues.	April 4 .. 15	1794	383
7	5555	Thurs.	Sept. 14 .. 25	1794	E	Sat.	March 24 .. April 4	1795	354
8 E	5556	Mon.	„ 3 .. 14	1795	D	Sat.	April 12 .. 23	1796 b	385
9	5557	Mon.	„ 22 .. Oct. 3	1796	B	Tues.	March 31 .. April 11	1797	353
10	5558	Thurs.	„ 10 .. 21	1797	A	Sun.	„ 21 .. April 1	1798	355
11 E	5559	Tues.	Aug. 31 .. Sept. 11	1798	G	Sat.	April 9 .. 20	1799	384
12	5560	Mon.	Sept. 19 .. 30	1799	F	Thurs.	March 29 .. April 10	1800	355
13	5561	Sat.	„ 8 .. 20	1800	E	Sun.	„ 17 .. 29	1801	353
14 E	5562	Tues.	Aug. 27 .. Sept. 8	1801	D	Sat.	April 5 .. 17	1802	384
15	5563	Mon.	Sept. 15 .. 27	1802	C	Thurs.	March 26 .. April 7	1803	355
16	5564	Sat.	„ 5 .. 17	1803	B	Tues.	„ 15 .. 27	1804 b	355
17 E	5565	Thurs.	Aug. 25 .. Sept. 6	1804	G	Sun.	April 2 .. 14	1805	383
18	5566	Tues.	Sept. 12 .. 24	1805	F	Thurs.	March 22 .. April 3	1806	354
19 E	5567	Sat.	„ 1 .. 13	1806	E	Thurs.	April 11 .. 23	1807	385

Molad 6 6 659. CYCLE 294. Days, 6939.

1	5568	Sat.	Sept. 21 .. Oct. 3	1807	D	Tues.	March 31 .. April 12	1808 b	355
2	5569	Thurs.	„ 10 .. 22	1808	B	Sat.	„ 20 .. April 1	1809	354
3 E	5570	Mon.	Aug. 30 .. Sept. 11	1809	A	Thurs.	April 7 .. 19	1810	383
4	5571	Sat.	Sept. 17 .. 29	1810	G	Tues.	March 28 .. April 9	1811	355
5	5572	Thurs.	„ 7 .. 19	1811	F	Sat.	„ 16 .. 28	1812 b	354
6 E	5573	Mon.	Aug. 26 .. Sept. 7	1812	D	Thurs.	April 3 .. 15	1813	383
7	5574	Sat.	Sept. 13 .. 25	1813	C	Tues.	March 24 .. April 5	1814	355
8 E	5575	Thurs.	„ 3 .. 15	1814	B	Tues.	April 13 .. 25	1815	385
9	5576	Thurs.	„ 23 .. Oct. 5	1815	A	Sat.	„ 1 .. 13	1816 b	354
10	5577	Mon.	„ 11 .. 23	1816	F	Tues.	March 20 .. April 1	1817	353
11 E	5578	Thurs.	Aug. 30 .. Sept. 11	1817	E	Tues.	April 9 .. 21	1818	385
12	5579	Thurs.	Sept. 19 .. Oct. 1	1818	D	Sat.	March 29 .. April 10	1819	354
13	5580	Mon.	„ 8 .. 20	1819	C	Thurs.	„ 18 .. 30	1820 b	355
14 E	5581	Sat.	Aug. 28 .. Sept. 9	1820	A	Tues.	April 5 .. 17	1821	383
15	5582	Thurs.	Sept. 15 .. 27	1821	G	Sat.	March 25 .. April 6	1822	354
16	5483	Mon.	„ 4 .. 16	1822	F	Thurs.	„ 15 .. 27	1823	355
17 E	5584	Sat.	Aug. 25 .. Sept. 6	1823	E	Tues.	April 1 .. 13	1824 b	383
18	5585	Thurs.	Sept. 11 .. 23	1824	C	Sun.	March 22 .. April 3	1825	355
19 E	5586	Tues.	„ 1 .. 13	1825	B	Sat.	April 10 .. 22	1826	384

MOLAD 1 23 174. CYCLE 295. DAYS, 6940.

1	5587	Mon.	Sept. 20 .. Oct. 2	1826	A	Thurs.	March 31 .. April 12	1827	35
2	5588	Sat.	" 10 .. 22	1827	G	Sun.	" 18 .. 30	1828 b	35
3 E	5589	Tues.	Aug. 28 .. Sept. 9	1828	E	Sat.	April 6 .. 18	1829	38
4	5590	Mon.	Sept. 16 .. 28	1829	D	Thurs.	March 27 .. April 8	1830	35
5	5591	Sat.	" 6 .. 18	1830	C	Tues.	" 17 .. 29	1831	35
6 E	5592	Thurs.	Aug. 27 .. Sept. 8	1831	B	Sun.	April 3 .. 15	1832 b	38
7	5593	Tues.	Sept. 13 .. 25	1832	G	Thurs.	March 23 .. April 4	1833	35
8 E	5594	Sat.	" 2 .. 14	1833	F	Thurs.	April 12 .. 24	1834	38
9	5595	Sat.	" 22 .. Oct. 4	1834	E	Tues.	" 2 .. 14	1835	35
10	5596	Thurs.	" 12 .. 24	1835	D	Sat.	March 21 .. April 2	1836 b	35
11 E	5597	Mon.	Aug. 31 .. Sept.12	1836	B	Thurs.	April 8 .. 20	1837	38
12	5598	Sat.	Sept. 18 .. 30	1837	A	Tues.	March 29 .. April 10	1838	35
13	5599	Thurs.	" 8 .. 20	1838	G	Sat.	" 18 .. 30	1839	35
14 E	5600	Mon.	Aug. 28 .. Sept. 9	1839	F	Sat.	April 6 .. 18	1840 b	38
15	5601	Mon.	Sept. 16 .. 28	1840	D	Tues.	March 25 .. April 6	1841	35
16	5602	Thurs.	" 4 .. 16	1841	C	Sat.	" 14 .. 26	1842	35
17 E	5603	Mon.	Aug. 24 .. Sept. 5	1842	B	Sat.	April 3 .. 15	1843	38
18	5604	Mon.	Sept. 13 .. 25	1843	A	Thurs.	March 23 .. April 4	1844 b	35
19 E	5605	Sat.	" 2 .. 14	1844	F	Tues.	April 10 .. 22	1845	38

MOLAD 4 15 769. CYCLE 296. DAYS, 6939.

1	5606	Thurs.	Sept. 20 .. Oct. 2	1845	E	Sat.	March 30 .. April 11	1846	35
2	5607	Mon.	" 9 .. 21	1846	D	Thurs.	" 20 .. April 1	1847	35
3 E	5608	Sat.	Aug. 30 .. Sept.11	1847	C	Tues.	April 6 .. 18	1848 b	38
4	5609	Thurs.	Sept. 16 .. 28	1848	A	Sat.	March 26 .. April 7	1849	35
5	5610	Mon.	" 5 .. 17	1849	G	Thurs.	" 16 .. 28	1850	35
6 E	5611	Sat.	Aug. 26 .. Sept. 7	1850	F	Thurs.	April 5 .. 17	1851	38
7	5612	Sat.	Sept. 15 .. 27	1851	E	Sun.	March 23 .. April 4	1852 b	35
8 E	5613	Tues.	" 2 .. 14	1852	C	Sat.	April 11 .. 23	1853	38
9	5614	Mon.	" 21 .. Oct. 3	1853	B	Thurs.	" 1 .. 13	1854	35
10	5615	Sat.	" 11 .. 23	1854	A	Tues.	March 22 .. April 3	1855	35
11 E	5616	Thurs.	" 1 .. 13	1855	G	Sun.	April 8 .. 20	1856 b	38
12	5617	Tues.	" 18 .. 30	1856	E	Thurs.	March 28 .. April 9	1857	35
13	5618	Sat.	" 7 .. 19	1857	D	Tues.	" 18 .. 30	1858	35
14 E	5619	Thurs.	Aug. 28 .. Sept. 9	1858	C	Tues.	April 7 .. 19	1859	38
15	5620	Thurs.	Sept. 17 .. 29	1859	B	Sat.	March 26 .. April 7	1860 b	35
16	5621	Mon.	" 5 .. 17	1860	G	Tues.	" 14 .. 26	1861	35
17 E	5622	Thurs.	Aug. 24 .. Sept. 5	1861	F	Tues.	April 3 .. 15	1862	38
18	5623	Thurs.	Sept. 13 .. 25	1862	E	Sat.	March 23 .. April 4	1863	35
19 E	5624	Mon.	" 2 .. 14	1863	D	Thurs.	April 9 .. 21	1864 b	38

Molad 7 8 284. CYCLE 297. Days, 6940.

1	5625	Sat.	Sept. 19 .. Oct. 1	1864	B	Tues.	March 30 .. April 11	1865	355
2	5626	Thurs.	„ 9 .. 21	1865	A	Sat.	„ 19 .. 31	1866	354
3 E	5627	Mon.	Aug. 29 .. Sept. 10	1866	G	Sat.	April 8 .. 20	1867	385
4	5628	Mon.	Sept. 18 .. 30	1867	F	Tues.	March 26 .. April 7	1868 b	353
5	5629	Thurs.	„ 5 .. 17	1868	D	Sat.	March 15 .. 27	1869	354
6 E	5630	Mon.	Aug. 25 .. Sept. 6	1869	C	Sat.	April 4 .. 16	1870	385
7	5631	Mon.	Sept. 14 .. 26	1870	B	Thurs.	March 25 .. April 6	1871	355
8 E	5632	Sat.	„ 4 .. 16	1871	A	Tues.	April 11 .. 23	1872 b	383
9	5633	Thurs.	„ 21 .. Oct. 3	1872	F	Sat.	March 31 .. April 12	1873	354
10	5634	Mon.	„ 10 .. 22	1873	E	Thurs.	„ 21 .. „ 2	1874	355
11 E	5635	Sat.	Aug. 31 .. Sept. 12	1874	D	Tues.	April 8 .. 20	1875	383
12	5636	Thurs.	Sept. 18 .. 30	1875	C	Sun.	March 28 .. April 9	1876 b	355
13	5637	Tues.	„ 7 .. 19	1876	A	Thurs.	„ 17 .. 29	1877	354
14 E	5638	Sat.	Aug. 27 .. Sept. 8	1877	G	Thurs.	April 6 .. 18	1878	385
15	5639	Sat.	Sept. 16 .. 28	1878	F	Tues.	March 27 .. April 8	1879	355
16	5640	Thurs.	„ 6 .. 18	1879	E	Sat.	„ 15 .. 27	1880 b	354
17 E	5641	Mon.	Aug. 25 .. Sept. 6	1880	C	Thurs.	April 2 .. 14	1881	383
18	5642	Sat.	Sept. 12 .. 24	1881	B	Tues.	March 23 .. April 4	1882	355
19 E	5643	Thurs.	„ 2 .. 14	1882	A	Sun.	April 10 .. 22	1883	383

Molad 3 0 879. CYCLE 298. Days, 6939.

1	5644	Tues.	Sept. 20 .. Oct. 2	1883	G	Thurs.	March 29 .. April 10	1884 b	354
2	5645	Sat.	„ 8 .. 20	1884	E	Tues.	„ 19 .. 31	1885	355
3 E	5646	Thurs.	Aug. 29 .. Sept. 10	1885	D	Tues.	April 8 .. 20	1886	385
4	5647	Thurs.	Sept. 18 .. 30	1886	C	Sat.	March 28 .. April 9	1887	354
5	5648	Mon.	„ 7 .. 19	1887	B	Tues.	„ 15 .. 27	1888 b	353
6 E	5649	Thurs.	Aug. 25 .. Sept. 6	1888	G	Tues.	April 4 .. 16	1889	385
7	5650	Thurs.	Sept. 14 .. 26	1889	F	Sat.	March 24 .. April 5	1890	354
8 E	5651	Mon.	„ 3 .. 15	1890	E	Thurs.	April 11 .. 23	1891	383
9	5652	Sat.	„ 21 .. Oct. 3	1891	D	Tues.	March 31 .. April 12	1892 b	355
10	5653	Thurs.	„ 10 .. 22	1892	B	Sat.	„ 20 .. „ 1	1893	354
11 E	5654	Mon.	Aug. 30 .. Sept. 11	1893	A	Sat.	April 9 .. 21	1894	385
12	5655	Mon.	Sept. 19 .. Oct. 1	1894	G	Tues.	March 28 .. April 9	1895	353
13	5656	Thurs.	„ 7 .. 19	1895	F	Sun.	„ 17 .. 29	1896 b	355
14 E	5657	Tues.	Aug. 27 .. Sept. 8	1896	D	Sat.	April 5 .. 17	1897	384
15	5658	Mon.	Sept. 15 .. 27	1897	C	Thurs.	March 26 .. April 7	1898	355
16	5659	Sat.	„ 5 .. 17	1898	B	Sun.	„ 14 .. 26	1899	353
17 E	5660	Tues.	Aug. 24 .. Sept. 5	1899	A	Sat.	April 1 .. 14	1900	384
18	5661	Mon.	Sept. 11 .. 24	1900	G	Thurs.	March 22 .. April 4	1901	355
19 E	5662	Sat.	„ 1 .. 14	1901	F	Tues.	April 9 .. 22	1902	383

Molad 5 17 394. CYCLE 299. Days, 6941.

1	5663	Thurs.	Sept. 19	.. Oct. 2	1902	E	Sun.	March 30	.. April 12	1903	355
2	5664	Tues.	„ 9	.. 22	1903	D	Thurs.	„ 18	.. 31	1904 b	354
3 E	5665	Sat.	Aug. 28	.. Sept.10	1904	B	Thurs.	April 7	.. 20	1905	385
4	5666	Sat.	Sept. 17	.. 30	1905	A	Tues.	March 28	.. April 10	1906	355
5	5667	Thurs.	„ 7	.. 20	1906	G	Sat.	„ 17	.. 30	1907	354
6 E	5668	Mon.	Aug. 27	.. Sept. 9	1907	F	Thurs.	April 3	.. 16	1908 b	383
7	5669	Sat.	Sept. 13	.. 26	1908	D	Tues.	March 24	.. April 6	1909	355
8 E	5670	Thurs.	„ 3	.. 16	1909	C	Sun.	April 11	.. 24	1910	383
9	5671	Tues.	„ 21	.. Oct. 4	1910	B	Thurs.	March 31	.. April 13	1911	354
10	5672	Sat.	„ 10	.. 23	1911	A	Tues.	„ 20	.. April 2	1912 b	355
11 E	5673	Thurs.	Aug. 30	.. Sept.12	1912	F	Tues.	April 9	.. 22	1913	385
12	5674	Thurs.	Sept. 19	.. Oct. 2	1913	E	Sat.	March 29	.. April 11	1914	354
13	5675	Mon.	„ 8	.. 21	1914	D	Tues.	„ 17	.. 30	1915	353
14 E	5676	Thurs.	Aug. 27	.. Sept. 9	1915	C	Tues.	April 5	.. 18	1916 b	385
15	5677	Thurs.	Sept. 15	.. 28	1916	A	Sat.	March 25	.. April 7	1917	354
16	5678	Mon.	„ 4	.. 17	1917	G	Thurs.	„ 15	.. 28	1918	355
17 E	5679	Sat.	Aug. 25	.. Sept. 7	1918	F	Tues.	April 2	.. 15	1919	383
18	5680	Thurs.	Sept. 12	.. 25	1919	E	Sat.	March 21	.. April 3	1920 b	354
19 E	5681	Mon.	Aug. 31	.. Sept.13	1920	C	Sat.	April 10	.. 23	1921	385

Molad 1 9 989. CYCLE 300. Days, 6940.

1	5682	Mon.	Sept. 20	.. Oct. 3	1921	B	Thurs.	March 31	.. April 13	1922	355
2	5683	Sat.	„ 10	.. 23	1922	A	Sun.	„ 19	.. April 1	1923	353
3 E	5684	Tues.	Aug. 29	.. Sept.11	1923	G	Sat.	April 6	.. 19	1924 b	384
4	5685	Mon.	Sept. 16	.. 29	1924	E	Thurs.	March 27	.. April 9	1925	355
5	5686	Sat.	„ 6	.. 19	1925	D	Tues.	„ 17	.. 30	1926	355
6 E	5687	Thurs.	Aug. 27	.. Sept. 9	1926	C	Sun.	April 4	.. 17	1927	383
7	5688	Tues.	Sept. 14	.. 27	1927	B	Thurs.	March 23	.. April 5	1928 b	354
8 E	5689	Sat.	„ 2	.. 15	1928	G	Thurs.	April 12	.. 25	1929	385
9	5690	Sat.	„ 22	.. Oct. 5	1929	F	Sun.	March 31	.. April 13	1930	353
10	5691	Tues.	„ 10	.. 23	1930	E	Thurs.	„ 20	.. April 2	1931	354
11 E	5692	Sat.	Aug. 30	.. Sept.12	1931	D	Thurs.	April 8	.. 21	1932 b	385
12	5693	Sat.	Sept. 18	.. Oct. 1	1932	B	Tues.	March 29	.. April 11	1933	355
13	5694	Thurs.	„ 8	.. 21	1933	A	Sat.	„ 18	.. 31	1934	354
14 E	5695	Mon.	Aug. 28	.. Sept.10	1934	G	Thurs.	April 5	.. 18	1935	383
15	5696	Sat.	Sept. 15	.. 28	1935	F	Tues.	March 25	.. April 7	1936 b	355
16	5697	Thurs.	„ 4	.. 17	1936	D	Sat.	„ 14	.. 27	1937	354
17 E	5698	Mon.	Aug. 24	.. Sept. 6	1937	C	Sat.	April 3	.. 16	1938	385
18	5699	Mon.	Sept. 13	.. 26	1938	B	Tues.	March 22	.. April 4	1939	353
19 E	5700	Thurs.	„ 1	.. 14	1939	A	Tues.	April 10	.. 23	1940 b	385

MOLAD 4 2 504. CYCLE 301. DAYS, 6939.

1	5701	Thurs.	Sept. 20	..	Oct. 3	1940	F	Sat.	March 30	..	April 12	1941	354
2	5702	Mon.	„ 9	..	22	1941	E	Thurs.	„ 20	..	April 2	1942	355
3 E	5703	Sat.	Aug. 30	..	Sept. 12	1942	D	Tues.	April 7	..	20	1943	383
4	5704	Thurs.	Sept. 17	..	30	1943	C	Sat.	March 26	..	April 8	1944 b	354
5	5705	Mon.	„ 5	..	18	1944	A	Thurs.	„ 16	..	29	1945	355
6 E	5706	Sat.	Aug. 26	..	Sept. 8	1945	G	Tues.	April 3	..	16	1946	383
7	5707	Thurs.	Sept. 13	..	26	1946	F	Sat.	March 23	..	April 5	1947	354
8 E	5708	Mon.	„ 2	..	15	1947	E	Sat.	April 11	..	24	1948 b	385
9	5709	Mon.	Sept. 21	..	Oct. 4	1948	C	Thurs.	„ 1	..	14	1949	355
10	5710	Sat.	„ 11	..	24	1949	B	Sun.	March 20	..	April 2	1950	353
11 E	5711	Tues.	Aug. 30	..	Sept. 12	1950	A	Sat.	April 8	..	21	1951	384
12	5712	Mon.	Sept. 18	..	Oct. 1	1951	G	Thurs.	March 28	..	April 10	1952 b	355
13	5713	Sat.	„ 7	..	20	1952	E	Tues.	„ 18	..	31	1953	355
14 E	5714	Thurs.	Aug. 28	..	Sept. 10	1953	D	Sun.	April 5	..	18	1954	383
15	5715	Tues.	Sept. 15	..	28	1954	C	Thurs.	March 25	..	April 7	1955	354
16	5716	Sat.	„ 4	..	17	1955	B	Tues.	„ 14	..	27	1956 b	355
17 E	5717	Thurs.	Aug. 24	..	Sept. 6	1956	G	Tues.	April 3	..	16	1957	385
18	5718	Thurs.	Sept. 13	..	26	1957	F	Sat.	March 23	..	April 5	1958	354
19 E	5719	Mon.	„ 2	..	15	1958	E	Thurs.	April 10	..	23	1959	383

MOLAD 6 19 19. CYCLE 302. DAYS, 6939.

1	5720	Sat.	Sept. 20	..	Oct. 3	1959	D	Tues.	March 30	..	April 12	1960 b	355
2	5721	Thurs.	„ 9	..	22	1960	B	Sat.	„ 19	..	April 1	1961	354
3 E	5722	Mon.	Aug. 29	..	Sept. 11	1961	A	Thurs.	April 6	..	19	1962	383
4	5723	Sat.	Sept. 16	..	29	1962	G	Tues.	March 27	..	April 9	1963	355
5	5724	Thurs.	„ 6	..	19	1963	F	Sat.	„ 15	..	28	1964 b	354
6 E	5725	Mon.	Aug. 25	..	Sept. 7	1964	D	Sat.	April 4	..	17	1965	385
7	5726	Mon.	Sept. 14	..	27	1965	C	Tues.	March 23	..	April 5	1966	353
8 E	5727	Thurs.	„ 2	..	15	1966	B	Tues.	April 12	..	25	1967	385
9	5728	Thurs.	„ 22	..	Oct. 5	1967	A	Sat.	March 31	..	April 13	1968 b	354
10	5729	Mon.	„ 10	..	23	1968	F	Thurs.	„ 21	..	April 3	1969	355
11 E	5730	Sat.	Aug. 31	..	Sept. 13	1969	E	Tues.	April 8	..	21	1970	383
12	5731	Thurs.	Sept. 18	..	Oct. 1	1970	D	Sat.	March 28	..	April 10	1971	354
13	5732	Mon.	„ 7	..	20	1971	C	Thurs.	„ 17	..	30	1972 b	355
14 E	5733	Sat.	Aug. 27	..	Sept. 9	1972	A	Tues.	April 4	..	17	1973	383
15	5734	Thurs.	Sept. 14	..	27	1973	G	Sun.	March 25	..	April 7	1974	355
16	5735	Tues.	„ 4	..	17	1974	F	Thurs.	„ 14	..	27	1975	354
17 E	5736	Sat.	Aug. 24	..	Sept. 6	1975	E	Thurs.	April 2	..	15	1976 b	385
18	5737	Sat.	Sept. 12	..	25	1976	C	Sun.	March 21	..	April 3	1977	353
19 E	5738	Tues.	Aug. 31	..	Sept. 13	1977	B	Sat.	April 9	..	22	1978	384

Molad 2 11 614. CYCLE 303. Days, 6940.

1	5739	Mon.	Sept. 19	..	Oct. 2	1978	A	Thurs.	March 30	..	April 12	1979	355
2	5740	Sat.	„ 9	..	22	1979	G	Tues.	„ 19	..	April 1	1980 b	355
3 E	5741	Thurs.	Aug. 29	..	Sept.11	1980	E	Sun.	April 6	..	19	1981	383
4	5742	Tues.	Sept. 16	..	29	1981	D	Thurs.	March 26	..	April 8	1982	354
5	5743	Sat.	„ 5	..	18	1982	C	Tues.	„ 16	..	29	1983	355
6 E	5744	Thurs.	Aug. 26	..	Sept. 8	1983	B	Tues.	April 4	..	17	1984 b	385
7	5745	Thurs.	Sept. 14	..	27	1984	G	Sat.	March 24	..	April 6	1985	354
8 E	5746	Mon.	„ 3	..	16	1985	F	Thurs.	April 11	..	24	1986	383
9	5747	Sat.	„ 21	..	Oct. 4	1986	E	Tues.	„ 1	..	14	1987	355
10	5748	Thurs.	„ 11	..	24	1987	D	Sat.	March 20	..	April 2	1988 b	354
11 E	5749	Mon.	Aug. 30	..	Sept.12	1988	B	Thurs.	April 7	..	20	1989	383
12	5750	Sat.	Sept. 17	..	30	1989	A	Tues.	March 28	..	April 10	1990	355
13	5751	Thurs.	„ 7	..	20	1990	G	Sat.	„ 17	..	30	1991	354
14 E	5752	Mon.	Aug. 27	..	Sept. 9	1991	F	Sat.	April 5	..	18	1992 b	385
15	5753	Mon.	Sept. 15	..	28	1922	D	Tues.	March 24	..	April 6	1993	353
16	5754	Thurs.	„ 3	..	16	1993	C	Sun.	„ 14	..	27	1994	355
17 E	5755	Tues.	Aug. 24	..	Sept. 6	1994	B	Sat.	April 2	..	15	1995	384
18	5756	Mon.	Sept. 12	..	25	1995	A	Thurs.	March 22	..	April 4	1996 b	355
19 E	5757	Sat.	„ 1	..	14	1996	F	Tues.	April 9	..	24	1997	383

Molad 5 4 129. CYCLE 304. Days, 6941.

1	5758	Thurs.	Sept. 19	..	Oct. 2	1997	E	Sat.	March 29	..	April 11	1998	354
2	5759	Mon.	„ 8	..	21	1998	D	Thurs.	„ 19	..	April 1	1999	355
3 E	5760	Sat.	Aug. 29	..	Sept.11	1999	C	Thurs.	April 7	..	20	2000 b	385
4	5761	Sat.	Sept. 17	..	30	2000	A	Sun.	March 26	..	April 8	2001	353
5	5762	Tues.	„ 5	..	18	2001	G	Thurs.	„ 15	..	28	2002	354
6 E	5763	Sat.	Aug. 25	..	Sept. 7	2002	F	Thurs.	April 4	..	17	2003	385
7	5764	Sat.	Sept. 14	..	27	2003	E	Tues.	March 24	..	April 6	2004 b	355
8 E	5765	Thurs.	„ 3	..	16	2004	C	Sun.	April 11	..	24	2005	383
9	5766	Tues.	„ 21	..	Oct. 4	2005	B	Thurs.	March 31	..	April 13	2006	354
10	5767	Sat.	„ 10	..	23	2006	A	Tues.	„ 21	..	April 3	2007	355
11 E	5768	Thurs.	Aug. 31	..	Sept.13	2007	G	Sun.	April 7	..	20	2008 b	383
12	5769	Tues.	Sept. 17	..	Oct. 30	2008	E	Thurs.	March 27	..	April 9	2009	354
13	5770	Sat.	„ 6	..	19	2009	D	Tues.	„ 17	..	30	2010	355
14 E	5771	Thurs.	Aug. 27	..	Sept. 9	2010	C	Tues.	April 6	..	19	2011	385
15	5772	Thurs.	Sept. 16	..	29	2011	B	Sat.	March 25	..	April 7	2012 b	354
16	5773	Mon.	„ 4	..	17	2012	G	Tues.	„ 13	..	26	2013	353
17 E	5774	Thurs.	Aug. 23	..	Sept. 5	2013	F	Tues.	April 2	..	15	2014	385
18	5775	Thurs.	Sept. 12	..	25	2014	E	Sat.	March 22	..	April 4	2015	354
19 E	5776	Mon.	„ 1	..	14	2015	D	Sat.	April 10	..	23	2016 b	385

MOLAD 7 20 724. CYCLE 305. DAYS, 6940.

1	5777	Mon.	Sept. 20	..	Oct. 3	2016	B	Tues.	March 29	..	April 11	2017	353
2	5778	Thurs.	„ 8	..	21	2017	A	Sat.	„ 18	..	31	2018	354
3 E	5779	Mon.	Aug. 28	..	Sept.10	2018	G	Sat.	April 7	..	20	2019	385
4	5780	Mon.	Sept. 17	..	30	2019	F	Thurs.	March 27	..	April 9	2020 b	355
5	5781	Sat.	„ 6	..	19	2020	D	Sun.	„ 15	..	28	2021	353
6 E	5782	Tues.	Aug. 25	..	Sept. 7	2021	C	Sat.	April 3	..	16	2022	384
7	5783	Mon.	Sept. 13	..	26	2022	B	Thurs.	March 24	..	April 6	2023	355
8 E	5784	Sat.	„ 3	..	16	2023	A	Tues.	April 10	..	23	2024 b	383
9	5785	Thurs.	„ 20	..	Oct. 3	2024	F	Sun.	March 31	..	April 13	2025	355
10	5786	Tues.	„ 10	..	23	2025	E	Thurs.	„ 20	..	April 2	2026	354
11 E	5787	Sat.	Aug. 30	..	Sept.12	2026	D	Thurs.	April 9	..	22	2027	385
12	5788	Sat.	Sept. 19	..	Oct. 2	2027	C	Tues.	March 29	..	April 11	2028 b	355
13	5789	Thurs.	„ 8	..	21	2028	A	Sat.	„ 18	..	31	2029	354
14 E	5790	Mon.	Aug. 28	..	Sept.10	2029	G	Thurs.	April 5	..	18	2030	383
15	5791	Sat.	Sept. 15	..	28	2030	F	Tues.	March 26	..	April 8	2031	355
16	5792	Thurs.	„ 5	..	18	2031	E	Sat.	„ 14	..	27	2032 b	354
17 E	5793	Mon.	Aug. 24	..	Sept. 6	2032	C	Thurs.	April 1	..	14	2033	383
18	5794	Sat.	Sept. 11	..	24	2033	B	Tues.	March 22	..	April 4	2034	355
19 E	5795	Thurs.	„ 1	..	14	2034	A	Tues.	April 11	..	24	2035	385

MOLAD 3 13 239. CYCLE 306. DAYS, 6939.

1	5796	Thurs.	Sept. 21	..	Oct. 4	2035	G	Sat.	March 30	..	April 12	2036 b	354
2	5797	Mon.	„ 9	..	22	2036	E	Tues.	„ 18	..	31	2037	353
3 E	5798	Thurs.	Aug. 28	..	Sept.10	2037	D	Tues.	April 7	..	20	2038	385
4	5799	Thurs.	Sept. 17	..	30	2038	C	Sat.	March 27	..	April 9	2039	354
5	5800	Mon.	„ 6	..	19	2039	B	Thurs.	„ 16	..	29	2040 b	355
6 E	5801	Sat.	Aug. 26	..	Sept. 8	2040	G	Tues.	April 3	..	16	2041	383
7	5802	Thurs.	Sept. 13	..	26	2041	F	Sat.	March 23	..	April 5	2042	354
8 E	5803	Mon.	„ 2	..	15	2042	E	Sat.	April 12	..	25	2043	385
9	5804	Mon.	„ 22	..	Oct. 5	2043	D	Tues.	March 30	..	April 12	2044 b	353
10	5805	Thurs.	„ 9	..	22	2044	B	Sun.	„ 20	..	„ 2	2045	355
11 E	5806	Tues.	Aug. 30	..	Sept.12	2045	A	Sat.	April 8	..	21	2046	384
12	5807	Mon.	Sept. 18	..	Oct. 1	2046	G	Thurs.	March 29	..	April 11	2047	355
13	5808	Sat.	„ 8	..	21	2047	F	Sun.	„ 16	..	29	2048 b	353
14 E	5809	Tues.	Aug. 26	..	Sept. 8	2048	D	Sat.	April 4	..	17	2049	384
15	5810	Mon.	Sept. 14	..	27	2049	C	Thurs.	March 25	..	April 7	2050	355
16	5811	Sat.	„ 4	..	17	2050	B	Tues.	„ 15	..	28	2051	355
17 E	5812	Thurs.	Aug. 25	..	Sept. 7	2051	A	Sun.	April 1	..	14	2052 b	383
18	5813	Tues.	Sept. 11	..	24	2052	F	Thurs.	March 21	..	April 3	2053	354
19 E	5814	Sat.	Aug. 31	..	Sept.13	2053	E	Thurs.	April 10	..	23	2054	385

MOLAD 6 5 834. CYCLE 307. DAYS, 6939.

1	5815	Sat.	Sept. 20	..	Oct. 3	2054	D	Tues.	March 31	..	April 13	2055		355
2	5816	Thurs.	„ 10	..	23	2055	C	Sat.	„ 19	..	April 1	2056 b		354
3 E	5817	Mon.	Aug. 29	..	Sept. 11	2056	A	Thurs.	April 6	..	19	2057		383
4	5818	Sat.	Sept. 16	..	29	2057	G	Tues.	March 27	..	April 9	2058		355
5	5819	Thurs.	„ 6	..	19	2058	F	Sat.	„ 16	..	29	2059		354
6 E	5820	Mon.	Aug. 26	..	Sept. 8	2059	E	Thurs.	April 2	..	15	2060 b		383
7	5821	Sat.	Sept. 12	..	25	2060	C	Tues.	March 23	..	April 5	2061		355
8 E	5822	Thurs.	„ 2	..	15	2061	B	Tues.	April 12	..	25	2062		385
9	5823	Thurs.	„ 22	..	Oct. 5	2062	A	Sat.	„ 1	..	14	2063		354
10	5824	Mon.	„ 11	..	24	2063	G	Tues.	March 19	..	April 1	2064 b		353
11 E	5825	Thurs.	Aug. 29	..	Sept. 11	2064	E	Tues.	April 8	..	21	2065		385
12	5826	Thurs.	Sept. 18	..	Oct. 1	2065	D	Sat.	March 28	..	April 10	2066		354
13	5827	Mon.	„ 7	..	20	2066	C	Thurs.	„ 18	..	31	2067		355
14 E	5828	Sat.	Aug. 28	..	Sept. 10	2067	B	Tues.	April 4	..	17	2068 b		383
15	5829	Thurs.	Sept. 14	..	27	2068	G	Sat.	March 24	..	April 6	2069		354
16	5830	Mon.	„ 3	..	16	2069	F	Thurs.	„ 14	..	27	2070		355
17 E	5831	Sat.	Aug. 24	..	Sept. 6	2070	E	Tues.	April 1	..	14	2071		383
18	5832	Thurs.	Sept. 11	..	24	2071	D	Sun.	March 21	..	April 3	2072 b		355
19 E	5833	Tues.	Aug. 31	..	Sept. 13	2072	B	Sat.	April 9	..	22	2073		384

MOLAD 1 22 349. CYCLE 308. DAYS, 6940.

1	5834	Mon.	Sept. 19	..	Oct. 2	2073	A	Thurs.	March 30	..	April 12	2074		355
2	5835	Sat.	„ 9	..	22	2074	G	Sun.	„ 18	..	31	2075		353
3 E	5836	Tues.	Aug. 28	..	Sept. 10	2075	F	Sat.	April 5	..	18	2076 b		384
4	5837	Mon.	Sept. 15	..	28	2076	D	Thurs.	March 26	..	April 8	2077		355
5	5838	Sat.	„ 5	..	18	2077	C	Tues.	„ 16	..	29	2078		355
6 E	5839	Thurs.	Aug. 26	..	Sept. 8	2078	B	Sun.	April 3	..	16	2079		383
7	5840	Tues.	Sept. 13	..	26	2079	A	Thurs.	March 22	..	April 4	2080 b		354
8 E	5841	Sat.	„ 1	..	14	2080	F	Thurs.	April 11	..	24	2081		385
9	5842	Sat.	„ 21	..	Oct. 4	2081	E	Tues.	„ 1	..	14	2082		355
10	5843	Thurs.	„ 11	..	24	2082	D	Sat.	March 21	..	April 3	2083		354
11 E	5844	Mon.	Aug. 31	..	Sept. 13	2083	C	Thurs.	April 7	..	20	2084 b		383
12	5845	Sat.	Sept. 17	..	30	2084	A	Tues.	March 28	..	April 10	2085		355
13	5846	Thurs.	„ 7	..	20	2085	G	Sat.	„ 17	..	30	2086		354
14 E	5847	Mon.	Aug. 27	..	Sept. 9	2086	F	Thurs.	April 4	..	17	2087		383
15	5848	Sat.	Sept. 14	..	27	2087	E	Tues.	March 24	..	April 6	2088 b		355
16	5849	Thurs.	„ 3	..	16	2088	C	Sat.	„ 13	..	26	2089		354
17 E	5850	Mon.	Aug. 23	..	Sept. 5	2089	B	Sat.	April 2	..	15	2090		385
18	5851	Mon.	Sept. 12	..	25	2090	A	Tues.	March 21	..	April 3	2091		353
19 E	5852	Thurs.	Aug. 31	..	Sept. 13	2091	G	Thurs.	April 9	..	22	2092 b		385

MOLAD 4 14 944. CYCLE 309. DAYS, 6939.

1	5853	Thurs.	Sept. 19	.. Oct. 2	2092	E	Sat.	March 29	.. April 11	2093	354
2	5854	Mon.	„ 8	.. 21	2093	D	Thurs.	„ 19	.. April 1	2094	355
3 E	5855	Sat.	Aug. 29	.. Sept. 11	2094	C	Tues.	April 6	.. 19	2095	383
4	5856	Thurs.	Sept. 16	.. 29	2095	B	Sat.	March 25	.. April 7	2096 b	354
5	5857	Mon.	„ 4	.. 17	2096	G	Thurs.	„ 15	.. 28	2097	355
6 E	5858	Sat.	Aug. 25	.. Sept. 7	2097	F	Thurs.	April 4	.. 17	2098	385
7	5859	Sat.	Sept. 14	.. 27	2098	E	Sun.	March 23	.. April 5	2099	353
8 E	5860	Tues.	„ 2	.. 15	2099	D	Sat.	April 10	.. 24	2100	384
9	5861	Mon.	„ 20	.. Oct. 4	2100	C	Thurs.	March 31	.. April 14	2101	355
10	5862	Sat.	„ 10	.. 24	2101	B	Tues.	„ 21	.. April 4	2102	355
11 E	5863	Thurs.	Aug. 31	.. Sept. 14	2102	A	Sun.	April 8	.. 22	2103	383
12	5864	Tues.	Sept. 18	.. Oct. 2	2103	G	Thurs.	March 27	.. April 10	2104 b	354
13	5865	Sat.	„ 6	.. 20	2104	E	Tues.	„ 17	.. 31	2105	355
14 E	5866	Thurs.	Aug. 27	.. Sept. 10	2105	D	Tues.	April 6	.. 20	2106	385
15	5867	Thurs.	Sept. 16	.. 30	2106	C	Sat.	March 26	.. April 9	2107	354
16	5868	Mon.	„ 5	.. 19	2107	B	Tues.	„ 13	.. 27	2108 b	353
17 E	5869	Thurs.	Aug. 23	.. Sept. 6	2108	G	Tues.	April 2	.. 16	2109	385
18	5870	Thurs.	Sept. 12	.. 26	2109	F	Sat.	March 22	.. April 5	2110	354
19 E	5871	Mon.	„ 1	.. 15	2110	E	Thurs.	April 9	.. 23	2111	383

MOLAD 7 7 459. CYCLE 310. DAYS, 6940.

1	5872	Sat.	Sept. 19	.. Oct. 3	2111	D	Tues.	March 29	.. April 12	2112 b	355
2	5873	Thurs.	„ 8	.. 22	2112	B	Sat.	„ 18	.. April 1	2113	354
3 E	5874	Mon.	Aug. 28	.. Sept. 11	2113	A	Sat.	April 7	.. 21	2114	385
4	5875	Mon.	Sept. 17	.. Oct. 1	2114	G	Tues.	March 26	.. April 9	2115	353
5	5876	Thurs.	„ 5	.. 19	2115	F	Sat.	„ 14	.. 28	2116 b	354
6 E	5877	Mon.	Aug. 24	.. Sept. 7	2116	D	Sat.	April 3	.. 17	2117	385
7	5878	Mon.	Sept. 13	.. 27	2117	C	Thurs.	March 24	.. April 7	2118	355
8 E	5879	Sat.	„ 3	.. 17	2118	B	Tues.	April 11	.. 25	2119	383
9	5880	Thurs.	„ 21	.. Oct. 5	2119	A	Sat.	March 30	.. April 13	2120 b	354
10	5881	Mon.	„ 9	.. 23	2120	F	Thurs.	„ 20	.. April 3	2121	355
11 E	5882	Sat.	Aug. 30	.. Sept. 13	2121	E	Tues.	April 7	.. 21	2122	383
12	5883	Thurs.	Sept. 17	.. Oct. 1	2122	D	Sun.	March 28	.. April 11	2123	355
13	5884	Tues.	„ 7	.. 21	2123	C	Thurs.	„ 16	.. 30	2124 b	354
14 E	5885	Sat.	Aug. 26	.. Sept. 9	2124	A	Thurs.	April 5	.. 19	2125	385
15	5886	Sat.	Sept. 15	.. 29	2125	G	Tues.	March 26	.. April 9	2126	355
16	5887	Thurs.	„ 5	.. 19	2126	F	Sat.	„ 15	.. 29	2127	354
17 E	5888	Mon.	Aug. 25	.. Sept. 8	2127	E	Thurs.	April 1	.. 15	2128 b	383
18	5889	Sat.	Sept. 11	.. 25	2128	C	Tues.	March 22	.. April 5	2129	355
19 E	5890	Thurs.	„ 1	.. 15	2129	B	Sun.	April 9	.. 23	2130	383

MOLAD 2 23 1054. CYCLE 311. DAYS, 6939.

1	5891	Tues.	Sept. 19 .. Oct. 3	2130	A	Thurs.	March 29 .. April 12	2131	354
2	5892	Sat.	„ 8 .. 22	2131	G	Tues.	„ 18 .. April 1	2132b	355
3 E	5893	Thurs.	Aug. 28 .. Sept.11	2132	E	Tues.	April 7 .. 21	2133	385
4	5894	Thurs.	Sept. 17 .. Oct. 1	2133	D	Sat.	March 27 .. April 10	2134	354
5	5895	Mon.	„ 6 .. 20	2134	C	Tues.	„ 15 .. 29	2135	353
6 E	5896	Thurs.	Aug. 25 .. Sept. 8	2135	B	Tues.	April 3 .. 17	2136 b	385
7	5897	Thurs.	Sept. 13 .. 27	2136	G	Sat.	March 23 .. April 6	2137	354
8 E	5898	Mon.	„ 2 .. 16	2137	F	Thurs.	April 10 .. 24	2138	383
9	5899	Sat.	Sept. 20 .. Oct. 4	2138	E	Tues.	March 31 .. April 14	2139	355
10	5900	Thurs.	„ 10 .. 24	2139	D	Sat.	„ 19 .. April 2	2140 b	354
11 E	5901	Mon.	Aug. 29 .. Sept.12	2140	B	Sat.	April 8 .. 22	2141	385
12	5902	Mon.	Sept. 18 .. Oct. 2	2141	A	Tues.	March 27 .. April 10	2142	353
13	5903	Thurs.	„ 6 .. 20	2142	G	Sun.	„ 17 .. 31	2143	355
14 E	5904	Tues.	Aug. 27 .. Sept.10	2143	F	Sat.	April 4 .. 18	2144b	384
15	5905	Mon.	Sept. 14 .. 28	2144	D	Thurs.	March 25 .. April 8	2145	355
16	5906	Sat.	„ 4 .. 18	2145	C	Sun.	„ 13 .. 27	2146	353
17 E	5907	Tues.	Aug. 23 .. Sept. 6	2146	B	Sat.	April 1 .. 15	2147	384
18	5908	Mon.	Sept. 11 .. 25	2147	A	Thurs.	March 21 .. April 4	2148 b	355
19 E	5909	Sat.	Aug. 31 .. Sept.14	2148	F	Tues.	April 8 .. 22	2149	383

MOLAD 5 16 569. CYCLE 312. DAYS, 6941.

1	5910	Thurs.	Sept. 18 .. Oct. 2	2149	E	Sun.	March 29 .. April 12	2150	355
2	5911	Tues.	„ 8 .. 22	2150	D	Thurs.	„ 18 .. April 1	2151	354
3 E	5912	Sat.	Aug. 28 .. Sept.11	2151	C	Thurs.	April 6 .. 20	2152 b	385
4	5913	Sat.	Sept. 16 .. 30	2152	A	Tues.	March 27 .. April 10	2153	355
5	5914	Thurs.	„ 6 .. 20	2153	G	Sat.	„ 16 .. 30	2154	354
6 E	5915	Mon.	Aug. 26 .. Sept. 9	2154	F	Thurs.	April 3 .. 17	2155	383
7	5916	Sat.	Sept. 13 .. 27	2155	E	Tues.	March 23 .. April 6	2156 b	355
8 E	5917	Thurs.	„ 2 .. 16	2156	C	Sun.	April 10 .. 24	2157	383
9	5918	Tues.	„ 20 .. Oct. 4	2157	B	Thurs.	March 30 .. April 13	2158	354
10	5919	Sat.	„ 9 .. 23	2158	A	Tues.	„ 20 .. April 3	2159	355
11 E	5920	Thurs.	Aug. 30 .. Sept.13	2159	G	Tues.	April 8 .. 22	2160 b	385
12	5921	Thurs.	Sept. 18 .. Oct. 2	2160	E	Sat.	March 28 .. April 11	2161	354
13	5922	Mon.	„ 7 .. 21	2161	D	Tues.	„ 16 .. 30	2162	353
14 E	5923	Thurs.	Aug. 26 .. Sept. 9	2162	C	Tues.	April 5 .. 19	2163	385
15	5924	Thurs.	Sept. 15 .. 29	2163	B	Sat.	March 24 .. April 7	2164 b	354
16	5925	Mon.	„ 3 .. 17	2164	G	Thurs.	„ 14 .. 28	2165	355
17 E	5926	Sat.	Aug. 24 .. Sept. 7	2165	F	Tues.	April 1 .. 15	2166	383
18	5927	Thurs.	Sept. 11 .. 25	2166	E	Sat.	March 21 .. April 4	2167	354
19 E	5928	Mon.	Aug. 31 .. Sept.14	2167	D	Sat.	April 9 .. 23	2168 b	385

MOLAD 1 9 84. CYCLE 313. DAYS, 6940.

1	5929	Mon.	Sept. 19 ..	Oct. 3	2168	B	Tues.	March 28 ..	April 11	2169	353
2	5930	Thurs.	„ 7 ..	21	2169	A	Sun.	„ 18 ..	April 1	2170	355
3 E	5931	Tues.	Aug. 28 ..	Sept.11	2170	G	Sat.	April 6 ..	20	2171	384
4	5932	Mon.	Sept. 16 ..	30	2171	F	Thurs.	March 26 ..	April 9	2172 b	355
5	5933	Sat.	„ 5 ..	19	2172	D	Sun.	„ 14 ..	28	2173	353
6 E	5934	Tues.	Aug. 24 ..	Sept. 7	2173	C	Sat.	April 2 ..	16	2174	384
7	5935	Mon.	Sept. 12 ..	26	2174	B	Thurs.	March 23 ..	April 6	2175	355
8 E	5936	Sat.	„ 2 ..	16	2175	A	Thurs.	April 11 ..	25	2176 b	385
9	5937	Sat.	„ 21 ..	Oct. 5	2176	F	Sun.	March 30 ..	April 13	2177	353
10	5938	Tues.	„ 9 ..	23	2177	E	Thurs.	„ 19 ..	April 2	2178	354
11 E	5939	Sat.	Aug. 29 ..	Sept.12	2178	D	Thurs.	April 8 ..	22	2179	385
12	5940	Sat.	Sept. 18 ..	Oct. 2	2179	C	Tues.	March 28 ..	April 11	2180 b	355
13	5941	Thurs.	„ 7 ..	21	2180	A	Sat.	„ 17 ..	31	2181	354
14 E	5942	Mon.	Aug. 27 ..	Sept.10	2181	G	Thurs.	April 4 ..	18	2182	383
15	5943	Sat.	Sept. 14 ..	28	2182	F	Tues.	March 25 ..	April 8	2183	355
16	5944	Thurs.	„ 4 ..	18	2183	E	Sat.	„ 13 ..	27	2184 b	354
17 E	5945	Mon.	Aug. 23 ..	Sept. 6	2184	C	Sat.	April 2 ..	16	2185	385
18	5946	Mon.	Sept. 12 ..	26	2185	B	Tues.	March 21 ..	April 4	2186	353
19 E	5947	Thurs.	Aug. 31 ..	Sept.14	2186	A	Tues.	April 10 ..	24	2187	385

MOLAD 4 1 679. CYCLE 314. DAYS, 6939.

1	5948	Thurs.	Sept. 20 ..	Oct. 4	2187	G	Sat.	March 29 ..	April 12	2188 b	354
2	5949	Mon.	„ 8 ..	22	2188	E	Thurs.	„ 19 ..	April 2	2189	355
3 E	5950	Sat.	Aug. 29 ..	Sept.12	2189	D	Tues.	April 6 ..	20	2190	383
4	5951	Thurs.	Sept. 16 ..	30	2190	C	Sat.	March 26 ..	April 9	2191	354
5	5952	Mon.	„ 5 ..	19	2191	B	Thurs.	„ 15 ..	29	2192 b	355
6 E	5953	Sat.	Aug. 25 ..	Sept. 8	2192	G	Tues.	April 2 ..	16	2193	383
7	5954	Thurs.	Sept. 12 ..	26	2193	F	Sat.	March 22 ..	April 5	2194	354
8 E	5955	Mon.	„ 1 ..	15	2194	E	Sat.	April 11 ..	25	2195	385
9	5956	Mon.	„ 21 ..	Oct. 5	2195	D	Thurs.	March 31 ..	April 14	2196 b	355
10	5957	Sat.	„ 10 ..	24	2196	B	Sun.	„ 19 ..	April 2	2197	353
11 E	5958	Tues.	Aug. 29 ..	Sept.12	2197	A	Sat.	April 7 ..	21	2198	384
12	5959	Mon.	Sept. 17 ..	Oct. 1	2198	G	Thurs.	March 28 ..	April 11	2199	355
13	5960	Sat.	„ 7 ..	21	2199	F	Tues.	„ 17 ..	April 1	2200	355
14 E	5961	Thurs.	Aug. 27 ..	Sept.11	2200	E	Sun.	April 4 ..	19	2201	383
15	5962	Tues.	Sept. 14 ..	29	2201	D	Thurs.	March 24 ..	April 8	2202	354
16	5963	Sat.	„ 3 ..	18	2202	C	Tues.	„ 14 ..	29	2203	355
17 E	5964	Thurs.	Aug. 24 ..	Sept. 8	2203	B	Tues.	April 2 ..	17	2204 b	385
18	5965	Thurs.	Sept. 12 ..	27	2204	G	Sat.	March 22 ..	April 6	2205	354
19 E	5966	Mon.	„ 1 ..	16	2205	F	Thurs.	April 9 ..	24	2206	383

Molad 6 18 194. CYCLE 315. Days, 6939.

1	5967	Sat.	Sept. 19	..	Oct. 4	2206	E	Tues.	March 30	..	April 14	2207	355
2	5968	Thurs.	„ 9	..	24	2207	D	Sat.	„ 18	..	April 2	2208 b	354
3 E	5969	Mon.	Aug. 28	..	Sept.12	2208	B	Thurs.	April 5	..	20	2209	383
4	5970	Sat.	Sept. 15	..	30	2209	A	Tues.	March 26	..	April 10	2210	355
5	5971	Thurs.	„ 5	..	20	2210	G	Sat.	„ 15	..	30	2211	354
6 E	5972	Mon.	Aug. 25	..	Sept. 9	2211	F	Sat.	April 3	..	18	2212 b	385
7	5973	Mon.	Sept. 13	..	28	2212	D	Tues.	March 22	..	April 6	2213	353
8 E	5974	Thurs.	„ 1	..	16	2213	C	Tues.	April 11	..	26	2214	385
9	5975	Thurs.	„ 21	..	Oct. 6	2214	B	Sat.	March 31	..	April 15	2215	354
10	5976	Mon.	„ 10	..	25	2215	A	Thurs.	„ 20	..	April 4	2216 b	355
11 E	5977	Sat.	Aug. 30	..	Sept.14	2216	F	Tues.	April 7	..	22	2217	383
12	5978	Thurs.	Sept. 17	..	Oct. 2	2217	E	Sat.	March 27	..	April 11	2218	354
13	5979	Mon.	„ 6	..	21	2218	D	Thurs.	„ 17	..	April 1	2219	355
14 E	5980	Sat.	Aug. 27	..	Sept.11	2219	C	Tues.	April 3	..	18	2220 b	383
15	5981	Thurs.	Sept. 13	..	28	2220	A	Sun.	March 24	..	April 8	2221	355
16	5982	Tues.	„ 3	..	18	2221	G	Thurs.	„ 13	..	28	2222	354
17 E	5983	Sat.	Aug. 23	..	Sept. 7	2222	F	Thurs.	April 2	..	17	2223	385
18	5984	Sat.	Sept. 12	..	27	2223	E	Sun.	March 20	..	April 4	2224 b	353
19 E	5985	Tues.	Aug. 30	..	Sept.14	2224	C	Sat.	April 8	..	23	2225	384

Molad 2 10 789. CYCLE 316. Days, 6940.

1	5986	Mon.	Sept. 18	..	Oct. 3	2225	B	Thurs.	March 29	..	April 13	2226	353
2	5987	Sat.	„ 8	..	23	2226	A	Tues.	„ 19	..	April 3	2227	355
3 E	5988	Thurs.	Aug. 29	..	Sept.13	2227	G	Sun.	April 5	..	20	2228 b	383
4	5989	Tues.	Sept. 15	..	30	2228	E	Thurs.	March 25	..	April 9	2229	354
5	5990	Sat.	„ 4	..	19	2229	D	Tues.	„ 15	..	30	2230	355
6 E	5991	Thurs.	Aug. 25	..	Sept. 9	2230	C	Tues.	April 4	..	19	2231	385
7	5992	Thurs.	Sept. 14	..	29	2231	B	Sat.	March 23	..	April 7	2232 b	354
8 E	5993	Mon.	„ 2	..	17	2232	G	Thurs.	April 10	..	25	2233	383
9	5994	Sat.	„ 20	..	Oct. 5	2233	F	Tues.	March 31	..	April 15	2234	355
10	5995	Thurs.	„ 10	..	25	2234	E	Sat.	„ 20	..	April 4	2235	354
11 E	5996	Mon.	Aug. 30	..	Sept.14	2235	D	Thurs.	April 6	..	21	2236 b	383
12	5997	Sat.	Sept. 16	..	Oct. 1	2236	B	Tues.	March 27	..	April 11	2237	355
13	5998	Thurs.	„ 6	..	21	2237	A	Sat.	„ 16	..	31	2238	354
14 E	5999	Mon.	Aug. 26	..	Sept.10	2238	G	Sat.	April 5	..	20	2239	385
15	6000	Mon.	Sept. 15	..	30	2239	F	Tues.	March 23	..	April 7	2240 b	353
16	6001	Thurs.	„ 2	..	17	2240	D	Sun.	„ 13	..	28	2241	355
17 E	6002	Tues.	Aug. 23	..	Sept. 7	2241	C	Sat.	April 1	..	16	2242	384
18	6003	Mon.	Sept. 11	..	26	2242	B	Thurs.	March 22	..	April 6	2243	355
19 E	6004	Sat.	„ 1	..	16	2243	A	Tues.	April 8	..	23	2244 b	383

MOLAD 5 3 304. CYCLE 317. DAYS, 6941.

1	6005	Thurs.	Sept. 18 .. Oct. 3	2244	F	Sat.	March 28 .. April 12	2245	354
2	6006	Mon.	„ 7 .. 22	2245	E	Thurs.	„ 18 .. April 2	2246	355
3 E	6007	Sat.	Aug. 28 .. Sept. 12	2246	D	Thurs.	April 7 .. 22	2247	385
4	6008	Sat.	Sept. 17 .. Oct. 2	2247	C	Sun.	March 25 .. April 9	2248 b	353
5	6009	Tues.	„ 4 .. 19	2248	A	Thurs.	„ 14 .. 29	2249	354
6 E	6010	Sat.	Aug. 24 .. Sept. 8	2249	G	Thurs.	April 3 .. 18	2250	385
7	6011	Sat.	Sept. 13 .. 28	2250	F	Tues.	March 24 .. April 8	2251	355
8 E	6012	Thurs.	„ 3 .. 18	2251	E	Sun.	April 10 .. 25	2252 b	383
9	6013	Tues.	„ 20 .. Oct. 5	2252	C	Thurs.	March 30 .. April 14	2253	354
10	6014	Sat.	„ 9 .. 24	2253	B	Tues.	„ 20 .. April 4	2254	355
11 E	6015	Thurs.	Aug. 30 .. Sept. 14	2254	A	Sun.	April 7 .. 22	2255	383
12	6016	Tues.	Sept. 17 .. Oct. 2	2255	G	Thurs.	March 26 .. April 10	2256 b	354
13	6017	Sat.	„ 5 .. 20	2256	E	Tues.	„ 16 .. 31	2257	355
14 E	6018	Thurs.	Aug. 26 .. Sept. 10	2257	D	Tues.	April 5 .. 20	2258	385
15	6019	Thurs.	Sept. 15 .. 30	2258	C	Sat.	March 25 .. April 9	2259	354
16	6020	Mon.	„ 4 .. 19	2259	B	Tues.	„ 12 .. 27	2260 b	353
17 E	6021	Thurs.	Aug. 22 .. Sept. 6	2260	G	Tues.	April 1 .. 16	2261	385
18	6022	Thurs.	Sept. 11 .. 26	2261	F	Sat.	March 21 .. April 5	2262	354
19 E	6023	Mon.	Aug. 31 .. Sept. 15	2262	E	Sat.	April 10 .. 25	2263	385

MOLAD 7 19 899. CYCLE 318. DAYS, 6940.

1	6024	Mon.	Sept. 20 .. Oct. 5	2263	D	Tues.	March 28 .. April 12	2264 b	353
2	6025	Thurs.	„ 7 .. 22	2264	B	Sat.	„ 17 .. April 1	2265	354
3 E	6026	Mon.	Aug. 27 .. Sept. 11	2265	A	Sat.	April 6 .. 21	2266	385
4	6027	Mon.	Sept. 16 .. Oct. 1	2266	G	Thurs.	March 27 .. April 11	2267	355
5	6028	Sat.	„ 6 .. 21	2267	F	Sun.	„ 14 .. 29	2268 b	353
6 E	6029	Tues.	Aug. 24 .. Sept. 8	2268	D	Sat.	April 2 .. 17	2269	384
7	6030	Mon.	Sept. 12 .. 27	2269	C	Thurs.	March 23 .. April 7	2270	355
8 E	6031	Sat.	„ 2 .. 17	2270	B	Tues.	April 10 .. 25	2271	383
9	6032	Thurs.	„ 20 .. Oct. 5	2271	A	Sat.	March 29 .. April 13	2272 b	354
10	6033	Mon.	„ 8 .. 23	2272	F	Thurs.	„ 19 .. April 3	2273	355
11 E	6034	Sat.	Aug. 29 .. Sept. 13	2273	E	Thurs.	April 8 .. 23	2274	385
12	6035	Sat.	Sept. 18 .. Oct. 3	2274	D	Sun.	March 27 .. April 11	2275	353
13	6036	Tues.	„ 6 .. 21	2275	C	Thurs.	„ 15 .. 30	2276 b	354
14 E	6037	Sat.	Aug. 25 .. Sept. 9	2276	A	Thurs.	April 4 .. 19	2277	385
15	6038	Sat.	Sept. 14 .. 29	2277	G	Tues.	March 25 .. April 9	2278	355
16	6039	Thurs.	„ 4 .. 19	2278	F	Sat.	„ 14 .. 29	2279	354
17 E	6040	Mon.	Aug. 24 .. Sept. 8	2279	E	Thurs.	„ 31 .. April 15	2280 b	383
18	6041	Sat.	Sept. 10 .. 25	2280	C	Tues.	„ 21 .. April 5	2281	355
19 E	6042	Thurs.	Aug. 31 .. Sept. 15	2281	B	Tues.	April 10 .. 25	2282	385

MOLAD 3 12 414. CYCLE 319. DAYS, 6939.

1	6043	Thurs.	Sept. 20	..	Oct. 5	2282	A	Sat.	March 30	..	April 14	2283	354
2	6044	Mon.	„ 9	..	24	2283	G	Tues.	„ 17	..	April 1	2284 b	353
3 E	6045	Thurs.	Aug. 27	..	Sept.11	2284	E	Tues.	April 6	..	21	2285	385
4	6046	Thurs.	Sept. 16	..	Oct. 1	2285	D	Sat.	March 26	..	April 10	2286	354
5	6047	Mon.	„ 5	..	20	2286	C	Thurs.	„ 16	..	31	2287	355
6 E	6048	Sat.	Aug. 26	..	Sept.10	2287	B	Tues.	April 2	..	17	2288 b	383
7	6049	Thurs.	Sept. 12	..	27	2288	G	Sat.	March 22	..	April 6	2289	354
8 E	6050	Mon.	„ 1	..	16	2289	F	Sat.	April 11	..	26	2290	385
9	6051	Mon.	„ 21	..	Oct. 6	2290	E	Tues.	March 30	..	14	2291	353
10	6052	Thurs.	„ 9	..	24	2291	D	Sun.	„ 19	..	April 3	2292 b	355
11 E	6053	Tues.	Aug. 29	..	Sept.13	2292	B	Sat.	April 7	..	22	2293	384
12	6054	Mon.	Sept. 17	..	Oct. 2	2293	A	Thurs.	March 28	..	April 12	2294	355
13	6055	Sat.	„ 7	..	22	2294	G	Sun.	„ 16	..	31	2295	353
14 E	6056	Tues.	Aug. 26	..	Sept.10	2295	F	Sat.	April 3	..	18	2296 b	384
15	6057	Mon.	Sept. 13	..	28	2296	D	Thurs.	March 24	..	April 8	2297	355
16	6058	Sat.	„ 3	..	18	2297	C	Tues.	„ 14	..	29	2298	355
17 E	6059	Thurs.	Aug. 24	..	Sept. 8	2298	B	Sun.	April 1	..	16	2299	383
18	6060	Tues.	Sept. 11	..	26	2299	A	Thurs.	March 20	..	April 5	2300	354
19 E	6061	Sat.	Aug. 30	..	Sept.15	2300	G	Thurs.	April 9	..	25	2301	385

MOLAD 6 4 1009. CYCLE 320. DAYS, 6939.

1	6062	Sat.	Sept. 19	..	Oct. 5	2301	F	Tues.	March 30	..	April 15	2302	355
2	6063	Thurs.	„ 9	..	25	2302	E	Sat.	„ 19	..	April 4	2303	354
3 E	6064	Mon.	Aug. 29	..	Sept.14	2303	D	Thurs.	April 5	..	21	2304 b	383
4	6065	Sat.	Sept. 15	..	Oct. 1	2304	B	Tues.	March 26	..	April 11	2305	355
5	6066	Thurs.	„ 5	..	21	2305	A	Sat.	„ 15	..	31	2306	354
6 E	6067	Mon.	Aug. 25	..	Sept.10	2306	G	Thurs.	April 2	..	18	2307	383
7	6068	Sat.	Sept. 12	..	28	2307	F	Tues.	March 22	..	April 7	2308 b	355
8 E	6069	Thurs.	„ 1	..	17	2308	D	Tues.	April 11	..	27	2309	385
9	6070	Thurs.	„ 21	..	Oct. 7	2309	C	Sat.	March 31	..	April 16	2310	354
10	6071	Mon.	„ 10	..	26	2310	B	Tues.	„ 19	..	April 4	2311	353
11 E	6072	Thurs.	Aug. 29	..	Sept.14	2311	A	Tues.	April 7	..	23	2312 b	385
12	6073	Thurs.	Sept. 17	..	Oct. 3	2312	F	Sat.	March 27	..	April 12	2313	354
13	6074	Mon.	„ 6	..	22	2313	E	Thurs.	„ 17	..	April 2	2314	355
14 E	6075	Sat.	Aug. 27	..	Sept.12	2314	D	Tues.	April 4	..	20	2315	383
15	6076	Thurs.	Sept. 14	..	30	2315	C	Sat.	March 23	..	April 8	2316 b	354
16	6077	Mon.	„ 2	..	18	2316	A	Thurs.	„ 13	..	29	2317	355
17 E	6078	Sat.	Aug. 23	..	Sept. 8	2317	G	Tues.	„ 31	..	April 16	2318	383
18	6079	Thurs.	Sept. 10	..	26	2318	F	Sun.	„ 21	..	April 6	2319	355
19 E	6080	Tues.	Aug. 31	..	Sept.16	2319	E	Sat.	April 8	..	24	2320 b	384

MOLAD 1 21 524. CYCLE 321. DAYS, 6940.

1	6081	Mon.	Sept. 18	.. Oct. 4	2320	C	Thurs.	March 29	.. April 14	2321	355
2	6082	Sat.	„ 8	.. 24	2321	B	Sun.	„ 17	.. April 2	2322	353
3 E	6083	Tues.	Aug. 27	.. Sept.12	2322	A	Sat.	April 5	.. 21	2323	384
4	6084	Mon.	Sept. 15	.. Oct. 1	2323	G	Thurs.	March 25	.. April 10	2324 b	355
5	6085	Sat.	„ 4	.. 20	2324	E	Tues.	„ 15	.. 31	2325	355
6 E	6086	Thurs.	Aug. 25	.. Sept.10	2325	D	Sun.	April 2	.. 18	2326	383
7	6087	Tues.	Sept. 12	.. 28	2326	C	Thurs.	March 22	.. April 7	2327	354
8 E	6088	Sat.	„ 1	.. 17	2327	B	Thurs.	April 10	.. 26	2328 b	385
9	6089	Sat.	„ 20	.. Oct. 6	2328	G	Tues.	March 31	.. April 16	2329	355
10	6090	Thurs.	„ 10	.. 26	2329	F	Sat.	„ 20	.. April 5	2330	354
11 E	6091	Mon.	Aug. 30	.. Sept.15	2330	E	Thurs.	April 7	.. 23	2331	383
12	6092	Sat.	Sept. 17	.. Oct. 3	2331	D	Tues.	March 27	.. April 12	2332 b	355
13	6093	Thurs.	„ 6	.. 22	2332	B	Sat.	„ 16	.. April 1	2333	354
14 E	6094	Mon.	Aug. 26	.. Sept.11	2333	A	Thurs.	April 3	.. 19	2334	383
15	6095	Sat.	Sept. 13	.. 29	2334	G	Tues.	March 24	.. April 9	2335	355
16	6096	Thurs.	„ 3	.. 19	2335	F	Sat.	„ 12	.. 28	2336 b	354
17 E	6097	Mon.	Aug. 22	.. Sept. 7	2336	D	Sat.	April 1	.. 17	2337	385
18	6098	Mon.	Sept. 11	.. 27	2337	C	Tues.	March 20	.. April 5	2338	353
19 E	6099	Thurs.	Aug. 30	.. Sept.15	2338	B	Tues.	April 9	.. 25	2339	385

MOLAD 4 14 39. CYCLE 322. DAYS, 6939.

1	6100	Thurs.	Sept. 19	.. Oct. 5	2339	A	Sat.	March 28	.. April 13	2340 b	354
2	6101	Mon.	„ 7	.. 23	2340	F	Thurs.	„ 18	.. April 3	2341	355
3 E	6102	Sat.	Aug. 28	.. Sept.13	2341	E	Tues.	April 5	.. 21	2342	383
4	6103	Thurs.	Sept. 15	.. Oct. 1	2342	D	Sat.	March 25	.. April 10	2343	354
5	6104	Mon.	„ 4	.. 20	2343	C	Thurs.	„ 14	.. 30	2344 b	355
6 E	6105	Sat.	Aug. 24	.. Sept. 9	2344	A	Thurs.	April 3	.. 19	2345	385
7	6106	Sat.	Sept. 13	.. 29	2345	G	Sun.	March 22	.. April 7	2346	353
8 E	6107	Tues.	„ 1	.. 17	2346	F	Sat.	April 10	.. 26	2347	384
9	6108	Mon.	„ 20	.. Oct. 6	2347	E	Thurs.	March 30	.. April 15	2348 b	355
10	6109	Sat.	„ 9	.. 25	2348	C	Tues.	„ 20	.. April 5	2349	355
11 E	6110	Thurs.	Aug. 30	.. Sept.15	2349	B	Sun.	April 7	.. 23	2350	383
12	6111	Tues.	Sept. 17	.. Oct. 3	2350	A	Thurs.	March 27	.. April 12	2351	354
13	6112	Sat.	„ 6	.. 22	2351	G	Tues.	„ 16	.. April 1	2352 b	355
14 E	6113	Thurs.	Aug. 26	.. Sept.11	2352	E	Sun.	April 3	.. 19	2353	383
15	6114	Tues.	Sept. 13	.. 29	2353	D	Thurs.	March 23	.. April 8	2354	354
16	6115	Sat.	„ 2	.. 18	2354	C	Tues.	„ 13	.. 29	2355	355
17 E	6116	Thurs.	Aug. 23	.. Sept. 8	2355	B	Tues.	April 1	.. 17	2356 b	385
18	6117	Thurs.	Sept. 11	.. 27	2356	G	Sat.	March 21	.. April 6	2357	354
19 E	6118	Mon.	Aug. 31	.. Sept.16	2357	F	Thurs.	April 8	.. 24	2358	383

MOLAD 7 6 634. CYCLE 323. DAYS, 6940.

1	6119	Sat.	Sept. 18 ..	Oct. 4	2358	E	Tues.	March 29 ..	April 14	2359	355
2	6120	Thurs.	„ 8 ..	24	2359	D	Sat.	„ 17 ..	April 2	2360 b	354
3 E	6121	Mon.	Aug. 27 ..	Sept.12	2360	B	Sat.	April 6 ..	22	2361	385
4	6122	Mon.	Sept. 16 ..	Oct. 2	2361	A	Tues.	March 25 ..	April 10	2362	353
5	6123	Thurs.	„ 4 ..	20	2362	G	Sat.	„ 14 ..	30	2363	354
6 E	6124	Mon.	Aug. 24 ..	Sept. 9	2363	F	Sat.	April 2 ..	18	2364 b	385
7	6125	Mon.	Sept. 12 ..	28	2364	D	Thurs.	March 23 ..	April 8	2365	355
8 E	6126	Sat.	„ 2 ..	18	2365	C	Tues.	April 10 ..	26	2366	383
9	6127	Thurs.	Sept. 20 ..	Oct. 6	2366	B	Sat.	March 30 ..	April 15	2367	354
10	6128	Mon.	„ 9 ..	25	2367	A	Thurs.	„ 19 ..	April 4	2368 b	355
11 E	6129	Sat.	Aug. 29 ..	Sept.14	2368	F	Tues.	April 6 ..	22	2369	383
12	6130	Thurs.	Sept. 16 ..	Oct. 2	2369	E	Sun.	March 27 ..	April 12	2370	355
13	6131	Tues.	„ 6 ..	22	2370	D	Thurs.	„ 16 ..	April 1	2371	354
14 E	6132	Sat.	Aug. 26 ..	Sept.11	2371	C	Thurs.	April 4 ..	20	2372 b	385
15	6133	Sat.	Sept. 14 ..	30	2372	A	Tues.	March 25 ..	April 10	2373	355
16	6134	Thurs.	„ 4 ..	20	2373	G	Sat.	„ 14 ..	30	2374	354
17 E	6135	Mon.	Aug. 24 ..	Sept. 9	2374	F	Thurs.	April 1 ..	17	2375	383
18	6136	Sat.	Sept. 11 ..	27	2375	E	Tues.	March 21 ..	April 6	2376 b	355
19 E	6137	Thurs.	Aug. 31 ..	Sept.16	2376	C	Sun.	April 8 ..	24	2377	383

MOLAD 2 23 149. CYCLE 324. DAYS, 6939.

1	6138	Tues.	Sept. 18 ..	Oct. 4	2377	B	Thurs.	March 28 ..	April 13	2378	354
2	6139	Sat.	„ 7 ..	23	2378	A	Tues.	„ 18 ..	April 3	2379	355
3 E	6140	Thurs.	Aug. 28 ..	Sept.13	2379	G	Tues.	April 6 ..	22	2380 b	385
4	6141	Thurs.	Sept. 16 ..	Oct. 2	2380	E	Sat.	March 26 ..	April 11	2381	354
5	6142	Mon.	„ 5 ..	21	2381	D	Tues.	„ 14 ..	30	2382	353
6 E	6143	Thurs.	Aug. 24 ..	Sept. 9	2382	C	Tues.	April 3 ..	19	2383	385
7	6144	Thurs.	Sept. 13 ..	29	2383	B	Sat.	March 22 ..	April 7	2384 b	354
8 E	6145	Mon.	„ 1 ..	17	2384	G	Thurs.	April 9 ..	25	2385	383
9	6146	Sat.	„ 19 ..	Oct. 5	2385	F	Tues.	March 30 ..	April 15	2386	355
10	6147	Thurs.	„ 9 ..	25	2386	E	Sat.	„ 19 ..	April 4	2387	354
11 E	6148	Mon.	Aug. 29 ..	Sept.14	2387	D	Sat.	April 7 ..	23	2388 b	385
12	6149	Mon.	Sept. 17 ..	Oct. 3	2388	B	Tues.	March 26 ..	April 11	2389	353
13	6150	Thurs.	„ 5 ..	21	2389	A	Sun.	„ 16 ..	April 1	2390	355
14 E	6151	Tues.	Aug. 26 ..	Sept.11	2390	G	Sat.	April 4 ..	20	2391	384
15	6152	Mon.	Sept. 14 ..	30	2391	F	Thurs.	March 24 ..	April 9	2392 b	355
16	6153	Sat.	„ 3 ..	19	2392	D	Sun.	„ 12 ..	28	2393	353
17 E	6154	Tues.	Aug. 22 ..	Sept. 7	2393	C	Sat.	„ 31 ..	April 16	2394	384
18	6155	Mon.	Sept. 10 ..	26	2394	B	Thurs.	„ 21 ..	April 6	2395	355
19 E	6156	Sat.	Aug. 31 ..	Sept.16	2395	A	Tues.	April 7 ..	23	2396 b	383

MOLAD 5 15 744. CYCLE 325. DAYS, 6941.

1	6157	Thurs.	Sept. 17 ..	Oct. 3	2396	F	Sun.	March 28 ..	April 13	2397	355
2	6158	Tues.	„ 7 ..	23	2397	E	Thurs.	„ 17 ..	April 2	2398	354
3 E	6159	Sat.	Aug. 27 ..	Sept.12	2398	D	Thurs.	April 6 ..	22	2399	385
4	6160	Sat.	Sept. 16 ..	Oct. 2	2399	C	Tues.	March 26 ..	April 11	2400 b	355
5	6161	Thurs.	„ 5 ..	21	2400	A	Sat.	„ 15 ..	31	2401	354
6 E	6162	Mon.	Aug. 25 ..	Sept.10	2401	G	Thurs.	April 2 ..	18	2402	383
7	6163	Sat.	Sept. 12 ..	28	2402	F	Tues.	March 23 ..	April 8	2403	355
8 E	6164	Thurs.	„ 2 ..	18	2403	E	Sun.	April 9 ..	25	2404 b	383
9	6165	Tues.	„ 19 ..	Oct. 5	2404	C	Thurs.	March 29 ..	April 14	2405	354
10	6166	Sat.	„ 8 ..	24	2405	B	Tues.	„ 19 ..	April 4	2406	355
11 E	6167	Thurs.	Aug. 29 ..	Sept.14	2406	A	Tues.	April 8 ..	24	2407	385
12	6168	Thurs.	Sept. 18 ..	Oct. 4	2407	G	Sat.	March 27 ..	April 12	2408 b	354
13	6169	Mon.	„ 6 ..	22	2408	E	Tues.	„ 15 ..	31	2409	353
14 E	6170	Thurs.	Aug. 25 ..	Sept.10	2409	D	Tues.	April 4 ..	20	2410	385
15	6171	Thurs.	Sept. 14 ..	30	2410	C	Sat.	March 24 ..	April 9	2411	354
16	6172	Mon.	„ 3 ..	19	2411	B	Thurs.	„ 13 ..	29	2412 b	355
17 E	6173	Sat.	Aug. 23 ..	Sept. 8	2412	G	Tues.	„ 31 ..	April 16	2413	383
18	6174	Thurs.	Sept. 10 ..	26	2413	F	Sat.	„ 20 ..	April 5	2414	354
19 E	6175	Mon.	Aug. 30 ..	Sept.15	2414	E	Sat.	April 9 ..	25	2415	385

MOLAD 1 8 259. CYCLE 326. DAYS, 6940.

1	6176	Mon.	Sept. 19 ..	Oct. 5	2415	D	Tues.	March 27 ..	April 12	2416 b	353
2	6177	Thurs.	„ 6 ..	22	2416	B	Sun.	„ 17 ..	April 2	2417	355
3 E	6178	Tues.	Aug. 27 ..	Sept.19	2417	A	Sat.	April 5 ..	21	2418	384
4	6179	Mon.	Sept. 15 ..	Oct. 1	2418	G	Thurs.	March 26 ..	April 11	2419	355
5	6180	Sat.	„ 5 ..	21	2419	F	Sun.	„ 13 ..	29	2420 b	353
6 E	6181	Tues.	Aug. 23 ..	Sept. 8	2420	D	Sat.	April 1 ..	17	2421	384
7	6182	Mon.	Sept. 11 ..	27	2421	C	Thurs.	March 22 ..	April 7	2422	355
8 E	6183	Sat.	„ 1 ..	17	2422	B	Thurs.	April 11 ..	27	2423	385
9	6184	Sat.	Sept. 21 ..	Oct. 7	2423	A	Sun.	March 29 ..	April 14	2424 b	353
10	6185	Tues.	„ 8 ..	24	2424	F	Thurs.	„ 18 ..	April 3	2425	354
11 E	6186	Sat.	Aug. 28 ..	Sept.13	2425	E	Thurs.	April 7 ..	23	2426	385
12	6187	Sat.	Sept. 17 ..	Oct. 3	2426	D	Tues.	March 28 ..	April 13	2427	355
13	6188	Thurs.	„ 7 ..	23	2427	C	Sat.	„ 16 ..	April 1	2428 b	354
14 E	6189	Mon.	Aug. 26 ..	Sept.11	2428	A	Thurs.	April 3 ..	19	2429	383
15	6190	Sat.	Sept. 13 ..	29	2429	G	Tues.	March 24 ..	April 9	2430	355
16	6191	Thurs.	„ 3 ..	19	2430	F	Sat.	„ 13 ..	29	2431	354
17 E	6192	Mon.	Aug. 23 ..	Sept. 8	2431	E	Sat.	April 1 ..	17	2432 b	385
18	6193	Mon.	Sept. 11 ..	27	2432	C	Tues.	March 20 ..	April 5	2433	353
19 E	6194	Thurs.	Aug. 30 ..	Sept.15	2433	B	Tues.	April 9 ..	25	2434	385

MOLAD 4 0 854. CYCLE 327. DAYS, 6939.

1	6195	Thurs.	Sept. 19 .. Oct. 5	2434	A	Sat.	March 29 .. April 14	2435	354
2	6196	Mon.	„ 8 .. 24	2435	G	Thurs.	„ 18 .. April 3	2436 b	355
3E	6197	Sat.	Aug. 28 .. Sept. 13	2436	E	Tues.	April 5 .. 21	2437	383
4	6198	Thurs.	Sept. 15 .. Oct. 1	2437	D	Sat.	March 25 .. April 10	2438	354
5	6199	Mon.	„ 4 .. 20	2438	C	Thurs.	„ 15 .. 31	2439	355
6E	6200	Sat.	Aug. 25 .. Sept. 10	2439	B	Tues.	April 1 .. 17	2440 b	383
7	6201	Thurs.	Sept. 11 .. 27	2440	G	Sat.	March 21 .. April 6	2441	354
8E	6202	Mon.	Aug. 31 .. Sept. 16	2441	F	Sat.	April 10 .. 26	2442	385
9	6203	Mon.	Sept. 20 .. Oct. 6	2442	E	Thurs.	March 31 .. April 16	2443	355
10	6204	Sat.	„ 10 .. 26	2443	D	Sun.	„ 18 .. April 3	2444 b	353
11E	6205	Tues.	Aug. 28 .. Sept. 13	2444	B	Sat.	April 6 .. 22	2445	384
12	6206	Mon.	Sept. 16 .. Oct. 2	2445	A	Thurs.	March 27 .. April 12	2446	355
13	6207	Sat.	„ 6 .. 22	2446	G	Tues.	„ 17 .. April 2	2447	355
14E	6208	Thurs.	Aug. 27 .. Sept. 12	2447	F	Sun.	April 3 .. 19	2448 b	383
15	6209	Tues.	Sept. 13 .. 29	2448	D	Thurs.	March 23 .. April 8	2449	354
16	6210	Sat.	„ 2 .. 18	2449	C	Tues.	„ 13 .. 29	2450	355
17E	6211	Thurs.	Aug. 23 .. Sept. 8	2450	B	Tues.	April 2 .. 18	2451	385
18	6212	Thurs.	Sept. 12 .. 28	2451	A	Sat.	March 21 .. April 6	2452 b	354
19E	6213	Mon.	Aug. 31 .. Sept. 16	2452	F	Thurs.	April 8 .. 24	2453	383

MOLAD 6 17 369. CYCLE 328. DAYS, 6939.

1	6214	Sat.	Sept. 18 .. Oct. 4	2453	E	Tues.	March 29 .. April 14	2454	355
2	6215	Thurs.	„ 8 .. 24	2454	D	Sat.	„ 18 .. April 3	2455	354
3E	6216	Mon.	Aug. 28 .. Sept. 13	2455	C	Thurs.	April 4 .. 20	2456 b	383
4	6217	Sat.	Sept. 14 .. 30	2456	A	Tues.	March 25 .. April 10	2457	355
5	6218	Thurs.	„ 4 .. 20	2457	G	Sat.	„ 14 .. 30	2458	354
6E	6219	Mon.	Aug. 24 .. Sept. 9	2458	F	Sat.	April 3 .. 19	2459	385
7	6220	Mon.	Sept. 13 .. 29	2459	E	Tues.	March 21 .. April 6	2460 b	353
8E	6221	Thurs.	Aug. 31 .. Sept. 16	2460	C	Tues.	April 10 .. 26	2461	385
9	6222	Thurs.	Sept. 20 .. Oct. 6	2461	B	Sat.	March 30 .. April 15	2462	354
10	6223	Mon.	„ 9 .. 25	2462	A	Thurs.	„ 20 .. April 5	2463	355
11E	6224	Sat.	Aug. 30 .. Sept. 15	2463	G	Tues.	April 6 .. 22	2464 b	383
12	6225	Thurs.	Sept. 16 .. Oct. 2	2464	E	Sat.	March 26 .. April 11	2465	354
13	6226	Mon.	„ 5 .. 21	2465	D	Thurs.	„ 16 .. April 1	2466	355
14E	6227	Sat.	Aug. 26 .. Sept. 11	2466	C	Tues.	April 3 .. 19	2467	383
15	6228	Thurs.	Sept. 13 .. 29	2467	B	Sun.	March 23 .. April 8	2468 b	355
16	6229	Tues.	„ 2 .. 18	2468	G	Thurs.	„ 12 .. 28	2469	354
17E	6230	Sat.	Aug. 22 .. Sept. 7	2469	F	Thurs.	April 1 .. 17	2470	385
18	6231	Sat.	Sept. 11 .. 27	2470	E	Sun.	March 20 .. April 5	2471	353
19E	6232	Tues.	Aug. 30 .. Sept. 15	2471	D	Sat.	April 7 .. 23	2472 b	384

MOLAD 2 9 964. CYCLE 329. DAYS, 6940.

1	6233	Mon.	Sept. 17	.. Oct. 3	2472	B	Thurs.	March 28	.. April 13	2473	355
2	6234	Sat.	„ 7	.. 23	2473	A	Tues.	„ 18	.. April 3	2474	355
3 E	6235	Thurs.	Aug. 28	.. Sept.13	2474	G	Sun.	April 5	.. 21	2475	383
4	6236	Tues.	Sept. 15	.. Oct. 1	2475	F	Thurs.	March 24	.. April 9	2476 b	354
5	6237	Sat.	„ 3	.. 19	2476	D	Tues.	„ 14	.. 30	2477	355
6 E	6238	Thurs.	Aug. 24	.. Sept. 9	2477	C	Tues.	April 3	.. 19	2478	385
7	6239	Thurs.	Sept. 13	.. 29	2478	B	Sat.	March 23	.. April 8	2479	354
8 E	6240	Mon.	„ 2	.. 18	2479	A	Thurs.	April 9	.. 25	2480 b	383
9	6241	Sat.	„ 19	.. Oct. 5	2480	F	Tues.	March 30	.. April 15	2481	355
10	6242	Thurs.	„ 9	.. 25	2481	E	Sat.	„ 19	.. April 4	2482	354
11 E	6243	Mon.	Aug. 29	.. Sept.14	2482	D	Thurs.	April 6	.. 22	2483	383
12	6244	Sat.	Sept. 16	.. Oct. 2	2483	C	Tues.	March 26	.. April 11	2484 b	355
13	6245	Thurs.	„ 5	.. 21	2484	A	Sat.	„ 15	.. 31	2485	354
14 E	6246	Mon.	Aug. 25	.. Sept.10	2485	G	Sat.	April 4	.. 20	2486	385
15	6247	Mon.	Sept. 14	.. 30	2486	F	Tues.	March 23	.. April 8	2487	353
16	6248	Thurs.	„ 2	.. 18	2487	E	Sun.	„ 12	.. 28	2488 b	355
17 E	6249	Tues.	Aug. 22	.. Sept. 7	2488	C	Sat.	„ 31	.. April 16	2489	384
18	6250	Mon.	Sept. 10	.. 26	2489	B	Thurs.	„ 21	.. April 6	2490	355
19 E	6251	Sat.	Aug. 31	.. Sept.16	2490	A	Tues.	April 8	.. 24	2491	383

MOLAD 5 2 479. CYCLE 330. DAYS, 6941.

1	6252	Thurs.	Sept. 18	.. Oct. 4	2491	G	Sat.	March 27	.. April 12	2492 b	354
2	6253	Mon.	„ 6	.. 22	2492	E	Thurs.	„ 17	.. April 2	2493	355
3 E	6254	Sat.	Aug. 27	.. Sept.12	2493	D	Tues.	April 4	.. 20	2494	383
4	6255	Thurs.	Sept. 14	.. 30	2494	C	Sun.	March 25	.. April 10	2495	355
5	6256	Tues.	„ 4	.. 20	2495	B	Thurs.	„ 13	.. 29	2496 b	354
6 E	6257	Sat.	Aug. 23	.. Sept. 8	2496	G	Thurs.	April 2	.. 18	2497	385
7	6258	Sat.	Sept. 12	.. 28	2497	F	Sun.	March 21	.. April 6	2498	353
8 E	6259	Tues.	Aug. 31	.. Sept.16	2498	E	Sat.	April 9	.. 25	2499	384
9	6260	Mon.	Sept. 19	.. Oct. 5	2499	D	Thurs.	March 29	.. April 15	2500	355
10	6261	Sat.	„ 8	.. 25	2500	C	Tues.	„ 19	.. April 5	2501	355
11 E	6262	Thurs.	Aug. 29	.. Sept.15	2501	B	Sun.	April 6	.. 23	2502	383
12	6263	Tues.	Sept. 16	.. Oct. 3	2502	A	Thurs.	March 26	.. April 12	2503	354
13	6264	Sat.	„ 5	.. 22	2503	G	Tues.	„ 15	.. April 1	2504 b	355
14 E	6265	Thurs.	Aug. 25	.. Sept.11	2504	E	Tues.	April 4	.. 21	2505	385
15	6266	Thurs.	Sept. 14	.. Oct. 1	2505	D	Sat.	March 24	.. April 10	2506	354
16	6267	Mon.	„ 3	.. 20	2506	C	Tues.	„ 12	.. 29	2507	353
17 E	6268	Thurs.	Aug. 22	.. Sept. 8	2507	B	Tues.	„ 31	.. April 17	2508 b	385
18	6269	Thurs.	Sept. 10	.. 27	2508	G	Sat.	„ 20	.. April 6	2509	354
19 E	6270	Mon.	Aug. 30	.. Sept.16	2509	F	Sat.	April 9	.. 26	2510	385

MOLAD 7 18 1074. CYCLE 331. DAYS, 6940.

1	6271	Mon.	Sept. 19	.. Oct. 6	2510	E	Tues.	March 28	.. April 14	2511	353
2	6272	Thurs.	„ 7	.. 24	2511	D	Sat.	„ 16	.. April 2	2512 b	354
3 E	6273	Mon.	Aug. 26	.. Sept.12	2512	B	Sat.	April 5	.. 22	2513	385
4	6274	Mon.	Sept. 15	.. Oct. 2	2513	A	Thurs.	March 26	.. April 12	2514	355
5	6275	Sat.	„ 5	.. 22	2514	G	Sun.	„ 14	.. 31	2515	353
6 E	6276	Tues.	Aug. 24	.. Sept.10	2515	F	Sat.	April 1	.. 18	2516 b	384
7	6277	Mon.	Sept. 11	.. 28	2516	D	Thurs.	March 22	.. April 8	2517	355
8 E	6278	Sat.	„ 1	.. 18	2517	C	Tues.	April 9	.. 26	2518	383
9	6279	Thurs.	„ 19	.. Oct. 6	2518	B	Sat.	March 29	.. April 15	2519	354
10	6280	Mon.	„ 8	.. 25	2519	A	Thurs.	„ 15	.. April 4	2520 b	355
11 E	6281	Sat.	Aug. 28	.. Sept.14	2520	F	Thurs.	April 7	.. 24	2521	385
12	6282	Sat.	Sept. 17	.. Oct. 4	2521	E	Sun.	March 26	.. April 12	2522	353
13	6283	Tues.	„ 5	.. 22	2522	D	Thurs.	„ 15	.. April 1	2523	354
14 E	6284	Sat.	Aug. 25	.. Sept.11	2523	C	Thurs.	April 3	.. 20	2524 b	385
15	6285	Sat.	Sept. 13	.. 30	2524	A	Tues.	March 24	.. April 10	2525	355
16	6286	Thurs.	„ 3	.. 20	2525	G	Sat.	„ 13	.. 30	2526	354
17 E	6287	Mon.	Aug. 23	.. Sept. 9	2526	F	Thurs.	„ 31	.. April 17	2527	383
18	6288	Sat.	Sept. 10	.. 27	2527	E	Tues.	„ 20	.. April 6	2528 b	355
19 E	6289	Thurs.	Aug. 30	.. Sept.16	2528	C	Tues.	April 9	.. 26	2529	385

MOLAD 3 11 589. CYCLE 332. DAYS, 6939.

1	6290	Thurs.	Sept. 19	.. Oct. 6	2529	B	Sat.	March 29	.. April 15	2530	354
2	6291	Mon.	„ 8	.. 25	2530	A	Tues.	„ 17	.. April 3	2531	353
3 E	6292	Thurs.	Aug. 27	.. Sept.13	2531	G	Tues.	April 5	.. 22	2532 b	385
4	6293	Thurs.	Sept. 15	.. Oct. 2	2532	E	Sat.	March 25	.. April 11	2533	354
5	6294	Mon.	„ 4	.. 21	2533	D	Thurs.	„ 18	.. April 1	2534	355
6 E	6295	Sat.	Aug. 25	.. Sept.11	2534	C	Tues.	April 2	.. 19	2535	383
7	6296	Thurs.	Sept. 12	.. 29	2535	B	Sat.	March 21	.. April 7	2536 b	354
8 E	6297	Mon.	Aug. 31	.. Sept.17	2536	G	Sat.	April 10	.. 27	2537	385
9	6298	Mon.	Sept. 20	.. Oct. 7	2537	F	Tues.	March 29	.. April 15	2538	353
10	6299	Thurs.	„ 8	.. 25	2538	E	Sat.	„ 18	.. April 4	2539	354
11 E	6300	Mon.	Aug. 28	.. Sept.14	2539	D	Sat.	April 6	.. 23	2540 b	385
12	6301	Mon.	Sept. 16	.. Oct. 3	2540	B	Thurs.	March 27	.. April 13	2541	355
13	6302	Sat.	„ 6	.. 23	2541	A	Sun.	„ 15	.. April 1	2542	353
14 E	6303	Tues.	Aug. 25	.. Sept.11	2542	G	Sat.	April 3	.. 20	2543	384
15	6304	Mon.	Sept. 13	.. 30	2543	F	Thurs.	March 23	.. April 9	2544 b	355
16	6305	Sat.	„ 2	.. 19	2544	D	Tues.	„ 13	.. 30	2545	355
17 E	6306	Thurs.	Aug. 23	.. Sept. 9	2545	C	Sun.	„ 31	.. April 17	2546	383
18	6307	Tues.	Sept. 10	.. 27	2546	B	Thurs.	„ 20	.. April 6	2547	354
19 E	6308	Sat.	Aug. 30	.. Sept.16	2547	A	Thurs.	April 8	.. 25	2548 b	385

MOLAD 6 4 104. CYCLE 333. DAYS, 6939.

1	6309	Sat.	Sept. 18 ..	Oct. 5	2548	F	Tues.	March 20 ..	April 15	2549		355
2	6310	Thurs.	„ 8 ..	25	2549	E	Sat.	„ 18 ..	April 4	2550		354
3 E	6311	Mon.	Aug. 28 ..	Sept.14	2550	D	Thurs.	April 5 ..	22	2551		383
4	6312	Sat.	Sept. 15 ..	Oct. 2	2551	C	Tues.	March 25 ..	April 11	2552	b	355
5	6313	Thurs.	„ 4 ..	21	2552	A	Sat.	„ 14 ..	31	2553		354
6 E	6314	Mon.	Aug. 24 ..	Sept.10	2553	G	Thurs.	April 1 ..	18	2554		383
7	6315	Sat.	Sept. 11 ..	28	2554	F	Tues.	March 22 ..	April 8	2555		355
8 E	6316	Thurs.	„ 1 ..	18	2555	E	Tues.	April 10 ..	27	2556	b	385
9	6317	Thurs.	„ 20 ..	Oct. 7	2556	C	Sat.	March 30 ..	April 16	2557		354
10	6318	Mon.	„ 9 ..	26	2557	B	Tues.	„ 18 ..	April 4	2558		353
11 E	6319	Thurs.	Aug. 28 ..	Sept.14	2558	A	Tues.	April 7 ..	24	2559		385
12	6320	Thurs.	Sept. 17 ..	Oct. 4	2559	G	Sat.	March 26 ..	April 12	2560	b	354
13	6321	Mon.	„ 5 ..	22	2560	E	Thurs.	„ 16 ..	April 2	2561		355
14 E	6322	Sat.	Aug. 26 ..	Sept.12	2561	D	Tues.	April 3 ..	20	2562		383
15	6323	Thurs.	Sept. 13 ..	30	2562	C	Sat.	March 23 ..	April 9	2563		354
16	6324	Mon.	„ 2 ..	19	2563	B	Thurs.	„ 12 ..	29	2564	b	355
17 E	6325	Sat.	Aug. 22 ..	Sept. 8	2564	G	Tues.	„ 30 ..	April 16	2565		383
18	6326	Thurs.	Sept. 9 ..	26	2565	F	Sun.	„ 20 ..	April 6	2566		355
19 E	6327	Tues.	Aug. 30 ..	Sept.16	2566	E	Sat.	April 8 ..	25	2567		384

MOLAD 1 20 699. CYCLE 334. DAYS, 6940.

1	6328	Mon.	Sept. 18 ..	Oct. 5	2567	D	Thurs.	March 28 ..	April 14	2568	b	355
2	6329	Sat.	„ 7 ..	24	2568	B	Sun.	„ 16 ..	April 2	2569		353
3 E	6330	Tues.	Aug. 26 ..	Sept.12	2569	A	Sat.	April 4 ..	21	2570		384
4	6331	Mon.	Sept. 14 ..	Oct. 1	2570	G	Thurs.	March 25 ..	April 11	2571		355
5	6332	Sat.	„ 4 ..	21	2571	F	Tues.	„ 14 ..	31	2572	b	355
6 E	6333	Thurs.	Aug. 24 ..	Sept.10	2572	D	Sun.	April 1 ..	18	2573		383
7	6334	Tues.	Sept. 11 ..	28	2573	C	Thurs.	March 21 ..	April 7	2574		354
8 E	6335	Sat.	Aug. 31 ..	Sept.17	2574	B	Thurs.	April 10 ..	27	2575		385
9	6336	Sat.	Sept. 20 ..	Oct. 7	2575	A	Tues.	March 30 ..	April 16	2576	b	355
10	6337	Thurs.	„ 9 ..	26	2576	F	Sat.	„ 19 ..	April 5	2577		354
11 E	6338	Mon.	Aug. 29 ..	Sept.15	2577	E	Thurs.	April 6 ..	23	2578		383
12	6339	Sat.	Sept. 16 ..	Oct. 3	2578	D	Tues.	March 27 ..	April 13	2579		355
13	6340	Thurs.	„ 6 ..	23	2579	C	Sat.	„ 15 ..	April 1	2580	b	354
14 E	6341	Mon.	Aug. 25 ..	Sept.11	2580	A	Thurs.	April 2 ..	19	2581		383
15	6342	Sat.	Sept. 12 ..	29	2581	G	Tues.	March 23 ..	April 9	2582		355
16	6343	Thurs.	„ 2 ..	19	2582	F	Sat.	„ 12 ..	29	2583		354
17 E	6344	Mon.	Aug. 22 ..	Sept. 8	2583	E	Sat.	„ 31 ..	April 17	2584	b	385
18	6345	Mon.	Sept. 10 ..	27	2584	C	Tues.	„ 19 ..	April 5	2585		353
19 E	6346	Thurs.	Aug. 29 ..	Sept.15	2585	B	Tues.	April 8 ..	25	2586		385

MOLAD 4 13 214. CYCLE 335. DAYS, 6939.

1	6347	Thurs.	Sept. 18	.. Oct. 5	2586	A	Sat.	March 28	.. April 14	2587		354
2	6348	Mon.	„ 7	.. 24	2587	G	Thurs.	„ 17	.. April 3	2588	b	355
3 E	6349	Sat.	Aug. 27	.. Sept.13	2588	E	Tues.	April 4	.. 21	2589		383
4	6350	Thurs.	Sept. 14	.. Oct. 1	2589	D	Sat.	March 24	.. April 10	2590		354
5	6351	Mon.	„ 3	.. 20	2590	C	Thurs.	„ 14	.. 31	2591		355
6 E	6352	Sat.	Aug. 24	.. Sept.10	2591	B	Thurs.	April 2	.. 19	2592	b	385
7	6353	Sat.	Sept. 12	.. 29	2592	G	Sun.	March 21	.. April 7	2593		353
8 E	6354	Tues.	Aug. 31	.. Sept.17	2593	F	Sat.	April 9	.. 26	2594		384
9	6355	Mon.	Sept. 19	.. Oct. 6	2594	E	Thurs.	March 30	.. April 16	2595		355
10	6356	Sat.	„ 9	.. 26	2595	D	Tues.	„ 19	.. April 5	2596	b	355
11 E	6357	Thurs.	Aug. 29	.. Sept.15	2596	B	Sun.	April 6	.. 23	2597		383
12	6358	Tues.	Sept. 16	.. Oct. 3	2597	A	Thurs.	March 26	.. April 12	2598		354
13	6359	Sat.	„ 5	.. 22	2598	G	Tues.	„ 16	.. April 2	2599		355
14 E	6360	Thurs.	Aug. 26	.. Sept.12	2599	F	Sun.	April 2	.. 20	2600		383
15	6361	Tues.	Sept. 12	.. 30	2600	E	Thurs.	March 22	.. April 9	2601		354
16	6362	Sat.	„ 1	.. 19	2601	D	Tues.	„ 12	.. 30	2602		355
17 E	6363	Thurs.	Aug. 22	.. Sept. 9	2602	C	Tues.	April 1	.. 19	2603		385
18	6364	Thurs.	Sept. 11	.. 29	2603	B	Sat.	March 20	.. April 7	2604	b	354
19 E	6365	Mon.	Aug. 30	.. Sept.17	2604	G	Thurs.	April 7	.. 25	2605		383

MOLAD 7 5 809. CYCLE 336. DAYS, 6940.

1	6366	Sat.	Sept. 17	.. Oct. 5	2605	F	Tues.	March 28	.. April 15	2606		355
2	6367	Thurs.	„ 7	.. 25	2606	E	Sat.	„ 17	.. April 4	2607		354
3 E	6368	Mon.	Aug. 27	.. Sept.14	2607	D	Sat.	April 5	.. 23	2608	b	385
4	6369	Mon.	Sept. 15	.. Oct. 3	2608	B	Tues.	March 24	.. April 11	2609		353
5	6370	Thurs.	„ 3	.. 21	2609	A	Sat.	„ 13	.. 31	2610		354
6 E	6371	Mon.	Aug. 23	.. Sept.10	2610	G	Sat.	April 2	.. 20	2611		385
7	6372	Mon.	Sept. 12	.. 30	2611	F	Thurs.	March 22	.. April 9	2612	b	355
8 E	6373	Sat.	„ 1	.. 19	2612	D	Tues.	April 9	.. 27	2613		383
9	6374	Thurs.	„ 19	.. Oct. 7	2613	C	Sat.	March 29	.. April 16	2614		354
10	6375	Mon.	„ 8	.. 26	2614	B	Thurs.	„ 19	.. April 6	2615		355
11 E	6376	Sat.	Aug. 29	.. Sept.16	2615	A	Tues.	April 5	.. 23	2616	b	383
12	6377	Thurs.	Sept. 15	.. Oct. 3	2616	F	Sun.	March 26	.. April 13	2617		355
13	6378	Tues.	„ 5	.. 23	2617	E	Thurs.	„ 15	.. April 2	2618		354
14 E	6379	Sat.	Aug. 25	.. Sept.12	2618	D	Thurs.	April 4	.. 22	2619		385
15	6380	Sat.	Sept. 14	.. Oct. 2	2619	C	Tues.	March 24	.. April 11	2620	b	355
16	6381	Thurs.	„ 3	.. 21	2620	A	Sat.	„ 13	.. 31	2621		354
17 E	6382	Mon.	Aug. 23	.. Sept.10	2621	G	Thurs.	„ 31	.. April 18	2622		383
18	6383	Sat.	Sept. 10	.. 28	2622	F	Tues.	„ 21	.. April 8	2623		355
19 E	6384	Thurs.	Aug. 31	.. Sept.18	2623	E	Sun.	April 7	.. 25	2624	b	383

Molad 2 22 324. CYCLE 337. Days, 6939.

1	6385	Tues.	Sept. 17 ..	Oct. 5	2624	C	Thurs.	March 27 ..	April 14	2625	354
2	6386	Sat.	„ 6 ..	24	2625	B	Tues.	„ 17 ..	April 4	2626	355
3 E	6387	Thurs.	Aug. 27 ..	Sept. 14	2626	A	Tues.	April 6 ..	24	2627	385
4	6388	Thurs.	Sept. 16 ..	Oct. 4	2627	G	Sat.	March 25 ..	April 12	2628 b	354
5	6389	Mon.	„ 4 ..	22	2628	E	Tues.	„ 13 ..	31	2629	353
6 E	6390	Thurs.	Aug. 23 ..	Sept. 10	2629	D	Tues.	April 2 ..	20	2630	385
7	6391	Thurs.	Sept. 12 ..	30	2630	C	Sat.	March 22 ..	April 9	2631	354
8 E	6392	Mon.	„ 1 ..	19	2631	B	Thurs.	April 8 ..	26	2632 b	383
9	6393	Sat.	„ 18 ..	Oct. 6	2632	G	Tues.	March 29 ..	April 16	2633	355
10	6394	Thurs.	„ 8 ..	26	2633	F	Sat.	„ 18 ..	April 5	2634	354
11 E	6395	Mon.	Aug. 28 ..	Sept. 15	2634	E	Sat.	April 7 ..	25	2635	385
12	6396	Mon.	Sept. 17 ..	Oct. 5	2635	D	Tues.	March 25 ..	April 12	2636 b	353
13	6397	Thurs.	„ 4 ..	22	2636	B	Sun.	„ 15 ..	April 2	2637	355
14 E	6398	Tues.	Aug. 25 ..	Sept. 12	2637	A	Sat.	April 3 ..	21	2638	384
15	6399	Mon.	Sept. 13 ..	Oct. 1	2638	G	Thurs.	March 24 ..	April 11	2639	355
16	6400	Sat.	„ 3 ..	21	2639	F	Sun.	„ 11 ..	29	2640 b	353
17 E	6401	Tues.	Aug. 21 ..	Sept. 8	2640	D	Sat.	„ 30 ..	April 17	2641	384
18	6402	Mon.	Sept. 9 ..	27	2641	C	Thurs.	„ 20 ..	April 7	2642	355
19 E	6403	Sat.	Aug. 30 ..	Sept. 17	2642	B	Tues.	April 7 ..	25	2643	383

Molad 5 14 919. CYCLE 338. Days, 6941.

1	6404	Thurs.	Sept. 17 ..	Oct. 5	2643	A	Sun.	March 27 ..	April 14	2644 b	355
2	6405	Tues.	„ 6 ..	24	2644	F	Thurs.	„ 16 ..	April 3	2645	354
3 E	6406	Sat.	Aug. 26 ..	Sept. 13	2645	E	Thurs.	April 5 ..	23	2646	385
4	6407	Sat.	Sept. 15 ..	Oct. 3	2646	D	Tues.	March 26 ..	April 13	2647	355
5	6408	Thurs.	„ 5 ..	23	2647	C	Sat.	„ 14 ..	April 1	2648 b	354
6 E	6409	Mon.	Aug. 24 ..	Sept. 11	2648	A	Thurs.	April 1 ..	19	2649	383
7	6410	Sat.	Sept. 11 ..	29	2649	G	Tues.	March 22 ..	April 9	2650	355
8 E	6411	Thurs.	„ 1 ..	19	2650	F	Sun.	April 9 ..	27	2651	383
9	6412	Tues.	„ 19 ..	Oct. 7	2651	E	Thurs.	March 28 ..	April 15	2652 b	354
10	6413	Sat.	„ 7 ..	25	2652	C	Tues.	„ 18 ..	April 5	2653	355
11 E	6414	Thurs.	Aug. 28 ..	Sept. 15	2653	B	Tues.	April 7 ..	25	2654	385
12	6415	Thurs.	Sept. 17 ..	Oct. 5	2654	A	Sat.	March 27 ..	April 14	2655	354
13	6416	Mon.	„ 6 ..	24	2655	G	Tues.	„ 14 ..	April 1	2656 b	353
14 E	6417	Thurs.	Aug. 24 ..	Sept. 11	2656	E	Tues.	April 3 ..	21	2657	385
15	6418	Thurs.	Sept. 13 ..	Oct. 1	2657	D	Sat.	March 23 ..	April 10	2658	354
16	6419	Mon.	„ 2 ..	20	2658	C	Thurs.	„ 13 ..	31	2659	355
17 E	6420	Sat.	Aug. 23 ..	Sept. 10	2659	B	Tues.	„ 30 ..	April 17	2660 b	383
18	6421	Thurs.	Sept. 9 ..	27	2660	G	Sat.	March 19 ..	April 6	2661	354
19 E	6422	Mon.	Aug. 29 ..	Sept. 16	2661	F	Sat.	April 8 ..	26	2662	385

Molad 1 7 434. CYCLE 339. Days, 6940.

1	6423	Mon.	Sept. 18	.. Oct. 6	2662	E	Tues.	March 27	.. April 14	2663		353
2	6424	Thurs.	„ 6	.. 24	2663	D	Sun.	„ 16	.. April 3	2664	b	355
3 E	6425	Tues.	Aug. 26	.. Sept. 13	2664	B	Sat.	April 4	.. 22	2665		384
4	6426	Mon.	Sept. 14	.. Oct. 2	2665	A	Thurs.	March 25	.. April 12	2666		355
5	6427	Sat.	„ 4	.. 22	2666	G	Sun.	„ 13	.. 31	2667		353
6 E	6428	Tues.	Aug. 23	.. Sept. 10	2667	F	Sat.	„ 31	.. April 18	2668	b	384
7	6429	Mon.	Sept. 10	.. 28	2668	D	Thurs.	„ 21	.. April 8	2669		355
8 E	6430	Sat.	Aug. 31	.. Sept. 18	2669	C	Thurs.	April 10	.. 28	2670		385
9	6431	Sat.	Sept. 20	.. Oct. 8	2670	B	Sun.	March 29	.. April 16	2671		353
10	6432	Tues.	„ 8	.. 26	2671	A	Thurs.	„ 17	.. April 4	2672	b	354
11 E	6433	Sat.	Aug. 27	.. Sept. 14	2672	F	Thurs.	April 6	.. 24	2673		385
12	6434	Sat.	Sept. 16	.. Oct. 4	2673	E	Tues.	March 27	.. April 14	2674		355
13	6435	Thurs.	„ 6	.. 24	2674	D	Sat.	„ 16	.. April 3	2675		354
14 E	6436	Mon.	Aug. 26	.. Sept. 13	2675	C	Thurs.	April 2	.. 20	2676	b	383
15	6437	Sat.	Sept. 12	.. 30	2676	A	Tues.	March 23	.. April 10	2677		355
16	6438	Thurs.	„ 2	.. 20	2677	G	Sat.	„ 12	.. 30	2678		354
17 E	6439	Mon.	Aug. 22	.. Sept. 9	2678	F	Thurs.	„ 30	.. April 17	2679		383
18	6440	Sat.	Sept. 9	.. 27	2679	E	Tues.	March 19	.. April 6	2680	b	355
19 E	6441	Thurs.	Aug. 29	.. Sept. 16	2680	C	Tues.	April 8	.. 26	2681		385

Molad 3 23 1029. CYCLE 340. Days, 6939.

1	6442	Thurs.	Sept. 18	.. Oct. 6	2681	B	Sat.	March 28	.. April 15	2682		354
2	6443	Mon.	„ 7	.. 25	2682	A	Tues.	„ 16	.. April 3	2683		353
3 E	6444	Thurs.	Aug. 26	.. Sept. 13	2683	G	Tues.	April 4	.. 22	2684	b	385
4	6445	Thurs.	Sept. 14	.. Oct. 2	2684	E	Sat.	„ 24	.. April 11	2685		354
5	6446	Mon.	„ 3	.. 21	2685	D	Thurs.	„ 14	.. April 1	2686		355
6 E	6447	Sat.	Aug. 24	.. Sept. 11	2686	C	Tues.	April 1	.. 19	2687		383
7	6448	Thurs.	Sept. 11	.. 29	2687	B	Sat.	March 20	.. April 7	2688	b	354
8 E	6449	Mon.	Aug. 30	.. Sept. 17	2688	G	Sat.	April 9	.. 27	2689		385
9	6450	Mon.	Sept. 19	.. Oct. 7	2689	F	Thurs.	March 30	.. April 17	2690		355
10	6451	Sat.	„ 9	.. 27	2690	E	Sun.	„ 18	.. April 5	2691		353
11 E	6452	Tues.	Aug. 28	.. Sept. 15	2691	D	Sat.	April 5	.. 23	2692	b	384
12	6453	Mon.	Sept. 15	.. Oct. 3	2692	B	Thurs.	March 26	.. April 13	2693		355
13	6454	Sat.	„ 5	.. 23	2693	A	Tues.	„ 16	.. April 3	2694		355
14 E	6455	Thurs.	Aug. 26	.. Sept. 13	2694	G	Sun.	April 3	.. 21	2695		383
15	6456	Tues.	Sept. 13	.. Oct. 1	2695	F	Thurs.	March 22	.. April 9	2696	b	354
16	6457	Sat.	„ 1	.. 19	2696	D	Tues.	„ 12	.. 30	2697		355
17 E	6458	Thurs.	Aug. 22	.. Sept. 9	2697	C	Tues.	April 1	.. 19	2698		385
18	6459	Thurs.	Sept. 11	.. 29	2698	B	Sat.	March 21	.. April 8	2699		354
19 E	6460	Mon.	Aug. 31	.. Sept. 18	2699	A	Thurs.	April 7	.. 26	2700		383

MOLAD 6 16 544. CYCLE 341. DAYS, 6939.

1	6461	Sat.	Sept. 17 ..	Oct. 6	2700	G	Tues.	March 28 ..	April 16	2701	355
2	6462	Thurs.	„ 7 ..	26	2701	F	Sat.	„ 17 ..	April 5	2702	354
3 E	6463	Mon.	Aug. 27 ..	Sept. 15	2702	E	Thurs.	April 4 ..	23	2703	383
4	6464	Sat.	Sept. 14 ..	Oct. 3	2703	D	Tues.	March 24 ..	April 12	2704 b	355
5	6465	Thurs.	„ 3 ..	22	2704	B	Sat.	„ 13 ..	April 1	2705	354
6 E	6466	Mon.	Aug. 23 ..	Sept. 11	2705	A	Sat.	April 2 ..	21	2706	385
7	6467	Mon.	Sept. 12 ..	Oct. 1	2706	G	Tues.	March 21 ..	April 9	2707	353
8 E	6468	Thurs.	Aug. 31 ..	Sept. 19	2707	F	Tues.	April 9 ..	28	2708 b	385
9	6469	Thurs.	Sept. 19 ..	Oct. 8	2708	D	Sat.	March 29 ..	April 17	2709	354
10	6470	Mon.	„ 8 ..	27	2709	C	Thurs.	„ 19 ..	April 7	2710	355
11 E	6471	Sat.	Aug. 29 ..	Sept. 17	2710	B	Tues.	April 6 ..	25	2711	383
12	6472	Thurs.	Sept. 16 ..	Oct. 5	2711	A	Sat.	March 25 ..	April 13	2712 b	354
13	6473	Mon.	„ 4 ..	23	2712	F	Thurs.	„ 15 ..	April 3	2713	355
14 E	6474	Sat.	Aug. 25 ..	Sept. 13	2713	E	Tues.	April 2 ..	21	2714	383
15	6475	Thurs.	Sept. 12 ..	Oct. 1	2714	D	Sun.	March 23 ..	April 11	2715	355
16	6476	Tues.	„ 2 ..	21	2715	C	Thurs.	„ 11 ..	30	2716 b	354
17 E	6477	Sat.	Aug. 21 ..	Sept. 9	2716	A	Thurs.	„ 31 ..	April 19	2717	385
18	6478	Sat.	Sept. 10 ..	29	2717	G	Sun.	„ 19 ..	April 7	2718	353
19 E	6479	Tues.	Aug. 29 ..	Sept. 17	2718	F	Sat.	April 7 ..	26	2719	384

MOLAD 2 9 59. CYCLE 342. DAYS, 6940.

1	6480	Mon.	Sept. 17 ..	Oct. 6	2719	E	Thurs.	March 27 ..	April 15	2720 b	355
2	6481	Sat.	„ 6 ..	25	2720	C	Tues.	„ 17 ..	April 5	2721	355
3 E	6482	Thurs.	Aug. 27 ..	Sept. 15	2721	B	Sun.	April 4 ..	23	2722	383
4	6483	Tues.	Sept. 14 ..	Oct. 3	2722	A	Thurs.	March 24 ..	April 12	2723	354
5	6484	Sat.	„ 3 ..	22	2723	G	Tues.	„ 13 ..	April 1	2724 b	355
6 E	6485	Thurs.	Aug. 23 ..	Sept. 11	2724	E	Tues.	April 2 ..	21	2725	385
7	6486	Thurs.	Sept. 12 ..	Oct. 1	2725	D	Sat.	March 22 ..	April 10	2726	354
8 E	6487	Mon.	„ 1 ..	20	2726	C	Thurs.	April 9 ..	28	2727	383
9	6488	Sat.	„ 19 ..	Oct. 8	2727	B	Tues.	March 29 ..	April 17	2728 b	355
10	6489	Thurs.	„ 8 ..	27	2728	G	Sat.	„ 18 ..	April 6	2729	354
11 E	6490	Mon.	Aug. 28 ..	Sept. 16	2729	F	Thurs.	April 5 ..	24	2730	383
12	6491	Sat.	Sept. 15 ..	Oct. 4	2730	E	Tues.	March 26 ..	April 14	2731	355
13	6492	Thurs.	„ 5 ..	24	2731	D	Sat.	„ 14 ..	April 2	2732 b	354
14 E	6493	Mon.	Aug. 24 ..	Sept. 12	2732	B	Sat.	April 3 ..	22	2733	385
15	6494	Mon.	Sept. 13 ..	Oct. 2	2733	A	Tues.	March 22 ..	April 10	2734	353
16	6495	Thurs.	„ 1 ..	20	2734	G	Sun.	„ 12 ..	31	2725	355
17 E	6496	Tues.	Aug. 22 ..	Sept. 10	2735	F	Sat.	March 30 ..	April 18	2736 b	384
18	6497	Mon.	Sept. 9 ..	28	2736	D	Thurs.	„ 20 ..	April 8	2737	355
19 E	6498	Sat.	Aug. 30 ..	Sept. 18	2737	C	Tues.	April 7 ..	26	2738	383

Molad 5 1 654. CYCLE 343. Days, 6941.

1	6499	Thurs.	Sept. 17	..	Oct. 6	2738	B	Sat.	March 27	..	April 15	2739	354
2	6500	Mon.	,, 6	..	25	2739	A	Thurs.	,, 16	..	April 4	2740 b	355
3 E	6501	Sat.	Aug. 26	..	Sept. 14	2740	F	Tues.	April 3	..	22	2741	383
4	6502	Thurs.	Sept. 13	..	Oct. 2	2741	E	Sun.	March 24	..	April 12	2742	355
5	6503	Tues.	,, 3	..	22	2742	D	Thurs.	,, 13	..	April 1	2743	354
6 E	6504	Sat.	Aug. 23	..	Sept. 11	2743	C	Thurs.	April 1	..	20	2744 b	385
7	6505	Sat.	Sept. 11	..	30	2744	A	Sun.	March 20	..	April 8	2745	353
8 E	6506	Tues.	Aug. 30	..	Sept. 18	2745	G	Sat.	April 8	..	27	2746	384
9	6507	Mon.	Sept. 18	..	Oct. 7	2746	F	Thurs.	March 29	..	April 17	2747	355
10	6508	Sat.	,, 8	..	27	2747	E	Tues.	,, 18	..	April 6	2748 b	355
11 E	6509	Thurs.	Aug. 28	..	Sept. 16	2748	C	Sun.	April 5	..	24	2749	383
12	6510	Tues.	Sept. 15	..	Oct. 4	2749	B	Thurs.	March 25	..	April 13	2750	354
13	6511	Sat.	,, 4	..	23	2750	A	Tues.	,, 15	..	April 3	2751	355
14 E	6512	Thurs.	Aug. 25	..	Sept. 13	2751	G	Tues.	April 3	..	22	2752 b	385
15	6513	Thurs.	Sept. 13	..	Oct. 2	2752	E	Sat.	March 23	..	April 11	2753	354
16	6514	Mon.	,, 2	..	21	2753	D	Tues.	,, 11	..	30	2754	353
17 E	6515	Thurs.	Aug. 21	..	Sept. 9	2754	C	Tues.	,, 31	..	April 19	2755	385
18	6516	Thurs.	Sept. 10	..	29	2755	B	Sat.	,, 19	..	April 7	2756 b	354
19 E	6517	Mon.	Aug. 29	..	Sept. 17	2756	G	Sat.	April 8	..	27	2757	385

Molad 7 18 169. CYCLE 344. Days, 6940.

1	6518	Mon.	Sept. 18	..	Oct. 7	2757	F	Tues.	March 27	..	April 15	2758	353
2	6519	Thurs.	,, 6	..	25	2758	E	Sat.	,, 16	..	April 4	2759	354
3 E	6520	Mon.	Aug. 26	..	Sept. 14	2759	D	Sat.	April 4	..	23	2760 b	385
4	6521	Mon.	Sept. 14	..	Oct. 3	2760	B	Thurs.	March 25	..	April 13	2761	355
5	6522	Sat.	,, 4	..	23	2761	A	Sun.	,; 13	..	April 1	2762	353
6 E	6523	Tues.	Aug. 23	..	Sept. 11	2762	G	Sat.	April 1	..	20	2763	384
7	6524	Mon.	Sept. 11	..	30	2763	F	Thurs.	March 21	..	April 9	2764 b	355
8 E	6525	Sat.	Aug. 31	..	Sept. 19	2764	D	Tues.	April 8	..	27	2765	383
9	6526	Thurs.	Sept. 18	..	Oct. 7	2765	C	Sat.	March 28	..	April 16	2766	354
10	6527	Mon.	,, 7	..	26	2766	B	Thurs.	,, 18	..	April 6	2767	355
11 E	6528	Sat.	Aug. 28	..	Sept. 16	2767	A	Thurs.	April 6	..	25	2768 b	385
12	6529	Sat.	Sept. 16	..	Oct. 5	2768	F	Sun.	March 25	..	April 13	2769	353
13	6530	Tues.	,, 4	..	23	2769	E	Thurs.	,, 14	..	April 2	2770	354
14 E	6531	Sat.	Aug. 24	..	Sept. 12	2770	D	Thurs.	April 3	..	22	2771	385
15	6532	Sat.	Sept. 13	..	Oct. 2	2771	C	Tues.	March 23	..	April 11	2772 b	355
16	6533	Thurs.	,, 2	..	21	2772	A	Sat.	,, 12	..	31	2773	354
17 E	6534	Mon.	Aug. 22	..	Sept. 10	2773	G	Thurs.	,, 30	..	April 18	2774	383
18	6535	Sat.	Sept. 9	..	28	2774	F	Tues.	,, 20	..	April 8	2775	355
19 E	6536	Thurs.	Aug. 30	..	Sept. 18	2775	E	Tues.	April 8	..	27	2776 b	385

MOLAD 3 10 764. CYCLE 345. DAYS, 6939.

1	6537	Thurs.	Sept. 18	.. Oct. 7	2776	C	Sat.	March 28	.. April 16	2777		354
2	6538	Mon.	„ 7	.. 26	2777	B	Tues.	„ 16	.. April 4	2778		353
3 E	6539	Thurs.	Aug. 26	.. Sept.14	2778	A	Tues.	April 5	.. 24	2779		385
4	6540	Thurs.	Sept. 15	.. Oct. 4	2779	G	Sat.	March 24	.. April 12	2780	b	354
5	6541	Mon.	„ 3	.. 22	2780	E	Thurs.	„ 14	.. April 2	2781		355
6 E	6542	Sat.	Aug. 24	.. Sept.12	2781	D	Tues.	April 1	.. 20	2782		383
7	6543	Thurs.	Sept. 11	.. 30	2782	C	Sat.	March 21	.. April 9	2783		354
8 E	6544	Mon.	Aug. 31	.. Sept.19	2783	B	Sat.	April 9	.. 28	2784	b	385
9	6545	Mon.	Sept. 19	.. Oct. 8	2784	G	Tues.	March 28	.. April 16	2785		353
10	6546	Thurs.	„ 7	.. 26	2785	F	Sat.	„ 17	.. April 5	2786		354
11 E	6547	Mon.	Aug. 27	.. Sept.15	2786	E	Sat.	April 6	.. 25	2787		385
12	6548	Mon.	Sept. 16	.. Oct. 5	2787	D	Thurs.	March 26	.. April 14	2788	b	355
13	6549	Sat.	„ 5	.. 24	2788	B	Sun.	„ 14	.. April 2	2789		353
14 E	6550	Tues.	Aug. 24	.. Sept.12	2789	A	Sat.	April 2	.. 21	2790		384
15	6551	Mon.	Sept. 12	.. Oct. 1	2790	G	Thurs.	March 23	.. April 11	2791		355
16	6552	Sat.	„ 2	.. 21	2791	F	Tues.	„ 12	.. 31	2792	b	355
17 E	6553	Thurs.	Aug. 22	.. Sept.10	2792	D	Sun.	„ 30	.. April 18	2793		383
18	6554	Tues.	Sept. 9	.. 28	2793	C	Thurs.	„ 19	.. April 7	2794		354
19 E	6555	Sat.	Aug. 29	.. Sept.17	2794	B	Thurs.	April 8	.. 27.	2795		385

MOLAD 6 3 279. CYCLE 346. DAYS, 6939.

1	6556	Sat.	Sept. 18	.. Oct. 7	2795	A	Tues.	March 28	.. April 16	2796	b	355
2	6557	Thurs.	„ 7	.. 26	2796	F	Sat.	„ 17	.. April 5	2797		354
3 E	6558	Mon.	Aug. 27	.. Sept.15	2797	E	Thurs.	April 4	.. 23	2798		383
4	6559	Sat.	Sept. 14	.. Oct. 3	2798	D	Tues.	March 25	.. April 13	2799		355
5	6560	Thurs.	„ 4	.. 23	2799	C	Sat.	„ 13	.. April 1	2800	b	354
6 E	6561	Mon.	Aug. 23	.. Sept.11	2800	A	Thurs.	„ 31	.. April 19	2801		383
7	6562	Sat.	Sept. 10	.. 29	2801	G	Tues.	„ 21	.. April 9	2802		355
8 E	6563	Thurs.	Aug. 31	.. Sept.19	2802	F	Tues.	April 10	.. 29	2803		385
9	6564	Thurs.	Sept. 20	.. Oct. 9	2803	E	Sat.	March 29	.. April 17	2804	b	354
10	6565	Mon.	„ 8	.. 27	2804	C	Tues.	„ 17	.. April 5	2805		353
11 E	6566	Thurs.	Aug. 27	.. Sept.15	2805	B	Tues.	April 6	.. 25	2806		385
12	6567	Thurs.	Sept. 16	.. Oct.5	2806	A	Sat.	March 26	.. April 14	2807		354
13	6568	Mon.	„ 5	.. 24	2807	G	Thurs.	„ 15	.. April 3	2808	b	355
14 E	6569	Sat.	Aug. 25	.. Sept.13	2808	E	Tues.	April 2	.. 21	2809		383
15	6570	Thurs.	Sept. 12	.. Oct. 1	2809	D	Sat.	March 22	.. April 10	2810		354
16	6571	Mon.	„ 1	.. 20	2810	C	Thurs.	„ 12	.. 31	2811		355
17 E	6572	Sat.	Aug. 22	.. Sept.10	2811	B	Tues.	„ 29	.. April 17	2812	b	383
18	6573	Thurs.	Sept. 8	.. 27	2812	G	Sun.	„ 19	.. April 7	2813		355
19 E	6574	Tues.	Aug. 29	.. Sept.17	2813	F	Sat.	April 7	.. 26	2814		384

MOLAD 1 19 874. CYCLE 347. DAYS, 6940.

1	6575	Mon.	Sept. 17 .. Oct. 6	2814	E	Thurs.	March 28 .. April 16	2815	355
2	6576	Sat.	„ 7 .. 26	2815	D	Sun.	„ 15 .. April 3	2816 b	353
3 E	6577	Tues.	Aug. 25 .. Sept.13	2816	B	Sat.	April 3 .. 22	2817	384
4	6578	Mon.	Sept. 13 .. Oct. 2	2817	A	Thurs.	March 24 .. April 12	2818	355
5	6579	Sat.	„ 3 .. 22	2818	G	Tues.	„ 14 .. April 2	2819	355
6 E	6580	Thurs.	Aug. 24 .. Sept.12	2819	F	Sun.	„ 31 .. April 19	2820 b	383
7	6581	Tues.	Sept. 10 .. 29	2820	D	Thurs.	„ 20 .. April 8	2821	354
8 E	6582	Sat.	Aug. 30 .. Sept.18	2821	C	Thurs.	April 19 .. 28	2822	385
9	6583	Sat.	Sept. 19 .. Oct. 8	2822	B	Tues.	March 30 .. April 18	2823	355
10	6584	Thurs.	„ 9 .. 28	2823	A	Sat.	„ 18 .. April 6	2824 b	354
11 E	6585	Mon.	Aug. 28 .. Sept.16	2824	F	Thurs.	April 5 .. 24	2825	383
12	6586	Sat.	Sept. 15 .. Oct. 4	2825	E	Tues.	March 26 .. April 14	2826	355
13	6587	Thurs.	„ 5 .. 24	2826	D	Sat.	„ 15 .. April 3	2827	354
14 E	6588	Mon.	Aug. 25 .. Sept.13	2827	C	Thurs.	April 1 .. 20	2828 b	383
15	6589	Sat.	Sept. 11 .. 30	2828	A	Tues.	March 22 .. April 10	2829	355
16	6590	Thurs.	„ 1 .. 20	2829	G	Sat.	„ 11 .. 30	2830	354
17 E	6591	Mon.	Aug. 21 .. Sept. 9	2830	F	Sat.	„ 31 .. April 19	2831	385
18	6592	Mon.	Sept. 10 .. 29	2831	E	Tues.	„ 18 .. April 6	2832 b	353
19 E	6593	Thurs.	Aug. 28 .. Sept.16	2832	C	Tues.	April 7 .. 26	2833	385

MOLAD 4 12 389. CYCLE 348. DAYS, 6939.

1	6594	Thurs.	Sept. 17 .. Oct. 6	2833	B	Sat.	March 27 .. April 15	2834	354
2	6595	Mon.	„ 6 .. 25	2834	A	Thurs.	„ 17 .. April 5	2835	355
3 E	6596	Sat.	Aug. 27 .. Sept.15	2835	G	Tues.	April 3 .. 22	2836 b	383
4	6597	Thurs.	Sept. 13 .. Oct. 2	2836	E	Sat.	March 23 .. April 11	2837	354
5	6598	Mon.	„ 2 .. 21	2837	D	Thurs.	„ 13 .. April 1	2838	355
6 E	6599	Sat.	Aug. 23 .. Sept.11	2838	C	Thurs.	April 2 .. 21	2839	385
7	6600	Sat.	Sept. 12 .. Oct. 1	2839	B	Sun.	March 20 .. April 8	2840 b	353
8 E	6601	Tues.	Aug. 30 .. Sept.18	2840	G	Sat.	April 8 .. 27	2841	384
9	6602	Mon.	Sept. 18 .. Oct. 7	2841	F	Thurs.	March 29 .. April 17	2842	355
10	6603	Sat.	„ 8 .. 27	2842	E	Tues.	„ 19 .. April 7	2843	355
11 E	6604	Thurs.	Aug. 29 .. Sept.17	2843	D	Sun.	April 5 .. 24	2844 b	383
12	6605	Tues.	Sept. 15 .. Oct. 4	2844	B	Thurs.	March 25 .. April 13	2845	354
13	6606	Sat.	„ 4 .. 23	2845	A	Tues.	„ 15 .. April 3	2846	355
14 E	6607	Thurs.	Aug. 25 .. Sept.13	2846	G	Sun.	April 2 .. 21	2847	383
15	6608	Tues.	Sept. 12 .. Oct. 1	2847	F	Thurs.	March 21 .. April 9	2848 b	354
16	6609	Sat.	Aug. 31 .. Sept.19	2848	D	Tues.	„ 11 .. 30	2849	355
17 E	6610	Thurs.	„ 21 .. Sept. 9	2849	C	Tues.	„ 31 .. April 19	2850	385
18	6611	Thurs.	Sept. 10 .. 29	2850	B	Sat.	„ 20 .. April 8	2851	354
19 E	6612	Mon.	Aug. 30 .. Sept.18	2851	A	Thurs.	April 6 .. 25	2852 b	383

MOLAD 7 4 984. CYCLE 349. DAYS, 6940.

1	6613	Sat.	Sept. 16	..	Oct. 5	2852	F	Tues.	March 27	..	April 15	2853	355
2	6614	Thurs.	„ 6	..	25	2853	E	Sat.	„ 16	..	April 4	2854	354
3 E	6615	Mon.	Aug. 26	..	Sept.14	2854	D	Sat.	April 5	..	24	2855	385
4	6616	Mon.	Sept. 15	..	Oct. 4	2855	C	Tues.	March 23	..	April 11	2856 b	353
5	6617	Thurs.	„ 2	..	21	2856	A	Sat.	„ 12	..	31	2857	354
6 E	6618	Mon.	Aug. 22	..	Sept.10	2857	G	Sat.	April 1	..	20	2858	385
7	6619	Mon.	Sept. 11	..	30	2858	F	Thurs.	March 22	..	April 10	2859	355
8 E	6620	Sat.	„ 1	..	20	2859	E	Tues.	April 8	..	27	2860 b	383
9	6621	Thurs.	„ 18	..	Oct. 7	2860	C	Sat.	March 28	..	April 16	2861	354
10	6622	Mon.	„ 7	..	26	2861	B	Thurs.	„ 18	..	April 6	2862	355
11 E	6623	Sat.	Aug. 28	..	Sept.16	2862	A	Tues.	April 5	..	24	2863	383
12	6624	Thurs.	Sept. 15	..	Oct. 4	2863	G	Sat.	March 24	..	April 12	2864 b	354
13	6625	Mon.	„ 3	..	22	2864	E	Thurs.	„ 14	..	April 2	2865	355
14 E	6626	Sat.	Aug. 24	..	Sept.12	2865	D	Thurs.	April 3	..	22	2866	385
15	6627	Sat.	Sept. 13	..	Oct. 2	2866	C	Sun.	March 22	..	April 10	2867	353
16	6628	Tues.	„ 1	..	20	2867	B	Thurs.	„ 10	..	29	2868 b	354
17 E	6629	Sat.	Aug. 20	..	Sept. 8	2868	G	Thurs.	„ 30	..	April 18	2869	385
18	6630	Sat.	Sept. 9	..	28	2869	F	Tues.	„ 20	..	April 8	2870	355
19 E	6631	Thurs.	Aug. 30	..	Sept.18	2870	E	Sun.	April 7	..	26	2871	383

MOLAD 2 21 499. CYCLE 350. DAYS, 6939.

1	6632	Tues.	Sept. 17	..	Oct. 6	2871	D	Thurs.	March 26	..	April 14	2872 b	354
2	6633	Sat.	„ 5	..	24	2872	B	Tues.	„ 16	..	April 4	2873	355
3 E	6634	Thurs.	Aug. 26	..	Sept.14	2873	A	Tues.	April 5	..	24	2874	385
4	6635	Thurs.	Sept. 15	..	Oct. 4	2874	G	Sat.	March 25	..	April 13	2875	354
5	6636	Mon.	„ 4	..	23	2875	F	Tues.	„ 12	..	31	2876 b	353
6 E	6637	Thurs.	Aug. 22	..	Sept.10	2876	D	Tues.	April 1	..	20	2877	385
7	6638	Thurs.	Sept. 11	..	30	2877	C	Sat.	March 21	..	April 9	2878	354
8 E	6639	Mon.	Aug. 31	..	Sept.19	2878	B	Thurs.	April 8	..	27	2879	383
9	6640	Sat.	Sept. 18	..	Oct. 7	2879	A	Tues.	March 28	..	April 16	2880 b	355
10	6641	Thurs.	„ 7	..	26	2880	F	Sat.	„ 17	..	April 5	2881	354
11 E	6642	Mon.	Aug. 27	..	Sept.15	2881	E	Sat.	April 6	..	25	2882	385
12	6643	Mon.	Sept. 16	..	Oct. 5	2882	D	Tues.	March 25	..	April 13	2883	353
13	6644	Thurs.	„ 4	..	23	2883	C	Sun.	„ 14	..	April 2	2884 b	355
14 E	6645	Tues.	Aug. 24	..	Sept.12	2884	A	Sat.	April 2	..	21	2885	384
15	6646	Mon.	Sept. 12	..	Oct. 1.	2885	G	Thurs.	March 23	..	April 11	2886	355
16	6647	Sat.	„ 2	..	21	2886	F	Sun.	„ 11	..	30	2887	353
17 E	6648	Tues.	Aug. 21	..	Sept. 9	2887	E	Sat.	„ 29	..	April 17	2888 b	384
18	6649	Mon.	Sept. 8	..	27	2888	C	Thurs.	„ 19	..	April 7	2889	355
19 E	6650	Sat.	Aug. 29	..	Sept.17	2889	B	Tues.	April 6	..	25	2890	383

Molad 5 14 14. CYCLE 351. Days, 6941.

1	6651	Thurs.	Sept.	16	..	Oct. 5	2890	A	Sun.	March	27	..	April 15	2891		355
2	6652	Tues.	„	6	..	25	2891	G	Thurs.	„	15	..	April 3	2892	b	354
3 E	6653	Sat.	Aug.	25	..	Sept. 13	2892	E	Thurs.	April	4	..	23	2893		385
4	6654	Sat.	Sept.	14	..	Oct. 3	2893	D	Tues.	March	25	..	April 13	2894		355
5	6655	Thurs.	„	4	..	23	2894	C	Sat.	„	14	..	April 2	2895		354
6 E	6656	Mon.	Aug.	24	..	Sept. 12	2895	B	Thurs.	„	31	..	April 19	2896	b	383
7	6657	Sat.	Sept.	10	..	29	2896	G	Tues.	„	21	..	April 9	2897		355
8 E	6658	Thurs.	Aug.	31	..	Sept. 19	2897	F	Sun.	April	8	..	27	2898		383
9	6659	Tues.	Sept.	18	..	Oct. 7	2898	E	Thurs.	March	28	..	April 16	2899		354
10	6660	Sat.	„	7	..	26	2899	D	Tues.	„	17	..	April 6	2900		355
11 E	6661	Thurs.	Aug.	27	..	Sept. 16	2900	C	Tues.	April	6	..	26	2901		385
12	6662	Thurs.	Sept.	16	..	Oct. 6	2901	B	Sat.	March	26	..	April 15	2902		354
13	6663	Mon.	„	5	..	25	2902	A	Tues.	„	14	..	April 3	2903		353
14 E	6664	Tues.	Aug.	24	..	Sept. 13	2903	G	Tues.	April	2	..	22	2904	b	385
15	6665	Thurs.	Sept.	12	..	Oct. 2	2904	E	Sat.	March	22	..	April 11	2905		354
16	6666	Mon.	„	1	..	21	2905	D	Thurs.	„	12	..	April 1	2906		355
17 E	6667	Sat.	Aug.	22	..	Sept. 11	2906	C	Tues.	„	30	..	April 19	2907		383
18	6668	Thurs.	Sept.	9	..	29	2907	B	Sat.	„	18	..	April 7	2908	b	354
19 E	6669	Mon.	Aug.	28	..	Sept. 17	2908	G	Sat.	April	7	..	27	2909		385

Molad 1 6 609. CYCLE 352. Days, 6941.

1	6670	Mon.	Sept.	17	..	Oct. 7	2909	F	Tues.	March	26	..	April 15	2910		353
2	6671	Thurs.	„	5	..	25	2910	E	Sun.	„	16	..	April 5	2911		355
3 E	6672	Tues.	Aug.	26	..	Sept. 15	2911	D	Sat.	April	3	..	23	2912	b	384
4	6673	Mon.	Sept.	13	..	Oct. 3	2912	B	Thurs.	March	24	..	April 13	2913		355
5	6674	Sat.	„	3	..	23	2913	A	Sun.	„	12	..	April 1	2914		353
6 E	6675	Tues.	Aug.	22	..	Sept. 11	2914	G	Sat.	„	31	..	April 20	2915		384
7	6676	Mon.	Sept.	10	..	30	2915	F	Thurs.	„	20	..	April 9	2916	b	355
8 E	6677	Sat.	Aug.	30	..	Sept. 19	2916	D	Thurs.	April	9	..	29	2917		385
9	6678	Sat.	Sept.	19	..	Oct. 9	2917	C	Sun.	March	28	..	April 17	2918		353
10	6679	Tues.	„	7	..	27	2918	B	Thurs.	„	17	..	April 6	2919		354
11 E	6680	Sat.	Aug.	27	..	Sept. 16	2919	A	Thurs.	April	5	..	25	2920	b	385
12	6681	Sat.	Sept.	15	..	Oct. 5	2920	F	Tues.	March	26	..	April 15	2921		355
13	6682	Thurs.	„	5	..	25	2921	E	Sat.	„	15	..	April 4	2922		354
14 E	6683	Mon.	Aug.	25	..	Sept. 14	2922	D	Thurs.	April	2	..	22	2923		383
15	6684	Sat.	Sept.	12	..	Oct. 2	2923	C	Tues.	March	22	..	April 11	2924	b	355
16	6685	Thurs.	„	1	..	21	2924	A	Sat.	„	11	..	31	2925		354
17 E	6686	Mon.	Aug.	21	..	Sept. 10	2925	G	Thurs.	„	29	..	April 18	2926		383
18	6687	Sat.	Sept.	8	..	28	2926	F	Tues.	„	19	..	April 8	2927		355
19 E	6688	Thurs.	Aug.	29	..	Sept. 18	2927	E	Tues.	April	7	..	27	2928	b	385

MOLAD 3 23 124. CYCLE 353. DAYS, 6939.

1	6689	Thurs.	Sept. 17	..	Oct. 7	2928	C	Sat.	March 27	..	April 16	2929	354
2	6690	Mon.	„ 6	..	26	2929	B	Tues.	„ 15	..	April 4	2930	353
3 E	6691	Thurs.	Aug. 25	..	Sept.14	2930	A	Tues.	April 4	..	24	2931	385
4	6692	Thurs.	Sept. 14	..	Oct. 4	2931	G	Sat.	March 23	..	April 12	2932 b	354
5	6693	Mon.	„ 2	..	22	2932	E	Thurs.	„ 13	..	April 2	2933	355
6 E	6694	Sat.	Aug. 23	..	Sept.12	2933	D	Tues.	„ 31	..	April 20	2934	383
7	6695	Thurs.	Sept. 10	..	30	2934	C	Sat.	„ 20	..	April 9	2935	354
8 E	6696	Mon.	Aug. 30	..	Sept.19	2935	B	Sat.	April 8	..	28	2936 b	385
9	6697	Mon.	Sept. 18	..	Oct. 8	2936	G	Thurs.	March 29	..	April 18	2937	355
10	6698	Sat.	„ 8	..	28	2937	F	Sun.	„ 17	..	April 6	2938	353
11 E	6699	Tues.	Aug. 27	..	Sept.16	2938	E	Sat.	April 5	..	25	2939	384
12	6700	Mon.	Sept. 15	..	Oct. 5	2939	D	Thurs.	March 25	..	April 14	2940 b	355
13	6701	Sat.	„ 4	..	24	2940	B	Tues.	„ 15	..	April 4	2941	355
14 E	6702	Thurs.	Aug. 5	..	Sept.14	2941	A	Sun.	April 2	..	22	2942	383
15	6703	Tues.	Sept. 12	..	Oct. 2	2942	G	Thurs.	March 22	..	April 11	2943	354
16	6704	Sat.	„ 1	..	21	2943	F	Tues.	„ 11	..	31	2944 b	355
17 E	6705	Thurs.	Aug. 21	..	Sept.10	2944	D	Tues.	„ 31	..	April 20	2945	385
18	6706	Thurs.	Sept. 10	..	30	2945	C	Sat.	„ 20	..	April 9	2946	354
19 E	6707	Mon.	Aug. 30	..	Sept.19	2946	B	Thurs.	April 7	..	27	2947	383

MOLAD 6 15 719. CYCLE 354. DAYS, 6939.

1	6708	Sat.	Sept. 17	..	Oct. 7	2947	A	Tues.	March 27	..	April 16	2948 b	355
2	6709	Thurs.	„ 6	..	26	2948	F	Sat.	„ 16	..	April 5	2949	354
3 E	6710	Mon.	Aug. 26	..	Sept.15	2949	E	Thurs.	April 3	..	23	2950	383
4	6711	Sat.	Sept. 13	..	Oct. 3	2950	D	Tues.	March 24	..	April 13	2951	355
5	6712	Thurs.	„ 3	..	23	2951	C	Sat.	„ 12	..	April 1	2952 b	354
6 E	6713	Mon.	Aug. 22	..	Sept.11.	2952	A	Sat.	April 1	..	21	2953	385
7	6714	Mon.	Sept. 11	..	Oct. 1	2953	G	Tues.	March 20	..	April 9	2954	353
8 E	6715	Thurs.	Aug. 30	..	Sept.19	2954	F	Tues.	April 9	..	29	2955	385
9	6716	Thurs.	Sept. 19	..	Oct. 9	2955	E	Sat.	March 28	..	April 17	2956 b	354
10	6717	Mon.	„ 7	..	27	2956	C	Thurs.	„ 18	..	April 7	2957	355
11 E	6718	Sat.	Aug. 28	..	Sept.17	2957	B	Tues.	April 5	..	25	2958	383
12	6719	Thurs.	Sept. 15	..	Oct. 5	2958	A	Sat.	March 25	..	April 14	2959	354
13	6720	Mon.	„ 4	..	24	2959	G	Thurs.	„ 14	..	April 3	2960 b	355
14 E	6721	Sat.	Aug. 24	..	Sept.13	2960	E	Tues.	April 1	..	21	2961	383
15	6722	Thurs.	Sept. 11	..	Oct. 1	2961	D	Sun.	March 22	..	April 11	2962	355
16	6723	Tues.	„ 1	..	21	2962	C	Thurs.	„ 11	..	31	2963	354
17 E	6724	Sat.	Aug. 21	..	Sept.10	2963	B	Thurs.	„ 30	..	April 19	2964 b	385
18	6725	Sat.	Sept. 9	..	29	2964	G	Sun.	„ 18	..	April 7	2965	353
19 E	6726	Tues.	Aug. 28	..	Sept.17	2965	F	Sat.	April 6	..	26	2966	384

Molad 2 8 234. CYCLE 355. Days, 6940.

1	6727	Mon.	Sept. 16	Oct. 6	2966	E	Thurs.	March 27	April 16	2967	353
2	6728	Sat.	„ 6	26	2967	D	Tues.	„ 6	April 5	2968 b	355
3 E	6729	Thurs.	Aug. 26	Sept. 15	2968	B	Sun.	April 3	23	2969	383
4	6730	Tues.	Sept. 13	Oct. 3	2969	A	Thurs.	March 23	April 12	2970	354
5	6731	Sat.	„ 2	22	2970	G	Tues.	„ 13	April 2	2971	355
6 E	6732	Thurs.	Aug. 23	Sept. 12	2971	F	Tues.	April 1	21	2972 b	385
7	6733	Thurs.	Sept. 11	Oct. 1	2972	D	Sat.	March 21	April 10	2973	354
8 E	6734	Mon.	Aug. 31	Sept. 20	2973	C	Thurs.	April 8	28	2974	383
9	6735	Sat.	Sept. 18	Oct. 8	2974	B	Tues.	March 29	April 18	2975	355
10	6736	Thurs.	„ 8	28	2975	A	Sat.	„ 17	April 6	2976 b	354
11 E	6737	Mon.	Aug. 27	Sept. 16	2976	F	Thurs.	April 4	24	2977	383
12	6738	Sat.	Sept. 14	Oct. 4	2977	E	Tues.	March 25	April 14	2978	355
13	6739	Thurs.	„ 4	24	2978	D	Sat.	„ 14	April 3	2979	354
14 E	6740	Mon.	Aug. 24	Sept. 13	2979	C	Sat.	April 2	22	2980 b	385
15	6741	Mon.	Sept. 12	Oct. 2	2980	A	Tues.	March 21	April 10	2981	353
16	6742	Thurs.	Aug. 31	Sept. 20	2981	G	Sun.	„ 11	31	2982	355
17 E	6743	Tues.	„ 21	Sept. 10	2982	F	Sat.	„ 30	April 19	2983	384
18	6744	Mon.	Sept. 9	29	2983	E	Thurs.	„ 19	April 8	2984 b	355
19 E	6745	Sat.	Aug. 29	Sept. 18	2984	C	Tues.	April 6	26	2985	383

Molad 5 0 829. CYCLE 356. Days, 6939.

1	6746	Thurs.	Sept. 16	Oct. 6	2985	B	Sat.	March 26	April 15	2986	354
2	6747	Mon.	„ 5	25	2986	A	Thurs.	„ 16	April 5	2987	355
3 E	6748	Sat.	Aug. 6	Sept. 15	2987	G	Tues.	April 2	22	2988 b	383
4	6749	Thurs.	Sept. 12	Oct. 2	2988	E	Sun.	March 23	April 12	2989	355
5	6750	Tues.	„ 2	22	2989	D	Thurs.	„ 12	April 1	2990	354
6 E	6751	Sat.	Aug. 22	Sept. 11	2990	C	Thurs.	April 1	21	2991	385
7	6752	Sat.	Sept. 11	Oct. 1	2991	B	Sun.	March 19	April 8	2992 b	353
8 E	6753	Tues.	Aug. 29	Sept. 18	2992	G	Sat.	April 7	27	2993	384
9	6754	Mon.	Sept. 17	Oct. 7	2993	F	Thurs.	March 28	April 17	2994	355
10	6755	Sat.	„ 7	27	2994	E	Tues.	„ 18	April 7	2995	355
11 E	6756	Thurs.	Aug. 28	Sept. 17	2995	D	Sun.	April 4	24	2996 b	383
12	6757	Tues.	Sept. 14	Oct. 4	2996	B	Thurs.	March 24	April 13	2997	354
13	6758	Sat.	„ 3	23	2997	A	Tues.	„ 14	April 3	2998	355
14 E	6759	Thurs.	Aug. 24	Sept. 13	2998	G	Tues.	April 3	23	2999	385
15	6760	Thurs.	Sept. 13	Oct. 3	2999	F	Sat.	March 22	April 12	3000	354
16	6761	Mon.	„ 1	22	3000	E	Tues.	„ 10	31	3001	353
17 E	6762	Thurs.	Aug. 20	Sept. 10	3001	D	Tues.	„ 30	April 20	3002	385
18	6763	Thurs.	Sept. 9	30	3002	C	Sat.	„ 19	April 9	3003	354
19 E	6764	Mon.	Aug. 29	Sept. 19	3003	B	Thurs.	April 5	26	3004 b	383

PART II

THE MUHAMMADAN CALENDAR

CHAPTER I

THE ARABIAN YEAR BEFORE MUḤAMMAD. ERA OF THE HIJRA. COMPUTATION OF TIME AS ESTABLISHED BY MUḤAMMAD.

1. It appears to be certain that from very ancient times till shortly after the commencement of the fifth century of the Christian Era the pagan Arabians made use of a purely Lunar year.* One of the practices of their religion, to which they attached the highest importance, was an annual pilgrimage to the Ka'ba, the sacred Temple at Mecca, which they believed to have been almost coeval with the world itself. They held that a representation of it was sent down from heaven after the expulsion of Ādam from Paradise; that a building was erected on the site by Seth after the death of Adam; and that it was rebuilt, at the command of God, by Abraham and Ishmael.†

The pilgrimage to this shrine was always made in the twelfth month of the year. The tenth day of that month was fixed for the Feast of Victims, when the animals which had been brought to Mecca to be sacrificed were slaughtered. This was the last of the days of the pilgrimage, and it must be understood that when, hereafter, the date of the pilgrimage is quoted it is to the date of this last day that reference is made.

2. Inasmuch as the Lunar year of twelve months is nearly eleven days shorter than the Solar year it follows that the commencement of the ancient Arabian year, and the time of the pilgrimage, became

* *Cf.* Caussin de Perceval, "Essai sur l'Histoire des Arabes avant L'Islamisme," tom. i. p. 241. Paris, 1847.

† For an account of the Ka'ba see Sale's translation of the Qu'rán, "Preliminary Discourse," section iv.

eleven days earlier in every successive Solar year, and as time went on must have run through all the seasons.* When, from this cause, the pilgrimage occurred before the harvests of the current year were gathered, and when those of the preceding year had been almost or perhaps entirely consumed, the pilgrims found great difficulty in obtaining food. To remedy this inconvenience, the Arabians endeavoured to remodel their year in such a manner that the pilgrimage should always take place in the Autumn, when both grain and fruit were abundant.

With this object in view they formed a Luni-Solar year by intercalating, from time to time, a thirteenth Lunar month at the end of their twelve Lunar months. This method of keeping, or rather of attempting to keep, the months in unison with the seasons, they had learned from the Jews who were settled at Yathrib.† They adopted it in A.D. 412, two hundred years before Islâm, or the Muslem religion, was introduced by Muḥammad.‡

3. The intercalated, or Embolismic, month was called Nasî, a word which properly signifies "retardation" or "postponement," for its effect, when it was employed at the end of any given year, was to postpone the commencement of the following year by one Lunar month,§ in this respect resembling the duplication of Adhâr by the Jews. Those to whom the duty of making and proclaiming the intercalation was committed were called Nasa'a; they belonged to the tribe Kinâna, and were known also as the Ḳalâmis, a plural form of the word Ḳalâmmas, which signifies a full-flowing sea, because they were possessed, as it were, of a sea of knowledge.‖

Different opinions have been held by Arabian writers as to the exact occasions when the Embolismic month was added to the year. Some have maintained that the intercalation was made nine times in every twenty-four years; others that it was done seven times in every nineteen years, according to the method adopted by the Jews about

* See *post*, Article 10.

† The ancient name of the city Al-Medina.

‡ Al-Bîrûnî, "Vestiges," pp. 14, 73. The word Islâm means "Submission," that is, to the will of God.

§ Graetz, in his "History of the Jews," vol. iii. p. 61, is probably wrong in deriving the word from the Hebrew Nasî, the name given to the Jewish Patriarch who communicated to the people the time when Festivals were to be observed.

‖ Al-Bîrûnî, pp. 13 and 73.

the middle of the fourth century.* Scaliger seems to take this for granted ("De Emend. Temporum," lib. ii. p. 110), and gives a Table showing the commencements of the years for three periods of seventy-six years each.

Some, again, say that the addition to the Lunar year was made whenever the error arising from the difference in the length of the lunar and solar year amounted to one month. This question may be left open for the present; it will be discussed in Chapter V., when the views of M. Caussin de Perceval upon the subject will be given.

In whatever way it may have been done it is generally believed that from the year 412 of the Christian Era an intercalation was made, and that the custom of making it was abolished by Muḥammad in the year before his death, which occurred on June 8, A.D. 632. He then established the system which is still in use among Muḥammadans of all nations.

4. In order to understand what the Prophet said with reference to this subject it will be necessary to refer to another practice. The pagan Arabians, from the most ancient times, had kept four months in the year as sacred. During these months it was not lawful to engage in war, or in any predatory expedition. These months were the first, the seventh, the eleventh, and the twelfth. Thus, while one of the sacred months, the seventh, was isolated in the middle of the year, there were three which were consecutive, the eleventh and the twelfth of one year with the first of the next year. The Arabians sometimes found this to be inconvenient. They did not appreciate the privilege of not being allowed to attack an enemy for three whole months at a time; and so the custom arose of effecting an exchange between the characters of the first and second months in the year, the sacredness of the first being transferred to the second, and the first receiving the secular character of the second.

The duty of declaring that this change was to be made was assigned to the Nasa'a, or Ḳalâmis. Their names have been preserved by al-Bîrûnî.† The change itself was called by the same name as the intercalation—Nasî—because, since it postponed the commencement of that sacred month which was the first month of the year, it post-

* It was certainly after A.D. 325, when the Council of Nicæa was held, at which time the Metonic Cycle was adopted by the Christians, and afterwards by the Jews.

† "Vestiges," p. 13.

poned, equally with an intercalation, the commencement of the year itself.

According to al-Bîrûnî the pagan Arabians had no special name for the intercalated month. When an intercalation took place the names of the months were simply shifted by one place: thus, if an intercalation occurred at the end of a given year the intercalated month was called by the name usually given to the first month of the year—Muḥarram; then the second month, usually called Ṣafar, became Muḥarram; the third month, usually called Rabî'u-l-avval, became Ṣafar, and so on. In this way all the names of the months were changed; and this went on till successive intercalations had passed through all the twelve months of the year, when Muḥarram returned both to its place and name.*

5. These, then, were the customs of the Nasî which were abolished by Muḥammad. He is reported to have said, in the course of an address delivered on the morning of the ninth day of the twelfth month, being the last day but one of the yearly pilgrimage, the day corresponding to Saturday, March 8, A.D. 632:—

"Certainly the Nasî is an impious addition, which has led the infidels into error. One year they authorise the Nasî,† another year they forbid it. They observe the divine precept with respect to the number of the sacred months, but in fact they profane that which God has declared to be inviolable, and sanctify that which God has declared to be profane. Assuredly time, in its revolution, has returned to such as it was at the creation of the heavens and the earth. In the eyes of God the number of the months is twelve. Among these twelve months four are sacred, namely, Rajab, which stands alone, and three others which are consecutive."

This passage from the address of the prophet, preserved by tradition, is reproduced in the Qu'rân, Sûrah ix. 36, 37:—

"Moreover, the complete number of months with God is twelve months, which were ordained in the book of God on the day when He created the heavens and the earth: of these, four are sacred. This is the right religion: therefore deal not unjustly with yourselves therein. Attack the infidels in all the months, as they attack you in all; and know that God is with those who fear Him. Verily, the transferring

* "Vestiges," p. 73.

† That is, they retard Muḥarram, either by transposition or by intercalation.

of a sacred month to another month is an additional infidelity. The unbelievers are led into an error thereby: they allow a month to be violated one year, and declare it sacred another year, that they may agree in the number of months which God hath commanded to be kept sacred; and they allow that which God hath forbidden."*

The character of the sacred months was sustained by Muḥammad to a certain extent, and their observance is enforced in several passages in the Qu'rân. His followers were not, however, forbidden altogether to wage war in these months. On the contrary, they were encouraged to "attack the infidels in all the months." In this respect the Prophet himself had set the example. In the year 631, the year preceding that in which he delivered his address, he had led an expedition against the Romans in the sacred month Rajab.† The violation of the sacred months which he forbade was engaging in warfare against any fellow-believers, against any who held these months to be sacred, full permission being given to attack those who did not hold the same views. Nevertheless, after the expedition against the Romans the sanctity of the four months came to consist rather in the idea that any offence committed while they were current was of far greater gravity than if committed at any other time.

THE ERA OF THE HIJRA.

6. The word Hijra‡ means "Departure," or "Flight," and the consequent "Separation of friends." The Era derives its name from the Flight of Muḥammad from Mecca to Medina. It is frequently said to have commenced with the day upon which Muḥammad fled from Mecca.§

* "The AlKoran of Mohammed," trans. by G. Sale, ch. ix. p. 153. London, 1844.

† Caussin de Perceval, "Histoire des Arabes," tom. iii. p. 304. Gibbon's "History," chap. l.

‡ Lat. and Ang., Hegira. Fr., Hégire. Ger., die Hegira; Epoche der Hedschra; die Aere der Flucht.

§ Thus, "L'Art de vérifier les Dates," pt. ii. tom. i. p. 53, "L'Hégire a pour epoque le jour que Mahomet s'enfuit de la Mecque à Medine; et ce jour repond, suivant l'usage civil, au Vendredi, 16 Juillet de l'an de Jésus Christ 622."

So, too, Professor Wilson in his Glossary: "The Flight of Mohammed from Mecca to Medina was constituted the commencement of the Mohammedan Era: this event took place on the night of Thursday the 15th of July, A.D. 622. The usual Era therefore reckons from the dawn of the 16th of July."

Woolhouse, "Measures, Weights, and Moneys of all Nations," p. 198, writes: "The Era of the Hegira is dated from the flight of Mahomet from Mecca to Medina, which was in the night of Thursday the 15th of July, A.D. 622, and it commenced on the day following."

By others it is said to commence with the day upon which he entered Medina after the Flight.* Both of these statements are wrong.

Gibbon, in his account, gives the year only, not the day of the year; but in Note 118 to Chalmer's edition of the "History of the Decline and Fall of the Roman Empire," the date of the Flight is made to be sixty-eight days after July 16, corresponding to September 22, A.D. 622. This is incorrect.

Historians in general assert that Muḥammad fled from Mecca at the commencement of the third month of the Arabian year, Rabî'u-l-avval. They do not agree as to the precise day. According to Ibn-Ishâk it was on the first or second day of the month; Abul'fêda says that it was on the eighth day.†

Al-Bîrûnî makes the date of the arrival at Medina to be Monday, the eighth day of Rabî'u-l-avval, corresponding according to the old Arabian Calendar to June 24, A.D. 622.‡

Crichton gives the date of the Flight as fifty-nine days after July 16.§

According to the calculation of M. Caussin de Perceval, "made after consideration of all the authorities most worthy of credit," Muḥammad fled from Mecca on the fourth day of Rabî'u-l-avval, corresponding to June 20, A.D. 622; and he entered the territory of Yathrib at the village of Coba, on Monday the twelfth day of the same month. He says that the distance from Mecca to Medina, by the road, cannot be traversed, even by a fugitive, in less than six or seven days.

* Bond, "Handy Book," p. 228. "The Era of the Mohammedans, called the Hegira, or Flight of the Prophet, dates from the day on which Mohammed entered Medina after his flight from Mecca, Friday, the 16th of July, 622 A.D."

Sault, in his translation of Strauchius, 2nd ed., 1704, p. 404, says: "The Epocha begins from the time of the Flight of Mahomet from Meccha, which, without contradiction, happened in the year of Christ 602" [a misprint for 622], "or in the year of the Julian Period 5355, on the 16th July, being the 6th Feria," Friday.

Playfair, in his Chronology published in 1784, escapes the error. At page 23 he says: "This flight happened in the fourteenth year after Mahomet was declared the prophet of God, and on the twelfth day of Rabi-al-Aoual, *i.e.* Prior, which is the third month of the Arabian year, yet the Mahometans compute their aera from the month of Mucharrem preceding, which answers to the 15th or 16th of July, A.D. 622."

† Ibn-Ishâk, "Ta'rîkh-al-khamîs," f. 143. Abul'fêda, "Vie de Mahomet, traduction de M. Desverges," p. 30. Both of these authorities are given in the text as quoted by M. Caussin de Perceval, "Histoire," tom. iii. p. 16.

‡ "Vestiges," p. 327.

§ "History of Arabia," 2nd ed. vol. i. p. 251. Edinburgh, 1854.

Burckhardt ("Travels in Arabia") states that caravans taking the direct route occupy ten or twelve days in passing from Mecca to Medina, which is three or four hours' additional march from Coba.

Besides the time occupied by the journey, there were the four days which Muḥammad passed in the cave on Mount Thour, which was three miles south of Mecca, and therefore on the side opposite to Medina.

Making allowance for this delay, and for the least possible time that could have been occupied in the actual Flight, Muḥammad, if he arrived at Medina on the twelfth, could not have left Mecca later than the second or third day of the month, which would be the date of the true Flight.

A very interesting account of the events which preceded and followed the Flight is given in Sir William Mure's "Life of Mahomet," and in "Mahomet and Islam," by the same author.

If the date given by al-Bîrûnî for the arrival of the Prophet at Medina were correct it would only allow four days for the journey and for the delay in the cave.

7. The date of the Flight must be carefully distinguished from the date of the commencement of the Era of the Hijra, instead of the two being confused together as is so frequently the case. Although the custom of referring to events according to the year of the Flight originated with Muḥammad, yet the Era of the Hijra was not officially instituted till seven years after his death, which took place in the third month of the eleventh year of the Era, June, A.D. 632,* and consequently seventeen years after the Flight.

Moreover, when the Era was instituted, by the Khalîfa 'Umar, its commencement was not made to coincide either with the day of the Flight or with the day upon which the prophet arrived at Medina. It was intended to commemorate the Flight, but in order that the change in the method of reckoning time might not alter the first day of the Arabian year, the Era was made to commence two months antecedent to the Flight, namely, with the first day of the month Muḥarram, the first day of the year current at the time of the Flight,

* Scaliger, "De Emend. Temp.," lib. ii. p. 136, C, is mistaken in placing the date of the prophet's death one year earlier than this. He says, "Anno Hegiræ X, obiit igitur anno Christi 631, circa xvi aut xvii Junii."

the day upon which the Festival of the New Year had from time immemorial been commemorated.*

This day corresponded to July 16, A.D. 622, according to Civil reckoning.

The error with respect to the Era, to which reference has been made above, consists in the assertion that this day was the day of the Prophet's Flight from Mecca; or, as others say, that it was the day of his arrival at Medina. It was neither the one nor the other.

8. The date for the commencement of the Era, Friday, July 16, A.D. 622, was, until M. Caussin de Perceval investigated the subject, almost if not quite universally adopted by chronologists. Strauchius says that "it is without contradiction." It will presently be explained how the date is sometimes given as Thursday, July 15, when time is reckoned according to the method of the Arabian astronomers. It will then be seen that these are only two names for the same day.†

M. de Perceval does not admit that the first year of the Hijra did really commence at the date which is usually assigned to it. There is every reason for thinking that he is right. Muḥammad did not abolish the current Arabian method of computing by Luni-Solar years with the intercalation of a thirteenth month every third year, until the end of the tenth year of the Flight, in the month corresponding to March, A.D. 632. Now these ten years, according to the Arabian Calendar, which was then in use, contained 3630 days, for three of them, at least, were Embolismic and had 384 days, while the remaining seven years had each 354 days. In making July 16, A.D. 622 to be the first day of the Era of the Hijra these ten years are computed according to Hijra reckoning, and made to contain only 3544 days, namely, six years of 354 days, and four years of 355 days; that being in accord with the method introduced by Muḥammad, as will be seen hereafter.

These ten years ought certainly to be reckoned in chronology

* Uluigh Beigh, "Epochæ Celebriores," trans. Gravius, 1650, p. 8. "Initium hujus Epochæ est principium Moharram illius anni, in quo propheta noster Mohammades Mostofa cui benedictio et pax sit, à Meccâ ad Medinam migrabat; et illud secundùm medium calculum est feria quinta, sed secundùm phasim Lunæ, dies Veneris."

† See *post*, Articles 15 and 16.

according to the Calendar which was in use during the period of time which they covered, and not according to a Calendar which was introduced after these years had expired.

9. M. Caussin de Perceval, on this account, makes the date of Muharram 1, A.H. 1, to be Monday, April 10, A.D. 622.

He considers that among the ten years in question, the first, the fourth, and the seventh were Embolismic, according to the Arabian Calendar. He deduces the following dates for their commencements:—

First year	Monday	April 19	A.D.	622	Emb.
Second ,,	Saturday	May 7	,,	623	
Third ,,	Thursday	April 26	,,	624	
Fourth ,,	Monday	April 15	,,	625	Emb.
Fifth ,,	Saturday	May 3	,,	626	
Sixth ,,	Thursday	April 23	,,	627	
Seventh ,,	Tuesday	April 12	,,	628	Emb.
Eighth ,,	Monday	May 1	,,	629	
Ninth ,,	Friday	April 20	,,	630	
Tenth ,,	Tuesday	April 9	,,	631	

According to this computation, the eighth year, which commenced with Monday, May 1, A.D. 629, would be the first of the future series of years in which no year was permitted to have more than twelve months.

M. de Perceval considers that the Tables which are usually published may be safely employed from this year forward, inclusive. In the Chronological Table at the end of this book, it will be seen that the commencement of years 8, 9, and 10 of the Hijra are in agreement with M. de Perceval's argument; but the preceding seven years are given according to the generally received chronology, and are coincident with the dates assigned by all historians hitherto for events which took place before they had elapsed.

During these first ten years, before the Arabian Calendar was abolished, it does not appear that the years were called the first, second, third, &c. of the Flight. Al-Bîrûnî says * that it was superfluous to denote them by numbers, because special names were given

* "Vestiges," p. 35.

to them by the people—names derived from some event which had happened to Muḥammad during each particular year.

The First was called	The year of the		permission.
Second	,,	,,	order for fighting.
Third	,,	,,	trial.
Fourth	,,	,,	congratulation on marriage.
Fifth	,,	,,	earthquake.
Sixth	,,	,,	enquiring.
Seventh	,,	,,	gaining victory.
Eighth	,,	,,	equality.
Ninth	,,	,,	exemption.
Tenth	,,	,,	farewell.

CHAPTER II

THE COMPUTATION OF TIME AS ESTABLISHED BY MUḤAMMAD

10. When the Prophet abolished the old Arabian Calendar the Muḥammadan year became exclusively Lunar. It was, and it still is, governed by the Moon alone, without any regard to the length of the Solar year, or to the seasons, which consequently "wander" through the year, coming later and later, according to Calendar dates, at every recurrence. For the Muḥammadan Lunar year of twelve months is, roughly speaking, eleven days shorter than the true Solar year; so that if at any given time the Spring season commences on the first day of the Muḥammadan year, it will not commence till the twelfth day in the next year, the twenty-third day in the next, the thirty-fourth in the year which follows, and so onwards, till it has wandered through all the months. In fact, in every thirty-three Muḥammadan years there are only thirty-two occurrences of each of the four seasons. This is according to the Civil, or established reckoning of the Calendar. Of course it is not so practically; the agriculturist sows his seed and reaps his harvest not by the Calendar of his religion, but under the influence of the Sun.

The Calendar itself is based on a Cycle of thirty years, each consisting of twelve months. There are two different methods of computing the commencement and the duration of these months. These two methods may be distinguished as the Civil or chronological, and the common or popular, sometimes called the practical, reckoning.

First, with respect to the Civil reckoning, by which all historical events are dated. Every year consists of twelve months; of these months, those which when all are arranged in numerical order are "uneven," as the first, the third, &c., have each thirty days; those which are "even," as the second, the fourth, &c., have twenty-nine days.

This arrangement would make the Cycle of thirty years to consist of 360 months, containing $6 \times 30 \times 30 + 6 \times 30 \times 29$, or 10620 days; but the months are intended to be Lunar, and to coincide as nearly as possible, after avoiding fractions of a day, with the length of a Lunation. Now, the mean length of a Lunation was estimated by the Arabian astronomers at 29d. 12h. 44m., and if this interval of time be multiplied by 360 it makes the 360 Lunar months, or the thirty years of the Cycle, to consist of 10631 days, indicating that the former number, 10620, is too short by eleven days.

In order that the whole number of 10631 days might be contained within the Cycle of thirty years it became necessary to increase the length of some of these years. This was done by adding one day to the length of each of eleven years. Those selected for the purpose are numbered in the Cycle thus :—2, 5, 7, 10, 13, 16, 18, 21, 24, 26, 29.*

The additional day in each of these years is intercalated at the end of the last month, which, therefore, has thirty instead of twenty-nine days. The last month in each of the other nineteen years has only twenty-nine days.

The intercalated day is called yaum Kabîsah, the intercalary year is 'am Kabîsah.

11. In order to judge how far the system of Kabîsah years tends to harmonise the Civil with the Lunar reckoning of time, it must be noticed that at the close of the second year, when Twenty-four Lunations are supposed to have elapsed, the mean Lunar time which has passed is, according to Muḥammadan computation, 708d. 17h. 36m. If, then, the Lunar years were all limited to 354 days, there would be in two such years 708 days only, and nearly three-fourths of another day would be required to equalise this number of days to the value of twenty-four Lunations. It is impossible to add three-quarters of a day, or any fraction of a day to a Calendar year, and accordingly one whole day is added at the end of the second year, making it Kabîsah.

At the close of five years, or sixty Lunations, the mean Lunar time that has elapsed is, by Muḥammadan computation, 1771d. 20h. 0m. But 5 × 354 days, together with the one day which was added to the second year, make only 1771 days. Five-sixths of a day more is required, therefore one whole day is added to the fifth year, which becomes Kabîsah; and the first five years of the Cycle have together 5 × 354 + 2, or 1772 days, being only four hours longer than sixty Muḥammadan Lunations.

* Uluigh Beigh, "Epochæ Celebriores," Gravius, p. 10, makes the fifteenth year to be Kabîsah instead of the sixteenth. He is followed by Meier Kornick, "System der Zeitrechnung in Chronologischen Tabellen," p. xxxiii. The sixteenth year is that which is generally received. Al-Bîrûnî has "fifteenth, or sixteenth."

By continuing this process, and tabulating the results, it will be seen that those years which are made Kabîsah are such as most nearly fulfil the condition of requiring an intercalated day. In fact, these days are added at the most fitting opportunities, when the Lunations elapsed exceed the number of days contained in the years by more than twelve hours.

LUNAR COMPUTATION FOR THE SYSTEM OF KABÎSAH YEARS

Years of Cycle.	Days elapsed c = 354.	Lunations.	Time elapsed by Muḥammadan computation.		
			Days.	H.	M.
1	c = 354	12	354	8	48
2 K	2c + 1 = 709	24	708	17	36
3	3c + 1 = 1063	36	1063	2	24
4	4c + 1 = 1417	48	1417	11	12
5 K	5c + 2 = 1772	60	1771	20	0
6	6c + 2 = 2126	72	2126	4	48
7 K	7c + 3 = 2481	84	2480	13	36
8	8c + 3 = 2835	96	2834	22	24
9	9c + 3 = 3189	108	3189	7	12
10 K	10c + 4 = 3544	120	3543	16	0
11	11c + 4 = 3898	132	3898	0	48
12	12c + 4 = 4252	144	4252	9	36
13 K	13c + 5 = 4607	156	4606	18	24
14	14c + 5 = 4961	168	4961	3	12
15	15c + 5 = 5315	180	5315	12	0
16 K	16c + 6 = 5670	192	5669	20	48
17	17c + 6 = 6024	204	6024	5	36
18 K	18c + 7 = 6379	216	6378	14	24
19	19c + 7 = 6733	228	6732	23	12
20	20c + 7 = 7087	240	7087	8	0
21 K	21c + 8 = 7442	252	7441	16	48
22	22c + 8 = 7796	264	7796	1	36
23	23c + 8 = 8150	276	8150	10	24
24 K	24c + 9 = 8505	288	8504	19	12
25	25c + 9 = 8859	300	8859	4	0
26 K	26c + 10 = 9214	312	9213	12	48
27	27c + 10 = 9568	324	9567	21	36
28	28c + 10 = 9922	336	9922	6	24
29 K	29c + 11 = 10277	348	10276	15	12
30	30c + 11 = 10631	360	10631	0	0

The result thus reached attains to considerable accuracy. The actual mean length of a Synodical month or Lunation is, by modern computation, 29d. 12h. 44m. 2·684s.; so that 360 mean Lunations contain 10631d. 0h. 16m. 6·24s. In other words, the Muḥammadan Cycle of thirty years terminates too soon by 16m. 6·24s., Lunar time, an error which amounts to a whole day in 2683 Lunar years nearly. It will therefore become necessary for the Muḥammadans to reform their Calendar by adding one day to their eighty-ninth or ninetieth Cycle.*

12. With respect to the common or popular reckoning—the beginning of each month is determined by actual observation; that is, by the first appearance of the crescent of the New Moon, which would not be visible till the evening of the first, or second, perhaps even of the third day after the actual Conjunction had taken place. If, through obscurity caused by clouds, the crescent is not visible on the third evening, no further postponement of the first day of the month takes place. The consequence of this is that the popular commencement of the month will differ in various places according to the time when the Moon may first become visible. For instance, in one place the crescent may be seen in the evening of the second day after the Conjunction; in another place the heavens may be covered with clouds, and the crescent not be visible till the third day. The commencement of the month may thus differ by a whole day in the same country.†

13. The Muḥammadan day is reckoned from Sunset to Sunset. The "day-time" is from Sunrise to Sunset, and as it is divided into twelve hours, these hours of necessity vary in length according to the season. If the Sun set at six o'clock the Civil day will commence at that hour,

* The ninetieth Cycle commences with the year of the Hijra 2671
= December 24, A.D. 3212, Julian Calendar,
= January 15, A.D. 3213, Gregorian Calendar.

† "It must be specially noted that variation of latitude and longitude sometimes causes a difference in the number of days in a month; for since the beginning of the Muhammadan month depends on the heliacal rising of the moon, the month may begin a day earlier at one place than at another, and therefore the following month may contain in one case a day more than in the other. Hence it is not right to lay down a law for all places in the world where Muhammadan reckoning is used, asserting that invariably months have alternately 29 and 30 days. No universal rule can be made, therefore, and each case can only be a matter of calculation." "The Indian Calendar," by R. Sewell and Sankara Bâlkṛishṇa Dikshit. Article 166, p. 103.

preceding the commencement of our own Civil day by six hours. The night-time of the hours which constitute a day precedes the day-time.

We are in the habit of speaking of a day and a night as forming a day, although it would be more strictly correct to speak of a half-night, a day, and a another half-night, namely, midnight to 6 a.m., 6 a.m. to 6 p.m., and 6 p.m. to midnight. The Muḥammadans would say that a night and a day form a day. Thus, the night immediately preceding our Sunday is commonly called by us Saturday night. By the Muḥammadans the same interval of time would be called Sunday night, or the night of Sunday. If any event happen here at 7 or 8 p.m. on Wednesday night, a Muḥammadan would speak of the same event as happening on Thursday night.

14. The hours are reckoned from one to twelve, and then from one to twelve again; Sunset being the close of the last hour. One hour after Sunset, which (when the Sun sets at 6 p.m.), we should call 7 o'clock in the evening, is with the Muḥammadans 1 o'clock in the night. Two hours after Sunset is 2 o'clock; and so on. Our 6 o'clock in the morning is 12 o'clock with them, and our Noon is 6 o'clock.

Lane says * that "the Egyptians set their watches, if necessary, at Sunset; or rather, a few minutes after; generally when they hear the call to evening prayer. Their watches, according to this system of reckoning time from Sunset to be always quite correct, should be set every evening as the days vary in length." This was written in 1833–35. The custom of setting watches at the time of evening prayer still prevails.

Lane further states that "a pocket almanac was annually printed at the Government press at Boolák. It comprises the period of a Solar year, commencing and terminating with the Vernal Equinox. It gives, for every day of the week, the day of the Muḥammadan, Coptic, Syrian, and European month. The Sun's place in the Zodiac, the time of Sunrise, Noon, and 'asr, that is about midway between Noon and nightfall."

The 'asr, to which he refers, is the time of afternoon prayer. The Prophet would not permit his followers to pray at exact Sunrise, Noon, or Sunset, because, he said, infidels worshipped the Sun at those times. Evening prayer is about four minutes after Sunset.

At the present time there is published a "Sudan Almanac, com-

* "Manners and Customs of the Modern Egyptians," ch. ix. p. 220, 5th ed. Lond., 1860.

piled at the Intelligence Division, War Office." The calculations for this Almanac are made at the office of the Nautical Almanac. It is for the current Gregorian year, and gives, for each month, the Phases of the Moon, the Arabic date corresponding to each day of the month, the day of the week, the mean time at Wadi Halfa at which the Moon rises and sets, the time of Sunrise and Sunset. It has a Column of Remarks, in which are noted both the Muḥammadan and Anglican Festivals and Fasts, and recent important events. At the end there are added some useful Notes, with Tables of Distances, the Latitudes and Longitudes of certain places in Egypt, and Measures, Weights, and Currency.

15. In considering Muḥammadan dates it is important to keep in mind the difference between the commencement of their day and of our own; otherwise confusion will occur. Hence arises a cause for dates which differ by a day being assigned to the same event, one historian referring to the Muḥammadan, another to the Christian day. A second cause for this is found in the fact that the Muḥammadans, like ourselves, have an Astronomical as well as a Civil day. The Astronomical commences earlier by six hours than the Civil day, namely, at the Noon which falls within the twenty-four hours of the preceding Civil day. With ourselves, on the contrary, the commencement of the Astronomical day is twelve hours later than the commencement of the Civil day, being reckoned from Noon of the Civil day.

As an instance of the discrepancy in dates which thus arises, nearly all modern chronologists give Friday, July 16, A.D. 622, as the date for the commencement of the Muḥammadan Era. Abu al-Hasan * and Uluigh Beigh † both give a day which corresponds to Thursday, July 15 in the same year. They are followed by Ideler.‡

Upon this point the authors of "L'Art de Vérifier les Dates" say: "Elle (*i.e.*, Hégire) a pour époque le jour que Mahomet s'enfuit de la Mecque à Medine §; et ce jour répond, suivant l'usage civil, au vendredi, 16 juillet de l'an de Jésus-Christ 622; mais les astronomes,

* Abu al-Hasan 'Alī Marrākushī. "Traité des Instruments Astronomiques des Arabe compose au treizième siècle, traduit de' l'Arabe par J. J. Sédillot." Paris, 1834–35.

† "Epochæ Celebriores," p. 10, and Table following p. 104.

‡ "Handbuch," ii. Band. pp. 483–4, 568, 629.

§ It has been already pointed out (Article 6) that this is incorrect. Muḥammadan Civil use.

et mêmes quelques historiens, la mettent au jeudi précédent, 15 juillet; ce qui avance d'un jour toute la suite de l'Hégire. C'est une observation qu'il ne faut point perdre de vue, en lisant les écrivains Arabes."*

Sédillot, in his notes on Abu al-Hasan, also explains the way in which the difference arises. Speaking of an example of a rule given by that author, in which Monday is found to be the initial day of a certain given year of the Hijra, he says: "L'Art de Vérifier les Dates donne le Mardi pour jour initial de la même année, parce que dans cet ouvrage on procède par années civiles au lieu que dans celui-ci † c'est par années astronomiques, et que l'année astronomique des Arabes commence un jour plus tôt que l'année civile, ou, pour parler plus exactement, commence au midi vrai du jour précédent. C'est ainsi que l'Art de Vérifier les Dates donne, avec tous les chronologistes, pour le premier jour de l'ère de l'Hégire, le vendredi 16 juillet 622 de J-X., à minuit, tandis que cette ère commence civilement le Jeudi 15 au soir, et astronomiquement le même jour à midi. Mais cela s'éclaircit en faisant attention que les Arabes commencent à compter Vendredi, ou leur sixième férie civile, le Jeudi au soir, et que le midi du Jeudi qui appartient à la cinquième férie civile commence la sixième férie astronomique. En un mot, les Astronomies ajoutent une unité au quatrième sans changer le férie." ‡

16. Suppose that some event occurred during the first twelve hours, Civil time, of our Friday, July 16, A.D. 622, that is to say, between the Midnight of July 15-16, and the Noon of July 16. These same twelve hours, according to the Muḥammadan Astronomical reckoning, are the last twelve of the preceding day, Thursday, July 15.

Now, in "L'Art de Vérifier les Dates," in Lacoine's "Tables de Concordance des Dates des Calendriers," in Playfair's "Chronology," in Rees' "Cyclopædia," in Woolhouse's "Measures, Weights, and Moneys," in Bond's "Handy Book," and in other books, as well as in the Chronological Table herewith, dates are given according to Common Civil, or historical time, unless it be otherwise specifically stated. On the other hand, in the work of Abu al-Hasan, in Uluigh Beigh, in the text of Ideler, in the "Tabella Chronologica of the Glossarium" of Du Cange, and by others, Muḥammadan dates are given according to Muḥammadan Astronomical reckoning of time.

* Pt. ii. tom. i. p. 53. † "Traité des Instruments." ‡ Sédillot, p. 88.

Thus it comes to pass that an event which occurred, say, on Friday, July 16, according to our common reckoning, is stated by these latter writers to have occurred on feria 5 (Thursday), July 15.*

Let it be quite understood that, under these circumstances, Chronologists do not differ as to the actual day upon which the event in question took place. They do but call the same day by different names, just as we, making use of ordinary Civil time might say that the Sun rises in the morning of July 13 at 4 o'clock, while our astronomers would give the time as July, 12d. 16h. The same Sunrise, the same day, the same hour, is identified, whichever of the two methods for marking the occurrence be adopted.

17. With reference to the Tables of Muḥammadan years, Woolhouse says: † "All the Tables which have hitherto been published of this kind, which extend beyond the year 1900 of the Christian Era, are erroneous, not excepting the celebrated French work 'L'Art de Vérifier les Dates,' so justly regarded as the greatest authority in chronological matters. The errors have probably arisen from a continued excess of 10 in the discrimination of the intercalary years, and they have been faithfully transcribed by other writers."

This is sweeping condemnation, and it cannot be accepted without inquiry, although it has received the endorsement of the "Encyclopædia Britannica." In that work the whole of Woolhouse's account of the Muḥammadan Calendar is transcribed word for word, together with his Chronological Table of the years of the Hijra. The source of this Table, but not the body of the text, is acknowledged by the encyclopædists.

In the first place—the latter part of the statement is not put by Woolhouse in the most intelligible form. His intention evidently is to refer to the ten days which were nominally dropped, as days of the month of October in A.D. 1582 by the Gregorian Calendar. He points to the error of maintaining the difference between the Julian and Gregorian reckoning as a constant of 10 days, instead of as a variable and increasing quantity. It changes to 11 after February 28 in A.D. 1700; to 12 in 1800; to 13 in 1900; to 14 in 2100, and so onwards.

* So Ideler, ii. p. 629, says: "Die Aere der Fluch wird aber mit dem Eintritt des Jahrs angefangen, nämlich mit dem 1 Moharrem, welcher ein Donnerstag war."

† "Measures, Weights, and Moneys of all Nations," 7th ed. p. 202.

Now it happens that the Table in "L'Art de Vérifier les Dates," which extends from A.D. 622 to A.D. 2000, A.H. 1 to 1421, is perfectly correct (8vo ed. 1818), with the exception of certain misprints, the majority of which are self-evident,* and of which not one occurs among the years included within the Table given by Woolhouse and the "Encyclopædia." This Table commences with A.D. 1845, and extends to A.D. 2047, A.H. 1261 to 1470, and it will hardly be believed, though a fact, that for the 155 years covered by both it is identical with that in "L'Art de Vérifier," which in the paragraph preceding his Table Woolhouse condemns as inaccurate.

The dates given by Woolhouse are also identical with those for the same years given by Bond in his "Handy Book," the fourth edition of which was published in 1899, the year before the seventh edition of Woolhouse was issued. Bond's Table commences with A.D. 1582, and extends to 1931, A.H. 991 to 1350.

Here, then, are two Tables, antecedent to that in Woolhouse, with which he is in accord. If, therefore, all those Tables which were published before his own be wrong, it follows that his own must be wrong also. This, however, is not the case.

There certainly are serious errors in many Tables. In the third edition of "L'Art de Vérifier,"† the Kabîsah years throughout the forty-seventh Cycle, A.H. 1381 to 1410, A.D. 1961 to 1989, are wrongly indicated. The asterisk by which they are marked is put one line too high, making the years 1381, 1384, 1386, 1389, 1392, 1395, 1397, 1400, 1403, 1405, and 1408 to be Kabîsah, instead of 1382, 1385, &c., so that the Christian date for Muharram 1, and the feria for these latter years, are wrong by one day. This error does not appear in the fourth edition.

The Table given by Dr. Rees in his "Cyclopædia,"‡ is wrong by one day from A.D. 1800 till 1899, both inclusive, except for the year

* The corrigenda are—

A.H.	57	for	F.9	read	F.6	A.H.	1095	for	A.D. 1283	read	1683
„	211	„	F.	„	F.6	„	1098	„	F.4	read	F.1
„	690	„	F.4	„	F.5	„	1157	„	4-13	„	4-15
„	691	„	F.5	„	F.2	„	1159	„	14-24	„	13-24
„	837	„	637	„	837	„	1162	„	11-12	„	11-22
„	1015	„	F.2	„	F.3	„	1168	„	7-17	„	7-18
„	1077	„	F.9	„	F.1	„	1187	„	14-15	„	14-25
„	1093	„	Indiction 6 read 5			„	1195	„	27-8	„	17-28

† Three vols. folio. The first volume was published in 1783; the second in 1784; the third in 1787; the Tables in 1792.

‡ Vol. xvii. *In loco* Hegira.

1801, where May 14 is right, perhaps by a fortunate misprint. From 1900 to 2000, at which year the Table stops, there is an error of two days. This evidently arises, as Woolhouse suggests, from an omission to notice that 1800 and 1900 were not Leap-years in the Gregorian Calendar. By crediting these years with 366 days the commencements of the years of the Hijra after 1799 up to 1899, inclusive, are all made one day earlier than they ought to be; while after that year, up to 2000 inclusive, the dates are two days earlier than they should be.

The dates up to 1751, inclusive, are given according to the Julian Calendar, and are correct. From 1752 the dates are according to the Gregorian Calendar, and are correct till 1800, with the exception of a misprint for A.H. 1197; for 1482, 17 Dec., read 1782, 7 Dec.

Marsden, in the "Philosophical Transactions" of the Royal Society,* gives Tables from A.D. 622 to A.D. 2000. These Tables are incorrect from 1800. The Hijra year 1215 is made to commence with "May 24, 1800, Sunday." It did commence with a Sunday, but that Sunday was May 25. May 24 was a Saturday, and could only have been a Sunday if the year 1800 had retained the Julian February 29. It makes the feriæ right, though the monthly dates are wrong. This applies also to the Table of Dr. Rees, where the feriæ are right. In Marsden's Table, as in that by Dr. Rees, the correct monthly date is given for A.H. 1216—Friday, May 14, 1801. Then the error of one day begins, and from 1900 onwards there is an error of two days.

With respect to the Table given by Gravius, "Ex traiditione Ulug Beigi," see *post*, Article 26.

The Muḥammadan Week.

18. Time is divided by Oriental, as by Western nations, into weeks of seven days. The following are the Arabic names of the week-days:—

Sunday	al-'aḥad	First day.
Monday	al-ithnân	Second day.
Tuesday	al-thulathâ	Third day.
Wednesday	al-'arbi'â	Fourth day.
Thursday	al-khamîs	Fifth day.
Friday	al-jumât	Day of Assembly.
Saturday	al-sabt	Seventh day.

* Vol. lxxviii., pt. ii. p. 428.

Friday is observed in the same way as Saturday by the Jews, and Sunday by the Christians.

Muḥammad established this day as a day of worship by Divine command, as he declared. In the "Traditions" * he says that Friday was ordered to be a day of worship both for Jews and Christians, but that they have acted contrary to the command. In the "Qu'rân," Sûrah lxii. which is entitled "The Assembly," we read: "O true believers, when ye are called to prayer on the Day of Assembly † hasten to the commemoration of God, and leave merchandising. This will be better for you, if ye knew it." ‡

Monday, Wednesday, Thursday, and Friday are considered to be fortunate days. Tuesday, Saturday, and Sunday are unfortunate and evil days. Compare with this the superstition still extant among ourselves, especially with sailors, that Friday is an unlucky day. Many actors consider it unlucky if a new play be put upon the stage for the first time upon a Friday. There are, apparently, still a few points upon which we are not very much wiser than our neighbours.

19. THE MUḤAMMADAN MONTHS.

When Muḥammad altered the form of the year the names of the months were not changed, although originally these names had reference, in at least some cases, to the seasons of the year in which they occurred under the old Calendar.

The conversion of the year into one which was purely Lunar, and therefore short of the true Solar, or Tropical year, by nearly eleven days, caused the months to retrogress through the four seasons in the course of about thirty-three years. Hence some of the names of the months have lost their former significance.

* The uninspired records of inspired sayings, Muḥammad was supposed to have received, in addition to the Qu'rân, further revelations from heaven which enabled him to make declarations concerning certain points connected with religion and morality. The "Traditions" contain records of what he did, what he ordered to be done, and what was done in his presence and not forbidden, or was done with his consent. Hughes, "A Dictionary of Islam." Lond., 1896.

† al-Jumât. It was upon this account that the name of the sixth day was changed from its former Arabian title al-'Arûba. One reason given for the sanctification of this day was that upon it God finished the work of creation. Sale.

‡ Sale's "al-Koran," 1884, p. 450.

They are as follows:—

1. Muḥarram.
2. Ṣafar.
3. Rabî'u-l-avval.
4. Rabî'u-l-âkhir, or th-thâni.
5. Jamâdâ-l-avval.
6. Jamâdâ-l-âkhir, or th-thâni.
7. Rajab.
8. Sha'bân.
9. Ramaḍân.
10. Shawwâl.
11. Ḍû-l-qa'dah.
12. Ḍû-l-ḥijjah.

The Arabic names are thus pronounced by the modern Egyptians:—

1. Moḥarram.
2. Ṣafar.
3. Rabeea-el-owwal.
4. Rabeea-el-tánee.
5. Gumád-el-owwal, or, Gumáda-el-oolà.
6. Gumád-el-tánee, or, Gumáda-t-tániyeh.
7. Regeb.
8. Shaabán.
9. Ramaḍán.
10. Showwál.
11. Zu-l-Kaadeh, or, El-Kaadeh.
12. Zu-l-Ḥeggeh, or, El-Ḥeggeh.

The months have thirty and twenty-nine days alternately, except in the Embolismic years, when the last month has thirty days.

20. The etymology of the names of the months as given below is taken from al-Birûnî, "Athár-ul-Bákiya," and from Hughes's "Dictionary of Islam."

(1) Muḥarram.—One of the four sacred months. Both in the pagan age, and under Muḥammad it was held to be unlawful—ḥarām—to go to war in this month.

The first ten days are observed in Persia in commemoration of the death of al-Husain, the grandson of Muḥammad who was murdered by Shamer, the general of the Cufians, October 10, A.D. 680. "On the annual festival of his martyrdom, in the devout pilgrimage to his sepulchre, his Persian votaries abandon their souls to the religious frenzy of sorrow and indignation." *

The tenth day is Ashûrâ, a day of fasting. Of this day the Prophet is reported to have said, "Hasten to do good works, for it is a grand and blessed day, on which God had mercy on Adam."

(2) Ṣafar.—So called, according to al-Bîrûnî, because during this month people procured their provisions, going out in a company which was called Ṣafariyya.

Hughes derives the name from Ṣafir, "empty," either because during this month the Arabians made warlike expeditions, leaving their homes deserted, or because they left "empty" those whom they attacked. Another derivation of the word is from Ṣafâr, "yellowness," † because when the month was first so called it fell in the Autumnal season when the leaves had begun to assume a yellow tint.

Ṣafar was considered to be the most inauspicious month of the year. It is said that in it Adam was removed from the Garden of Eden.

(3) and (4). Rabî 'u-l-avval, and Rabî 'u-l-âkhir.—These were the first and second months of the Spring season when they were first so named, from Rabî, Spring.

The 13th day of Rabî 'u-l-avval was called Maulûd 'n-Nabî, from Maulûd, "birth." It is observed in Turkey, Egypt, and some parts of India as the birthday of Muḥammad. He died upon the same day of the month, Monday, June 8, A.D. 632, year 11 of the Hijra.

(5) and (6). Jamâdâ-l-avval, and Jamâdâ-l-âkhir.—When the months were named these occurred in the Winter, and were so called, according to al-Bîrûnî, because then water freezes. Lane, in his Arabic Dictionary, gives the same derivation. Caussin de Perceval is of opinion that this derivation was invented at a later period when these months had

* Gibbon, "History of the Decline and Fall," &c., ch. l. The Festival of the death of al-Husain is fully described by Sir John Chardin in his "Travels," published in 10 vols. in 1711, and in 4 vols. in 1735, at Amsterdam. They have been translated from the French into English, German, and Flemish. He was knighted by Charles II.

† *Cf.* our word Saffron, which is derived from the Arabic, as are many of our words, *e.g.*, Saccharine, and especially words commencing with al, as Alcove, Algebra, Alembic, Alcohol Algorism, or Algorithm, Alkali, &c. Alchymist and chymist are not, as is sometimes supposed, Arabic words, but are derived from the Greek χεῦμα, from χεύειν—to pour.

really fallen back into the Winter. He shows that when they were first named Jamâdâ-l-avval commenced in March, and Jamâdâ-l-âkhir in April. He believes that they were named originally from jamâd, "hard," a term applied to land upon which rain had not fallen for some time. Hughes adopts the same view.

The 20th day of Jamâdâ-l-avval is the anniversary of the taking of Constantinople by the Ottomans* under Mahomet II., Tuesday, May 29, A.D. 1453, year of the Hij. 857, after a siege which had lasted for fifty-three days. The city then became the capital of the Turkish Empire.

(7) Rajab.—The second of the four sacred months, during which war was not permitted. The word means "honoured."

The first Friday night in this month, that is the night which we call Thursday night, is usually spent in prayer by devout Muḥammadans, in commemoration of the conception of the Prophet. The 26th is the night of His Ascension.

(8) Sha'bân.—This month was so called because in it the tribes were dispersed. In the pagan times, when the months were regulated by the Solar year, it fell partly in our June, partly in July. The tribes were scattered in their search for water.

On the 15th of this month is the Lailatu'n-nisf min Sha'bân, "the night of the middle of Sha'bân," when, Muḥammad said, "God places upon record all the actions which men are to perform during the year." He enjoined his followers to remain awake, to repeat prayers throughout the night, and to fast upon the next day. It is now generally spent in rejoicing instead of fasting, and is a favourite day for fireworks, as our November 5. In Persia and India it is called Shab-i-Barât, "night of record."

This day must not be confounded with Lailatu-l-ḳadr, which occurs in the next month.

(9) Ramaḍân.—Is so called, according to al-Bîrûnî, because "the stones are roasted by the intense heat." Hughes derives the word from ramz, "to burn," either because it occurred in the hot season when first named, in which he agrees with al-Bîrûnî, or because the solemn fast that is observed during the whole of this month is supposed to burn up the sins of men. It is not lawful to eat or drink anything

* "L'Art de Vérifier les Dates," pt. ii. tom. v. p. 251. Gibbon gives the same date. Francœur in his pamphlet "Sur le Calendrier des Mahométans," gives the first day of Jamâdâ-l-âkhir; this is probably due to a misprint. The correct date is well established.

at all in the daytime throughout this month, so long as a white thread can be distinguished from a black thread. The injunctions respecting it are given in the Qur'ân, Sûrah ii. 179: "The month of Ramaḍân shall ye fast, in which the Koran was sent down from heaven, a direction unto men, and declarations of direction, and the distinction between good and evil. Therefore, let him among you who shall be present in this month, fast the same month; but he who shall be sick, or on a journey, shall fast the like number of other days."*

The 27th day of Ramaḍân is Lailat-al-ḳadr, "the Night of Power," when the Qur'ân came down entire, in one volume, to the lowest heaven, whence it was revealed in separate portions to Muḥammad by the Angel Gabriel.† It is believed that during the hours of this night the whole animal and vegetable creation bow down in humble adoration of Almighty God.‡ It was said by Muḥammad to have been either on Ramaḍân 21, 23, 25, 27, or 29. The exact day was known only to himself and to some of his "companions." It was not made known to his followers generally.

Observance of this month, with the utmost strictness, is one of the great features of the religion of Islâm.

In India the Persianised form of the word is used—Ramazân.

(10) Shawwâl.—A curious derivation for the name of this month is given in the Arabic Lexicons, connected with the season when the female camels are impregnated.

On the 1st, 2nd, and 3rd days of the month the Festival of "Breaking the Fast," 'Idu-el-Fiṭr, is observed. It is also called 'Idu-Ramaḍân, and 'Idu-s-saighr, or the Little Festival. It comes immediately after the great Fast of Ramaḍân.

(11) Ḍû-l-qa'dah.—The month of truce. The third of the four sacred months. It was on the 5th day of this month that God took compassion on Adam, and sent down the Ka'ba from heaven.

(12) Ḍû-l-ḥijjah.—The month of pilgrimage. The fourth of the sacred months. The first ten days are especially sacred. On the last of these ten days the great Feast of Sacrifice, 'Idu-l-kabîr, is celebrated. In Turkey and Egypt it is called 'Idu Bairâm. It is enjoined in the

* Sale's trans., chap. ii. p. 22.

† *Ib.*, ch. ii. p. 13; ch. liii. p. 427; ch. xcvii. p. 495.

‡ *Cf.* the mediæval superstition with respect to Christmas Eve, which, according to Brande ("Popular Antiquities"), still prevailed in Western Devonshire in his time: "At twelve o'clock at night on Christmas Eve the oxen in their stalls are always found on their knees, as in an attitude of devotion."

Qur'ân, Sûrah xxii.: "Call to mind when we gave the site of the house of the Caaba for an abode unto Abraham, saying, Do not associate any thing with me; and cleanse my house for those who compass it, and who stand up, and who bow down to worship. And proclaim unto the people a solemn pilgrimage; let them come unto thee on foot, and on every lean camel, arriving from every distant road; that they may be witnesses of the advantages which accrue to them from the visiting this holy place, and may commemorate the name of GOD on the appointed days in gratitude for the brute cattle which he hath bestowed on them." *

Sale in his notes quotes Savary: "Before the time of Mohammed the Arabians went in pilgrimage to Mecca. They went there to celebrate the memory of Abraham and of Ishmael" [from whom they claimed descent]. "This was only a custom. Mohammed consecrated it by religious ceremonies, and enjoined it by a precept. Under religious motives he hid political views. He wished that Mecca should become a point of union for all the Mohammedans; that they should resort there to exchange the gold and the productions of their own countries for the aromatics of Arabia Felix. The great caravans which travel every year from Persia, Damascus, Morocco, and Cairo, unite at Mecca. During the time of the Pilgrimage an immense commerce is carried on in that city, and at Jidda, which is the port of it."

Crichton in his "History of Arabia," vol. ii. chap. vi., gives a full account of the Pilgrimage.

The "appointed days" to which reference is made in the quotation from the Qur'ân, above, are the first ten days of the month, or, according to Sale, the three days following the tenth.† The Hajj, or Pilgrimage, is a religious duty incumbent upon all true followers of Muḥammad. This word means "setting out," "going forward."

The Muḥammadan Fasts and Festivals are very fully described by Lane in "The Modern Egyptians," ch. xxiv.–xxvi. The history of the Hajj will be found in ch. iii., and of "The Return," in ch. xxiv.

Table 1 shows the number of days in each of the Muḥammadan months, and their serial enumeration as days of the year.

* Sale's trans., ch. xxii. p. 276.

† F.n. C, p. 24, Sûrah ii. 199. So also al-Bîrûnî, "Vestiges," p. 333. But Sale, in f.n. D to Sûrah xxii. p. 276, says, "The ten first days, or the tenth and the three following."

CHAPTER III

THE MUḤAMMADAN CYCLE

21. Insomuch as the Kabîsah, or intercalary years of the Cycle are those whose numerical order is

2, 5, 7, 10, 13, 16, 18, 21, 24, 26, 29,

and because the numerical position of any given year, H, in the Cycle, is indicated by the remainder when H has been divided by 30, it follows that if the remainder be one of the above numbers the year is Kabîsah, and has 355 days. If the remainder be any other than one of these numbers the year is common, and has 354 days.

If the remainder be zero, the year is the last of a Cycle.

When the numerical value of any given year, H, is divided by 30, the integral part of the quotient indicates the number of completed Cycles which have elapsed before the commencement of that Cycle to which the given year belongs. Thus:—Let the given year be Hij. 397; then $\left\{\frac{397}{30}\right\} = 13$, with a remainder 7. The given year is the seventh of the fourteenth Cycle, and is Kabîsah.

22. Every Cycle of 30 years consists of 19 which have 354 days, and 11 which have 355 days. Therefore, every Cycle contains 6726 + 3905, or 10631 days. The Muḥammadan Cycles, being of constant length, differ in this respect from the Jewish Civil Cycles of 19 years, which vary in length from 6939 to 6942 days, and from our own Gregorian Cycles of 19 years which vary from 6938 to 6940 days.

It is evident that, because 10631 is not a multiple of 7, the order of week-days with which the successive Cycles, and therefore the successive years commence, cannot recur until 7 × 10631 days, or 210 years have elapsed. This period of time is called a Great Cycle.

23. THE SIGN OF A CYCLE.

Let numerical values be attached to the days of the week as follows:—

Sunday.........	1	Thursday......	5
Monday........	2	Friday..........	6
Tuesday........	3	Saturday	7, or zero.
Wednesday....	4		

The numerical value of the week-day with which any Cycle, year, or month commences is called the SIGN of that Cycle, year, or month.

The division of 10631 by 7 shows that every Cycle contains 5 days more than an integral number of weeks. Consequently, if a Cycle commence with any given week-day, the next succeeding Cycle will commence 5 days later in the week. If, for example, a Cycle, C, commence with a Sunday, its completed weeks will terminate with a Saturday; the remaining five days will terminate with a Thursday, and the next Cycle, C + 1, will commence with a Friday.

To find the SIGN OF ANY GIVEN CYCLE.

It is known that the first Cycle commenced, according to Civil reckoning, with a Friday (July 16, A.D. 622). Its Sign was, therefore, 6. Because every Cycle contains 5 days more than an integral number of weeks, an addition of 5 must be made to the Sign of the first Cycle, for every revolution of the Cycle, and 7 must be rejected when the Sign thus found exceeds 7, since the Sign can never be greater than 7. Hence, for the

Second Cycle,	the Sign is	$6 + 5 = 11$, or 4	after	rejecting	7.
Third	,,	,,	$6 + 10 = 16$, or 2	,,	,,	14.
Fourth	,,	,,	$6 + 15 = 21$, or 7	,,	,,	14.
Fifth	,,	,,	$6 + 20 = 26$, or 5	,,	,,	21.

And, generally, for the nth Cycle, the Sign is

$$6 + 5\,(n - 1).$$

24. To find the SIGN OF ANY GIVEN YEAR.

Let H be the number representing the given year.

(1) If H be the first year in a Cycle there will be a remainder, 1, after dividing H by 30. The number of Cycles which have elapsed before the commencement of H will be $\frac{H-1}{30}$, and the number of the Cycle whose first year is H will be $\frac{H-1}{30}+1$.

The Sign of H, in this case, is the same as that of the Cycle in which it is the first year; and, by substituting $\frac{H-1}{30}+1$ for n in the last expression, it is found to be—

$$6+\frac{5(H-1)}{30}.$$

Thus, for the year 481. Dividing 481 by 30, the quotient is 16, with a remainder 1. This year is therefore the first in the seventeenth Cycle, and its Sign is $6+\frac{5\times 480}{30}=86$, or 2 when 7×12 is rejected. The first day of the year is therefore Monday.

(2) If the given year, H, be not the first in a Cycle the problem becomes general:—To find the Sign of any given year.

Unless H be the last year in a Cycle there will be a remainder after dividing H by 30. If H be the last year in a Cycle there will be no remainder; in that case the quotient must be diminished by unity, and the remainder then becomes 30. (See *post*, Article 25.)

Let the remainder be R; then R – 1 years have elapsed since the preceding Cycle terminated, and before the given year, H, commenced.

A certain number of these R – 1 years will be Kabîsah, having each 355 days, while the rest of the years are Common with 354 days. In the first place let all the years be treated as though they all were Common. Each of them will then have to be treated as containing 4 days more than an integral number of weeks; and because they are R – 1 in number, they will together contain 4 (R – 1) days more than an integral number of weeks. Consequently, in the first instance, 4 (R – 1) must be added to the Sign of the first year of the Cycle, that is, to the Sign of the Cycle to which the year H belongs.

But some of these R – 1 years are Kabîsah. For each of these years which may occur among the R – 1 there must be made a further addition of unity to the Sign of the first year of the Cycle.

Let the number of days to be thus added on account of those years amongst the R − 1 which are Kabîsah be B; and let N be the number of completed Cycles which have elapsed before the commencement of the year H; that is to say, let N be the integral part of the quotient when H is divided by 30, or $N = \left\{\frac{H}{30}\right\}$, so that the year H belongs to the Cycle whose number is N + 1. Then, because the Sign of the *n*th Cycle is 6 + 5 (*n* − 1), (Article 23), the Sign of the Cycle whose number is N + 1 will be 6 + 5 N, and the Sign of the year H will be

$$6 + 5N + 4(R - 1) + B.$$

Example.—For the year 1047.

$N = \left\{\frac{H}{30}\right\} = \left\{\frac{1047}{30}\right\} = 34$, and $R = 27$. Therefore 34 completed Cycles, together with 26 years, have elapsed before the given year 1047 commences.

During the 26 years there are 10 which are Kabîsah, namely, those whose numerical order in the Cycle is 2, 5, 7, 10, 13, 16, 18, 21, 24, and 26; so that B = 10, and the Sign for 1047 is—

$$6 + (5 \times 34) + (4 \times 26) + 10,$$

or 3, after 41 × 7 is rejected. The year commences with a Tuesday.

(3) With respect to the value of B in the formula, 6 + 5 N + 4 (R − 1) + B.

There is no necessity for ascertaining the number of Kabîsah years by counting. M. Francœur found that the number in *n* years reckoned from the commencement of any period, that is from the commencement of any Cycle, is expressed by $\left\{\frac{11n + 14}{30}\right\}$, or the integral part of the quotient when 11*n* + 14 is divided by 30. He says that he arrived at this result by feeling his way and by trials.*

The problem which he desired to solve is similar to that of which an explanation is given in the Note at the end of Chapter VIII. of "The Jewish Calendar," page 237, for the formula of Dr. Gauss, $e = \left\{\frac{12H + 17}{19}\right\}$, where *e* is the number of Common years which occur in H years of the Jewish Era.

In the present case it is required to find an expression, a function

* "Par tâtonnements, et à l'aide d'essais;" in a pamphlet published in Paris "Sur le Calendrier des Mahométans," being "Extrait des Additions à la Connaisance des Temps, pour 1844."

of one variable, n, which shall have the property of giving, for the successive values $n = 0, 1, 2, 3$, &c., certain integral values fixed in advance, fractions being neglected.

Following the same method as that employed in the Note on the formula of Dr. Gauss, it is clear, in the first place, that there is no Kabîsah year in a Cycle before the second year is reached; therefore

B must = 0, when n = either 0 or 1.

One Kabîsah year occurs, and only one, before the fifth year is reached, therefore

B must = 1, when n = either 2, 3, or 4.

Two Kabîsah years occur before the seventh year is reached; therefore

B must = 2, when n = either 5 or 6.

Proceeding thus, and tabulating the results, the two first columns of the Table which follows are obtained.

In order to find an expression, a function of n, of which the integral part will give these required values to B, it is natural to take for its first term, $\left\{\frac{11n}{30}\right\}$, because there are eleven Kabîsah years in every Cycle of thirty years, and the question is—What increment, x, may be made to the numerator, $11n$, in order that the expression $\left\{\frac{11n + x}{30}\right\}$ may fulfil the required condition?

These increments, for the values of B corresponding to the successive values of n, appear in the fourth and fifth columns of the following Table; the fourth containing the least possible, and the fifth the greatest possible that can be made in each case. They are obtained in the same way as that described in the Note on the formula of Dr. Gauss. Thus:—When $n = 13$, that is when 13 years of the Cycle have elapsed, five Kabîsah years have occurred, and B, or $\left\{\frac{11n + x}{30}\right\}$ must = 5. In order that the integral part of $\left\{\frac{11n + x}{30}\right\}$ may have this value, x cannot be less than 7 nor greater than 36; for $\left\{\frac{11n + x}{30}\right\}$ would only be 4 if x were anything less than 7, and would be 6, or more than 6 if x were greater than 36.

Now it appears from the fifth column that the lowest of all the maxima increments that can be made is 14, and from the fourth column that 14 is also the highest of all the possible minima increments. The former is for the fifteenth, the latter is for the twenty-sixth year. The increment, therefore, can neither be less nor greater than 14, that is, it must be 14, and we have—

$$\left\{\frac{11n + x}{30}\right\} = \left\{\frac{11n + 14}{30}\right\}.$$

In the present case, $n = \mathrm{R} - 1$, and so we have—

$$\mathrm{B} = \left\{\frac{11\,(\mathrm{R} - 1) + 14}{30}\right\}.$$

Years of the Cycle. $n =$	No. of K. years in n. B =	$11n$.	Increments that may be made to $11n$.	
			Least.	Greatest.
1	0	11	0	18
2 K.	1	22	8	37
3	1	33	0	26
4	1	44	0	15
5 K.	2	55	5	34
6	2	66	0	23
7 K.	3	77	13	42
8	3	88	2	31
9	3	99	0	20
10 K.	4	110	10	39
11	4	121	0	28
12	4	132	0	17
13 K.	5	143	7	36
14	5	154	0	25
15	5	165	0	14
16 K.	6	176	4	33
17	6	187	0	22
18 K.	7	198	12	41
19	7	209	1	30
20	7	220	0	19
21 K.	8	231	9	38
22	8	242	0	27
23	8	253	0	16
24 K.	9	264	6	35
25	9	275	0	24
26 K.	10	286	14	43
27	10	297	3	32
28	10	308	0	21
29 K.	11	319	11	40
30	11	330	0	29

If then the formula of M. Francœur be employed, the Sign of any given year, H, will be—

$$6 + 5\,N + 4\,(R + 1) + \left\{\frac{11\,(R - 1) + 14}{30}\right\},$$

after rejecting from the sum the highest possible multiple of 7.

Thus :—For H 835.

$$N = \left\{\frac{835}{30}\right\} = 27. \quad R = 25. \quad R - 1 = 24.$$

And—

$$B = \left\{\frac{264 + 14}{30}\right\} = 9.$$

The required Sign is, therefore—
$6 + (5 \times 27) + (4 \times 24) + 9 = 246 = 1$, when 7×35 is rejected. The year commences with a Sunday.

25. In Article 24 (2) it was said that if H be the last year in a Cycle there will no remainder when H is divided by 30. In this case $R - 1$ would be negative, which cannot be allowed, for it is evident that $R - 1$ must be a positive integer; or, in the case of a first year of a Cycle, zero, if the formula for B is employed.

For example: Let $H = 30$; then $R = 0$, and $R - 1 = -1$. B would become $\left\{\frac{-11 + 14}{30}\right\} = \left\{\frac{3}{30}\right\} = 0$, which is absurd, for we know that in this case $B = 11$.

The difficulty is at once met by diminishing the integral part, N, of the quotient by unity, and in that way making the remainder 30. We then have $R - 1 = 29$.

Thus, for $H = 240$. Here $N = \left\{\frac{240}{30}\right\} = 8$, and there is no remainder; but if N be called 7 the remainder is 30. The latter alternative must be chosen. Then, $R - 1 = 29$, and $B = \left\{\frac{11 \times 29 + 14}{30}\right\} = 11$. The Sign of the year, or $6 + 5\,N + 4\,(R - 1) + B$, is $6 + (5 \times 7) + 116 + 11 = 168$, which becomes 7 when 7×23 is rejected. The year 240 commenced with a Saturday.

When H is the first year of a Cycle, the division of H by 30 leaves a remainder 1, and $R - 1 = 0$. Therefore, B, or $\left\{\frac{11 \times 0 + 14}{30}\right\} = 0$. The two last terms of the expression vanish, and the Sign is $6 + 5N$ where N is the number of Cycles which have elapsed before the year H commences. But if n be the number of the Cycle whose first year is H, then $n = N + 1$, or $N = n - 1$, and the Sign is $6 + 5(n - 1)$, as shown in Article 23.

26. Table II. shows the Sign for each year in a Great Cycle of 210 years. After that period, the series of week-days with which the successive years commence is repeated.

This Table differs from that which is given by Gravius in his version of Uluigh Beigh. He takes for the first day of the Era Thursday, feria 5, July 15, whereas the Table follows the usually accepted Civil date, Friday, feria 6, July 16. The Signs in the Table, therefore, exceed by unity those given by Uluigh Beigh. There is, however, an exception to this, for he makes the fifteenth year of the Cycle to be Kabîsah instead of the sixteenth. The effect of this is to increase by unity the Sign for year 16, and the Signs for all years of the form $30n + 16$ in his Table, so that his sixteenth line is the same as that in Table II. herewith.

27. The Signs of the Months.

The months consist of 30 and 29 days alternately, that is to say, of 2 days and of 1 day more, respectively, than an integral number of weeks. If, therefore, the Sign of the first month in any year be known, the successive additions to it of 2 and 1, alternately, will give the Signs of the remaining eleven months.

The Sign of the first month of any year is, of course, the Sign of the year.

Thus:—If in a given year the first day, or Muḥarram 1, fall upon a Friday, feria 6, the Sign for Muḥarram will be 6. This month has 30 days; its last is therefore a Saturday. The second month will commence with a Sunday, feria 1. The Sign, 1, is obtained by the addition of 2 to 6, and the rejection of 7. The second month has 29 days; it, therefore, terminates with a Sunday, and the third month commences with a Monday, feria 2. The Sign, 2, is obtained by the addition of 1 to the Sign of the first month.

Example.—The Signs of the months of the year 931.

The Sign for Muḥarram, which is the Sign of the year, must first be found.

$\frac{931}{30} = 31$, with remainder 1. This year is therefore the first in the 32nd Cycle, and its Sign is $6 + 5\,(32 - 1) = 161$ or 7, when 7×22 is rejected.

The Sign for Muḥarram is therefore 7, and we have, Sign of—

1st month	7	....	Saturday.
2nd ,,	7 + 2 or 2	....	Monday.
3rd ,,	2 + 1 ,, 3	....	Tuesday.
4th ,,	3 + 2 ,, 5	....	Thursday.
5th ,,	5 + 1 ,, 6	....	Friday.
6th ,,	6 + 2 ,, 1	....	Sunday.
7th ,,	1 + 1 ,, 2	....	Monday.
8th ,,	2 + 2 ,, 4	....	Wednesday.
9th ,,	4 + 1 ,, 5	....	Thursday.
10th ,,	5 + 2 ,, 7	....	Saturday.
11th ,,	7 + 1 ,, 1	....	Sunday.
12th ,,	1 + 2 ,, 3	....	Tuesday.

Table III. shows the Sign for each month of any given year according to the Sign of the year, that is, according to the week-day with which Muḥarram commences.

CHAPTER IV

THE REDUCTION OF MUḤAMMADAN TO CHRISTIAN DATES, AND THE REVERSE

28. When the Julian date corresponding to the first day of any Muḥammadan year is known, it is easy to continue establishing the correspondence for any number of succeeding years.

The Muḥammadan Common year of 354 days terminates 11 days sooner than a Common Christian year of 365 days, and 12 days sooner than a Bissextile year of 366 days.

A Kabîsah year, having 355 days, terminates 10 days earlier than a Common Christian year, and 11 days earlier than a Bissextile year.

Hence, the commencements of the successive Muḥammadan years retrogress from the successive Julian or Gregorian dates by

11 days after a Common year,
10 days after a Kabîsah year,
12 days after a Christian Bissextile year.

When a Muḥammadan year follows next after a Kabîsah year which coalesces with a Bissextile year, the effect of the combination is that the advance caused by the former neutralises the retrogression caused by the latter; that is to say, the retrogression which would be decreased from 11 to 10 by the Kabîsah year, and increased from 11 to 12 by the Bissextile, remains at 11.

The Julian dates corresponding to Muḥarram 1 for the years of the first Cycle may, by way of example, be traced in this manner, starting from the known fact that the first day of the first year of the Era corresponded to July 16, A.D. 622, being the day whose serial number in that Common year was 197.

The Muḥammadan Kabisah years are marked K; the Julian Bissextile years are marked B.

Years of Hijra.	Muḥarram 1. Serial Number of Day in Julian Year.		Julian Month and Day.		A.D.
1		197	July	16	622
2 K	197 — 11 =	186	July	5	623
3	186 — 10 =	176	June	24	624 B
4	176 — 12 =	164	June	13	625
5 K	164 — 11 =	153	June	2	626
6	153 — 10 =	143	May	23	627
7 K	143 — 11 =	132	May	11	628 B
8	132 — 11 =	121	May	1	629
9	121 — 11 =	110	April	20	630
10 K	110 — 11 =	99	April	9	631
11	99 — 10 =	89	March	29	632 B
12	89 — 12 =	77	March	18	633
13 K	77 — 11 =	66	March	7	634
14	66 — 10 =	56	February	25	635
15	56 — 11 =	45	February	14	636 B
16 K	45 — 12 =	33	February	2	637
17	33 — 10 =	23	January	23	638
18 K	23 — 11 =	12	January	12	639
19	12 — 10 =	2	January	2	640 B
20	2 — 12, or 368 — 12 =	356	December	21	640 B
21 K	356 — 12 =	344	December	10	641
22	344 — 10 =	334	November	30	642
23	334 — 11 =	323	November	19	643
24 K	323 — 11 =	312	November	7	644 B
25	312 — 11 =	301	October	28	645
26 K	301 — 11 =	290	October	17	646
27	290 — 10 =	280	October	7	647
28	280 — 11 =	269	September	25	648 B
29 K	269 — 12 =	257	September	14	649
30	257 — 10 =	247	September	4	650

The method of procedure is simple. In forming the column of figures for the serial numbers of the Julian days with which the Hijra years commence, 11 is subtracted from that number, in the line above, which stands in a line where neither K nor B appear, and also when both K and B appear, in order to obtain the serial number for the line after such appearance. When K appears alone in a line 10 is subtracted. When B appears alone 12 is subtracted.

Care must be taken to observe that this direction applies only to the serial number of the day, not to the number which notifies the day of the month. Thus: if, for year 3 in the Table, 10 days were subtracted from July 5 (= June 35), the initial day would result as June 25, whereas it should be June 24, obtained by subtracting 10 from the serial number, 186, of July 5.

It will be noticed that the years 19 and 20 of the Hijra both commence in A.D. 640. Hij. 19 commences with January 2; it has 354 days, and therefore its last day is January (2 + 353) = January 355 = December 20, the year 640 being Bissextile. By subtracting 12 from 2, as in the Table, the serial number − 10 is obtained. This indicates that the days of the year, 640 B., have to be reckoned backwards, or that 10 is to be subtracted from 366, giving the serial number 356. When negative values are thus given to the days of the year, December 31 must be reckoned as zero, December 30 as − 1, December 21 as − 10.

29. In forming a Chronological Table of the correspondence between Muḥammadan and Christian years, which may be done by the method just described, it will be well to check the results by finding, in an independent way, the date corresponding to the initial days of the first years in the successive Muḥammadan Cycles.

In doing this it will be found convenient to perform the work throughout according to Julian reckoning; the Julian dates may, afterwards, be reduced to Gregorian when necessary.

In every Cycle of thirty Muḥammadan years there are 10631 days; the first day of any Cycle will therefore be found by the addition of this number of days to the date of the first day of the next preceding Cycle. Now, every period of four consecutive Julian years contains 1461 days, and because 10631 divided by 1461 gives a quotient 7 and a remainder 404, therefore the addition of seven quadriennial periods (or twenty-eight Julian years), and 404 days to the date of any Cycle will give the date of the next Cycle.

It is true that 404 days contain one Common Julian year + 39 days, or one Bissextile year + 38 days, and the result would therefore be the same if the addition to the date of the first day of any Cycle were 29 years + 39 days in the one case, and 29 years + 38 days in the other case.

It will however be found, in practice, that there is more liability to error in thus accomplishing the work than if the method first suggested be employed.

The Sign of the Cycle, or feria for its initial day is found by the rule given in Article 23.

Commencing with the first day of the first Cycle, or Friday, July 16, A.D. 622, the initial days of the successive Cycles may be found to any extent that may be desired, as follows:—

H. 1, commences on day	197 = July 16, A.D.		622, feria 6.
Add	404		28
	601		650
Subtract	365 days in A.D. 650		
H. 31, commences on day	236 = August 24,		651, feria 4.
Add	404		28
	640		679
Subtract	365 days in A.D. 679		
H. 61, commences on day	275 = October 1,		680, feria 2.
Add	404		28
	679		708, Bis.
Subtract	366 days in A.D. 708		
H. 91, commences on day	313 = November 9,		709, feria 7.
Add	404		28
	717		737
Subtract	365 days in A.D. 737		
H. 121, commences on day	352 = December 18,		738, feria 5.
Add	404		28
	756		766
Subtract	365 days in A.D. 766		
	391		
Subtract	365 days in A.D. 767		
	26		

H. 151, commences on day	26	= January 26,	768,	feria 3.
Add	404		28	
	430		796	
Subtract	366	days in A.D. 796		
H. 181, commences on day	64	= March 5,	797,	feria 1.
Add	404		28	
	468		825	
Subtract	365	days in A.D. 825		
H. 211, commences on day	103	= April 13,	826,	feria 6.

This method may be continued to any extent. It is unnecessary to give the results here in a tabulated form as they are all contained in the extended Chronological Table at the end of this book. In that Table Julian dates for Muḥarram 1 are given until A.D. 1582 inclusive; from 1583 both Julian and Gregorian dates are noted.

30. The Julian dates for Muḥarram 1 in the successive Muḥammadan years cannot recur, in regular sequence, until a period of time has elapsed which is a common multiple of four Julian years and thirty Muḥammadan years, that is to say, of 1461 and 10631 days. These two numbers have no common measure greater than unity; the period will therefore consist of 1461 × 10631 days, or 42524 Julian years, 43830 Muḥammadan years, measured from the commencement of July 16, A.D. 622.

The Julian time, therefore, which will have elapsed since the commencement of the Christian Era, before the Cycle of correspondence recurs, will be 42524y. + 621y. + 196d., or, 43145y. + 196d. It will be upon the next day to this, namely July 16, in A.D. 43146, that the year of the Hijra 43831, the first year of the 1462nd Cycle, will have its initial day on the same Julian monthly date as Muḥarram 1 in the first year of the Era of the Hijra.

The corresponding Gregorian date will be 322 days, or one year all but 43 days in advance of the Julian, that is, June 3, A.D. 43147. This day will be a Tuesday.

The same thing may be proved in another way. Let J be the Julian year in which a Cycle of 30 years will commence with July 16, or the 197th day of the year if J be a Common year.

The Julian time which will have elapsed since the commencement of the Christian Era will be—

$$(J - 1) \text{ years} + 196 \text{ days} \ldots\ldots\ldots\ldots \quad \text{(I.)}$$

Let H be the number of the Muḥammadan Cycle, which commences with July 16. Then, because every Cycle contains, in Julian time, 28y. + 404d., and because the Era of the Hijra commenced when 621y. + 196d. of the Christian Era had elapsed, the Julian time elapsed before the commencement of the Cycle H will be—

$$621\text{y.} + 196\text{d.} + (H - 1)(28\text{y.} + 404\text{d.}) \ldots\ldots\ldots \quad \text{(II.)}$$

Equating (I.) and (II.) we have—

$$J = 622\text{y.} + (H - 1)\, 28\text{y.} + (H - 1)\, 404\text{d} \ldots\ldots\ldots \quad \text{(III.)}$$

Because J represents an integral number of years the second side of this equation must also represent an integral number of years, therefore (H – 1) 404d. is an integral number of years.

The least number of days which contain an integral number of Julian years is 1461; and, because 1461 and 404 have no common measure, H – 1 must be a multiple of 1461. Let $H - 1 = 1461p$, where p may be any positive integer.

If $p = 1$, $H - 1 = 1461$, and equation (III.) becomes

$$\begin{aligned} J &= 622\text{y.} + (28\text{y.} \times 1461) + (404\text{d.} \times 1461) \\ &= 622\text{y.} + 40908\text{y.} + 1616\text{y.} \\ &= 43146\text{y.} \end{aligned}$$

It is, therefore, in A.D. 43146, which is not a Leap-year, that the Cycle of correspondence begins to recur with the 197th day, or July 16; and the time elapsed since the commencement of the Era of the Hijra before this day is 43145y. + 196d. – (621y. + 196d.), or 42524 Julian years.

31. The Muḥammadan date corresponding to January 1, in each of the successive Julian years, may be found in the same manner as the Julian dates for Muḥarram 1, described in Article 28.

It is first necessary to establish the date for the January 1 which first occurred after the commencement of the Era of the Hijra, namely, January 1, A.D. 623.

The first day of the Era corresponded to the 197th day of A.D. 622. There are required 168 more days to complete this year, and 169 to reach January 1, 623. Consequently, Muḥarram (1 + 169) will be the day required in Hij. 1, or the 22nd day of the sixth month.

Starting from this point, the successive dates for January 1 are found by the additions of 11, 10, or 12, precisely as described in Article 28, and the following Table can be formed:—

A.D.	Serial Number of Day in Muhammadan Year.	Month and Day.	Year of Hijra.
	January 1.		
623	170	Sixth, 22	1
624 B	170 + 11 = 181	Seventh, 4	2 K
625	181 + 11 = 192	Seventh, 15	3
626	192 + 11 = 203	Seventh, 26	4
627	203 + 11 = 214	Eighth, 7	5 K
628 B	214 + 10 = 224	Eighth, 17	6
629	224 + 12 = 236	Eighth, 29	7 K
630	236 + 10 = 246	Ninth, 10	8
631	246 + 11 = 257	Ninth, 21	9
632 B	257 + 11 = 268	Tenth, 2	10 K
633	268 + 11 = 279	Tenth, 13	11
634	279 + 11 = 290	Tenth, 24	12
635	290 + 11 = 301	Eleventh, 6	13 K
636 B	301 + 10 = 311	Eleventh, 16	14
637	311 + 12 = 323	Eleventh, 28	15
638	323 + 11 = 334	Twelfth, 9	16 K
639	334 + 10 = 344	Twelfth, 19	17
640 B	344 + 11 = 355	Twelfth, 30	18 K
641	355 + 11 = 366 } or 12 }	First, 12	19
			20
642	12 + 11 = 23	First, 23	21 K
643	23 + 10 = 33	Second, 3	22
644 B	33 + 11 = 44	Second, 14	23
645	44 + 12 = 56	Second, 26	24 K
646	56 + 10 = 66	Third, 7	25
647	66 + 11 = 77	Third, 18	26 K
648 B	77 + 10 = 87	Third, 28	27
649	87 + 12 = 99	Fourth, 10	28
650	99 + 11 = 110	Fourth, 21	29 K
651	110 + 10 = 120	Fifth, 2	30
652 B	120 + 11 = 131	Fifth, 13	31
653	131 + 12 = 143	Fifth, 25	32 K
654	143 + 10 = 153	Sixth, 5	33
655	153 + 11 = 164	Sixth, 16	34
656 B	164 + 11 = 175	Sixth, 27	35 K
	&c.	&c.	

This Table may easily be continued, if it be desired. A check upon results at intervals of 30 Muḥammadan years, can be obtained from the Julian dates of Muḥarram 1, which have been already found (Article 29), or at any other intervals by taking such dates from the Chronological Table, in the following way, the work being done in a tabulated form:—

July 16 = day 197 of A.D. 622, corresponds to Muḥarram 1 of Hij. 1. The number of days required to complete the Christian year 622 is 168. If one more day be added, making 169, January 1 of A.D. 623 is reached; this number is called the *complement* to 197. It must be remembered that the number of days required to reach January 1 in any year $y + 1$ is one more than the number required to complete the year y. In fact, it makes up the serial number of any given day either to 366 or 367, according to whether the year have 365 or 366 days. Thus, for line 2 in the following computation, the serial number for August 24 in the Common year 651 is 236, and $(365 + 1) - 236 = 130$. In line 3 the serial number is 275 for October 1 in the Bissextile year 650, and $(366 + 1) - 275 = 92$.

Just as the 130th day after August 24 is January 1, so the 130th after Muḥarram 1 has the serial number required for the day in the year of the Hijra which corresponds to this January 1.

Julian date of Muḥarram 1 in the Hijra Year of Column 5.			Days required to reach January 1.	Muḥammadan date of January 1 in A.D. of Column 8.			A.D.
A.D.	Month and Day of Month.	Day of the Year.		Year of Hijra.	Day of the Year.	Month and Day of Month.	
622	July 16	197	169	1	170	Sixth, 22	623
651	August 24	236	130	31	131	Fifth, 13	652
680 B	October 1	275	92	61	93	Fourth, 4	681
709	November 9	313	53	91	54	Second, 24	710
738	December 18	352	14	121	15	First, 15	739
768 B	January 26	26	341	151	342	Twelfth, 17	769
797	March 5	64	302	181	303	Eleventh, 8	798
826	April 13	103	263	211	264	Ninth, 28	827

General Rules for the Reduction of Muḥammadan to Christian Dates; and the Reverse.

32. Several methods of finding the Christian date corresponding to the first day of a Muḥammadan year, and the reverse, have been proposed, but the rules as generally given are not infallible. They will find, as is sometimes stated, the day "on or about which" the correspondence takes place. Correct results may be obtained in certain instances, but reliance cannot invariably be placed upon the rules; too frequently they fail to find the exact day.

Some of these rules will be examined presently, and the reasons for their failure be pointed out. Meantime, there is a direct method, which may be called "the method of days elapsed," producing an absolutely correct result if ordinary care be employed. It is simply to ascertain the number of days that have elapsed, reckoning from the commencement of the given Era, before the day is reached whose date in the Christian Era is required; add to this number the number of days in the Christian Era elapsed before the given Era commenced. The sum gives the Serial number in the Christian Era of the day next before the required date.

The work of an example will explain this: The Christian date corresponding to Muḥarram 1, A.H. 1315 is required.

Here 1314 years, or 43 Cycles + 24 years of the Hijra have elapsed before the given date is reached. The number of days is—

$$(10631 \times 43) + (354 \times 24) + \left\{\frac{11 \times 24 + 14}{30}\right\},$$
$$= 457133 + 8496 + 9 = 465638.$$

The time elapsed from the commencement of the Christian Era up to the close of July 15, A.D. 662, is 621y. + 196d., or

$$621 \times 365 + \left\{\frac{621}{4}\right\} + 196 = 227016 \text{ days.}$$

This number of days must be added to the number elapsed before the first day of the given Hijra year, 1315, is reached; the sum is 692654. The next day, with the serial number 692655 in the Christian Era, is the day corresponding to Muḥarram 1, A.H. 1315.

A Table of Serial days will show that this is June 2, A.D. 1897, (Gregorian); but if no such Table is at hand the date will be found in the usual way, thus:—

Every 4 Julian years contain 1461 days; 692655 divided by 1461 gives a quotient 474, and a remainder 141. Therefore 4 × 474, or 1896 Julian years + 141 days are contained in the 692655 days. The Julian date required is therefore the 141st day of A.D. 1897, or May 21. The Gregorian date, 12 days later, is June 2.

Example 2.—Muḥarram 1, A.H. 1179.

$$355\,(H-1)\ \ldots\ldots\ldots\ldots = 417012$$

$$\left\{\frac{11\,(H-1)+14}{30}\right\}\ldots\ldots = 432$$

$$\text{Jan. 1, A.D. 1 to July 15, 622} = 227016$$

$$\begin{array}{r} 1461)644460(441 \\ 644301 \\ \hline 159 \end{array}$$

The day required is the 160th in the Julian year (4 × 441 + 1), or June 9, A.D. 1765. The Gregorian date is June (9 + 11) = June 20.

33. The reverse process for finding the Muḥammadan date corresponding to any given Christian date is equally simple.

Example.—Required the Muḥammadan date corresponding to January 1, A.D. 2000.

The years may, in the first instance, be conveniently treated as Julian.

The number of days elapsed before January 1, 2000 (Julian), is reached is—

$$1999 \times 365 + \left\{\frac{1999}{4}\right\} = 729635 + 499 = 730134$$

$$\text{Subtract days elapsed before Era of Hijra commenced} = 227016$$

$$503118$$

Dividing this number of days by 10631, the number of days in a Cycle, the quotient is 47, and the remainder is 3461; that is to say, the days in question contain 47 × 30, or 1410 Muḥammadan years and 3461 days. Dividing 3461 by 354, it is found that this number of days contains 9 Muḥammadan Common years and 275 days. But three of these nine years are Kabīsah, namely, the 2nd, the 5th, and the 7th, and as only 354 days were allowed to each year, whereas three of these years ought to have been credited with 355 days, it is evident that 3 must be subtracted from the remainder 275. So that the 3461 days contain 9 years of the Hijra and 272 days.

It appears, then, that 1410y. + 9y. + 272d. of the Hijra have elapsed when the Julian year 1999 terminates. The next day of the Hijra Era, or the 273rd of A.H. 1420, will correspond to January 1, A.D. 2000 (Julian).

As the Muḥammadan months are of 30 and 29 days alternately, the first nine months contain 266 days, and the 273rd day is the 7th of the tenth month Shawwâl.

The Gregorian year 2000 commences 13 days earlier than the Julian, therefore the required date, according to New Style, is 13 days earlier than Shawwal 7, that is, the date is Ramaḍân 24, A.H. 1420.

Example 2.—Required the Muḥammadan date for February 28, A.D. 1896, New Style.

It will be convenient to work by Julian years. The Julian date, corresponding to the Gregorian February 28 in 1896, is February 16.

The number of days elapsed since the commencement of the Christian Era before February 16, 1896, commences is—

$$1895 \times 365 + \left\{\frac{1895}{4}\right\} + 46 = 692194$$

Subtract days elapsed before the Era of the Hijra commenced 227016

465178

10631)465178(43 Cycles = 1290 years
457133

354)8045(22 Common years
7788

257

Subtract $\left\{\frac{11 \times 22 + 14}{30}\right\}$ ... 8

249

Hence, the Muḥammadan time elapsed before the Julian February 16, which is the Gregorian February 28, in A.D. 1896 is (1290 + 22) years + 249 days. The next day, or the 250th of the year, is the date required, namely, Ramaḍân 14, A.H. 1313.

CHAPTER V

THE METHODS AND RULES ADOPTED BY CERTAIN AUTHORS

34. M. Francœur, in his treatise, "Sur le Calendrier des Mahometans,"* describes a method of reducing Muḥammadan to Julian dates, which, though perhaps a little complicated, gives correct results. With certain modifications which may render it more easily intelligible it is as follows :—

(1) Let H be the given year of the Hijra, and J the Julian date corresponding to Muḥarram 1 in that year.

Divide H by 30. Let C be the quotient and r the remainder, so that $H = 30\,C + r$.

The years which have elapsed before H commences are $H - 1$, and $H - 1 = 30\,C + r - 1$.

(2) This interval of times contains 30 Cycles of 10631 days, and $r - 1$ additional years which contain $354\,(r - 1) + K$ days, where $K = \left\{\frac{11\,(r - 1) + 14}{30}\right\}$, or $\left\{\frac{11r + 3}{30}\right\}$ if r be greater than 11.

Hence the time elapsed from the commencement of the Era, before Muḥarram 1 in the year H is reached, is in days—

$$10631\,C + 354\,(r - 1) + K.$$

(3) If, instead of reckoning the days from the commencement of the Era—that is, from July 16, A.D. 622, inclusive—they be reckoned from January 1 in that year, an addition must be made of 196 days, and the serial number of Muḥarram 1 in the year H, reckoned from this base, will be—

$$10631\,C + 354\,(r - 1) + K + 197.$$

* Additions à la Connaisance des Temps, pour 1844.

(4) To avoid any difficulty which may arise from Leap-years, it may be better to reckon from January 1, A.D. 621, that being the first year of a Julian quadriennial period. If this be done, a further addition of 365 days must be made, and the expression becomes—

$$10631\text{ C} + 354r + \text{K} + 208.$$

(5) Every Julian quadriennial period contains 1461 days, and on dividing the expression by this number it becomes—

$$7\text{ C} + \frac{404\text{ C} + 354r + \text{K} + 208}{1461}.$$

Let the integral part of the fraction in this expression be Q, and the remainder be R. Then the Julian time elapsed from January 1, 621, to the required day, inclusive, is 4 (7 C + Q) years + R days. To this must be added 620 Julian years when the date is reckoned from the commencement of the Christian Era, so that—

$$\text{J} = 620\text{y.} + 4\,(7\text{ C} + \text{Q})\text{y.} + \text{Rd.}$$

(6) If R be less than 365 it will be the number of the day in the year next after 620 + 4 (7 C + Q), that is to say, in the Julian year 621 + 4 (7 C + Q); but if R be greater than 365, and it be possible to subtract from it 365, or 730, or 1095 days, this subtraction must be made, and the equivalent years, either 1, 2, or 3 must be added to 621 + 4 (7 C + Q).

(7) René Martin, in commenting upon Francœur's method,* points out a slight advantage which amounts to this:—If R be less than 365 the date will fall in a year of the form 620 + 4 (7 C + Q) + 1, that is, of the form $4n + 1$; if R be greater than 365, so that either 1, 2, or 3 years have to be added, the date will fall in a year which will be of the form $4n + 2$, or $4n + 3$, or $4n$. It is only in the last case that the date falls in a Bissextile year; therefore the subtraction of 365, or of 2 × 365, or of 3 × 365 will always show by the remainder the actual serial number of the required day, that is, the serial number as a day of the year. There can be no need ever to consider whether 366 ought to be subtracted from R. In other, words the remainder, after dividing by the constant, 365, invariably shows the serial number required. In the case of a date falling in a Bissextile year, care will, of course, be taken to assign to it its right monthly title. Thus, if the

* Page 102 of his "Mémoire."

remainder be 61, the day will be March 1 in a Bissextile, though it is March 2 in a Common year.

Example.—Required the Julian date of the first day of A.H. 1256.

(1) Dividing 1256 by 30, we have C = 41, and $r = 26$.

(2) $10631\,C + 354\,(r-1) + \left\{\frac{11r+3}{30}\right\}$

$= 435871 + 8850 + 9$

$= 444730.$

(3) 444730 + 197 = 444927.

(4) Add for A.D. 621, 365 days ; sum = 445292.

(5) Divide by 1461, and divide the remainder by 365.

```
1461)445292(304 periods of 4 years, or 1216y.
     444144
     ------
 365)1148(3 years
     1095
     ----
       53 days.
```

J is therefore the 53rd day, or February 22 in the Julian year 621 + 1216 + 3, or A.D. 1840.

The Gregorian date will be 12 days later, or day 65, which, in the Bissextile year 1840, is March 5.

35. M. Francœur's reverse method, for finding the Muḥammadan date corresponding to January 1 in any given Julian year, J, is with certain modifications, as follows :—

(1) January 1 in the year 623 of our Era corresponded to the 170th day of the first year of the Hijra,* therefore, since the commencement of the Era of the Hijra, (J – 623) Julian years + 169 days have elapsed before January 1 in the year J is reached; or, if January 1 be taken into the account, this will be increased by one day and will become (J – 623) years + 170 days.

```
* July 16, or day 197 of A.D. 622 = day   1 of A.H. 1.
                  168                   168
                  ---                   ---
  Dec. 31, or day 365   ,,    ,,  = day 169   ,,   ,,
          January 1 of A.D. 623 = day 170   ,,   ,,
```

(2) $J - 623$ may be put into the form $4q + r$, where q and r are both known, and r may equal either 0, 1, 2, or 3.

When $r = 0$, $k = 0$. When $r = 1$, $k = 365$. When $r = 2$, $k = 731$. When $r = 3$, $k = 1096$.*

(3) There are 1461 days in every 4 Julian years, so that if $(4q + r)$ years + 170 days be reduced to days, the number of days will be $1461q + k + 170$, where k is the number of days in r years. This expression gives the number of the day in the Era of the Hijra, counted from the commencement, which corresponds to January 1 in the Julian year J.

(4) If $1461q + k + 170$ be divided by 10631, the quotient, Q, will indicate the number of Cycles, and the remainder, R (which may be zero, or any integral number less than 10631), the number of days. These days must be reduced to Common years by dividing by 354, and from the remaining days there must be subtracted the number of intercalary days which occur in such of the $\left\{\frac{R}{354}\right\}$ years as are Kabîsah. Let the final remainder be n. Then the required date will be the nth day of the year of the Hijra $30\,Q + \left\{\frac{R}{354}\right\} + 1$. The addition of unity being made because the nth day belongs to the year next after $30\,Q + \left\{\frac{R}{354}\right\}$.

Example.—Required the Muḥammadan date corresponding to January 1, A.D. 1840.

The given Christian date must be first taken as Julian.

$$J - 623 = 1840 - 623 = 1217 = 4 \times 304 + 1,$$

* M. Francœur does not show how these values of k are obtained; they may be ascertained thus: The Julian years, commencing with 623, are reckoned by quadriennial periods; the first of these periods consists of the years 623, 624, 625, 626. The first of these years is Common, and has 365 days; the second is a Bissextile year, and has 366 days; the third and fourth are both Common years.

The four current years of every succeeding period will be of the same forms, that is, will have a similar number of days. In other words, if (k) be the number of days contained in the (r) years which may have to be added to the $4q$ years, then—

$$\begin{aligned} \text{if } r &= 0, k = 0 \\ r &= 1, k = 365 \\ r &= 2, k = 365 + 366 = 731 \\ r &= 3, k = 365 + 366 + 365 = 1096. \end{aligned}$$

that is— $q = 304$; $r = 1$; $\therefore k = 365$.

$$1461q + k + 170 = 444144 + 365 + 170 = 444679.$$

```
10631)444679(41 = Q = 1230 years
      435871
      ------
   354) 8808 = R (24 Common years
        8496
        ----
         312
```

Subtract $\left\{\dfrac{11 \times 24 + 14}{30}\right\} = 9$

303 days.

The date required is the 303rd day of the Hijra year (1230 + 24 + 1), or A.H. 1255. This is the 8th day of the eleventh month, for there are 295 days in the first ten months.

The Gregorian January 1 of 1840 occurs 12 days earlier than the Julian, and therefore corresponds to the 291st day of A.H. 1255, or the 25th of the tenth month.

This result is correct. It may be verified by adding 52 days to both sides for the Julian, and 64 for the Gregorian date. This will give the Julian and Gregorian dates corresponding to Muḥarram 1, A.H. 1256.

```
    January  1, 1840 = 303rd of H. 1255
            52          52
            --          --
    January 53, 1840 = 355 of H. 1255
or— February 22, 1840 =  1 of H. 1256.
```

Also, for the Gregorian date,

January (1 + 64) = March 5, 1840 = (291 + 64)th of H. 1255
= 1 of H. 1256.

The Chronological Table shows that this correspondence of dates is correct.

Example 2.—Required the Muḥammadan date corresponding to March 31, Easter Sunday, A.D. 1499.

March 31 is the 90th day in the year 1499, therefore, when the Muḥammadan date corresponding to January 1 has been found it will be necessary to add to it 89 days.

$$1499 - 623 = 876 = 4 \times 219,$$

that is— $q = 219;\ r = 0,\ \therefore k = 0.$

$$1461q + k + 170 = 319959 + 170 = 320129 \text{ days.}$$

```
10631)319959(30 Cycles = 900 years
       318930
       ------
        354)1199(3 Common years
            1062
            ----
             137
Subtract {(11 × 3 + 14)/30} =   1
            --
             136
```

The date for January 1, 1499, is therefore the 136th day of A.H. (900 + 3 + 1). To this must be added 89 days for March 31, and the required date is the 225th day, or the 18th of the eighth month in A.H. 904.

Examination of Certain Inaccurate Rules.

36. The rules which are given by some writers for finding the correspondence between Muḥammadan and Julian years, depend upon the ratio which exists between Civil Muḥammadan and mean Julian years. In other instances, upon the ratio between mean Julian and mean Muḥammadan years. The latter ratio is obtained as follows:—

Thirty Muḥammadan years contain always 10631 days, and four Julian years contain always 1461 days.

Let H represent one Muḥammadan mean year, and J one mean Julian year, then—

$$H : J :: \frac{10631}{30} : \frac{1461}{4} :: 21262 : 21915$$

$$\therefore H = J \times \frac{21262}{21915} = J \times \cdot 970203. \ldots$$

and— $$J = H \times \frac{21915}{21262} = H \times 1 \cdot 103071. \ldots$$

* If G be a mean Gregorian year, $H : G :: \frac{10631}{30} : \frac{146097}{400}$

$$:: 425240 : 438291$$

$$\therefore H = G \times \cdot 9702227. \ldots$$

Observe that neither this ratio, nor that of H to J can be expressed as a finite decimal.

From this it follows that if any number of Muḥammadan mean years be multiplied by ·970203 . . . they will be reduced to their equivalent in mean Julian years.

Now the ratio which exists between the lengths of the mean years of the two Eras does not exist between the lengths of the Civil years; but dating is always effected by means of Civil years; consequently, when this ratio is employed to establish the correspondence of dates a source of error is at once introduced.

There is, however, one exception to this: if the Muḥammadan years be, in number, 30, or any multiple of 30, it matters not whether they be treated as Civil or as mean years. The same thing applies to Julian years if they be, in number, 4 or any multiple of 4.

Consider the case if any other number of Muḥammadan years than $30n$ be thus treated. The first two years of every Cycle contain together 709 days, if they be computed as though they were mean years they will be made to contain $2 \times 354\frac{11}{30}$ days, or 708d. 17h. 36m. Here the error decreases the interval of time. The first four years of a Cycle contain 1417 days; if treated as mean years they will be credited with 1417d. 11h. 12m., an increase on the true interval. And so it goes on. Sometimes, when the length of a given number of Civil years is computed as though they were mean years, the interval will be made too long; sometimes it will be made too short.

So again with Julian years. A.D. 622 is generally taken as the base in computing the correspondence, and as both 622 and 623 are Common years there must always be an error of 6h., or of 12h., or of 18h., unless the computed years exceed $4n$, in number, by 2.

37. The first erroneous rule which will be considered is that given by Ciccolini in his "Mémoire," published in "Correspondance Astronomique du Baron du Zach," tom. xi. No. 6.*

He employs the formula—

$$J = \frac{354\,(H-1) + \left\{\dfrac{11\,(H-1)+15}{30}\right\} + 196}{365{\cdot}25} + 621$$

where J is the interval of time in Julian years and days elapsed before the commencement of the Muḥammadan year H.

* It is also given by Francœur in Férussac "Bulletin des Sciences Mathematiques," 1825, p. 159, and by René Martin, who quotes from Francœur in his "Mémoire," p. 76.

It will be seen at once that the two first terms of the numerator in the fraction are intended to represent, in days, the interval of Muhammadan Civil time elapsed from the commencement of the Era in July, A.D. 622, up to the close of the year H − 1. The addition of 196 days to the numerator carries the time back to January 1, A.D. 622. The number of days, thus found, is reduced to Julian mean years and days by dividing the whole by 365·25. To the interval of mean Julian time thus obtained there are added 621 Julian Civil years, and the whole sum is supposed to be expressed by J in Julian Civil time.

Ciccolini directs that if there be any fraction of a day remaining after the division by 365·25 it is to be regarded as a whole day.

It is impossible that such a formula can invariably produce a correct result. In the first place the number of intercalary days in H−1 years is wrongly expressed; it ought to be $\left\{\frac{11(H-1)+14}{30}\right\}$. The substitution of 15 for 14 causes the expression to fail when H = 16 years, or any number of years of the form $30n + 16$, that is, when H−1=15, or $30n + 15$.

But suppose this error to be corrected: the formula will still sometimes fail on account of the confusion between mean and Civil years.

It so happens that in the particular example given by Ciccolini the result is not affected by either error, for H is not of the form $30n+16$, and the last of the Julian years elapsed, A.D. 1773, is of the form $4n + 1$, so that the period from A.D. 622, inclusive, contains a number of years which is a multiple of 4. The number of days which they contain, expressed by the numerator of the fraction in the formula, may therefore be correctly reduced to periods of 4 years by dividing by 1461, or to a group of single years by dividing by 365·25.

The example he gives is—To find the Julian date corresponding to the first day of A.H. 1188.

$$354(H-1) = 354 \times 1187 = 420198$$

$$\left\{\frac{11(H-1)+15}{30}\right\} = \left\{\frac{13072}{30}\right\} = 435$$

Add 196

$$365{\cdot}25)420829(1152 \text{ years}$$
$$420768$$

61 days.

To the 1152 years add 621, and the time elapsed from the commencement of the Christian Era before the commencement of A.H. 1188 is 1773 years and 61 days. The first day of that year will, therefore, be the 62nd, or March 3 in A.D. 1774. The corresponding Gregorian date is March 14. This date is correct.

But now test the formula for A.H. 49, first making the correction of 14 for 15 in the expression for the Kabîsah years—

$$354 \times 48 = 16992$$

$$\left\{\frac{11 \times 48 + 14}{30}\right\} = 18$$

$$\text{Add } 196$$

$$365{\cdot}25)17206{\cdot}00(47 \text{ years}$$

$$17166{\cdot}75$$

$$39{\cdot}25 \text{ days.}$$

The decimal of a day is, by the direction in the rule, to be reckoned as a whole day. Therefore, 47 + 621, or 668 years and 40 days have elapsed before the commencement of A.H. 49. The date required is, therefore, by the rule, the 41st day, or February 10, in A.D. 669. This is wrong; it ought to be February 9.

Further tests will show that the formula, even when corrected for the Kabîsah years, if taken together with the directions concerning the decimals of a day, will fail, whenever the decimal part of the remainder is ·25; but it succeeds when the decimal part is ·50 or ·75 or when there is no decimal in the remainder.

The decimal part of the remainder will be ·25 whenever the quotient is 3, or any number of the form $4n + 3$; and because 621 is to be added to the quotient to give the number of Julian years elapsed, the decimal will be ·25 whenever the Julian years elapsed amount to 624, or to any number of the form $4n$, that is, when the Julian year in which Muḥarram 1 occurs is of the form $4n + 1$.

It is necessary to correct the rule by striking out the direction concerning the decimal of a day, and substituting the words—If the fractional part of the remainder after dividing by 365·25 be ·25, this decimal is to be neglected; but if it be ·50 or ·75, these decimals of a day are to be reckoned as a whole day.

If trial be made it will be found that the rules, after correcting the expression for the Kabîsah years, gives wrong results for the first day of A.H. 923, the quotient being 895; for 1125, quotient 1091; for 1154, quotient 1119; for 1158, quotient 1123, &c. All these quotients are of the form $4n + 3$. The correct Julian dates are, respectively, January 24, 1517; January 17, 1713; March 8, 1741; and January 23, 1745. All these years are of the form $4n + 1$.

38. For the reverse process—To find the Muḥammadan date corresponding to January 1 in any given Christian year—Ciccolini employs the formula—

$$H = \frac{(J - 622)\ 365{\cdot}25}{10631} \times 30 + \frac{R}{354} - \left\{\frac{11r + 15}{30}\right\} - 196.$$

He directs that if there be any fraction in the product of (J − 622) and 365·25, it is to be ignored.

H is the interval of Hijra time elapsed before January 1 in the given Christian year is reached.

J is the given Christian year.

R is the remaining number of days after the integral part of (J − 622) 365·25 has been divided by 10631.

r is the quotient arising from the division of R by 354.

The first part of this formula is not expressed in the usual Algebraical manner. Indeed, it would not be readily understood without the assistance of the example which Ciccolini gives. This example shows that not the whole fraction is to be multiplied by 30, as the formula implies, but only the integral part of the quotient arising from the division by 10631. In fact, multiplication by 30 is simply to reduce Cycles to years.

The substitution of 14 for 15 in the expression for Kabîsah years must be made as before.

The example attached is—To find the Muḥammadan date corresponding to the Julian January 1, A.D. 1774.

Notice that (J − 622) is really (J − 1 − 621). In the example the Julian time elapsed since the commencement of the Era of the Hijra is (1773 − 621) years − 196 days; but the 196 days are subtracted as the last term in the formula—

$$\frac{(1774 - 622)\ 365{\cdot}25}{10631} = 39 \text{ Cycles} = 1170 \text{ years, with remainder } 6159 \text{ days.}$$

$$\frac{6159}{354} = 17 \text{ years, with remainder } 141 \text{ days}$$

$$\left(\frac{11 \times 17 + 14}{30}\right) = 6 \text{ days}$$

$$\begin{aligned} H &= (1170 + 17) \text{ years} + (141 - 6 - 196) \text{ days} \\ &= 1187\text{y.} - 61\text{d.} = 1186\text{y.} + 293\text{d.} \end{aligned}$$

The next day, which corresponds to January 1, A.D. 1774, is the 294th in A.H. 1187, or S̲hawwâl 28.

The formula is successful for this year, although 1774 – 622, or 1152, is an interval of time measured in actual current Julian years while 365·25 is the length of a mean year. This, however, leads to no confusion here, because 1152 is an integral number of quadriennial periods, namely 288, and 288 × 1461 = 1152 × 365·25. There is, in fact, no decimal in the product.

The direction given with the formula states that if there be any decimal it is to be ignored; but it will be found that when the decimal is ·75 the formula fails. This will be the case for all Julian years of the form $4n + 1$. The decimal ·75 must not be ignored: it must be reckoned as one day.

Thus, for January 1, A.D. 633.

$$(633 - 622)\, 365{\cdot}25 = 4017{\cdot}75 \text{ days.}$$

If the ·75 be ignored, we have $\frac{4017}{354} = 11$ years, with remainder 123 days. The Kabîsah days in 11 years are 4. Therefore—

$$\begin{aligned} H &= 11 \text{ years} + (123 - 4 - 196) \text{ days.} \\ &= 10 \text{ years} + 277 \text{ days.} \end{aligned}$$

The next day is the 278th in A.H. 11. This is wrong; it ought to be the 279th, or the 19th of the tenth month.

That the latter day is correct may be proved by adding 75 to 279, which brings us to the 354th, or last day of A.H. 11; the same being a Common year. If one more day be added, the first of A.H. 12 is reached. Also, January 1, with the addition of 75 + 1 days, is January 77, or March 18, which is the correct Julian date for the first day of A.H. 12.

The rule is inaccurate; it should be corrected thus:—If the fractions

·25, or ·50 occur in the product of (J – 622) and 365·25 they are to be ignored; if ·75 occur it is to be reckoned as one whole day.

39. Le Boyer gives a rule which, though ingenious, is somewhat cumbersome.* It is founded on the difference in length, expressed in hours, between 30 mean Muḥammadan, and the same number of mean Julian years. Through this use of mean time it frequently fails. It is given in an elaborate manner in ten separate paragraphs, but the reasons for the various directions are not very clearly stated. The last paragraph admits the liability to failure, stating that if the date found does not fall to the proper week-day, as indicated by the Sign of the year, it must be amended.†

The rule, as now given, is not a direct translation of Le Boyer's words, but is put in a more familiar form, and explanations are added where necessary. The numbers refer to his paragraphs.

(1) Let H be the given year of the Hijra; then, H – 1 years have elapsed before the initial day of H is reached.

Let H – 1 = C + *n*, where C is the number of completed Cycles, and *n* the number of years beyond C.

(2, 3) A mean Julian year of 365·25 days exceeds a mean Muḥammadan year of 354d. 8h. 48m. by 10d. 21h. 12m. Therefore 30 mean Julian years exceed one Cycle by 7836 hours; and 30 C mean Julian years will be 7836 C hours longer than C Cycles.‡ Also *n* mean Julian will exceed *n* mean Muḥammadan years by *x* hours, if *x* be the fourth term in the proportion 30 : *n* : : 7836 : *x*.

(4) H – 1 Julian years will, therefore, exceed H – 1 Muḥammadan years by (7836 C + *x*) hours. Fractions of an hour, if there be any in *x*, are ignored.

(5) Reduce these hours to Julian mean years by dividing by 8766, that being the number of hours in 365·25 days. Retain the quotient, Q. Let R be the remainder.

(6, 7) If the remaining R hours be more than sufficient to form 196 days, that is, be more than 4704, the quotient, Q, is to be increased by unity.

* "Traité complet du Calendrier," pp. 283-287. Nantes et Paris, 1822.

† "Si le dernier jour trouvé de cette manière ne s'accordait pas avec la férie trouvée par le problème précédent pour le jour initial de l'année donnée, il faudrait l'y ramener."

‡ Notice here that the C Cycles are of actual Civil length, while the Julian years are measured by the mean length of the year.

Subtract Q, (or Q + 1 if Q has been increased) from H − 1, and add 622 to the remainder. The sum is the number of the Julian year in which the initial day of H occurs. Observe, here, that if 621 were added to Q, which would be more natural, the sum would show the number of completed Julian years elapsed from the commencement of A.D. 1, before the date corresponding to the first day of H is reached.

(8) Divide the R hours remaining after the quotient Q was obtained by 24, so reducing them to days. Retain the quotient, q, and let r be the remainder. If r be less than 12 it is ignored, but if r exceed 12 the quotient, q, is to be increased by unity. I have found, after trials, that this should be—If r amount to, or exceed, 12, the quotient must be increased by unity.

(9) This direction is as follows:—"The initial day of the first year" [of the Era] "is distant from January 1 by 196 days; therefore the number found by (8)" [that is, the quotient, q, or $q + 1$ if q has been increased] "must be subtracted from 196. If the subtraction cannot be made, 365 days are to be added to 196, and the remainder will always * indicate the day with which the last of the completed years of the Hijra terminates."

This is equivalent to stating that the quotient, q (or $q + 1$), will show the number of days by which the Julian date corresponding to the last day of H + 1 falls short of July 16 in the Julian year (H − 1) − Q + 622, which has been found by (6, 7); but July 16 is the 197th day of the year, or is 196 days beyond January 1; therefore, $196 - q$ will be the serial number of the last day of H − 1 in the stated Julian year, and the next day will correspond to the first day of H. If, however, q (or $q + 1$) be greater than 196, then 196 must be augmented by 365, making 561, and $561 - q$ will, it is said, "always" indicate the serial number of the last day of H − 1, because July 16 in any year, Y + 1, is beyond January 1 in the year Y by 196 + 365 days.

Here, surely, there is a serious error, or, at least, a serious omission. First, with regard to the subtraction of q (or $q + 1$ if q be increased) from 196 if it be possible. It is true that July 16 is 196 days beyond January 1 in a Julian Common year, but it is the 198th day of a

* "La reste sera toujours le jour . . ." This should certainly be "généralement," or "très souvent."

Bissextile year, and is 197 days beyond January 1 in such a year. This would point to the fact that, if the monthly Julian date corresponding to Muḥarram 1 should occur in a Julian year of the form $4n$, the quotient, q (or $q + 1$), should be subtracted from 197 rather than from 196.

Again: If q (or $q + 1$) should be greater than 196, so that 365 has to be added to 196, which will be the case when Muḥarram 1 corresponds to any day later than July 16, then, if Muḥarram 1 fall in a Julian year, Y, of the form $4n + 3$, the next year will be Bissextile, and q (or $q + 1$) ought to be subtracted from 197 + 365, or, for it is the same thing, from 196 + 366, because July 16 is 197 days beyond January 1 in the year Y + 1.

The rule frequently fails upon this account when Muḥarram 1 corresponds to any day in a Julian year of the form $4n$, or to any day after July 16 in a year of the form $4n + 3$.

The rule does not thus fail invariably, because the error arising from the employment of mean time will sometimes compensate the error of subtracting q from 196 + 365 instead of from 197 + 366.

Examples will presently be given.

(10) This paragraph, with respect to the necessary correction if the day found have the wrong feria, has been quoted in the footnote at the commencement of this Article. The week-day for the Julian date will be found by means of the Sunday Letter for the year, and the Sign of the year H, or feria of its first day by the rule given in Article 24 (2). If the two do not agree the date found is wrong, and must be "remedied" so that the week-day may coincide with the Sign.

Le Boyer gives as an example of his method the work required for finding the Julian date corresponding to the first day of A. H. 1127.

(1) $H - 1 = 1126 = 30 \times 37 + 16$.

(2) 30×37 mean Julian years exceed the same number of mean Muḥammadan years by 7836×37, or 289932 hours.

(3) Also, $30 : 16 :: 7836 : x$.

$$\therefore x = 4179\text{h. } 6\text{m.}; \text{ but the minutes are ignored.}$$

(4) 1126 mean Julian years, therefore, exceed 1126 mean Muḥammadan years by 289932 + 4179, or 294111 hours.

(5) Dividing 294111 by 8766, the quotient Q = 33, and the remainder R = 4833.

(8) Dividing 4833 by 24, the quotient $q = 201$; the remainder, $r = 9$ hours, is ignored because less than 12.

(6, 7) Because R, or 4833 hours, is more than 196 days, the quotient Q is increased by unity to 34, which being subtracted from H – 1, or 1126, leaves 1092. To this there is added 622, giving 1714 for the Julian year in which the first day of H occurs.

(9) 201 cannot be subtracted from 196, which is therefore to be augmented by 365, and 196 + 365 – 201 = 360. Hence, the last day of H – 1 corresponds to the Julian day whose serial number is 360 in A.D. 1714; that is, December 26. The next day, December 27, corresponds to Muḥarram 1 of A.H. 1127.

(10) This result is correct. The Julian Sunday Letter for A.D. 1714 is C, and as December 1 is always F, December 27 in this year is a Monday. Also, the Sign for A.H. 1127, or feria for Muḥarram 1, is found by the rule in Article 24 (2) to be 2, or Monday.

It happens in this particular case that the use of mean instead of actual time does not affect the result, because the final remainder, 9, is ignored by the rule. The actual number of days in 1126 Julian years, commencing with A.D. 622, is 1126 × 365 + 281,* or 411271. The actual number in 1126 Muḥammadan years is (10631 × 37) + (354 × 16) + 6, or 399017. The actual excess of the Julian years is, therefore, 12254 days, or (8 × 1461 + 566) days = 33 years + 201 days. The work in the example makes the excess to be 33 years + 201 days + 9 hours, and the 9 hours being ignored by the rule the excess is the same in both cases.

The rule, however, is not always so successful, even for years in which Muḥarram 1 does not occur in a Julian year of the form $4n$, or $4n + 3$.

* The formula for the intercalated days in n years, reckoned from A.D. 622 as the first, is not $\left\{\frac{n}{2}\right\}$ but $\left\{\frac{n+1}{2}\right\}$, for in the first three years there is one which is Bissextile, and in the remaining $n - 3$ years there are $\left\{\frac{n-3}{4}\right\}$. The whole number is therefore $1 + \left\{\frac{n-3}{4}\right\}$, or $\left\{\frac{n+1}{4}\right\}$

Consider, for example, A.H. 136. Its initial day corresponds to July 7, A.D. 753, of the form $4n + 1$, but the rule finds July 8 for the first day.

H − 1 = 135 = 4 Cycles + 15 years.

30 : 15 : : 7836 : 3918.

```
Excess for 4 Cycles = 7836 × 4 = 31344 hours
   ,,     15 years.............. =  3918   ,,
                                 ------
                            8766)35262(4 years
                                 35064
                                 ------
                                 24)198(8 days
                                    192
                                    ---
                                      6 hours, ignored.
```

To find the year...135 − 4 + 622 = 753, A.D.

To find the day...196 − 8 = 188 = July 7 = last day of A.H. 135. Therefore, first day of A.H. 136 is July 8, which is wrong by one day.

The reason for the failure: The actual number of days contained in 135 Julian years commencing with July 16, 622, is 49309. The actual number in 135 Muḥammadan years is 47839. The Julian excess is, therefore, 1470 days, or 1461 + 9, that is, 4 years + 9 days. The work in the example makes the excess to be 4 years + 8 days + 9 hours, but the 9 hours are ignored, and the excess is one day short of the true measure.

Take another case, A.H. 152. Its first day corresponds to January 14, A.D. 769.

The actual number of days in the 151 elapsed Muḥammadan years is 53509. In the 151 Julian years commencing with July 16, 622, it is 55153. The real Julian excess is, therefore, 1644 days, or 4 years + 183 days. If the work be done it will be found that the rule makes the excess to be 4 years + 182 days + 9 hours, and the 9 hours are ignored. Thus, working by mean time makes the excess to be one day less than it actually is, and January 15, instead of January 14, is found for the required date.

Consider next the failure of the rule when Muḥarram 1 occurs in a Julian Bissextile year. The correct date for the first day of A.H. 36 is June 30, A.D. 656.

Here H − 1 = 35 = 30 + 5.

Excess for 1 Cycle = 7836 hours
„ 5 years = 1306 „

8766)9142(1 year
8766

24)376(15 days = *q*
360

16

The remainder 16 is greater than 12, therefore *q* is to be increased by unity, and we have—

For the year: 35 − 1 + 622 = 656, A.D.

For the day: 196 − 16 = 180 = June 28 in a Leap-year. The next day, June 29, ought to correspond to Muḥarram 1, but it does not. If 16 had been subtracted from 197, the remainder would have been 181 = June 29, and the next day, June 30, is the correct date.

The year 36 of the Hijra is of the form $30n + 6$; the rule fails for all years of this form which fulfil the condition of their initial day occurring in a Julian year of the form $4n$. There are eighteen such years in the first 82 Cycles, besides H. 36, namely; 156, 366, 576, 696, 786, 846, 906, 1116, 1126, 1146, 1566, 1656, 1776, 1866, 1986, 2106, 2196, and 2316.

There are other forms of the Muḥammadan years for which the rule fails under the same condition, but it does not fail for every form because in some cases the computation made by mean time makes the Julian excess to be one day less than it actually is. When that is so, compensation is made for the error of subtracting *q* from 196, or from 561, instead of from 197, or 572. In other words, if the computation make the Julian excess to appear as *t* days, whereas the actual excess is $t + 1$ days, then $196 - t$ gives the same result as $197 - (t + 1)$, and $561 - t$ is the same as $562 - (t + 1)$.

For example: Muḥarram 1, A.H. 362 (of the form $30n + 2$), corresponds to October 12, A.D. 972 (of the form $4n$). Working by the rule, the Julian excess appears to be 10 years + 276 days. The actual time elapsed during the 361 years commencing with July 16, A.D. 622 is—

Julian....................	$361 \times 365 + 90 = 131855$ days
Muḥammadan	$10631 \times 12 + 354 = 127926$,,
Actual Julian excess..............	3929 ,,

or, 10 years + 277 days.

Here, $561 - 276 = 285 = 562 - 277 =$ October 11. And the next day, October 12, is the correct date.

Next, with respect to the error when the initial day of the Muḥammadan year occurs after July 16 in a Julian year of the form $4n + 3$.

Muḥarram 1, A.H. 1367 (of the form $30n + 17$), corresponds to November 2, A.D. 1947 (of the form $4n + 3$). Let the date be found by the rule :—

H − 1 = 1366 = 45 Cycles + 16 years.

$$7836 \times 45 = 352620$$
$$30 : 16 :: 7836 : x = 4179$$
$$8766)356799(40 = Q$$
$$350640$$
$$24)6159(256 = q$$
$$6144$$
$$15$$

Because q is greater than 196, Q is increased from 40 to 41 ; and because r is greater than 12, q is increased from 256 to 257.

Hence we have—

For the year ....1366 − 41 + 622 = 1947, A.D.
For the day ....561 − 257 = 304 = October 31.

The next day is November 1. This is short of the correct date by one day.

If the fact that there are 366 days in the year commencing with July 16, 1947, and terminating with July 15, 1948, had been recognised, the subtraction of 257 would have been made from 562 ; the remainder would have been 305, and the correct date for the next day would have been found.

The other Muḥammadan years which, being of the form $30n + 17$, fulfil the necessary conditions for failure of the rule, are 497, 827, 1037, 1577, 1907, and 2447.

There are eight years of the form $30n$ for which the rule fails, namely, 390, 600, 930, 1140, 1470, 1800, 2010, and 2340.

There are ten of the form $30n + 4$; 64, 394, 534, 604, 724, 934, 1264, 1334, 1804, 2344.

It fails in years of other forms. The above are mentioned in order that the truth of what has been said may be tested.

Now, the question might very naturally be asked—Why, if this be the case, should not the rule be corrected by adding the words, "When the date for Muḥarram 1 is found by the computation to fall in a Julian year of the form $4n$, or, after July 16 in a Julian year of the form $4n + 3$, the quotient q (or $q + 1$), must be subtracted from 197, or from 562"?

Unfortunately this would not be sufficient to meet the error. If it were done the rule would still fail when the computation made by mean time renders the days elapsed one less than the actual number. Provision for this contingency would have to be made by a saving clause to the effect that reliance cannot be placed upon the result obtained until the true Julian excess has been ascertained, and this excess must be found by computing the actual number of days elapsed. If it agree with the excess found by the rule the date is correct; if it do not agree, the date is incorrect.

How much more simple to compute the actual number of days elapsed, and obtain the date by the method recommended in Article 31.

40. Le Boyer gives an alternative rule which produces a correct result because actual time elapsed is employed. It is, in fact, practically similar to that described in Article 31, though somewhat more complicated.

(1) Find the number of days in the Muḥammadan years elapsed before the given year is reached.

(2) Divide the number by 365; the quotient, Q, will show the equivalent number of Julian Common years, and the remainder, r gives the number of surplus days.

(3) The Q years of 365 days will contain a certain number of

intercalary days, namely, the integral part of $Q + 1$ divided by 4, or $\left\{\frac{Q+1}{4}\right\}$*. This number of days must be subtracted from r, or, if that cannot be done, Q must be diminished by unity and r be augmented by 365. The subtraction can then be made.

(4) The final remainder shows the number of days elapsed beyond July 15, and if this remainder be increased by 196 the sum will show the serial number of the last day of the year H in the Julian year $Q + 622$.

(5) The next day is that required.

Example.—Required the Julian date corresponding to A.H. 828.

$$H - 1 = 827 = 27 \text{ Cycles} + 17 \text{ years.}$$

$$\text{Days elapsed} = 10631 \times 27 + 354 \times 17 + \left\{\frac{11 \times 17 + 14}{30}\right\}$$

$$= 287037 + 6018 + 6 = 293061$$

$$365)293061(802 = Q$$
$$292730$$
$$\overline{331} = r$$
$$\left\{\frac{802 + 1}{4}\right\} = 200$$
$$\overline{131}$$

Therefore 802 years + 131 days have elapsed beyond July 15, A.D. 622. By the addition of 196 days we have 802y. + 327d. beyond the termination of A.D. 621. That is, 1423y. + 327d. since the commencement of the Christian Era, before the required date is reached, which is the 328th day, or November 23, in the year 1426.

It seems unfortunate that, while Le Boyer had at his command a rule which gives accurate results, he should have adopted in the first instance one which frequently fails, and which must therefore be condemned.

41. Amongst the rules given by English authors the first that will be examined is that by Sir N. H. Nicolas in his "Notitia Historica."† His words are, "To ascertain precisely the day on which any year of

* See footnote, p. 427.

† First published in 1824, and again, as vol. xliv. of Lardner's "Cabinet Cyclopædia," in 1833, under the title "The Chronology of History." A new edition was issued by Dr. Lardner in 1840.

the Hejira begins would require elaborate Tables, which may be found in 'L'Art de Vérifier les Dates,' and in Playfair's 'System of Chronology'; but by the following calculations the fact will be ascertained with tolerable accuracy:—Multiply the years elapsed by 970203; cut off six decimals; add 622·54, and the sum will be the year of the Christian Era, and decimal of the day following, in Old Style."

It may, in the first place, be noticed that neither the authors of "L'Art de Vérifier les Dates," nor Playfair give any Tables for finding the dates; moreover, they give no rules; but they do give Chronological Tables containing the dates after they have been found.

No example is attached, and the rule is so badly expressed that, at first reading, it is difficult to understand what is intended. What can be the meaning of the words, "and decimal of the day following"? The decimal of a day, as the expression is usually understood, means some part of a day; that is certainly not what is intended. And—"the day following"—what does that mean?

Precisely the same rule appears in "The Companion to the British Almanac,"* where an example is attached. It is also given by Bond in his "Handy-Book of Rules and Tables,"† but in a more definite form (see *post*, Article 42). With the help thus afforded the rule may be interpreted:—

Multiply the number of Muḥammadan years which have elapsed before the given date is reached by ·970203, add 622·54 to the product. The integral part of the sum will show the Julian year in which the required day occurs, and the decimal part, when reduced to days, will give the serial number of the last day of the preceding Muḥammadan year; therefore, the following day will be that of the required date. When the decimal part of the sum has been reduced to days, any decimals of a day which may remain are to be ignored.

In the "Companion to the British Almanac" the following words are added after the rule:—"By the table, p. 23, the day of the week on which any Mahometan year begins is shewn; and as, by table p. 32, 33, the day of the week answering to any day of our Calendar may be also known, a comparison of these two will serve to correct the result of the above rule, if it should be a day in error, as will sometimes be the case, on account of the clashing of the Mahometan and Christian leap years."

* For 1830, p. 22.

† Page 231, 4th edition.

This is a wise provision, equivalent to an acknowledgment that the rule sometimes fails. We are not told how to ascertain when the Julian Bissextile years "clash" with the Muḥammadan Kabîsah years.

Example 1.—Required the Julian date of the first day of A.H. 527.*

H − 1 = 526.

$$526 \times {\cdot}970203 = 510{\cdot}326778$$
$$\text{Add } 622{\cdot}54$$
$$1132{\cdot}866778$$
$${\cdot}866778 \times 365 = 316{\cdot}37397.$$

The last day of H − 1 is therefore the 316th, or November 11, in A.D. 1132, and the next day, November 12, is the required date. This is correct.

Example 2.—The Julian date of the first day of A.H. 107.

H − 1 = 106.

$$106 \times {\cdot}970203 = 102{\cdot}841518$$
$$\text{Add } 622{\cdot}54$$
$$725{\cdot}381518$$
$${\cdot}381518 \times 365 = 139{\cdot}254070.$$

The last day of A.H. 106 is therefore the 139th, or May 19 in A.D. 725, and the first day of A.H. 107 is May 20. This is wrong; the first day was Saturday, May 19.

The reason why the rule frequently fails is evident. The whole of the Muḥammadan Civil years elapsed are treated as though they were mean years, and the Julian years elapsed since July 15, A.D. 622, are treated in the same way. This is evident from the direction to multiply the Muḥammadan years elapsed, or H − 1, by ·970203 (see Article 36). On the other hand 622 Julian Civil years are added to the number of mean years elapsed, and the sum is held to represent a total expressed in Civil years. Hence, unless the number of Julian years elapsed be of the form $4n$, there may be an error of 6, 12, or 18 hours, and when this is added to the decimal of a day which is ignored an error of one day may easily occur.

* This is the example given in "The Companion to the British Almanac." I find that authors who give a rule which is not infallible, generally select for their example a year with respect to which the rule is successful.

With reference to the addition of 622·54: this is done in order that the integral part of the sum may show the actual Julian year in which the required date occurs. It is equivalent to adding 622 years + 196 days.* It leads to an unfortunate use of integers and decimals, for, as in the last example, the figures 725·381518 are not to be read according to their proper meaning, namely 725 years + 139 days, so that the date would be the 139th day in A.D. 726, but they are to be read as though they were written 724·381518.

Sir H. Nicolas says that the date "will be found with tolerable accuracy." But tolerable accuracy is not sufficient for the purpose in view. The rule must be condemned.

42. The rule as given by Bond in a more definite form, to which reference has been made, is stated by him as follows:—

"Multiply the years of the Hegira elapsed by ·970203, and add 622·540000 (*sic*), the *whole numbers* in the result will then represent the year required, and the decimals will give the day of the year. [N.B.—When the Julian year has been found, give the year-letter, that the day of the week may be verified.]

"Multiply the remaining decimals of the preceding sum by 365, the *whole numbers* will then represent the number of days of the Julian Common year from the 1st of January, Leap-years not being recognised. N.B.—As certain years which follow intercalary Mohammadan years require one day to be added to the sum, for the day of the year, it is necessary to ascertain what position the *preceding* year held in the Cycle, to know whether it had been reckoned as an intercalary year." The italics are Bond's.

Three pages further on, the author adds in a note: "The addition of one day will also be required in certain other years when the Julian and Mohammadan intercalary years clash. But this can easily be set right by advancing the Julian date, and taking care always to make the day of the week of the Julian date correspond to the day represented by the *feria* belonging to the Mahommadan date."

The note amounts to this:—After all the trouble has been taken the date found may be wrong by one day; the result must, therefore, be tested by other means, and if it be found wrong the date must be altered accordingly to suit the exigencies of the case.

* Accurately, 196 days = $\cdot 5\dot{3}6\ 986\ 30\dot{1}\ \dot{3}$ of a Common year.

The term "year-letter" is used by Bond for that one of the Dominical Letters which indicates the initial day of the year, according to the following arrangement:—

G Monday.	C Friday.
F Tuesday.	B Saturday.
E Wednesday.	A Sunday.
D Thursday.	

It is nothing more than another way of saying that the Sunday Letter for the year must be found, for, if January 1 be a Monday, the Sunday Letter must be G; if January 1 be a Tuesday, the Sunday Letter can be no other than F; and so onwards. The year-letter changes after February 28 in Bissextile years, just as the Sunday Letter changes.

The intimation that after multiplying the decimals of a year by 365 "the whole numbers will represent the number of days from the 1st of January" is vague. One day measured from January 1, would surely be January 2, and 355 days from January 1 would be January 356, or December 22 in a Common year, December 21 in a Leap-year. But, from the example which Mr. Bond gives, it appears that the 355th day from January 1 is December 21 in the Common year 1682. Hence, it would seem that "from 1st of January" is intended to mean "from the commencement of the year."

No reason is assigned for the non-recognition of Leap-years, or why the decimal of a Leap-year should be multiplied by 365 in order to reduce it to days. We do not multiply the decimal of a guinea by 20 to bring it into shillings; if we desire to obtain the true value we must recognise the twenty-first shilling of the guinea, but we are not to recognise the fact that a Leap-year has one day more than a Common year.

The example given by Mr. Bond is—Required the Julian date corresponding to the first day of A.H. 1094.

Here $H - 1 = 1093$.

$$1093 \times \cdot 970203 = 1060 \cdot 431879$$

$$\text{Add } \quad 622 \cdot 54$$

$$1682 \cdot 971879$$

$$\cdot 971879 \times 365 = 354 \cdot 735835.$$

The decimals are ignored, and 354 is increased by unity because

A.H. 1094 is the fourteenth year in a Cycle and, therefore, follows a Kabîsah year. This brings the required date to the 355th day, or December 21 in A.D. 1682.

This is the correct date for Muḥarram 1, A.H. 1094, but it is impossible to admit that it is reached in a legitimate manner. The calculation is made with a view to finding what interval of time had elapsed from the commencement of the Christian Era to the close of the day which corresponds to the last day of the Muḥammadan year 1093. This interval of time is actually 614339 days, or 1681 years + 354 days. By the employment of the ratio between mean Julian and Muḥammadan years the calculation makes the interval to be 1681y. + 354d. + 18 hours, nearly. The 18 hours are ignored, and, by way of compensation, one day is added, making 1681y. + 355d. The next day, or December 22, in A.D. 1682, would therefore be the day which corresponds to Muḥarram 1, A.H. 1094; but, by some method of reasoning which is not explained, the correspondence is made with December 21.

But, independent of this difficulty, it is acknowledged by Mr. Bond, as well as by others who employ as a foundation the rule of Sir H. Nicolas, that it is subject to failure, and that its results must be verified by other means. The rule must be condemned.

43. Professor Wilson, in his "Glossary of Judicial and Revenue Terms for British India," * gives three different rules. Of the first he says: "The rule given by Major Jervis, from Professor Carlysle, for finding the corresponding years of the Hijra and the Christian Era, is only an approximation: multiply the Centuries of the year by 3, and add to the product for the years over the Century as many times as it may be divided by 33, deduct the total from the whole number, and add to the reminder 621; thus—Required the year of our Lord corresponding to the year H. 1396; then, 13 × 3 = 39, to which add 2, the quotient of 96 divided by 33, making 41; then 1396 − 41 = 1355 + 621 = A.D. 1976."

This is certainly a very rough measurement of time. The result can hardly be called an "approximation." The excess of one hundred Julian, above the same number of Muḥammadan years is taken to be three Julian years, and the excess of thirty-three Julian years to be

* P. 227. London, 1885.

one year. No account is taken of any of those Hijra years elapsed which are less than 33, or more than 33*n*, in number. No attempt is made to establish the day, but only the year, in which correspondence occurs.

Professor Wilson himself says: "That this is not correct in cases where the number in excess of the Centuries is a trifle less than 33, or a trifle more than any of its multiples, is evident from a comparison with the standard tables: for instance, the year 1132 should be according to this rule A.D. 1720, but it begins 14th November, 1719,* according to the tables: so 1198 should be 1784, but in the table it begins 26th November, 1783.* The result, however, is near enough for general purposes, requiring correction only as to the period at which the year commences."

Further comment is unnecessary. The rule is worthless.

44. Professor Wilson's second rule. "Multiply the Hijra year by 970203, cut off six decimals, add 622·54, and the sum will be the year of the Christian Era, and decimal of the day following, in Old Style: thus, A.H. 1215 × 970203 = 1178·796645, leaving 1178 + 622·54 = 1800·54. The Hijra year commences on the 25th May, so that this is only an approximation."

This is evidently intended for the rule given by Sir H. Nicolas, which is interpreted in a manner absolutely ridiculous. The example shows that not the number of Hijra years elapsed, but one more than this number is to be multiplied by 970203, and not only are six decimals to be "cut off" from the product—they are to be altogether erased. Hence the first day of every year of the Hijra must correspond to July 16. To add to the confusion, the date for the commencement of A.H. 1215 is given as May 25; this is according to the Gregorian Calendar; the Julian date is May 13. The rule expressly states that the date will be found in Old Style.

Of all the rules that have been considered this—if under Wilson's interpretation it can be called a rule—is the most absurd.

45. Professor Wilson's third rule is given also by T. P. Hughes in his "Dictionary of Islam," a well-known and standard work. "A more simple form, and one which also shows the day on or about which the concurrence of the Mohammadan and Christian year com-

*. These are Gregorian dates.

mences, is the following: Multiply the Hijra year by 2·977, the difference between 100 solar, and as many lunar Mohammadan years; divide the product by 100, and deduct the quotient from the Hijra year; add to the result 621·569 (the decimal being the equivalent of the 15th July, plus 12 days for the change of the Kalendar); and the quotient will be the Christian year from the date at which the Mohammadan year begins. Thus—Hij. 1269 × 2·977 = 37778,* which divided by 100 = 37·778, and 1269 − 37·778 = 1231·222 + 621·569 = 1852·791, or 9 months and 15 days, *i.e.*, the 15th of October, which is the commencement of the Hijra year 1269."

The arithmetical equations in this example are expressed, as in that attached to the second rule, in a remarkable manner; but let that pass.

The word "Solar" should be replaced by "mean Gregorian"; that the latter is intended is evident from the difference assigned between 100 of each of such years.†

The direction to "add 621·569," the decimal including 12 days for the change of Style, indicates that the rule as it stands is only intended to apply to those years of the Hijra which have their commencement within the period beginning with March 1, A.D. 1800, and ending with February 28, 1900. It is remarkable that the rule should make no provision for the years from A.D. 622 to 1799, teeming as they do with important events in Arabian and Ottoman history: still more remarkable that this should have escaped the notice of Hughes who quotes the rule. The rule omits to state the fact, though it is one that ought not to be left unnoticed.

The rule says that after adding 621·509 "the quotient will be the Christian year from the date at which the Mohammadan year begins." When one amount is added to another it is more usual to call the result the sum. This, however, is no doubt an oversight. The rest of the sentence is unintelligible. Its probable meaning is—The integral part of the sum will show the year, and the decimal part, when reduced to days, will show the day of the year in the Gregorian Calendar with which the first day of the given Muḥammadan year corresponds.

* *Sic.* The omission of the point before the digit 8 may be due to a misprint. The product is 3777·813.

† The Commissioners of Pope Gregory took, for the mean length of the year, 365·2425 days. The difference between 100 such years and 100 mean Muḥammadan days is 1087·5817 days, or 2·97769 . . . mean Gregorian years. Julian years are not employed in this rule.

With respect to the example attached to the rule: the same unfortunate use of decimals and integers occurs as that to which reference was made in the comments on the rule of Sir H. Nicolas (Article 41). We are instructed to read 1852·791 as indicating the 289th day of the year 1852—a date which would be properly indicated by 1851·791, or 1851 years + ·791 of the next year. This next year, 1852, is a Leap-year, and ·791 × 366 = 289·506. The 289th day of a Leap-year is October 15, and thus the correct date is reached by ignoring the decimal ·506 of a day, which, if it were taken into the account, would advance the date to October 16.

The rule, if read in connection with the example, virtually says that these decimals are to be ignored; but it will be found in other cases that they have to be considered. Thus, for A.H. 1260, we have, following the rule—

$$1260 - \frac{1260 \times 2{\cdot}977}{100} = 1260 - 37{\cdot}5102 = 1222{\cdot}4898$$

$$\begin{array}{r} \text{Add } \underline{621{\cdot}569} \\ 1844{\cdot}0588 \end{array}$$

The year 1844 is Bissextile, and ·0588 × 366 = 21·5208. This gives the Gregorian date as January 21, A.D. 1844. It ought to be Monday, January 22, which may be obtained by noticing that ·5208 advances the date by one day.

It is unnecessary to multiply examples. If trial be made, it will be found that sometimes the decimals must be ignored, sometimes they must be reckoned as one day. The rule will find "on, or about which" day correspondence takes place, but it will not do more. Reliance cannot be placed in it.

46. The last rule to be examined is that given by W. H. Woolhouse in "Measures, Weights, and Moneys of all Nations."* It is copied, verbatim, by the "Encyclopædia Britannica," and is the only rule given in that work.

"For the computation of the Christian date, the ratio of a mean year of the Hegira to a solar year is—

$$\frac{\text{Year of Hegira}}{\text{Mean solar year}} = \frac{354\frac{11}{30}}{365{\cdot}24222} = 0{\cdot}970244.$$

* P. 200, seventh edition, 1890.

The year 1 began 16 July, 622, Old Style, or 19 July, 622, according to the New or Gregorian Style. Now the day of the year answering to the 19th of July is 200, which, in parts of the solar year, is 0·5476, and the number of years elapsed = Y – 1. Therefore, as the intercalary days are distributed with considerable regularity in both Calendars, the date of the commencement of the year Y expressed in Gregorian years is—

$$0·970224\,(Y - 1) + 622·5476$$

or—

$$0·970224 + 621·5774.$$

This formula gives the following rule for calculating the date of the commencement of any year of the Hegira, according to the Gregorian or New Style.

"Rule.—Multiply 970244 by the year of the Hegira, cut off six decimals from the product, and add 621·5774. The sum will be the year of the Christian Era, and the day of the year will be found by multiplying the decimal figures by 365. The result may sometimes differ a day from the truth as the intercalary days do not occur simultaneously; but as the day of the week can always be accurately obtained, the error, if any, can be readily adjusted."

The example attached is—To find the date on which A.H. 1362 commences.

$$1362 \times ·970224 = 1321·445088$$
$$\text{Add } 621·5774$$
$$1943·0225$$
$$·0225 \times 365 = 8·2125.$$

"The date is the 8th day, or 8 January, of the year 1943." It is hardly necessary to observe that in the example supplied the rule finds the correct date. This, however, as is admitted by Mr. Woolhouse, will not always be the case.

The reasons why the rule sometimes fails are similar to those already described. The ratio of a mean Muḥammadan to a mean Tropical year (called a Solar year), is employed, the length of the latter being taken as 365·24222 days.* Insomuch as dates are not given

* This is the length assigned by Woolhouse at p. 145. More accurately it is 365·24219862.

either by mean Tropical or by mean Muḥammadan or mean Gregorian years there does not appear to be any particular cause for taking this ratio. Moreover, if mean years must be employed, it would simplify matters if the value of a mean Gregorian year, namely, 365·2425 days, were taken.

The rule is, in part, founded upon the assumption that "intercalary days are distributed with considerable regularity in both calendars," although "the result may sometimes differ a day from the truth as the intercalary days do not occur simultaneously." They are so far removed from occurring simultaneously that in 1200 Gregorian years there are 291 which are Bissextile, while in the 1236 Muḥammadan years which, roughly, they contain, there are 454 which are Kabîsah.

In the first two hundred years of the Hijra there are fifteen Kabîsah years which commence in a Leap-year; eighteen which include a February 29; and two which both commence in a Leap-year and also include February 29.

The rule says that "the day of the year will be found by multiplying the decimal figures by 365." This will not always be the case when the decimal represents a part of a Bissextile year. It is true that the date found, ignoring the decimals of a day, will sometimes be the same whether the factor employed be 365 or 366; while, on the other hand, the use of 365 for a Leap-year will sometimes cause an error of one day. Thus, for A.H. 1417, which will commence with May 19, A.D. 1996, it does not matter which multiplier is used; the one gives the day as 140·4549, the other gives 140·8368. The integral part of the product is the same in both cases. For A.H. 1244, which commenced with July 14, 1828, the day found will be 195·6604, or July 13, if 365 be used, but 196·1964, or July 14 if the proper multiplier, 366, be used.

The variation from other rules made by finding the nominal date according to the Gregorian Calendar in preference to the Julian is far from being an improvement. The Christian date for the commencement of any year, if it occurred before the change of Style,* must be reduced to the Julian Calendar which was then in use. It is true that this may easily be done, but the method of doing it may not be known by every reader. It would, therefore, have been well to add that a

* October 5, 1582, for Rome. September 14, 1752, for England.

certain number of days must be subtracted from the Gregorian date found, in order to obtain the date according to the Calendar in use before the change.

From	July 16, 622,	to end of February,	700,	subtract	3
„	March 1, 700	„	900	„	4
„	„ 900	„	1000	„	5
„	„ 1000	„	1100	„	6
„	„ 1100	„	1300	„	7
„	„ 1300	„	1400	„	8
„	„ 1400	„	1500	„	9
„	„ 1500	„	1700	„	10
„	„ 1700,	to September 13,	1752	„	11

This rule, then, like all others which employ mean time, whether Tropical, Julian, or Gregorian, requires verification, and very frequently correction of its results.

47. The reverse rule for finding the Muḥammadan date corresponding to the first day of any Julian year is given by Sir N. H. Nicolas thus :—

"Subtract 622 from the current year; multiply by 1·0307; cut off four decimals, and add ·46. The sum will be the year, and decimal of the day, Old Style."

The same rule is given by Crichton in his "History of Arabia." *

No explanation of the figures used is afforded; the reason for them is, however, easily traced.

The factor 1·0307 is derived from the ratio of a mean Julian to a mean Muḥammadan year (Article 36). "Cut off four decimals" means no more than "put the point in the right place," and is unnecessary. The addition of ·46 is made because only 621 years and 196 days of the Christian Era had elapsed when that of the Hijra commenced, consequently, when 622 years are subtracted, too much by 169 days, or ·46 of a Common Julian year, has been taken away, and this interval of time must be replaced. "Decimal of the day" should be "the decimal of the year will show the day."

* In a note attached to a "Table of Arabian Months and Weeks," vol. i. ch. v. p. 204. Edinburgh, 1834.

The rule frequently fails on account of the use of mean time. Thus:—

Example 1.—Required the Muḥammadan date corresponding to January 1, A.D. 1682 (Julian).

$$1682 - 622 = 1060$$
$$1060 \times 1{\cdot}0307 = 1092{\cdot}542$$
$$\text{Add} \quad {\cdot}46$$
$$1093{\cdot}002$$

1093 is a Kabîsah year, for it = 30 × 36 + 13, therefore, we have for the day of the year, ·002 × 355 = ·71. If this decimal of a day be reckoned as a whole day the date will be Muḥarram 1, A.H. 1093. If the decimal be ignored the date will be the last day of the previcus year 1092. Both are wrong; the correct date is Muḥarram 2, A.H. 1093.

Example 2.—January 1, A.D. 1705.

$$1705 - 622 = 1083$$
$$1083 \times 1{\cdot}0307 = 1116{\cdot}2481$$
$$\text{Add} \quad {\cdot}46$$
$$1116{\cdot}7081$$

1116 is a Common year, = 30 × 37 + 6, therefore we have for the day ·7081 × 354 = 250·6674. If the decimal of a day be ignored the date found is the 250th day, or Ramaḍân 14, A.H. 1116. If the decimal be reckoned as one day, the date is Ramaḍân 15. Both are wrong; the correct date is Ramaḍân 16.

The rule must be rejected as being imperfect.

48. Bond has a variation upon this rule which entirely vitiates the result.

"Deduct 622 from the given year of our Lord, multiply the sum (*sic*) by 1·0307, and add 1·4600. The whole numbers in the result will be the year required." If it were not that he gives an example, it might be thought that the direction to add 1·46, instead of ·46, was due to a misprint.

His example is that which I have purposely taken as (1) in the last Article. He gives it thus:—

"A.D. 1682 – 622 = 1060

1060 × 1·0307 = 1092·542

He adds 1·46

1094·002 = 1094 of the Hegira

which began on the 21st of December, 1682."

Having thus found the year of the Hijra to be 1094 (instead of 1093) he leaves the question of the day in this year entirely unconsidered.

Now let us endeavour to verify the year which he gives, namely, A.H. 1094.

It is a fact that December 21, 1682, corresponded to Muḥarram 1, A.H. 1094. We, therefore, have—

Day 355 of A.D. 1682 = Day 1 of A.H. 1094
= Day 356 of A.H. 1093 K.
Day (355–354) ,, ,, = Day (356–354) ,, ,, ,,

or January 1, 1682, corresponds to Muharram 2, 1093. Bond advances the Hijra date by one whole year because he adds 1·46 instead of ·46.

If this error be corrected his rule becomes the same as that of Nicolas, and frequently fails.

Professor Wilson gives the same rule with another variation.

"Subtract 622 from the current year; multiply the result by 1·0307; cut off four decimals, and add ·46; the sum will be the year, which when it has a surplus decimal requires the addition of 1. Thus, 1852 – 622 = 1230; 1230 × 1·0307 = 1267·7610 + ·46 = 1268·22. Add, therefore, 1, and we have the equivalent Hijra year 1269."

No attempt is made to find the day corresponding to January 1. Moreover, this day did not occur in A.H. 1269 at all, but in A.H. 1268. This is easily proved:

Muḥarram 1, 1268, corresponded to October 15, 1851
Muḥarram 78 ,, ,, December 31 ,,
Muḥarram 79 ,, ,, January 1, 1852

The date required is, therefore, the 79th day of A.H. 1268, or Rabī 'u-l-avval 20.

As all these rules fail, nothing remains but to resort to the method of "Days Elapsed," Article 32.

Mr. Woolhouse and the "Encyclopædia Britannica" give no rule for finding the Muḥammadan date corresponding to January 1.

CHAPTER VI

THE ARABIAN YEAR BEFORE ISLÂM. THE USUALLY ACCEPTED DATE FOR THE ERA OF THE HIJRA IS INCORRECT

49. In Chapter I., Article 3, reference was made to the investigations of M. Caussin de Perceval, and the results at which he had arrived with regard both to the year of the pagan Arabians in the "times of ignorance"—as the period before Islâm was introduced is called by Muḥammadan writers—and also with regard to the true commencement of the Era of the Hijra.

His views upon these subjects are so important, and are maintained by such powerful arguments, that it will be well to consider them in some detail. I think that there can be little doubt that his opinion is correct, and especially that the generally accepted date for the commencement of the Era, Friday, July 16, A.D. 622, is erroneous. This date has been obtained by assuming that the method of reckoning time introduced by the Khalîfa 'Umar, some years after the death of Muḥammad, was actually in use for ten years before his death. This is analagous to the method of reckoning the commencement of the Christian Era. It is said to have commenced upon a Saturday, with the Sunday Letter B. Now January 1, A.D. 1, would undoubtedly have been a Saturday, and the Sunday Letter for the year would have been B if the Julian Leap-years had always been regularly observed. We know, however, that this regularity of observance was broken, and that A.D. 4, by the Edict of Augustus, was made to be a Common year. When, therefore, an event is said to have happened on Saturday, January 1, A.D. 4, it must be understood to mean that the day upon which the event happened would have been Saturday if Leap-years had been counted regularly. So it is with the Hijra: the Era would have commenced with Friday, July 16, A.D. 622, if the reckoning of time had been observed at that date in the same way as that in which it came to be observed some seventeen or eighteen years later.

50. M. Caussin de Perceval's discussion is contained in the "Mémoire sur le Calendrier Arabe avant L'Islamisme," published in the *Journal Asiatique*, series iv. tom. i. pp. 342–349, Paris, 1843; and again in his "Essai sur L'Histoire des Arabes avant L'Islamisme," tom. i. pp. 241–248 and 413–417. Paris, 1848.

He says that the Muḥammadan writers, who ascribe to the pagan Arabians the use of an intercalated month, and a Luni-Solar Calendar, during the two Centuries which preceded the introduction of Islâm, are not in agreement as to the way in which the Embolism was practised. Mas'ûdî and Abul'fêda say that a month was added every third year; according to Haji Khalîfa, seven months were added in the course of nineteen years [this was the method adopted by the Jews in the middle of the fourth century]; while al-Bîrûnî, Maḳrîzî, and Muḥammad al-Jarkasî say that nine months were intercalated in every period of twenty-four years.

He examines the three methods, and shows how extremely improbable it is that the pagan Arabians, who were very ignorant, could have invented a Cycle of twenty-four years; and, moreover, that such a period would have made the commencement of every fresh Cycle to have become later and later by 4d. 18h. 18m., because

24 Lunar years + 9 Lunar months = 297 Lunations = 8770d. 13h. 48m.,
while 24 Solar years = 8765d. 19h. 30m.

As an actual matter of fact, the years of the pagan Arabians, instead of being too long, were too short; this does away with the idea of a twenty-four years' Cycle. Makrîzî and Muhammad al-Jarkasî rely upon a statement made by al-Bîrûnî; it will be found at page 14 of Dr. Sachau's translation of the "Athâr-ul-Bâkiya": "He (*i.e.*, Hudfaifa, the first of those who held the office of Intercalator) had taken this system of intercalation from the Jews nearly two hundred years before Islâm; the Jews, however, intercalated 9 months in twenty-four years. In consequence their months were fixed, and came always in at their proper times, wandering in a uniform course through the year without retrograding and without advancing. This state of things remained till the Prophet made his Farewell pilgrimage."* Nevertheless, the same author, in a subsequent passage, page 73, says that when the Arabs found the months coming too early, in spite of the intercalation, then they added a second intercalation.

It is very clear that al-Bîrûnî made some mistake. The Jews of Yathrib did not employ a twenty-four years' Cycle at the time when they instructed the Arabs in the system of intercalation, and if such a Cycle had been employed by the Arabs they could never have found the months arriving too early with respect to the seasons.

51. As regards the Cycle of nineteen years, M. de Perceval says there is no doubt that the Arabs adopted a system of intercalation from the Jews, and it is quite true that the Jews did employ this Cycle; but it was not used by them till towards the end of the fourth Century, and would be still novel at the commencement of the fifth, when the system of Embolism was introduced among the Arabs. He thinks it unlikely that they had become sufficiently familiar with it to communicate it to the Arabs. ("Mémoire," p. 366.) They were, he says, much less enlightened than the Jews of Palestine, and were accustomed, like other foreign Jewish communities, to receive from the Rabbis of Jerusalem a notification of the years when an Embolismic month was to be introduced.

This is true, so far as it goes. The Jews did receive such instruction up to the time of Hillel II., but when he published his Calendar and made known the method of computing the years, the foreign communities became independent of Jerusalem; they were able to make the calculations for themselves.† M. de Perceval's argument, founded upon this point, does not appear to have any very great weight, though it is worth consideration. He himself only puts it in the form of a question, and, not affirming that it was impossible for the Jews of Yathrib to have become acquainted with the Cycle, only asserts that it is doubtful whether they were able to communicate it to the Arabs.

Far greater emphasis may be given to his deduction that if the nineteen years' Cycle, which is very nearly exact, had been employed

* M. de Perceval always refers to the original Arabic MS. of al-Bîrûnî in the Library of the Arsenal.

† See "The Jewish Calendar," Chap I. Art. 13; and Graetz' "History of the Jews," vol. ii. p. 579, English ed. by Bella Löwy.

the time for the celebration of the annual pilgrimage to Mecca would have remained fixed to the autumnal months, and not have been disturbed in the way that it certainly was disturbed.

The conclusion at which he arrives is that, although the Arabs learned from the Jews to intercalate a thirteenth month, yet they did not copy the Jewish method exactly, but were content to add one month at the end of every third year, thus making every third year to consist of thirteen Lunations instead of twelve.

This intercalated month, as well as the act of intercalation itself, they called Nasî, "retardation," because the Embolism effected at the end of a year retarded the commencement of the next year.

52. M. de Perceval then shows that this addition would not bring back the commencement of the fourth year to precisely the same point in the Tropical year, for, he says,

3 Solar years = 1095d. 17h. 28m. 15s.,*

while two Arabian years of twelve Lunations and one of thirteen would amount together to 1092d. 15h. 8m., the difference being 3d. 2h. 20m. 15s. (There is a misprint in the French text with respect to the minutes in the difference, vingt-huit for vingt ("Mémoire," p. 368); it is repeated in the "Essai," tom i. p. 242). The result would be that after every series of three years the commencement of a first year of a new triennial series would be earlier than the Tropical Solar year by 3d. 2h. and a fraction.

The Arabs, and their Nasa'a, or Ḳalâmis, were too ignorant of astronomy to detect this error until it had attained to an amount that would force itself into consideration. Meantime they believed that they had accomplished their object, which was to keep the annual pilgrimage to the Autumn. Thinking that the months were now permanently fixed in coincidence with the seasons, they gave to them names, of which five at least had reference to the time of the year to which they then corresponded; of the remaining seven names four indicate the sacred character of the months to which they belong. These names were—

* 1095d. 17h. 26m. 43s. would be more correct for the length of three Tropical years between A.D. 400 and A.D. 600.

Rabî'u-l-avval }
Rabî'u-l-âkher } Spring showers; verdure.
Jamâdâ-l-avval }
Jamâdâ-l-âkhir } Drought.
Ramaḍân, Great heat.

For the sacred months the names were—

Muḥarram, which signifies "Inviolable."
Rajab, Reverence.
Dû-l-qa'dah, Month of Repose, or Peace.
Dû-l-ḥijjah, Month of the Pilgrimage.

The great Feast of Sacrifices which terminated the ceremonies of the Pilgrimage was fixed, from very ancient times, at the tenth day of this month.

Throughout the period during which the Embolism was made, A.D. 412–632, just as in the ancient purely Lunar Calendar, there were three consecutive months which were sacred, the eleventh and twelfth of one year with the first of the succeeding year, and one, Rajab, which was always isolated in the middle of the year. This month was regarded as the most inviolable of the four, and was consecrated to fasting and penitence.

53. Although the error, which amounted to 3d. 2h. 20m. 15s. at the end of every triennial period, caused the coincidence between the months and the seasons to grow less and less every year till at last such coincidence ceased to exist, yet the names of the months derived from the seasons were retained when the system of Intercalation was abolished by Muḥammad, and have, in fact, been retained to the present time. There is a similar example in the old Roman Calendar; September, October, November, and December were originally, as their names imply, the seventh, eighth, ninth, and tenth months of the year. These four months retained their names when the Decemviri, about the year B.C. 450, attempted to reform the Calendar, and made January and February to be the two first instead of the two last months in the year.

For some length of time the Pilgrimage would continue to be maintained at a convenient season of the year—the Autumn—after the harvests had been gathered. According to the computation of M. de Perceval it occurred, during the first twenty-two years of the Institution of the Nasî, once in November and twenty-one times in October. During the next twenty-nine years it fell in September, so that for more than half a century the object of the Intercalation was attained. The date, gradually becoming earlier in the year, then retrogressed to August, July, and June.

In the one hundred and twenty-ninth year of the Institution of the Nasî, A.D. 541, it occurred at the time of the Summer Solstice, June 22. This is proved by a passage in Procopius, "De Bello Persico," lib. ii. cap. xvi. In that year Belisarius was sent to defend the eastern portion of the Roman Empire against the attacks of Chosroes (or Nushirvan), King of Persia. He was encamped with his army beyond the Euphrates, within six miles of the City of Nisibis. Here he assembled his generals to deliberate on a plan of campaign. Two officers in command of a division, formed from the permanent garrisons in Syria and Phœnicia, declared that it would not be safe for the forces under their command to join the proposed expedition against Nisibis, because, if they did so, Syria and Phœnicia would be exposed to the attacks of the Arabs under their ruler (al-Mundhir III.). Belisarius pointed out that their fears were without foundation on account of the approach of the Summer Solstice, when the Arabs had consecrated two entire months to the practice of their religion, during which they made no use of arms.*

Evidently this must have been near to the time of the annual Pilgrimage, for that is the only time of the year when the Arabs observed two consecutive months as sacred.

Moreover, if Belisarius were right in saying that there were then two—not three—consecutive sacred months, the time is limited to the eleventh and twelfth months of the year, for it was only Muḥarram which ever had its inviolability postponed.

M. Caussin de Perceval concludes from these facts that in the year A.D. 541, the one hundred and twenty-ninth of the Institution of the Nasî, the Pilgrimage occurred on June 22. By the day of the Pilgrimage is meant the last or great day, the Feast of Sacrifices.

At length, in the year 220 of the Nasî, A.D. 631, the last year in which intercalation of a month was employed, the Pilgrimage took place in the beginning of March. The original object for which the

* *Cf.* also Gibbon's "History," cap. xlii.

system had been adopted was entirely frustrated, and we may well be astonished that the Arabs had so long persisted in a method of intercalation which had proved to be so erroneous.

54. The year in which Muḥammad abolished the Nasî, the tenth of the Hijra, which commenced on April 9, A.D. 631, and ended on March 28, A.D. 632, affords a fixed point of departure from which the preceding Arabian years may be calculated on the assumption that the intercalation took place at the end of every third year. The date of the Pilgrimage in that year is known to have been March 9. It may safely be assumed that it would have been an Embolismic year if the system had not been abolished. Indeed this must have been the case unless either of the two preceding years, the eighth and ninth of the Hijra, had had thirteen months, of which there is no probability. Muḥammad became master of Mecca in the year 8 of the Hijra, and then suppressed most of the pagan institutions; no doubt he would have suppressed the Nasî also if it had been employed during either of the two years in question.

If, then, the year 10 of the Hijra, ending in March, A.D. 632, were an Embolismic year, there must have elapsed from the time of the Institution of the Nasî up to the commencement of that year in April, A.D. 631, 219 years, or 73 triennial periods. If the error in the Arabian computation had amounted to exactly three days in every three years, then the year of the Institution would have commenced exactly 219 days earlier than April 9, on which day the year 10 of the Hijra commenced. That is, the year 1 of the Nasî would have commenced on November 14. But the error really was 3d. 2h. 20m. 15s., and the fraction of a day when multiplied by 73 gives the product 7d. 2h. 38m. 15s. Consequently the first year of the Nasî commenced seven days later than November 14, that is, on November 21, A.D. 412.

Again, if the year 220 of the Nasî were Embolismic, or rather, if it would have been Embolismic had the system not been abolished, then the first year must have been Embolismic, and, having thirteen months, would have terminated on December 8, A.D. 413. The tenth day of its twelfth month would have been October 21, A.D. 413.

The second year of the Nasî, commencing on December 9, 413, would terminate on November 27, 414. The third year, commencing November 28, would terminate on November 17, 415; each of these years had twelve Lunar months.

The fourth year of the Institution, being the second in which the Nasî was employed, commenced on November 18, 415, and terminated on December 5, 416. The tenth day of its twelfth month would be October 19.

In this way the years may successively be traced. M. Caussin de Perceval gives the following Table, showing the dates according to his view.

It will be noticed that only those years which were Embolismic are stated, with a few exceptions, including the last ten, for all of which, being years within the Era of the Hijra, the commencements and dates of the Pilgrimage are given. In order to avoid any confusion, I have marked these years as Com., for Common years; M. de Perceval prints them in italic characters.

Years of the Institution of the Nasi.	Commencement of the Year. A.D.	Tenth Day of Pilgrimage. A.D.
1 } Nasi }	November 21, 412 „ 10, 413	October 21, 413
Com. 2	December 9, 413	November 9, 414
Com. 3	November 28, 414	October 29, 415
4	„ 18, 415	„ 19, 416
7	„ 15, 418	„ 16, 419
10	„ 12, 421	„ 13, 422
13	„ 9, 424	„ 10, 425
16	„ 6, 427	„ 7, 428
19	„ 3, 430	„ 4, 431
22	October 31, 433	„ 1, 434
25	„ 28, 436	September 28, 437
28	„ 25, 439	„ 25, 440
31	„ 22, 442	„ 22, 443
34	„ 18, 445	„ 18, 446
37	„ 15, 448	„ 15, 449
40	„ 12, 451	„ 12, 452
43	„ 9, 454	„ 9, 455
46	„ 6, 457	„ 6, 458
49 } Nasi }	„ 3, 460 September 22, 461	„ 3, 461
Com. 50	October 21, 461	September 21, 462
Com. 51	„ 11, 462	„ 11, 463
52	September 30, 463	August 31, 464
55	„ 27	„ 28, 467
58	„ 24	„ 25, 470
61	„ 21	„ 22, 473
64	„ 17	„ 18, 476
67	„ 14	„ 15, 479
70	„ 11	„ 12, 482
73	„ 8	„ 9, 485
76	„ 5	„ 6, 488
79	„ 2	„ 3, 491
82	August 30	July 31, 494
85	„ 27	„ 28, 497
88	„ 24	„ 25, 500

Years of the Institution of the Nasi.	Commencement of the Year. A.D.	Tenth Day of Pilgrimage. A.D.
91	August 21, 502	July 22, 503
94	„ 17, 505	„ 16, 506
97	„ 14, 508	„ 15, 509
100	„ 11, 511	„ 12, 512
103	„ 8, 514	„ 9, 515
106	„ 5, 517	„ 6, 518
109	„ 2, 520	„ 3, 521
112	July 30, 523	June 30, 524
115	„ 27, 526	„ 27, 527
118	„ 24, 529	„ 24, 530
121	„ 21, 532	„ 21, 533
124	„ 17, 535	„ 17, 536
127 }	„ 14, 538	„ 14, 539
Nasi }	„ 3, 539	
Com. 128	August 1, 539	July 2, 540
Com. 129	July 21, 540	June 22, 541
130	„ 11, 541	„ 11, 542
133	„ 8, 544	„ 8, 545
136	„ 5, 547	„ 5, 548
139	„ 2, 550	„ 2, 551
142	June 29, 553	May 30, 554
145	„ 26, 556	„ 27, 557
148	„ 23, 559	„ 24, 560
151	„ 20, 562	„ 21, 563
154	„ 16, 565	„ 17, 566
157	„ 13, 568	„ 14, 569
160	„ 10, 571	„ 11, 572
163	„ 7, 574	„ 8, 575
166	„ 4, 577	„ 5, 578
169	„ 1, 580	„ 2, 581
172	May 29, 583	April 29, 584
175	„ 26, 586	„ 26, 587
178	„ 23, 589	„ 23, 590
181	„ 20, 592	„ 20, 593
184	„ 16, 595	„ 16, 596
187	„ 13, 598	„ 13, 599
190	„ 10, 601	„ 10, 602
193	„ 7, 604	„ 7, 605
196	„ 4, 607	„ 4, 608
199	„ 1, 610	„ 1, 611
202	April 28, 613	March 28, 614
205	„ 25, 616	„ 25, 617
208	„ 22, 619	„ 22, 620

Hijra.	Years of the Institution of the Nasi.	Commencement of the Year. A.D.	Tenth Day of Pilgrimage. A.D.
I.	211	April 19, 622	March 19, 623
	Nasi	" 8, 623	
II.	Com. 212	May 7, 623	April 7, 624
III.	Com. 213	April 26, 624	March 26, 625
IV.	214	" 15, 625	" 15, 626
	Nasi	" 4, 626	
V.	Com. 215	May 3, 626	April 3, 627
VI.	Com. 216	April 23, 627	March 23, 628
VII.	217	" 12, 628	" 12, 629
	Nasi	" 2, 629	
VIII.	Com. 218	May 1, 629	April 1, 630
IX.	Com. 219	April 20, 630	March 20, 631
X.	220	" 9, 631	" 9, 632

55. It will be seen, from this Table, that M. de Perceval makes the commencement of each suggested Embolismic year to be three days earlier than that of the preceding Embolismic year, except for the years:

34	A.D.	445	94	A.D.	505	154	A.D.	565
64	"	475	124	"	535	184	"	595
						214	"	625

The commencement of each of these years is earlier by four days than the commencement of the next preceding Embolismic year; for, the error in three years being 3d. 2h. 20m. 15s., the accumulation of the hours, minutes, and seconds in ten times three, or thirty years, amounts to 23h. 22m. 30s., or very nearly one whole day.

The Table also shows that, if the computation be correct, the usually accepted date for the Era of the Hijra is incorrect. Instead of commencing on Friday, July 16, A.D. 622, it commenced on Monday, April 19, in that year. The coincidence between M. de Perceval's dates and the usually accepted commencements for the years of the Hijra does not occur till the year 8, which commenced on Monday, May 1, A.D. 629.

He holds that the truth of this Table is confirmed by certain known facts: First, when the Nasi was instituted the Pilgrimage was in the

Autumn; the object of the Intercalation was to keep it always at that convenient season. Secondly, there is the passage in Procopius proving that in the 129th year of the Institution, A.D. 541, the Pilgrimage, that is, the tenth day of the twelfth month of the year, occurred on or about the day of the Summer Solstice, June 22. Thirdly, that in the tenth year of the Hijra, the year when the Nasî was abolished, the Pilgrimage occurred on March 9, A.D. 632.

Again: In the first year of the Hijra, which he places as coincident with April 19, 622, to March 19, 623, there is a record that the heat was very great during the month Rabî'u-l-avval, when Muḥammad fled from Mecca and arrived at Medina.* According to the Table, the middle of this month, the third month of the year which commenced on April 19, would coincide with the first days of July.

Also: in the fifth year of the Hijra, May 3, 626, to April 22, 627, the tribesmen who were besieging Medina in the month Shawwâl, the tenth of the year, suffered much from the cold and inclemency of the weather.† This month, according to the Table, would extend from January 23 to February 22.

56. Besides the important testimony which M. Caussin de Perceval brings forward in order to establish his view concerning the true commencement of the Era, he insists strongly upon another point. Reference was made to this in Chapter I., Article 4. He maintains that the privilege of transposing the sacred character of Muḥarram to Safar, when the warlike tendencies of the Arab tribes made the change expedient, was entrusted to the Nasa'a or Ḳalâmis; and, that the declaration that this exchange between the two months might be effected, was proclaimed at the same time as the Nasî, or intercalation of a month, namely, at the close of the Pilgrimage when the pilgrims were about to quit Mecca.

Thus the office of the Nasa'a had a double character, partly civil or political, partly religious. They were invested with two functions which were very closely connected, and which, under a certain point of view, might be resolved into one. For, suppose that they intercalated a month at the end of three Lunar years, that is, immediately before the commencement of the sacred month Muḥarram in the

* "La chaleur était alors très-incommode." "Sirat al Rasul," fol. 84.

† ". . . eut beaucoup à souffir du froid el des intempéries de la saison." *Ibid.*, fol. 179. The "Sirat al-Rasul," or "Life of the Prophet," was written by 'Abd-al-Malek Ibn Hishâm.

fourth year; there would be a postponement of Muḥarram; only two sacred months would come together consecutively. Suppose again that on some occasion during the course of the three Lunar years, of which the last was Embolismic, they had transferred the sacred character of Muḥarram to Safar; this would equally make a postponement; the arrival of the sacred month would be retarded by twenty-nine or thirty days.

Hence this transfer was called by the same name as the Intercalation—Nasî.

57. M. de Perceval concludes his "Mémoire" in the *Journal Asiatique* with the following summary:—

The names of the Arabian months as still in use were adopted, more than two Centuries before the Era of the Hijra, at the same time that a system of triennial intercalation was introduced.

The object of this system was to keep the month of the Pilgrimage in the Autumn, but this object was frustrated by the erroneous method of intercalation.

The pagan Arabians, before the time when they adopted intercalation, had four sacred months, three of which were consecutive; to avoid this inconvenience the sacred character of Muḥarram was sometimes transferred to Safar.

The term Nasî, of which the proper meaning is "retardation," was applied equally to the intercalation, to the intercalary month, and to the postponement of Muḥarram in whichever way that postponement might have been effected.

Muḥammad abolished both practices in the tenth year of the Hijra, A.D. 632.

For a long time the date of the Pilgrimage had ceased to coincide with the Autumnal months, which were originally considered as the most favourable for its accomplishment. The intercalation had therefore become, so far, a useless practice, and Muḥammad suppressed it without inconvenience and without opposition.

CHAPTER VII

MAHMUD EFFENDI ON THE ARABIAN CALENDAR BEFORE ISLÂM

58. Although a great majority of chronologers have maintained the opinion that the pagan Arabians employed a Luni-Solar Calendar for two hundred years before Islâm, yet, as it is only right to state, cogent reasons have been given for the opposite view, namely, that the year was purely Lunar.

In A.D. 1858 Mahmud Effendi, afterwards Mahmud Pasha, an Egyptian astronomer, published both in the *Journal Asiatique*, and in the form of a pamphlet,* a "Mémoire sur Le Calendrier Arabe avant L'Islamisme, et sur La Naissance et L'Age du Prophète Mohammad." In the introduction he refers to the difference of opinion which has always existed as to the character of the pagan Arabian Calendar. He says that no Arabian writers commenced their labours till two or three Centuries after the Era of the Hijra commenced, so that it is easy to understand the difficulty of establishing with certainty the ancient chronology of the country. Among European scholars, Pococke, Gagnier, Golius, Prideaux, Caussin de Perceval, and others, are of opinion that a Luni-Solar year was employed. Silvestre de Sacy takes the view, which Ideler also seems to adopt, that a purely Lunar year was in use.

Mahmud says that he makes no attempt at criticising either one or the other opinion; nevertheless, his object is to show that the former view is positively incorrect, and that a purely Lunar year was always employed.

He does not admit that the Nasî, or "retardation," had anything

* Paris, "Imprimerie Impériale," 1858.

to do with the intercalation of a month, but maintains that the word should only be understood with reference to the occasional postponement of the sacred character of the month Muḥarram to the month Ṣafar.

He endeavours to fix the Julian dates of the death of Ibrahîm, the infant son of the Prophet; the day of Muḥammad's entry into Medina after the flight from Mecca; the date of his birth; and the Arabian dates corresponding to those of the Lunar Eclipse which occurred on November 20, A.D. 625, and of the Summer Solstice, June 20, A.D. 541. He thus brings up to five the number of epochs upon which he grounds his researches.

59. First, with respect to the death of Ibrahîm. He quotes from Bokhârî * that an Eclipse of the Sun occurred on the day when this infant son of the Prophet, by his slave and concubine Mary the Copt, died † at Medina in the tenth year of the Hijra, which commenced April 10, A.D. 631, and ended March 28, 632. Some biographers place this event in the month Rabî'u-l-avval; others in Ramaḍân. Again, in the chapter on the Children of the Prophet in the "al-Sirat al-ḥalabîyah," ‡ it is stated that in the year 8 of the Hijra in the month Ḍû-l-hijjah, Mary the Copt became the mother of Ibrahîm, the son of the Prophet, and that he died in the year 10. Writers are not in agreement as to his exact age when he died. Some say that he lived for one year, ten months, and six days; § others, that when he died he was only eighteen months old. All, however, agree in stating that there was an Eclipse of the Sun on the day of his death; and all are in accord as to his birth having taken place in the month Dû-l-hijjah.‖

Now, it is certain that an Eclipse of the Sun, visible at Medina, occurred on January 27, A.D. 632.¶ Mahmud, therefore, rejects the tradition that Ibrahîm lived for eighteen months only, since, by counting from the 25th day of Ḍû-l-hijjah in the year 8, to the 29th

* P. 58, No. 301, "Supplément des Manuscrits de la Bibliothèque Impériale de Paris." Also No. 213, "Supplément des Manuscrits Arabes."

† For an account of his birth and death, see Muir's "Mahomet and Islâm," chap. xxxi.

‡ No. 596, "Supplément des Manuscrits Arabes."

§ Mas'ûdî, in "Manuscrits Arabes," No. 714, fol. 286, says that he lived for 1y. 10m. 8d.

‖ Thus, M. Caussin de Perceval, "Essai sur l'Histoire des Arabes," vol. iii. p. 267, writes: "Mohammad rentra à Médine à la fin du mois de dhoul-càda, peu de jours après, c'est-à-dire dans les commencements du mois de dhoul-hedja (fin de Mars 630), Marie la Copte, son esclave et sa concubine, accoucha d'un fils."

¶ "L'Art de Verifier les Dates," pt. ii. tom. i. p. 310.

day of Shawwâl in the year 10, there is an interval of one year, ten months, and six days.*

If this were the correct age of Ibrahîm when he died, the correspondence between January 27, A.D. 632, and Shawwâl 29, H. 10, is Astronomically established.

It need hardly be pointed out that the argument is hypothetical. But it is not a hypothetical impossibility. It simply depends upon which of the traditions as to the age of the child be correct.

60. Next, with respect to the date of the Prophet's arrival at Medina after his flight from Mecca.

Mahmud quotes from the author of "al-Sirat al-halabîyah"† the tradition that al-Ḥâfiz-Ibn-Nâsir-al-Dîn recounts that Ibn 'Abbâs, the cousin and companion of the Prophet, says that he arrived at Medina ‡ on the day of the Âshûrâ, at the time of the Jewish Fast. The Prophet inquired why the Jews fasted on that day, and was told that it was the day on which Pharaoh was overwhelmed by the waters and Moses saved by God. The Prophet replied, "I, even more than the Jews, ought to respect the memory of Moses"; and he ordered that a Fast should be observed upon that day.

Before any conclusion can be derived from this tradition it is necessary to understand what is here meant by the word Âshûrâ. With the Muhammadans it was the tenth day of the first month, Muharram, and it appears that the Jews in Arabia also called the tenth day of their first month, Tishrî, by the same name. If we are

* There is no dispute as to the commencement of the year 10 of the Hijra on Tuesday, April 9, A.D. 631, according to Civil reckoning, or Monday, April 8, by Astronomical time. This gives the following dates for the commmencements of the months in that year:—

Muḥarram 1	=	April 8, Astron. reckoning.
Safar 1	=	May 8
Rabi'u-l-avâal 1	=	June 6
Rabi'u-l-âkhir 1	=	July 5
Jamâdâ-l-avval 1	=	August 4
Jamâdâ-l-âkhir 1	=	September 3
Rajab 1	=	October 2
Sha'bân 1	=	November 1
Shawwâl 1	=	December 30

Therefore Shawwâl 29 corresponds to January 27, A.D. 632.

† "Supplément des Manuscrits," &c., No. 596, fol. 210, vol. ii.

‡ By Medina is to be understood either the city itself, or the village of Coba in the immediate neighbourhood.

to understand that Âshûrâ, as said to have been used by Ibn 'Abbâs, means this day, then the tradition would contradict the generally received opinion that the Flight took place in the month Rabî'u-l-avval, an opinion which is founded upon equally authentic traditions.

The author of the "al-Sirat al-halabîyah" recognises this difficulty. He says, as quoted by Mahmud: "The observance by the Jews of a fast upon that day raises a difficulty; for, if Âshûrâ was, in conformity with Ibn-'Abbâs, the tenth or the ninth day of Muḥarram, how could it fall in the month Rabî'u-l-avval, in which assuredly Muḥammad made his entrance into Medina? The difficulty is removed by the consideration that the year being Solar and not Lunar with the Jews, the Âshûrâ which was on the tenth day of Muḥarram, and which, in the old times, corresponded to the day when Pharaoh was overwhelmed, would not always answer to that tenth day; it is simply found to be the same day as that upon which Moḥammad made his entry into Medina. In fact, if that day had been the day of Âshûrâ, the tenth of Muḥarram, the prophet would not have had to ask what day it was." The same author adds: "In support of this interpretation we are able to cite a passage from the work entitled 'al-mujam al-kabîr' by al-Ṭabarânî,—Khârijah, the son of Zaid, tells that his father, the companion of the prophet, said, 'The day of Âshûrâ is not that which the people wish to indicate; it was the day on which they used to cover up the Ka'ba, and on which the Ethiopians * came; this day is shifted from month to month throughout the year; the determination of the day was entrusted to a certain Jew, and after his death to Zaid the son of Thâbit.'"

Mahmud says that this tradition proves the day of Âshûrâ, which is in question, to have been a day fixed according to the Luni-Solar year: but, in which month, and on what day of the month?

Al-Bîrûnî writes: † "Some people say that Âshûrâ is an Arabized Hebrew word, viz., Âshûr, *i.e.*, the 10th of the Jewish month Tishrî, in which falls the fasting Kippûr; that the date of this fasting was compared with the months of the Arabs, and that it was fixed on the tenth day of their first month, as it—with the Jews—falls on the 10th of their first month."

Mahmud quotes this passage, and concludes that Muḥammad

* That is the Abyssinian Christian army.

† Sachau, trans., p. 327. Mahmud quotes from the original MS.

entered Medina on the tenth day of the Jewish month Tishrî, the day of the Jewish Fast Kippûr, which is prescribed in their Law, and which is strictly observed to the present time.

Hence, he finds that it is only necessary to compute the tenth day of Tishrî in A.D. 622, which he makes to correspond with Monday, September 20,* the eighth day of the Lunar month counting from the first appearance of the Moon. The true Conjunction took place on Sunday, September 11, at about one hour and a half after Midnight (Medina local time), and the crescent would not be visible before the night of Sunday, September 12–13. From this it follows that Monday, September 13, would be the first day of the Arabian Lunar month.

Now, traditions inform us that it was either upon the 2nd, the 8th, or the 12th of the month Rabî'u-l-avval that the Prophet entered Medina, and that the day was a Monday. Of these days only the 8th was a Monday, and Mahmud is convinced that the entry into Medina occurred, accordingly, on Monday, the eighth day of Rabî'u-l-avval, corresponding to September 20, A.D. 622, and to Tishrî 10 in the year of the world (*i.e.*, the Jewish year), 4383.

It may be remembered that M. Caussin de Perceval makes the day June 28, so that there is a difference of twelve weeks between the two computations.

Al-Bîrûnî asserts † that the tradition is altogether unfounded. The assertion that Pharaoh was overwhelmed in the sea on the day of Âshûrâ is refuted by the Thora itself. "The event occurred on the seventh of the days of unleavened bread, Nîsân 21. The beginning of the Jewish Passover after the arrival of the prophet in Medina was a Tuesday, the 22nd Adhâr ‡ Era of the Seleucidæ 933, coinciding with Ramaḍân 17, and the day on which Pharaoh was drowned was Ramaḍân 23."

Mahmud, however, refuses to accept the computation of al-Bîrûnî, although he speaks in high terms of the value and importance of his work. §

* See, by the same author, "Mémoire sur le Calendrier judaïque," in tom. xxvi. des Mémoires des Savants étrangers de l'Académie Royale de Belgique.

† Pp. 327, 328.

‡ Not the Jewish month of that name, but the Syrian month, the sixth in the Syrian year.

§ "Cet ouvrage, precieux par son ancienneté et par les riches matériaux qu'il renferme, m'a été très utile, et je ne puis que remercier ici M. Reinaud de m'avoir engagé à le consulter et de m'en avoir fait sentir l'importance." Footnote, p. 12 of the "Mémoire."

61. The third date which Mahmud Effendi desires to establish is that of the birth of the Prophet. There is a want of direct evidence upon this point, but Mahmud gives a number of quotations from Arabian writers which bear upon the subject. In the first volume of "al-Sîrat-al-ḥalabîyah,* we read as follows: "Kotâdah states that the prophet said, 'Monday is the day on which I was born.' Ibn-Bakkâr and Ibn-'Asâkir say that the birth took place at the break of day. Sa'îd ibn Musaiyib reports that the prophet was born in the middle of the day. This day was the twelfth of Rabî'u-l-avval, and was in the spring-time. The night before the twelfth is adopted generally in the cities, and at Mecca in particular, especially when the people wish to visit the place of his birth. Others say that he was born on the tenth of the month, and Historians assert that it was on the eighth."

According to these three opinions Muḥammad was born on the 8th, 10th, or 12th of Rabî'u-l-avval.

In al-Jafr al-kabîr † we are told, "It is certain that the prophet was born on a Monday in the month Rabî'u-l-avval, the month Nîsân in the year of the Elephants, ‡ in the time of Nushirvan" [Chosroes, King of Persia]. "He received his prophetic mission forty years and one day after his birth, and accomplished his flight to Medina when he was fifty-three years of age."

The Syriac month Nîsân in the year of the Elephants corresponds to April. This confirms the testimony that Muḥammad was born in the Spring.

Mas'ûdî, in the Murûj-al-ḍahab places the birth in the year 882 of the Era of the Seleucidæ, corresponding to A.D. 571.

M. Caussin de Perceval says § that Chosroes had reigned forty complete years when Muḥammad was born. He commenced his reign in A.D. 531, so that the Prophet was born in the course of the year 571. Ideler states ‖ that, according to al-Makîn, Muḥammad was born on Nîsân 22 (Syriac month) in the year of the Seleucidæ 882. This day, according to Mahmud, corresponds to April 22, A.D. 571.

* No. 596, "Supplément des Manuscrits de la Bibliothèque Imp.," fol. 47.

† No. 1174, "Manuscrits Arabes, ancien fonds," fol. 4, by Imâm-Shams-al-Dîn Muḥammad.

‡ A.D. 571, the year in which the Abyssinian Christians came to Mecca with their elephants to besiege the city.

§ "Essai sur l'Histoire des Arabes," vol. i. p. 283.

‖ "Handbuch," vol. ii. p. 498.

M. Silvestre de Sacy, on the authority of Gagnier, gives the date as Nîsân 20, corresponding to April 20, in the same year.

There appears, then, to be a general agreement in the opinion that Muḥammad was born in April, A.D. 571; and the Eastern astronomers fix the birth as having taken place soon after a Conjunction of the planets Jupiter and Saturn, which occurred in the constellation Scorpio.

The calculations of Mahmud show that this Conjunction took place on March 29 or 30, A.D. 571. It was called by the Arabians "The Conjunction of the Muslem religion," or simply "The Conjunction of religion."

Much additional testimony is quoted in the "Mémoire," and Mahmud has no hesitation in concluding that Muḥammad was born on Monday, the ninth day of Rabî'u-l-avval, corresponding to April 20, A.D. 571.

62. In the second part of the "Mémoire" the object of Mahmud is to ascertain, from the correspondence of dates thus found, the system of the Calendar in use in Arabia Petræa, and particularly at Mecca and Medina, before the introduction of Islâm.

He holds that the three following dates are established:—

(1) That of the death of Ibrahîm, when the Sun was eclipsed,
January 27, 632 = Shawwâl 29, year of Hijra 10.

(2) Entry of Muḥammad into Medina after the flight from Mecca,
Monday, September 20, 622 = 8 Rabî'u-l-avval,
= 10 Tishrî, A.M. 4383.

(3) Birth of Muḥammad, Monday, April 20, 571,
= 9 Rabî'u-l-avval.

He finds, by comparison of (3) and (2), that from Monday, April 20, 571, to Monday, September 20, 622, which he says is an interval of 18780 days, the Arabians reckoned one day less than a certain number of complete years, for the period commences on 9 Rabî'u-l-avval, and ends on 8 Rabî'u-l-avval.

There appears to be some error here; the interval according to the given Julian dates is 18781 days, for—

From April 20, inclusive, to end of A.D. 571 =	256	days
A.D. 572 to 621, both inclusive = 50 × 365 + 13 =	18263	,,
January 1, 622, to September 19, inclusive...... =	262	,,
	18781	days

This error of one day will not, however, effect the result obtained by Mahmud. It may have escaped his notice that there are 13 Leap-years in the period A.D. 572–621.

The ordinary Arabian year, as employed before Islâm according to his view, contained twelve Lunations, and, from time to time, a thirteenth was intercalated. Five different systems for their Calendar have been suggested:—

1. That 9 months were intercalated in the course of every 24 years
2. That 7 " " " 19 "
3. That 1 month was " " " 3 "
4. That 1 " " " " 2 "
5. That the system employed was purely Lunar; that is, no intercalation was ever made.

By the First	system, 1 mean	year	= 365·441 days
" Second	"	"	= 365·246 "
" Third	"	"	= 364·211 "
" Fourth	"	"	= 369·132 "
" Fifth	"	"	= 354·367* "

One of these five systems must have been in use at Mecca when the Flight took place. The question to be answered is, Which of the systems was employed? Mahmud maintains that it was the last, because only in the last case will the division of 18780 [18781] days by each of these five numbers give an integral number of years less one day.

The results obtained by the respective divisions are—

1	51·3899 years
2	51·4174 "
3	51·5635 "
4	50·8761 "
5	52·9959 "

The division of 18781 days by 354·367 gives the quotient 52·99869, differing from 53 complete mean years by ·00131. If the interval be taken as consisting of 18780 days, then the quotient differs from 53 years by ·0041. The value of one day expressed in decimals of 354·367 is ·0028.

Mahmud says that the result of the division gives exactly

* More accurately, 354·3670644.

(*rigoureusement*) 53 years all but one day. This is certainly very nearly, though not absolutely, correct.

He arrives at the same conclusion, namely, that a purely Lunar year was employed, by a comparison between (1) and (2) of the dates which he considers to be established. These are—

April 20, A.D. 571 = Rabî'u-l-avval 9,
January 27, 632 = Shawwâl 29.

The number of days in this interval of time is 22197; for—

From April 20, 571, inclusive, to end of the year =	256 days
A.D. 572 to 631, both inclusive = 60 × 365 + 15 =	21915 ,,
January 1, 632, to January 26, inclusive .... =	26 ,,
	22197 days

Also, from Rabî'u-l-avval 9 to Shawwâl 29 is an interval of 226 days, according to Mahmud Effendi, and he says that 22197 days ought to give 226 days more than an integral number of completed years; adding that, in fact, if 22197 be divided by 354·367 (the duration of a mean vague Lunar year), the quotient is 62 years, and the remainder is 226 days. This ought to be 226·246 days.

His conclusion does not appear to be obtained correctly. In computing the Julian period from April 20, 571, to January 27, 632, one of the terminal days is properly taken into the account; in other words, the days are reckoned from the commencement of the one to the commencement of the other, or from the end of the one to the end of the other; but, in computing that the interval from Rabî'u-l-avval 9 to Shawwâl 29 consists of 226 days, neither of the terminal days is taken into consideration. If these days were reckoned in the same way as the Julian days they would be 227 in number, for we have—

From commencement of Rabî'u-l-avval 9 to end of the month =	22 days
3 months of 29 days + 3 months of 30 days = 87 + 90 ....=	177 ,,
Shawwâl 1 to commencement of Shawwâl 29 ....=	28 ,,
	227 days

Now the remainder, 226·246, obtained by dividing 22197 by 354·367 is treated by Mahmud as representing 226 days. To justify his conclusion that a purely Lunar year was employed the remainder ought to be 227 days. It is true that the difference consists only in the decimal of a day, and this decimal may arise from the fact that for the division the mean length of twelve Lunar months is taken, whereas the dividend is taken as representing the exact number of days contained in the period under discussion. Slight errors must of necessity arise when mean time is thus treated in connection with absolute time.

Mahmud takes no notice of this fact, and he takes no notice of the decimal, but is quite content in giving his remainder as 226; and the result convinces him that a purely Lunar year was in use both at Mecca and Medina for sixty-two years before the tenth year of the Hijra.

63. He next proceeds to examine the passage quoted from Procopius by M. Caussin de Perceval. He compares the date of the Solar Eclipse of January 27, A.D. 632, when Ibrahîm died, with that of the Lunar Eclipse, which is known to have occurred on November 20, 625. It will be remembered that he considers the former date to correspond to Shawwâl 29, year of the Hijra 10, so that the New Moon of the next month, Dû-l-qa'dah, must have occurred on January 28. He says, with respect to the Lunar Eclipse of November 20, 625, that the Eclipse occurred in the Arabian month, Jamâdâ-l-âkhir, so that the day of the New Moon for that month must have been November 6.

From these two New Moons of January 28, A.D. 632, and November 6, A.D. 625, he reckons backwards to the Summer Solstice of A.D. 541, and maintains that it could not have occurred when two sacred months came together, but must have been in the isolated sacred month, Rajab. He suggests that there is a mistake, which he ascribes to an error made by the transcribers of Procopius, who have substituted "two entire months," *δύο μάλιστα μῆνας*, for "one entire month," *ἕνα μάλιστα μῆνα*. In that case the New Moon of Rajab would be either soon before or soon after the Summer Solstice in A.D. 541, and June 10 would be the day of the New Moon either of the month Rajab or of the preceding month, Jamâdâ-l-âkhir.

From this he concludes that either Procopius was wrong in stating that Belisarius spoke of two months, or else that the transcribers have caused the error; for, he says, if it were the month Rajab to which Belisarius referred, then the interval of time elapsed between the New

Moon of that month and the New Moons of January 28, 632, and November 6, 625, would be compatible with a purely Lunar year. Moreover, if the month Rajab be accepted as coming immediately after the Summer Solstice of A.D. 541, it would be verified by the dates given above for the birth of Muḥammad and for the Flight.

And so we have, says Mahmud, five epochs, each determined independently of the others, which when combined two and two produce ten resultants, or intervals of time, the lapse of which conforms exclusively to a purely Lunar system; and the perfect accord of all these results is assuredly a certain proof of the mistake made by those who maintain the use of a Luni-Solar Calendar by the pagan Arabians.

These views are worthy of consideration, but they are certainly not free from objections.

CHAPTER VIII

THE OTTOMAN FINANCIAL CALENDAR

64. On the twenty-fifth day of the last month of the year of the Hijra 1086, corresponding to March 1, A.D. 1676 (Julian Calendar), a Solar Calendar based upon Julian years was adopted in Turkey for financial purposes.

The years were made to commence always on the day corresponding to the Julian March 1. The twelve months were of the same length as the Julian months to which they respectively corresponded, so that in intercalary years it was the last day of the Financial year which corresponded to February 29.

The months, therefore, were as follows:—

First	had 31	days,	corresponding to	March.
Second	„ 30	„	„	April.
Third	„ 31	„	„	May.
Fourth	„ 30	„	„	June.
Fifth	„ 31	„	„	July.
Sixth	„ 31	„	„	August.
Seventh	„ 30	„	„	September.
Eighth	„ 31	„	„	October.
Ninth	„ 30	„	„	November.
Tenth	„ 31	„	„	December.
Eleventh	„ 31	„	„	January.
Twelfth	„ 28	„	„	February.

In intercalary years the twelfth month had 29 days.

Some inconvenience arose from the use of this Calendar, for it attempted to preserve the Hijra method of enumerating the current years. This could not be done without having recourse to a proceeding which must, in all probability, have sometimes led to mistakes. The Muḥammadan Lunar years are, on an average, eleven days shorter than the Julian years, and, therefore, in order to preserve for the Financial Calendar the Hijra enumeration, the annual name of one Financial year was entirely suppressed, or omitted, from time to time.

This had to be done once in about every thirty-three years, but the framers of this Calendar did not wait, before making the suppression, till thirty-three years had elapsed. The first year of the Calendar, called 1086, commenced with the 350th day of Hij. 1086, and as it had 365 days it ended with the fifth day of Hij. 1088. It therefore included the whole of the year Hij. 1087 within its compass, and when the second Financial year commenced Hijra 1088 had also commenced, and was already five days old.

If, then, the annual name of any year was to be omitted it was very suitable that the first year to be so treated should be 1087, and accordingly there was no such year in the Financial Calendar. The first year was called 1086; the second was called 1088.

The next year of which the annual name was dropped was that which would have been numbered as 1121; this was after an interval of thirty-three years. The year 1120 was followed by 1122.

Thirty-two years were then allowed to pass, and 1153 was followed by 1155.

The remaining years of which the annual numerical names were suppressed were 1188, 1221, and 1255.

With respect to intercalary years:—The first was 1090. It commenced with March 1, A.D. 1679. The next year, 1091, commenced with March 1, A.D. 1680; consequently, 1090 included the February 29 of A.D. 1680. It therefore consisted of 366 days. After this every fourth year had the intercalated day, namely, 1094, 1098, . . . 1118.

There was no year with the number 1121; so that the next Leap-year to 1118 was not 1122, but 1123; and then 1127, 1131, . . . 1151.

There was no year with the number 1154; so that the next Leap-year to 1151 was 1156.

In the same way, the next to 1184 was 1189. The next to 1217 was 1222; and the next to 1254 was 1259.

But before the year 1259 was reached a modification of these arrangements was effected, and a New Financial Calendar which is still in use was adopted in Turkey.

The New Calendar starts from the year 1256, which commenced with the Julian March 1, Gregorian March 13, A.D. 1840. No alteration was made in the form of the years, which retain their Julian character of 365 and 366 days. They still commence on the Julian March 1 (corresponding now to the Gregorian March 14). The months retain the same number of days as in the former Calendar. The numbers representing certain years are no longer suppressed; the years run on consecutively from 1256.

The consequence is that at the present time, A.D. 1900, there is a difference of 2 between the numbers representing the current years of the Hijra and of the Financial Calendar. The former is Hij. 1318, which commenced with the Julian April 18, Gregorian May 1, 1900; the latter is 1316, which commenced with Julian March 1, Gregorian March 14, in the same year, 1900.

GENERAL TABLES.

Table I.

SERIAL ENUMERATION OF DAYS IN THE MUḤAMMADAN YEAR.

Day of the Month.	Muḥarram.	Ṣafar.	Rabí'u I.	Rabí'u II.	Jamádá I.	Jamádá II.	Rajab.	Sha'bán.	Ramaḍán.	Shawwal.	Dú-l-qa'dah.	Dú-l-ḥijjah.
1	1	31	60	90	119	149	178	208	237	267	296	326
2	2	32	61	91	120	150	179	209	238	268	297	327
3	3	33	62	92	121	151	180	210	239	269	298	328
4	4	34	63	93	122	152	181	211	240	270	299	329
5	5	35	64	94	123	153	182	212	241	271	300	330
6	6	36	65	95	124	154	183	213	242	272	301	331
7	7	37	66	96	125	155	184	214	243	273	302	332
8	8	38	67	97	126	156	185	215	244	274	303	333
9	9	39	68	98	127	157	186	216	245	275	304	334
10	10	40	69	99	128	158	187	217	246	276	305	335
11	11	41	70	100	129	159	188	218	247	277	306	336
12	12	42	71	101	130	160	189	219	248	278	307	337
13	13	43	72	102	131	161	190	220	249	279	308	338
14	14	44	73	103	132	162	191	221	250	280	309	339
15	15	45	74	104	133	163	192	222	251	281	310	340
16	16	46	75	105	134	164	193	223	252	282	311	341
17	17	47	76	106	135	165	194	224	253	283	312	342
18	18	48	77	107	136	166	195	225	254	284	313	343
19	19	49	78	108	137	167	196	226	255	285	314	344
20	20	50	79	109	138	168	197	227	256	286	315	345
21	21	51	80	110	139	169	198	228	257	287	316	346
22	22	52	81	111	140	170	199	229	258	288	317	347
23	23	53	82	112	141	171	200	230	259	289	318	348
24	24	54	83	113	142	172	201	231	260	290	319	349
25	25	55	84	114	143	173	202	232	261	291	320	350
26	26	56	85	115	144	174	203	233	262	292	321	351
27	27	57	86	116	145	175	204	234	263	293	322	352
28	28	58	87	117	146	176	205	235	264	294	323	353
29	29	59	88	118	147	177	206	236	265	295	324	354
30	30	—	89	—	148	—	207	—	266	—	325	*

* In Embolismic years the thirtieth day of the twelfth month is the 355th day of the year.

TABLE II.

SIGNS OF THE YEARS FOR THE CYCLE OF 210 YEARS.

R.	0	30	60	90	120	150	180
1	6	4	2	7	5	3	1
2	3	1	6	4	2	7	5
3	1	6	4	2	7	5	3
4	5	3	1	6	4	2	7
5	2	7	5	3	1	6	4
6	7	5	3	1	6	4	2
7	4	2	7	5	3	1	6
8	2	7	5	3	1	6	4
9	6	4	2	7	5	3	1
10	3	1	6	4	2	7	5
11	1	6	4	2	7	5	3
12	5	3	1	6	4	2	7
13	2	7	5	3	1	6	4
14	7	5	3	1	6	4	2
15	4	2	7	5	3	1	6
16	1	6	4	2	7	5	3
17	6	4	2	7	5	3	1
18	3	1	6	4	2	7	5
19	1	6	4	2	7	5	3
20	5	3	1	6	4	2	7
21	2	7	5	3	1	6	4
22	7	5	3	1	6	4	2
23	4	2	7	5	3	1	6
24	1	6	4	2	7	5	3
25	6	4	2	7	5	3	1
26	3	1	6	4	2	7	5
27	1	6	4	2	7	5	3
28	5	3	1	6	4	2	7
29	2	7	5	3	1	6	4
30	7	5	3	1	6	4	2

(Table II.)

EXPLANATION OF TABLE OF SIGNS OF THE YEARS.

CYCLE OF 210 MUḤAMMADAN YEARS.

Sunday	= 1
Monday	= 2
Tuesday	= 3
Wednesday	= 4
Thursday	= 5
Friday	= 6
Saturday	= 7

Divide the given year, H, by 210; consider only the remainder. If the remainder be less than 30, the Sign of the year, indicating the week-day on which it commences, will be found in the first column under the heading 0, and in the same line with the remainder itself, which appears in the vertical argument under the heading R.

If the remainder be greater than 30, one of the columns headed 30, 60, 90, &c., must be used, according to the magnitude of the remainder, and that horizontal line in which the amount above 30, 60, 90, &c. appears in the vertical argument. Where the horizontal and vertical lines intersect will be found the character required.

Ex.—H. 1033.

1033 ÷ 210 gives a remainder 193 = 180 + 13. In the column headed 180, and in line with 13, the character 4 is found. Therefore the year commences with a Wednesday.

Table III

SIGNS OF THE MONTHS.

Muḥarram	1. Sun.	2. Mon.	3. Tues.	4. Wed.	5. Thurs.	6. Fri.	7. Sat.
Ṣafar	3. Tues.	4. Wed.	5. Thurs.	6. Fri.	7. Sat.	1. Sun.	2. Mon.
Rabi'u-l-avval	4. Wed.	5. Thurs.	6. Fri.	7. Sat.	1. Sun.	2. Mon.	3. Tues.
Rabi'u-ṯh-thânî ..	6. Fri.	7. Sat.	1. Sun.	2. Mon.	3. Tues.	4. Wed.	5. Thurs.
Jamâdâ-l-âkhir ..	7. Sat.	1. Sun.	2. Mon.	3. Tues.	4. Wed.	5. Thurs.	6. Fri.
Jamâdâ-ṯh-thânî ..	2. Mon.	3. Tues.	4. Wed.	5. Thurs.	6. Fri.	7. Sat.	1. Sun.
Rajab	3. Tues.	4. Wed.	5. Thurs.	6. Fri.	7. Sat.	1. Sun.	2. Mon.
Sha'bân	5. Thurs.	6. Fri.	7. Sat.	1. Sun.	2. Mon.	3. Tues.	4. Wed.
Ramaḍân	6. Fri.	7. Sat.	1. Sun.	2. Mon.	3. Tues.	4. Wed.	5. Thurs.
Shawwâl	1. Sun.	2. Mon.	3. Tues.	4. Wed.	5. Thurs.	6. Fri.	7. Sat.
Ḍû-l-qa'dah	2. Mon.	3. Tues.	4. Wed.	5. Thurs.	6. Fri.	7. Sat.	1. Sun.
Ḍû-l-hijjah	4. Wed.	5. Thurs.	6. Fri.	7. Sat.	1. Sun.	2. Mon.	3. Tues.
Next Year.							
Muḥ. after common year	5. Thurs.	6. Fri.	7. Sat.	1. Sun.	2. Mon.	3. Tues.	4. Wed.
Muḥ. after Kabîsah year	6. Fri.	7. Sat.	1. Sun.	2. Mon.	3. Tues.	4. Wed.	5. Thurs.

(Table III.)

EXPLANATION OF TABLE OF SIGNS OF THE MONTHS.

The Table is to be read as follows:—If, in any given year of the Hijra, Muḥarram 1 occur on the first day of the week—Sunday, then Safar will begin on the third day—Tuesday; Rabi'u I. will begin on the fourth day—Wednesday; and so on. The first column will be used.

If Muḥarram 1 occur on a fourth day—Wednesday, then Ṣafar will begin on a sixth day—Friday; and so on. The fourth column will be used.

The last two lines of the Table show that if a Common year commence with a first day of the week—Sunday, then the next year will commence with a fifth day—Thursday; if, in a Common year, Muḥarram 1 occur upon a second day—Monday, then the next Muḥarram 1 will be upon a sixth day—Friday, and so on. But if a Kabīsah year commence with a first day—Sunday, then the next year will commence with a sixth day—Friday.

For a Common year of 354 days occupies 50 weeks and 4 days; so that, if it commence on a Sunday, its fifty weeks end with a Saturday, and it occupies also Sunday, Monday, Tuesday, and Wednesday of the next week. But if a Kabīsah year commence on a Sunday it will occupy Thursday also, in its fifty-first week, and the next year will commence with a Friday.

Table IV.

NUMBER OF DAYS ELAPSED AT THE CLOSE OF EACH YEAR IN A MUḤAMMADAN CYCLE.

Year of Cycle.	Days Elapsed.	Year of Cycle.	Days Elapsed.
1	354	16 K	5670
2 K	709	17	6024
3	1063	18 K	6379
4	1417	19	6733
5 K	1772	20	7087
6	2126	21 K	7442
7 K	2481	22	7796
8	2835	23	8150
9	3189	24 K	8505
10 K	3544	25	8859
11	3898	26 K	9214
12	4252	27	9568
13 K	4607	28	9922
14	4961	29 K	10277
15	5315	30	10631

CHRONOLOGICAL TABLE.

A.H.		Date of Muḥarram 1.			A.D.	A.H.		Date of Muḥarram 1.			A.D.
1	1	Friday	July	16	622	46	16 K	Friday	March	13	666
2	2 K	Tuesday	„	5	623	47	17	Wednesday	„	3	667
3	3	Sunday	June	24	624	48	18 K	Sunday	Feb.	20	668
4	4	Thursday	„	13	625	49	19	Friday	„	9	669
5	5 K	Monday	„	2	626	50	20	Tuesday	Jan.	29	670
6	6	Saturday	May	23	627	51	21 K	Saturday	„	18	671
7	7 K	Wednesday	„	11	628	52	22	Thursday	„	8	672
8	8	Monday	„	1	629	53	23	Monday	Dec.	27	„
9	9	Friday	April	20	630	54	24 K	Friday	„	16	673
10	10 K	Tuesday	„	9	631	55	25	Wednesday	„	6	674
11	11	Sunday	March	29	632	56	26 K	Sunday	Nov.	25	675
12	12	Thursday	„	18	633	57	27	Friday	„	14	676
13	13 K	Monday	„	7	634	58	28	Tuesday	„	3	677
14	14	Saturday	Feb.	25	635	59	29 K	Saturday	Oct.	23	678
15	15	Wednesday	„	14	636	60	30	Thursday	„	13	679
16	16 K	Sunday	„	2	637						
17	17	Friday	Jan.	23	638	61	1	Monday	„	1	680
18	18 K	Tuesday	„	12	639	62	2 K	Friday	Sept.	20	681
19	19	Sunday	„	2	640	63	3	Wednesday	„	10	682
20	20	Thursday	Dec.	21	„	64	4	Sunday	Aug.	30	683
21	21 K	Monday	„	10	641	65	5 K	Thursday	„	18	684
22	22	Saturday	Nov.	30	642	66	6	Tuesday	„	8	685
23	23	Wednesday	„	19	643	67	7 K	Saturday	July	28	686
24	24 K	Sunday	„	7	644	68	8	Thursday	„	18	687
25	25	Friday	Oct.	28	645	69	9	Monday	„	6	688
26	26 K	Tuesday	„	17	646	70	10 K	Friday	June	25	689
27	27	Sunday	„	7	647	71	11	Wednesday	„	15	690
28	28	Thursday	Sept.	25	648	72	12	Sunday	„	4	691
29	29 K	Monday	„	14	649	73	13 K	Thursday	May	23	692
30	30	Saturday	„	4	650	74	14	Tuesday	„	13	693
						75	15	Saturday	„	2	694
31	1	Wednesday	Aug.	24	651	76	16 K	Wednesday	April	21	695
32	2 K	Sunday	„	12	652	77	17	Monday	„	10	696
33	3	Friday	„	2	653	78	18 K	Friday	March	30	697
34	4	Tuesday	July	22	654	79	19	Wednesday	„	20	698
35	5 K	Saturday	„	11	655	80	20	Sunday	„	9	699
36	6	Thursday	June	30	656	81	21 K	Thursday	Feb.	26	700
37	7 K	Monday	„	19	657	82	22	Tuesday	„	15	701
38	8	Saturday	„	9	658	83	23	Saturday	„	4	702
39	9	Wednesday	May	29	659	84	24 K	Wednesday	Jan.	24	703
40	10 K	Sunday	„	17	660	85	25	Monday	„	14	704
41	11	Friday	„	7	661	86	26 K	Friday	„	2	705
42	12	Tuesday	April	26	662	87	27	Wednesday	Dec.	23	„
43	13 K	Saturday	„	15	663	88	28	Sunday	„	12	706
44	14	Thursday	„	4	664	89	29 K	Thursday	„	1	707
45	15	Monday	March	24	665	90	30	Tuesday	Nov.	20	708

A.H.		Date of Muharram 1.			A.D.
91	1	Saturday	Nov.	9	709
92	2 K	Wednesday	Oct.	29	710
93	3	Monday	„	19	711
94	4	Friday	„	7	712
95	5 K	Tuesday	Sept.	26	713
96	6	Sunday	„	16	714
97	7 K	Thursday	„	5	715
98	8	Tuesday	Aug.	25	716
99	9	Saturday	„	14	717
100	10 K	Wednesday	„	3	718
101	11	Monday	July	24	719
102	12	Friday	„	12	720
103	13 K	Tuesday	„	1	721
104	14	Sunday	June	21	722
105	15	Thursday	„	10	723
106	16 K	Monday	May	29	724
107	17	Saturday	„	19	725
108	18 K	Wednesday	„	8	726
109	19	Monday	April	28	727
110	20	Friday	„	16	728
111	21 K	Tuesday	„	5	729
112	22	Sunday	March	26	730
113	23	Thursday	„	15	731
114	24 K	Monday	„	3	732
115	25	Saturday	Feb.	21	733
116	26 K	Wednesday	„	10	734
117	27	Monday	Jan.	31	735
118	28	Friday	„	20	736
119	29 K	Tuesday	„	8	737
120	30	Sunday	Dec.	29	„
121	1	Thursday	„	18	738
122	2 K	Monday	„	7	739
123	3	Saturday	Nov.	26	740
124	4	Wednesday	„	15	741
125	5 K	Sunday	„	4	742
126	6	Friday	Oct.	25	743
127	7 K	Tuesday	„	13	744
128	8	Sunday	„	3	745
129	9	Thursday	Sept.	22	746
130	10 K	Monday	„	11	747
131	11	Saturday	Aug.	31	748
132	12	Wednesday	„	20	749
133	13 K	Sunday	„	9	750
134	14	Friday	July	30	751
135	15	Tuesday	„	18	752
136	16 K	Saturday	July	7	753
137	17	Thursday	June	27	754
138	18 K	Monday	„	16	755
139	19	Saturday	„	5	756
140	20	Wednesday	May	25	757
141	21 K	Sunday	„	14	758
142	22	Friday	„	4	759
143	23	Tuesday	April	22	760
144	24 K	Saturday	„	11	761
145	25	Thursday	„	1	762
146	26 K	Monday	March	21	763
147	27	Saturday	„	10	764
148	28	Wednesday	Feb.	27	765
149	29 K	Sunday	„	16	766
150	30	Friday	„	6	767
151	1	Tuesday	Jan.	26	768
152	2 K	Saturday	„	14	769
153	3	Thursday	„	4	770
154	4	Monday	Dec.	24	„
155	5 K	Friday	„	13	771
156	6	Wednesday	„	2	772
157	7 K	Sunday	Nov.	21	773
158	8	Friday	„	11	774
159	9	Tuesday	Oct.	31	775
160	10 K	Saturday	„	19	776
161	11	Thursday	„	9	777
162	12	Monday	Sept.	28	778
163	13 K	Friday	„	17	779
164	14	Wednesday	„	6	780
165	15	Sunday	Aug.	26	781
166	16 K	Thursday	„	15	782
167	17	Tuesday	„	5	783
168	18 K	Saturday	July	24	784
169	19	Thursday	„	14	785
170	20	Monday	„	3	786
171	21 K	Friday	June	22	787
172	22	Wednesday	„	11	788
173	23	Sunday	May	31	789
174	24 K	Thursday	„	20	790
175	25	Tuesday	„	10	791
176	26 K	Saturday	April	28	792
177	27	Thursday	„	18	793
178	28	Monday	„	7	794
179	29 K	Friday	March	27	795
180	30	Wednesday	„	16	796

A.H.		Date of Muḥarram 1.			A.D.
181	1	Sunday	March	5	797
182	2 K	Thursday	Feb.	22	798
183	3	Tuesday	„	12	799
184	4	Saturday	„	1	800
185	5 K	Wednesday	Jan.	20	801
186	6	Monday	„	10	802
187	7 K	Friday	Dec.	30	„
188	8	Wednesday	„	20	803
189	9	Sunday	„	8	804
190	10 K	Thursday	Nov.	27	805
191	11	Tuesday	„	17	806
192	12	Saturday	„	6	807
193	13 K	Wednesday	Oct.	25	808
194	14	Monday	„	15	809
195	15	Friday	„	4	810
196	16 K	Tuesday	Sept.	23	811
197	17	Sunday	„	12	812
198	18 K	Thursday	„	1	813
199	19	Tuesday	Aug.	22	814
200	20	Sunday	„	11	815
201	21 K	Wednesday	July	30	816
202	22	Monday	„	20	817
203	23	Friday	„	9	818
204	24 K	Tuesday	June	28	819
205	25	Sunday	„	17	820
206	26 K	Thursday	„	6	821
207	27	Tuesday	May	27	822
208	28	Saturday	„	16	823
209	29 K	Wednesday	„	4	824
210	30	Monday	April	24	825
211	1	Friday	„	13	826
212	2 K	Tuesday	„	2	827
213	3	Sunday	March	22	828
214	4	Thursday	„	11	829
215	5 K	Monday	Feb.	28	830
216	6	Saturday	„	18	831
217	7 K	Wednesday	„	7	832
218	8	Monday	Jan.	27	833
219	9	Friday	„	16	834
220	10 K	Tuesday	„	5	835
221	11	Sunday	Dec.	26	„
222	12	Thursday	„	14	836
223	13 K	Monday	„	3	837
224	14	Saturday	Nov.	23	838
225	15	Wednesday	„	12	839

A.H.		Date of Muḥarram 1.			A.D.
226	16 K	Sunday	Oct.	31	840
227	17	Friday	„	21	841
228	18 K	Tuesday	„	10	842
229	19	Sunday	Sept.	30	843
230	20	Thursday	„	18	844
231	21 K	Monday	„	7	845
232	22	Saturday	Aug.	28	846
233	23	Wednesday	„	17	847
234	24 K	Sunday	„	5	848
235	25	Friday	July	26	849
236	26 K	Tuesday	„	15	850
237	27	Sunday	„	5	851
238	28	Thursday	June	23	852
239	29 K	Monday	„	10	853
240	30	Saturday	„	2	854
241	1	Wednesday	May	22	855
242	2 K	Sunday	„	10	856
243	3	Friday	April	30	857
244	4	Tuesday	„	19	858
245	5 K	Saturday	„	8	859
246	6	Thursday	March	28	860
247	7 K	Monday	„	17	861
248	8	Saturday	„	7	862
249	9	Wednesday	Feb.	24	863
250	10 K	Sunday	„	13	864
251	11	Friday	„	2	865
252	12	Tuesday	Jan.	22	866
253	13 K	Saturday	„	11	867
254	14	Thursday	„	1	868
255	15	Monday	Dec.	20	„
256	16 K	Friday	„	9	869
257	17	Wednesday	Nov.	29	870
258	18 K	Sunday	„	18	871
259	19	Friday	„	7	872
260	20	Tuesday	Oct.	27	873
261	21 K	Saturday	„	16	874
262	22	Thursday	„	6	875
263	23	Monday	Sept.	24	876
264	24 K	Friday	„	13	877
265	25	Wednesday	„	3	878
266	26 K	Sunday	Aug.	23	879
267	27	Friday	„	12	880
268	28	Tuesday	„	1	881
269	29 K	Saturday	July	21	882
270	30	Thursday	„	11	883

A.H.		Date of Muharram 1.			A.D.
271	1	Monday	June	29	884
272	2 K	Friday	„	18	885
273	3	Wednesday	„	8	886
274	4	Sunday	May	28	887
275	5 K	Thursday	„	16	888
276	6	Tuesday	„	6	889
277	7 K	Saturday	April	25	890
278	8	Thursday	„	15	891
279	9	Monday	„	3	892
280	10 K	Friday	March	23	893
281	11	Wednesday	„	13	894
282	12	Sunday	„	2	895
283	13 K	Thursday	Feb.	19	896
284	14	Tuesday	„	8	897
285	15	Saturday	Jan.	28	898
286	16 K	Wednesday	„	17	899
287	17	Monday	„	7	900
288	18 K	Friday	Dec.	26	„
289	19	Wednesday	„	16	901
290	20	Sunday	„	5	902
291	21 K	Thursday	Nov.	24	903
292	22	Tuesday	„	13	904
293	23	Saturday	„	2	905
294	24 K	Wednesday	Oct.	22	906
295	25	Monday	„	12	907
296	26 K	Friday	Sept.	30	908
297	27	Wednesday	„	20	909
298	28	Sunday	„	9	910
299	29 K	Thursday	Aug.	29	911
300	30	Tuesday	„	18	912
301	1	Saturday	„	7	913
302	2 K	Wednesday	July	27	914
303	3	Monday	„	17	915
304	4	Friday	„	5	916
305	5 K	Tuesday	June	24	917
306	6	Sunday	„	14	918
307	7 K	Thursday	„	3	919
308	8	Tuesday	May	23	920
309	9	Saturday	„	12	921
310	10 K	Wednesday	„	1	922
311	11	Monday	April	21	923
312	12	Friday	„	9	924
313	13 K	Tuesday	March	29	925
314	14	Sunday	„	19	926
315	15	Thursday	„	8	927
316	16 K	Monday	Feb.	25	928
317	17	Saturday	„	14	929
318	18 K	Wednesday	„	3	930
319	19	Monday	Jan.	24	931
320	20	Friday	„	13	932
321	21 K	Tuesday	„	1	933
322	22	Sunday	Dec.	22	„
323	23	Thursday	„	11	934
324	24 K	Monday	Nov.	30	935
325	25	Saturday	„	19	936
326	26 K	Wednesday	„	8	937
327	27	Monday	Oct.	29	938
328	28	Friday	„	18	939
329	29 K	Tuesday	„	6	940
330	30	Sunday	Sept.	26	941
331	1	Thursday	„	15	942
332	2 K	Monday	„	4	943
333	3	Saturday	Aug.	24	944
334	4	Wednesday	„	13	945
335	5 K	Sunday	„	2	946
336	6	Friday	July	23	947
337	7 K	Tuesday	„	11	948
338	8	Sunday	„	1	949
339	9	Thursday	June	20	950
340	10 K	Monday	„	9	951
341	11	Saturday	May	29	952
342	12	Wednesday	„	18	953
343	13 K	Sunday	„	7	954
344	14	Friday	April	27	955
345	15	Tuesday	„	15	956
346	16 K	Saturday	„	4	957
347	17	Thursday	March	25	958
348	18 K	Monday	„	14	959
349	19	Saturday	„	3	960
350	20	Wednesday	Feb.	20	961
351	21 K	Sunday	„	9	962
352	22	Friday	Jan.	30	963
353	23	Tuesday	„	19	964
354	24 K	Saturday	„	7	965
355	25	Thursday	Dec.	28	„
356	26 K	Monday	„	17	966
357	27	Saturday	„	7	967
358	28	Wednesday	Nov.	25	968
359	29 K	Sunday	„	14	969
360	30	Friday	„	4	970

A.H.			Date of Muḥarram 1.			A.D.
361	1		Tuesday	Oct.	24	971
362	2	K	Saturday	,,	12	972
363	3		Thursday	,,	2	973
364	4		Monday	Sept.	21	974
365	5	K	Friday	,,	10	975
366	6		Wednesday	Aug.	30	976
367	7	K	Sunday	,,	19	977
368	8		Friday	,,	9	978
369	9		Tuesday	July	29	979
370	10	K	Saturday	,,	17	980
371	11		Thursday	,,	7	981
372	12		Monday	June	26	982
373	13	K	Friday	,,	15	983
374	14		Wednesday	,,	4	984
375	15		Sunday	May	24	985
376	16	K	Thursday	,,	13	986
377	17		Tuesday	,,	3	987
378	18	K	Saturday	April	21	988
379	19		Thursday	,,	11	989
380	20		Monday	March	31	990
381	21	K	Friday	,,	20	991
382	22		Wednesday	,,	9	992
383	23		Sunday	Feb.	26	993
384	24	K	Thursday	,,	15	994
385	25		Tuesday	,,	5	995
386	26	K	Saturday	Jan.	25	996
387	27		Thursday	,,	14	997
388	28		Monday	,,	3	998
389	29	K	Friday	Dec.	23	,,
390	30		Wednesday	,,	13	999
391	1		Sunday	,,	1	1000
392	2	K	Thursday	Nov.	20	1001
393	3		Tuesday	,,	10	1002
394	4		Saturday	Oct.	30	1003
395	5	K	Wednesday	,,	18	1004
396	6		Monday	,,	8	1005
397	7	K	Friday	Sept.	27	1006
398	8		Wednesday	,,	17	1007
399	9		Sunday	,,	5	1008
400	10	K	Thursday	Aug.	25	1009
401	11		Tuesday	,,	15	1010
402	12		Saturday	,,	4	1011
403	13	K	Wednesday	July	23	1012
404	14		Monday	,,	13	1013
405	15		Friday	,,	2	1014
406	16		Tuesday	June	21	1015
407	17	K	Sunday	,,	10	1016
408	18	K	Thursday	May	30	1017
409	19		Tuesday	,,	20	1018
410	20		Saturday	,,	9	1019
411	21	K	Wednesday	April	27	1020
412	22		Monday	,,	17	1021
413	23		Friday	,,	6	1022
414	24	K	Tuesday	March	26	1023
415	25		Sunday	,,	15	1024
416	26	K	Thursday	,,	4	1025
417	27		Tuesday	Feb.	22	1026
418	28		Saturday	,,	11	1027
419	29	K	Wednesday	Jan.	31	1028
420	30		Monday	,,	20	1029
421	1		Friday	,,	9	1030
422	2	K	Tuesday	Dec.	29	,,
423	3		Sunday	,,	19	1031
424	4		Thursday	,,	7	1032
425	5	K	Monday	Nov.	26	1033
426	6		Saturday	,,	16	1034
427	7	K	Wednesday	,,	5	1035
428	8		Monday	Oct.	25	1036
439	9		Friday	,,	14	1037
430	10	K	Tuesday	,,	3	1038
431	11		Sunday	Sept.	23	1039
432	12		Thursday	,,	11	1040
433	13	K	Monday	Aug.	31	1041
434	14		Saturday	,,	21	1042
435	15		Wednesday	,,	10	1043
436	16	K	Sunday	July	29	1044
437	17		Friday	,,	19	1045
438	18	K	Tuesday	,,	8	1046
439	19		Monday	June	28	1047
440	20		Thursday	,,	16	1048
441	21	K	Monday	,,	5	1049
442	22		Saturday	May	26	1050
443	23		Wednesday	,,	15	1051
444	24	K	Sunday	,,	3	1052
445	25		Friday	April	23	1053
446	26	K	Tuesday	,,	12	1054
447	27		Sunday	,,	2	1055
448	28		Thursday	March	21	1056
449	29	K	Monday	,,	10	1057
450	30		Saturday	Feb.	28	1058

A.H.		Date of Muḥarram 1.			A.D.
451	1	Wednesday	Feb.	17	1059
452	2 K	Sunday	,,	6	1060
453	3	Friday	Jan.	26	1061
454	4	Tuesday	,,	15	1062
455	5 K	Saturday	,,	4	1063
456	6	Thursday	Dec.	25	,,
457	7 K	Monday	,,	13	1064
458	8	Saturday	,,	3	1065
459	9	Wednesday	Nov.	22	1066
460	10 K	Sunday	,,	11	1067
461	11	Friday	Oct.	31	1068
462	12	Tuesday	,,	20	1069
463	13 K	Saturday	,,	9	1070
464	14	Thursday	Sept.	29	1071
465	15	Monday	,,	17	1072
466	16 K	Friday	,,	6	1073
467	17	Wednesday	Aug.	27	1074
468	18 K	Sunday	,,	16	1075
469	19	Friday	,,	5	1076
470	20	Tuesday	July	25	1077
471	21 K	Saturday	,,	14	1078
472	22	Thursday	,,	4	1079
473	23	Monday	June	22	1080
474	24 K	Friday	,,	11	1081
475	25	Wednesday	,,	1	1082
476	26 K	Sunday	May	21	1083
477	27	Friday	,,	10	1084
478	28	Tuesday	April	29	1085
479	29 K	Saturday	,,	18	1086
480	30	Thursday	,,	8	1087
481	1	Monday	March	27	1088
482	2 K	Friday	,,	16	1089
483	3	Wednesday	,,	6	1090
484	4	Sunday	Feb.	23	1091
485	5 K	Thursday	,,	12	1092
486	6	Tuesday	,,	1	1093
487	7 K	Saturday	Jan.	21	1094
488	8	Thursday	,,	11	1095
489	9	Monday	Dec.	31	,,
490	10 K	Friday	,,	19	1096
491	11	Wednesday	,,	9	1097
492	12	Sunday	Nov.	28	1098
493	13 K	Thursday	,,	17	1099
494	14	Tuesday	,,	6	1100
495	15	Saturday	Oct	26	1101
496	16 K	Wednesday	Oct.	15	1102
497	17	Monday	,,	5	1103
498	18 K	Friday	Sept.	23	1104
499	19	Wednesday	,,	13	1105
500	20	Sunday	,,	2	1106
501	21 K	Thursday	Aug.	22	1107
502	22	Tuesday	,,	11	1108
503	23	Saturday	July	31	1109
504	24 K	Wednesday	,,	20	1110
505	25	Monday	,,	10	1111
506	26 K	Friday	June	28	1112
507	27	Wednesday	,,	18	1113
508	28	Sunday	,,	7	1114
509	29 K	Thursday	May	27	1115
510	30	Tuesday	,,	16	1116
511	1	Saturday	,,	5	1117
512	2 K	Wednesday	April	24	1118
513	3	Monday	,,	14	1119
514	4	Friday	,,	2	1120
515	5 K	Tuesday	March	22	1121
516	6	Sunday	,,	12	1122
517	7 K	Thursday	,,	1	1123
518	8	Tuesday	Feb.	19	1124
519	9	Saturday	,,	7	1125
520	10 K	Wednesday	Jan.	27	1126
521	11	Monday	,,	17	1127
522	12	Friday	,,	6	1128
523	13 K	Tuesday	Dec.	25	,,
524	14	Sunday	,,	15	1129
525	15	Thursday	,,	4	1130
526	16 K	Monday	Nov.	23	1131
527	17	Saturday	,,	12	1132
528	18 K	Wednesday	,,	1	1133
529	19	Monday	Oct.	22	1134
530	20	Friday	,,	11	1135
531	21 K	Tuesday	Sept.	29	1136
532	22	Sunday	,,	19	1137
533	23	Thursday	,,	8	1138
534	24 K	Monday	Aug.	28	1139
535	25	Saturday	,,	17	1140
536	26 K	Wednesday	,,	6	1141
537	27	Monday	July	27	1142
538	28	Friday	,,	16	1143
539	29 K	Tuesday	,,	4	1144
540	30	Sunday	June	24	1145

A.H.		Date of Muḥarram 1.			A.D.
541	1	Thursday	June	13	1146
542	2 K	Monday	„	2	1147
543	3	Saturday	May	22	1148
544	4	Wednesday	„	11	1149
545	5 K	Sunday	April	30	1150
546	6	Friday	„	20	1151
547	7 K	Tuesday	„	8	1152
548	8	Sunday	March	29	1153
549	9	Thursday	„	18	1154
550	10 K	Monday	„	7	1155
551	11	Saturday	Feb.	25	1156
552	12	Wednesday	„	13	1157
553	13 K	Sunday	„	2	1158
554	14	Friday	Jan.	23	1159
555	15	Tuesday	„	12	1160
556	16 K	Saturday	Dec.	31	„
557	17	Thursday	„	21	1161
558	18 K	Monday	„	10	1162
559	19	Saturday	Nov.	30	1163
560	20	Wednesday	„	18	1164
561	21 K	Sunday	„	7	1165
562	22	Friday	Oct.	28	1166
563	23	Tuesday	„	17	1167
564	24 K	Saturday	„	5	1168
565	25	Thursday	Sept.	25	1169
566	26 K	Monday	„	14	1170
567	27	Saturday	„	4	1171
568	28	Wednesday	Aug.	23	1172
569	29 K	Sunday	„	12	1173
570	30	Friday	„	2	1174
571	1	Tuesday	July	22	1175
572	2 K	Saturday	„	10	1176
573	3	Thursday	June	30	1777
574	4	Monday	„	19	1778
575	5 K	Friday	„	8	1179
576	6	Wednesday	May	28	1180
577	7 K	Sunday	„	17	1181
578	8	Friday	„	7	1182
579	9	Tuesday	April	26	1183
580	10 K	Saturday	„	14	1184
581	11	Thursday	„	4	1185
582	12	Monday	March	24	1186
583	13 K	Friday	„	13	1187
584	14	Wednesday	„	2	1188
585	15	Sunday	Feb.	19	1189
586	16 K	Thursday	Feb.	8	1190
587	17	Tuesday	Jan.	29	1191
588	18 K	Saturday	„	18	1192
589	19	Thursday	„	7	1193
590	20	Monday	Dec.	27	„
591	21 K	Friday	„	16	1194
592	22	Wednesday	„	6	1195
593	23	Sunday	Nov.	24	1196
594	24 K	Thursday	„	13	1197
595	25	Tuesday	„	3	1198
596	26 K	Saturday	Oct.	23	1199
597	27	Thursday	„	12	1200
598	28	Monday	„	1	1201
599	29 K	Friday	Sept.	20	1202
600	30	Wednesday	„	10	1203
601	1	Sunday	Aug.	29	1204
602	2 K	Thursday	„	18	1205
603	3	Tuesday	„	8	1206
604	4	Saturday	July	28	1207
605	5 K	Wednesday	„	16	1208
606	6	Monday	„	6	1209
607	7 K	Friday	June	25	1210
608	8	Wednesday	„	15	1211
609	9	Sunday	„	3	1212
610	10 K	Thursday	May	23	1213
611	11	Tuesday	„	13	1214
612	12	Saturday	„	2	1215
613	13 K	Wednesday	April	20	1216
614	14	Monday	„	10	1217
615	15	Friday	March	30	1218
616	16 K	Tuesday	„	19	1219
617	17	Sunday	„	8	1220
618	18 K	Thursday	Feb.	25	1221
619	19	Tuesday	„	15	1222
620	20	Saturday	„	4	1223
621	21 K	Wednesday	Jan.	24	1224
622	22	Monday	„	13	1225
623	23	Friday	„	2	1226
624	24 K	Tuesday	Dec.	22	„
625	25	Sunday	„	12	1227
626	26 K	Thursday	Nov.	30	1228
627	27	Tuesday	„	20	1229
628	28	Saturday	„	9	1230
629	29 K	Wednesday	Oct.	29	1231
630	30	Monday	„	18	1232

A.H.		Date of Muḥarram 1.			A.D.
631	1	Friday	Oct.	7	1233
632	2 K	Tuesday	Sept.	26	1234
633	3	Sunday	,,	16	1235
634	4	Thursday	,,	4	1236
635	5 K	Monday	Aug.	24	1237
636	6	Saturday	,,	14	1238
637	7 K	Wednesday	,,	3	1239
638	8	Monday	July	23	1240
639	9	Friday	,,	12	1241
640	10 K	Tuesday	,,	1	1242
641	11	Sunday	June	21	1243
642	12	Thursday	,,	9	1244
643	13 K	Monday	May	29	1245
644	14	Saturday	,,	19	1246
645	15	Wednesday	,,	8	1247
646	16 K	Sunday	April	26	1248
647	17	Friday	,,	16	1249
648	18 K	Tuesday	,,	5	1250
649	19	Sunday	March	26	1251
650	20	Thursday	,,	14	1252
651	21 K	Monday	,,	3	1253
652	22	Saturday	Feb.	21	1254
653	23	Wednesday	,,	10	1255
654	24 K	Sunday	Jan.	30	1256
655	25	Friday	,,	19	1257
656	26 K	Tuesday	,,	8	1258
657	27	Sunday	Dec.	29	,,
658	28	Thursday	,,	18	1259
659	29 K	Monday	,,	6	1260
660	30	Saturday	Nov.	26	1261
661	1	Wednesday	,,	15	1262
662	2 K	Sunday	,,	4	1263
663	3	Friday	Oct.	24	1264
664	4	Tuesday	,,	13	1265
665	5 K	Saturday	,,	2	1266
666	6	Thursday	Sept.	22	1267
667	7 K	Monday	,,	10	1268
668	8	Saturday	Aug.	31	1269
669	9	Wednesday	,,	20	1270
670	10 K	Sunday	,,	9	1271
671	11	Friday	July	29	1272
672	12	Tuesday	,,	18	1273
673	13 K	Saturday	,,	7	1274
674	14	Thursday	June	27	1275
675	15	Monday	,,	15	1276
676	16 K	Friday	June	4	1277
677	17	Wednesday	May	25	1278
678	18 K	Sunday	,,	14	1279
679	19	Friday	,,	3	1280
680	20	Tuesday	April	22	1281
681	21 K	Saturday	,,	11	1282
682	22	Thursday	,,	1	1283
683	23	Monday	March	20	1284
684	24 K	Friday	,,	9	1285
685	25	Wednesday	Feb.	27	1286
686	26 K	Sunday	,,	16	1287
687	27	Friday	,,	6	1288
688	28	Tuesday	Jan.	25	1289
689	29 K	Saturday	,,	14	1290
690	30	Thursday	,,	4	1291
691	1	Monday	Dec.	24	1291
692	2 K	Friday	,,	12	1292
693	3	Wednesday	,,	2	1293
694	4	Sunday	Nov.	22	1294
695	5 K	Thursday	,,	10	1295
696	6	Tuesday	Oct.	30	1296
697	7 K	Saturday	,,	19	1297
698	8	Thursday	,,	9	1298
699	9	Monday	Sept.	28	1299
700	10 K	Friday	,,	16	1300
701	11	Wednesday	,,	6	1301
702	12	Sunday	Aug.	26	1302
703	13 K	Thursday	,,	15	1303
704	14	Tuesday	,,	4	1304
705	15	Saturday	July	24	1305
706	16 K	Wednesday	,,	13	1306
707	17	Monday	,,	3	1307
708	18 K	Friday	June	21	1308
709	19	Wednesday	,,	11	1309
710	20	Sunday	May	31	1310
711	21 K	Thursday	,,	20	1311
712	22	Tuesday	,,	9	1312
713	23	Saturday	April	28	1313
714	24 K	Wednesday	,,	17	1314
715	25	Monday	,,	7	1315
716	26 K	Friday	March	26	1316
717	27	Wednesday	,,	16	1317
718	28	Sunday	,,	5	1318
719	29 K	Thursday	Feb.	22	1319
720	30	Tuesday	,,	12	1320

A.H.		Date of Muḥarram 1.			A.D.
721	1	Saturday	Jan.	31	1321
722	2 K	Wednesday	„	20	1322
723	3	Monday	„	10	1323
724	4	Friday	Dec.	30	„
725	5 K	Tuesday	„	18	1324
726	6	Sunday	„	8	1325
727	7 K	Thursday	Nov.	27	1326
728	8	Tuesday	„	17	1327
729	9	Saturday	„	5	1328
730	10 K	Wednesday	Oct.	25	1329
731	11	Monday	„	15	1330
732	12	Friday	„	4	1331
733	13 K	Tuesday	Sept.	22	1332
734	14	Sunday	„	12	1333
735	15	Thursday	„	1	1334
736	16 K	Monday	Aug.	21	1335
737	17	Saturday	„	10	1336
738	18 K	Wednesday	July	30	1337
739	19	Monday	„	20	1338
740	20	Friday	„	9	1339
741	21 K	Tuesday	June	27	1340
742	22	Sunday	„	17	1341
743	23	Thursday	„	6	1342
744	24 K	Monday	May	26	1343
745	25	Saturday	„	15	1344
746	26 K	Wednesday	„	4	1345
747	27	Monday	April	24	1346
748	28	Friday	„	13	1347
749	29 K	Tuesday	„	1	1348
750	30	Sunday	March	22	1349
751	1	Thursday	„	11	1350
752	2 K	Monday	Feb.	28	1351
753	3	Saturday	„	18	1352
754	4	Wednesday	„	6	1353
755	5 K	Sunday	Jan.	26	1354
756	6	Friday	„	16	1355
757	7 K	Tuesday	„	5	1356
758	8	Sunday	Dec.	25	„
759	9	Thursday	„	14	1357
760	10 K	Monday	„	3	1358
761	11	Saturday	Nov.	23	1359
762	12	Wednesday	„	11	1360
763	13 K	Sunday	Oct.	31	1361
764	14	Friday	„	21	1362
765	15	Tuesday	„	10	1363
766	16 K	Saturday	Sept.	28	1364
767	17	Thursday	„	18	1365
768	18 K	Monday	„	7	1366
769	19	Saturday	Aug.	28	1367
770	20	Wednesday	„	16	1368
771	21 K	Sunday	„	5	1369
772	22	Friday	July	26	1370
773	23	Tuesday	„	15	1371
774	24 K	Saturday	„	3	1372
775	25	Thursday	June	23	1373
776	26 K	Monday	„	12	1374
777	27	Saturday	„	2	1375
778	28	Wednesday	May	21	1376
779	29 K	Sunday	„	10	1377
780	30	Friday	April	30	1378
781	1	Tuesday	„	19	1379
782	2 K	Saturday	„	7	1380
783	3	Thursday	March	28	1381
784	4	Monday	„	17	1382
785	5 K	Friday	„	6	1383
786	6	Wednesday	Feb.	24	1384
787	7 K	Sunday	„	12	1385
788	8	Friday	„	2	1386
789	9	Tuesday	Jan.	22	1387
790	10 K	Saturday	„	11	1388
791	11	Thursday	Dec.	31	„
792	12	Monday	„	20	1389
793	13 K	Friday	„	9	1390
794	14	Wednesday	Nov.	29	1391
795	15	Sunday	„	17	1392
796	16 K	Thursday	„	6	1393
797	17	Tuesday	Oct.	27	1394
798	18 K	Saturday	„	16	1395
799	19	Thursday	„	5	1396
800	20	Monday	Sept.	24	1397
801	21 K	Friday	„	13	1398
802	22	Wednesday	„	3	1399
803	23	Sunday	Aug.	22	1400
804	24 K	Thursday	„	11	1401
805	25	Tuesday	„	1	1402
806	26 K	Saturday	July	21	1403
807	27	Thursday	„	10	1404
808	28	Monday	June	29	1405
809	29 K	Friday	„	18	1406
810	30	Wednesday	„	8	1407

A.H.		Date of Muḥarram 1.			A.D.
811	1	Sunday	May	27	1408
812	2 K	Thursday	„	16	1409
813	3	Tuesday	„	6	1410
814	4	Saturday	April	25	1411
815	5 K	Wednesday	„	13	1412
816	6	Monday	„	3	1413
817	7 K	Friday	March	23	1414
818	8	Wednesday	„	13	1415
819	9	Sunday	„	1	1416
820	10 K	Thursday	Feb.	18	1417
821	11	Tuesday	„	8	1418
822	12	Saturday	Jan.	28	1419
823	13 K	Wednesday	„	17	1420
824	14	Monday	„	6	1421
825	15	Friday	Dec.	26	„
826	16 K	Tuesday	„	15	1422
827	17	Sunday	„	5	1423
828	18 K	Thursday	Nov.	23	1424
829	19	Tuesday	„	13	1425
830	20	Saturday	„	2	1426
831	21 K	Wednesday	Oct.	22	1427
832	22	Monday	„	11	1428
833	23	Friday	Sept.	30	1429
834	24 K	Tuesday	„	19	1430
835	25	Sunday	„	9	1431
836	26 K	Thursday	Aug.	28	1432
837	27	Tuesday	„	18	1433
838	28	Saturday	„	7	1434
839	29 K	Wednesday	July	27	1435
840	30	Monday	„	16	1436
841	1	Friday	„	5	1437
842	2 K	Tuesday	June	24	1438
843	3	Sunday	„	14	1439
844	4	Thursday	„	2	1440
845	5 K	Monday	May	22	1441
846	6	Saturday	„	12	1442
847	7 K	Wednesday	„	1	1443
848	8	Monday	April	20	1444
849	9	Friday	„	9	1445
850	10 K	Tuesday	March	29	1446
851	11	Sunday	„	19	1447
852	12	Thursday	„	7	1448
853	13 K	Monday	Feb.	24	1449
854	14	Saturday	„	14	1450
855	15	Wednesday	„	3	1451

A.H.		Date of Muḥarram 1.			A.D.
856	16 K	Sunday	Jan.	23	1452
857	17	Friday	„	12	1453
858	18 K	Tuesday	„	1	1454
859	19	Sunday	Dec.	22	„
860	20	Thursday	„	11	1455
861	21 K	Monday	Nov.	29	1456
862	22	Saturday	„	19	1457
863	23	Wednesday	„	8	1458
864	24 K	Sunday	Oct.	28	1459
865	25	Friday	„	17	1460
866	26 K	Tuesday	„	6	1461
867	27	Sunday	Sept.	26	1462
868	28	Thursday	„	15	1463
869	29 K	Monday	„	3	1464
870	30	Saturday	Aug.	24	1465
871	1	Wednesday	„	13	1466
872	2 K	Sunday	„	2	1467
873	3	Friday	July	22	1468
874	4	Tuesday	„	11	1469
875	5 K	Saturday	June	30	1470
876	6	Thursday	„	20	1471
877	7 K	Monday	„	8	1472
878	8	Saturday	May	29	1473
879	9	Wednesday	„	18	1474
880	10 K	Sunday	„	7	1475
881	11	Friday	April	26	1476
882	12	Tuesday	„	15	1477
883	13 K	Saturday	„	4	1478
884	14	Thursday	March	25	1479
885	15	Monday	„	13	1480
886	16 K	Friday	„	2	1481
887	17	Wednesday	Feb.	20	1482
888	18 K	Sunday	„	9	1483
889	19	Friday	Jan.	30	1484
890	20	Tuesday	„	18	1485
891	21 K	Saturday	„	7	1486
892	22	Thursday	Dec.	28	„
893	23	Monday	„	17	1487
894	24 K	Friday	„	5	1488
895	25	Wednesday	Nov.	25	1489
896	26 K	Sunday	„	14	1490
897	27	Friday	„	4	1491
898	28	Tuesday	Oct.	23	1492
899	29 K	Saturday	„	12	1493
900	30	Thursday	„	2	1494

A.H.		Date of Muḥarram 1.			A.D.
901	1	Monday	Sept.	21	1495
902	2 K	Friday	„	9	1496
903	3	Wednesday	Aug.	30	1497
904	4	Sunday	„	19	1498
905	5 K	Thursday	„	8	1499
906	6	Tuesday	July	28	1500
907	7 K	Saturday	„	17	1501
908	8	Thursday	„	7	1502
909	9	Monday	June	26	1503
910	10 K	Friday	„	14	1504
911	11	Wednesday	„	4	1505
912	12	Sunday	May	24	1506
913	13 K	Thursday	„	13	1507
914	14	Tuesday	„	2	1508
915	15	Saturday	April	21	1509
916	16 K	Wednesday	„	10	1510
917	17	Monday	March	31	1511
918	18 K	Friday	„	19	1512
919	19	Wednesday	„	9	1513
920	20	Sunday	Feb.	26	1514
921	21 K	Thursday	„	15	1515
922	22	Tuesday	„	5	1516
923	23	Saturday	Jan.	24	1517
924	24 K	Wednesday	„	13	1518
925	25	Monday	„	3	1519
926	26 K	Friday	Dec.	23	„
927	27	Wednesday	„	12	1520
928	28	Sunday	„	1	1521
929	29 K	Thursday	Nov.	20	1522
930	30	Tuesday	„	10	1523
931	1	Saturday	Oct.	29	1524
932	2 K	Wednesday	„	18	1525
933	3	Monday	„	8	1526
934	4	Friday	Sept.	27	1527
935	5 K	Tuesday	„	15	1528
936	6	Sunday	„	5	1529
937	7 K	Thursday	Aug.	25	1530
938	8	Tuesday	„	15	1531
939	9	Saturday	„	3	1532
940	10 K	Wednesday	July	23	1533
941	11	Monday	„	13	1534
942	12	Friday	„	2	1535
943	13 K	Tuesday	June	20	1536
944	14	Sunday	„	10	1537
945	15	Thursday	May	30	1538
946	16 K	Monday	May	19	1539
947	17	Saturday	„	8	1540
948	18 K	Wednesday	April	27	1541
949	19	Monday	„	17	1542
950	20	Friday	„	6	1543
951	21 K	Tuesday	March	25	1544
952	22	Sunday	„	15	1545
953	23	Thursday	„	4	1546
954	24 K	Monday	Feb.	21	1547
955	25	Saturday	„	11	1548
956	26 K	Wednesday	Jan.	30	1549
957	27	Monday	„	20	1550
958	28	Friday	„	9	1551
959	29 K	Tuesday	Dec.	29	„
960	30	Sunday	„	18	1552
961	1	Thursday	„	7	1553
962	2 K	Monday	Nov.	26	1554
963	3	Saturday	„	16	1555
964	4	Wednesday	„	4	1556
965	5 K	Sunday	Oct.	24	1557
966	6	Friday	„	14	1558
967	7 K	Tuesday	„	3	1559
968	8	Sunday	Sept.	22	1560
969	9	Thursday	„	11	1561
970	10 K	Monday	Aug.	31	1562
971	11	Saturday	„	21	1563
972	12	Wednesday	„	9	1564
973	13 K	Sunday	July	29	1565
974	14	Friday	„	19	1566
975	15	Tuesday	„	8	1567
976	16 K	Saturday	June	26	1568
977	17	Thursday	„	16	1569
978	18 K	Monday	„	5	1570
979	19	Saturday	May	26	1571
980	20	Wednesday	„	14	1572
981	21 K	Sunday	„	3	1573
982	22	Friday	April	23	1574
983	23	Tuesday	„	12	1575
984	24 K	Saturday	March	31	1576
985	25	Thursday	„	21	1577
986	26 K	Monday	„	10	1578
987	27	Saturday	Feb.	28	1579
988	28	Wednesday	„	17	1580
989	29 K	Sunday	„	5	1581
990	30	Friday	Jan.	26	1582

A.H.		Date of Muharram 1.			A.D.
991	1	Tues.	Jan.	15 .. 25	1583
992	2 K	Sat.	"	4 .. 14	1584
993	3	Thurs.	Dec.	24, 1584 .. Jan. 3	1585
994	4	Mon.	"	13 .. 23	"
995	5 K	Fri.	"	2 .. 12	1586
996	6	Wed.	Nov.	22 .. Dec. 2	1587
997	7 K	Sun.	"	10 .. 20	1588
998	8	Fri.	Oct.	31 .. Nov. 10	1589
999	9	Tues.	"	20 .. 30	1590
1000	10 K	Sat.	"	9 .. 19	1591
1001	11	Thurs.	Sept.	28 .. Oct. 8	1592
1002	12	Mon.	"	17 .. 27	1593
1003	13 K	Fri.	"	6 .. 16	1594
1004	14	Wed.	Aug.	27 .. Sept. 6	1595
1005	15	Sun.	"	15 .. 25	1596
1006	16 K	Thurs.	"	4 .. 14	1597
1007	17	Tues.	July	25 .. Aug. 4	1598
1008	18 K	Sat.	"	14 .. 24	1599
1009	19	Thurs.	"	3 .. 13	1600
1010	20	Mon.	June	22 .. July 2	1601
1011	21 K	Fri.	"	11 .. 21	1602
1012	22	Wed.	"	1 .. 11	1603
1013	23	Sun.	May	20 .. 30	1604
1014	24 K	Thurs.	"	9 .. 19	1605
1015	25	Mon.	April	29 .. May 2	1606
1016	26 K	Sat.	"	18 .. 28	1607
1017	27	Thurs.	"	7 .. 17	1608
1018	28	Mon.	Mar.	27 .. April 6	1609
1019	29 K	Fri.	"	16 .. 26	1610
1020	30	Wed.	"	6 .. 16	1611
1021	1	Sun.	Feb.	23 .. Mar. 4	1612
1022	2 K	Thurs.	"	11 .. 21	1613
1023	3	Tues.	"	1 .. 11	1614
1024	4	Sat.	Jan.	21 .. 31	1615
1025	5 K	Wed.	"	10 .. 20	1616
1026	6	Mon.	Dec.	30, 1616 .. Jan. 9	1617
1027	7 K	Fri.	"	19 .. 29	"
1028	8	Wed.	"	9 .. 19	1618
1029	9	Sun.	Nov.	28 .. Dec. 8	1619
1030	10 K	Thurs.	"	16 .. 26	1620
1031	11	Tues.	"	6 .. 16	1621
1032	12	Sat.	Oct.	26 .. Nov. 5	1622
1033	13 K	Wed.	"	15 .. 25	1623
1034	14	Mon.	"	4 .. 14	1624
1035	15	Fri.	Sept.	23 .. Oct. 3	1625

A.H.		Date of Muharram 1.			A.D.
1036	16 K	Tues.	Sept.	12 .. 22	1626
1037	17	Sun.	"	2 .. 12	1627
1038	18 K	Thurs.	Aug.	21 .. 31	1628
1039	19	Tues.	"	11 .. 21	1629
1040	20	Sat.	July	31 .. Aug. 10	1630
1041	21 K	Wed.	"	20 .. 30	1631
1042	22	Mon.	"	9 .. 19	1632
1043	23	Fri.	June	28 .. July 8	1633
1044	24 K	Tues.	"	17 .. 27	1634
1045	25	Sun.	"	7 .. 17	1635
1046	26 K	Thurs.	May	26 .. June 5	1636
1047	27	Tues.	"	16 .. 26	1637
1048	28	Sat.	"	5 .. 15	1638
1049	29 K	Wed.	April	24 .. May 4	1639
1050	30	Mon.	"	13 .. 23	1640
1051	1	Fri.	"	2 .. 12	1641
1052	2 K	Tues.	Mar.	22 .. April 1	1642
1053	3	Sun.	"	12 .. 22	1643
1054	4	Thurs.	Feb.	29 .. Mar. 10	1644
1055	5 K	Mon.	"	17 .. 27	1645
1056	6	Sat.	"	7 .. 17	1646
1057	7 K	Wed.	Jan.	27 .. Feb. 6	1647
1058	8	Mon.	"	17 .. 27	1648
1059	9	Fri.	"	5 .. 15	1649
1060	10 K	Tues.	Dec.	25, 1649 .. Jan. 4	1650
1061	11	Sun.	"	15 .. 25	"
1062	12	Thurs.	"	4 .. 14	1651
1063	13 K	Mon.	Nov.	22 .. Dec. 2	1652
1064	14	Sat.	"	12 .. 22	1653
1065	15	Wed.	"	1 .. 11	1654
1066	16 K	Sun.	Oct.	21 .. 31	1655
1067	17	Fri.	"	10 .. 20	1656
1068	18 K	Tues.	Sept.	29 .. Oct. 9	1657
1069	19	Sun.	"	19 .. 29	1658
1070	20	Thurs.	"	8 .. 18	1659
1071	21 K	Mon.	Aug.	27 .. Sept. 6	1660
1072	22	Sat.	"	17 .. 27	1661
1073	23	Wed.	"	6 .. 16	1662
1074	24 K	Sun.	July	26 .. Aug. 5	1663
1075	25	Fri.	"	15 .. 25	1664
1076	26 K	Tues.	"	4 .. 14	1665
1077	27	Sat.	June	24 .. July 4	1666
1078	28	Thurs.	"	13 .. 23	1667
1079	29 K	Mon.	June	1 .. 11	1668
1080	30	Sat.	May	22 .. June 1	1669

A.H.		Date of Muḥarram 1.	A.D.
1081	1	Wed. May 11 .. 21	1670
1082	2 K	Sun. April 30 .. May 10	1671
1083	3	Fri. „ 19 .. 29	1672
1084	4	Tues. „ 8 .. 18	1673
1085	5 K	Sat. Mar. 28 .. April 7	1674
1086	6	Thurs. „ 18 .. 28	1675
1087	7 K	Mon. „ 6 .. 16	1676
1088	8	Sat. Feb. 24 .. Mar. 6	1677
1089	9	Wed. „ 13 .. 23	1678
1090	10 K	Sun. „ 2 .. 12	1679
1091	11	Fri. Jan. 23 .. Feb. 2	1680
1092	12	Tues. „ 11 .. 21	1681
1093	13 K	Sat. Dec. 31, 1681 .. Jan 10	1682
1094	14	Thurs. „ 21 .. 31	„
1095	15	Mon. „ 10 .. 20	1683
1096	16 K	Fri. Nov. 28 .. Dec. 8	1684
1097	17	Wed. „ 18 .. 28	1685
1098	18 K	Sun. „ 7 .. 17	1686
1099	19	Fri. Oct. 28 .. Nov. 7	1687
1100	20	Tues. „ 16 .. 26	1688
1101	21 K	Sat. „ 5 .. 15	1689
1102	22	Thurs. Sept. 25 .. Oct. 5	1690
1103	23	Mon. „ 14 .. 24	1691
1104	24 K	Fri. „ 2 .. 12	1692
1105	25	Wed. Aug. 23 .. Sept. 2	1693
1106	26 K	Sun. „ 12 .. 22	1694
1107	27	Fri. „ 2 .. 12	1695
1108	28	Tues. July 21 .. 31	1696
1109	29 K	Sat. „ 10 .. 20	1697
1110	30	Thurs. June 30 .. July 10	1698
1111	1	Mon. „ 19 .. 29	1699
1112	2 K	Fri. „ 7 .. 18	1700
1113	3	Wed. May 28 .. June 8	1701
1114	4	Sun. „ 17 .. 28	1702
1115	5 K	Thurs. „ 6 .. 17	1703
1116	6	Tues. April 25 .. May 6	1704
1117	7 K	Sat. „ 14 .. 25	1705
1118	8	Thurs. „ 4 .. 15	1706
1119	9	Mon. Mar. 24 .. April 4	1707
1120	10 K	Fri. „ 12 .. 23	1708
1121	11	Wed. „ 2 .. 13	1709
1122	12	Sun. Feb. 19 .. Mar. 2	1710
1123	13 K	Thurs. „ 8 .. 19	1711
1124	14	Tues. Jan. 29 .. Feb. 9	1712
1125	15	Sat. „ 17 .. 28	1713
1126	16 K	Wed. Jan. 6 .. 17	1714
1127	17	Mon. Dec. 27, 1714 .. Jan. 7	1715
1128	18 K	Fri. „ 16 .. 27	„
1129	19	Wed. „ 5 .. 16	1716
1130	20	Sun. Nov. 24 .. Dec. 5	1717
1131	21 K	Thurs. „ 13 .. 24	1718
1132	22	Tues. „ 3 .. 14	1719
1133	23	Sat. Oct. 22 .. Nov. 2	1720
1134	24 K	Wed. „ 11 .. 22	1721
1135	25	Mon. „ 1 .. 12	1722
1136	26 K	Fri. Sept. 20 .. Oct. 1	1723
1137	27	Wed. „ 9 .. 20	1724
1138	28	Sun. Aug. 29 .. Sept. 9	1725
1139	29 K	Thurs. „ 18 .. 29	1726
1140	30	Tues. „ 8 .. 19	1727
1141	1	Sat. July 27 .. Aug. 7	1728
1142	2 K	Wed. „ 16 .. 27	1729
1143	3	Mon. „ 6 .. 17	1730
1144	4	Fri. June 25 .. July 6	1731
1145	5 K	Tues. „ 13 .. 24	1732
1146	6	Sun. „ 3 .. 14	1733
1147	7 K	Thurs. May 23 .. June 3	1734
1148	8	Tues. „ 13 .. 24	1735
1149	9	Sat. „ 1 .. 12	1736
1150	10 K	Wed. April 20 .. May 1	1737
1151	11	Mon. „ 10 .. 21	1738
1152	12	Fri. Mar. 30 .. April 10	1739
1153	13 K	Tues. „ 18 .. 29	1740
1154	14	Sun. „ 8 .. 19	1741
1155	15	Thurs. Feb. 25 .. Mar. 8	1742
1156	16 K	Mon. „ 14 .. 25	1743
1157	17	Sat. „ 4 .. 15	1744
1158	18 K	Wed. Jan. 23 .. Feb. 3	1745
1159	19	Mon. „ 13 .. 24	1746
1160	20	Fri. „ 2 .. 13	1747
1161	21 K	Tues. Dec. 22, 1747 .. Jan. 2	1748
1162	22	Sun. „ 11 .. 22	„
1163	23	Thurs. Nov. 30 .. Dec. 11	1749
1164	24 K	Mon. „ 19 .. 30	1750
1165	25	Sat. „ 9 .. 20	1751
1166	26 K	Wed. Oct. 28 .. Nov. 8	1752
1167	27	Mon. „ 18 .. 29	1753
1168	28	Fri. „ 7 .. 18	1754
1169	29 K	Tues. Sept. 26 .. Oct. 7	1755
1170	30	Sun. „ 15 .. 26	1756

A.H.		Date of Muḥarram 1.	A.D.
1171	1	Thurs. Sept. 4 .. 15	1757
1172	2 K	Mon. Aug. 24 .. Sept. 4	1758
1173	3	Sat. „ 14 .. 25	1759
1174	4	Wed. „ 2 .. 13	1760
1175	5 K	Sun. July 22 .. Aug. 2	1761
1176	6	Fri. „ 12 .. 23	1762
1177	7 K	Tues. „ 1 .. 12	1763
1178	8	Sun. June 20 .. July 1	1764
1179	9	Thurs. „ 9 .. 20	1765
1180	10 K	Mon. May 29 .. June 9	1766
1181	11	Sat. „ 19 .. 30	1767
1182	12	Wed. „ 7 .. 18	1768
1183	13 K	Sun. April 26 .. May 7	1769
1184	14	Fri. „ 16 .. 27	1770
1185	15	Tues. „ 5 .. 16	1771
1186	16 K	Sat. Mar. 24 .. April 4	1772
1187	17	Thurs. „ 14 .. 25	1773
1188	18 K	Mon. „ 3 .. 14	1774
1189	19	Sat. Feb. 21 .. Mar. 4	1775
1190	20	Wed. „ 10 .. 21	1776
1191	21 K	Sun. Jan. 29 .. Feb. 9	1777
1192	22	Fri. „ 19 .. 30	1778
1193	23	Tues. „ 8 .. 19	1779
1194	24 K	Sat. Dec. 28, 1779 .. Jan. 8	1780
1195	25	Thurs. „ 17 .. 28	„
1196	26 K	Mon. „ 6 .. 17	1781
1197	27	Sat. Nov. 26 .. Dec. 7	1782
1198	28	Wed. „ 15 .. 26	1783
1199	29 K	Sun. „ 3 .. 14	1784
1200	30	Fri. Oct. 24 .. Nov. 4	1785
1201	1	Tues. „ 13 .. 24	1786
1202	2 K	Sat. „ 2 .. 13	1787
1203	3	Thurs. Sept. 21 .. Oct. 2	1788
1204	4	Mon. „ 10 .. 21	1789
1205	5 K	Fri. Aug. 30 .. Sept. 10	1790
1206	6	Wed. „ 20 .. 31	1791
1207	7 K	Sun. „ 8 .. 19	1792
1208	8	Fri. July 29 .. Aug. 9	1793
1209	9	Tues. „ 18 .. 29	1794
1210	10 K	Sat. „ 7 .. 18	1795
1211	11	Thurs. June 26 .. July 7	1796
1212	12	Mon. „ 15 .. 26	1797
1213	13 K	Fri. „ 4 .. 15	1798
1214	14	Wed. May 25 .. June 5	1799
1215	15	Sun. „ 13 .. 25	1800
1216	16 K	Thurs. May 2 .. 14	1801
1217	17	Tues. April 22 .. May 4	1802
1218	18 K	Sat. „ 11 .. 23	1803
1219	19	Thurs. Mar. 31 .. April 12	1804
1220	20	Mon. „ 20 .. April 1	1805
1221	21 K	Fri. „ 9 .. 21	1806
1222	22	Wed. Feb. 27 .. Mar. 11	1807
1223	23	Sun. „ 16 .. 28	1808
1224	24 K	Thurs. „ 4 .. 16	1809
1225	25	Tues. Jan. 25 .. Feb. 6	1810
1226	26 K	Sat. „ 14 .. 26	1811
1227	27	Thurs. „ 4 .. 16	1812
1228	28	Mon. Dec. 23, 1812 .. Jan. 4	1813
1229	29 K	Fri. „ 12 .. 24	„
1230	30	Wed. „ 2 .. 14	1814
1231	1	Sun. Nov. 21 .. Dec. 3	1815
1232	2 K	Thurs. „ 9 .. 21	1816
1233	3	Tues. Oct. 30 .. Nov. 11	1817
1234	4	Sat. „ 19 .. 31	1818
1235	5 K	Wed. „ 8 .. 20	1819
1236	6	Mon. Sept. 27 .. Oct. 9	1820
1237	7 K	Fri. „ 16 .. 28	1821
1238	8	Wed. „ 6 .. 18	1822
1239	9	Sun. Aug. 26 .. Sept. 7	1823
1240	10 K	Thurs. „ 14 .. 26	1824
1241	11	Tues. „ 4 .. 16	1825
1242	12	Sat. July 24 .. Aug. 5	1826
1243	13 K	Wed. „ 13 .. 25	1827
1244	14	Mon. „ 2 .. 14	1828
1245	15	Fri. June 21 .. July 3	1829
1246	16 K	Tues. „ 10 .. 22	1830
1247	17	Sun. May 31 .. June 12	1831
1248	18 K	Thurs. „ 19 .. 31	1832
1249	19	Tues. „ 9 .. 21	1833
1250	20	Sat. April 28 .. May 10	1834
1251	21 K	Wed. „ 17 .. 29	1835
1252	22	Mon. „ 6 .. 18	1836
1253	23	Fri. Mar. 26 .. April 7	1837
1254	24 K	Tues. „ 15 .. 27	1838
1255	25	Sun. „ 5 .. 17	1839
1256	26 K	Thurs. Feb. 22 .. Mar. 5	1840
1257	27	Tues. „ 11 .. 23	1841
1258	28	Sat. Jan. 31 .. Feb. 12	1842
1259	29 K	Wed. „ 20 .. Feb. 1	1843
1260	30	Mon. „ 10 .. 22	1844

A.H.		Date of Muḥarram 1.			A.D.
1261	1	Fri.	Dec. 29, 1844	.. Jan. 10	1845
1262	2 K	Tues.	,,	18 .. 30	,,
1263	3	Sun.	,,	8 .. 20	1846
1264	4	Thurs.	Nov.	27 .. Dec. 9	1847
1265	5 K	Mon.	,,	15 .. 27	1848
1266	6	Sat.	,,	5 .. 17	1849
1267	7 K	Wed.	Oct.	25 .. Nov. 6	1850
1268	8	Mon.	,,	15 .. 27	1851
1269	9	Fri.	,,	3 .. 15	1852
1270	10 K	Tues.	Sept.	22 .. Oct. 4	1853
1271	11	Sun.	,,	12 .. 24	1854
1272	12	Thurs.	,,	1 .. 13	1855
1273	13 K	Mon.	Aug.	20 .. Sept. 1	1856
1274	14	Sat.	,,	10 .. 22	1857
1275	15	Wed.	July	30 .. Aug. 11	1858
1276	16 K	Sun.	,,	19 .. 31	1859
1277	17	Fri.	,,	8 .. 20	1860
1278	18 K	Tues.	June	27 .. July 9	1861
1279	19	Sun.	,,	17 .. 29	1862
1280	20	Thurs.	,,	6 .. 18	1863
1281	21 K	Mon.	May	25 .. June 6	1864
1282	22	Sat.	,,	15 .. 27	1865
1283	23	Wed.	,,	4 .. 16	1966
1284	24 K	Sun.	April	23 .. May 5	1867
1285	25	Fri.	,,	12 .. 24	1868
1286	26 K	Tues.	,,	1 .. 13	1869
1287	27	Sun.	Mar.	22 .. April 3	1870
1288	28	Thurs.	,,	11 .. 23	1871
1289	29 K	Mon.	Feb.	28 .. Mar. 11	1872
1290	30	Sat.	,,	17 .. Mar. 1	1873
1291	1	Wed.	,,	6 .. 18	1874
1292	2 K	Sun.	Jan.	26 .. Feb. 7	1875
1293	3	Fri.	,,	16 .. 28	1876
1294	4	Tues.	,,	4 .. 16	1877
1295	5 K	Sat.	Dec. 24, 1877	.. Jan. 5	1878
1296	6	Thurs.	,,	14 .. 26	,,
1297	7 K	Mon.	,,	3 .. 15	1879
1298	8	Sat.	Nov.	22 .. Dec. 4	1880
1299	9	Wed.	,,	11 .. 23	1881
1300	10 K	Sun.	Oct.	31 .. Nov. 12	1882
1301	11	Fri.	,,	21 .. Nov. 2	1883
1302	12	Tues.	,,	9 .. 21	1884
1303	13 K	Sat.	Sept.	28 .. Oct. 10	1885
1304	14	Thurs.	,,	18 .. 30	1886
1305	15	Mon.	,,	7 .. 19	1887
1306	16 K	Fri.	Aug.	26 .. Sept. 7	1888
1307	17	Wed.	,,	16 .. 28	1889
1308	18 K	Sun.	,,	5 .. 17	1890
1309	19	Fri.	July	26 .. Aug. 7	1891
1310	20	Tues.	,,	14 .. 26	1892
1311	21 K	Sat.	,,	3 .. 15	1893
1312	22	Thurs.	June	23 .. July 5	1894
1313	23	Mon.	,,	12 .. 24	1895
1314	24 K	Fri.	May	31 .. June 12	1896
1315	25	Wed.	,,	21 .. June 2	1897
1316	26 K	Sun.	,,	10 .. 22	1898
1317	27	Fri.	April	30 .. May 12	1899
1318	28	Wed.	,,	18 .. May 1	1900
1319	29 K	Sat.	,,	7 .. 20	1901
1320	30	Thurs.	Mar.	28 .. April 10	1902
1321	1	Mon.	,,	17 .. 30	1903
1322	2 K	Fri.	,,	5 .. 18	1904
1323	3	Wed.	Feb.	23 .. Mar. 8	1905
1324	4	Sun.	,,	12 .. 25	1906
1325	5 K	Thurs.	,,	1 .. 14	1907
1326	6	Tues.	Jan.	22 .. Feb. 4	1908
1327	7 K	Sat.	,,	10 .. 23	1909
1328	8	Thurs.	Dec. 31, 1909	.. Jan. 13	1910
1329	9	Mon.	,,	20, 1910 .. Jan. 2	1911
1330	10 K	Fri.	,,	9 .. 22	,,
1331	11	Wed.	Nov.	28 .. Dec. 11	1912
1332	12	Sun.	,,	17 .. 30	1913
1333	13 K	Thurs.	,,	6 .. 19	1914
1334	14	Tues.	Oct.	27 .. Nov. 9	1915
1335	15	Sat.	,,	15 .. 28	1916
1336	16 K	Wed.	,,	4 .. 17	1917
1337	17	Mon.	Sept.	24 .. Oct. 7	1918
1338	18 K	Fri.	,,	13 .. 26	1919
1339	19	Wed.	,,	2 .. 15	1920
1340	20	Sun.	Aug.	22 .. Sept. 4	1921
1341	21 K	Thurs.	,,	11 .. 24	1922
1342	22	Tues.	,,	1 .. 14	1923
1343	23	Sat.	July	20 .. Aug. 2	1924
1344	24 K	Wed.	,,	9 .. 22	1925
1345	25	Mon.	June	29 .. July 12	1926
1346	26 K	Fri.	,,	18 .. July 1	1927
1347	27	Wed.	,,	7 .. 20	1928
1348	28	Sun.	May	27 .. June 9	1929
1349	29 K	Thurs.	,,	16 .. 29	1930
1350	30	Tues.	,,	6 .. 19	1931

A.H.		Date of Muharram 1.			A.D.
1351	1	Sat.	April	24 .. May 7	1932
1352	2 K	Wed.	,,	13 .. 26	1933
1353	3	Mon.	,,	3 .. 16	1934
1354	4	Fri.	Mar.	23 .. April 5	1935
1355	5 K	Tues.	,,	11 .. 24	1936
1356	6	Sun.	,,	1 .. 14	1937
1357	7 K	Thurs.	Feb.	18 .. Mar. 3	1938
1358	8	Tues.	,,	8 .. 21	1939
1359	9	Sat.	Jan.	28 .. Feb. 10	1940
1360	10 K	Wed.	,,	16 .. 29	1941
1361	11	Mon.	,,	6 .. 19	1942
1362	12	Fri.	Dec.	26, 1942 .. Jan. 8	1943
1363	13 K	Tues.	,,	15 .. 28	,,
1364	14	Sun.	,,	4 .. 17	1944
1365	15	Thurs.	Nov.	23 .. Dec. 6	1945
1366	16 K	Mon.	,,	12 .. 25	1946
1367	17	Sat.	,,	2 .. 15	1947
1368	18 K	Wed.	Oct.	21 .. Nov. 3	1948
1369	19	Mon.	,,	11 .. 24	1949
1370	20	Fri.	Sept.	30 .. Oct. 13	1950
1371	21 K	Tues.	,,	19 .. Oct. 2	1951
1372	22	Sun.	,,	8 .. 21	1952
1373	23	Thurs.	Aug.	28 .. Sept. 10	1953
1374	24 K	Mon.	,,	17 .. 30	1954
1375	25	Sat.	,,	7 .. 20	1955
1376	26 K	Wed.	July	26 .. Aug. 8	1956
1377	27	Mon.	,,	16 .. 29	1957
1378	28	Fri.	,,	5 .. 18	1958
1379	29 K	Tues.	June	24 .. July 7	1959
1380	30	Sun.	,,	13 .. 26	1960
1381	1	Thurs.	,,	2 .. 15	1961
1382	2 K	Mon.	May	22 .. June 4	1962
1383	3	Sat.	,,	12 .. 25	1963
1384	4	Wed.	April	30 .. May 13	1964
1385	5 K	Sun.	,,	19 .. May 2	1965
1386	6	Fri.	,,	9 .. 22	1966
1387	7 K	Tues.	Mar.	29 .. April 11	1967
1388	8	Sun.	,,	18 .. 31	1968
1389	9	Thurs.	,,	7 .. 20	1969
1390	10 K	Mon.	Feb.	24 .. Mar. 9	1970
1391	11	Sat.	,,	14 .. 27	1971
1392	12	Wed.	,,	3 .. 16	1972
1393	13 K	Sun.	Jan.	22 .. Feb. 4	1973
1394	14	Fri.	,,	12 .. 25	1974
1395	15	Tues.	,,	1 .. 14	1975
1396	16 K	Sat.	Dec.	21, 1975 .. Jan. 3	1976
1397	17	Thurs.	,,	10 .. 23	,,
1398	18 K	Mon.	Nov.	29 .. Dec. 12	1977
1399	19	Sat.	,,	19 .. Dec. 2	1978
1400	20	Wed.	,,	8 .. 21	1979
1401	21 K	Sun.	Oct.	27 .. Nov. 9	1980
1402	22	Fri.	,,	17 .. 30	1981
1403	23	Tues.	,,	6 .. 19	1982
1404	24 K	Sat.	Sept.	25 .. Oct. 8	1983
1405	25	Thurs.	,,	14 .. 27	1984
1406	26 K	Mon.	,,	3 .. 16	1985
1407	27	Sat.	Aug.	24 .. Sept. 6	1986
1408	28	Wed.	,,	13 .. 26	1987
1409	29 K	Sun.	,,	2 .. 14	1988
1410	30	Fri.	July	22 .. Aug. 4	1989
1411	1	Tues.	,,	11 .. 24	1990
1412	2 K	Sat.	June	30 .. July 13	1991
1413	3	Thurs.	,,	19 .. July 2	1992
1414	4	Mon.	,,	8 .. 21	1993
1415	5 K	Fri.	May	28 .. June 10	1994
1416	6	Wed.	,,	18 .. 31	1995
1417	7 K	Sun.	,,	6 .. 19	1996
1418	8	Fri.	April	26 .. May 9	1997
1419	9	Tues.	,,	15 .. 28	1998
1420	10 K	Sat.	,,	4 .. 17	1999
1421	11	Thurs.	Mar.	24 .. April 6	2000
1422	12	Mon.	,,	13 .. 26	2001
1423	13 K	Fri.	,,	2 .. 15	2002
1424	14	Wed.	Feb.	20 .. Mar. 5	2003
1425	15	Sun.	,,	9 .. 22	2004
1426	16 K	Thurs.	Jan.	28 .. Feb. 10	2005
1427	17	Tues.	,,	18 .. 31	2006
1428	18 K	Sat.	,,	7 .. 20	2007
1429	19	Thurs.	Dec.	28, 2007 .. Jan. 10	2008
1430	20	Mon.	,,	16 .. 29	,,
1431	21 K	Fri.	,,	5 .. 18	2009
1432	22	Wed.	Nov.	25 .. Dec. 8	2010
1433	23	Sun.	,,	14 .. 27	2011
1434	24 K	Thurs.	,,	2 .. 15	2012
1435	25	Tues.	Oct.	23 .. Nov. 5	2013
1436	26 K	Sat.	,,	12 .. 25	2014
1437	27	Thurs.	,,	2 .. 15	2015
1438	28	Mon.	Sept.	20 .. Oct. 3	2016
1439	29 K	Fri.	,,	9 .. 22	2017
1440	30	Wed.	Aug.	30 .. Sept. 12	2018

A.H.		Date of Muḥarram 1.		A.D.
1441	1	Sun.	Aug. 19 .. Sept. 1	2019
1442	2 K	Thurs.	„ 7 .. 20	2020
1443	3	Tues.	July 28 .. Aug. 10	2021
1444	4	Sat.	„ 17 .. 30	2022
1445	5 K	Wed.	„ 6 .. 19	2023
1446	6	Mon.	June 25 .. July 8	2024
1447	7 K	Fri.	„ 14 .. 27	2025
1448	8	Wed.	„ 4 .. 17	2026
1449	9	Sun.	May 24 .. June 6	2027
1450	10 K	Thurs.	„ 12 .. 25	2028
1451	11	Tues.	„ 2 .. 15	2029
1452	12	Sat.	April 21 .. May 4	2030
1453	13 K	Wed.	„ 10 .. 23	2031
1454	14	Mon.	Mar. 30 .. April 12	2032
1455	15	Fri.	„ 19 .. April 1	2033
1456	16 K	Tues.	„ 8 .. 21	2034
1457	17	Sun.	Feb. 26 .. Mar. 11	2035
1458	18 K	Thurs.	„ 15 .. 28	2036
1459	19	Tues.	„ 4 .. 17	2037
1460	20	Sat.	Jan. 24 .. Feb. 6	2038
1461	21 K	Wed.	„ 13 .. 26	2039
1462	22	Mon.	„ 3 .. 16	2040
1463	23	Fri.	Dec. 22, 2040 .. Jan. 4	2041
1464	24 K	Tues.	„ 11 .. 24	„
1465	25	Sun.	„ 1 .. 14	2042
1466	26 K	Thurs.	Nov. 20 .. Dec. 3	2043
1467	27	Tues.	„ 9 .. 22	2044
1468	28	Sat.	Oct. 29 .. Nov. 11	2045
1469	29 K	Wed.	„ 18 .. 31	2046
1470	30	Mon.	„ 8 .. 21	2047
1471	1	Fri.	Sept. 26 .. Oct. 9	2048
1472	2 K	Tues.	„ 15 .. 28	2049
1473	3	Sun.	„ 5 .. 18	2050
1474	4	Thurs.	Aug. 25 .. Sept. 7	2051
1475	5 K	Mon.	„ 13 .. 26	2052
1476	6	Sat.	„ 3 .. 16	2053
1477	7 K	Wed.	July 23 .. Aug. 5	2054
1478	8	Mon.	„ 13 .. 26	2055
1479	9	Fri.	„ 1 .. 14	2056
1480	10 K	Tues.	June 20 .. July 3	2057
1481	11	Sun.	„ 10 .. 23	2058
1482	12	Thurs.	May 30 .. June 12	2059
1483	13 K	Mon.	„ 18 .. 31	2060
1484	14	Sat.	„ 8 .. 21	2061
1485	15	Wed.	April 27 .. May 10	2062
1486	16 K	Sun.	April 16 .. 29	2063
1487	17	Fri.	„ 5 .. 18	2064
1488	18 K	Tues.	Mar. 25 .. April 7	2065
1489	19	Sun.	„ 15 .. 28	2066
1490	20	Thurs.	„ 4 .. 17	2067
1491	21 K	Mon.	Feb. 21 .. Mar. 5	2068
1492	22	Sat.	„ 10 .. 23	2069
1493	23	Wed.	Jan. 30 .. Feb. 12	2070
1494	24 K	Sun.	„ 19 .. Feb. 1	2071
1495	25	Fri.	„ 9 .. 22	2072
1496	26 K	Tues.	Dec. 28, 2072 .. Jan. 10	2073
1497	27	Sun.	„ 18 .. 31	„
1498	28	Thurs.	„ 7 .. 20	2074
1499	29 K	Mon.	Nov. 26 .. Dec. 9	2075
1500	30	Sat.	„ 15 .. 28	2076
1501	1	Wed.	„ 4 .. 17	2077
1502	2 K	Sun.	Oct. 24 .. Nov. 6	2078
1503	3	Fri.	„ 14 .. 27	2079
1504	4	Tues.	„ 2 .. 15	2080
1505	5 K	Sat.	Sept. 21 .. Oct. 4	2081
1506	6	Thurs.	„ 11 .. 24	2082
1507	7 K	Mon.	Aug. 31 .. Sept. 13	2083
1508	8	Sat.	„ 20 .. Sept. 2	2084
1509	9	Wed.	„ 9 .. 22	2085
1510	10 K	Sun.	July 29 .. Aug. 11	2086
1511	11	Fri.	„ 19 .. Aug. 1	2087
1512	12	Tues.	„ 7 .. 20	2088
1513	13 K	Sat.	June 26 .. July 9	2089
1514	14	Thurs.	„ 16 .. 29	2090
1515	15	Mon.	„ 5 .. 18	2091
1516	16 K	Fri.	May 24 .. June 6	2092
1517	17	Wed.	„ 14 .. 27	2093
1518	18 K	Sun.	„ 3 .. 16	2094
1519	19	Fri.	April 23 .. May 6	2095
1520	20	Tues.	„ 11 .. 24	2096
1521	21 K	Sat.	Mar. 31 .. April 13	2097
1522	22	Thurs.	„ 21 .. April 3	2098
1523	23	Mon.	„ 10 .. 23	2099
1524	24 K	Fri.	Feb. 27 .. Mar. 12	2100
1525	25	Wed.	„ 16 .. Mar. 2	2101
1526	26 K	Sun.	„ 5 .. 19	2102
1527	27	Fri.	Jan. 26 .. Feb. 9	2103
1528	28	Tues.	„ 15 .. 29	2104
1529	29 K	Sat.	„ 3 .. 17	2105
1530	30	Thurs.	Dec. 24, 2105 .. Jan. 7	2106

A.H.		Date of Muharram 1.			A.D.
1531	1	Mon.	Dec.	13 .. 27	2106
1532	2 K	Fri.	„	2 .. 16	2107
1533	3	Wed.	Nov.	21 .. Dec. 5	2108
1534	4	Sun.	„	10 .. 24	2109
1535	5 K	Thurs.	Oct.	30 .. Nov. 13	2110
1536	6	Tues.	„	20 .. Nov. 3	2111
1537	7 K	Sat.	„	8 .. 22	2112
1538	8	Thurs.	Sept.	28 .. Oct. 12	2113
1539	9	Mon.	„	17 .. Oct. 1	2114
1540	10 K	Fri.	„	6 .. 20	2115
1541	11	Wed.	Aug.	26 .. Sept. 9	2116
1542	12	Sun.	„	15 .. 29	2117
1543	13 K	Thurs.	„	4 .. 18	2118
1544	14	Tues.	July	25 .. Aug. 8	2119
1545	15	Sat.	„	13 .. 27	2120
1546	16 K	Wed.	„	2 .. 16	2121
1547	17	Mon.	June	22 .. July 6	2122
1548	18 K	Fri.	„	11 .. 25	2123
1549	19	Wed.	May	31 .. June 14	2124
1550	20	Sun.	„	20 .. June 3	2125
1551	21 K	Thurs.	„	9 .. 23	2126
1552	22	Tues.	April	29 .. May 13	2127
1553	23	Sat.	„	17 .. May 1	2128
1554	24 K	Wed.	„	6 .. 20	2129
1555	25	Mon.	Mar.	27 .. April 10	2130
1556	26 K	Fri.	„	16 .. 30	2131
1557	27	Wed.	„	5 .. 19	2132
1558	28	Sun.	Feb.	22 .. Mar. 8	2133
1559	29 K	Thurs.	„	11 .. 25	2134
1560	30	Tues.	„	1 .. 15	2135
1561	1	Sat.	Jan.	21 .. Feb. 4	2136
1562	2 K	Wed.	„	9 .. 23	2137
1563	3	Mon.	Dec.	30, 2137 .. Jan 13	2138
1564	4	Fri.	„	19, 2138 .. Jan. 2	2139
1565	5 K	Tues.	„	8 .. 22	„
1566	6	Sun.	Nov.	27 .. Dec. 11	2140
1567	7 K	Thurs.	„	16 .. 30	2141
1568	8	Tues.	„	6 .. 20	2142
1569	9	Sat.	Oct.	26 .. Nov. 9	2143
1570	10 K	Wed.	„	14 .. 28	2144
1571	11	Mon.	„	4 .. 18	2145
1572	12	Fri.	Sept.	23 .. Oct. 7	2146
1573	13 K	Tues.	„	12 .. 26	2147
1574	14	Sun.	„	1 .. 15	2148
1675	15	Thurs.	Aug.	21 .. Sept. 4	2149
1576	16 K	Mon.	Aug.	10 .. 24	2150
1577	17	Sat.	July	31 .. Aug. 14	2151
1578	18 K	Wed.	„	19 .. Aug. 2	2152
1579	19	Mon.	„	9 .. 23	2153
1580	20	Fri.	June	28 .. July 12	2154
1581	21 K	Tues.	„	17 .. July 1	2155
1582	22	Sun.	„	6 .. 20	2156
1583	23	Thurs.	May	26 .. June 9	2157
1584	24 K	Mon.	„	15 .. 29	2158
1585	25	Sat.	„	5 .. 19	2159
1586	26 K	Wed.	April	23 .. May 7	2160
1587	27	Mon.	„	13 .. 27	2161
1588	28	Fri.	„	2 .. 16	2162
1589	29 K	Tues.	Mar.	22 .. April 5	2163
1590	30	Sun.	„	11 .. 25	2164
1591	1	Thurs.	Feb.	28 .. Mar. 14	2165
1592	2 K	Mon.	„	17 .. Mar. 3	2166
1593	3	Sat.	„	7 .. 21	2167
1594	4	Wed.	Jan.	27 .. Feb. 10	2168
1595	5 K	Sun.	„	15 .. 29	2169
1596	6	Fri.	„	5 .. 19	2170
1597	7 K	Tues.	Dec.	25, 2170 .. Jan. 8	2171
1598	8	Sun.	„	15 .. 29	„
1599	9	Thurs.	„	3 .. 17	2172
1600	10 K	Mon.	Nov.	22 .. Dec. 6	2173
1601	11	Sat.	„	12 .. 26	2174
1602	12	Wed.	„	1 .. 15	2175
1603	13 K	Sun.	Oct.	20 .. Nov. 3	2176
1604	14	Fri.	„	10 .. 24	2177
1605	15	Tues.	Sept.	29 .. Oct. 13	2178
1606	16 K	Sat.	„	18 .. Oct. 2	2179
1607	17	Thurs.	„	7 .. 21	2180
1608	18 K	Mon.	Aug.	27 .. Sept. 10	2181
1609	19	Sat.	„	17 .. 31	2182
1610	20	Wed.	„	6 .. 20	2183
1611	21 K	Sun.	July	25 .. Aug. 8	2184
1612	22	Fri.	„	15 .. 29	2185
1613	23	Tues.	„	4 .. 18	2186
1614	24 K	Sat.	June	23 .. July 7	2187
1615	25	Thurs.	„	12 .. 26	2188
1616	26 K	Mon.	„	1 .. 15	2189
1617	27	Sat.	May	22 .. June 5	2190
1618	28	Wed.	„	11 .. 25	2191
1619	29 K	Sun.	April	29 .. May 13	2192
1620	30	Fri.	„	19 .. May 3	2193

A.H.		Date of Muharram 1.			A.D.
1621	1	Tues.	April	8 .. 22	2194
1622	2 K	Sat.	Mar.	28 .. April 11	2195
1623	3	Thurs.	„	17 .. 31	2196
1624	4	Mon.	„	6 .. 20	2197
1625	5 K	Fri.	Feb.	23 .. Mar. 9	2198
1626	6	Wed.	„	13 .. 27	2199
1627	7 K	Sun.	„	2 .. 16	2200
1628	8	Fri.	Jan.	22 .. Feb. 6	2201
1629	9	Tues.	„	11 .. 26	2202
1630	10 K	Sat.	Dec.	31, 2202 .. Jan. 15	2203
1631	11	Thurs.	„	21, 2203 .. Jan. 5	2204
1632	12	Mon.	„	9 .. 24	„
1633	13 K	Fri.	Nov.	28 .. Dec. 13	2205
1634	14	Wed.	„	18 .. Dec. 3	2206
1635	15	Sun.	„	7 .. 22	2207
1636	16 K	Thurs.	Oct.	26 .. Nov. 10	2208
1637	17	Tues.	„	16 .. 31	2209
1638	18 K	Sat.	„	5 .. 20	2210
1639	19	Thurs.	Sept.	25 .. Oct. 10	2211
1640	20	Mon.	„	13 .. 28	2212
1641	21 K	Fri.	„	2 .. 17	2213
1642	22	Wed.	Aug.	23 .. Sept. 7	2214
1643	23	Sun.	„	12 .. 27	2215
1644	24 K	Thurs.	July	31 .. Aug. 15	2216
1645	25	Tues.	„	21 .. Aug. 5	2217
1646	26 K	Sat.	„	10 .. 25	2218
1647	27	Thurs.	June	30 .. July 15	2219
1648	28	Mon.	„	18 .. July 3	2220
1649	29 K	Fri.	„	7 .. 22	2221
1650	30	Wed.	May	28 .. June 12	2222
1651	1	Sun.	„	17 .. June 1	2223
1652	2 K	Thurs.	„	5 .. 20	2224
1653	3	Tues.	April	25 .. May 10	2225
1654	4	Sat.	„	14 .. 29	2226
1655	5 K	Wed.	„	3 .. 18	2227
1656	6	Mon.	Mar.	23 .. April 7	2228
1657	7 K	Fri.	„	12 .. 27	2229
1658	8	Wed.	„	2 .. 17	2230
1659	9	Sun.	Feb.	19 .. Mar. 6	2231
1660	10 K	Thurs.	„	8 .. 23	2232
1661	11	Tues.	Jan.	28 .. Feb. 12	2233
1662	12	Sat.	„	17 .. Feb. 1	2234
1663	13 K	Wed.	„	6 .. 21	2235
1664	14	Mon.	Dec.	27, 2235 .. Jan. 11	2236
1665	15	Fri.	„	15 .. 30	„
1666	16 K	Tues.	Dec.	4 .. 19	2237
1667	17	Sun.	Nov.	24 .. Dec. 9	2238
1668	18 K	Thurs.	„	13 .. 28	2239
1669	19	Tues.	„	2 .. 17	2240
1670	20	Sat.	Oct.	22 .. Nov. 6	2241
1671	21 K	Wed.	„	11 .. 26	2242
1672	22	Mon.	„	1 .. 16	2243
1673	23	Fri.	Sept.	19 .. Oct. 4	2244
1674	24 K	Tues.	„	8 .. 23	2245
1675	25	Sun.	Aug.	29 .. Sept. 13	2246
1676	26 K	Thurs.	„	18 .. Sept. 2	2247
1677	27	Tues.	„	7 .. 22	2248
1678	28	Sat.	July	27 .. Aug. 11	2249
1679	29 K	Wed.	„	16 .. 31	2250
1680	30	Mon.	„	6 .. 21	2251
1681	1	Fri.	June	24 .. July 9	2252
1682	2 K	Tues.	„	13 .. 28	2253
1683	3	Sun.	„	3 .. 18	2254
1684	4	Thurs.	May	23 .. June 7	2255
1685	5 K	Mon.	„	11 .. 26	2256
1686	6	Sat.	„	1 .. 16	2257
1687	7 K	Wed.	April	20 .. May 5	2258
1688	8	Mon.	„	10 .. 25	2259
1689	9	Fri.	Mar.	29 .. April 13	2260
1690	10 K	Tues.	„	18 .. April 2	2261
1691	11	Sun.	„	8 .. 23	2262
1692	12	Thurs.	Feb.	25 .. Mar. 12	2263
1693	13 K	Mon.	„	14 .. 29	2264
1694	14	Sat.	„	3 .. 18	2265
1695	15	Wed	Jan.	23 .. Feb. 7	2266
1696	16 K	Sun.	„	12 .. 27	2267
1697	17	Fri.	„	2 .. 17	2268
1698	18 K	Tues.	Dec.	21, 2268 .. Jan. 5	2269
1699	19	Sun.	„	11 .. 26	„
1700	20	Thurs.	Nov.	30 .. Dec. 15	2270
1701	21 K	Mon.	„	19 .. Dec. 4	2271
1702	22	Sat.	„	8 .. 23	2272
1703	23	Wed.	Oct.	28 .. Nov. 12	2273
1704	24 K	Sun.	„	17 .. Nov. 1	2274
1705	25	Fri.	„	7 .. 22	2275
1706	26 K	Tues.	Sept.	25 .. Oct. 10	2276
1707	27	Sun.	„	15 .. 30	2277
1708	28	Thurs.	„	4 .. 19	2278
1709	29 K	Mon.	Aug.	24 .. Sept. 8	2279
1710	30	Sat.	„	13 .. 28	2280

A.H.		Date of Muḥarram 1.			A.D.
1711	1	Wed.	Aug.	2 .. 17	2281
1712	2 K	Sun.	July	22 .. Aug. 6	2282
1713	3	Fri.	„	12 .. 27	2283
1714	4	Tues.	June	30 .. July 15	2284
1715	5 K	Sat.	„	19 .. July 4	2285
1716	6	Thurs.	„	9 .. 24	2286
1717	7 K	Mon.	May	29 .. June 13	2287
1718	8	Sat.	„	18 .. June 2	2288
1719	9	Wed.	„	7 .. 22	2289
1720	10 K	Sun.	April	26 .. May 11	2290
1721	11	Fri.	„	16 .. May 1	2291
1722	12	Tues.	„	4 .. 19	2292
1723	13 K	Sat.	Mar.	24 .. April 8	2293
1724	14	Thurs.	„	14 .. 29	2294
1725	15	Mon.	„	3 .. 18	2295
1726	16 K	Fri.	Feb.	20 .. Mar. 6	2296
1727	17	Wed.	„	9 .. 24	2297
1728	18 K	Sun.	Jan.	29 .. Feb. 13	2298
1729	19	Fri.	„	19 .. Feb. 3	2299
1730	20	Tues.	„	8 .. 23	2300
1731	21 K	Sat.	Dec.	27, 2300 .. Jan. 12	2301
1732	22	Thurs.	„	17, 2301 .. Jan. 2	2302
1733	23	Mon.	„	6 .. 22	„
1734	24 K	Fri.	Nov.	25 .. Dec. 11	2303
1735	25	Wed.	„	14 .. 30	2304
1736	26 K	Sun.	„	3 .. 19	2305
1737	27	Fri.	Oct.	24 .. Nov. 9	2306
1738	28	Tues.	„	13 .. 29	2307
1739	29 K	Sat.	„	1 .. 17	2308
1740	30	Thurs.	Sept.	21 .. Oct. 7	2309
1741	1	Mon.	„	10 .. 26	2310
1742	2 K	Fri.	Aug.	30 .. Sept. 15	2311
1743	3	Wed.	„	19 .. Sept. 4	2312
1744	4	Sun.	„	8 .. 24	2313
1745	5 K	Thurs.	July	28 .. Aug. 13	2314
1746	6	Tues.	„	18 .. Aug. 3	2315
1747	7 K	Sat.	„	6 .. 22	2316
1748	8	Thurs.	June	26 .. July 12	2317
1749	9	Mon.	„	15 .. July 1	2318
1750	10 K	Fri.	„	4 .. 20	2319
1751	11	Wed.	May	24 .. June 9	2320
1752	12	Sun.	„	13 .. 29	2321
1753	13 K	Thurs.	„	2 .. 18	2322
1754	14	Tues.	April	22 .. May 8	2323
1755	15	Sat.	„	10 .. 26	2324

A.H.		Date of Muḥarram 1.			A.D.
1756	16 K	Wed.	Mar.	30 .. April 15	2325
1757	17	Mon.	„	20 .. April 5	2326
1758	18 K	Fri.	„	9 .. 25	2327
1759	19	Wed.	Feb.	27 .. Mar. 14	2328
1760	20	Sun.	„	15 .. Mar. 3	2329
1761	21 K	Thurs.	„	4 .. 20	2330
1762	22	Tues.	Jan.	25 .. Feb. 10	2331
1763	23	Sat.	„	14 .. 30	2332
1764	24 K	Wed.	„	2 .. 18	2333
1765	25	Mon.	Dec.	23, 2333 .. Jan. 8	2334
1766	26 K	Fri.	„	12 .. 28	„
1767	27	Wed.	„	2 .. 18	2335
1768	28	Sun.	Nov.	20 .. Dec. 6	2336
1769	29 K	Thurs.	„	9 .. 25	2337
1770	30	Tues.	Oct.	30 .. Nov. 15	2338
1771	1	Sat.	„	19 .. Nov. 4	2339
1772	2 K	Wed.	„	7 .. 23	2340
1773	3	Mon.	Sept.	27 .. Oct. 13	2341
1774	4	Fri.	„	16 .. Oct. 2	2342
1775	5 K	Tues.	„	5 .. 21	2343
1776	6	Sun.	Aug.	25 .. Sept. 10	2344
1777	7 K	Thurs.	„	14 .. 30	2345
1778	8	Tues.	„	4 .. 20	2346
1779	9	Sat.	July	24 .. Aug. 9	2347
1780	10 K	Wed.	„	12 .. 28	2348
1781	11	Mon.	„	2 .. 18	2349
1782	12	Fri.	June	21 .. July 7	2350
1783	13 K	Tues.	„	10 .. 26	2351
1784	14	Sun.	May	30 .. June 15	2352
1785	15	Thurs.	„	19 .. June 4	2353
1786	16 K	Mon.	„	8 .. 24	2354
1787	17	Sat.	April	28 .. May 14	2355
1788	18 K	Wed.	„	16 .. May 2	2356
1789	19	Mon.	„	6 .. 22	2357
1790	20	Fri.	Mar.	26 .. April 11	2358
1791	21 K	Tues.	„	15 .. 31	2359
1792	22	Sun.	„	4 .. 20	2360
1793	23	Thurs.	Feb.	21 .. Mar. 9	2361
1794	24 K	Mon.	„	10 .. 26	2362
1795	25	Sat.	Jan.	31 .. Feb. 16	2363
1796	26 K	Wed.	„	20 .. Feb. 5	2364
1797	27	Mon.	„	9 .. 25	2365
1798	28	Fri.	Dec.	29, 2365 .. Jan. 14	2366
1799	29 K	Tues.	„	18, 2366 .. Jan. 3	2367
1800	30	Sun.	„	8 .. 24	„

A.H.		Date of Muharram 1.	A.D.	A.H.		Date of Muharram 1.	A.D.
1801	1	Thurs. Nov 26 .. Dec. 12	2368	1846	16 K	Thurs. July 24 .. Aug. 9	2412
1802	2 K	Mon. „ 15 .. Dec. 1	2369	1847	17	Tues. „ 14 .. 30	2413
1803	3	Sat. „ 5 .. 21	2370	1848	18 K	Sat. „ 3 .. 19	2414
1804	4	Wed. Oct. 25 .. Nov. 10	2371	1849	19	Thurs. June 23 .. July 9	2415
1805	5 K	Sun. „ 13 .. 29	2372	1850	20	Mon. „ 11 .. 27	2416
1806	6	Fri. „ 3 .. 19	2373	1851	21 K	Fri. May 31 .. June 16	2417
1807	7 K	Tues. Sept. 22 .. Oct. 8	2374	1852	22	Wed. „ 21 .. June 6	2418
1808	8	Sun. „ 12 .. 28	2375	1853	23	Sun. „ 10 .. 26	2419
1809	9	Thurs. Aug. 31 .. Sept. 16	2376	1854	24 K	Thurs. April 28 .. May 14	2420
1810	10 K	Mon. „ 20 .. Sept. 5	2377	1855	25	Tues. „ 18 .. May 4	2421
1811	11	Sat. „ 10 .. 26	2378	1856	26 K	Sat. „ 7 .. 23	2422
1812	12	Wed. July 30 .. Aug. 15	2379	1857	27	Thurs. Mar. 28 .. April 13	2423
1813	13 K	Sun. „ 18 .. Aug. 3	2380	1858	28	Mon. „ 16 .. April 1	2424
1814	14	Fri. „ 8 .. 24	2381	1859	29 K	Fri. „ 5 .. 21	2425
1815	15	Tues. June 27 .. July 13	2382	1860	30	Wed. Feb. 23 .. Mar. 11	2426
1816	16 K	Sat. „ 16 .. July 2	2383	1861	1	Sun. „ 12 .. 28	2427
1817	17	Thurs. „ 5 .. 21	2384	1862	2 K	Thurs. „ 1 .. 17	2428
1818	18 K	Mon. May 25 .. June 10	2385	1863	3	Tues. Jan. 21 .. Feb. 6	2429
1819	19	Sat. „ 15 .. 31	2386	1864	4	Sat. „ 10 .. 26	2430
1820	20	Wed. „ 4 .. 20	2387	1865	5 K	Wed. Dec. 30, 2430 .. Jan. 15	2431
1821	21 K	Sun. April 22 .. May 8	2388	1866	6	Mon. „ 20, 2431 .. Jan. 5	2432
1822	22	Fri. „ 12 .. 28	2389	1867	7 K	Fri. „ 8 .. 24	„
1823	23	Tues. „ 1 .. 17	2390	1868	8	Wed. Nov. 28 .. Dec. 14	2433
1824	24 K	Sat. Mar. 21 .. April 6	2391	1869	9	Sun. „ 17 .. Dec. 3	2434
1825	25	Thurs. „ 10 .. 26	2392	1870	10 K	Thurs. „ 6 .. 22	2435
1826	26 K	Mon. Feb. 27 .. Mar. 15	2393	1871	11	Tues. Oct. 26 .. Nov. 11	2436
1827	27	Sat. „ 17 .. Mar. 5	2394	1872	12	Sat. „ 15 .. 31	2437
1828	28	Wed. „ 6 .. 22	2395	1873	13 K	Wed. „ 4 .. 20	2438
1829	29 K	Sun. Jan. 26 .. Feb. 11	2396	1874	14	Mon. Sept. 24 .. Oct. 10	2439
1830	30	Fri. „ 15 .. 31	2397	1875	15	Fri. „ 12 .. 28	2440
1831	1	Tues. „ 4 .. 20	2398	1876	16 K	Tues. „ 1 .. 17	2441
1832	2 K	Sat. Dec. 24, 2398 .. Jan. 9	2399	1877	17	Sun. Aug. 22 .. Sept. 7	2442
1833	3	Thurs. „ 14 .. 30	„	1878	18 K	Thurs. „ 11 .. 27	2443
1834	4	Mon. „ 2 .. 18	2400	1879	19	Tues. July 31 .. Aug. 16	2444
1835	5 K	Fri. Nov. 21 .. Dec. 7	2401	1880	20	Sat. „ 20 .. Aug. 5	2445
1836	6	Wed. „ 11 .. 27	2402	1881	21 K	Wed. „ 9 .. 25	2446
1837	7 K	Sun. Oct. 31 .. Nov. 16	2403	1882	22	Mon. June 29 .. July 15	2447
1838	8	Fri. „ 20 .. Nov. 5	2404	1883	23	Fri. „ 17 .. July 3	2448
1839	9	Tues. „ 9 .. 25	2405	1884	24 K	Tues. „ 6 .. 22	2449
1840	10 K	Sat. Sept. 28 .. Oct. 14	2406	1885	25	Sun. May 27 .. June 12	2450
1841	11	Thurs. „ 18 .. Oct. 4	2407	1886	26 K	Thurs. „ 16 .. June 1	2451
1842	12	Mon. „ 6 .. 22	2408	1887	27	Tues. „ 5 .. 21	2452
1843	13 K	Fri. Aug. 26 .. Sept. 11	2409	1888	28	Sat. April 24 .. May 10	2453
1844	14	Wed. „ 16 .. Sept. 1	2410	1889	29 K	Wed. „ 13 .. 29	2454
1845	15	Sun. „ 5 .. 21	2411	1890	30	Mon. „ 3 .. 13	2455

A.H.		Date of Muḥarram 1.	A.D.
1891	1	Fri. Mar. 22 .. April 7	2456
1892	2 K	Tues. „ 11 .. 27	2457
1893	3	Sun. „ 1 .. 17	2458
1894	4	Thurs. Feb. 18 .. Mar. 6	2459
1895	5 K	Mon. „ 7 .. 23	2460
1896	6	Sat. Jan. 27 .. Feb. 12	2461
1897	7 K	Wed. „ 16 .. Feb. 1	2462
1898	8	Mon. „ 6 .. 22	2463
1899	9	Fri. Dec. 26, 2463 .. Jan. 11	2464
1900	10 K	Tues. „ 14 .. 30	„
1901	11	Sun. „ 4 .. 20	2465
1902	12	Thurs. Nov. 23 .. Dec. 9	2466
1903	13 K	Mon. „ 12 .. 28	2467
1904	14	Sat. „ 1 .. 17	2468
1905	15	Wed. Oct. 21 .. Nov. 6	2469
1906	16 K	Sun. „ 10 .. 26	2470
1907	17	Fri. Sept. 30 .. Oct. 16	2471
1908	18 K	Tues. „ 18 .. Oct. 4	2472
1909	19	Sun. „ 8 .. 24	2473
1910	20	Thurs. Aug. 28 .. Sept. 13	2474
1911	21 K	Mon. „ 17 .. Sept. 2	2475
1912	22	Sat. „ 6 .. 22	2476
1913	23	Wed. July 26 .. Aug. 11	2477
1914	24 K	Sun. „ 15 .. 31	2478
1915	25	Fri. „ 5 .. 21	2479
1916	26 K	Tues. June 23 .. July 9	2480
1917	27	Sun. „ 13 .. 29	2481
1918	28	Thurs. „ 2 .. 18	2482
1919	29 K	Mon. May 22 .. June 5	2483
1920	30	Sat. „ 11 .. 27	2484
1921	1	Wed. April 30 .. May 16	2485
1922	2 K	Sun. „ 19 .. May 5	2486
1923	3	Fri. „ 9 .. 25	2487
1924	4	Tues. Mar. 28 .. April 13	2488
1925	5 K	Sat. „ 17 .. April 2	2489
1926	6	Thurs. „ 7 .. 23	2490
1927	7 K	Mon. Feb. 24 .. Mar. 12	2491
1928	8	Sat. „ 14 .. Mar. 1	2492
1929	9	Wed. „ 2 .. 18	2493
1930	10 K	Sun. Jan. 22 .. Feb. 7	2494
1931	11	Fri. „ 12 .. 28	2495
1932	12	Tues. „ 1 .. 17	2496
1933	13 K	Sat. Dec. 20, 2496 .. Jan. 5	2497
1934	14	Thurs. „ 10 .. 26	„
1935	15	Mon. Nov. 29 .. Dec. 15	2498

A.H.		Date of Muḥarram 1.	A.D.
1936	16 K	Fri. Nov. 18 .. Dec. 4	2499
1937	17	Wed. „ 7 .. 24	2500
1938	18 K	Sun. Oct. 27 .. Nov. 13	2501
1939	19	Fri. „ 17 .. Nov. 3	2502
1940	20	Tues. „ 6 .. 23	2503
1941	21 K	Sat. Sept. 24 .. Oct. 11	2504
1942	22	Thurs. „ 14 .. Oct. 1	2505
1943	23	Mon. „ 3 .. 20	2506
1944	24 K	Fri. Aug. 23 .. Sept. 9	2507
1945	25	Wed. „ 12 .. 29	2508
1946	26 K	Sun. „ 1 .. 18	2509
1947	27	Fri. July 22 .. Aug. 8	2510
1948	28	Tues. „ 11 .. 28	2511
1949	29 K	Sat. June 29 .. July 16	2512
1950	30	Thurs. „ 19 .. July 6	2513
1951	1	Mon. „ 8 .. 25	2514
1952	2 K	Fri. May 28 .. June 14	2515
1953	3	Wed. „ 17 .. June 3	2516
1954	4	Sun. „ 6 .. 23	2517
1955	5 K	Thurs. April 25 .. May 12	2518
1956	6	Tues. „ 15 .. May 2	2519
1957	7 K	Sat. „ 3 .. 20	2520
1958	8	Thurs. Mar. 24 .. April 10	2521
1959	9	Mon. „ 13 .. April 30	2522
1960	10 K	Fri. „ 2 .. 19	2523
1961	11	Wed. Feb. 20 .. Mar. 9	2524
1962	12	Sun. „ 8 .. 25	2525
1963	13 K	Thurs. Jan. 28 .. Feb. 14	2526
1964	14	Tues. „ 18 .. Feb. 4	2527
1965	15	Sat. „ 7 .. 24	2528
1966	16 K	Wed. Dec. 26, 2528 .. Jan. 12	2529
1967	17	Mon. „ 16, 2529 .. Jan. 2	2530
1968	18 K	Fri. „ 5 .. 22	„
1969	19	Wed. Nov. 25 .. Dec. 12	2531
1970	20	Sun. „ 13 .. 30	2532
1971	21 K	Thurs. „ 2 .. 19	2533
1972	22	Tues. Oct. 23 .. Nov. 9	2534
1973	23	Sat. „ 12 .. 29	2535
1974	24 K	Wed. Sept. 30 .. Oct. 17	2536
1975	25	Mon. „ 20 .. Oct. 7	2537
1976	26 K	Fri. „ 9 .. 26	2538
1977	27	Wed. Aug. 30 .. Sept. 16	2539
1978	28	Sun. „ 18 .. Sept. 4	2540
1979	29 K	Thurs. „ 7 .. 24	2541
1980	30	Tues. July 28 .. Aug. 14	2542

A.H.		Date of Muḥarram 1.		A.D.
1981	1	Sat.	July 17 .. Aug. 3	2543
1982	2 K	Wed.	,, 5 .. 22	2544
1983	3	Mon.	June 25 .. July 12	2545
1984	4	Fri.	,, 14 .. June 1	2546
1985	5 K	Tues.	,, 3 .. 20	2547
1986	6	Sun.	May 23 .. June 9	2548
1987	7 K	Thurs.	,, 12 .. 29	2549
1988	8	Tues.	,, 2 .. 19	2550
1989	9	Sat.	April 21 .. May 8	2551
1990	10 K	Wed.	,, 9 .. 26	2552
1991	11	Mon.	Mar. 30 .. April 16	2553
1992	12	Fri.	,, 19 .. April 5	2554
1993	13 K	Tues.	,, 8 .. 25	2555
1994	14	Sun.	Feb. 26 .. Mar. 14	2556
1995	15	Thurs.	,, 14 .. Mar. 3	2557
1996	16 K	Mon.	,, 3 .. 20	2558
1997	17	Sat.	Jan. 24 .. Feb. 11	2559
1998	18 K	Wed.	,, 13 .. 30	2560
1999	19	Mon.	,, 2 .. 19	2561
2000	20	Fri.	Dec. 22, 2561 .. Jan. 8	2562
2001	21 K	Tues.	,, 11 .. 28	,,
2002	22	Sun.	,, 1 .. 18	2563
2003	23	Thurs.	Nov. 19 .. Dec. 6	2564
2004	24 K	Mon.	,, 8 .. 25	2565
2005	25	Sat.	Oct. 29 .. Nov. 15	2566
2006	26 K	Wed.	,, 18 .. Nov. 4	2567
2007	27	Mon.	,, 7 .. 24	2568
2008	28	Fri.	Sept. 26 .. Oct. 13	2569
2009	29 K	Tues.	,, 15 .. Oct. 2	2570
2010	30	Sun.	,, 5 .. 22	2571
2011	1	Thurs.	Aug. 24 .. Sept. 10	2572
2012	2 K	Mon.	,, 13 .. 30	2573
2013	3	Sat.	,, 3 .. 20	2574
2014	4	Wed.	July 23 .. Aug. 9	2575
2015	5 K	Sun.	,, 11 .. 28	2576
2016	6	Fri.	,, 1 .. 18	2577
2017	7 K	Tues.	June 20 .. July 7	2578
2018	8	Sun.	,, 10 .. 27	2579
2019	9	Thurs.	May 29 .. June 15	2580
2020	10 K	Mon.	,, 18 .. June 4	2581
2021	11	Sat.	,, 8 .. 25	2582
2022	12	Wed.	April 27 .. May 14	2583
2023	13 K	Sun.	,, 15 .. May 2	2584
2024	14	Fri.	,, 5 .. 22	2585
2025	15	Tues.	Mar. 25 .. April 11	2586
2026	16 K	Sat.	Mar. 14 .. 31	2587
2027	17	Thurs.	,, 3 .. 20	2588
2028	18 K	Mon.	Feb. 20 .. Mar. 9	2589
2029	19	Sat.	,, 10 .. 27	2590
2030	20	Wed.	Jan. 30 .. Feb. 16	2591
2031	21 K	Sun.	,, 19 .. Feb. 5	2592
2032	22	Fri.	,, 8 .. 25	2593
2033	23	Tues.	Dec. 28, 2593 .. Jan. 14	2594
2034	24 K	Sat.	,, 17, 2594 .. Jan. 3	2595
2035	25	Thurs.	,, 7 .. 24	,,
2036	26 K	Mon.	Nov. 25 .. Dec. 12	2596
2037	27	Sat.	,, 15 .. Dec. 2	2597
2038	28	Wed.	,, 4 .. 21	2598
2039	29 K	Sun.	Oct. 24 .. Nov. 10	2599
2040	30	Fri.	,, 13 .. Oct. 31	2600
2041	1	Tues.	,, 2 .. 20	2601
2042	2 K	Sat.	Sept. 21 .. Oct. 9	2602
2043	3	Thurs.	,, 11 .. 29	2603
2044	4	Mon.	Aug. 30 .. Sept. 17	2604
2045	5 K	Fri.	,, 19 .. Sept. 6	2605
2046	6	Wed.	,, 9 .. 27	2606
2047	7 K	Sun.	July 29 .. Aug. 16	2607
2048	8	Fri.	,, 18 .. Aug. 5	2608
2049	9	Tues.	,, 7 .. 25	2609
2050	10 K	Sat.	June 26 .. July 14	2610
2051	11	Thurs.	,, 16 .. July 4	2611
2052	12	Mon.	,, 4 .. 22	2612
2053	13 K	Fri.	May 24 .. June 11	2613
2054	14	Wed.	,, 14 .. June 1	2614
2055	15	Sun.	,, 3 .. 21	2615
2056	16 K	Thurs.	April 21 .. May 9	2616
2057	17	Tues.	,, 11 .. 29	2617
2058	18 K	Sat.	Mar. 31 .. April 18	2618
2059	19	Thurs.	,, 21 .. April 8	2619
2060	20	Mon.	,, 9 .. 27	2620
2061	21 K	Fri.	Feb. 26 .. Mar. 16	2621
2062	22	Wed.	,, 16 .. Mar. 6	2622
2063	23	Sun.	,, 5 .. 23	2623
2064	24 K	Thurs.	Jan. 25 .. Feb. 12	2624
2065	25	Tues.	,, 14 .. Feb. 1	2625
2066	26 K	Sat.	,, 3 .. 21	2626
2067	27	Thurs.	Dec. 24, 2626 .. Jan. 11	2627
2068	28	Mon.	,, 13 .. 31	,,
2069	29 K	Fri.	,, 1 .. 19	2628
2070	30	Wed.	Nov. 21 .. Dec. 9	2629

A.H.		Date of Muharram 1.			A.D.
2071	1	Sun.	Nov.	10 .. 28	2630
2072	2 K	Thurs.	Oct.	30 .. Nov. 17	2631
2073	3	Tues.	„	19 .. Nov. 6	2632
2074	4	Sat.	„	8 .. 26	2633
2075	5 K	Wed.	Sept.	27 .. 15	2634
2076	6	Mon.	„	17 .. Oct. 5	2635
2077	7 K	Fri.	„	5 .. 23	2636
2078	8	Wed.	Aug.	26 .. Sept. 13	2637
2079	9	Sun.	„	15 .. Sept. 2	2638
2080	10 K	Thurs.	„	4 .. 22	2639
2081	11	Tues.	July	24 .. Aug. 11	2640
2082	12	Sat.	„	13 .. 31	2641
2083	13 K	Wed.	„	2 .. 20	2642
2084	14	Mon.	June	22 .. July 10	2643
2085	15	Fri.	„	10 .. 28	2644
2086	16 K	Tues.	May	30 .. June 17	2645
2087	17	Sun.	„	20 .. June 7	2646
2088	18 K	Thurs.	„	9 .. 27	2647
2089	19	Tues.	April	28 .. May 16	2648
2090	20	Sat.	„	17 .. May 5	2649
2091	21 K	Wed.	„	6 .. 24	2650
2092	22	Mon.	Mar.	27 .. April 14	2651
2093	23	Fri.	„	15 .. April 2	2652
2094	24 K	Tues.	„	4 .. 22	2653
2095	25	Sun.	Feb.	22 .. Mar. 12	2654
2096	26 K	Thurs.	„	11 .. 29	2655
2097	27	Tues.	„	1 .. 19	2656
2098	28	Sat.	Jan.	20 .. Feb. 7	2657
2099	29 K	Wed.	„	9 .. 27	2658
2100	30	Mon.	Dec.	30, 2658 .. Jan. 17	2659
2101	1	Fri.	„	19, 2659 .. Jan. 6	2660
2102	2 K	Tues.	„	7 .. 25	„
2103	3	Sun.	Nov.	27 .. Dec. 15	2661
2104	4	Thurs.	„	16 .. Dec. 4	2662
2105	5 K	Mon.	„	5 .. 23	2663
2106	6	Sat.	Oct.	25 .. Nov. 12	2664
2107	7 K	Wed.	„	14 .. Nov. 1	2665
2108	8	Mon.	„	4 .. 22	2666
2109	9	Fri.	Sept.	23 .. Oct. 11	2667
2110	10 K	Tues.	„	11 .. 29	2668
2111	11	Sun.	„	1 .. 19	2669
2112	12	Thurs.	Aug.	21 .. Sept. 8	2670
2113	13 K	Mon.	„	10 .. 28	2671
2114	14	Sat.	July	30 .. Aug. 17	2672
2115	15	Wed.	„	19 .. Aug. 6	2673
2116	16 K	Sun.	July	8 .. 26	2674
2117	17	Fri.	June	28 .. July 16	2675
2118	18 K	Tues.	„	16 .. July 4	2676
2119	19	Sun	„	6 .. 24	2677
2120	20	Thurs.	May	26 .. June 13	2678
2121	21 K	Mon.	„	15 .. June 2	2679
2122	22	Sat.	„	4 .. 22	2680
2123	23	Wed.	April	23 .. May 11	2681
2124	24 K	Sun.	„	12 .. 30	2682
2125	25	Fri.	„	2 .. 20	2683
2126	26 K	Tues.	Mar.	21 .. April 8	2684
2127	27	Sun.	„	11 .. 29	2685
2128	28	Thurs.	Feb.	28 .. Mar. 18	2686
2129	29 K	Mon.	„	17 .. Mar 7	2687
2130	30	Sat.	„	7 .. 25	2688
2131	1	Wed.	Jan.	26 .. Feb. 13	2689
2132	2 K	Sun.	„	15 .. Feb. 2	2690
2133	3	Fri.	„	5 .. 23	2691
2134	4	Tues.	Dec.	25, 2691 .. Jan. 12	2692
2135	5 K	Sat.	„	13 .. 31	„
2136	6	Thurs.	„	3 .. 21	2693
2137	7 K	Mon.	Nov.	22 .. Dec. 10	2694
2138	8	Sat.	„	12 .. 30	2695
2139	9	Wed.	Oct.	31 .. Nov. 18	2696
2140	10 K	Sun.	„	20 .. Nov. 7	2697
2141	11	Fri.	„	10 .. 28	2698
2142	12	Tues.	Sept.	29 .. Oct. 17	2699
2143	13 K	Sat.	„	17 .. Oct. 5	2700
2144	14	Thurs.	„	7 .. 26	2701
2145	15	Mon.	Aug.	27 .. Sept. 15	2702
2146	16 K	Fri.	„	16 .. Sept. 4	2703
2147	17	Wed.	„	5 .. 24	2704
2148	18 K	Sun.	July	25 .. Aug. 13	2705
2149	19	Fri.	„	15 .. Aug. 3	2706
2150	20	Tues.	„	4 .. 23	2707
2151	21 K	Sat.	June	22 .. July 11	2708
2152	22	Thurs.	„	12 .. July 1	2709
2153	23	Mon.	„	1 .. 20	2710
2154	24 K	Fri.	May	21 .. June 9	2711
2155	25	Wed.	„	10 .. 29	2712
2156	26 K	Sun.	April	29 .. May 18	2713
2157	27	Fri.	„	19 .. May 8	2714
2158	28	Tues.	„	8 .. 27	2715
2159	29 K	Sat.	Mar.	27 .. April 15	2716
2160	30	Thurs.	„	17 .. April 5	2717

A.H.		Date of Muharram 1.			A.D.
2161	1	Mon.	Mar.	6 .. 25	2718
2162	2 K	Fri.	Feb.	23 .. Mar. 14	2719
2163	3	Wed.	„	13 .. Mar. 3	2720
2164	4	Sun.	„	1 .. 20	2721
2165	5 K	Thurs.	Jan.	21 .. Feb. 9	2722
2166	6	Tues.	„	11 .. 30	2723
2167	7 K	Sat.	Dec.	31, 2723 .. Jan. 19	2724
2168	8	Thurs.	„	20, 2724 .. Jan. 8	2725
2169	9	Mon.	„	9 .. 28	„
2170	10 K	Fri.	Nov.	28 .. Dec. 17	2726
2171	11	Wed.	„	18 .. Dec. 7	2727
2172	12	Sun.	„	6 .. 25	2728
2173	13 K	Thurs.	Oct.	26 .. Nov. 14	2729
2174	14	Tues.	„	16 .. Nov. 4	2730
2175	15	Sat.	„	5 .. 24	2731
2176	16 K	Wed.	Sept.	23 .. Oct. 12	2732
2177	17	Mon.	„	13 .. Oct. 2	2733
2178	18 K	Fri.	„	2 .. 21	2734
2179	19	Wed.	Aug.	23 .. Sept. 11	2735
2180	20	Sun.	„	11 .. 30	2736
2181	21 K	Thurs.	July	31 .. Aug. 19	2737
2182	22	Tues.	„	21 .. Aug. 9	2738
2183	23	Sat.	„	10 .. 29	2739
2184	24 K	Wed.	June	28 .. Aug. 17	2740
2185	25	Mon.	„	18 .. July 7	2741
2186	26 K	Fri.	„	7 .. 26	2742
2187	27	Wed.	May	28 .. June 16	2743
2188	28	Sun.	„	16 .. June 4	2744
2189	29 K	Thurs.	„	5 .. 24	2745
2190	30	Tues.	April	25 .. May 14	2746
2191	1	Sat.	„	14 .. May 3	2747
2192	2 K	Wed.	„	2 .. 21	2748
2193	3	Mon.	Mar.	23 .. April 11	2749
2194	4	Fri.	„	12 .. 31	2750
2195	5 K	Tues.	„	1 .. 20	2751
2196	6	Sun.	Feb.	19 .. Mar. 9	2752
2197	7 K	Thurs.	„	7 .. 26	2753
2198	8	Tues.	Jan.	28 .. Feb. 16	2754
2199	9	Sat.	„	17 .. Feb. 5	2755
2200	10 K	Wed.	„	6 .. 25	2756
2201	11	Mon.	Dec.	26, 2756 .. Jan. 14	2757
2202	12	Fri.	„	15, 2757 .. Jan. 3	2758
2203	13 K	Tues.	„	4 .. 23	„
2204	14	Sun.	Nov.	24 .. Dec. 13	2759
2205	15	Thurs.	„	12 .. Dec. 1	2760
2206	16 K	Mon.	Nov.	1 .. 20	2761
2207	17	Sat.	Oct.	22 .. Nov. 10	2762
2208	18 K	Wed.	„	11 .. 30	2763
2209	19	Mon.	Sept.	30 .. Oct. 19	2764
2210	20	Fri.	„	19 .. Oct. 8	2765
2211	21 K	Tues.	„	8 .. 27	2766
2212	22	Sun.	Aug.	29 .. Sept. 17	2767
2213	23	Thurs.	„	17 .. Sept. 5	2768
2214	24 K	Mon.	„	6 .. 25	2769
2215	25	Sat.	July	27 .. Aug. 15	2770
2216	26 K	Wed.	„	16 .. Aug. 4	2771
2217	27	Mon.	„	5 .. 24	2772
2218	28	Fri.	June	24 .. July 13	2773
2219	29 K	Tues.	„	13 .. July 2	2774
2220	30	Sun.	„	3 .. 22	2775
2221	1	Thurs.	May	22 .. June 10	2776
2222	2 K	Mon.	„	11 .. 30	2777
2223	3	Sat.	„	1 .. 20	2778
2224	4	Wed.	April	20 .. May 9	2779
2225	5 K	Sun.	„	8 .. 27	2780
2226	6	Fri.	Mar.	29 .. April 17	2781
2227	7 K	Tues.	„	18 .. April 6	2782
2228	8	Sun.	„	8 .. 27	2783
2229	9	Thurs.	Feb.	25 .. Mar. 15	2784
2230	10 K	Mon.	„	13 .. Mar. 4	2785
2231	11	Sat.	„	3 .. 22	2786
2232	12	Wed.	Jan.	23 .. Feb. 11	2787
2233	13 K	Sun.	„	12 .. 31	2788
2234	14	Fri.	„	1 .. 20	2789
2235	15	Tues.	Dec.	21, 2789 .. Jan. 9	2790
2236	16 K	Sat.	„	10 .. 29	„
2237	17	Thurs.	Nov.	30 .. Dec. 19	2791
2238	18 K	Mon.	„	18 .. Dec. 7	2792
2239	19	Sat.	„	8 .. 27	2793
2240	20	Wed.	Oct.	28 .. Nov. 16	2794
2241	21 K	Sun.	„	17 .. Nov. 5	2795
2242	22	Fri.	„	6 .. 25	2796
2243	23	Tues.	Sept.	25 .. Oct. 14	2797
2244	24 K	Sat.	„	14 .. Oct. 3	2798
2245	25	Thurs.	„	4 .. 23	2799
2246	26 K	Mon.	Aug.	23 .. Sept. 11	2800
2247	27	Sat.	„	13 .. Sept. 1	2801
2248	28	Wed.	„	2 .. 21	2802
2249	29 K	Sun.	July	22 .. Aug. 10	2803
2250	30	Fri.	„	11 .. 30	2804

A.H.		Date of Muḥarram 1.			A.D.
2251	1	Tues.	June	30 .. July 19	2805
2252	2 K	Sat.	„	19 .. July 8	2806
2253	3	Thurs.	„	9 .. 28	2807
2254	4	Mon.	May	28 .. June 16	2808
2255	5 K	Fri.	„	17 .. June 5	2809
2256	6	Wed.	„	7 .. 26	2810
2257	7 K	Sun.	April	26 .. May 15	2811
2258	8	Fri.	„	15 .. May 4	2812
2259	9	Tues.	„	4 .. 23	2813
2260	10 K	Sat.	Mar.	24 .. April 12	2814
2261	11	Thurs.	„	14 .. April 2	2815
2262	12	Mon.	„	2 .. 21	2816
2263	13 K	Fri.	Feb.	19 .. Mar. 10	2817
2264	14	Wed.	„	9 .. 28	2818
2265	15	Sun.	Jan.	29 .. Feb. 17	2819
2266	16 K	Thurs.	„	18 .. Feb. 6	2820
2267	17	Tues.	„	7 .. 26	2821
2268	18 K	Sat.	Dec.	27,2821 .. Jan. 15	2822
2269	19	Thurs.	„	17,2822 .. Jan. 5	2823
2270	20	Mon.	„	6 .. 25	„
2271	21 K	Fri.	Nov.	24 .. Dec. 13	2824
2272	22	Wed.	„	14 .. Dec. 3	2825
2273	23	Sun.	„	3 .. 22	2826
2274	24 K	Thurs.	Oct.	23 .. Nov. 11	2827
2275	25	Tues.	„	12 .. 31	2828
2276	26 K	Sat.	„	1 .. 20	2829
2277	27	Thurs.	Sept.	21 .. Oct. 10	2830
2278	28	Mon.	„	10 .. 29	2831
2279	29 K	Fri.	Aug.	29 .. Sept. 17	2832
2280	30	Wed.	„	19 .. Sept. 7	2833
2281	1	Sun.	„	8 .. 27	2834
2282	2 K	Thurs.	July	28 .. Aug. 16	2835
2283	3	Tues.	„	17 .. Aug. 5	2836
2284	4	Sat.	„	6 .. 25	2837
2285	5 K	Wed.	June	25 .. July 14	2838
2286	6	Mon.	„	15 .. July 4	2839
2287	7 K	Fri.	„	3 .. 22	2840
2288	8	Wed.	May	24 .. June 12	2841
2289	9	Sun.	„	13 .. June 1	2842
2290	10 K	Thurs.	„	2 .. 21	2843
2291	11	Tues.	April	21 .. May 10	2844
2292	12	Sat.	„	10 .. 29	2845
2293	13 K	Wed.	Mar.	30 .. April 18	2846
2294	14	Mon.	„	20 .. April 8	2847
2295	15	Fri.	„	8 .. 27	2848
2296	16 K	Tues.	Feb.	25 .. Mar. 16	2849
2297	17	Sun.	„	15 .. Mar. 6	2850
2298	18 K	Thurs.	„	4 .. 23	2851
2299	19	Tues.	Jan.	25 .. Feb. 13	2852
2300	20	Sat.	„	13 .. Feb. 1	2853
2301	21 K	Wed.	„	2 .. 21	2854
2302	22	Mon.	Dec.	23,2854 .. Jan. 11	2855
2303	23	Fri.	„	12 .. 31	„
2304	24 K	Tues.	Nov.	30 .. Dec. 19	2856
2305	25	Sun.	„	20 .. Dec. 9	2857
2306	26 K	Thurs.	„	9 .. 28	2858
2307	27	Tues.	Oct.	30 .. Nov. 18	2859
2308	28	Sat.	„	18 .. Nov. 6	2860
2309	29 K	Wed.	„	7 .. 26	2861
2310	30	Mon.	Sept.	27 .. Oct. 16	2862
2311	1	Fri.	„	16 .. Oct. 5	2863
2312	2 K	Tues.	„	4 .. 23	2864
2313	3	Sun.	Aug.	25 .. Sept. 13	2865
2314	4	Thurs.	„	14 .. Sept. 2	2866
2315	5 K	Mon.	„	3 .. 22	2867
2316	6	Sat.	July	23 .. Aug. 11	2868
2317	7 K	Wed.	„	12 .. 31	2869
2318	8	Mon.	„	2 .. 21	2870
2319	9	Fri.	June	21 .. July 10	2871
2320	10 K	Tues.	„	9 .. 28	2872
2321	11	Sun.	May	30 .. June 18	2873
2322	12	Thurs.	„	19 .. June 7	2874
2323	13 K	Mon.	„	8 .. 27	2875
2324	14	Sat.	April	27 .. May 16	2876
2325	15	Wed.	„	16 .. May 5	2877
2326	16 K	Sun.	„	5 .. 24	2878
2327	17	Fri.	Mar.	26 .. April 14	2879
2328	18 K	Tues.	„	14 .. April 2	2880
2329	19	Sun.	„	4 .. 23	2881
2330	20	Thurs.	Feb.	21 .. Mar. 12	2882
2331	21 K	Mon.	„	10 .. Mar. 1	2883
2332	22	Sat.	Jan.	31 .. Feb. 19	2884
2333	23	Wed.	„	19 .. Feb. 7	2885
2334	24 K	Sun.	„	8 .. 27	2886
2335	25	Fri.	Dec.	29,2886 .. Jan. 17	2887
2336	26 K	Tues.	„	18,2887 .. Jan. 6	2888
2337	27	Sun.	„	7 .. 26	„
2338	28	Thurs.	Nov.	26 .. Dec. 15	2889
2339	29 K	Mon.	„	15 .. Dec. 4	2890
2340	30	Sat.	„	5 .. 24	2891

A.H.		Date of Muḥarram 1.	A.D.
2341	1	Wed. Oct. 24 .. Nov. 12	2892
2342	2 K	Sun. „ 13 .. Nov. 1	2893
2343	3	Fri. „ 3 .. 22	2894
2344	4	Tues. Sept. 22 .. Oct. 11	2895
2345	5 K	Sat. „ 10 .. 29	2896
2346	6	Thurs. Aug. 31 .. Sept. 19	2897
2347	7 K	Mon. „ 20 .. Sept. 8	2898
2348	8	Sat. „ 10 .. 29	2899
2349	9	Wed. July 29 .. Aug. 18	2900
2350	10 K	Sun. „ 18 .. Aug. 7	2901
2351	11	Fri. „ 8 .. 28	2902
2352	12	Tues. June 27 .. July 17	2903
2353	13 K	Sat. „ 15 .. July 5	2904
2354	14	Thurs. „ 5 .. 25	2905
2355	15	Mon. May 25 .. June 14	2906
2356	16 K	Fri. „ 14 .. June 3	2907
2357	17	Wed. „ 3 .. 23	2908
2358	18 K	Sun. April 22 .. May 12	2909
2359	19	Fri. „ 12 .. May 2	2910
2360	20	Tues. „ 1 .. 21	2911
2361	21 K	Sat. Mar. 20 .. April 9	2912
2362	22	Thurs. „ 10 .. 30	2913
2363	23	Mon. Feb. 27 .. Mar. 19	2914
2364	24 K	Fri. „ 16 .. Mar. 8	2915
2365	25	Wed. „ 6 .. 26	2916
2366	26 K	Sun. Jan. 25 .. Feb. 14	2917
2367	27	Fri. „ 15 .. Feb. 4	2918
2368	28	Tues. „ 4 .. 24	2919
2369	29 K	Sat. Dec. 24, 2919 .. Jan. 13	2920
2370	30	Thurs. „ 13, 2920 .. Jan. 2	2921
2371	1	Mon. „ 2 .. 22	„
2372	2 K	Fri. Nov. 21 .. Dec. 11	2922
2373	3	Wed. „ 11 .. Dec. 1	2923
2374	4	Sun. Oct. 30 .. Nov. 19	2924
2375	5 K	Thurs. „ 19 .. Nov. 8	2925
2376	6	Tues. „ 9 .. 29	2926
2377	7 K	Sat. Sept. 28 .. Oct. 18	2927
2378	8	Thurs. „ 17 .. Oct. 7	2928
2379	9	Mon. „ 6 .. 26	2929
2380	10 K	Fri. Aug. 26 .. Sept. 15	2930
2381	11	Wed. „ 16 .. Sept. 5	2931
2382	12	Sun. „ 4 .. 24	2932
2383	13 K	Thurs. July 24 .. Aug. 13	2933
2384	14	Tues. „ 14 .. Aug. 3	2934
2385	15	Sat. „ 3 .. 23	2935

A.H.		Date of Muḥarram 1.	A.D.
2386	16 K	Wed. June 21 .. July 11	2936
2387	17	Mon. „ 11 .. July 1	2937
2388	18 K	Fri. May 31 .. June 20	2938
2389	19	Wed. „ 21 .. June 10	2939
2390	20	Sun. „ 9 .. 29	2940
2391	21 K	Thurs. April 28 .. May 18	2941
2392	22	Tues. „ 18 .. May 8	2942
2393	23	Sat. „ 7 .. 27	2943
2394	24 K	Wed. Mar. 26 .. April 15	2944
2395	25	Mon. „ 16 .. April 5	2945
2396	26 K	Fri. „ 5 .. 25	2946
2397	27	Wed. Feb. 23 .. Mar. 15	2947
2398	28	Sun. „ 12 .. Mar. 3	2948
2399	29 K	Thurs. Jan. 31 .. Feb. 20	2949
2400	30	Tues. „ 21 .. Feb. 10	2950
2401	1	Sat. „ 10 .. 30	2951
2402	2 K	Wed. Dec. 30, 2951 .. Jan. 19	2952
2403	3	Mon. „ 19, 2952 .. Jan. 8	2953
2404	4	Fri. „ 8 .. 28	„
2405	5 K	Tues. Nov. 27 .. Dec. 17	2954
2406	6	Sun. „ 17 .. Dec. 7	2955
2407	7 K	Thurs. „ 5 .. 25	2956
2408	8	Tues. Oct. 26 .. Nov. 15	2957
2409	9	Sat. „ 15 .. Nov. 4	2958
2410	10 K	Wed. „ 4 .. 24	2959
2411	11	Mon. Sept. 23 .. Oct. 13	2960
2412	12	Fri. „ 12 .. Oct. 2	2961
2413	13 K	Tues. „ 1 .. 21	2962
2414	14	Sun. Aug. 22 .. Sept. 11	2963
2415	15	Thurs. „ 10 .. 30	2964
2416	16 K	Mon. July 30 .. Aug. 19	2965
2417	17	Sat. „ 20 .. Aug. 9	2966
2418	18 K	Wed. „ 9 .. 29	2967
2419	19	Mon. June 28 .. July 18	2968
2420	20	Fri. „ 17 .. July 7	2969
2421	21 K	Tues. „ 6 .. 26	2970
2422	22	Sun. May 27 .. June 16	2971
2423	23	Thurs. „ 15 .. June 4	2972
2424	24 K	Mon. „ 4 .. 24	2973
2425	25	Sat. April 24 .. May 14	2974
2426	26 K	Wed. „ 13 .. May 3	2975
2427	27	Mon. „ 2 .. 22	2976
2428	28	Fri. Mar. 22 .. April 11	2977
2429	29 K	Tues. „ 11 .. 31	2978
2430	30	Sun. „ 1 .. 21	2979

A.H.		Date of Muḥarram 1.	A.D.	A.H.		Date of Muḥarram 1.	A.D.
2431	1	Thurs. Feb. 18 .. Mar. 9	2980	2446	16 K	Sat. „ 7 .. 27	2994
2432	2 K	Mon. „ 6 .. 26	2981	2447	17	Thurs. Aug. 28 .. Sept. 17	2995
2433	3	Sat. Jan. 27 .. Feb. 16	2982	2448	18 K	Mon. „ 16 .. Sept. 5	2996
2434	4	Wed. „ 16 .. Feb. 5	2983	2449	19	Sat. „ 6 .. 26	2997
2435	5 K	Sun. „ 5 .. 25	2984	2450	20	Wed. July 26 .. Aug. 15	2998
2436	6	Fri. Dec. 25, 2984 .. Jan. 14	2985	2451	21 K	Sun. „ 15 .. Aug. 4	2999
2437	7 K	Tues. „ 14, 2985 .. Jan. 3	2986	2452	22	Fri. „ 4 .. 25	3000
2438	8	Sun. „ 4 .. 24	„	2453	23	Tues. June 23 .. July 14	3001
2439	9	Thurs. Nov. 23 .. Dec. 13	2987	2454	24 K	Sat. „ 12 .. July 3	3002
2440	10 K	Mon. „ 11 .. Dec. 1	2988	2455	25	Thurs. „ 2 .. 23	3003
2441	11	Sat. „ 1 .. 21	2989	2456	26 K	Mon. May 21 .. June 11	3004
2442	12	Wed. Oct. 21 .. Nov. 10	2990	2457	27	Sat. „ 11 .. June 1	3005
2443	13 K	Sun. „ 10 .. 30	2991	2458	28	Wed. April 30 .. May 21	3006
2444	14	Fri. Sept. 29 .. Oct. 19	2992	2459	29 K	Sun. „ 19 .. May 10	3007
2445	15	Tues. „ 18 .. Oct. 8	2993	2460	30	Fri. „ 8 .. 29	3008

PART III

BRIEF EXPLANATORY NOTES ON THE ORIGIN AND USE OF THE JULIAN AND GREGORIAN CALENDARS.

PART III

NOTES ON THE CHRISTIAN CALENDAR.

1. THE ANCIENT ROMAN CALENDAR.

The Calendars, both Civil and Ecclesiastical, of all Christian countries are founded upon that of the Romans. Romulus had made the year to consist of only 304 days, divided into ten months of nearly equal length, of which the first was Martius, followed by Aprilis, Maius, Junius, Quintilis, Sextilis, September, October, November, and December. The names of the fifth and sixth months were afterwards changed to Julius and Augustus in honour of the two first Emperors of Rome.

Numa Pompilius added two months to the year of Romulus, Januarius at the beginning, and Februarius at the end of the year. He made his twelve months to be Lunar, consisting of 30 and 29 days alternately, so that this year contained 354 days, but he added one more day, making 355, in deference to the popular superstition that uneven numbers were more fortunate than even. This Lunar year was more than ten whole days shorter than the true Solar year, and so, with a view to harmonising the two, Numa ordered that in the course of every eight years ninety days should be intercalated, namely, a month of 22 days in every second and sixth year, and one of 23 days in every fourth and eighth year. The intercalations were to be made after February 23, thus dividing that month into two portions. This arrangement made the period of eight years to consist of 8 × 355 + 90, or 2930 days, so that the mean length of the year was 366d. 6h., involving an error of one day in excess, which was corrected by causing every third period of eight years to receive only three instead of four intercalated months, and these months were each to have 22 days. In this way twenty-four years were made to contain 8766 days, and the mean length of the Civil year was reduced to 365d. 6h.

It is far from certain that these regulations were carried into practical effect. The care of the Calendar, with its intercalations, was committed to the Pontifices, or Priests, and in process of time they inserted or refrained from inserting extra days and months to suit their own convenience—to hasten or delay the annual elections—so that they might cause a friendly magistrate to remain longer in office, or compel one whom they disliked to vacate his post before the proper term of service was reached.

In the time of the Decemviri, about the year 304 of the Foundation of Rome, B.C. 450, the number of days in the month was altered, and, while January was still retained as the first month of the year, February was placed as the second. This arrangement continued in force till the great and important correction which was affected by Julius Cæsar.

2. In the year of the Foundation of Rome 708, B.C. 46, Julius Cæsar found that the Pontifices had again caused the Calendar to fall into confusion. In his capacity as Pontifex Maximus he considered it his duty to effect a reform. He committed the charge of the work to Sosigenes, an astronomer of Alexandria, who assumed for the length of the Solar year 365d. 6h.; but, insomuch as fractions of a day could not be admitted into Civil reckoning, he adopted for his Calendar the Egyptian year of 365 days, with the correction that every fourth year was to consist of 366 days. This extra day was obtained by duplicating the day called in the Roman Calendar *dies sextus ante Kalendas Martias*—the sixth day before the Kalends of March—corresponding to February 24. The first portion of this doubled day was called *dies bissextus ante Kalendas Martias*, the second portion retained the original name. Hence is derived the term Bissextilis, which is not a Classical word, but appears to have been used first by the Venerable Bede for a year which receives the intercalated day, now commonly called a Leap-year.

3. Cæsar decreed that in future the Civil year should commence with the Kalends of January, that is, January 1. His decree came into force on that day in the year 709 of the Foundation, corresponding to B.C. 45. He had ordered that the uneven months, January, March, May, July, September, and November, should each have 31 days, and the other months 30 days, with the exception of February, which in Common years was to have 29 days, but in every fourth year it was to have 30. This arrangement was altered by Augustus, who took away a day from February both in Common and Bissextile years, and added it to August, in order that the month now bearing his name might have as many days as July, which had been so called in honour of his uncle Julius. At the same time, September and November were reduced to 30 days, and 31 were given to October and December. In this way the months were arranged as they exist at present.

The year of 365d. 6h. is called the mean Julian year, and the Calendar which has this year for its basis is called the Julian Calendar.

4. The Gregorian Correction.

The mean length of the Tropical or true Solar year is 365d. 5h. 48m. 46s., consequently a mean Julian year is too long by 11m. 14s. This error amounts to three whole days in between 384 and 385 years. It had long been recognised by astronomers that an error existed, and the authorities of the Church had been repeatedly urged to correct it. In or about A.D. 1576 a scheme for a new Calendar had been prepared by Luigi Lilio Ghiraldi, better known as Aloysius Lilius, a physician of Naples. He had found that the Vernal Equinox in that year occurred on the day called March 11, for every preceding year of the Calendar having been too long, the day of the Equinox was reached too soon. In other words, the Julian Calendar called the day on which the Equinox occurred March 11, whereas it ought to have been called March 21.

Now, it had been decided by the Council of Nicæa, in A.D. 325, that Easter Sunday should be the first Sunday after that fourteenth day of the Moon,* which happens upon or next after March 21, because it was believed that March 21 would always be the day of the Equinox. If then the Equinox occurred on the day called March 11, instead of on the day called March 21, the date of Easter might be seriously affected; this was, indeed, frequently the case.

* Called in the English Prayer Book the "Full Moon." It ought to be called the fourteenth day of the artificial, or Ecclesiastical Moon, which is supposed to move uniformly in the heavens, and to be "Full" on its fourteenth day.

For instance—in A.D. 1557 the true Equinox occurred on Wednesday, March 10. There had been a New Moon on Monday, March 1; the fourteenth day of this Moon was Sunday, March 14; the following Sunday, March 21, ought to have been Easter Day, if the decree of the Fathers had been observed. But Easter was not observed in that year until April 18, for the next fourteenth day of the Moon after March 21 occurred on Tuesday, April 13, and the following Sunday was April 18. This was four weeks later than it ought to have been.*

Aloysuis Lilius died before having the opportunity of bringing his computations to the notice of the authorities. His system was, however, submitted to Pope Gregory XIII. by his brother Antonio, and the Pope wisely determined to take action at once. He appointed commissioners to carry out the work, and to frame rules which were to be observed in future by the Church. The new Calendar was completed before February, 1581, for on the twenty-third day of that month a Papal Bull was issued abolishing the Julian Calendar, giving a general description of the correction, and announcing that a full explanation would be shortly published.

The first thing required was to alter the monthly names of the Calendar days in such a way that the day of the Equinox might in future be called March 21. With this object the Pope decreed that the following year, A.D. 1582, should be shortened by ten days. This was done by omitting from the Calendar the monthly names of the days from October 5 to October 14, both inclusive, that is to say, the day next after Thursday, October 4, was to be called Friday, October 15, instead of Friday, October 5, which was its designation in the Julian Calendar. This reduction in the length of the year 1582 was intended to compensate the accumulated error due to the excess in length of all the previous years since A.D. 325.

In the next place, because the mean years of 365d. 6h. would still be too long, the Bull enacted that every 400 years should be shortened by three days. This was to be done by ceasing to intercalate a day in all those Centurial years which are not multiples of 400. In other words, all such years as 1700, 1800, 1900, 2100, &c., were no longer to have 29 days in the month of February, as in the Julian Calendar, but were to be made Common years of 365 days. In this way 400

* Stöffler, "Calendarium Romanum Magnum," Prop. xxxix. fol. 70.

Gregorian years are reduced in length from 146100 to 146097 days, which gives, for the mean length of the Gregorian year, 365d. 5h. 49m. 12s. This interval of time is 26s. longer than the mean length of the Tropical year, so that there still remains an error amounting to an excess of one day all but two seconds in 3323 years.

5. The Gregorian Calendar, the reckoning of time by which is frequently called New Style, was at once accepted in Spain, Portugal, and part of Italy. In France the change was made in December of the same year, 1582, and in other countries on the Continent of Europe at various later dates. In England the use of the Julian Calendar was retained until 1752; in that year eleven nominal days were removed from the Calendar, namely, September 3 to September 13, both inclusive, so that Wednesday, September 2, was followed by Thursday, September 14. Russia, Greece, and Bulgaria are now the only Christian countries in which the old Julian Calendar is still employed.

6. To find the number of days by which the Gregorian Calendar has shortened the previous Julian years at any given date.

Ten days were dropped from the year 1582, and afterwards one day of February is taken away from every Julian Centurial year, which is not of the form $400n$.

Let C be the number of completed Centuries in the given date. The Centuries must be treated as commencing not with January 1, but with March 1, and let it be remembered that any Century, as the nth, commences with the year $100\,(n-1)+1$. Then, because none of the intercalated days were removed from the first sixteen Centuries, but that one day is taken from every subsequent Centurial year which is not a multiple of 400, the total number of days dropped by the Gregorian Calendar before any given date will be—

$$10 + (C - 16) - \left\{\frac{C - 16}{4}\right\}.$$

It is by this number of days that the Gregorian dating for any given day is in advance of the Julian.

It is most important to bear in mind that the intercalary day of those Centurial years which are not of the form $400n$ is not dropped until February 28 has elapsed, so that, if the given date in such a

Centurial year be before February 29, the months of January and February must be treated as though they belonged to the preceding year.

Example 1.

Find the Gregorian date coinciding with the Julian February 7, 1900.

Here 1900 is not of the form $400n$, therefore February 7 must be treated as though it belonged to the year 1899, and we have $C = 18$.

The number of days by which the Gregorian date is in advance of the Julian is, therefore—

$$10 + (18 - 16) - \left\{\frac{18 - 16}{4}\right\} = 10 + 2 - 0 = 12.$$

The Gregorian date is, therefore, February (7 + 12), or 19.

Example 2.

Find the Gregorian date corresponding to the Julian August 10, A.D. 3100.

$$\text{Here } C = 31\,;\ C - 16 = 15\,;\ \text{and } \left\{\frac{C - 16}{4}\right\} = 3.$$

$$\therefore 10 + (C - 16) - \left\{\frac{C - 16}{4}\right\} = 10 + 15 - 3 = 22.$$

The required date is August 10 + 22 = September 1.

7. The Moon of the Calendar.

In A.D. 325 the Council of Nicæa ordained that Easter should be observed everywhere on the Sunday next following that fourteenth day of the Moon which occurs upon or next after March 21. The Council did not say how the fourteenth day of the Moon was to be found, but ordained that the duty of determining at what date Easter Sunday would occur should be committed to the Bishop of Alexandria; he was to communicate his decision to the Bishop of Rome, who, in turn, was to inform all other Bishops.

The Ecclesiastical authorities at Rome had long been dissatisfied with this arrangement. They considered that it was derogatory to the See of Rome, and that they were themselves quite as capable of determining the date as any Alexandrian Bishop.

Hence it was that in A.D. 437 a great effort was made by Hilarius, then Archdeacon of Rome and afterwards Pope, to obtain a correct Calendar and a Cycle of his own, and thus render the Western Church independent of Alexandria. He employed Victorinus of Aquitaine for the purpose, and ordained that the Moon which governed the date of Easter should not be either the true or the mean Moon of the heavens, but should be an artificial Moon supposed to move regularly, and that the Full Moon should be accounted as occurring on its fourteenth day. These Moons were to be computed by means of the Metonic Cycle,* on the assumption that 235 Lunations are equivalent to 19 Solar years. This artificial Moon was afterwards adopted by Pope Gregory for his reformed Calendar, and is still employed by the Church.

8. THE DOMINICAL LETTERS.

These Letters are the first seven of the Alphabet. They are placed in the Calendar, in recurring consecutive order, against the days of the months throughout the year. Insomuch as their number coincides with the number in the week it comes to pass that some one or other of them will be the Letter by which the same week-day will be marked throughout every Common year. .

The first day of the year, January 1, no matter upon which day of the week it may fall, is invariably marked by the Letter A; the second day by B; the third by C, and so forwards until G is reached for the seventh day. The series of Letters then recommences, and goes on continually throughout the year until December 31 is reached, to which A will again fall, because 365, the number of days in a Common year, exceeds by unity an exact multiple of 7. The result is that two consecutive days are marked by the same Letter, A, namely December 31 in every year, and January 1 in the next year.

This is invariably the case whether the year be Bissextile or not, because the intercalated day in February, when it occurs, is entirely ignored so far as the Letters are concerned; that is to say, no Letter is ever attached to it. Hence, the Letter attached to March 1 is the next in alphabetical order to that for February 28, whether it be in a Leap-year or in a Common year. Consequently there is no interference with the sequence of the Letters which are attached to the days of the twelve months of the year.

* See *post*, Article 10.

The Sunday Letter for a Common year is that which belongs to the day in January upon which the first Sunday in the year occurs. Thus, if January 1 be a Sunday, A, which always marks that day, will be the Sunday Letter. If January 2 be a Sunday, B will be the Sunday Letter for the year, and so onwards.

In the case of a Leap-year there is a difference; such a year must of necessity have two Letters which indicate its Sundays, one from the beginning of the year up to the intercalated day, and the other for the remainder of the year after the intercalated day. This will be made more clear by the following illustration:—Let January 1 be a Sunday; then in a Common year A will be the Sunday Letter throughout the year; February 26 will be a Sunday, and March 5 will be a Sunday, both these days are marked by A. In a Leap-year, if February 26 be a Sunday, March 4 is a Sunday, but the Letter which is always attached to March 4 is G, and G will be the Sunday Letter for the rest of the year. Thus the two Sunday Letters for a Leap-year, in which January 1 is a Sunday, are A and G.

The initials of the words in the following old "memoria technica" indicate the Letter which is attached to the first day of each of the twelve months, A to January 1, D to February 1, D again to March 1, &c.

At Dover Dwells George Brown Esquire
Good Caleb Finch And David Friar.

In the Julian Calendar the Cycle of the Dominical Letters, often called erroneously the Cycle of the Sun, repeats itself after every twenty-eight years. When this interval of time has elapsed the days of the week fall to the same days of the months as before, and have the same Letters attached to them, with the same Letters in pairs for Leap-years. In the Gregorian Calendar a period of four hundred years is required to complete a Cycle of the Dominical Letters.

9. Rules for finding the Sunday Letter of any year.

Let the Letters be numbered in arithmetical order as they stand in the Alphabet, thus—

A	B	C	D	E	F	G.
1	2	3	4	5	6	7.

(1) For the years B.C.

To the number representing the given year add a fourth part of this number diminished by unity, neglecting fractions. Add also 3. Divide the sum by 7. The remainder is the numerical value of the Sunday Letter for the year.

In Leap-years the Letter thus found is for January and February. The Letter for the remaining ten months is that which precedes in the Alphabet the one that has been found.

(2) For the Julian Calendar.

To the number representing the given year add its fourth part, neglecting fractions. From the sum subtract 3. Divide the remainder by 7, and subtract the remainder so obtained from 7. The result gives the numerical value of the Letter required.

In Leap-years the Letter thus found is for the last ten months of the year. The Letter for January and February is that which follows next in alphabetical order.

(3) For the Gregorian Calendar.

To the number representing the given year add its fourth part, neglecting fractions. From the sum subtract 3, and also the total number of days dropped from the Calendar previous to the given date. Divide the remainder by 7, and subtract the remainder so obtained from 7. The result is the number of the Sunday Letter.

In Leap-years the Letter thus found is for the last ten months of the year, just as in the Julian Calendar. The Letter for January and February is the next in alphabetical order.

Example 1.—Find the Sunday Letter for B.C. 201.

$$201 + \left\{\frac{201 - 1}{4}\right\} + 3 = 254.$$

The remainder, after dividing 254 by 7 is 2. Therefore, the Letter for January and February is B, and for the rest of the year it is A.

Example 2.—A.D. 1004, Julian.

$$1004 + \left\{\frac{1004}{4}\right\} - 3 = 1252.$$

The remainder, after dividing by 7, is 6.

$7 - 6 = 1 =$ A, for the last ten months, and therefore B for January and February.

Example (3).—A.D. 4892, Gregorian.

$$4892 + \left\{\frac{4892}{4}\right\} - 3 - \left(10 + (48 - 16) - \left\{\frac{48 - 16}{4}\right\}\right)$$
$$= 4892 + 1223 - 3 - (10 + 32 - 8) = 6078.$$

The remainder, after dividing 6078 by 7, is 2, and $7 - 2 = 5$; therefore E is the Letter for the last ten months of the year, and F for January and February.

The Dominical Letters are used for finding the week-day of any given date, and insomuch as they have always been attached, respectively, to the same days of the year both in the Julian and Gregorian Calendars, their use is the same in both Calendars. They will be found, attached to the days of the year, in the Calendar of the English Prayer Book. Thus, for example, F is attached to September 8 and December 29, both in the Julian and Gregorian Calendars. It must, however, be remembered that September 8 and December 29, &c., do not fall to the same week-day in both Calendars. September 8, 1902, for instance, will be a Monday in the Gregorian Calendar, but in the Julian it will be a Sunday. Hence, in seeking the week-day for any given date the question must be considered whether that date is under Old or New Style.

Example 1.—Required the week-day for December 25, A.D. 1004.

The Sunday Letter for this year, which comes under Old Style, has been found above to be A, for the last ten months. By the Calendar in the Prayer Book it is seen that A is attached to December 24, which was therefore a Sunday, and December 25 must have been Monday.

Example 2.—Required the week-day for December 25, A.D. 4892.

The Sunday Letter for this year, Gregorian, has been found above to be E during the last ten months. This Letter is attached to December 21, which will therefore be a Sunday in A.D. 4892, and December 25 will therefore be a Thursday.

Example 3.—To what week-day will January 1, A.D. 2049, fall in Russia, if the Julian Calendar will then be still employed in that country?

By Rule 2, Article 9, the Julian Sunday Letter for 2049, is found to be D. This Letter belongs to January 4, which will therefore be a Sunday in Russia, and January 1 will, therefore, be a Thursday.

Notice that the particular day which is called January 1, 2049, in

Russia, is called January 14 in countries where the Gregorian Calendar is used. The Gregorian Sunday Letter for 2049 is C, which is always attached to January 10, therefore January 14 is a Thursday. In fact, any particular day in time, as, for instance, the day when the "Sun enters Aries" in this present year, 1901, has the same week-day name both in the Julian and Gregorian Calendars; but it has a different monthly name; in the Julian Calendar it is called Thursday, March 8, in the Gregorian it is called Thursday, March 21.

10. The Golden Numbers.

In the year 432 B.C. Meton, an Athenian astronomer, found that 235 Lunations are very nearly, though not exactly, equal in duration to 19 Solar years. This discovery was held to be of so great importance that it was ordered to be engraved in letters of gold on a marble tablet which was placed in one of the Temples at Athens. The Cycle of nineteen years is called the Metonic Lunar Cycle, and the number indicating the position of any year in this Cycle is called the Golden Number of the year.

This Cycle was adopted by the Christian Church for the purpose of finding the date of Easter, and remained in use by the Roman Church till the time of the reformation of the Calendar by Pope Gregory, A.D. 1582, when another system was adopted by that Church. It is still employed by the Anglican Church.

11. To find the Golden Number for any year of the Christian Era. Add 1 to the number representing the given year, and divide the sum by 19. The remainder is the Golden Number for the year. If there be no remainder the year is the last in a Cycle, and the Number is XIX.

To find the Golden Number for any year before the Christian Era. Subtract 2 from the number representing the given year, and divide the remainder by 19. Subtract the remainder from 19. The final remainder is the Number required. If there be no remainder the Number is XIX., as above.

12. How the Golden Numbers are Employed.

The computists of the Ecclesiastical Calendar assumed for the length of the artificial Lunar year twelve months of 30 and 29 days alternately, with certain modifications, of which the chief was that a

Lunation was always attributed to the month in which it terminated. Thus—if an artificial Lunation terminated in an "uneven month," as January or March, it was made to be one of 30 days, but if it terminated in an "even" month, as February or April, it was one of 29 days. It is quite possible that two artificial Lunations might terminate in the same month, and thus two Lunations of 30 days, or two of 29 days might follow each other. Suppose that August 1 were the last day of an artificial Lunation; as it terminates in this "even" month it would be reckoned as having had 29 days. The next Lunation, commencing with August 2, must also terminate in August, whether it be of 29 or 30 days, but because it terminates in August it has 29 days, and its last day is August 30. Thus there are two Lunations of 29 days both terminating in August.

An artificial Lunar year consisted of 354 days, or twelve Lunations, and, in order to complete nineteen Calendar, or Julian, years, seven additional Lunar months were added during the course of the Cycle. Six of these consisted of 30 days, and one, at the end of the Cycle, of 29 days. This gives the equation $(12 \times 19) + 7$, or 235 Lunations $= (19 \times 354) + (6 \times 30) + 29$, or 6935 days. But in every Leap-year the particular Lunation which includes February 29 will be, in reality, one day longer than its supposed length. If either the first, second, or third year of the Cycle of nineteen years should be a Leap-year, there would be five such years in the Cycle; if the fourth were a Leap-year there would be only four. In the former case there would be 6940 days in 235 Lunations, in the latter case there would be 6939. The mean length of the Cycle was therefore $\frac{3 \times 6940 + 6939}{4}$, or $6939\frac{3}{4}$ days, which is the exact length of nineteen mean Julian years. When four such periods had elapsed the fraction would be eliminated and 4×235, or 940 artificial Lunations would be exactly equal to 76 Civil Julian years: but not to 76 mean Tropical years.

Before the Gregorian correction the first day of every artificial Lunation was indicated in the Calendar by affixing to that day one of the Golden Numbers. These Numbers were arranged as it was believed that they would have been placed at the time of the Nicæan Council, A.D. 325. Thus—it was computed that January 1 in that year was the first day of the artificial Moon, and accordingly III was affixed to January 1, the year 325 being the third in a Cycle. This was intended to convey the fact that in every subsequent year whose

Golden Number was III the first day of the artificial Moon would fall to that monthly date. Precisely in the same way the other Golden Numbers were placed against those days of the months to which it was computed that the first days of the Moon would fall in perpetuity, according to the position of the year in the Cycle. Thus, the Number XII was affixed to January 22, February 20, March 22, April 20, &c., indicating that in every year whose Golden Number was XII the first day of the Ecclesiastical Moon fell to those dates.

In this way all the 235 days of the year which were the computed first days of Lunations received their proper Number. Twelve of the Numbers appeared twelve times, and seven, namely, III, V, VIII, XI, XIII, XIV, and XIX, appeared thirteen times. They will be thus found in the Calendar of any English Prayer Book published before A.D. 1783. This left 130 days in a Common year, 131 in a Leap-year, without the affix of any Golden Number. In other words, there are this number of days in the year upon which the first day of an artificial Lunation never occurs. This alone will indicate the difference between the artificial Moon of the Calendar and the true Moon of the heavens, for, of course, there is no day of the year, including February 29, upon which at some time or other the true Moon of the heavens will not be New.

13. How Easter Day was Determined under the Old Calendar.

The earliest date at which Easter can occur is March 22, and this can only be the case when March 21 is the fourteenth day of the Calendar Moon, and is a Saturday.

The latest possible date for Easter is April 25, and this is only the case when the fourteenth day of the Moon falls to April 18, and when that day is a Sunday.

March 21 and April 18 are called "The Paschal Limits."

There are consequently only thirty-five days of the year, namely, March 22 to April 25, both inclusive, upon which Easter can occur; and, because Easter governs all the other movable Feasts, there are only thirty-five possible forms for the annual Almanac.* These facts hold good both for the Julian and the Gregorian Calendar.

* If the true Moon of the heavens were employed for finding Easter there would be thirty-six possible forms of the Almanac.

Easter Day, for any given year, H, was determined under the old Calendar in the following manner:—

(1) Divide H + 1 by 19. The remainder is the Golden Number, N, for the year H.

(2) Search the Calendar from March 21 to April 18, both inclusive, for the day to which N is affixed. That day will be the first day of the Moon which governs Easter.

(3) Count thirteen days beyond this day, so that the fourteenth day of the Moon is reached.

(4) The following Sunday, found by means of the Sunday Letter for the year, will be Easter Day.

Example.—A.D. 1196.

(1) There is no remainder after dividing 1196 by 19, therefore the Golden Number for the year is XIX.

(2) This Number is affixed to April 4 in the Calendar of the old Prayer Books. April 4 is therefore the first day of the Paschal Moon.

(3) $4 + 13 = 17$. Therefore April 17 is the fourteenth day of the Moon.

(4) The Sunday Letter for the year is found by Rule 2, Article 9, to be F, which first appears (in any Calendar, old or new) against April 21, pointing out that day as the first Sunday after the fourteenth day of the Moon which occurs next after March 21. April 21 was, therefore, kept as Easter Sunday in the year 1196.

14. The determination of Easter by these rules made it recur, under the old Calendar, in regular sequence after every 28×19, or 532 years. This period of time was called the Paschal Cycle, and was used by the Church for more than a thousand years before the reform of the Calendar in 1582. It was, of course, erroneous, for the reasons pointed out in Article 4, but was nevertheless employed by the Anglican Church till the year 1783.

15. How Easter is Determined by Means of the Golden Numbers under the Gregorian Calendar.

When the Tables for finding Easter, which are given in the Prayer Book, were formed, a change in the places of the Golden Numbers had to be effected; this was rendered necessary by the correction which had been effected in the Calendar. March 21, for instance, had become the name of the day which had previously been called March 10; and the day which had previously been called March 21 had now become April 1. Clearly, the Numbers must assume different positions to those which they had formerly held. Accordingly, such new arrangement was made. It is given in the Prayer Book, under the heading "A Table to Find Easter Day from the present time* till the year 1899 inclusive.".

Moreover, for the purpose of finding Easter, it is more convenient that the fourteenth rather than the first day of the Moon should be indicated; and, because no one would require to know the fourteenth day of the artificial Moon at any other time of the year, it was ordered that the fourteenth days in the respective years should be marked by their proper Golden Number from March 21 to April 18 only, both inclusive. Although, therefore, the Numbers are attached to certain days throughout the whole year in the English Prayer Books published before 1783, they only appear against nineteen days in March and April in Prayer Books published since September 14, 1782.

Again: because 235 Lunations of the artificial Moon are not exactly equal either to nineteen true Solar years, or to 235 Lunations of the true Moon, thus causing an error in the Metonic Cycle, and, further, because the reformed Calendar shortens every 400 Julian years by three days, it was found that it would become necessary to make further changes in the places of the Numbers after the lapse of certain periods. This shifting is effected in the following manner:—After the year 1783 the places are advanced one day in the Calendar at every completed Century which is not a multiple of either 300 or 400, such as 1900, 2200, 2500, &c.; and they are set back one day at every completed Century which is a multiple of both 300 and 400, that is, at every Century which is of the form 1200*n*, such as 2400, 3600, &c.

By this means compensation is made for the error in the Metonic Cycle, which puts the date of the artificial New Moon nearly one day forward of the date of the true Moon in about 300 years, but the corrected Calendar shortens every year which is of the form 300*n* by one day. This lengthening by the error in the Cycle, and shortening by the dropping of a day, compensate each other, so that there is no need to shift the places of the Numbers for those years which are multiples of 300.

* "From the present time" is from the date of the correction, namely, September 14, 1782.

Neither is it necessary to change the places for those completed Centuries which are of the form 400n, for (1) these years do not lose the intercalated day, and (2) the Metonic error, having been compensated in those years which are of the form 300n, will not yet amount to one whole day.

But it is necessary to shift the places forward by one day for those completed Centuries, after 1782, which are of the form 100n, or 200n, because such years do lose the intercalated day, and the day which would have been called March 21 is now called, in the one case March 22, in the other March 23. Therefore the Number which was affixed to March 21 must be shifted after 100 years to March 22, and 100 years later to March 23. In neither case does the Metonic error compensate for the loss of the intercalated day, because it does not yet amount to one whole day.

Lastly, it is necessary to shift the places by one day backwards at every completed Century which is of the form 1200n, because, being also of the form 300n, the Metonic error now amounts to one whole day, and puts the artificial Moon one day too forward; this error is not compensated by any loss of a day in the Calendar because a year of the form 400n does not lose the intercalated day, and compensation must be made by shifting the Numbers backwards.

It must always be understood that the object of these alterations is to keep the fourteenth day of the artificial Moon as near as possible to the day of the true Full Moon of the heavens.

16. The Prayer Book provides Tables, showing to which days the Numbers are to be affixed, for two periods only, namely, from 1753 to 1899, both inclusive, and from 1900 to 2199, both inclusive. It is, however, easy to form additional Tables by following the directions which have just been given.

The Numbers are used in the same way as that described for the old Calendar in Article 13, with the exception that there is now no necessity to count thirteen days beyond that to which the Number is attached.

Example.—Required the date of Easter in A.D. 2198.

1. The remainder, after dividing 2198 + 1, by 19 gives XIV for the Golden Number.

2. The Prayer Book Table, for the period 1900 to 2199, affixes XIV to March 22.

3. The Sunday Letter for 2198 is found by Rule 3, Article 9, to be G. The first Sunday after March 22 is therefore March 25, which will be Easter Day in A.D. 2198.

17. THE JULIAN PERIOD.

This is a Period of 7980 years, being the continued product of the three numbers 28, 19, and 15, of which the first is the number of years in the Dominical Cycle under the Julian Calendar, the second the number of years in the Metonic Cycle, and the last the number in the Roman Indiction.

Insomuch as these three numbers have no common measure it is impossible that during the Period covered by their product there can occur any two years which shall both possess the same number of position in each of the three Cycles. Thus, if there be a year whose number in the Dominical Cycle is 3, in the Metonic Cycle XVI, and in the Indiction 5, there cannot be any other year during the Period of 7980 years which fulfils the same conditions.

The first year of the Period was that year B.C. which, if the Cycles be continued backwards, was the first in each of the three Cycles. This was the year 4713 B.C. The Period, therefore, commenced at Noon on January 1 in this year, according to Astronomical computation, but for Chronological purposes it commenced twelve hours earlier, at the preceding Midnight.

The invention of this Period is generally ascribed to Joseph Scaliger, and it is said that he gave to it its name in honour of his father Julius Cæsar Scaliger.

The years of the Julian Period must not be confused with the years of Julius Cæsar of which the first was 45 B.C.

To reduce the years of the Julian Period to the common Christian reckoning; and the reverse.

Let P be the given year of the Julian Period,
and Y be the corresponding year in the Christian reckoning.

For the years B.C.,

$$P = 4714 - Y; \text{ and } Y = 4714 - P.$$

For the Christian Era, or A.D.,

$$P = 4713 + Y; \text{ and } Y = P = 4713.$$

Example.

Julian Period 3981 = B.C. (4714 − 3981) = 733 B.C.
B.C. 40 = Jul. Per. (4714 − 40) = 4674 J.P.

Julian Period 5214 = A.D. (5214 − 4713) = A.D. 501
A.D. 499 = Jul. Per. (4713 + 499) = 5212 J.P

18. It may be well to note here that—

(1) The initial letters B.C. do not mean "Before the Birth of Christ," but "Before the Christian Era." This Era did not commence till four years and one week after the date generally accepted as that of the Nativity.

(2) In Chronology and History there is no year which is called either A.D. 0, or B.C. 0; the year next preceding the first of the Christian Era is the year B.C. 1. But astronomers, for the sake of greater convenience in reckoning the lapse of time, call the year next preceding the first of the Christian Era the year A.D. 0; the Chronological year B.C. 2 corresponds to the Astronomical year B.C. 1, which is equivalent to A.D. − 1, and so on.

Hence the number of any given year before the Christian Era is, in Chronology, always greater by unity than its number in Astronomy. So it is that in the Nautical Almanac, the Table, which gives the days elapsed since the commencement of the Julian Period, states that number to be 1721058 up to the Noon of January 1, A.D. 0. A similar Table in a Chronological work would give that as the number of days elapsed up to the Midnight at which January 1 in the year B.C. 1 commences.

(3) For convenience in reckoning dates, either Chronologically or Astronomically, Leap-years are assumed to have occurred regularly every fourth year, according to the Julian Calendar, since the commencement of the second year of the Julian Period; the first year of this Period, B.C. 4713, being itself accounted as a Leap-year. Hence, in Chronology the years B.C. 1, 5, 9, . . . 4713, and all years B.C. of the form $4n + 1$ are reckoned as Leap-years, while the corresponding Astronomical years are A.D. 0, B.C. 4, 8 . . . 4712, or, if preferred, A.D. 0, − 4, − 8, &c. Since the commencement of the Christian Era the Leap-years both in Chronology and Astronomy are all, in the Julian Calendar, of the form $4n$.

(4) A Century commences Chronologically with the Midnight at

which January 1 commences in a Civil year of the form $100n + 1$, where n may be zero, or any positive integer. A completed Century terminates with the Midnight at which December 31 terminates in a Civil year of the form $100n$. The years and the Centuries commence and terminate Astronomically twelve hours later, namely at Noon.

INDICES

INDICES

JEWISH CALENDAR.

TABLES AND COMPUTATIONS IN THE TEXT.

GENERAL TABLES, *see* CONTENTS.

MUHAMMADAN CALENDAR.

TABLES IN THE TEXT.

GENERAL TABLES, *see* CONTENTS.

JULIAN AND GREGORIAN CALENDARS.

AUTHORS CONSULTED AND EDITIONS TO WHICH REFERENCE IS MADE IN THE TEXT.

ACTES DU ONZIÈME CONGRÈS INTERNATIONAL DES ORIENTALISTES. Paris. 1897. Quatrième Section ... ... Paris. Imprim. Nat. 1898

AL-BÎRÛNI, ATHÂR-UL-BÂKIYÂ. This book was written in A.D. 1000. The English translation of the MS. is by Dr. C. E. Sachau, under the title, The Chronology of Ancient Nations, or Vestiges of the Past. Published for the Oriental Translation Fund ... ... London. 1879

L'ART DE VÉRIFIER LES DATES. La Nouvelle Ed. in 8vo. ... ... Paris. 1818–1844

BANNISTER, J. T. The Temples of the Hebrews ... ... London. 1861

BENDAVID, LAZARUS. Zur Berechnung und Geschicte des Jüdischen Kalenders ... ... Berlin. 1817

BEVERIDGE, W. Institutiones Chronologicæ .. .. Londini. 1721

BOND, J. J. Handy-Book of Rules and Tables for Verifying Dates with the Christian Era. 4th Ed. ... ... London. 1889

CORRESPONDANCE ASTRONOMIQUE, &c., du Baron du Zach. Tom i. ... Gênes. 1818

CRELLE JOURNAL FÜR DIE MATHEMATIK. Band xxvi. ... ... Berlin. 1843

CRICHTON, A. History of Arabia. 2nd Ed. ... ... Edinburgh. 1854

EWALD, H. The History of Israel. Translated from the German. Edited by Russell Martineau. 3rd Ed. ... ... London. 1876

" Antiquities of Israel. Translated by H. S. Solly ... London. 1876

FRANCŒUR, L. B. Sur le Calendrier des Mahométans ... ... Paris. 1844

" Théorie du Calendrier. (Manuels-Roret) ... ... Paris. 1842

FRANKIUS, J. G. Novum Systema Chronologiæ Fundamentalis ... Goettingæ. 1778

GRAETZ, H. History of the Jews. Edited, and in part translated by, Bella Löwy ... ... London. 1891

GUMPACH, J. Über den Altjüdischen Kalendar ... ... Brüssel. 1848

HAMBURGER. Real-Encyclopädie für Bibel und Talmud ... ... Strelitz. 1866–1883

HUGHES, T. P. A Dictionary of Islâm ... ... London. 1896

IDELER, LUDWIG. Handbuch der Mathematischen und Technischen Chronologie ... ... Berlin. 1825

JEWISH YEAR-BOOK. Edited by Joseph Jacobs ... ... London. Annual.

JOSEPHUS, Genuine Works of, translated according to Havercamp's accurate Edition, by W. Whiston ... ... Glasgow. n.d.

JOURNAL ASIATIQUE. Series iv. tom. i. ... ... Paris. 1843

KORNICK, MEIER. System den Zeitrechnung in Chronologischen Tabellen Berlin. 1825

LACOINE, EMILE. Tables de Concordance des Dates des Calendriers. ... Paris. 1891

LANE, E. W. Manners and Customs of the Modern Egyptians. 5th Ed. London. 1860
LE BOYER, J. Traité complet du Calendrier ... ... Nantes. 1822
LEWISOHN. Geschichte der Jüdischen Kalenderwersen ... ... Leipzig. 1856
LINDO, E. H. A Jewish Calendar for Sixty-four Years ... ... London. 1838
LOEB, ISIDORE. Tables du Calendrier Juif ... ... Paris. 1886
MAIMONIDES, R. MOSES. Kiddusch hachodesh. Latin version by L. de Compiegne de Veil, under the title, Tractatus de Consecratione Calendarum, et de Ratione Intercalandi ... ... Londini. 1683
MAHMUD EFFENDI. Mémoire sur le Calendrier Arabe avant L'Islamisme Paris. 1858
MARTIN, RENÉ. Mémoire sur le Calendrier Hebraïque ... ... Angers. 1863
,, Mémoire sur le Calendrier Musulman ... ... Paris. 1857
MONATLICHE CORRESPONDENZ VON FREYHERNN VON ZACH. Band V. ... Gotha. 1802
NESSELMANN, G. H. F. Beiträge zur Chronologie. In the Crelle Journal, Band xxvi. ... ... Berlin. 1823
NICOLAS, SIR HARRIS. The Chronology of History. In Lardner's Cabinet Cyclopædia. A new Ed. ... ... London. 1840
PARKHURST, J. Hebrew Lexicon ... ... London. 1823
PERCEVAL, CAUSSIN DE. Essai sur L'Histoire des Arabes avant L'Islamisme ... ... Paris. 1847
PETAVIUS (Père Petau). Rationarii Temporum ... ... Franequeræ. 1700
,, De Doctrina Temporum ... ... Venetiis. 1757
PRIDEAUX, H. The Old and New Testaments connected in History. 16th Ed. ... ... London. 1808
RICCIOLI. Chronologia Reformata ... ... Bononiæ. 1669
SALE, G. The Al-Koran of Mohammed, translated into English ... London. 1844
SCAFF-HERZOG ENCYCLOPÆDIA OF RELIGIOUS KNOWLEDGE... ... ... New York. 1891
SCALIGER. De Emendatione Temporum ... ... Genevæ. 1629
SCHWARZ, ADOLF. Der Jüdische Kalendar ... ... Berlin. 1872
SEDILLOT, J. J. Abu-al-Hasan 'Alī Marrâkushī, Traité des Instruments Astronomiques des Arabes, traduit ... ... Paris. 1834-1835
SELDEN, J. De Anno Civile et Calendaris veteris Ecclesiæ seu Reipublicæ Judaicæ dissertatio... ... ... Londini. 1644
SMITH, W. Dictionary of the Bible ... ... London. 1863
STÖFFLER. Calendarium Romanum Magnum ... ... Oppenheim. 1518
STRAUCHIUS, G. Breviarium Chronologicum, done into English by R. Sault ... ... London. 1704
ULUGH BEIGH. Epochæ Celebriores. Eas publicavit, et commentariis illustravit J. Gravius ... ... Londini. 1650
WHEATLEY, C. B. A Rational Illustration of the Book of Common Prayer ... ... London. 1853
WILSON. Glossary of Judicial and Revenue Terms for British India... London. 1885
WOOLHOUSE, W. S. B. Measures, Weights, and Moneys of all Nations. 7th Ed. ... ... London. 1890

LIST OF SUBSCRIBERS

Acret, C. H. J.
Aitken, G.
Ambrose, W., K.C.
Andrew, J.
Baker, C.
Baker, W. F.
Bartrum, C. O.
Bell, Edward.
Bell, J. C.
Bell, Miss, and G. B.
Belton, J.
Blockley, H. E.
Bond, E., M.P.
Bond, Mrs.
Carrington, J. B.
Champneys, Basil.
Chouler, C.
Claudet, F.
Clarke, Mrs. C.
Coates, C. J.
Coates, Joseph.
Corbett, C. Newberry, M.D.
Collins, E.
Cow, J.
Craigie, Major P. G.
Crispe, J. H.
Crump, E. C.
Dalton, R. N.
d'Ambrumenil, B. N.
Delbridge, Miss.
Drummond, Captain A. M.
Edis, R.
Essex, A.
Evans, W. Norman, M.D.
Fletcher, J. S., J.P., L.C.C.
Gilchrist, P. C., F.R.S.
Gilchrist, Mrs. P. C.
Glyn, C. H.
Greaves, Mrs.
Griffiths, Mrs. G.
Griffiths, H. I.
Hackworth, R.
Harben, Sir Henry, J.P., Mayor of Hampstead.
Hart, W. H.
Harvest, Mrs.
Hepburn, James.
Hoare, E. Brodie, M.P.

Hoare, Sir Samuel, Bart., M.P.
Hoare, Miss.
Hopkins, Mrs. Manley.
Howard, Mrs. C.
Humphreys, F.
Husband, Miss.
Jay, Mrs. Hastings.
Jessop, E., M.D.
Johnston, C.
Johnston, Mrs.
Kennedy, James.
Kinns, Rev. S., Ph.D.
Klein, W. G.
Lake, E. E.
Lister, I. S.
Lister, Miss.
Luard, Miss.
Lyon, B. A.
MacInnes, Mrs.
Marston, E.
Martelli, Mrs.
Mayor, Miss E.
Monro, F. J.
Mullins, E. G., L.C.C.
Negretti, H. P. J.
Nevinson, Mrs. S. C., and Miss.
Parker, F. C.
Parker, H. S.
Payne, E. S.
Pinches, Miss.
Pollock, Mrs.
Pooley, H. F.
Potter, G. W.
Prance, Reginald H.
Prance, R. Hart.
Preston, C. Sansome.
Preston, T. Sansome.
Randall, T. Gurney.
Reed, C. H.
Roberts, Miss E. T.
Rooth, Mrs. Goodwin.
Rose, H. C., M.D.
Ryalls, C. W., LL.D.
Scott, Mrs. F. W.
Skoyles, Mrs. R.
Stamp, E. B.
Stedall, H.
Stedman, M. H.
Temple, Sir R., Bart., P.C., G.C.S.I., etc.
Tremlett, Rev. F. W., D.D.
Tulloch, H. M.
Underwood, A. S., and Mrs.
Warren, Mrs.
Weaver, F. P., M.D., J.P.
Weekley, C.
Wightman, C.
Wilkins, Mrs. M. F.
Wilson, R.
Wilson, Maryon-, Sir S. P., Bart.
Woodcock, E. H.
Woodd-Smith, B., D.L., J.P. (the late).